Television Finales

Television and Popular Culture
Robert J. Thompson, *Series Editor*

Director's Choice

For over twenty years, our Television and Popular Culture series has been publishing award-winning titles in all areas of television studies. *Television Finales: From "Howdy Doody" to "Girls"* is the natural Director's Choice title this season, as it brings together more than seventy compulsively readable essays by a broad range of today's leading television scholars and critics. It represents the excellence, diversity, accessibility, and vitality that Syracuse University Press strives for in this and all its series.

Alice Randel Pfeiffer
Director, Syracuse University Press

Television FINALES

From *Howdy Doody* to *Girls*

Edited by
Douglas L. Howard
and David Bianculli

Syracuse University Press

∞ The paper used in this publication meets the minimum requirements
of the American National Standard for Information Sciences—Permanence
of Paper for Printed Library Materials, ANSI Z39.48-1992.

For a listing of books published and distributed by Syracuse University Press,
visit www.SyracuseUniversityPress.syr.edu.

ISBN: 978-0-8156-3604-5 (hardcover)   978-0-8156-1105-9 (paperback)   978-0-8156-5447-6 (e-book)

Library of Congress Cataloging-in-Publication Data
Names: Howard, Douglas L., 1966– editor. | Bianculli, David, editor.
Title: Television finales : from Howdy Doody to Girls / edited by Douglas L. Howard and David Bianculli.
Description: First edition. | Syracuse, New York : Syracuse University Press, 2018. | Series: Television and
    popular culture | Includes bibliographical references and index.
Identifiers: LCCN 2018031406 (print) | LCCN 2018041442 (ebook) | ISBN 9780815654476 (E-book) |
    ISBN 9780815636045 | ISBN 9780815636045 (hardback : alk. paper) | ISBN 9780815611059
    (paperback : alk. paper) | ISBN 9780815654476 (e-book)
Subjects: LCSH: Television series—History and criticism.
Classification: LCC PN1992.8.S4 (ebook) | LCC PN1992.8.S4 T456 2018 (print) | DDC 791.45/75–dc23
LC record available at https://lccn.loc.gov/2018031406

Manufactured in the United States of America

This book is dedicated to David Lavery, author, scholar, teacher, mentor, and friend. Almost all of the authors in this book were influenced by David in some way, and generations of scholars worldwide will, we are sure, continue to be influenced by his work. This collection, in fact, was also one of David's ideas, and all of the authors in this volume have worked diligently to see it through to completion. We hope that it does justice to his vision for the project.

Contents

Contents by Year

Contents by Genre

Drama

Soap Opera

Science Fiction

Horror

Western

Medical Drama

Police Drama/Crime Drama/Police Procedural

Acknowledgments

Douglas L. Howard: I thank all of the authors for their inspired contributions to this collection as well as for their patience through this rather lengthy process. I am so grateful to have had the opportunity to work with such talented writers and accomplished scholars and to bring them together for this book.

Thanks to David Bianculli for so many interesting discussions about beginnings and endings on television and for his keen insights into the scope of this project.

Thanks to Lynnette Porter, a true inspiration, for her contributions to this book as well as to popular-culture studies in general.

Thanks as well to my colleagues at Suffolk County Community College for their collegiality and friendship and for giving me the opportunity to take part in this project. I would particularly like to recognize the members of the English Department on the Ammerman campus for all of their suggestions and conversations about the book; the faculty and staff in the Huntington Library, who helped out with research questions and interlibrary loans; and the college administration for seeing the value of this work and giving me the time to do it.

Thanks to Deborah Manion and Bob Thompson at Syracuse University Press for their continued enthusiasm and support for this project.

Thanks to Annie Barva for her incredible editorial work.

Thanks to my good friend Pat Tierney, *Fugitive* fan and TV buff, for more than thirty years of conversations about the good, the bad, and the ridiculous on the small screen as well as for many recent conversations about this collection. I have no doubt that he could beat Lieutenant Gerard in a footrace.

Thanks to my family for all of their love and support. Thanks in particular to Jennifer and Carolyn for all of those iced teas that kept me awake and car-ride conversations that kept me sane and to Ginger and Olive, who often sat next to me while I edited.

And, finally, thanks to the late David Lavery for asking me to be a part of this book and for putting out a call for papers on *The Sopranos* many years ago that changed my life.

David Bianculli: Thanks to the late David Lavery for starting this ball rolling. And thanks to Douglas Howard for carrying it, and me, over the goal line.

Television Finales

Introduction

This Is the Series' End, My Only Friend?
(With Apologies to The Doors)

DOUGLAS L. HOWARD

Let's begin at the end. After all, this entire book is about endings, and if you are reading this, you're admittedly here for the end, not the beginning. And why shouldn't you be? As part of this culture, you have been spoon-fed endings with your strained peas and your mashed bananas, socialized into a world of milestones, holidays, and step-up ceremonies that are as much endings as they are entry items on the universal "Rites-of-Passage Check-list." (Damn, that sounds cynical.) Just think about all of those final exams that your teachers spent months telling you about, all of those videogame walkthroughs/cheats, movie spoilers, March Madness brackets, horoscopes, weather reports, and book/film/TV reviews that you still turn to on a regular basis, or all that time that you spent in line for *Return of the Jedi* (Richard Marquand, 1983), *Return of the King* (Peter Jackson, 2003), and *Deathly Hallows, Part 2* (David Yates, 2011). Those things exist because they speak to the need for finality, the desire for narrative completion, the increasing general anxiety to know how it all works out. It's not about the journey. Like Phil Collins in that "Don't Lose My Number" video in the 1980s, you, too, smack your neck as you wonder about the one true question that really matters: "So how does it end?"

As another point of cultural unity, television is all about the end, too. From the moment that you grab that remote and push that button, you insert yourself into a different world of time and imaginative space, one that is incessantly populated by arbitrary beginnings and endings. The detailed television grid that you surf—with colorful boxes that visually illustrate the length, the boundaries, the life span of each program—in fact tempts you with nothing but moments of chronological and narrative entry. Regardless

1

of where you wind up and how much of that choice you control or delay—and with DVRs you can control or delay quite a bit—the inevitable, inescapable truth is still the same: the program must end. You actively choose to devote your attention to a narrative that will conclude by time if not by structure or story line. To engage it is to accept and even ask for a moment of closure, a moment that you can hasten with streaming video by fast-forwarding or by taking advantage of the ultimate self-destruct option and turning off the TV entirely.

Even within the confines of the episodes themselves—and confines, of course, presuppose and are defined by clearly demarcated limits—we regularly confront multiple endings, as David Lavery points out in his *Buffy* essay on "narrative eschatology"; the very nature of television narrative turns on this series of "mini-apocalypses": "the distinctly televisual ends, allowing for commercial breaks, that come within the narrative itself; the ending of each episode . . . ; the endings of narrative arcs; the ending of each season" (2003). Just as we plan our viewing in anticipation of and around these ends, we often reschedule our lives for them, from that bathroom break during commercials[1] to that unplanned binge watch, brought on by our sudden investment in the narrative and our insatiable need to know what happens. As with life, perhaps, the ends are what give meaning to our watching.

This book specifically focuses on the global endings and those narratives that do conclude or appear to conclude, the final episodes of television series: the finales. They are the stuff of watercooler conversation and blogging buzz. They have become, as Joanne Morreale describes the ending of *Seinfeld* (1989–98), "cultural spectacles" and occasions for the shows themselves, whether their producers have made the decision or declining ratings have made it for them,[2] "to call attention to their departure" (2003, 274). Why are there so many? The cut-and-dried answer here would be that the end sells.

---

1. As a case in point about bathroom breaks and rescheduling lives, roughly "a million New Yorkers [used] their bathrooms at the end of the [*M*A*S*H* finale in 1983], sending an additional 6.7 million gallons of water into the city's sewers" ("The Last Episode of 'M-A-S-H'" 1983).

2. As Jason Mittell insightfully notes in his book *Complex TV* (2015), television shows end in a number of different ways, many of which are unplanned: "actual finales are quite rare for American television series" (319). Mittell goes on to define these other types of endings—"the stoppage," "the wrap-up," "the conclusion," and "the cessation"—before arriving at "the finale," which he defines as "a conclusion with a going-away party" (322).

Finales on television mean ratings and advertising dollars.³ Look for a list of "most-watched television programs," and you'll probably find a healthy handful of last episodes and/or sporting-event finals such as the Super Bowl, a game that, among other things, marks the end of the NFL season.⁴ *Business Insider*'s rundown of most-watched broadcasts, which leaves out "all live broadcasts," includes the finales for *The Fugitive* (1963–67), *Seinfeld*, *Cheers* (1982–93), and *M*A*S*H* (1972–83) as well as the final episodes of the miniseries *The Winds of War* (1983), *The Thorn Birds* (1983), and *Roots* (1977) (Lynch 2017). Television shows such as *The Walking Dead* (2010–) have even taken to cutting their seasons in half, giving them the chance to drum up interest in a "midseason finale" (as opposed to an episode 7, 8, or 9) and to reap the rewards of some extra audience attention in November or December as well as in March or April.

The other side of this equation, though, is that the end sells because we want it, because it fulfills some kind of psychological need within us. (We can't even blame the networks for creating this desire—even if they feed into it now—because the network executives were initially more interested in syndication than in conclusion, if *The Fugitive* finale is any indication [for more on that episode, please see chapter 21]). Whether beginnings and endings are fictional and illusory or not and whether we perceive them as such or not, we still crave and enjoy them because they help us to compartmentalize and consider moments in time in more digestible packages. Literary critic Frank Kermode famously talks about our "imaginative investments in coherent patterns" and how "the provision of the end" helps us, "in the middest," to coordinate "the origins" and "the middle" (2000, 17).⁵ Jungian analyst and film critic Christopher Hauke makes a similar point, that "the human psyche cannot tolerate gaps in meaning and coherence" (2014, 127) and that it turns to and relies on narrative as a way of making sense of an often chaotic and fragmented existence. Historian Hayden White says something

---

3. Rebecca Williams agrees that the media industry's goals for "the promotion of finales" are rather straightforward: "attract high audience figures and appease advertisers" (2015, 200).

4. *MASH4077TV*'s "Most-Watched Television Broadcasts in U.S. History" list, for example, includes nine Super Bowls and, of course, the last episode of *M*A*S*H* ("Super Bowl 50" 2016).

5. Although Kermode could not have "imagine[d] his narratology being applied to television" (2000, 17), Lavery (2003) seems to relish the application in his *Buffy* essay as well as how Kermode's discussion of "season" has a unique double meaning in context.

along the same lines in "The Value of Narrativity in the Representation of Reality" (1980) when he states that narrative may be a way for us to "[fashion] human experience into a form assimilable to structures of meaning that are generally human rather than culture-specific" (5). For White, the attempt to impose a narrative structure on real events in history works as a kind of wish fulfillment: "In this world [of historical narrative], reality wears the mask of a meaning, the completeness and fullness of which we can only imagine, never experience. Insofar as historical stories can be completed, can be given narrative closure, can be shown to have had a plot all along, they give to reality the odor of the *ideal*" (24).

As a human creation, a work of art, and a fictional representation of reality, television, too, provides us with the opportunity to fulfill that wish and create narrative closure where reality might be more resistant to it. Here, we don't just get a "whiff of the ideal"; we get to take a deep breath and see it played out in front of us. And we don't have to cherry-pick historical or biographical details to direct or redirect the story toward its end. The writers, directors, producers, and actors do that for us and, if only for a half-hour or an hour, show us worlds where the rules that we want to believe actually do apply. People who appear to be real (or, at the very least, share some tiny emotional or psychological similarity with our species) take part in events that unfold for particular reasons toward specific ends—ends or "cultural spectacles" that celebrate the narrative dream come to (some kind of) life.

The narrative dream that lives, of course, paradoxically hinges on "the end of our elaborate plans, the end of everything that stands" (The Doors [1967] 1988), at least for the shows that we enjoy. It requires that final episode, the end of days for those characters and the lives that they have led (and a vision of our own), to make it work. In the same way that Lavery talks about "little deaths" and "mini-apocalypses" in his discussion of *Buffy*, C. Lee Harrington identifies the various ways in which critical analyses of finales have "[employed] a *discourse* of death and dying in [their] consideration of textual mourning" (2013, 580, emphasis in original). According to Rebecca Williams, "fans themselves continue to draw on [these discourses as well]" (2015, 204). Harrington's and Williams's work begs the question: Why would we want to see something that we love end and metaphorically or literally die if the payoff is little more than psychological comfort and the (re) affirmation of an illusory order? Perhaps such comforts and illusions are hard to come by, cannot be overestimated, and are worth the price of apocalypse.

If we follow the paradox a little farther down the rabbit hole, however, we find that television endings, in particular very good or great ones, can offer both us and the shows themselves the prospect of even more than that. Because all series will eventually end, the "good death" or "model ending" becomes the ultimate goal of any TV finale, as Harrington explains, because it will "live on in the public (and industry) imagination" (2013, 584).⁶ Not only does the good death create an interest in rewatching the series and bringing it back to life over and over again,⁷ but it also becomes the subject of critical and fan discussion, debate, and analysis as well as the stuff of academic study in a book like this one—staples of the afterlife in the televisual Valhalla.⁸

And this is the great irony of the series' ending, the ideal that we long for, the one that establishes order and gives meaning to the whole: it never satisfies the dream, the desire that gives rise to it. For all of the neat narrative conclusions that television tries to offer us through these endings, some sense of reality (or some need to make more money from a successful premise) often finds its way in. One of the themes that recur throughout this book and these essays is that television finales are not so final. So many quality television dramas have worked this way, through open-ended closure, by leaving some of the central tensions unresolved in their last moments, by leaving their antiheroes alive and capable of more mischief, or by leaving us to wonder, as in *The Sopranos* finale (2007), exactly how the narrative ends and what becomes of the main characters.⁹ But long before such narrative experimentation became fashionable—and I encourage you to look at Mark Dawidziak's chapter on *The Dick Van Dyke Show* (1961–66) in this regard—and

6. Inasmuch as no series' fan wants to have his or her "love" betrayed by a "bad death" or a flawed ending, Claire Burdfield, in a recent *CSTonline* piece, talks about how some viewers have even taken to watching the finale first so that they can decide "whether they want to watch [the rest of it]" and spare themselves that disappointment. Where the pilot was once the measure of what viewers could expect from a show, Burdfield notes, "finales have increasingly become a way of judging a television series' worthiness" (2016).

7. Mittell even uses the term *resurrection* to describe "an already concluded show [that] returns [such as *Firefly* (2002–3) or *Veronica Mars* (2004–7)], either on television or in another medium" (2015, 321).

8. As Rebecca Williams notes, fans may choose to actively reject a finale, whether they perceive it as good or bad, and keep the world of that show alive through various alternatives, including social media, fanfiction, and conventions: "Fandom does not end once a television series ceases to produce and air new episodes" (2015, 195).

9. Although Ryan Engley believes that television is "aligned with the death drive," he argues that contemporary television has been successful precisely because it undermines finality: through its "creative uses of failure[, it] endlessly defers narrative closure" (2016, 74).

even with shows that aren't trying to mess with our desire for order, our sense of the real (or a network's need to go back to the well) undermines the finality of the narrative and leaves the window open for our imaginations (and, of course, for the writers, producers, and dedicated, die-hard fans) to consider what comes after the ending. Richard Kimble goes home after his exoneration; Hawkeye Pierce comes back from the war; Jerry, George, Elaine, and Kramer wake up in prison, and then . . . ? The reboots, restarts, and revivals of shows such as *Veronica Mars*, *Gilmore Girls* (2000–2007, 2016), and *The X-Files* (1993–2002, 2016) clearly demonstrate that there's always more story to tell, that the imposition of narrative structure, even in the fictional world, is problematic, that the end on television is never the end.

In that spirit, this book of endings doesn't really end. In some ways, it stands as the start or the middle of a conversation rather than as the end of one inasmuch as finales typically leave us to discuss their meaning, impact, significance, and success. We hope that it will inspire you to revisit your own conversations about these final episodes and, perhaps, to take yet another look at them, all moments that arguably stand out as milestones for the medium. The book brings together an unusual collection of critical voices, with essays from leading television and media scholars as well as from renowned journalists and TV critics, all with their own unique take on these memorable moments. The chapters are organized alphabetically by show title, but we have offered you chronological and genre listings in case you would rather follow those groupings or orders instead. Feel free to jump around to your personal favorites or to read about something that you may have overlooked. Although spoilers abound, there are also opportunities to learn about and later watch some really great television as well as some endings that may shock, disturb, frustrate, and baffle. So let's get to what you came here for. Without further ado, this is the end or, at least, the first of many . . .

References

Burdfield, Claire. 2016. "Avoiding Disappointment—Judging a TV Show by Its Finale." *CSTonline*, May 12. At https://cstonline.net/avoiding-disappointment -judging-a-tv-show-by-its-finale-by-claire-burdfield/.
The Doors. 1967. "The End." *The Doors*. Elektra, 1988. CD.
Engley, Ryan. 2016. "The Greatest Trick the Devil Ever Played: Desire, Drive, and the Twist Ending." In *Cinematic Cuts: Theorizing Film Endings*, edited by Sheila Kunkle, 59–79. Albany: State Univ. of New York Press.

Harrington, C. Lee. 2013. "The *Ars Moriendi* of US Serial Television: Towards a Good Textual Death." *International Journal of Cultural Studies* 16, no. 6: 579–95.

Hauke, Christopher. 2014. *Visible Mind: Movie, Modernity, and the Unconscious.* New York: Routledge.

Kermode, Frank. 2000. *The Sense of an Ending: Studies in the Theory of Fiction with a New Epilogue.* New York: Oxford Univ. Press.

"The Last Episode of 'M-A-S-H' Was a Royal Flush. . . ." 1983. UPI, Mar. 14, 1983. At http://www.upi.com/Archives/1983/03/14/The-last-episode-of-M-A-S-H-was -a-royal-flush/3459416466000/.

Lavery, David. 2003. "Apocalyptic Apocalypses: The Narrative Eschatology of *Buffy the Vampire Slayer.*" *Slayage: The Online International Journal of Buffy Studies* 3, no. 1. At http://www.whedonstudies.tv/uploads/2/6/2/8/26288593/lavery _slayage_3.1.pdf.

Lynch, John. 2017. "The 20 Most-Watched TV Episodes of All Time." *Business Insider*, Oct. 1, 2017. At http://www.businessinsider.com/most-watched-episodes -2016-9.

Mittell, Jason. 2015. *Complex TV: The Poetics of Contemporary Storytelling.* New York: New York Univ. Press.

Morreale, Joanne. 2003. "Sitcoms Say Good-bye: The Cultural Spectacle of *Seinfeld*'s Last Episode." In *Critiquing the Sitcom: A Reader*, edited by Joanne Morreale, 274–85. Syracuse, NY: Syracuse Univ. Press.

"Super Bowl 50 Tops *M*A*S*H* Finale in Viewers." 2016. *MASH4077TV*, Feb. 20. At http://www.mash4077tv.com/2016/02/super-bowl-50-tops-mash-finale -in-viewers/.

White, Hayden. 1980. "The Value of Narrativity in the Representation of Reality." *Critical Inquiry* 7, no. 1: 5–27.

Williams, Rebecca. 2015. *Post-object Fandom: Television, Identity, and Self-Narrative.* New York: Bloomsbury.

1

As the World Turns

Season 52, Episode 181 (or 13,858)

SAM FORD

For almost all types of fictional television series, the finale is an inevitable conclusion, one that the producers and the viewers alike are often working toward from the first seconds of the premiere episode. Not so with the US soap opera. Soaps are commonly referred to as "worlds without end" (Museum 1997), predicated upon "the impossibility of closure" (Allen 1985, 13). Even more emphatically, Tania Modleski writes, "It is not only that successful soap operas do not end, it is also that they cannot end" (1979, 12).

The finale of a US soap, then, is a particularly complicated narrative moment—a final text destined to be unsatisfactory, created by a production team whose career has built around avoiding such moments and engaged with by an audience whose pleasures in viewing have been shaped by the idea that such a moment would not come.[1]

There is perhaps no better finale to illustrate these tensions than the last installment, episode 13,858, of the lives of the residents of Oakdale, Illinois, on CBS's long-running soap opera *As the World Turns* (*ATWT*).

Although this iconic daytime drama proved impossible to end satisfactorily, the storytelling model of *ATWT* initially proved difficult to begin as well. With the show's debut, series creator Irna Phillips took an approach to the soap opera that focused on character over plot. Typical scenes in early episodes involved couples, relatives, and friends talking in living rooms, kitchens, and bedrooms. Very little "happened" in the average scene. As Robert LaGuardia puts it, "The activities on *As the World Turns* were very,

---

1. For more on coping and understanding the textual death of serialized dramas, see Harrington 2013.

very slow" (1983, 105). Before launching, Phillips got Proctor & Gamble to agree not to cancel the show for its first year—a prescient move because that slow storytelling style took significant time to begin picking up viewers but then gained momentum rapidly, catapulting from the low ratings of its first year to being the top-rated soap by the end of its second year on air (LaGuardia 1983, 106).

And *ATWT* was the exemplar US soap in all sorts of respects. It was the first soap opera, with its debut in 1956, to expand beyond fifteen-minute daily episodes (beating *The Edge of Night* [1956–84], which also debuted the same day at thirty minutes, by a time slot or so). It was the highest-rated soap for twenty years, from 1958 to 1978, at the height of the genre's popularity. Its finale marked the end of the true soap opera in that it was the last daytime drama still being produced by an actual soap company (Proctor & Gamble). And it was the fullest realization of the vision of the mother of the soap opera genre, Irna Phillips. As the Museum of Television and Radio describes its influence, "The conversations over cups of coffee, recaps of previous events, pregnant pauses, and long close-ups preceding fade-out that were introduced on *As the World Turns* are all clichés now, but at the time they were the strikingly original building blocks of Phillips's new, visual style of soap-opera storytelling" (1997, 132).

By 2010, longtime viewers had watched hundreds, if not thousands, of actors pass through Oakdale—as well as the twists and turns of multiple generations of characters. In some cases, a host of actors had taken their pass at the same role. (For instance, thirteen different actors were billed as playing Tom Hughes [Ford 2011]). And *ATWT*, like all its daytime sisters, had been an early stop in the careers of various film and TV stars—for instance, Martin Sheen, James Earl Jones, Dana Delany, Meg Ryan, Marisa Tomei, Courteney Cox, Stephen Weber, William Fichtner, Ming-Na, Parker Posey, Jason Biggs, James Van Der Beek, and Julianne Moore.

Through those characters and their stories, *ATWT* also tackled many contemporary concerns and social issues throughout its fifty-four years—divorce, rape (in particular marital rape), incest, interracial marriage between white and black characters, an interracial child fathered in Vietnam by an American soldier, the first gay male character in daytime TV, the first gay male kiss on daytime TV, end-of-life family tensions, miscarriages, cancer, Alzheimer's, HIV/AIDS, and a wide range of other social issue stories.

More powerfully, *ATWT* had retained its history more completely than those other daytime dramas. In the final year before its cancellation in 2010, the series could boast in its ensemble an actor who had debuted on the premiere episode in 1956 (Helen Wagner); four actors who had started with the show in the 1960s (Don Hastings, Eileen Fulton, Marie Masters, and Larry Bryggman); two actors whose run had begun in the 1970s (Kathryn Hays and Colleen Zenk); and a range of others whose faces first appeared in Oakdale in the 1980s, 1990s, and early 2000s.

The deep relationship soap opera fans feel with "their story" (as many viewers have described their preferred soap opera) is driven by this intimate, daily connection with faces who have been in Oakdale for decades. *ATWT*'s intergenerational fan base either had been watching the series for a significant portion of its run or had the show handed down to them from previous generations of viewers, such as family members or caretakers, who had passed down the wisdom of Oakdale lore like town elders, or, in later years, had caught up through online fan discussion sites (Ford 2008). In many cases, those fans had been with the series or had ties to the series for a much longer duration than most members of the writing team at the show's helm as the finale neared.

This kind of dedication led to a feeling of ownership over the soap that for many fans was more powerful and significant than the authorial direction of any one writing team.[2] Some fans had been particularly disappointed in the show's initial lack of concern to build toward a finale. When news broke of the show's cancellation nine months prior to the final episode, executive producer Chris Goutman said, "We still have exciting stories in the works, and we're sticking to them. We're not ready to start inviting back old favorites and do the nostalgia thing. . . . We just continue to tell good stories. . . . There will be plenty of time to bring in whomever we want from the past" (quoted in Newcomb 2009). The statement was particularly infuriating to some fans; some of those longtime viewers expressed their feeling that the series' current state paled in comparison to certain previous eras. (Soap operas, after all, don't "jump the shark" just once but jump the shark and back over many times through decades.)

ATWT's writers eventually took a range of steps to remember the series' history—for instance, commemorating the show's fifty-fourth and final anniversary via a story line celebrating the twenty-fifth wedding anniversary of

---

2. For more on this phenomenon, see Harrington and Bielby 1994 and Ford 2015.

characters Bob and Kim Hughes and the return of daughter Frannie (played by Julianne Moore) and bringing back Larry Bryggman's character, John Dixon, a longtime icon of the show, for twelve episodes at the series' end, after a six-year hiatus. But those frustrations that the show didn't dedicate itself to a nine-month-long finale persisted.

In this complex, intricate backstory came the final installment of *As the World Turns* on September 17, 2010.[3] The original plan was to have Helen Wagner's character, Nancy Hughes, whose "Good morning, dear" were the first lines of the series, close out the run with "Good night, dear." Unfortunately, Wagner passed away on May 1 of that year, having made her final appearance on the show a month earlier.

The finale was instead narrated by the character Dr. Bob Hughes, played by Don Hastings, at that point the senior-most member of the cast. The finale was framed around characters' retirement or slowing down from work to focus on new romantic entanglements or their families. Powerful female executive Lucinda Walsh, in her midseventies, vows to trust her daughter, Lily, with the reins of her company and to quit meddling in Lily's life—in order to focus on rekindling her former romance with recently returned exhusband, Dr. John Dixon. Mother-and-son business partners Barbara and Paul Ryan mutually plan to absolve their tense working relationship so that Paul can concentrate on his family while Barbara concentrates on her new marriage with a much younger man. The longest-running couple on the show—Tom and Margo Hughes—decide to slow down their work lives to cope with empty-nest syndrome when their son, Casey, leaves town to start a new life with his fiancée. And, for his part, Bob is stepping down as the hospital's chief of staff, so he and his wife (local TV executive Kim Hughes) can finally enjoy retirement. These vows to slow it down are particularly poignant because, for many of these actors, this cancellation signaled the end of their regular appearances on TV screens and thus a very real retirement.

Meanwhile, the rekindled romance between Lucinda and John ends with John getting one last chance to needle a former fiancée (from the mid-1990s), Lisa, while directly referencing going to their hotel suite to re-create an iconic hot-tub scene between Lucinda and him from the 1980s. Multiple couples who had battled adversity for months or years are finally together and happy (albeit fearing "normalcy") at show's end or demonstrate at least the hope of reconciliation. A heart-transplant recipient asks his girlfriend to

---

3. All references to the final *ATWT* episode come from Goutman [2010] 2012.

marry him—while the lover of the heart donor is given the chance to listen to the heartbeat of the man he'll now never be able to be with. And decades-old rivals Kim and Susan hug as Kim prepares to leave town.

But these moments, try as they might, are unsatisfactory. Longtime viewers have been trained to expect that any moment of happiness is a signal that something ominous is around the corner (Flitterman-Lewis 1992). In this case, they were left to ponder all the stories never to be resolved. (What happened to Kirk and Samantha when they disappeared off that pier in the late 1990s? Will Craig's murderous acts never catch up to him? And what of the fates of hundreds of other characters who didn't return to get a bit of finality or of the other thousands of loose ends left dangling since 1956?) And fans wondered why there weren't many months dedicated more fully to wrapping up fifty-four years of history.

Most of all, longtime fans had to cope with the fact that these characters and families alongside whom they had aged suddenly ceased to exist simultaneously.[4] Our world would keep turning, but *Oakdale's* had stopped. For decades, soaps had mimicked real life in the sense that both the series and the fandom were intergenerational and that aging, change, and death had come gradually. If soaps help their viewers ponder and cope with the passage of time in everyday life, a soap's end perhaps poses deeper questions about the stability of the cornerstones of life and society, those we had always presumed—like Oakdale—would outlive us all.

References

Allen, Robert C. 1985. *Speaking of Soap Operas*. Chapel Hill: Univ. of North Carolina Press.

Flitterman-Lewis, Sandy. 1992. "All's Well That Doesn't End—Soap Opera and the Marriage Motif." In *Private Screenings: Television and the Female Consumer*, edited by Lynn Spiegel and Denise Mann, 216–25. Minneapolis: Univ. of Minnesota Press.

Ford, Sam. 2008. "Soap Operas and the History of Fan Discussion." *Transformative Works and Cultures* 1. At http://journal.transformativeworks.org/index.php/twc/article/view/42/50.

———. 2011. "Growing Old Together: Following *As the World Turns'* Tom Hughes through the Years." In *The Survival of Soap Opera: Transformations for a New*

4. For more on the phenomenon of fans aging alongside characters, see Ford 2011 and Harrington and Brothers 2011.

Media Era, edited by Sam Ford, Abigail De Kosnik, and C. Lee Harrington, 86–100. Jackson: Univ. Press of Mississippi.

———. 2015. "Social Media Ownership." In *The International Encyclopedia of Digital Communication and Society*, 1–10. West Sussex, UK: Wiley.

Goutman, Christopher, dir. [2010] 2012. "Episode 181 (or Episode 13,858)." *As the World Turns*, season 52. Written by Jean Passanante and Lucky Gold. Aired Sept. 17, 2010, CBS. On *As the World Turns—Farewell to Oakdale*. New York: SoapClassics. DVD.

Harrington, C. Lee. 2013. "The *Ars Moriendi* of U.S. Serial Television: Towards a Good Textual Death." *International Journal of Cultural Studies* 16, no. 6: 579–95.

Harrington, C. Lee, and Denise D. Bielby. 1994. *Soap Fans: Pursuing Pleasure and Making Meaning in Everyday Life*. Philadelphia: Temple Univ. Press.

Harrington, C. Lee, and Denise Brothers. 2011. "Constructing the Older Audience: Age and Aging in Soaps." In *The Survival of Soap Opera: Transformations for a New Media Era*, edited by Sam Ford, Abigail De Kosnik, and C. Lee Harrington, 300–314. Jackson: Univ. Press of Mississippi.

LaGuardia, Robert. 1983. *Soap World*. New York: Priam.

Modleski, Tania. 1979. "The Search for Tomorrow in Today's Soap Operas: Notes on a Feminine Form." *Film Quarterly* 33, no. 1: 12–21.

Museum of Television and Radio. 1997. *Worlds without End: The Art and History of the Soap Opera*. New York: Harry N. Abrams.

Newcomb, Roger. 2009. "Executive Producer Chris Goutman on *ATWT*'s Cancellation." *We Love Soaps*, Dec. 14. At http://www. welovesoaps.net/2009/12 /executive-producer-chris-goutman-on.html.

2

Ashes to Ashes

Episode 8

KAREN HELLEKSON

As the sequel to stylish British time-travel cop drama *Life on Mars* (2006–7, BBC One),[1] *Ashes to Ashes* (2008–10, BBC One) had big shoes to fill: the big question behind the first show had been answered, so the spin-off couldn't simply retread the same ground. And when it came time to end *Ashes to Ashes* after three seasons, season-level closure had to be combined with closure on the level of the entire milieu. For me, viewing the finale provided an explosion of understanding that called into question everything I had seen before; I excitedly felt that I would have to rewatch the entire two series with this new knowledge in mind to truly understand the texts. Indeed, from the beginning, showrunners Matthew Graham and Ashley Pharoah, who cocreated both shows for BBC One, had planned the finale of *Ashes to Ashes* to close out the entire canon: "Series three unifies *Life on Mars* and *Ashes to Ashes* and makes them one show. By the time you get halfway through series three of *Ashes to Ashes*, you will actually feel like you're watching series five of *Life on Mars*!" (Wilkes 2009).

The finale of *Ashes to Ashes* is startling because, although it remains true to the characters and the milieu, it introduces a metaphysical aspect that ponders the meaning of life, death, and an afterlife—an aspect so radical that rewatching all the episodes of both *Life on Mars* and *Ashes to Ashes* is in order so that the contents might be reinterpreted in light of the new information. Both shows, with their heavily researched re-creations of past eras—the mid-1970s for *Life on Mars*, the early 1980s for *Ashes*

---

1. *Editors' note*: For a discussion of the *Life on Mars* (UK) finale, see chapter 33 by Trisha Dunleavy.

to Ashes—mix nostalgia evoked by music and costume with eye-opening reminders of exactly how overtly sexist and racist the world used to be. They are cop dramas with a twist: not just a police procedural but the analysis of an inner psyche being tested by inexplicable happenings.

To recap: the hero of *Life on Mars*, Sam Tyler (John Simm), a Manchester police officer in 2006, finds himself inexplicably back in 1973 after being struck by a car.[2] The voiceover in the opening credits of season 1 summarizes the program's central mystery: "Am I mad, in a coma, or back in time? Whatever's happened, it's like I've landed on a different planet. Now maybe if I can work out the reason, I can get home." Many individual episodes focus on an event that Tyler interprets as a sort of test: if he can pass it, he can return home. *Life on Mars*'s finale closes out the story: Tyler, who has indeed been in a coma, commits suicide in the present to assure his return to the past.

Ashes to Ashes returns to the milieu set up in *Life on Mars*.[3] Point-of-view character Detective Inspector Alex Drake (Keeley Hawes), a police psychologist with the London Metropolitan Police and briefly mentioned in the *Life on Mars* finale, is shot in 2008 and finds herself in 1981. Like Tyler, she tries to find meaning in this experience: her season 3 opening voiceover states, "Is it real or in my mind? Either way, I have to solve the mystery of what all this means and fight to get home, because time is running out." Like Tyler, she finds herself working with Detective Chief Inspector (DCI) Gene Hunt (Philip Glenister) and two other familiar faces, detectives Ray Carling (Dean Andrews) and Chris Skelton (Marshall Lancaster), although the venue has changed, with a move from Manchester to London. And like Tyler, she seems to receive messages from devices such as telephones, televisions, and radios, as though someone from her present is attempting to contact her in the past and these devices permit the two worlds to be bridged.

From the beginning, *Ashes to Ashes* alludes to *Life on Mars*. Drake stands in for the audience: she is aware of Tyler's case, and, in fact, at the time of her move into the past she is reviewing Tyler's file, helpfully stamped "SUICIDE," so there can be no doubt. In a review of the premiere of *Ashes to Ashes*, one TV critic writes, "In a fascinating piece of postmodernism, the viewer adopts the same perspective as Drake with regards to Hunt and

2. All references to *Life on Mars* come from Graham, Pharoah, and Jordan 2006–7, the original television broadcasts.

3. All references to *Ashes to Ashes* come from Graham and Pharoah 2008–10, the original television broadcasts.

his returning (and wonderfully restyled) colleagues Chris Skelton and Ray Carling. Like us, Drake possesses the knowledge of how Tyler facilitated his return to the present day, so understandably seeks to use his tried and tested methods to speed up her return" (Rawson-Jones 2008).

Drake's knowledge provides valuable background information about the milieu—not only for Drake in the context of the program itself but also for the viewers. We know from the outset that Tyler had been in a coma, so we infer that the same is true of Drake. Pushing Tyler and Drake into the past provides new ground, stripping what it means to be a cop down to its essentials by removing accountability, rules, and modern forensics (it's not for nothing that there's a *High Noon* film poster in Hunt's office), even as Drake appears to have an edge because she has knowledge of elements of the future, including details of cases as well as more general cultural knowledge—not to mention an excellent understanding of motivation and psychology. Drake knows everything about the future, including what happened to Sam Tyler. She should be in a position of power. Yet she knows nothing. Graham notes, "We wanted to play with the idea that the audience knew exactly what was going on, so we thought let's have a character who, like the audience, knows what's happening. . . . And then the next stage of the three-year plan is to undermine that, so that you realise you don't know what's going on and nor does Alex" (Wylie 2008). Drake's frantic attempts to find out what is going on—what she thinks is the truth—lead her to do some detective work on her own time as she seeks to learn what happened to Tyler in the past. She comes to believe that Hunt killed Tyler and is covering it up, which makes Hunt dishonorable and not worthy of Drake's regard or love.

The finale of *Ashes to Ashes* is foregrounded in the first episode of the third and final season. Drake is in a coma, but she's in a coma in the past, dreaming she is in the present. A TV playing in her room mentions that human remains have been found. A clock turns over to the time 9:06, there's a brief blackout, and then Drake awakens in the past. In the final episode of the series, Drake, following a trail of clues and egged on by the mysterious and sinister DCI Jim Keats (Daniel Mays), uncovers the body of a policeman. Visual evidence links this body's dump site to the site shown on the TV in the future's hospital room. However, when Drake checks the ID buried with the body, it's not Tyler, as she had assumed. It's Gene Hunt.

Drake has discovered the revelatory truth: this past world is a holding place, a kind of purgatory, for dead cops. Gene Hunt is the ferryman who tries to see them safely on, and Jim Keats, the devil himself, opposes him (Wilde 2007; Lund 2010; Wollaston 2010; Wylie 2010b; Yan 2010). In this milieu, the dead or comatose cops can fight crime and perhaps redeem themselves. But this revelation means that Drake has to face the truth about herself: the clock turns over to 9:06, and "the moment of it [the screen] plunging to black and then Gene slapping her awake, that's literally the moment" of Drake's death (Wylie 2010a).

Graham explains in an interview in the *Guardian*:

> The place that Alex finds herself in is a plane between heaven and Earth. . . . When we [Graham and Pharoah] discussed the philosophy behind it we decided that, seeing as how the cosmos was infinite, everybody who dies can afford to go to some kind of purgatory plane that is relevant and significant to them. So we liked the idea that coppers with issues would go to a place designed for coppers. And a coppers' paradise surely has to be *The Sweeney*, or *The French Connection* if you're an American. That's the place where you've got all the freedoms and, therefore, all the chances to make all the big mistakes that could lead you to hell. But all the good decisions would lead you to heaven. (Wylie 2010b)

The *Ashes to Ashes* finale comes full circle. *Life on Mars* is set in Manchester and *Ashes to Ashes* in London, but for the finale they return to the Manchester cops' hangout, the Railway Arms pub, complete with the familiar barkeep, and we learn that this is the gateway to—somewhere, perhaps heaven. Drake is not the only cop caught in this purgatory: all her close associates are too, as is hinted at in season 3's fifth episode, when Carling and Woman Police Constable Shaz Granger (Montserrat Lombard) take the stage at a talent show and sing the folk song "Danny Boy," with the telling words "And I am dead, as dead I well may be." However, hints are sprinkled liberally throughout the show, so the surprise should not come out of left field, as Graham describes: "Ash [Pharoah] has always said that he never wanted the ending to be unguessable because that would be a cheat. And so all the afterlife stuff is kind of seeded in. And Gene throughout *Ashes* has cradled dying coppers. In series two he cradled two dying coppers. So those kind of things are all there to be taken as clues" (quoted in Wylie 2010a). Carling, Granger, and Skelton pass into the Railway Arms, a bright white light illuminating the street when the door opens, and it remains for Drake to step through the door next, as (we now know) Sam Tyler did a few years earlier.

One major question *Ashes to Ashes* asks is, If both Tyler and Drake are in comas, how can they both be hallucinating in this shared milieu? The finale, in addition to closing out Drake's personal story line, provides an all-encompassing answer to this looming question. The finale closes off the possibility of any future spin-offs because the answer—that this past world is a sort of purgatory for dead cops, with the characters ferried there by Gene Hunt—shuts down any further discourse in terms of television programming. Yet this answer opens up the text to endless possibilities, with the potential for endless spin-offs that we will never see: in the finale, yet another confused refugee from the future (he mentions something about his iPhone) enters Hunt's office. Hunt's work is not yet done and, indeed, may never be done.

The *Ashes to Ashes* finale is unique in television in that it provides an overarching ultimate answer to not one but two television programs as well as satisfying closure on the level of individual character arc and the season-long story arc. Unlike the finale of the US version of *Life on Mars* (2008–9), where the past is all a dream, the result of a faulty stasis-sleep device for futuristic travelers to Mars, there's no bait and switch: the happenings, even if not real per se, are meaningful, and the stakes (as the character of Keats, the devil, makes clear) are high. With its metaphysical finale, *Ashes to Ashes* closes out the *Life on Mars–Ashes to Ashes* milieu and changes the terms of engagement: both shows must now be viewed again, revisited with this new information in mind, because many of the cop characters, not just Tyler and Drake, must also be dead, and it's Hunt's job to guide them. For me, the most satisfying thing about the finale is the way it melds the two shows and recasts the stakes of both. In the end, the *Ashes to Ashes* finale indicates to us that the shows are not ultimately about Tyler and Drake. They are about Gene Hunt.

References

Graham, Matthew, and Ashley Pharoah, creators. 2008–10. *Ashes to Ashes*. Kudos Film and Television. Original broadcasts on BBC One.

Graham, Matthew, Ashley Pharoah, and Tony Jordan, creators. 2006–7. *Life on Mars*. Kudos Film and Television. Original broadcasts on BBC One.

Lund, Anthony. 2010. "*Ashes to Ashes*: The Series Finale Review." *News Blaze*, May 21. At http://newsblaze.com/entertainment/tv/ashes-to-ashes-series-finale -review-contains-spoilers_13877/.

Rawson-Jones, Ben. 2008. "Cult Spy: *Ashes to Ashes*: The Verdict." *Digital Spy*, Jan. 20. At http://www.digitalspy.com/tv/ashes-to-ashes/news/a85879/cult-spy -ashes-to-ashes-the-verdict/.

Wilde, Jon. 2007. "*Life on Mars*: The Perfect Finale." *Guardian*, Apr. 11. At https://www.theguardian.com/culture/tvandradioblog/2007/apr/11/lifeonmars theperfectfinal.

Wilkes, Neil. 2009. "*Ashes* Finale Will Explain *Life on Mars*." *Digital Spy*, Dec. 9. At http://www.digitalspy.com/tv/ashes-to-ashes/news/a190555/ashes-finale-will-explain-life-on-mars/.

Wollaston, Sam. 2010. "*Ashes to Ashes* Ends and Everything Becomes Less Clear." *Guardian*, May 21. At https://www.theguardian.com/tv-and-radio/2010/may/21/ashes-to-ashes-final-episode.

Wylie, Ian. 2008. "*Mars* to *Ashes*: The Writers Talk." *Life of Wylie*, Apr. 15. At https://lifeofwylie.com/2008/04/15/mars-to-ashes-the-writers-talk/.

———. 2010a. "*Ashes to Ashes*: The Answers." *Life of Wylie*, May 23. At https://lifeofwylie.com/2010/05/23/ashes-to-ashes-the-answers/.

———. 2010b. "*Ashes to Ashes*: Co-creator Matthew Graham Says Goodbye to Gene Hunt." *Guardian*, May 21. At https://www.theguardian.com/tv-and-radio/tvandradioblog/2010/may/21/ashes-to-ashes-final-episode.

Yan, Jack. 2010. "The Final[e] of *Ashes to Ashes*: A Cultural Phenomenon." *Lucire*, May 21. At http://lucire.com/insider/20100521/the-nal-of-ashes-to-ashes-a-cultural-phenomenon/.

3

Babylon 5

"Sleeping in Light"

ENSLEY F. GUFFEY

In television studies, the auteur theory of the creator/showrunner as the single, guiding vision behind a television series is slowly falling out of favor. With *Babylon 5* (1994–98), however, J. Michael Straczynski may be the exception that proves the rule, and the vision he realized was truly revolutionary. For Straczynski had plotted out the entire series, often in acute detail, before the first shot of the pilot episode was ever filmed and would go on to write 92 of the series' 110 episodes. Straczynski's idea was to translate the traditional five-act structure of a play or novel (exposition, rising action, climax, falling action, and denouement) into a five-season television narrative. Though television shows today regularly employ multiepisode or multiseason story arcs, in the late 1980s and early 1990s, when Straczynski was creating, pitching, and producing *Babylon 5*, American television shows were still largely episodic in structure, with stories that reverted to the status quo ante every week.

Planning a show that would tell a single story over the course of five years in a business that routinely canceled shows without notice was considered impossible. Nor was a narrative requiring viewer memory to stretch over five years thought to be either practical or possible. Added to these concerns was the fact that Straczynski planned to base the action of his show largely on an immobile space station rather than on a far-ranging starship, the model proven to be successful by the ongoing *Star Trek* franchise. Further, at the heart of the story was a kind of galactic United Nations that was almost as ineffective as the real thing and a recent history in which Earth and the human race as a whole had come to the brink of extinction by starting a war with the wrong people. Straczynski combined these impossibilities with a set of self-imposed criteria that only increased the obstacles in his way:

1. It [the show] would have to be good science fiction.
2. It would have to be good *television*, and rarely are SF [science fiction] shows both good SF *and* good TV; there're [*sic*] generally one or the other.
3. It would have to be an adult approach to SF, and attempt to do for television SF what *Hill Street Blues* did for cop shows.
4. It would have to be affordable, done on a reasonable budget.
5. It would have to look unlike anything ever seen before on TV, and present not just individual stories, but present those stories against a much broader canvas.

The result was *Babylon 5*. (Straczynski 1991)

Straczynski also took advantage of the still nascent Internet to connect with fans, beginning as early as 1991, when the show was still in preproduction. His regular postings in newsgroups and bulletin boards on USENET, GEnie, and CompuServe created an anticipatory buzz about the series well before the pilot aired in February 1993 and again before the first season began in January 1994. Straczynski continued to post throughout *Babylon 5*'s original run, and the series became the first television show to make Internet advertising and online interaction with fans an integral part of its ongoing promotional campaigns. In turn, Straczynski was one of the first creator/showrunners to regularly communicate and build a rapport with fans through the Internet, a practice he has continued throughout his career. Add to all of these factors the show's use of then state-of-the-art, computer-generated imagery, and *Babylon 5* takes its place as one of the most groundbreaking and important shows in television history.

Beyond the televisual, *Babylon 5* emerged during an era of tremendous transition in the United States. With the fall of the Soviet Union in 1991, the decades-long Cold War came to an end, and the United States found itself the only superpower left standing. Combined with the quick, efficient, and decisive victory in the Gulf War of 1990–91 and a booming economy, it seemed that the United States could do anything. Yet the decade that would see *Babylon 5* go into production would also see this early confidence challenged and checked by bursting economic bubbles, the rise of global terrorist movements, and the inability of the United States to prevent a new, wider-spread proliferation of nuclear weapons. Around world, it seemed that old choices were having new, often unforeseen consequences, while both individuals and nation-states were asking themselves who they were and what they wanted. American culture and the entertainment industry were also undergoing tremendous changes. The emergence of the Internet has already been mentioned, but television was also being transformed by the emergence of affordable, easy-to use VCR recorders and tapes, the acceleration of technologies to make televisions lighter and sharper, and the newly pervasive adoption of cable television nationwide. Taken all together, the possibilities and problems in the United States and the world were enormous, exciting, terrifying, and often befuddling.

In these troubled waters, Straczynski asked two fundamental questions: "Who are you?" and "What do you want?"

These questions comprise the core themes of *Babylon 5*. As the cast of characters repeatedly answer these questions for both themselves as individuals and for the larger communities to which they belong, *Babylon 5* uses their answers to examine the universal verities of choices, consequences, and responsibility on both the microscale and the macroscale. The central stories told in the series concern an eternally recurring war between two ancient races, the Vorlons and the Shadows, both of whom were old and powerful when Earth's dominant life forms were single-celled prokaryotes, and running in tandem with this galactic plotline is a more localized one, where the multisystem Earth Alliance (EA) degenerates into a neofascist police state and, eventually, outright civil war. As the series opens, the initial moves in the latest Shadow War have begun, with the ancient races using the younger ones, including humans, as their proxies.

At the center of both stories is John Sheridan (played by Bruce Boxleitner), and it is Sheridan's choices, their consequences, and the manner in which he takes responsibility for both that drive the last four seasons of the series. Sheridan is a mythoheroic leader, even to the point of dying and being reborn to continue the struggle against the forces of darkness, yet he remains throughout unapologetically human. In the series finale, "Sleeping in Light" (5.22), Sheridan's story is coming to a close.[1] Twenty years after the events depicted in the rest of *Babylon 5*, the ultimate consequence of what was perhaps the greatest of John Sheridan's choices comes due. "Sleeping in Light" is about endings, but it is also about beginnings. The tale of John Sheridan is ending, but he is survived by his wife, Delenn (Mira Furlan), a son (never seen), and a group of friends and comrades in arms who make up the rest of the series' main cast. The lives of these people and of all the people they will influence will continue after Sheridan is gone, and Straczynski uses this

---

1. All references to "Sleeping in Light" come from Straczynski [1998] 2004b.

sweetly melancholy episode to underline the fact that although one story may end, others continue, and new ones begin while the great story, the universal story, always goes on.

"Sleeping in Light" is also a deeply extradiegetic, metatextual work, for the finale is as much Straczynski talking to his collaborators, his audience, and perhaps especially his naysayers as it is an epilogue to the main narrative. As the episode opens, Sheridan has been plagued by dreams, which appear to the viewer as black-and-white flashbacks to scenes shown in season 4, where Sheridan's seemingly miraculous resurrection was revealed to have been a resuscitation by the ancient—indeed the very first—sentient being in the galaxy, Lorien (Wayne Alexander). Sheridan, on the very border between life and death, was given some of Lorien's life force, but his condition was so severe that even this powerful being could not fully restore Sheridan's natural life span. In choosing to return to the world and to life, Sheridan literally chose to live on borrowed time. He was given twenty years, and as "Sleeping in Light" opens, that time has passed.

Having chosen to live, however, and well knowing this day would come, Sheridan took responsibility for that choice and its consequences long ago, and the tolling of the bell finds him prepared. He summons his old friends, all of those who were with him throughout the events of *Babylon 5*, to his home for one final celebration and good-bye. The viewer, too, is invited to this gathering. As Straczynski reveals what has become of beloved characters in the intervening years and even some of what their futures hold, the viewer becomes progressively aware that he or she, too, is saying good-bye to them and to the show that many had lived with for five years and that others had obsessively caught up with on reruns or by circulating videotapes. This story is done, and Straczynski's preplotting allows him to elegantly tie up the loose ends, leave room for more stories in the same narrative universe, and put a true period to *Babylon 5*.

The explosive destruction of the space station *Babylon 5* itself—foreshadowed as far back as the season 1 episode "Signs and Portents" (1.13)—is revealed to be a great irony. Everything that Sheridan and his friends and allies have done has changed the space station from a thriving, exciting place at the very heart of things, home to 250,000 people of various species, to an almost deserted backwater that is rarely visited. The station is now slated for decommissioning and destruction lest it become a hazard to navigation. As Sheridan notes, he and the station remain connected to the very last. During Sheridan's visit in the finale, he meets up with Security Chief Zack Allen (Jeff Conaway), who says, "We did everything we said we were gonna do, and nobody can take that away from us, or this place." Straczynski admitted that he was speaking through Zack, talking directly about the act of telling the story itself and of having managed to do what so many people believed to be impossible (Straczynski 2004a). It is a shared moment between Straczynski, his characters, and the viewers, each aware from his or her own perspective of what has been accomplished, of a story told all the way to the end. After this last visit to the station, Sheridan pilots his one-man ship to the location of his great victory over both the Shadows and the Vorlons and is consumed in a burst of brilliant white light. The great hero passes "beyond the rim" to begin a new story. His mysterious death leaves him a legend, and his friends take up his legacy.

At the end of the fourth act of "Sleeping in Light," the surviving main characters visit the empty *Babylon 5* station one last time for the decommissioning ceremony. The last person seen aboard is a technician who pulls a massive breaker switch that turns out all of the interior lights and who is played by J. Michael Straczynski himself, turning out the lights on his show. To Christopher Franke's swelling score, the station is ripped apart by scuttling charges as warships from each of the races encountered during the series stands by as a guard of honor for the place where their galaxy was remade. It is perhaps the most complete and perfect ending possible. The station is no more, but what transpired there, the great story that the *place* allowed to be told, has grown too big for even "a self-contained world five miles long" and continues on in larger spaces. So, too, was *Babylon 5* the series a new beginning for American television, and though it ended, it did so deliberately and opened the way for a new kind of storytelling in an ever-expanding field.

References

Straczynski, J. Michael. 1991. "Well, Now That the Official Announcement. . . ." *JMSNews*, J. Michael Straczynski Message Archive, Nov. 20. At http://jms news.com/msg.aspx?id=1-7689&topic=Spiderman.

———. 2004a. "Commentary to 'Sleeping in Light.'" *Babylon 5: The Complete Fifth Season*. Burbank, CA: Warner Home Video. DVD.

———, dir. [1998] 2004b. "Sleeping in Light." *Babylon 5*, season 5, episode 22. Written by J. Michael Straczynski. Aired Nov. 25, 1998, TNT. On *Babylon 5: The Complete Fifth Season*. Burbank, CA: Warner Home Video. DVD.

4

Barney Miller

"Landmark"

DAVID SCOTT DIFFRIENT

The series finale of ABC's Emmy Award–winning workplace comedy *Barney Miller* (1975–82) bears a title that metaphorically connotes this pioneering program's historical significance. Spread out over a trio of half-hour episodes (airing over three consecutive weeks in May 1982), "Landmark" was indeed a televisual milestone that reflected in miniature the entire series' groundbreaking use of place and space as well as its social relevance as a politically sophisticated TV show about crime in New York City.[1] Set entirely inside the Greenwich Village offices of the fictional Twelfth Precinct, this extended finale—like the 167 episodes preceding it—focuses on a close-knit group of ethnically diverse characters: fellow detectives whose lives outside the walls of the drab squad room are verbally referenced but never shown.[2] Joining Captain Barney Miller (Hal Linden) inside this cramped and cluttered precinct station is a middle-aged foursome—Detective Stanley Thaddeus "Wojo" Wojciehowicz (Max Gail), Sergeant Ron Nathan Harris (Ron Glass), Detective Arthur Dietrich (Steve Landesberg), and Officer Carl Levitt (Ron Carey)—whose commitment to the profession of law enforcement is rivaled only by their loyalty to the titular protagonist, a sensitive, levelheaded leader of men who learns of the precinct building's status as a historical landmark in the opening minutes of this finale.

---

1. All references to "Landmark, Parts 1, 2, and 3" come from Arnold [1982] 2015a, [1982] 2015b and Sheehan [1982] 2015.

2. According to Vincent Brook, *Barney Miller* is "the definitive example of the platoon approach" to multiethnic casting and representation: "one Black, one Asian, one Puerto Rican, one Pole, one Jew" (2003, 61).

Because city officials are willing to sell the building to the highest bidder, the detectives and their captain are forced to reckon with imminent reassignment and relocation. Thus, like the viewer, they are asked to go their separate ways and leave behind an almost "hallowed" place where, according to a spokeswoman from the State Division for Historic Preservation, Theodore Roosevelt (former head of New York's Board of Police Commissioners) once hung his hat and gun decades earlier (between 1895 and 1897). Figuratively "haunted" by that historical figure, the station also bears the ghostly imprint of those who are present in spirit if not in flesh: dead or departed detectives, such as Sergeant Nick Yemana (Jack Soo), Sergeant Philip K. Fish (Abe Vigoda), Sergeant Miguel "Chano" Amanguale (Gregory Sierra), and Detective Janice Wentworth (Linda Lavin), who through the use of archival clips from past episodes appear fleetingly in the final scene as Barney's nostalgic recollections of happier times.

Before returning to those last moments of "Landmark," it will be helpful to first foreground *Barney Miller*'s unique textual features as an unconventional "cop comedy"—one that consistently ranked among the most-watched television programs of the late 1970s and early 1980s—and as a cultural distillation of the social milieu in which it was produced and initially broadcast. Because several scenes in the finale in 1982 harken back to previous episodes while alluding to contemporaneous events in the nation's history, I use "Landmark" in a synecdochal fashion here—that is, as a metarepresentation of the entire series' thematic preoccupations and aesthetic characteristics and as a lens onto the larger landscape of law enforcement during that time period. Significantly, *Barney Miller*'s eight-season network run coincided with a widely reported fiscal crisis that drastically decreased the number of sworn officers in the New York Police Department (NYPD). As Robert J. Kane and Michael D. White point out in their recent publication *Jammed Up* (2013), more than 11,000 police officers in the city's five boroughs were laid off during the late 1970s, a trend that was reversed at the beginning of the next decade when "the department hired 12,000 new and formerly employed police officers" (11–12). Ironically, that hiring spree brought an attendant rise in organizational misconduct (e.g., drug use, abuse of power, selective enforcement, etc.) within the increasingly scandal-ridden NYPD. According to Kane and White, the problem of police misconduct played out against a backdrop of "increasing crime and disorder in New York City" and was exacerbated by the minimal screening procedures and incomplete background checks being used to reverse the attrition rates of the previous decade (2013, 61). Although series creators Danny Arnold and Theodore J.

Flicker made few overt attempts to address these factors in *Barney Miller*,[3] the show's dingy, ramshackle setting—the drab olives, mustards, and grays of the station interior—hints at the austerity measures and personnel cutbacks that were being implemented by city officials during its first five seasons.

In the words of Jack Norrell (Al Ruscio), the wealthy businessman who ultimately buys the Twelfth Precinct building, it looks like "a pile of junk." Though it is aesthetically offensive in its current state, Norrell plans to restore the station to its former glory—albeit as a converted dentist office—and seeks to take advantage of the 25 percent tax credit that he will receive for doing so. This new owner of the precinct building clearly represents the moneyed class, a member of New York's socioeconomic elite who puts his own self-interests before the needs of the local community. As a counterimage to Norell, Howard Spangler (Philip Sterling), another businessman, is brought in to the station by Wojo for having attacked some cleaning people outside his apartment. Spangler, who had been kidnapped three years earlier by a rebel group of political agitators while he was doing business in South America, simply snapped upon hearing the cleaning crew speak to one another in Spanish. This is one of many instances in *Barney Miller* when the "outside world"—the global sphere of international conflicts, foreign-relations crises, and even terrorism—filters into the interior space of the station. Other examples of this occur in the season 7 episode "Agent Orange," in which former marine Wojo investigates the effects that herbicidal warfare might have had on another Vietnam War veteran, and in the season 8 opener, "Paternity," in which Detective Dietrich and Captain Miller debate the effectiveness of the Polish Solidarity movement. According to Dietrich, this act of national civil disobedience and resistance is playing right into the hands of the Russians, but Barney believes that Poland's trade union has successfully gained "quite a few concessions from the government: greater freedom of speech, assembly, access to the media, religion" (Arnold [1981]

---

3. On occasion, *Barney Miller* made reference to the NYPD layoffs and cutbacks of the mid-1970s. For example, the season 2 episode "The Social Worker" features a scene in which Barney tells his wife, Liz, that "everybody's having a tough time getting a job these days" (Pitlik [1975] 2008). Two years later, in the season 4 episode "Quo Vadis?" Liz tells her husband, "It's getting worse and worse. There are fewer and fewer of you out there. And there are more and more of them [criminals]." Anticipating the couple's eventual separation, she goes on to muse, "I really wonder sometimes what it would be like to live somewhere else . . . such as Long Island, Connecticut, Sweden. . . . It's very law-abiding there this time of year" (March [1978] 2014).

2015c). Few sitcoms, then or today, engage such serious topics and certainly not in such a thoughtful way.

Once Spangler is brought into the precinct, he is deposited in "the cage," a small holding cell located next to the iconic chalkboard where the detectives sign in for their daily shifts. Finding himself yet again behind bars, Spangler rails against the "imperialist pigs who sit on the backs of the workers," an indication that this former CEO of a multinational company became politically conscious and self-critical during his years as a hostage. His presence in this episode casts in relief the comparatively narrower mindset of Norell, the other representative of the corporate world, who lets greed—the desire for material accrual—obscure his understanding of the station's *nonmonetary* worth to the citizens of New York, a city that is "decaying and rotting away," according to Noel Cadey (another character played by Philip Sterling) in the season 4 episode "The Inauguration."[4] That dichotomy within "Landmark" is a structuring principle of the entire series, which pivots on scenes in which class antagonisms and disparities between the rich and the poor are the basis for its spatially contained yet far-reaching, observational humor. Tellingly, Spangler resists leaving the holding cell when he is released on bail, rejecting the idea of returning to his own office, which he describes as a "tiny little cubicle with no window and no air." Rather than crawl back "to the big bosses who feed off the flesh of the peasants," he wishes to remain where he is. His desire to stay put is later echoed by the detectives' own hesitancy in leaving their home away from home, the claustrophobic precinct station that on more than one occasion has been compared to a cagelike prison.

Fans of *Barney Miller* might recognize the two actors playing these wealthy characters as intratextual linkages to previous episodes and different roles. Before assuming the role of the capitalist turned anticapitalist Spangler in "Landlord," Sterling had appeared as Mr. Buckholtz in the season 2 episode "Discovery," Noel Cadey in the season 4 episode "Inauguration," Mitchell Warner in the season 5 episode "The Spy," Judge Philip Paul Gibson in the season 6 episode "The Judge," and Frank Rilling, an agent working for the Federal Bureau of Investigation, in the season 8 episode

4. Cadey's description of New York as a city that is "decaying and rotting away" is reminiscent of a comment from another aggrieved character in the season 3 episode "Strike, Part 1": "You know the city's dying out there, there's nothing you guys can do about it. They're killing each other off, one by one, and it's going to be the end." He then puts an anti-NYPD spin on that comment, stating, "The public hates cops. I know. I hate cops, I'm part of the public" (Morris [1977] 2009).

"Games." Similarly, Ruscio had appeared as the foul-smelling, disheveled-looking apartment manager Mr. Seldiz in the season 4 episode "Atomic Bomb" and as the cash-strapped Mr. Becker in the season 5 episode "The Counterfeiter." In the latter episode, Becker shows up at the station to turn in $36 of counterfeit money but is dismayed to find out that he will not be reimbursed for his efforts as a good citizen. Before exiting, he remarks, "You know, they never tell you about these little things in civics class. All they ever tell you is you should vote in every election and that everybody is entitled to a little justice." Quoting the famous lawyer Clarence Darrow, Harris responds, "There is no justice in or out of court" (Gail [1979] 2014). This is just one of the many social critiques embedded in this satirical police procedural, which differs considerably from other TV cop shows of the 1970s, such as *McCloud* (1970–77), *Streets of San Francisco* (1972–77), *Kojak* (1973–78), *Baretta* (1975–78), and *Starsky & Hutch* (1975–79), in terms of its content and its form.

Like the classic anthology series *Police Story* (1973–79) and the more critically acclaimed drama *Hill Street Blues* (1981–87) after it, *Barney Miller* has been celebrated for its realistic portrayal of actual police work, which is often mundane and unglamorous, lacking the "action" associated with the programs mentioned earlier.[5] In their study of the effects that such TV series had on both the general viewing public and police officers themselves, Rita J. Simon and Fred Fejes explain that "accurate" portrayals are those that present "the complexities of police work as well as the boredom, the noncriminal aspects of their job" (1987, 64). Despite its grounding in the quotidian aspects of the daily police grind, however, *Barney Miller*'s frequent recasting of character actors such as Al Ruscio and Philip Sterling in different supporting roles or minor parts sometimes breaks the "spell" or "illusion" of realism, reflexively reminding audiences of the text's fictionality. Indeed, the setting of this workplace comedy is little more than a soundstage littered with the professional "props" of police work (e.g., paperwork spread atop debris-filled desks, filing cabinets stuffed with criminal records, etc.), in addition to call-back objects such as Wojo's autographed baseball (a relic of the World Series of 1936 that he uses as a paperweight) that trigger memories of past episodes. And yet, despite the series' theatrical artifice, which is further accentuated by the sound of spectatorial laughter (initially

---

5. In the words of Dan Savage, the jobs of the detectives on *Barney Miller* are "tedious . . . all paperwork and bad coffee, no car chases, no shoot-outs" (2013, 93).

provided by an in-studio audience but in later seasons manufactured by way of a pre-recorded laugh track), many police officers of the 1970s and 1980s believed *Barney Miller* to be the most realistic televisual treatment of their profession (Pollock 2011, 4).

The show's verisimilitude can be attributed in part to the unflinching way in which taboo or risqué subjects are broached during the detectives' sometimes brutally honest conversations. Plotlines and passages of dialogue from particular episodes touch on everything from suicide (e.g., "Smog Alert," "Fire '77") to the illegal drug trade (e.g., "Ramon," "You Dirty Rat," "Hash," "Dorsey," "Altercation"), the plight of young women being exploited in prostitution rings (e.g., "The Courtesans," "Massage Parlor," "Kidnapping," "Call Girl," "Games"), and the often dehumanizing treatment of individuals with mental health problems (e.g., "Thanksgiving Story," "Hunger Strike"). Other "mature" subjects—ranging from political corruption (e.g., "Graft" and "Doomsday") and unionization/worker unrest (e.g., "Strike, Part 1" and "Strike, Part 2") to marital separation/divorce (e.g., "Toys") and domestic abuse and sexual molestation (e.g., "Rape," "The Dentist")—became part of the national prime-time conversation of American audiences during the run of this program, which furthermore offered up one of the first "coming out" story arcs in the medium's history: that of Officer Zitelli (Dino Natali), a sympathetic administrative assistant at Police Headquarters who faces bigotry, harassment, and homophobic slurs (e.g., "fairy," "fruit," "faggot") inside and outside the precinct station.

Although Zitelli does not appear in "Landmark," two other gay characters—Marty Morrison (Jack DeLeon) and Darryl Driscoll (Ray Stewart)—are among the many friends of the station who show up near the end. Joining the same-sex couple are the gruff jewelry store owner Bruno Bender (Stanley Brock) and his wife, Naomi (Mari Gorman), both of whom had appeared in more than half a dozen episodes prior to this one. Barney is genuinely touched to see the local entrepreneur and many others, including petty thieves Leon Roth (Ralph Manza) and Arthur Duncan (J. J. Barry) as well as members of the neighborhood's homeless community, Sam Belinkoff (Walter Janowitz) and Ray Brewer (John Dullaghan), who turn up to wish him well in his future endeavors as newly promoted deputy inspector. In a manner that anticipates the inclusion of several "call-back guests" (or, rather, courtroom character witnesses) in the series finale of NBC's *Seinfeld* (1989–98), this penultimate scene in *Barney Miller* uses actor cameos as conduits to the past, oft-recycled reminders of how far the series had come since its first season, when many of these performers first appeared.

One sign of its growth as a politically progressive series set in a demographically mixed Greenwich Village was creator Danny Arnold's willingness to work with the National Gay Task Force, a New York–based organization that called for more fully realized and *realistic* lesbian, gay, bisexual, and transgender characters on television. Throughout the sixth, seventh, and eighth seasons of *Barney Miller*, Arnold and the show's other writers sought to tone down the stereotypically flamboyant behavior of Marty and Darryl, residents of the once bohemian, now gentrified "Village" who were initially portrayed as mincing, limp-wristed lispers but then became much less stereotyped as the series neared its conclusion. In a sense, the couple's appearance in "Landmark" suggests that these men have been "promoted," brought into (and embraced by) the ranks of a more tolerant society, in much the same way that the diminutive brown-nosing Officer Levitt is finally made sergeant before he and the other detectives part company in the episode's closing minutes. The finale's inclusion of these minor characters is a reminder that the creators of *Barney Miller* attempted to counter ethnic, racial, and sexual stereotypes with three-dimensional representations. It was an admirable effort that extended to the show's main cast of beleaguered male protagonists, in particular Ron Harris, a fastidiously attired, snobby African American detective who pursues a publishing career as a novelist, both on and off the clock, and yet has experienced discrimination and has even been shot at by police officers who mistake him for a criminal (in the season 5 episode "The Harris Incident"). But that progressive attitude toward the main characters did not always accommodate feminists' concerns about the latent misogyny of a program that frequently reduced women to the hookers/housewives binary.

At one point during the finale, Captain Miller tries to comfort his men by telling them, "It's just a building! And a damn lousy one at that!" He reminds them that they "sweat like pigs in the summertime [and] freeze [their] tails off in the winter." "I've got a bathroom that's an embarrassment. The roof leaks. You really want my opinion?" Before waiting for a response, he states, "We should have been out of here years ago!" The idea that the Twelfth Precinct might one day be shut down was first introduced in "Protection," an episode in the series' second season (originally broadcast in December 1975) that reflects some of the setbacks faced by the NYPD during its downsizing period. Not until *Barney Miller*'s series finale, however, does the threat of the station's closing become real. Nevertheless, a comment made by a neighborhood store owner in that earlier episode both anticipates and neatly sums ups many fans' feelings about this low-key yet highly praised TV comedy. "You will be missed," the man tells the detectives, words that continue to reverberate more than thirty-five years after the lights of this landmark building—and landmark television program—were turned off.

References

Arnold, Danny, dir. [1982] 2015a. "Landmark, Part 2." *Barney Miller*, season 8, episode 21. Written by Frank Dungan and Jeff Stein. Aired May 13, 1982, ABC. On *Barney Miller: The Final Season*. Los Angeles: Shout! Factory, 2015. DVD.

————, dir. [1982] 2015b. "Landmark, Part 3." *Barney Miller*, season 8, episode 22. Written by Frank Dungan, Jeff Stein, and Tony Sheehan. Aired May 20, 1982, ABC. On *Barney Miller: The Final Season*. Los Angeles: Shout! Factory, 2015. DVD.

————, dir. [1981] 2015c. "Paternity." *Barney Miller*, season 8, episode 1. Written by Nat Mauldin and Danny Arnold. Aired Oct. 29, 1981, ABC. On *Barney Miller: The Final Season*. Los Angeles: Shout! Factory. DVD.

Brook, Vincent. 2003. *Something Ain't Kosher Here: The Rise of the "Jewish" Sitcom*. New Brunswick, NJ: Rutgers Univ. Press.

Gail, Max, dir. [1979] 2014. "The Counterfeiter." *Barney Miller*, season 5, episode 19. Written by Frank Dungan and Jeff Stein. Aired Feb. 8, 1979, ABC. On *Barney Miller: The Complete Fifth Season*. Los Angeles: Shout! Factory. DVD.

Kane, Robert J., and Michael D. White. 2013. *Jammed Up: Bad Cops, Police Misconduct, and the New York City Police Department*. New York: New York Univ. Press.

March, Alex, dir. [1978] 2014. "Quo Vadis?" *Barney Miller*, season 4, episode 19. Written by Tony Sheehan, Douglas Wyman, and Tony Sheehan. Aired Mar. 2, 1978, ABC. On *Barney Miller: The Complete Fourth Season*. Los Angeles: Shout! Factory. DVD.

Morris, Jeremiah, dir. [1977] 2009. "Strike, Part 1." *Barney Miller*, season 3, episode 21. Written by Reinhold Weege, Larry Balmagia, and Dennis Koenig. Aired Mar. 24, 1977, ABC. On *Barney Miller: The Complete Third Season*. Culver City, CA: Sony Pictures Home Entertainment. DVD.

Pitlik, Noam, dir. [1975] 2008. "The Social Worker." *Barney Miller*, season 2, episode 2. Written by Danny Arnold, Chris Hayward, and Arne Sultan. Aired Sept. 18, 1975, ABC. On *Barney Miller: The Complete Second Season*. Culver City, CA: Sony Pictures Home Entertainment. DVD.

Pollock, Joycelyn M. 2011. *Crime and Justice in America: An Introduction to Criminal Justice*. London: Routledge.

Savage, Dan. 2013. *American Savage: Insights, Slights, and Fights on Faith, Sex, Love, and Politics*. New York: Plume.

Sheehan, Tony, dir. [1982] 2015. "Landmark, Part 1." *Barney Miller*, season 8, episode 20. Written by Tony Sheehan. Aired May 6, 1982, ABC. On *Barney Miller: The Final Season*. Los Angeles: Shout! Factory. DVD.

Simon, Rita J., and Fred Fejes. 1987. "Real Police on Television Supercops." In *Television in Society*, edited by Arthur Asa Berger, 63–69. New Brunswick, NJ: Transaction.

5

Battlestar Galactica

"Daybreak"

MARTHA P. NOCHIMSON

A television series makes an implicit contract with an audience that governs whatever may happen afterward. Betraying that seminal understanding with viewers is the one truly unforgivable sin of serial television. The time that serial creators are most likely to lose control is when they are bringing the show to a close. Putting a period on a series, especially one that has been on-air for many years, can bring enough pressure to lead a writer to "jump the shark" and make a profound and basic creative misjudgment.[1]

David Chase, who as the benchmark creator and writer in American television today is a credible authority on serialization, defines "shark jumping" in a way that cuts to the heart of the matter. A show that has jumped the shark has gone where it cannot and should not go (personal conversation, Aug. 5, 2010). This is a simple formulation, and almost certainly all series television writers would agree. Unfortunately, there are no recipes or even established standards for determining "cannot" and "should not"; it is completely a matter of the empowered hand on the helm and a keen sense of a show's basic identity. Break concentration, and the series will jump.

1. The phrase "jumping the shark" originally comes from the September 20, 1977, episode of *Happy Days* (1974–84), when the Fonz (Henry Winkler) goes waterskiing and literally jumps over a shark. As a catch-phrase for television, it typically signals the demise of a show, although *Happy Days* itself stayed on for seven more years after Fonzie's infamous jump. *Wikipedia* credits Sean Connolly, roommate of radio personality Jon Hein at the University of Michigan, for coining the phrase in 1985 when the two "were talking about favorite television shows that had gone downhill" ("Jumping the Shark" 2016).

This was the lamentable case with the finale of *Battlestar Galactica* (2004–9).[2] What happened? The problem with the finale wasn't a matter of an alien intervention (read: network interference). Ronald D. Moore, the show's creator, was still in charge as his series wound down to its final season; nevertheless, he drove his show where it could not and should not go with an abandon that cries out for analysis. The series began with a unique energy and innovative intelligence that make it all the more regrettable that Moore's extreme carelessness in his fourth—and final—season "frakked up."

The *Battlestar Galactica* (*BSG*) under discussion here is an adaptation of an earlier television series of the same name (1978–79) created by Glen Larson, so the contract with the audience was that the version beginning in 2004 would be a new *BSG*. At first, Moore, along with his key collaborator, David Eick, delivered with interest on the deal. The original series was a mind-numbing cliché. In telling of the hostilities between the last few thousand human beings left in the universe and some robot enemies, the Cylons, who came from out of nowhere to exterminate us, it reduced women and people of color to secondary status, at best, and defined masculinity as the capacity to wage war. There was never any other point of view but that of the (white) heroes and never any alternative but violent combat. Old *BSG* imagined a postapocalyptic world tied to every snoozable pop-culture prejudice. New *BSG* made a much more exciting use of the story premise.

New *BSG* honed in on the obvious fact that when the attacking Cylons nuked the known human-governed planets, they violently cut the human race off from all its old traditions. The episodes of new *BSG* were designed to explore how, under these circumstances, people would carry on. In their desire for stability, would they cling more tightly to old prejudices and venerable repressive conventions? Or would they try new ways of organizing society? To ramp up the conflicts that emerged around this new theme, Moore and Eick also created a new relationship between the Cylons and the remnants of the human race.

New *BSG* retained the basic premise of Cylon/human enmity but, with a stroke of creative ingenuity, repositioned the Cylons as creations of the human community, à la *Frankenstein*.[3] (The first frame of the pilot episode

---

2. All references to episodes of *Battlestar Galactica*, including the final episode, come from *Battlestar Galactica* 2005a, 2005b, 2006, 2008, 2009a, 2009b.

3. Despite the obvious parallels, there is (astonishingly) no discussion of Mary Shelley's novel of 1818 in the commentary tracks and podcasts that accompany the DVD box sets of *Battlestar Galactica*.

began, in fact, with the statement, "The Cylons were created by Man.") With this new genesis for the Cylons, the writers made a contract with the audience that in a postapocalyptic world humanity would ponder its responsibility for the problems it faced. Commander William Adama (Edward James Olmos), the military leader in charge of the survival of humanity in new *BSG*, openly questioned the claims of our species in the human/Cylon battle on the basis of our clear failure to own up to our obligations to the new kind of being we had invented.

The Cylons, like Victor Frankenstein's creature, were now the abused children of humanity, taking their revenge for a long history of cruel treatment. Some Cylons remained the metallic robots of the original *BSG*, but the primary Cylons in the story were given humanoid faces and bodies as well as humanlike passions and intellect. If they could feel, desire, and think, was there any rationale to their subordinate status within human culture? Stimulating? Very. In the face-off between twelve models of humanoid Cylons (aided by their metallic, robotlike sidekicks) and the noticeably flawed and self-doubting humans, new *BSG* put an end to the absurdly idealized "frat boy" boosters of the original. As part of the delicious questioning of human superiority, the show made it clear that under pressure from the Cylon attack, the upper class abandoned thousands of their fellow humans for their own convenience as they made plans for their survival.

For three years, the series paid respect to the understanding it had established with its viewers that we could count on it for piercing moral and ethical questions. But plot turns at the end of the third season began a painful process of breaking the contract and going where *BSG* could not and should not go.

The worst of these turns was the belated introduction at the end of season 3 of the mystery of five Cylon models called the Final Five. From first to last, the search for their identities and the boring, belated insertion of their backstories into the final episodes of this season, too late in the day for such large-chunk exposition, took over the show as a futile digression, a case of bad narrative driving out good. The Final Five were carelessly defined and often contradicted *BSG*'s established history. Where we had been told that "the Cylons were created by Man," we were now to understand that the Final Five had created the humanoid Cylons two thousand years earlier, and there was no attempt to reconcile the two versions. Moreover, while sometimes the Final Five were Cylons with more authority than any of the other models, at other times all humanoid Cylons were equals—whatever the plot of the particular episode called for. Some of the Final Five were characters we already knew, who were unbelievable in their new roles; some weren't and were boring as they took over big portions of the episodes. On the podcast for "Crossroads II," the finale of season 3, Moore's explanation of why certain characters turned out to be part of the Final Five (Moore 2008b) may seem compelling to some. Others will find it a rationalization with barely a whisper of validity. Most will wonder about this revisionist history.

In the end, those problems paled beside the mistake of choosing the surprises associated with these characters as the basis of the dramatic reversals that would determine the closure of the show. Surprise, as Alfred Hitchcock knew well, is the most fragile and temporary way to heighten the interest of a narrative. The surprise identities of the Final Five were no exception. Once the big reveal was over, the entire story line fell flat and never recovered. At least as bad was that the Final Five broke the original contract with the viewers that the show would investigate human responsibility. The Cylons turned out to be the children of the Final Five, not the children of humanity; but then the Cylons *were* sometimes still referred to as the progeny of mankind. The paradoxes of human/Cylon relationships were replaced by this inconsistency and by redundant recriminations and counterrecriminations about Cylon-on-Cylon behavior. For numerous flimsy reasons, the bickering Cylons began to make decisions that gave humans the undisputed upper hand and restored the clear superiority of humanity characteristic of original *BSG*, which new *BSG* had once fascinatingly questioned.

At the same time that the problems and paradoxes of the human/Cylon controversy were thrown out the airlock, the voices of the women and other dissidents who had made the show so compelling were silenced. By the final episode, the once vibrant human women were dead, leaving no foregrounded female characters but the female Cylons, now cut down to size as subordinate to a newly male-dominated human culture. The death of every human woman who had been featured in any capacity in any episode was, although apparently the writers did not intend this, a cruel return to the old cultural lesson for women that ambition equals death. And not just one kind of ambition. The contingent of deceased females covered a wide range of achieving women, including the pious official priestess of Kobol, Elosha (Lorena Gale); fighter pilot Captain Louanne "Kat" Katraine (Lucianna Karo), second only to Starbuck (Katee Sackhoff) for moxie; as well as the cold, callous lesbian Admiral Helena Cain (Michelle Forbes). There is also the completely unmotivated suicide of the innovative Anastasia Dualla (Kayndyse McClure), who runs rings around Adama in the season 2 episode "Home, Part I," only to be reduced, in the end, to the "tragic mulatta," the beautiful mixed-race black woman who epitomizes the doom of "her kind." And, for its big closing act, the show ostentatiously killed the two most important (and accomplished) human women on the show, Laura Roslin (Mary McDonnell) and Starbuck.

The valiant Starbuck is expunged from the show, in any previously recognizable form, before the last season—in fact, near the end of season 3 in an episode called "Maelstrom." Her death in that show put the character on a slippery slope and served as a preview of Moore's careless approach to narrative in general in season 4. For all her smarts and courage, we are made to understand, Starbuck is fatally neurotic because of a terrible relationship with a sadistic mother and, for that reason, courts her own destruction by stupidly flying her plane into the gravitational force field of a planet while chasing a phantom enemy spaceship and in this way blowing herself up. Demonization of the mother–daughter relationship is an old sexist cliché that frequently involves the destruction of the daughter, as is the case in "Maelstrom." The fact that Starbuck reappeared in the last episode of season 3, "Crossroads, Part 2"—without explanation of how this was possible—made matters even worse. Theoretically an undead being in the final season who was neither human nor Cylon, perhaps an angel—and one felt that Moore had no idea what she was, either—Starbuck was dead as far as her original identity was concerned, purged of her hallmark vibrant energy of human femininity. Once gutted, her character lost definition in the fourth season, and in "Daybreak, Part 3," the final series episode, she literally became nothing. After the human remnant found a planet to colonize, we last see Starbuck in a breezy meadow in midconversation with Lee Adama, a farewell moment that perversely works against Starbuck's power and the chemistry between these two actors: no matter what Starbuck and Lee ever said to each other, they always seemed to be saying, "I love you." Yet in Starbuck's ultimate moments, this feisty gal just faded away. When the camera leaves her momentarily for Lee's face, he turns to gaze on her, only to find her gone. Some may have found this moment poignant; others will have found it an insult to a dynamic girl.

The destruction of Laura Roslin was a more complex betrayal of the original premises of the series. Since Roslin was diagnosed in the pilot with incurable cancer that had gone beyond the point of treatment because she hadn't had mammograms, her death in the last episode might be said to be narratively justified—and a real public service that drove home the need for regular breast checkups. And yet Roslin's cancer had already been declared in remission when the plot made it expedient; at that time, a transfusion of Cylon blood cured her illness. Somehow she never got another transfusion.

Moreover, as she descended toward death, Roslin was made to explicitly disavow all that she had achieved after the holocaust—if only she had spent more time living!—a knife in the heart of *BSG*'s initial promise to give us a more enlightened picture of women.

In another repudiation of the contract, all validity was removed from social dissent when Tom Zarek (Richard Hatch) and Felix Gaeta (Allesandro Juliani), a crew member once loyal to Adama, mutiny and reveal their social ideals to be nothing but self-delusion. What happened to the questioning in the first three years of the executive decisions that were made by the upper class at the expense of thousands of people who were left to die in order allow the leadership to continue making its plans for the future?

In the final season, when Bill Adama learns that his best friend, Saul Tigh, is "one of them," in a fit of drunken self-loathing he asks the question, "What was it all for?" Alas, it is a question all too pertinent to the new *BSG* as a whole.

Like pearls that have fallen off the ruptured string of a necklace, a few inventive and fascinating moments continued to pop up in the last season. Felix Gaeta's self-delusions about his part in the mutiny before his execution are a brilliant study in hysterical denial. A charming and warmly erotic scene between Bill Adama and a Laura Roslin who is bald from belated cancer treatments not only offers a rare television affirmation of the continuing sexuality of men and women well into middle age but is also a precedent-setting rejection of worn-out clichés about women and illness. But for the most part, the final episodes, "Daybreak 1, 2 and 3," were larded with collages of outrageously revisionist backstory.[4] Podcasts about the final episodes reveal that the writers never looked again at the initial episodes while they were trying to write a series finale (Moore, Eick, and Rymer 2009), and their strange lack of understanding that they needed to have the facts of the miniseries pilot in mind as they ended the show led them to work at cross purposes to their own creation.

---

4. One of the most glaring revisionist gaffes as *BSG* ends occurs when in a flashback Bill Adama is shown being given a lie detector test for his promotion. One of the questions is, "Are you a Cylon?" Disgusted by the entire procedure, Adama tears off the electrodes and leaves, an act that ultimately saves him from the Cylon holocaust. What is most significant about the question for our purposes, however, is that Moore had obviously forgotten that at that point no humans knew that there were Cylons who were indistinguishable in appearance from human beings. There would have been no way an interrogator could have asked that question.

In "Daybreak 3," *Galactica* and all the ships in its entourage land on an Earth-like planet, and the passengers and crew disembark into the sunlit grass, suddenly free of all the tensions associated with the human condition. Whereas everyone had a point of view when the series began, no one has one when it ends. The tensions between the Final Five and the other Cylons disappear as the humanoid Cylons agree to stay (happily) with the humans, and the metallic Centurian Cylons are given some of the spaceships as parting gifts as they go off (happily) on their own. A Cylon/human couple walks off into the sunrise with their child toward a future of domesticity that saves the world: their child, half human, half Cylon, becomes the mother of the future human race. The remaining pesky technology is sent into the sun of that planetary system on the basis of some vague consensus that the remaining humans don't want any more advanced engineering. "Our brains have outraced our hearts" is the lesson, and apparently this means that the wiser, surviving humans will become "happy farmers." We all know how farming unifies people and makes everyone kind to animals as well. To add insult to injury, this clichéd agricultural fix is tinged by the "white man's burden" as the once idealistic Lee Adama fails to see the problem in his idea that the human newcomers will peacefully integrate their culture with that of the native peoples on this newly discovered planet by giving them language. Are we to suppose that human brains won't start racing again as our heroes civilize "primitive" peoples?

The cherry on top of this saccharine-coated racism is that Gaius Baltar (James Callis), guilty several times over of genocide, is "revirginized" as he decides to stop being humanity's last remaining brilliant scientist and go back to his peasant roots—which he has spent a lifetime denying—taking Model 6 (Tricia Helfer), also guilty of the same atrocities, with him. This purification by vegetable is quite chilling in its full implications. On the final episode commentary track, with no thought to the fact that they are talking about two mass murderers, Moore, Eick, and key director Michael Rymer congratulate themselves for effectively managing an affectionate ending for Baltar and 6 (Moore, Eick, and Rymer 2009), which seems to them an achievement in complexity, and some may think it is. But others may be appalled.

American television pioneered the series format, which at its best complicates the previous week's solutions and reconsiders everything from multiple perspectives. This, if one believes their podcasts, is what Moore and Eick wanted. At its worst, the American television series achieves bogus closure by going where it cannot and should not when it hauls out an oversimplifying deus ex machina or becomes incoherent when each new episode develops amnesia about what is already in place. Moore and Eick apparently quite blindly ended up doing both in *Battlestar Galactica*.

In their podcasts for the final season, Moore and Eick speak proudly of having gone with their instincts when they designed the finale (Moore, Eick, and Rymer 2009).[5] Following inspiration is a valid modus operandi in the proper hands—it is the strategy of the great David Lynch—but Moore and Eick demonstrated in the fourth season of *Battlestar Galactica* that they could not sustain the enormous powers of concentration such a method requires, nor did they have the genius that produces a coherence that comes from a source deep within the imagination. Instinct had worked for them as long as they let it bounce off the foundational exposition they had established. Although every word spoken by Moore and Eick testifies to their good intentions, in the end they blindly threw a hodgepodge of inventions at the screen thinking they were at their creative peak. If we are to believe their commentaries, they never knew that they were breeching the extraordinary contract with which they had initiated *Battlestar Galactica*.

References

Battlestar Galactica: Season One. 2005a. Based on *Battlestar Galactica* by Glen A. Larson. Universal City, CA: Universal Studios. DVD.

Battlestar Galactica: Season 2.0. 2005b. Based on *Battlestar Galactica* by Glen A. Larson. Universal City, CA: Universal Studios. DVD.

Battlestar Galactica: Season 2.5. 2006. Based on *Battlestar Galactica* by Glen A. Larson. Universal City, CA: Universal Studios. DVD.

Battlestar Galactica: Season Three. 2008. Based on *Battlestar Galactica* by Glen A. Larson. Universal City, CA: Universal Studios. DVD.

Battlestar Galactica: Season 4.0. 2009a. Including *Razor*. Based on *Battlestar Galactica* by Glen A. Larson. Universal City, CA: Universal Studios. DVD.

Battlestar Galactica: Season 4.5. 2009b. Based on *Battlestar Galactica* by Glen A. Larson. Universal City, CA: Universal Studios. DVD.

5. Calling the finale a "work of art" in their podcast, Moore, Eick, and Rymer claim that the flashbacks in the finale were an invention that honored the theme of cyclical history in the show and that the purpose of these characters' appearance in the finale was to tell us, after four years of episodes, who these *Galactica* people "really are" (Moore, Eick, and Rymer 2009). Some viewers may wonder how experienced television writers could make this claim with straight faces. Even more are going to wonder how Moore and Eick could begin to claim that the finale bookends the beginning when, by their own words, they admit to neither remembering the beginning nor taking steps to refresh their memories.

"Jumping the Shark." 2016. *Wikipedia*, last modified Nov. 3. At https://en.wikipe dia.org/wiki/Jumping_the_shark.

Moore, Ronald. 2008b. Podcast commentary. On *Battlestar Galactica: Season Three*. Universal City, CA: Universal Studios. DVD.

Moore, Ronald, David Eick, and Michael Rymer. 2009. Podcast commentary. On *Battlestar Galactica: Season 4.5*. Universal City, CA: Universal Studios. DVD.

6

Boston Legal

"Made in China"/"Last Call"

BARBARA VILLEZ

As life goes on, there are many things that remain unknown. One has to become comfortable with the impossibility of mastering everything. The question of accepting is at the heart of the two-part finale of *Boston Legal* (2004–8, ABC),[1] the David E. Kelley legal dramedy that brought viewers into the offices of a Boston law firm to follow the exploits of its offbeat yet brilliant attorneys. The ending had been prepared for several weeks. Viewers learn that the firm is having financial difficulties, and then it is clear that it is going broke. Denny Crane (William Shatner), whose behavior has always been eccentric, turns out to be at an advancing stage of Alzheimer's and will soon no longer be able to live on his own. These two elements alone would obviously bring major changes to the characters' lives. However, creator Kelley would not let his protagonists go out without a fight, and, actually, the finale contains, as usual, a number of legal battles. If there is a message here, it is that some things cannot be controlled. Viewers are invited to think about the consequences of these particular changes, and the series ends not with a bang or with a whimper, for that matter, but with some thought-provoking arguments—a last chance at some first-class pleading.

The last two episodes, broadcast together, are titled "Made in China" and "Last Call."[2] As far as the title of the first part goes, Finley, the firm that was slated as the potential buyer of Crane, Poole and Schmidt, has been bought up by a huge Chinese law firm. This makes Denny Crane, Shirley

---

1. The finale of *Boston Legal* was a two-hour special shown on ABC, December 8, 2008.

2. All references to "Last Call" and "Made in China" come from D'Elia [2008] 2009a and [2008] 2009b.

Schmidt (Candice Bergen), Alan Shore (James Spader), and the others at the firm suddenly employees of the Chinese. And in his "last call" on the show, Shore has to deal with a variety of issues: obtaining a court order permitting the use of an experimental drug, fighting an injunction against a same-sex marriage, and struggling to prevent the Chinese takeover of the firm.

The series finale thus brings a share of new problems to the characters. All of them contribute to conveying a sense of loss of control and a sense of disorder. Denny Crane's loss of memory because of Alzheimer's has brought him to the stage of serious trouble, including being arrested for climbing, naked, into his neighbor's bed in the middle of the night. When asked what he remembers happening that particular evening, he cannot answer, and his teary eyes convey his worst fears becoming reality. In a previous episode, he made a formal request for permission to use an experimental drug, which was refused by the state court hierarchy. This episode takes him to the Supreme Court, with his best friend and colleague, Alan Shore, representing him.

Courtroom drama is ideal for giving the opposing sides of a conflict equal (or almost equal) time to present their principal arguments, so the case against Denny makes it possible to hear reasons to forbid a person from benefitting from experimental drugs. On several occasions, the finale refers to the millions of people in the United States who are afflicted with Alzheimer's and brings home the magnitude of the problem far beyond Denny's personal fictional story. Opposing counsel, pleading the case against authorization to use a drug not approved by the Food and Drug Administration, even if it could provide a chance to slow down the Alzheimer's process, has equally solid arguments. Even Shore seems impressed by the strength of her presentation. She argues that permission to use nontested drugs would discourage the testing process. She goes on to warn against unscrupulous pharmaceutical companies, seeking profits and new markets rather than finding cures. These companies would abandon expensive testing if it became possible to "peddle drugs." Her position against big business is difficult to counter and could strike any viewer as reasonable, even winning her their sympathy. Her arguments also pose a considerable challenge to Shore, who has to plead right after her. The arguments used in the Supreme Court scenes are wonderful opportunities for Kelley to maintain public awareness of issues that concern the viewers and their families.

Besides corporate interests, Kelley takes a jab at hypocrisy itself in this finale: rampant hypocrisy, a menace to good application of the law. This particular theme has already been dealt with in various episodes, but here the word itself is used repeatedly, and the illustration is quite unexpected, strengthening its impact on the audience. Denny, in his concern that he will need someone to make decisions for him if he continues to lose his capacity to do so, proposes marriage to Alan Shore. Denny relies on several arguments to persuade him: their close friendship and mutual trust, spousal privilege, Alan's legal expertise, and Denny's money, which would become more easily transferable to Alan. Alan had said in the past that he might like to open a legal aid clinic one day to help the poor, who cannot afford top lawyers. Isn't it a sign of hypocrisy that people go to law school to help people and end up being too expensive for those who need to have access to their competence? "Think of all the poor people you could help [rather than] the Iraq War or Wall Street bailout," Denny says to convince Alan to marry him.

Alan finally agrees, and they go for a marriage license. The city clerk denounces their "engagement" to the Massachusetts Chapter of the Gay and Lesbian League, who bring a motion for an injunction against this marriage. At court, Alan lashes out against the league's hypocritical opposition to their union based on the pretext that they are "blatant heterosexuals." People marry for many reasons, he says, not just sex. The league belittles their marriage as a mere tax-evasion scheme. Alan admits that Denny has in mind this "clean and efficient" means of transferring property but insists that their decision to marry goes far beyond financial considerations. They are friends who love each other, and to say they cannot get married because they do not want to have sex with each other is pure hypocrisy. Alan also objects to the league's suggestion that Denny get a proxy to help him when he loses his autonomy, answering that it is his prerogative to have a caring partner instead of someone with power of attorney. The judge, agreeing with Alan's arguments, denies the motion for an injunction, which is a victory for Alan and Denny, of course, but a victory against hypocrisy as well.

Money and honor are also linked to the subject of the Chinese takeover of the firm. How hypocritical is it for the United States to criticize China's politics on human rights and yet accept its money? Paul Lewiston (René Auberjonois), one of the partners of the firm, presents Denny Crane and Shirley Schmidt to several of the Chinese firm's lawyers, announcing that the Chinese have acquired Finley and thus are the new owners of both American firms. Crane and Schmidt refuse to hide their disapproval. Denny hisses that the Chinese will not get his firm and then, in keeping with his personal style, attacks the Chinese lawyers with a paintball gun. Shirley says little for the moment but will later try to remove her name from the firm. Lewiston then reminds her that her name belongs to the firm and that such business transformations are the new way of the world: "Do you know how many companies in this country are owned and operated by the Chinese?" If this argument is intended to prove that the Chinese buyout is a good option, it only depresses Shirley, and it is quite unlikely to produce a positive effect on the audience.

A more potent argument proposed to appease Crane and Schmidt is that the Chinese will assure a smooth transition, allowing the company to become solvent again and saving a significant number of jobs. The fear of having to fire colleagues is, of course, a major concern to viewers living in a time of financial crisis. This argument, however, is clearly a puff of smoke, and the first to go will be Crane, Shore, and probably Schmidt. How many unknown starting lawyers will follow? The audience is reminded of China's "track record on human rights," of its policies toward Tibet, and of its general handling of pro-democracy activists, student dissidents, and journalists. Having missed out on the festivities, Alan learns late about the buyout and refuses to believe the Chinese are interested in acquiring an American law firm. Denny corrects him: "They're buying everything. It's a Communist invasion." Here again, audiences are invited, with a spark of humorous exaggeration, to consider the legal consequences of globalization, second to the much more debated economic or cultural questions of the day.

Disorder resides in other subthemes of the finale, such as the disintegration of Shirley and Carl Sack's (John Larroquette) wedding rehearsal. The priest and the rabbi cannot work together. They are unable to hide their disapproval of the marriage. To them, this marriage is a mistake on religious grounds, even for a mature couple, neither of whom is getting married for the first time. The bickering between these two men of faith quickly becomes contagious, and the future spouses start taking sides. Efforts at diplomacy but continuing criticisms of each other's religion follow at the office the next day, mixed with Shirley's Freudian slips, giving the audience a slight apprehension that the marriage will indeed not take place. The atmosphere is decidedly chaotic.

In his courtroom dramas—especially *The Practice* (ABC, 1997–2004) and *Ally McBeal* (Fox, 1997–2002)—David Kelley has always given privileged time, in both concise and convincing ways, to courtroom closing arguments for their quality as final arguments and conclusions in order to bring ideas to the viewers' attention with the most impact. In this regard, the finale of *Boston Legal* is actually more of a closing than an ending because it operates more as a process than as a final verdict. Audiences are invited to draw their own conclusions on the issues discussed. The finale leaves open a number of questions rather than giving complete closure to banal worries such as who ends up with whom or who leaves town and says good-bye.

The final episodes also offer multiple opportunities to go to court, bringing the audience the pleasure of observing talented lawyering skills. The injunction against Denny and Alan's marriage is one such moment when Alan demonstrates his adversarial skills. Later, in the Supreme Court scenes, at the sound of "Oyea, oyea, oyea" and the sight of the nine justices taking their places, audiences are privy to the thrill felt by Denny and Alan ("God, it's good to be back") as well as to the ritual and authority of this court. Here, in a very compressed scene, with sharp attacks against the justices, Shore manages to bring the Court's recent record back to viewers' attention and, as in other episodes, to express Kelley's criticisms of this judicial body. In answer to Justice Antonin Scalia's comments that the brief counsel has provided for the court contains very little case law, Shore retorts: "That is because there is none, but your court is not big on precedent either." He goes on to argue: "The little guy is due in this court" because he has been losing out with a Court that has allowed corporations to win all the antitrust cases of the past years. Scalia, in an effort to cut short Shore's irreverence, reminds him that it is getting late and he has vacation plans, to which Shore quips, "And speaking for all Americans, I authorize you to stay away as long as you like." Shore concludes his case for authorization to use the experimental drug by saying, "The law cannot say to a man, 'You have no right to save yourself.' If the law says that, then it has to change. This drug is not Denny Crane's last hope; you are." The silence of the courtroom, the camera on several judicial faces, and the music, chosen for its slow thoughtful mood, all enhance the message that the law also exists to bring relief to citizens, not just to keep them under control. Like all closings, this one "dramatizes the transformation of private desire into public right" (Burns 1999, 71).

Shore's colleagues have recognized his talents on many occasions, but in these last scenes alone four of his colleagues express their admiration at four different moments. Shirley Schmidt tells him he is "really something" after he has argued with the Chinese to maintain the litigation team. Jerry Espenson (Christian Clemenson) tells Katie Lloyd (Tara Summers), his colleague and perhaps future girlfriend, that watching Shore practice law is a treat: "There will never be anyone ever like him." Even Paul Lewiston, who has been exasperated by Shore's flippant behavior throughout the series, encourages the Chinese to reconsider firing Shore. Lewiston has been retained by the Chinese company to head the "new" litigation team, and as he tries to compose the department, he tells them that in his opinion Alan Shore is the best and that any firm would want to have him. Nevertheless, the Chinese have different criteria, and they begrudge Shore the insults for which audiences, on the contrary, have come to admire him.

The best moment of pleading occurs when Shore reacts to Shirley's announcement that the Chinese have decided to fire the litigation team, which includes herself, Shore, Crane, Espenson, Lloyd, and Sack. He suggests that they fire their new bosses. Impressed but skeptical, Sack responds, "I know you're good, but how exactly would that work?" Alan asks him to arrange a meeting, and the scene begins with him, followed by all the others, walking out of the elevator, with a rhythm and music indicating the coming confrontation. A sort of Maypole dance takes place as the American law team enters the room bowing to each Chinese lawyer, who bows back, even though, as Shirley tells Alan, it is not the Chinese who bow, but the Japanese. Smiles on the Chinese lawyers' faces are replaced by surprise as Alan informs them they are fired: "Sue us. American juries will prefer the American defendants. Do you think they will prefer you? Cases depend on who the juries like better, not on law. Here's a tip: Americans love to deal on fear—ask W, ask Dick, ask Rummy. Fear sells. Fear works. The fear I'll be working on is China, active Communists made in China. . . . We control litigation. Do what you want with corporate tax or whatever, but leave the litigation to us." When he has finished, there is a split second of silence as everyone waits for the reaction of the Chinese, who suddenly applaud. They, too, recognize his skill and the quality of the legal performance they have just witnessed.

The second part of the *Boston Legal* finale is entitled "Last Call." The phrase *last call* refers to a specified time, usually established by local laws, for the final purchase of alcoholic beverages in a bar or pub and an announcement of the last chance for drinks. This episode is the viewers' last chance to appreciate Alan Shore's impressive adversarial skills. Shore indeed excels in legal performance and rhetoric, and audiences have had frequent evidence of this excellence in past episodes. He has shown them that lawyering is a craft that relies on creative thinking and a mastery of language. It is thus fitting that the finale of the show offers several last courtroom battles to judge his talented oral arguments. The importance of performance in adversarial trials shows a concern for informing the public through stories as well as for delivering evidence and debate to juries (Mulcahy 2011, 85). Television is an effective means to bring the public into the forum of courtroom reasoning and to implicate citizens in their judicial system—in part because most people just do not attend trials.

A closing in law also has the meaning of completion. There is a sense of satisfaction and of a new order of things. *Boston Legal* ends with some battles won and some lost; most, but not all, of the chaos has been settled. The lesson seems double: to learn to accept what one has no power to change and yet not to throw in the towel. A good fight is a right afforded by the American legal system, even though Kelley has suggested in other shows that the use of this right has gone too far. The Chinese have won the battle of the takeover. Lewiston reminds Shirley that business, the firm, is bigger than any of its individual parts. Audiences see how hard it may be to defeat such big interests, but they are warned to remain vigilant. Some colleagues of the firm will keep their jobs, at least for a while. Others will have to go. Such things are inevitable. Crane and Shore will probably not be retained; this is not resolved in the end.

Denny will get his drug, but no legal decision can bring about a cure for the disease. The product in question is just a glimmer of hope to control the progression of his condition. In this situation, too, there is little else to do than accept it and prepare the practical side of life as much as possible. Acceptance and hope for a scientific breakthrough, however, are not incompatible.

Denny and Alan are married in a double wedding ceremony with Shirley and Carl. The ceremony is performed by Justice Scalia, of all people, which offers an opportunity for more biting humor but also a sort of truce to end the show on. Jerry and Katie end their date with a kiss, a promise of a relationship. Her acceptance of him, her seeing him as a brilliant lawyer, a kind, sweet man who just happens to have Tourette's, has also been a subject Kelley has dealt with in past series.

Before the finale ends, two Chinese lawyers go out on the terrace to enjoy a brandy, a cigar, and conversation, as Denny and Alan have done at the end of every episode of the four-year series. The Chinese seem to be practicing for their new role and their new American life. But, in typical Kelley style, the scene also reminds viewers of the Goldilocks tale, especially when Alan and Denny do finally return to the terrace after the wedding: "Someone has been here. . . . They could at least have cleaned up the mess," a symbolic presage of the results of Chinese takeovers.

Alan warns Denny that they will face ridicule and abuse because of their marriage, but Crane feels that sealing their relationship is worth the risk. The camera leaves them on the terrace and turns slowly from them to the empty, dimly lit offices and then to the names of the firm on the entrance wall: Crane's name has been replaced, and the firm is now announced as

"Chang, Poole and Schmidt." Shirley, it seems, will play along for a while. Other developments are left open, but viewers can suppose from a previous scene that she will follow her own advice: to do what she loves to do "because a life—personal or professional—without passion, you're dead."

The series closes but also opens up to future possibilities. These lives cannot just stop here in viewers' imaginations. Things will happen that no one will see. There is a quick wink at audiences when Denny jokes that his and Alan's union could be the subject of a new TV series. Alan puts in, "On a new network," to which Denny adds, "One that cares." Could this be a poke at the station that dropped *Boston Legal*? A new series (perhaps titled *Alan Shore and Denny Crane: Husband and Mad Cow*[3]), like some of Kelley's older programs, could see itself as a public-education resource on the law in society.

Finally, Denny asks Alan, What will they do? Should they stay with the firm or start a new one? Puffing on his cigar, Alan answers: "We don't have to decide tonight." Thus the show ends, and the audience does not have to think about that either.

References

Burns, R. P. 1999. *A Theory of the Trial*. Princeton, NJ: Princeton Univ. Press.

D'Elia, Bill, dir. [2008] 2009a. "Last Call." *Boston Legal*, season 5, episode 13. Story by David E. Kelley and Susan Dickes. Teleplay by David E. Kelley. Aired Dec. 8, 2008, ABC. On *Boston Legal: Season Five*. Beverly Hills, CA: Twentieth Century Fox Home Entertainment. DVD.

———, dir. [2008] 2009b. "Made in China." *Boston Legal*, season 5, episode 12. Story by David E. Kelley, Susan Dickes, and Lauren Mackenzie. Teleplay by David E. Kelley. Aired Dec. 8, 2008. On *Boston Legal: Season Five*. Beverly Hills, CA: Twentieth Century Fox Home Entertainment. DVD.

Mulcahy, Linda. 2011. *Legal Architecture: Justice, Due Process, and the Place of Law*. London: Routledge.

---

3. *Mad cow* is the term Denny has used in the show to refer to his Alzheimer's.

7

Breaking Bad

"Felina"

K. DALE KOONTZ

Historically, a standby of network television has been the telling of simple binary stories of good guys vanquishing bad guys. While especially prominent in the popular television Westerns of the 1950s and 1960s (think *Gunsmoke* [1955–75] and *Bonanza* [1959–73]), this traditional structure has served as the cornerstone for many other genres as well, including shows focusing on superheroes, detectives, and police officers. In addition to this "White Hat/Black Hat" structure, many shows have relied heavily on the relationship between the hero and his partner or, if the power structure is more skewed, between the hero and his faithful sidekick. Sometimes the hero acts outside of the strict bounds of the law, which was the case especially following the turbulent real-life events in the United States in the late 1960s and 1970s, but the hero always operates from a deep core of decency and morality. In the first decade of the new millennium, Vince Gilligan had a vastly different perception of heroes, sidekicks, and Westerns. Paul MacInnes (2012) reported that Gilligan, having honed his skills on *The X-Files* (1993–2002), a show that revels in twisty mysteries and long arcs, pitched his new idea as being the story of a man who transforms from Mr. Chips to Scarface.[1] Intrigued and willing to take a chance on a show with such an

---

1. Interestingly, actors Bryan Cranston (Walter White) and Aaron Paul (Jesse Pinkman) had worked with Gilligan in his *X-Files* days, albeit on different episodes. Impressed by Cranston's ability to find the humanity in a deranged, unsympathetic character in the episode "Drive" (*X-Files*, 6.2), Gilligan had hoped to work with Cranston again, and Cranston, impressed with the pilot script of *Breaking Bad*, wanted in. Paul was in a later episode of *X-Files* ("Lord of the Flies," 9.5), and he had also auditioned for the role of the oldest son on *Malcolm in the Middle* (2000–2006), the show that first brought fame to Cranston.

odd premise, AMC greenlit *Breaking Bad* (2008–13), and television history was made.

Although protagonists who possess antiheroic qualities had been seen before, never had a man like Walter White anchored a television show. At the beginning of his journey, Walt is a likable, middle-aged nebbish whose incredible skills in chemistry have never quite panned out in terms of financial success, so he is supporting his growing family through his meager income as a high school chemistry teacher. His life is a struggle, but a mundane one until he is galvanized into action following his diagnosis of Stage III lung cancer. Determined to leave a nest egg for his family, Walt forms an unequal partnership with former student Jesse Pinkman to manufacture and sell the purest methamphetamine on the planet. Over the course of five seasons, Walt's pride and hubris grow like another type of cancer, and his financial success comes at the expense of both the guilty and the innocent as he transforms from mild and frustrated chemistry teacher to furious and vengeful "Heisenberg," the meth kingpin of Duke City.

By the time *Breaking Bad* was debuted, television viewers were accustomed to seeing lead characters undertake what Joseph Campbell identified as the "hero's journey," but Walt's transformative road is a darker one that leads to the Underworld.[2] Walt also has little in common with characters such as Tony Soprano, who begins *The Sopranos* (1999–2007) already firmly established as an antihero. What Gilligan gives viewers is an unprecedented thrill ride with a once-decent man who willingly chooses to descend into depravity and violence. Although Walt has multiple opportunities to step off this path, every time he is faced with that choice, he doubles down and becomes more corrupt, corroded, and cruel. During the series' original broadcast, while a vocal minority of fans persisted in viewing all of Walt's actions as laudable (many in this minority blamed Walt's wife, Skyler, for his actions), most found themselves enmeshed in a sticky conundrum. This man, who has taken truly monstrous actions—including causing the death of his brother-in-law, watching a helpless girl choke to death, and poisoning

2. Joseph Campbell (1904–87) was best known for his work in comparative mythology. In one of his most influential works, *The Hero's Journey* (1990), he identifies a number of common milestones in the narrative structure of heroic myths told in an array of widely different societies. He theorizes that there is such a thing as a "narrative monomyth" in which these common elements can be viewed as variations on a single epic story, regardless of the differences in details. For example, Homer's *Odyssey* and George Lucas's *Star Wars* share any number of common points.

an innocent child—is the centerpiece of the show and is positioned as the one to cheer for. With *Breaking Bad*, viewers are confronted with the horrifying result of staring too long into Nietzsche's abyss.[3] Many of the estimated 10.3 million viewers who tuned in to watch the original broadcast of the final episode, "Felina," on September 29, 2013 (O'Connell 2013), were not quite prepared to face an existentialist crisis via the television screen.[4] In light of the remarkable surge in viewers, owing in large part to the emergence of streaming technology at the time,[5] it must have been tempting to continue the show, but Gilligan was convinced that the story needed to come to a full and satisfying end. Shouldering his responsibilities, like Travis Coates in *Old Yeller*,[6] Gilligan served as both writer and director for the nigh-perfect "Felina."

Walt begins his journey into darkness by telling himself that his motives are pure—he is doing all of this for his family, a motive that helps viewers side with him. However, his selfish, violent actions over time cause him to lose everything that he claims to be fighting to save—his family despises him, and the family home has been confiscated. For all of the money Walt has managed to accumulate—a king's ransom—it does neither him nor his family any good. In "Felina," Walt rashly decides to return to New Mexico from his secure hideout in the rural Northeast and tie up some loose

3. Friedrich Nietzsche (1844–1900) was a German philosopher and scholar who wrote in his book *Beyond Good and Evil* (1886) that "he who fights with monsters should be careful lest he thereby become a monster. And if thou gaze long into an abyss, the abyss will also gaze into thee." (1954, 446). In other words, one must be very careful to not employ the methods of evil when fighting evil, for evil is taking the measure of its opponent and is always seeking an advantage.

4. All references to "Felina" come from Gilligan 2013.

5. As described in the news segment "The One Who Binges" (2014), *Breaking Bad* benefitted hugely from streaming technology and "binge-watching." It was also shot on film rather than being shot digitally. As Michael Slovis, the director of photography for forty-four episodes of *Breaking Bad* explains in *Wanna Cook?*, the transfer of digital footage to higher-resolution formats is limited by the camera that was originally used (Guffey and Koontz 2014, 194). However, when a show is shot on film, transferring those images to other formats is easy to accomplish.

6. *Old Yeller* (1956) is a children's novel by author Fred Gipson. A year after its publication, it was made into a Disney movie (Robert Stevenson, 1957) and has scarred generations of children since that time because its dramatic climax involves a young man (Travis) being forced to shoot the family pet, who has contracted rabies by fighting off a wolf who was trying to attack the family. A little like Stephen King's *Cujo* (1981; film: Lewis Teague, 1983) if that book/film had been aimed at a preteen audience.

ends.[7] He secures his family's financial future by cold-heartedly forcing his former partners to serve as accomplices to transfer the blood money. With that done, it is time to settle other scores, for nothing has ever truly mattered to Walt other than achieving his own goals.

"Felina" beautifully encapsulates the larger themes Gilligan used throughout *Breaking Bad*. Walt's actions created the very enemies he now intends to ruthlessly destroy with a personal touch. Knowing that the cancer will kill him even if he survives the night, Walt is determined to make sure his victims know who is responsible for their fate. This pathological need to be the top dog is woven throughout the episode—it is evident in his phone call to Lydia, his execution of Jack and Jack's horde of neo-Nazis, and his conversation with Skyler. Walt finally speaks the truth about his motives when he admits that he did all of this for his own gratification, not for his family. But he makes this confession when it is too late to matter. Walt is no hero, and here at the end it is doubtful that he is even an antihero. Rather, he is the villain of the piece. It is a measure of the depth of Walt's fall from grace that he can be identified as the villain of *Breaking Bad* given the other choices for this position (Hector Salamanca, Tuco, Gus Fring, entire drug cartels, and murderous neo-Nazis who imprison Jesse as a meth-cooking slave). They all, of course, are terrible people, but they all are brought into the orbit of those Walt loves by Walt himself. Of course, Walt's own hands are dipped in the blood of innocents as well, through his own actions, which result in the deaths of hundreds.[8]

The relationship between Walt and Jesse is key to appreciating *Breaking Bad*. Jesse has been Walt's lead into the meth world, his partner, and his surrogate son. Eager to please, Jesse has compromised his own morals to please Walt, only to have his loyalty repaid repeatedly with scorn, pain, and betrayal. Jesse's moment of breaking free from Walt occurs when he refuses to act as the wounded Walt's cat's-paw any longer. Walt has saved

7. The car Walt steals for his homeward trek has a Marty Robbins cassette tape containing Robbins's hit "El Paso," which tells the story of a doomed cowboy and his Mexican love, Felina, a story that echoes Walt's return to his love, meth. Fans tried mightily to make something more of the title, beyond its being an anagram for *finale*, repeatedly claiming that it stands for "Blood, Meth, and Tears" based on the periodic table. That's a nice try and an understandable one, but lithium ("Li" on the periodic table) is not involved in the process of meth manufacture.

8. Presuming one includes the crash of commercial airline flight Wayfarer 515. If that event is removed from the tally, twenty-four deaths can be laid directly at Walt's feet.

Jesse's life through the use of one of his overly elaborate contraptions[9] (a recurring motif in *Breaking Bad* is Walt's need to complicate matters in an effort to be the smartest guy in the room), but Jesse finally walks away. Left alone, Walt staggers to the meth lab and pats the cooking tank as he gazes at his distorted reflection in the tank's metal skin. The chemistry never failed him. His strength depleted, Walt slumps to the ground, leaving behind a bloody handprint, and dies with his eyes finally wide open to what is going on around him. He dies on his own terms, which can be read as being more than he deserves (plenty of fans wanted to see him taken into custody and forced to pay for his crimes that way), but he dies nonetheless.[10]

In the end, *Breaking Bad* is far more than a cautionary tale about pride. Gilligan created a new type of story with Walt's journey as viewers became deeply invested in the tortuous path taken by a deeply flawed man who can list stubbornness and a near-pathological need to be the smartest guy in the room among his character traits. We cheered for Walt, then we faltered as we realized the depths to which he was capable of plumbing, but at that point any justification we may have constructed to excuse Walt's actions had ceased to matter. We were with Walt, and Walt was in us. In *Breaking Bad*, the abyss stared back.

References

Campbell, Joseph. 1990. *The Hero's Journey: Joseph Campbell on His Life and Work*. San Francisco: Harper & Row.

Gilligan, Vince, dir. 2013. "Felina." *Breaking Bad*, season 5, episode 16. Written by Vince Gilligan. Directed by Vince Gilligan. Aired Sept. 29, AMC. iTunes. Accessed Sept. 16, 2014.

Guffey, Ensley F., and K. Dale Koontz. 2014. *Wanna Cook? The Complete Unofficial Companion to "Breaking Bad."* Toronto: ECW Press.

9. The execution of Walt's plan—which involves a number of other "executions"—is perhaps the single flaw in "Felina." Walt drives into a den of neo-Nazis, who take great care to pat him down for weapons and who know his propensity for death-dealing gizmos, but somehow they never think to open the trunk of the land yacht Walt drives and conveniently parks in close proximity to their evil clubhouse.

10. A few hardcore fans insist that Walt is not really dead, and even Cranston toyed with this idea. Nonetheless, Walt is definitely as dead as Jacob Marley in *A Christmas Carol*. Gilligan has made that abundantly clear, as does the shooting script. See Sepinwall 2009 and Snierson 2013.

MacInnes, Paul. 2012. "*Breaking Bad* Creator Vince Gilligan: The Man Who Turned Walter White from Mr. Chips into Scarface." *Guardian*, May 12. At http://www .theguardian.com/tv-and-radio/2012/may/19/vince-gilligan-breaking-bad.

Nietzsche, Friedrich. 1954. *The Philosophy of Nietzsche*. Translated by Helen Zimmern. New York: Random House.

O'Connell, Michael. 2013. "TV Ratings: *Breaking Bad* Finale Smashes Records with 10.3 Million Viewers." *Hollywood Reporter*, Sept. 30. At http://www .hollywoodreporter.com/live-feed/tv-ratings-breaking-bad-finale-639093.

"The One Who Binges: *Breaking Bad* Is Most Binge-Watched Show, Study Says." 2014. *NBC News*, June 25. At http://www.nbcnews.com/tech/internet/one-who -binges-breaking-bad-most-binge-watched-show-study-n139821.

Sepinwall, Alan. 2009. "*Breaking Bad*: Bryan Cranston/Vince Gilligan Q&A." *NJ.com*, Mar. 6. At http://www.nj.com/entertainment/tv/index.ssf/2009/03 /breaking_bad_bryan_cranstonvin.html.

Snierson, Dan. 2013. "*Breaking Bad*: Creator Vince Gilligan Explains Series Finale." *EW*, Sept. 30. At http://insidetv.ew.com/2013/09/30/breaking-bad-finale -vince-gilligan/.

8

Buffy the Vampire Slayer

"Chosen"

ELIZABETH L. RAMBO

Buffy the Vampire Slayer, created by Joss Whedon based on his script for the movie of the same title released in 1992, ran for seven seasons: from 1997 to 2001 on the WB network and from 2001 to 2003 on UPN. The show starred Sarah Michelle Gellar as Buffy Summers, Alyson Hannigan as Willow Rosenberg, Nicholas Brendon as Xander Harris—Buffy's two best friends—and Anthony Stewart Head as Buffy's mentor or "watcher," Rupert Giles. These four remained essential. In retrospect, the thirteen-episode first season is the weakest, but when *Buffy* debuted in March 1997, one hundred years after the publication of Bram Stoker's novel *Dracula*, its genre mix of horror, comedy, action, and drama and its girl-power teen heroine were refreshing surprises. Critics responded with almost universal praise, and *Buffy*'s ratings for the struggling WB network were strong enough to bring *Buffy* back for season 2 (Garron 1998) and then for three more seasons, with one hundred episodes total. *Buffy*'s sixth and seventh seasons on UPN were marked by controversy and a darker tone overall, but the final episode, "Chosen," aired on May 20, 2003, was the biggest ratings success of the year ("*Buffy* Finale" 2003).[1]

The basic premise of *Buffy the Vampire Slayer* is famously summed up in the opening voiceover of the first two seasons: "In every generation there is a Chosen One. She alone will stand against the vampires, the demons, and the forces of darkness. She is the Slayer" (Whedon 1997). The show was frequently compared with contemporary series featuring young women with supernatural powers, such as *Charmed* (1998–2006), *Xena: Warrior*

---

1. All references to "Chosen" come from Whedon 2003.

Princess (1995–2001), and *Joan of Arcadia* (2003–5), and later to the extraordinary but merely human protagonists of *Alias* (2001–6) and *Veronica Mars* (2004–7). However, *Buffy* outlasted many of these shows (except *Charmed*) and continues to attract new fans and attention from pop-culture scholars. What distinguishes *Buffy the Vampire Slayer* from these and other shows or films about young "chosen ones"—a trope that has become so embedded in pop culture that Gina Dalfonzo (2013) calls it "the formula that's ruining teen movies"?

First, critics and fans alike note *Buffy*'s flipped script in which the ditzy blonde is the action hero rather than the victim or damsel in distress. Fifteen years after the series' end, this scenario may seem commonplace, but it was groundbreaking in the late 1990s. Series creator Joss Whedon explains, "Nobody ever expected that [the cute, sexy blonde] could take care of herself, or turn around and become a superhero. And not just a superhero, but a hero in the classical sense" (Longworth 2011, 53). In the years since *Buffy*'s final episode, most fantasies about "chosen ones" have had male protagonists (e.g., Harry Potter, Percy Jackson, Clark Kent/Superman), and few female characters have been given the kind of agency Buffy repeatedly claims for herself. According to Whedon, the question to ask about such TV shows and films is this: "[Are] there female characters who are being empowered, who are driving the narrative? The *Twilight* thing and a lot of these franchise attempts coming out, everything rests on what this girl will do, but she's completely passive, or not really knowing what the hell is going on. And . . . a lot of what's taking on the oeuvre of *Buffy*, is actually a reaction against it. Everything is there—except for the Buffy. A lot of things aimed at the younger kids is just *Choosing Boyfriends: The Movie*" (Hibberd 2013, 27). Buffy and her friends always insist that they make their own decisions—the results aren't always positive—but although fans frequently debate which vampire, Angel (David Boreanaz) or Spike (James Marsters), is most worthy of Buffy's love, Buffy herself always has something more important to think about: saving the world.

In terms of style and structure, *Buffy the Vampire Slayer* is repeatedly picked out for its distinctive writing, use of metaphor, and seasonal narrative-arc structure. Credit for the writing style goes to Joss Whedon, who generally wrote the opening and closing episodes as well as at least one other episode of each season. These Whedon-penned episodes are frequently praised for their unique qualities: "Hush" (4.10) has no dialogue for about twenty-nine minutes and is the only *Buffy* episode nominated for an Emmy for writing; "Restless" (4.22) is a surreal dream episode; "The Body" (5.16) is an unusually realistic dramatization of death (Wilcox 2005, "Death"); and "Once More, with Feeling" (6.7) is a musical episode. All four were also directed by Joss Whedon. In seasons 4 through 6, *Buffy* also broke new ground by introducing TV's first long-term lesbian couple, Willow and Tara, who first kiss onscreen in "The Body." Jane Espenson and other *Buffy* staff writers note that Whedon reviewed and often rewrote parts or all of every script (Dumars 2000). Linguist Michael Adams (2003) documents how *Buffy*'s particular word usages—for example, using the term *much* as an interrogative adverb, as in "Morbid much?"; adding a suffix such as *-age* to other terms, as in *slayage* (killing vampires or demons); and using names well known in pop culture as verbs ("I cannot believe that you of all people are trying to Scully me!")—rapidly entered popular usage and appeared in other TV shows, movies, novels, and popular journalism. In this way, at least, *Buffy* affected popular culture far beyond its relatively limited fan base during its broadcast run.

The unifying metaphor of the first three seasons of *Buffy the Vampire Slayer* is "high school is hell," with Buffy's Sunnydale High built literally over a gateway to the demonic depths that attracts not only vampires but also various other evil creatures. Although some of these metaphorical demons may have been a bit on the nose (many viewers were unhappy with Willow's "addiction" to dark magic in season 6), most were presented with enough "emotional resonance" to carry the audience along (Whedon 2008a). In addition to each episode's metaphorical demon(s)—for example, the vengeful Anyanka of "The Wish" (Greenwalt [1998] 2008) in season 3—Whedon structured each season around a longer narrative that would conclude at the season's end, allowing a sense of closure if the show were not renewed but also giving a shape and greater sense of purpose to each individual episode. Although *Buffy* was not the first TV series to have season-long narrative arcs as well as stand-alone episodes,[2] scholars have noted that each season—and the seven seasons together—in some sense follow the classic "hero's journey" structure, lending further coherence to the entire series (Wilcox 2005, "Pain"; Fritts 2009; Hawkins 2009; Frankel 2012).

In each season of *Buffy*, the unifying metaphor is sometimes linked with the primary villain to be defeated, the "big bad," along with the individual

---

2. As far as recent television shows, credit for the season-long (and series-long) narrative arc in genre TV goes to J. Michael Straczynski and *Babylon 5* (1994–98) (see chapter 3 in this volume).

episodes' "little bads." When Buffy and her gang graduate from high school and move on to college, the metaphorical opponents become more diversified and, at times, less metaphorical. College (season 4) isn't quite as hellish as high school; the issue becomes finding one's identity and the balance between independence and cooperation. In season 5, the last season shown on the WB, Buffy begins to embrace her calling as Slayer and faces her greatest ordeals yet, ending with her self-sacrificial death to save her sister and (of course) the world. "The Gift" (Whedon [2001] 2008b) would have been a fitting finale for the series if arrangements had not been made to bring *Buffy* back for two more seasons on a different network, UPN. David Lavery (2003) classifies "The Gift" as one of only two *Buffy* episodes that are "closurey (at the level of expectation), resolving major, multiple plot entanglements." The other, of course, is the season 7 finale, "Chosen."

Television characters have been brought back from the dead, but rarely (if ever) with as much personal and external difficulty as Buffy the Vampire Slayer is. In season 6, the "growing up" theme (Springer 2002) made for a metaphorically grim struggle for all the characters as they fight themselves and a trio of twisted geeks who seem to embody "the banality of evil" (Arendt [1963] 2006), but in the end the real threat turns out to be Willow. Season 7, the final season, is "about power" (Solomon [2002] 2008). It is also about going "back to the beginning" (Solomon [2002] 2008) with many references throughout the season to previous seasons as well as with narrative elements that involve searching for historical origins. (Nikki Stafford's book *Bite Me: The Unofficial Guide to "Buffy the Vampire Slayer"* [2007] provides a comprehensive guide to these callbacks.)

Through all six previous seasons, Buffy has been the "one girl" with power (with one or two exceptions). In season 7, she faces her ultimate opponent, "the First Evil," a force that originally appeared in season 2 and now intends to destroy every potential slayer and to release hell on earth along with thousands of extrastrong vampires called "Turok-Han." For much of season 7, the issue seems to be whether Buffy is strong enough to defeat this almost omnipotent enemy, who can appear as any dead person and can often read people's thoughts. "The First" is described by its corrupted, misogynistic priest, Caleb, as "everywhere. You're in the hearts of little children, in the souls of the rich, you're the fire that makes people kill and hate. . . . They're just sinners. You are Sin" ("Touched" [Solomon 2003]). Although Buffy and her comrades save and train as many potential Slayers as they can, it seems unlikely that they will be prepared to face the First Evil and its minions. The tide begins to turn in Buffy's favor at last when she finds an ancient Slayer weapon, called a "scythe" (it looks more like an ornate battle ax with a sharpened handle), and she is inspired with an unusual way to use this weapon after encounters with the shamans who created the First Slayer ("Get It Done" [Petrie 2003]), an equally ancient and mysterious female "Guardian" ("End of Days" [Grabiak 2003]), and the "First" itself.

Dozens of "Potentials," along with Giles, Willow, Xander, Spike, Faith (Eliza Dushku), Anya (Emma Caulfield Ford), and Andrew (Tom Lenk), a convert from the evil trio of season 6, have gathered in Buffy's house, training half-heartedly in this frail outpost against what seems likely to be a final apocalypse. Early in "Chosen," the First Evil, appearing in Buffy's likeness, tauntingly reminds her that she is "the one . . . alone," but Buffy comes up with a revolutionary plan, which she presents to the Potentials the next day: "So here's the part where you make a choice: What if you could have that power—now? In every generation, one slayer is born, because a bunch of men who died thousands of years ago made up that rule. So I say we change the rule. I say my power should be our power. . . . Slayers. Every one of us. Make your choice. Are you ready to be strong?"

The full version of this speech is heard in voiceover as the group waits to attack the First Evil's forces in the halls and beneath Sunnydale High School, where everything began. As Willow casts the spell that will empower the Potentials, we see not only each of the girls in Sunnydale but also other girls around the world receiving their Slayer power and rising to meet challenges. As a finale, then, "Chosen" once again flips the script, turning the story of Buffy the Vampire Slayer as *the* powerful "chosen one" into a story of sharing power, a story of all of us—especially all women—making our own choices. Susan Payne-Mulliken and Valerie Renegar make a strong case for this final feminist metaphor of shared power in their essay "Buffy Never Goes It Alone" (2009). As Buffy, along with her surviving friends and newly empowered Slayers, contemplates the crater that was once Sunnydale, California, "Chosen" provides a satisfactory "closurey" finale for seven seasons of *Buffy the Vampire Slayer* while also opening the possibility for more. "Buffy, what are we gonna do now?" asks Dawn, and Buffy's enigmatic smile is our answer: whatever we decide to do. Though there *is* another hellmouth: in Cleveland.

References

Adams, Michael. 2003. *Slayer Slang: A "Buffy the Vampire Slayer" Lexicon*. New York: Oxford Univ. Press.

Arendt, Hannah. [1963] 2006. *Eichmann in Jerusalem: A Report on the Banality of Evil*. New York: Penguin Classics.

"*Buffy* Finale a Big Hit with Young, Devoted Fans." 2003. *Calgary Herald*, May 23.

Dalfonzo, Gina. 2013. "The Formula That's Ruining Teen Movies." *Atlantic*, Aug. 27. At http://www.theatlantic.com/entertainment/archive/2013/08/the-formula-thats-ruining-teen-movies/279080/.

Dumars, Denise. 2000. "*Buffy the Vampire Slayer*: Writer Jane Espenson." *Mania: Beyond Entertainment*, Jan. 24. At http://www.javascrypt.com/spikeschip/text/cinescape1.txt.

Frankel, Valerie Estelle. 2012. *Buffy and the Heroine's Journey*. Jefferson, NC: McFarland.

Fritts, David. 2009. "*Buffy*'s Seven Season Initiation." In *"Buffy" Meets the Academy: Essays on the Episodes and Scripts as Texts*, edited by Kevin K. Durand, 32–44. Jefferson, NC: McFarland.

Garron, Barry. 1998. "The Frog That Crowed." *Broadcasting & Cable* 128, no. 2: 3, 10.

Grabiak, Marita, dir. 2003. "End of Days." *Buffy the Vampire Slayer*, season 7, episode 13. Written by Jane Espenson and Douglas Petrie. Aired May 13, UPN. Original broadcast.

Greenwalt, David, dir. [1998] 2008. "The Wish." *Buffy the Vampire Slayer*, season 3, episode 9. Written by Marti Noxon. Aired Dec. 8, 1998, WB. On *Buffy the Vampire Slayer: The Complete Third Season*. Los Angeles: Twentieth Century Fox. DVD.

Hawkins, Paul. 2009. "Season Six and the Supreme Ordeal." In *"Buffy" Goes Dark: Essays on the Final Two Seasons of "Buffy the Vampire Slayer" on Television*, edited by Lynne Y. Edwards, Elizabeth L. Rambo, and James B. South, 183–97. Jefferson, NC: McFarland.

Hibberd, James. 2013. "Joss Whedon: The *EW* Interview." *Entertainment Weekly*, Aug. 30.

Lavery, David. 2003. "Apocalyptic Apocalypses: The Narrative Eschatology of *Buffy the Vampire Slayer*." *Slayage: The Online International Journal of Buffy Studies* 3, no. 1 [9]. At http://www.whedonstudies.tv/uploads/2/6/2/8/26288593/lavery_slayage_3.1.pdf.

Longworth, James. 2011. "Joss Whedon, Feminist." In *Joss Whedon: Conversations*, edited by David Lavery and Cynthia Burkhead, 42–63. Jackson: Univ. Press of Mississippi.

Payne-Mulliken, Susan, and Valerie Renegar. 2009. "Buffy Never Goes It Alone: The Rhetorical Construction of Sisterhood in the Final Season." In *"Buffy" Meets the Academy: Essays on the Episodes and Scripts as Texts*, edited by Kevin K. Durand, 57–77. Jefferson, NC: McFarland.

Petrie, Doug, dir. 2003. "Get It Done." *Buffy the Vampire Slayer*, season 7, episode 15. Written by Doug Petrie. Aired Feb. 18, UPN. Original broadcast.

Solomon, David, dir. 2003. "Touched." *Buffy the Vampire Slayer*, season 7, episode 20. Written by Rebecca Rand Kirshner. Aired May 6, UPN. Original broadcast.

———, dir. [2002] 2008. "Lessons." *Buffy the Vampire Slayer*, season 7, episode 1. Written by Joss Whedon. Aired Sept. 24, 2002, UPN. On *Buffy the Vampire Slayer: The Complete Seventh Season*. Los Angeles: Twentieth Century Fox. DVD.

Springer, Matt. 2002. "Growing Up." Marti Noxon Interview. *Official UK Buffy Magazine*, May.

Stafford, Nikki. 2007. *Bite Me! The Unofficial Guide to "Buffy the Vampire Slayer."* The Chosen Edition. Toronto: ECW Press.

Whedon, Joss, dir. 1997. "Welcome to the Hellmouth." *Buffy the Vampire Slayer*, season 1, episode 1. Written by Joss Whedon. Aired Mar. 10, WB. Original broadcast.

———, dir. 2003. "Chosen." *Buffy the Vampire Slayer*, season 7, episode 22. Written by Joss Whedon. Aired May 20, UPN. Original broadcast.

———. 2008a. "Audio Commentary on 'Innocence.'" On *Buffy the Vampire Slayer: The Complete Second Season*. Los Angeles: Twentieth Century Fox. DVD.

———, dir. [2001] 2008b. "The Gift." *Buffy the Vampire Slayer*, season 5, episode 22. Written by Joss Whedon. Aired May 22, 2001, WB. *Buffy the Vampire Slayer: The Complete Fifth Season*. Los Angeles: Twentieth Century Fox. DVD.

Wilcox, Rhonda. 2005. *Why Buffy Matters: The Art of "Buffy the Vampire Slayer."* London: I. B. Tauris, 2005.

9

Carnivàle

"New Canaan, CA"

ERIKA JOHNSON-LEWIS

HBO aired the first twelve-episode season of *Carnivàle* in the fall of 2003. The series returned for its second season in January 2005, more than a year after the first-season run. Originally intending to run *Carnivàle* for six seasons divided into three parts, HBO canceled it in May 2005, citing its high production costs and low ratings as the primary reasons. This abrupt cancellation in itself isn't a particularly noteworthy occurrence in the television industry. Series are canceled for these reasons all the time. Some series, such as *Firefly* (2002–3), *Freaks and Geeks* (1999–2000), and *Deadwood* (2004–6) were canceled well before their time. But perhaps because I experienced them after they were canceled, with the knowledge that they were doomed to end too soon, I did not experience the same kind of disappointment I did once *Carnivàle* ended. I was never angry that I would not see what happened to Lindsey Weir after she skipped out on the academic summit or that I would not see Al Swearengen monologue to a decaying skull again. *Carnivàle* was different. When it was canceled, I was angry. I felt betrayed, frustrated, and confused. I thought maybe writing about *Carnivàle* for this collection might help me understand where my sense of frustration and annoyance came from. I realize this might sound a little grandiose and melodramatic, but it is in keeping with the grandiosity the series tried to convey.

Carnivàle, created by Daniel Knauf, entered the television landscape during an upswing in serialized narratives that was spurred on by the success of series such as *Lost* (2004–10) and at the high point of HBO's "not TV" domination of the airwaves with series such as *The Sopranos* (1999–2007), *The Wire* (2002–8), and *Sex and the City* (1998–2004) and with limited miniseries such as *Angels in America* (2003). It also tapped into the apocalypse/end-of-the-world theme that emerged in the wake of the terrorist attacks of September 11, 2001. Given how it conforms to these trends, we can easily understand how it fared so well during its first season. However, season 2 saw a marked drop in viewership, perhaps owing in large part to the series' year-long hiatus. Season 2 also saw a change in the storytelling pace that, on the one hand, was more intense, with early revelations about Ben's and Justin's natures, but, on the other, was much slower as, after these revelations, the narrative meandered around without a clear, central driving purpose. The audience gets the sense that there will be a dramatic confrontation between Ben and Justin, but so many intervening unrelated or deliberately confusing elements are added to the mix that what is meant to drive the plot feels like an afterthought, and when the confrontation finally occurs at the end of the season, it lacks energy.[1]

While on the air, *Carnivàle* was known for its Byzantine plot and its high-quality visual aesthetics. Though the characters were often covered in dust and grime, *Carnivàle* was visually stunning. The plotting and character developments in the first season were deliberately and tantalizingly slow and ponderous. The opening sequence, which it may be even better known for, pulls the viewer in with its lush colors, religiously charged imagery, vintage film footage, and dramatic music. The series opens with the promise of an epic story, the struggle between light and dark, good and evil, and the end of the world.

The show follows the story of Ben Hawkins, who has mysterious healing powers, and Brother Justin Crowe, a Methodist charismatic preacher who has a somewhat disturbing relationship with his sister, Iris. Ben joins up with a traveling carnival, and we follow them as they move westward through the dust-covered western landscape and Brother Justin begins to build a cult-like following through his successful radio sermons. Accompanying Ben and Justin are a colorful cast of "carney" folk: a crippled former baseball player and ride mechanic, a tarot card reader and her catatonic mother, a scheming bearded lady, a snake charmer, the peep-show family, and Samson, who runs the operation for the mysterious and never seen "Management." Woven through the group's day-to-day travels is the specter of an impending epic battle between good and evil. Samson's opening monologue in "Milfay" (episode 1) explains: "Before the beginning, after the great war between Heaven and Hell, God created the Earth and gave dominion over it to the crafty ape he called man. And to each generation was born a creature of light and a

---

1. All references to *Carnivàle* come from *Carnivàle* 2004, 2006.

creature of darkness. And great armies clashed by night in the ancient war between good and evil. There was magic then, nobility, and unimaginable cruelty. And so it was until the day that a false sun exploded over Trinity, and man forever traded away wonder for reason." Part of *Carnivàle*'s appeal is the promise of this coming apocalypse; unlike in many other TV series, there is a promise of an end built into the show's core premise.

But *Carnivàle*'s ending offers no sense of closure or finality. The promised apocalypse never arrives. *Carnivàle* instead leaves its audience with little sense of finality or completion. Given its disappointing end, what makes *Carnivàle*'s "season finale that wasn't" an interesting example for this collection? It is instructive of the limits of long-form serialized narratives on television, and it provides some indication as to what serial narratives require to be counted as successful. For my purposes here, I focus on two primary points.

As noted earlier, the season 2 finale, "New Canaan," retroactively became the series finale only after it aired. It was written, produced, and aired with the expectation that season 3 would at some point appear. From what Knauf has discussed about the series, he intended it to run for six seasons in three books. Knauf's planning indicates he felt fairly confident about his story, his audience, and HBO's willingness to see the project through.[2] And, indeed, throughout season 1 the ratings implied it was a gamble that would pay off. But after its year-long hiatus, the second season saw a marked decline in ratings and share, which leads us to the first lesson of the *Carnivàle* finale: don't leave mythologically and narratively dense series off the air for more than a year; or, if it ain't broke, don't fix it.

The second lesson of *Carnivàle*'s failed ending concerns the nature and relationship of series finales to season finales. If *Carnivàle*'s ending was successful in achieving anything, it was to underscore the importance of season endings to include some kind of narrative completion while also leaving open the obvious continuation of the narrative in subsequent seasons. Even if a series is canceled, the season finale could still offer its audience a formal sense of closure. This is especially important for *Carnivàle* because it is, for all intents and purposes, a show about the end of days, the final battle between good and evil, the triumph of reason over wonder, when the "false sun exploded over Trinity." Its ending should have been "a big deal." This

2. For more on Knauf's plans for the series, see VanDerWerff 2013a and 2013b as well as Morton 2014.

is perhaps doubly so because *Carnivàle*'s complex mythology, which made *Lost*'s narrative feel positively lucid, begs for moments of clarity and comprehension. The purpose of a series finale, as opposed to a season finale, is to bring the entire narrative to a more formal end—to say, "Sorry, we're closed," or to smile quietly with the knowledge that you have defeated evil, for the time being at least. Even the series finale of *Lost*, which I personally found disappointing, offered its audience an emotional release, despite many things being left unexplained. *Carnivàle* left us with an unconscious and possibly bleeding-to-death Ben, a probably dead Jonesy, a now evil Sofie, and a lot of dying corn. All of this might have been perfectly acceptable if in the opening episode of season 3 some of these issues were resolved, but none of these events explains or furthers the mythology established in earlier episodes. We can glean that Sofie is more important than we previously realized. She is the Omega, but what that means and what her relationship is to the creature-of-light/creature-of-darkness mythology is obscured because we know that only males can be avatars. The confrontation between Justin and Ben happens quickly, and the side plots concerning the carnies don't seem to relate in any real way to the larger cosmological events. *Carnivàle*'s final episode fails as both a season finale and a series finale. However, despite this narrative failure, the ending of the series is instructive as a test case for what not to do.

References

Carnivàle: The Complete First Season. 2004. New York: HBO Home Video. DVD.

Carnivàle: The Complete Second Season. 2006. New York: HBO Home Video. DVD.

Morton, Lisa. 2014. "Interview: Daniel Knauf." *Nightmare Magazine*, Aug. 27. At http://www.nightmare-magazine.com/nonfiction/interview-daniel-knauf/.

VanDerWerff, Todd. 2013a. "Daniel Knauf Opens up about *Carnivàle*'s Long, Weird Journey (1 of 2)." *AV/TV Club*, Feb. 21. At https://tv.avclub.com/daniel-knauf-opens-up-about-carnivale-s-long-weird-jou-1798236466.

———. 2013b. "Daniel Knauf Tells Us His Plan for the End of *Carnivàle*." *AV/TV Club*, Feb. 22. At https://tv.avclub.com/daniel-knauf-tells-us-his-plan-for-the-end-of-carnivale-1798236491.

10

Cheers

"One for the Road"

MITCHELL E. SHAPIRO

Cheers (1982–93) was part of NBC's long-running "Must-See TV" Thursday-night lineup before NBC was "Must-See TV." When *Cheers* first premiered in the fall of 1982, NBC was in third place of a three-network universe—Fox wasn't to arrive until four years later in 1986, and cable networks would not really be significant competition until the turn of the century. Although most programs that had ratings like those of *Cheers*' first season would have been summarily canceled—it ranked seventy-fourth out of seventy-seven programs for the 1982–83 season—*Cheers* was brought back for a second season because it received high praise from the critics and the Emmy establishment. If NBC shows weren't generating audiences, at least this one (along with *Hill Street Blues* [1981–87]) was getting favorable press. NBC Entertainment president Brandon Tartikoff and his boss, Chairman Grant Tinker, made *Cheers* the lowest-rated comedy series ever picked up for a second season and then did it again for season 3 (Shapiro and Jicha 2015, 7–10).

Cheers was a trailblazer of NBC's transformation into "the Quality Network," as it came to be known for almost two decades starting in the mid-1980s. Everything changed in 1984. *The Cosby Show* (1984–92) became one of the hottest newcomers in years, energizing Thursday's lineup, which is when that lineup came to be christened "Must-See TV." Tens of millions of viewers brought to the network at the start of the night by *The Cosby Show* fed into *Family Ties* (1982–89) at 8:30, *Cheers* at 9:00, *Night Court* (1984–92) at 9:30, and *Hill Street Blues* at 10:00 Eastern Standard Time.

Cheers, which had languished so deep into the Nielsen rankings that it didn't make the cut in many newspaper ratings reports, jumped into the top fifteen in its first *Cosby*-fueled season, then into the top five through the rest of the decade, until it peaked at number one in 1990–91, a rarity for a show so deep into its run (Shapiro and Jicha 2015, 7–10).

The setting for *Cheers* was a neighborhood bar in Boston. Although the series broke no new ground with the workplace humor concept, the writing was brilliant, the characters were rich and well fleshed out, and the superlative cast, none of whom was really well known to the audience at that time, eventually racked up more than a dozen individual Emmys to accompany the series' four Emmy awards as television's outstanding comedy. By the end of its eleven-season run in the spring of 1993, *Cheers* had racked up twenty-eight Emmys and was nominated for Best Comedy Series each year (Shapiro and Jicha 2015, 7–10).

Created by the team of Glen Charles, James Burrows, and Les Charles, *Cheers* is similar in format to their earlier series *Taxi* (1978–83). Almost every scene in *Cheers* is set in the bar; in *Taxi*, it is the garage. The humor is derived from the interactions between the different employees and patrons of the bar Cheers. On rare occasions, the action will take place in the home of one of the regular characters or in Melville's, the fancy seafood restaurant that sits atop the bar.

The central character is bar owner Sam Malone, a washed-up former pitcher for the Boston Red Sox. Ted Danson, who had a long list of television credits as minor or guest characters, plays Malone. He is wonderful as the handsome, not-too-smart womanizer who purchases the bar after his baseball career ends. Shelley Long plays the first of Danson's leading ladies, Diane Chambers. Diane is a graduate student studying classic literature. She is pretentious and always thinks working as a barmaid beneath her, but she needs the money. She doesn't really get along with the other employees or the patrons of the bar. However, she and Sam develop a love/hate relationship.

One of the elements that *Cheers* introduced and perfected within the sitcom form is the serialized nature of the relationship between Sam and Diane. Up until that time, sitcoms were considered to be episodic—each episode stood on its own. The audience did not need to watch all episodes to follow the plot in one episode. Although some sitcoms did have "history" in the series story line and would refer back to earlier moments in the series as plot devices, there was still a "stand-alone" quality to each episode. With *Cheers*, each episode was able to stand on its own, but the show also introduced an over-reaching story arc that continued through each episode of the series—the "will they or won't they get together" story line. This continued throughout the series' run and was arguably something that held the audience's interest.

Shelley Long left the series after the sixth season to pursue a career in feature films. Her departure was set up through having her end her engagement to Sam in order to move to Los Angeles and pursue a writing career. Her replacement was Kirstie Alley, who played Rebecca Howe. Alley's character starts out as a strong, independent woman who is brought in to manage the bar by its new owners (Sam gives it away after Diane leaves him). She is a different kind of foil for Sam. Initially, Sam tries to seduce her, without success. She dates only rich, successful men, and these relationships always end in failure. After each of these failed relationships, her character becomes less confident and more needy. Sam eventually regains ownership of the bar, and Rebecca begs him to allow her to stay on as manager, which he does.

Other original cast members include George Wendt as Norm Peterson, John Ratzenberger as Cliff Clavin, Rhea Perlman as Carla Tortelli, and Nicholas Colasanto as Coach Ernie Pantusso. Norm Peterson is a regular customer at the bar and an accountant. Although Norm is married, he seems to spend almost all of his time at the bar. Norm's wife, Vera, is one of those television characters whom the audience never sees but is often referred to. Cliff Clavin works for the postal service as a carrier and is a know-it-all who really doesn't know much of anything. He lives with his mother (another character who is never seen). Carla Tortelli is the sharp-mouthed waitress who idolizes Sam, and Coach is Sam's former not-too-bright pitching coach who now works as a bartender. In *Cheers'* fifth season, the character of Carla was spun-off into another series, *The Tortellis* (1987). It lasted only five months, and she returned to *Cheers*.

During the course of *Cheers'* run, two other significant characters were added. Woody Harrelson played Woody Boyd, a sweet, simple-minded young man who replaces Coach as a bartender. Nicholas Colasanto passed away in real life, and the writers wrote the same fate for his character, Coach. Kelsey Grammer portrayed Frasier Crane, a psychiatrist and snooty know-it-all. Frasier was initially brought in as a love-interest for Diane after Sam and Diane's first breakup. Although Diane eventually leaves Frasier at the altar to go back to Sam, Frasier is kept on for the remainder of the series.

The final episode of *Cheers* aired on May 20, 1993.[1] It became a national event. There was tremendous buildup and much anticipation for it. In fact, NBC devoted almost the whole night to it. The night began with a one-hour

---

1. All references to the final episode, "One for the Road," come from Burrows [1993] 2009.

season finale of *Seinfeld* (1989–98) at 8:00 p.m. After a "pregame" show, hosted by Bob Costas, NBC aired the extended ninety-eight-minute final episode of *Cheers* from 9:00 to 11:00 p.m. The network followed up by airing a live episode of *The Tonight Show Starring Jay Leno* from the Bull & Finch Pub in Boston, the pub that the Cheers bar was supposedly based on. The cast of *Cheers* showed up for this tribute unexpectedly inebriated, making for quite an interesting tribute.

The finale was a perfect ending to this wonderful series. Written by the series creators, Glen and Les Charles, and directed by the other third of the creative team, James Burrows, the episode answered all questions and tied up all loose ends that the series had developed throughout its run. Even Shelley Long returned to bring closure to Sam and Diane's relationship.

The episode begins with Rebecca Howe being proposed to by her current beau, Don the plumber (Tom Berenger). She wants to accept but can't bring herself to do it—she can't picture herself married to a plumber. Meanwhile, Sam is struggling with where his life is going—he's trying to abstain from drinking and sex. The patrons in the bar are watching television and see Diane win a Cable Ace award for writing. After winning the award, she phones Sam. She informs him that she is now married with three kids. To save face with her, he pretends to be married with four kids and casually invites her to drop by and go to dinner (this is really sort of a false invite as he knows she is in Los Angeles and the bar is in Boston). Surprisingly, Diane shows up at the bar with husband in tow, expecting to dine with Sam and his "wife." Quick-thinking Sam grabs Rebecca and begs her to pretend to be his wife. She agrees, and the four of them go to dinner. While at dinner, Dan shows up and again proposes to Rebecca. She accepts, and he carries her out of the restaurant. Having caught Sam in the deception, Diane begins to gloat, when no sooner does a man enter the restaurant proclaiming to be her supposed husband's lover. The two men leave, and Sam and Diane are left alone with the realization that they are still in love with each other.

The next day they enter the bar and announce that they are back together, moving to California, and getting married. Norm and the other patrons are stunned and wonder what will become of them. Sam gets angry and basically tells them all that he's "not their mother" and that they need to get their own lives.

On the plane waiting to take off, both Sam and Diane start to have doubts and realize that they are not really right for each other and a marriage will not work. She returns to Los Angeles; he returns to the bar. At the bar, he apologizes to his friends for the way he treated them. They are insulted and leave, only to return a minute later and let him know that they were playing a practical joke on him—Diane had called them earlier and told them of the breakup. They proceed to sit around, philosophize, and tell each other how much they mean to one another. They then leave one at a time. Sam locks the door, turns out the lights, and is left by himself, alone in the bar with his one true love, Cheers—"I'm the luckiest son of a bitch on Earth." Suddenly there is a knock on the door. Sam says, "Sorry, we're closed." Fade out.

What happened to the other characters? Rebecca and Dan get married. Woody is elected to the Boston City Council and helps get Norm a new job. Cliff gets a promotion at work, and Carla goes on as usual. Oh yes, Frasier. He goes on to a spin-off series playing a radio talk-show host in Seattle. The new series, *Frasier* (1993–2004), goes on for another eleven years, winning the Emmy for Best Comedy Series a record five times. Kelsey Grammer also holds the distinction of having played the same character longer than anyone in the history of television (with the arguable exception of James Arness as Matt Dillon on *Gunsmoke*). Most of the cast of *Cheers* made guest appearances on *Frasier* as their *Cheers* characters.

The finale of *Cheers* garnered 84.4 million viewers, the second-largest audience for any episode of any television series in American history—only the finale of *M*A*S*H* (1972–83) ever had a larger audience ("NBC Wins May Sweeps" 1993).

References

Burrows, James, dir. [1993] 2009. "One for the Road." *Cheers*, season 11, episode 25. Written by Glen Charles and Les Charles. Aired May 20, 1993, NBC. On *Cheers: The Final Season*. Hollywood: Paramount. DVD.

"NBC Wins May Sweeps: Cheers Ratings No. 2 All Time." 1993. *Toronto Star*, May 30.

Shapiro, Mitchell E., and Tom Jicha. 2015. *The Top 100 American Situation Comedies: An Objective Ranking*. Jefferson, NC: McFarland.

11

The Colbert Report

"Episode 1,447"

KEITH BRAND

The Colbert Report (the *t* in "Colbert" is silent) first aired on Comedy Central on October 17, 2005. The premise of the show was that a fictional character named Stephen Colbert was the host of a political talk show. That character was modeled after any number of political pundits, but perhaps most pointedly on Bill O'Reilly, the host of the Fox Network's show *The O'Reilly Factor* (1996–2017). Colbert, in his guise as an arrogant conservative host, would deliver the news with a satirical wink. He would then interview various guests, often skewering their answers, again with a sly nod to the audience.

Colbert began his comedy career with the Chicago improvisational company Second City, where he met Amy Sedaris and subsequently left to work on the show *Exit 57* (1995–96) for HBO. Although receiving good reviews, *Exit 57* lasted only twelve episodes. Colbert then worked as a cast member for *The Dana Carvey Show* (1996–), along with Steve Carell, Louis C. K., and Robert Smigel. The fictional Steven Colbert character made his first appearance there in 1996. Colbert also had brief stints on *Good Morning America* (1975–) as a correspondent and *Saturday Night Live* (1975–), where he voiced half of the animated Ambiguously Gay Duo.

Stephen Colbert joined *The Daily Show* (1996–) in its second season in 1997, hosted by Craig Kilborn. When Jon Stewart took over the program in 1999, he asked Colbert to give his character a sharper political edge. After a few years, Stewart and Colbert pitched *The Colbert Report* to Comedy Central, and the program debuted in 2005. Although similar in format to Jon Stewart's *The Daily Show*, *The Colbert Report* masterly employed Colbert's conservative persona to parody the news of the day, always delivered with a knowing glance.

The Report, as it was often referred to, opened with a montage of iconic American images, including an animated bald eagle. During the opening, Colbert would appear as the defender of mainstream values, often holding an American flag. The burst of images was delivered over the raucous beat of the song "Baby Mumbles" by the band Cheap Trick.

After a rabidly cheering audience welcomed the host, Colbert would launch into his spin on the news of the day. That segment would lead into "The Word," a parody of Bill O'Reilly's "Talking Points Memo." The show sometimes featured "The Colbert Report Special Report," where the host could devote the rest of the show to a special topic. But usually he would feature an interview with a newsworthy guest. If the guest was politically or socially liberal, the Colbert character would mock his or her viewpoint, again with a sly wink. Although *The Colbert Report*'s knowing satire might have been aimed at conservatives, an interesting study done by Jody Baumgartner and Jonathan Morris (2008) concludes that Colbert's attempts to satirize those ideologies and personalities may very well have assisted in spreading their messages. Apparently, the comedy blocked the program's implicit message.

By the time Stephen Colbert ended *The Report* in December 2014, he had delivered 1,447 episodes of often brilliant political satire, picking up two Peabody Awards and breaking Jon Stewart's run of Emmy Award wins for Outstanding Variety, Music, or Comedy Series in 2013. At the same time, he had amassed many fans across the political spectrum, collectively referred to as the "Colbert Nation." At its height, the program had 1.2 million viewers, sometimes beating *The Tonight Show Starring Jay Leno* (1992–2004) in the key eighteen- to forty-nine-year-old age demographic.

In between the show's debut in 2005 and its swan song in 2014, Colbert also managed to make headlines by starting his own Super Pac, which he called "Americans for a Better Tomorrow, Tomorrow," and attempted to run for president. In 2006, he hosted the White House Correspondents Dinner only a few months after the show's premiere. While the video of his performance went viral, the actual audience watched in stunned silence. Both NASA and Ben & Jerry's were admirers enough to name a treadmill and pint of ice cream, respectively, after Colbert. As an enduring legacy, his invented and oft-used word *truthiness* officially entered the lexicon courtesy of *Merriam-Webster* in 2006.

The December 18, 2014, finale began like most previous *Colbert Report*s:[1] the Stephen Colbert character began the show with his characteristic take on world news, including a piece about a truck from a Texas plumbing company showing up on the battlefield in Syria. This was followed by a segue into "The Word" segment, which for that evening's episode was focused on his legacy, complete with on-screen bullet points that added to the satire. This led to a scene in which he killed death and gained immortality. Although these segments were amusing, they could have appeared on any of the series' previous programs.

In the show's moving conclusion, Colbert began the segment by boasting about his immortality while pensively sitting on his futuristic desk. After a few quips about attempting to finish items on his bucket list, which evolved into items he would like to eat out of a bucket, Colbert began his final goodbye. With a series of piano chords as the introduction, he began to sing an upbeat version of "We'll Meet Again," the iconic and popular World War II–era dirge written by Ross Parker and Hughie Charles and made popular by Vera Lynn in 1939. Many will remember this song from the final scene of *Dr. Strangelove* (Stanley Kubrick, 1964).

As Colbert began earnestly singing, he stood and moved from behind his desk toward the center of the set, where he was joined by Jon Stewart, who entered to thunderous cheers that never subsided throughout the segment. Holding hands, they strolled toward a grand piano, which revealed the singer-songwriter Randy Newman, still playing and singing "We'll Meet Again." The camera then cut to groups of singers, mostly recognizable personalities. The first group consisted of Willie Nelson, Bryan Cranston, Doris Kearns Goodwin, and National Institutes of Health director Francis Collins.

On a program that prided itself on sharp satire, what was interesting about this segment was the singers' various levels of commitment to the segment's conceit. In some instances, it looked as if participants were singing a different song, feeling lost, or even wondering, "What am I doing here?" Other guests committed fully to the moment. Andy Cohen, the Bravo network host and producer, passionately sang along, while Samantha Power, the US ambassador to the United Nations, provided an endearing contrast with some strange dance moves.

---

1. All references to the *Colbert Report* finale come from Hoskinson 2014.

When a cut was made to a group featuring Katie Couric, Andrew Sullivan, Ken Burns, Ric Ocasek, and the dancer David Hallberg, Gloria Steinem accidently walked through the shot looking a bit lost. Apparently realizing that anything could happen at this point, Hallberg and Couric embraced and started dancing in the crowded space. In some of the groups, a measure of comic relief was unwittingly provided as various individuals angled themselves to ensure their faces were seen during the onstage chaos.

After a number of in-studio singers were featured, the finale cut to pre-taped scenes with guests who for various reasons couldn't attend the "live" event, all still singing "We'll Meet Again." In the first of these scenes, the staff of *The Colbert Report* joined in from their midtown Manhattan head-quarters. This segment continued with members of Pussy Riot, the outspoken Russian punk band; Vince Gilligan chained in a basement somewhere in Hollywood; Bill Clinton tweeting the lyrics to the song; a large group of service members in Afghanistan; and director J. J. Abrams. And in a thoroughly meta-addition to this cast, both Tek Janson, an animated Colbert character, and Esteban Colberto, his Spanish equivalent, also sang along. Oh yes, even Smaug the dragon made an appearance.

In a return to the studio, the camera panned across close to one hundred political, entertainment, sports, diplomatic, business, and media celebrities. Before the final stanza of the song, there was a cut to a long shot of the audience, the three studio cameras disseminating the words of the song on each of the teleprompters. As the song came to an end and the cheering continued, a circle wipe to black enveloped the screen, while the sound faded to a faint echo. The entire charming sendoff lasted four and a half minutes.

But that wasn't all. In the penultimate segment, Colbert had a chat about his future with none other than Santa Claus, Abraham Lincoln (as a unicorn), and Alex Trebek, the host of the game show *Jeopardy* (1964–). After taking off in Santa's sleigh, they returned for a final segment where Colbert thanked a number of people who had assisted in the creation and long run of the program before exiting to the strains of the Neutral Milk Hotel song "Holland, 1945."

Although most of the finale kept Colbert in character, the "We'll Meet Again" segment was delightfully off-script. Warm and sincere where his character was not, it seemed like a welcome break from the satire. With its mix of political eccentrics, Hollywood actors, media celebrities, and military and sports figures, the lineup was impressively eclectic. And as we move into an era of increasingly deep ideological and political fault lines, it's one we likely won't see again.

References

Baumgartner, Jody C., and Jonathan S. Morris. 2008. "One 'Nation,' under Stephen? The Effects of *The Colbert Report* on American Youth." *Journal of Broadcasting & Electronic Media* 52, no. 4: 622–43.

Hoskinson, Jim, dir. 2014. "Episode 1,447." *The Colbert Report*, season 11. Written by Stephen Colbert and others. Aired Dec. 18, Comedy Central. Original broadcast.

12

Dark Shadows

Episode 1,245

JEFF THOMPSON

Something rare in television is the last episode of a soap opera. Daytime serials, at least at the peak of their popularity, seem eternal, with their beginnings shrouded in 1950s/1960s antiquity and their endings nowhere in sight, at least for years or even decades. When a soap opera such as *Guiding Light* (1952–2009), *As the World Turns* (1956–2010), or *One Life to Live* (1968–2013) ends, a cultural institution is lost. Soaps are daytime fixtures that two or three generations of family members have watched together.

Although ABC's series *Dark Shadows*, created by Syracuse University graduate Dan Curtis, lasted only five years, from 1966 to 1971—a mere moment compared to the runs experienced by *Search for Tomorrow* (1951–86) and *Another World* (1964–99), seven times longer—the groundbreaking gothic serial seemed to pack two hundred years' worth of stories and melodrama into its highly rated run. Supernatural story lines took place in 1795, 1840, 1897, 1968, and many other time periods, and the enduring popularity of *Dark Shadows* is timeless. *Dark Shadows* is one of the very few soap operas ever to be rerun in syndication and the *only* soap opera to be released in its entirety (1,225 episodes) on VHS and DVD, to spawn extensive merchandising and three feature films, and to sustain a yearly fan convention, the Dark Shadows Festival, which has lasted seven times longer than the TV series itself.

In 1969, at the height of the popularity of *Dark Shadows*, more than 18 million viewers were watching the daily adventures of the vampire Barnabas Collins (Jonathan Frid), the witch Angelique (Lara Parker), and the werewolf Quentin Collins (David Selby) (Thompson 2009, 57). By late 1970, however, the viewership had fallen off to 12 million (Scott and Pierson 2000,

104)—although that is still quite a successful number for a television program in 1971 and even very impressive for a TV show in 2018. Nevertheless, some of the audience—as well as executive producer Dan Curtis himself—"became disenchanted" with the TV show, in Curtis's words (quoted in Thompson 2009, 23). Curtis, his frequent director Lela Swift, and his writers Sam Hall, Gordon Russell, and others had pitted Barnabas Collins, Victoria Winters (Alexandra Moltke), and Elizabeth Collins Stoddard (Joan Bennett) against ghosts, vampires, witches, werewolves, *Frankenstein*-like creations, Lovecraftian elder gods called Leviathans, and a phoenix fire creature in time periods stretching from the seventeenth and eighteenth centuries to the then future year of 1995, and the show had begun repeating itself (e.g., two phoenix story lines, two *Turn of the Screw*–style hauntings, two journeys into Parallel Time).

"When we were doing *Dark Shadows*," actress and author Lara Parker recalled in an interview in 2010, "we were certain that each show would be seen only once and never again. It has such a cult following now, but for us, it was just a job. Later, we realized that we had created something unique and remarkable that has never really been duplicated on TV since."[1] From November 1967 until January 1971, Parker played the "plum role" (in Frid's words to her at the time) of Angelique Bouchard Collins, the scorned witch who places the vampire curse on Barnabas after he chooses Josette DuPres (Kathryn Leigh Scott) over her. However, in the final three months of *Dark Shadows*, Parker and Frid stopped playing Angelique and Barnabas and began portraying Catherine Harridge and Bramwell Collins, star-crossed lovers in the world of 1841 in Parallel Time. "Finally, after five years, I was being allowed to play the heroine," Parker remembered, "but it was not as satisfying as I thought it would be. I experienced discontent because I missed the Angelique character."

Many *Dark Shadows* fans also may have missed the witch and the vampire, but the Bramwell–Catherine love story, reminiscent of Emily Brontë's Heathcliff–Cathy love story in *Wuthering Heights*, served as a reward for the fans who had always wanted to see Frid's and Parker's characters as a couple. Throughout the run of *Dark Shadows*, the fickle Barnabas pursued Josette (Scott), Vicki (Moltke), Maggie (Scott again), Roxanne (Donna Wandrey), and other love interests, while Angelique—not to mention the

---

1. Lara Parker, telephone interview by Jeff Thompson, Nov. 26, 2010; all quotations from Parker come from this interview.

long-suffering Dr. Julia Hoffman (Grayson Hall)—languished unwanted and unloved. "The whole show was about yearning and longing for love," Parker observed: "Even the 'monsters' on the show wanted love."

Dark Shadows ended like it had begun, in its pre-Barnabas months, as a mildly mysterious soap opera patterned after the gothic-romance novels popular in the 1960s and 1970s (the vampires, werewolves, and Leviathans had come later). Granted, the Parallel Time story line set in 1841 featured a vengeful ghost (Louis Edmonds) and a terrifying family ritual patterned after Shirley Jackson's story "The Lottery," but at its heart were interpersonal relationships, family dynamics, and soap-operatic plot devices, such as Catherine's illicit pregnancy, Melanie's secret parentage, and Daphne's terminal illness (Thompson 2009, 63). The actresses of *Dark Shadows*—Parker, Bennett, Hall, Nancy Barrett, Kathleen Cody, and (in her first acting job) Kate Jackson—took center stage in the TV show's final story.

In a way, *Dark Shadows* "ended" not on April 2, 1971, but on January 27, 1971. Episode 1,198 featured the final appearances of the present-day characters Elizabeth, Barnabas, Angelique, Julia, and Stokes (Thayer David). In that episode, set in 1841, Angelique dies, and the time travelers Barnabas, Julia, and Stokes return to their own time, 1971, where they find that they have changed history and prevented the destruction of the Collinwood mansion and the Collins family. The saga ends happily for the core characters; then the story again shifts back in time, not to 1841 but to an 1841 in an alternate universe known on the TV show as Parallel Time. Now, as they had done many times before, the *Dark Shadows* repertory actors took on new roles very different from their present-day characters.

The 1,225th and final episode of *Dark Shadows*—labeled by ABC as "Episode #1245"—was videotaped at the show's New York City studio on March 24, 1971, and telecast on Friday, April 2 (Scott 2001, 302).[2] Written by Sam Hall and directed by Lela Swift, the last episode was unusual in that it featured ten characters instead of the usual five or six—Bramwell Collins (Jonathan Frid), Catherine Harridge Collins (Lara Parker), Morgan Collins (Keith Prentice), Flora Collins (Joan Bennett), the ghost of Brutus Collins (Louis Edmonds), Julia Collins (Grayson Hall), Kendrick Young (John Karlen), Melanie Collins Young (Nancy Barrett), Ben Stokes (Thayer David), and the servant Harris (writer Gordon Russell in a walk-on role).

2. All references to the final episode of *Dark Shadows* come from Swift [1971] 2012.

In the episode, featuring opening narration by Hall and closing narration by David, a pregnant Catherine and her lover, Bramwell, spend the night in a room haunted by the vicious ghost of Brutus Collins, who possesses Catherine and tries to kill Bramwell. Catherine and Bramwell survive the night, defeat the ghost, and end Brutus's curse, only to be terrorized further by Catherine's husband, Morgan, who has been driven insane by Catherine's infidelity. Morgan abducts Catherine at gunpoint. In a struggle with Bramwell and Kendrick, Morgan falls to his death from a turret at Collinwood. Meanwhile, Melanie recovers from her illness and makes plans to move to Boston with her husband, Kendrick. After first planning to leave Collinwood as well, Bramwell and Catherine decide to remain at the family manor at the urging of a very forgiving Flora. "Their love became a living legend," the closing narration reveals, and "the dark shadows at Collinwood were but a memory of the distant past."

"There was a crazy, happy-go-lucky feeling on the set" on the last day of taping, Lara Parker remembered: "No one was that unhappy. We felt a sort of relief that the show was ending because we all thought we would be moving on to nighttime TV and movies. Also, we were looking forward to doing the movie [*Night of Dark Shadows*], so the last day didn't really feel like an ending." Indeed, just five days after the taping of the last episode, director Dan Curtis began filming the MGM movie *Night of Dark Shadows* (1971)—a follow-up to *House of Dark Shadows* (1970)—at the Lyndhurst estate in Tarrytown, New York (Thompson 2010, 26). In addition to David Selby and Kate Jackson, the film starred five of the actors (including Parker) who had appeared in episode 1,245.

Lara Parker remembered that playwright Neil Simon was visiting the *Dark Shadows* studio on the last day of taping: "Keith Prentice [as Morgan Collins] had to do a fall in the episode, so he kept practicing pratfalls in front of Neil Simon to impress him and maybe get a part in a play!" Parker, now an author and an educator, called *Dark Shadows* "an iconic symbol of horror and gothic romance" and observed, "For many fans, *Dark Shadows* is something that made their adolescence bearable." Now, fifty-plus years later, those fans are the devotees who flock to the Dark Shadows Festivals in New York and Los Angeles to meet Parker, Selby, Scott, Cody, and many other stars who have meant so much to them over the years. Meanwhile, *Dark Shadows* has been resurrected twice by Dan Curtis (1991, 2004) and once by Tim Burton (2012), but it is the innovative original that has endured and flourished as a cult classic in TV syndication; on video, DVD, and Netflix;

on Syfy; and as a new series of CD audio dramas featuring the original stars voicing their famous characters.

Immediately after ABC-TV canceled *Dark Shadows* and replaced it with *Password* (1961–75), the gothic serial found an afterlife not only in the feature film *Night of Dark Shadows* but also in the daily *Dark Shadows* newspaper comic strip, in a series of Gold Key comic books, in the last five of Dan Ross's series of thirty-two *Dark Shadows* gothic novels for Paperback Library, and in fanzines of the 1970s, such as *The World of Dark Shadows* and *Inside the Old House*. Millions of *Dark Shadows* fans of all ages were suffering from withdrawal symptoms after the cancellation, and many were not satisfied with the abrupt conclusion that had left the show in Parallel Time instead of returning it to "their" time (i.e., 1971) and "their" characters (i.e. the present-day Collins family: Elizabeth, Roger, Carolyn, Barnabas, and so on).

Therefore, on October 9, 1971, a full six months after the final episode of *Dark Shadows* had aired, *TV Guide* featured the article "Here's What *Really* Happened to Barnabas & Co." (Hall 1971). The three-page feature was written by Sam Hall, who had scripted 316 episodes of the TV series (Thompson 2010, 21). The article was a scorecard of "an estate full of troubled characters" (Hall 1971) and what might have happened to them if *Dark Shadows* had continued or if the last episode had shown the characters of 1971 one last time.

In the article, Hall (1971) decreed happiness for Elizabeth, Carolyn, Amy, and Maggie and Joe; endless wandering and searching for the immortal Quentin; and death for Roger, Sabrina, and Chris. Even the creature like Frankenstein's monster, Adam, who had not been seen since early December 1968, received a long-overdue wrap-up to his abruptly ended story: "He had become a successful, sophisticated man," and he and Carolyn "parted warm friends." As for Barnabas Collins, the article revealed that when Dr. Julia Hoffman was stricken by a serious illness, Barnabas "realized how much he loved her and promised her that if she lived, they would marry." According to Hall,

> They were married in Singapore. Barnabas felt they must never return to Collinsport. Angelique must not find them—for she would never allow Julia to live. So they stayed on. Julia began working with an Asian doctor and experimented with a new treatment which she was positive would take away the curse of Barnabas's vampirism. They began the treatments. They were successful. Barnabas Collins at last could walk in the light of

day—walk with the woman he loved, but walk with an ever-present fear—a fear that Angelique would find them and destroy the only happiness he has had in his life. No audience will see these stories playing out. But for those for whom our characters were real, these are merely signposts pointing a direction the characters might have gone.

In thinking about the finale, I have always wished that when Barnabas, Julia, and Stokes left 1841 and returned to 1971, Professor Stokes would have stayed behind and crossed over to 1841 Parallel Time. Every other time trip had included a character from "our" world and "our" present time (e.g., Vicki, Barnabas, Julia, Eve), and that element was missing from 1841 Parallel Time. Professor Stokes would have provided a link to "our" world as he observed and participated in the world of 1841 Parallel Time. As it was, the only link to "our" band of time was that the Bramwell Collins character was the son of the Parallel Time Barnabas (never a vampire) and the Parallel Time Josette (never a suicide). At least *Dark Shadows* came to a definite conclusion in its final episode and did not end on a cliff-hanger, as so many daytime and nighttime series have done.

References

Hall, Sam. 1971. "Here's What *Really* Happened to Barnabas & Co." *TV Guide*, Oct. 9.

Scott, Kathryn Leigh. 2001. *"Dark Shadows" Memories*. Los Angeles: Pomegranate Press.

Scott, Kathryn Leigh, and Jim Pierson, eds. 2000. *"Dark Shadows" Almanac*. Millennium ed. Los Angeles: Pomegranate Press.

Swift, Lela, dir. [1971] 2012. Episode 1,245. *Dark Shadows*, season 6. Written by Sam Hall. Aired Apr. 2, 1971, ABC. On *Dark Shadows: Collection 26*. Orland Park, IL: MPI Home Video. DVD.

Thompson, Jeff. 2009. *The Television Horrors of Dan Curtis: "Dark Shadows," "The Night Stalker," and Other Productions, 1966–2006*. Jefferson, NC: McFarland.

13

Dawson's Creek

"All Good Things . . . Must Come to an End"

LORI BINDIG YOUSMAN

Dawson's Creek (1998–2003) emerged out of a historical and cultural moment when the media turned their attention to the growing teen population. With 76 million youth becoming teens during the late 1990s, the demographic was its largest since the 1950s. Disposable income and their numbers made teens prime targets for an endless parade of products pushed across media properties. Industry deregulation allowed for increased media concentration, conglomeration, and synergy, which produced a plethora of film and television vehicles aimed at teens. New technological advancements led to niche cable, satellite, and Internet platforms designed to capture the hearts and wallets of American teens and their global counterparts (Wee 2010).

Launching in the midst of the teen boom in 1995, the WB was initially conceived as a family-friendly television network. After two years of struggling, it adopted the strategy of a competitor, Fox, and began courting young viewers through teen programming (Osgerby 2010). As part of this approach, it purchased a series by the $100-million-grossing *Scream*-franchise writer Kevin Williamson. Williamson's relationship with the WB marked a new trend in feature-film writers, directors, and producers aligning themselves with teen-branded networks (Wee 2010).

The WB premiered *Dawson's Creek* on January 20, 1998, to much success. Over the first season, the show ranked number one among teens and eighteen- to thirty-four-year-olds (Sharkey 1998), which quickly helped stabilize the fledgling network. The show also launched the careers of little-known actors James Van Der Beek, Katie Holmes, Joshua Jackson, and Michelle Williams and served as a training ground for many of contemporary television's power players (Goldberg 2015). Although a clear descendant of *Beverly Hills, 90210* (1990–2000), *Dawson's Creek* revolutionized the teen genre through its unique tone and style. Unlike earlier teen programs, which were straightforward and earnest, *Dawson's Creek* featured hyperarticulate characters who were ironic and self-aware and who engaged in metacommentary through reflexive and intertextual references. This sophisticated approach resulted in Williamson being hailed as an "authorial voice" and *Dawson's Creek* being labeled as "quality television" (Hills 2004), and it paved the way for the critical reception of subsequent teen television shows and teen television auteurs (Bindig and Bergstrom 2008).

Over six seasons, *Dawson's Creek* followed the lives of Dawson (a burgeoning filmmaker), Joey (a tomboy from the wrong side of the creek), Pacey (a good-natured smart aleck), and Jen (the beautiful "bad girl" from New York) as they navigated the trials and tribulations of growing up. Accompanied by a musical soundtrack featuring Warner Bros. artists and a bevy of integrated brands and cross-promotional initiatives, the story lines generally revolved around the heterosexual romantic relationships of exclusively white main characters who conformed to traditional standards of beauty. When Jack (a gay teen) was added to the cast, the show sensitively depicted his coming-out narrative and was responsible for the first gay kiss on prime-time network television. Overall, *Dawson's Creek* continued to be a fan favorite and remained the top program for twelve- to seventeen-year-old girls through its sixth and final season (Campbell 2003).

Although the series includes a total of 128 episodes, the show was slated to end with episode 22, season 6, "Joey Potter and the Capeside Redemption." However, the WB asked Williamson, who had left *Dawson's Creek* during its second season to work on other projects, to return for the finale to "show how everyone ended up" (Bierly 2014). Williamson agreed to pen the series finale, which would consist of two back-to-back, hour-long episodes (episode 23, "All Good Things . . . ," and episode 24, ". . . Must Come to an End") set five years into the future.[1] The finale, which aired on May 14, 2003, became the highest-rated episode of the series, with 7.8 million viewers (Fernandez 2015). Years after airing, the *Dawson's Creek* finale is ranked number 16 on *TV Guide*'s roster of most unforgettable finales (*TV's Most Unforgettable Finales* 2011) and is listed among *Entertainment Weekly*'s ten most iconic television series finales ("The Art of Saying Goodbye" 2014).

Although *Dawson's Creek* explored "first love, first sex, first everything," Williamson noted that "they hadn't dealt with the death of a core member of

---

1. All references to the *Dawson's Creek* finale come from Prange 2003a, 2003b.

their group" (quoted in Bierly 2014). Therefore, Williamson's finale tells the story of a professionally frustrated Dawson's reunion with his high school friends when he returns to Capeside for his mother's wedding. Joey realizes she still loves both Dawson and Pacey but is encouraged by Jen to finally choose her romantic destiny. Jen's unexpected death prompts Doug, Jack's closeted boyfriend, to come to terms with his sexuality and join Jack in raising Jen's orphaned daughter, Amy. The finale ends with Dawson writing the "perfect" ending for his television show and sharing with a happy Joey and Pacey the news of an upcoming meeting with Steven Spielberg, his idol. Williamson's narrative provides a solid framework, but it is his authorial voice, reflexivity, and referentiality that are vital to positioning the finale as a gratifying natural conclusion to a beloved series.

From the very beginning, Williamson was always forthcoming that *Dawson's Creek* was rooted in his own experience (Bierly 2014) and personality (Williamson 2003). Therefore, it is not surprising that much of the titular character's finale story line is a pastiche of Williamson's life. When the episode opens, Dawson is running his own autobiographical teen soap, *The Creek*, much like Williamson with *Dawson's Creek*. Although his show is a hit, Dawson is unfulfilled in Hollywood, which reflects Williamson's dissatisfaction with his own career at the time of writing the finale (Goldberg 2015). Just as Williamson was given only a few days to complete the final hour of the series, Dawson has time constraints in completing his show's finale. Likewise, Dawson's struggle over the ending of *The Creek* epitomizes the uncertainty Williamson experienced when determining the fate of the characters on *Dawson's Creek*.

Williamson also used *The Creek* to imbue the finale with the self-reflexive metacommentary that *Dawson's Creek* was known for. When Joey's boyfriend, Christopher, complains that "the teen hyperbole, it's hard on the stomach. And the writers must sit around with a thesaurus just seeking out four-syllable ways to abuse the English language," Williamson winkingly addressed the criticism the series received over the years (Bierly 2014). Williamson wittily acknowledged fan desire for a satisfying resolution to the series' prolonged love triangle when Christopher mocks, "Will Sam and Colby ever get together? Will Sam choose Petey? Will Sam choose Colby? Find out next week as we continue to beat a dead dog all the way into syndication!" Williamson alluded to several of the well-known production challenges the series encountered by means of Dawson and his assistant's discussion of *The Creek*'s mumbling actors, a network-dictated euphemism, and a character's outing. When a writer from *The Creek* notes, "This show is about twisting the convention," Williamson not only referenced the way *Dawson's Creek*'s season 1 finale defied convention (Williamson 2003) but also suggested a similarly unexpected ending for the series as a whole.

Williamson was able to integrate the unique aesthetic style of *Dawson's Creek* into the series finale through musical and visual references. For example, the finale features a number of songs used throughout the series. In particular, the inclusion of Edwin McCain's "I'll Be," Sarah McLachlan's "Angel," and Beth Nielsen Chapman's "Say Goodnight" summon their original context in the iconic season 1 finale (Goldberg 2015) and thus subtly show how they acted as foreshadowing for the series finale. Beyond supplementing story lines and heightening emotion, these songs are reminders of the integral role music played in the show's cross-promotional strategies, including official soundtracks marketed to teen viewers. Similarly, the *Dawson's Creek* finale highlights a visual mainstay of the series by incorporating an overhead shot of Dawson and Joey chastely lying next to each other in Dawson's bed. This shot, which originated in the pilot and "established a feel [for the show]," references all the other moments these characters shared in Dawson's room. In addition to its use in storytelling, Williamson felt this visual reference was necessary because "he thought it was important to see them in bed in that famous pose one last time" (Stupin and Williamson 2003). Williamson also paired musical and visual references together in the finale through the appearance of Pacey's "home movies." The video, which is an extended version of the season 1 title sequence, allows the audience to revisit the literal beginning of the series. Because Alanis Morissette's song "Hand in My Pocket" was originally intended for (but never used in) the opening credits, combining it with the home-movie footage functions intertextually in the series finale as a "fun message to the fans" (Williamson 2003).

Beyond its reflexive and aesthetic references, the finale of *Dawson's Creek* reiterates and extends the series' groundbreaking representation of gay characters. When the finale reveals Doug as Jack's love interest, it plays upon the character's origins—specifically the many quips questioning Doug's sexuality—while surprising viewers with an unexpected gay character, just like Jack's introduction in the second season. Doug's uncertainty mirrors Jack's own journey for acceptance over the course of the series. When Jack says, "You know, we do live in a post–*Will & Grace* world. I mean, do you really think people still care who you sleep with?" Williamson recognized the crucial role that television programming, in particular *Dawson's Creek*, was playing in the increasing visibility and acceptance of the gay community. Though the finale revisits Jack's past hardships when he speaks of being "tired of being first" and of "reeducating" Capeside, it also presents new obstacles with his concerns over Amy being "the only kid with a gay parent." Nevertheless, the finale replicates the previous outcome when Doug comes to terms with his sexuality and publicly kisses Jack. At the same time, by having Jack and Doug raise Amy together, the finale pushes the boundaries of mainstream television, just as Jack's landmark first kiss did years earlier.

Williamson's authorship, reflexivity, and referentiality carry through to the final minutes of *Dawson's Creek*. The penultimate scene of the finale reveals Dawson's ending for *The Creek*, which features Dawson and Joey doppelgängers, Colby and Sam, as they stand in a replica of Dawson's childhood bedroom trying to discern what they mean to each other. The dialogue recited by *The Creek*'s actors includes memorable verbal references that bookend the series. When Sam tells Colby, "I don't want to wait for my life to be over. I want to know right now. What will it be?" she makes an intertextual nod to Paula Cole's lyrics heard in the *Dawson's Creek* theme song at the beginning of every episode. Colby's response, "You and me. Always," jumps to the series end, echoing dialogue heard moments earlier in Dawson and Joey's last scene together. In between these lines, Colby kisses Sam, reminding viewers of Dawson and Joey's kiss in the season 4 finale, which is an intentional reproduction of the seminal season 1 finale. Thus, the "TV show within a show" is simultaneously a playful self-reference and a microsummation of Dawson and Joey's relationship—a journey from friendship to romance to eternal "soul mates." Even more significantly, *The Creek* serves as an alternate ending, in which Dawson and Joey are able to be together "always," despite the ultimate pairing of Joey and Pacey in the "real" world of *Dawson's Creek*. Thus, rather than being "polarizing" (Bierly 2014), Williamson's finale placates fans of both couples.

Williamson revealed Joey's choice in the last scene by showing a happy Joey and Pacey talking to Dawson following the finale of *The Creek*. For Pacey, Joey's choice allows him to move beyond being "the jokester who never got anything right" (quoted in Ross 2015) and restores his relationship with Dawson. In honoring the "fan favorite pairing" of Joey and Pacey (Goldberg 2015), Williamson also acknowledged how the show had "evolved over time" (quoted Ross 2015) and provided his final "twist on the teen genre" (Goldberg 2015). The scene also represents Williamson's final authorial stamp: "I wanted to say something about soul mates and what I believe soul mates can be, and that's why I ultimately did it both ways. We find our soul mates in our best friends. We find our soul mates in our partners. It's not always a romantic love. Pacey and Joey are soul mates. Dawson and Joey are soul mates. Pacey and Dawson are soul mates. . . . Everyone got their fulfillment" (quoted in Ross 2015).

The significance of the *Dawson's Creek* finale is rooted in Williamson's desire for the finale to "celebrate the show." He wanted the finale to "celebrate what it was that made people want to tune in to begin with and really honor fans and give them a taste of what it used to be" (quoted in Ross 2015). As a result, the finale functions as a coda to the entire series—simultaneously providing an epic new story line while adhering to the program's foundational themes, tone, and style. By successfully employing authorship, reflexivity, and referentiality, the very devices that made the series revolutionary, the finale achieves what Williamson set out to do and celebrates the essence of *Dawson's Creek*.

References

"The Art of Saying Goodbye." 2014. *Entertainment Weekly*, Apr. 10. At http://www.ew.com/article/2014/04/10/art-saying-goodbye.

Bierly, Mandi. 2014. "Kevin Williamson Looks Back at the 'Dawson's Creek' Series Finale: The Art of Saying Goodbye." *Entertainment Weekly*, Apr. 15. At http://www.ew.com/article/2014/04/15/kevin-williamson-dawsons-creek-finale.

Bindig, Lori, and Andrea M. Bergstrom. 2008. *"The O.C.": A Critical Understanding*. Lanham, MD: Lexington Books.

Campbell, Richard. 2003. *Media and Culture*. Boston: Bedford/St. Martin's.

Fernandez, Maria Elena. 2015. "Showrunner Greg Berlanti Explains How Joey and Pacey Found Love on *Dawson's Creek*." *Vulture*, Oct. 26. At http://www.vulture.com/2015/10/joey-pacey-dawsons-creek.html.

Goldberg, Lesley. 2015. "*Dawson's Creek* Writers Reunion: Why Joey Didn't End Up with Dawson and 19 More Highlights." *Hollywood Reporter*, June 6. At http://www.hollywoodreporter.com/live-feed/dawsons-creek-writers-reunion-why-800624.

Hills, Matt. 2004. "*Dawson's Creek*: 'Quality Teen TV' and 'Mainstream Cult'?" In *Teen TV*, edited by Glyn Davis and Kay Dickinson, 54–67. London: British Film Institute.

Osgerby, Bill. 2004. *Youth Media*. New York: Routledge.

Prange, Greg, dir. 2003a. "All Good Things. . . ." *Dawson's Creek*, season 6, episode 23. Written by Kevin Williamson and Maggie Freidman. Aired May 14, 2003. On *Dawson's Creek: The Series Finale*. Culver City, CA: Sony Pictures. DVD.

———, dir. 2003b. ". . . Must Come to an End." *Dawson's Creek*, season 6, episode 24. Written by Kevin Williamson and Maggie Freidman. Aired May 14, 2003. On *Dawson's Creek: The Series Finale*. Culver City, CA: Sony Pictures. DVD.

Ross, Robyn. 2015. "Dawson Was This Close to Ending Up with Joey and 9 More Things We Learned at the *Dawson's Creek* Reunion." *TV Guide.com*, June 6. At http://www.tvguide.com/news/dawsons-creek-reunion/.

Sharkey, Betsy. 1998. "Ad Rates Jump for WB's Tuesday Nite." *Media Week*, Mar. 2.

Stupin, Paul, and Kevin Williamson. 2003. "Commentary." On *Dawson's Creek: The Series Finale*. Culver City, CA: Sony Pictures. DVD.

TV's Most Unforgettable Finales. 2011. TV Guide Network, May 22.

Wee, Valerie. 2010. *Teen Media*. Jefferson, NC: McFarland.

Williamson, Kevin. 2003. "Commentary." On *Dawson's Creek: The Series Finale*. Culver City, CA: Sony Pictures. DVD.

14

Dexter

"Remember the Monsters?"

SUE TURNBULL AND RENEE MIDDLEMOST

It ends like this. A bearded Dexter Morgan (Michael C. Hall) stares stony-eyed and silent into the camera. In the final moments of the last episode, Dexter is working as a lumberjack somewhere northern, drab, and cold. It's a long way from sunny Miami, where for eight seasons on the subscriber-based cable network Showtime from 2006 to 2013 a pastel-clad Dexter cheerfully analyzed blood spatter by day and stalked serial killers by night, dismembering them in his "kill room" and neatly disposing of them at sea over the side of his powerboat, mischievously christened *Slice of Life.*

Absent too from this final, chilling scene is Dexter's jovial voiceover commentary, ensuring the viewer is inside and giving him or her access to Dexter's inner life and raison d'être. Finally, Dexter has nothing to say since he has lost everything he once valued. This would include the spectral shade of his foster father, Harry (James Remar), who served as his ethical guide; his potty-mouthed adopted sister, Deb (Jennifer Carpenter); his lover, the beautiful poisoner Hannah (Yvonne Strahovski), who accepts him for what he is; and his young son, Harrison (played by a number of child actors), who knows Dexter only as a devoted father. He has also lost his sense of humor. Gone are the wry observations about people and their predicaments. Most important of all and spelling the ultimate death knell for the series as a whole, Dexter has apparently lost his desire to kill, becoming "human" at last. Contemplating Dexter's dismal face in that final midshot, it is clear that, although redemption may have been achieved, it has come at considerable cost—not least the fan reception of this final season and the last episode.

In his book *Complex TV* (2015), Jason Mittell outlines the challenges of bringing to a close a long-form drama series and the various strategies it might involve. As Mittell wisely observes, the "discursive prominence of finales raises the narrative stakes of anticipation and expectation for viewers, and thus finales frequently produce disappointment and backlash when they inevitably fail to please everyone" (322). With Dexter about to take a break from the police force, the finale of *Dexter*, "Remember the Monsters?" (8.12), would appear to have been heading for what Mittell identifies as "a conclusion with a going-away party" (322), until, that is, it all goes pear-shaped, and the bleak finale outlined earlier ensues.[1]

The *Dexter* finale is therefore notable for being one of the most hated long-form series' endings of recent times, particularly among those viewers identifying as fans. In their thorough examination of the series, Stephen Tropiano and Holly Van Buren (2015) note that despite an apparent consensus that *Dexter* had over time diminished in impact, there was a glimmer of hope among critics and fans that the finale would see a return to form. This was not to be. The conclusion was greeted by disappointment, followed by anger. What is striking about this reception is the frequent repetition of the adage "Dexter *deserved* better. The fans *deserve* better" (see, e.g., Moore 2013 and Rys 2013). Other complaints came from fans who felt their loyalty had been betrayed and their time had been wasted.

In an age of media convergence where the creators (producers, directors, writers, showrunners) are able to interact with their core audience in the online space, it could be argued that creative teams now have a responsibility to the fans of a show as well as to the creative vision of the production itself (McGee 1990). Fans' heightened sense of ownership over a TV text such as *Dexter* has been attributed to what Art Herbig and Andrew Herrmann identify as its "polymediated narrative" (2016, 749); that is, the flow of content about a series in other media contexts may eventually affect what appears on screen. In the *Dexter* case, the apparent disregard for fans' expectations for the finale led to feelings of betrayal, anger, and disappointment that were palpably evident in the online space within moments of its screening (see Peitzman 2013).

Executive producer Sara Colleton defended the finale, claiming that the creative team had indeed considered the response fans might have to their conclusion, but "if we tried to factor in an assortment of opinions it would dilute the process" (quoted in Hibberd 2013). Ultimately, Colleton and showrunner Scott Buck executed the narrative arc they said they had

---

1. All references to "Remember the Monsters?" come from Shill 2013.

planned from the beginning of the series, stating that a scenario in which Dexter would die was "never on the table" (quoted in Masters 2013).

Another notable critique of the *Dexter* finale was that it apparently abandons the Dark Passenger at the core of Dexter's compulsion to kill, suggesting that he is "cured by love." Or as Kristen Dos Santos stated, "The finale's series of events really made no sense whatsoever . . . because suddenly, being a serial killer was a choice?" (2014).

However, for some prescient viewers it was clear that in Dexter's beginning was his end. Pondering what might happen to *Dexter* when the series was but three seasons old, David Lavery (2010) was alert to the signs. While season 1, as Lavery points out, had drawn substantially on Jeff Lindsay's novel *Darkly Dreaming Dexter* (2004) with a narrative arc involving Dexter's brother (Christian Camargo), a.k.a. the Ice Truck Killer, in season 2, suspected by the evil Sergeant Doakes (Erik King) of being the Bay Harbor Butcher, Dexter himself becomes the quarry. Having disposed of Doakes, Dexter is ready for a season 3 in which the viewer is confronted with the first suggestion that Dexter might be "humanized." By the final episode of this season, Dexter is contemplating marriage and fatherhood with the expectant Rita (Julie Benz) and her two children, Astor and Cody.

For Lavery, Dexter's domestication at this point clearly signals a "master narrative" at work and announces it to be nothing more or less than the "humanization of Dexter Morgan" (2010, 47). Interestingly, James Manos Jr., who wrote the pilot and choreographed the first season before leaving the show, also raised this possibility. In an interview by Douglas Howard, Manos suggested that the "whole trick" would be to "have Dexter be put into situations, first and foremost human situations, the more human, the more uncomfortable he would be in them," with the "irony of the piece" being that Dexter might become so human that he "would lose his serial killer thing" (Howard 2010, 19).

By the end of season 4, however, involving Dexter's deadly dance with the consummate serial killer Trinity (John Lithgow), culminating in the murder of Rita, the "humanization" narrative seems to have been ditched in favor of two seasons in which Dexter engages in yet more dalliances with dangerous killers and odd allies. In the opinion of both critics and fans, this is the moment in the middle when the series began to sag. For Jason Mittell, the problem for the series as a whole is a function of the character of Dexter as an antihero (2015, 145–48.) Like Tony Soprano or Don Draper, Dexter is an amoral Machiavellian character whose "stable façade" has to be maintained in order for the show's premise to work. In effect, this means that in seasons 5 and 6 the show begins to suffer from what Mittell describes as "overt stagnation," given that the character of Dexter is allowed little room to move or change. According to Mittell, it is only during the seventh season, after Dexter's adopted sister Deb has discovered his secret life and begins to challenge his worldview, transforming their relationship in the process, that the series regains its narrative complexity and drive (2015, 147).

There is, in fact, evidence to suggest that season 7 was always intended to be the last. According to Colleton, "From the very beginning, when I first started developing the pilot, I always knew it would be a seven-year arc for the series" (quoted in Pellissier 2013). As it was, despite an apparent consensus that the series might have been running out of steam, ratings remained high enough for Showtime to commission an eighth season. It is therefore possible to argue that the end of season 7, when Deb chooses Dexter rather than the law and in a surprise move kills her superior officer, LaGuerta (Lauren Luna Vélez), in order to save her adopted brother, might well have been a more effective place to stop.

In the end, *Dexter* is all about families, the ones that make us (for better and worse) and the ones we make ourselves. Dexter's impulse to kill, as we discover in season 1, is a product of his witnessing the horrific murder and dismemberment of his mother. Season 1 ends with him killing his brother, Brian, the Ice Truck Killer, in order to save his adopted sister's life because Brian does not share Dexter's guiding moral code. Season 8 involves the invention of a Dr. Frankenstein "mother" figure for Dexter in the character of psychotherapist Dr. Vogel (Charlotte Rampling), a story line that demands rather a great deal of retroactive continuity in order to put Vogel in the picture as the architect of Dexter's code. Rather than the code being Harry's (the ethical solution arrived at by Dexter's adopted father), it is in fact Vogel's.

In the end, Vogel herself chooses Dexter over her "real" son, the sociopathic Saxon (Darri Ingolfsson), whose life Dexter spares as an act of humanity that has disastrous outcomes. Saxon slits Vogel's throat with the observation that she chose the wrong son, effectively casting Dexter as his brother and rival before going on to shoot Deb, who dies as a result of her wound. In recognizing his responsibility for Deb's death, Dexter comes to the inevitable conclusion that since he "destroy[s] everyone [he] love[s]" (8.12), he cannot join Hannah and Harrison in Argentina to form a new family because of the threat he will inevitably pose to them. This final choice reveals that Dexter is truly human after all in his empathy and concern for the well-being of those he loves.

Although several years have passed since the conclusion aired, a sense of dissatisfaction over the finale still persists among fans of *Dexter*, as is evident in subsequent developments. In the aftermath of the finale, the possibility of alternate endings was debated online, and an interview with former executive producer, writer, showrunner Clyde Phillips was circulated in 2009, discussing the ending he had planned for *Dexter* (Dos Santos 2013). This ending involved Dexter awaking to find he is strapped to a gurney in the Florida State Penitentiary moments before being put to death by lethal injection. As Dexter prepares to die, he sees before him the images of those whose lives he has taken, both directly (Brian, Trinity) and indirectly (Deb, Rita, LaGuerta). But would this have been a satisfying way to bid farewell to our favorite serial killer? Is this the ending Dexter deserved?

As yet another expression of this dissatisfaction, the satirical web periodical *Unreal Times* even claimed that Indian fans of *Dexter* had submitted an online petition to Showtime asking for a new series based on the country's very real Vyapam Scam.[2] According to the petition, more than a year after the series ended, fans had still not come to terms with "what could easily be the lousiest ending to a crime mystery series," and the idea of basing a series on the Vyapam Scam was "God handing [the producers] a premise on a platter . . . a series like *Dexter deserves* a much better closure" (Kumar 2015, our emphasis). Like much speculation around Dexter's future, the proposed season on the Vyapam Scam was pure fiction, but it speaks to fans' authentic desire for a more satisfying farewell.

There was also fan speculation that Showtime might be ready to revisit Dexter's story when the network disseminated a Thanksgiving tweet in 2015 suggesting that "his knife's freshly sharpened." The *Hollywood Reporter* sought and received confirmation from Showtime, however, that there was no current plan to reboot the series (Goldberg 2015), although network head David Nevins has stated in numerous interviews (see, e.g., Goldberg 2014) that *Dexter* would be one program he would consider reviving in the future, but only if Michael C. Hall's involvement were assured.

And so the fate of an exiled and alone Dexter may still hang in the balance. Never say never.

---

2. The Vyapam Scam exposed corruption at the highest level of government in India, involving the taking of bribes in order to modify the results of examinations for thousands of "highly coveted government jobs and admissions to state-run medical colleges" (Sethi 2015). Hundreds of arrests followed, and many of those trying to expose the scandal were found dead.

References

Dos Santos, Kristen. 2013. "Chills! Former *Dexter* Producer Clyde Phillips Reveals How He Planned to End the Series." *E! News*, Sept. 22. At https://www.eon line.com/news/461558/chills-former-dexter-producer-clyde-phillips-reveals -how-he-planned-to-end-the-series

———. 2014. "Apparently Michael C. Hall Hated the *Dexter* Finale, Too." *E! News*, Dec. 3. At http://www.eonline.com/au/news/603188/apparently-michael -c-hall-hated-the-dexter-finale-too.

Goldberg, Lesley. 2014. "*Dexter* Spinoff 'Would Have to Involve' Michael C. Hall, Showtime Boss Says." *Hollywood Reporter*, Jan. 16. At http://www.hollywood reporter.com/live-feed/dexter-spinoff-would-have-involve-671620.

———. 2015. "There Are No Current Plans for a *Dexter* Revival, Showtime Says." *Hollywood Reporter*, Nov. 30. At http://www.hollywoodreporter.com /live-feed/dexter-revival-844204.

Herbig, Art, and Andrew F. Herrmann. 2016. "Polymediated Narrative: The Case of the *Supernatural* Episode 'Fan Fiction.'" *International Journal of Communication* 10:748–65.

Hibberd, James. 2013. "*Dexter* Final Season: 10 Biggest Fan Gripes." *Entertainment Weekly*, Sept. 20. At http://www.ew.com/article/2013/09/20/dexter-final -season-gripes.

Howard, Douglas L. 2010. "An Interview with *Dexter* Writer and Developer James Manos, Jr." In *"Dexter": Investigating Cutting Edge Television*, edited by Douglas L. Howard, 3–13. London: I. B. Tauris.

Kumar, Ashwin. 2015. "*Dexter* Fans Urge Showtime Networks for Show Reboot Based on Vyapam Scam." *Unreal Times*, July 23. At http://www.theunreal times.com/2015/07/23/dexter-fans-urge-showtime-networks-for-show-reboot -based-on-vyapam-scam/.

Lavery, David. 2010. "'Serial' Killer: *Dexter*'s Narrative Strategies." In *"Dexter": Investigating Cutting Edge Television*, edited by Douglas L. Howard, 43–48. London: I. B. Tauris.

Lindsay, Jeff. 2004. *Darkly Dreaming Dexter*. London: Orion.

Masters, Megan. 2013. "*Dexter* Series Finale post Mortem: EP Reveals Why [Spoiler] Had to Live and [Spoiler] Had to Die, Talks Alt Endings, and Dissects That Final Scene." *TVLine*, Sept. 22. At http://tvline.com/2013/09/22 /dexter-series-finale-spoilers-deb-dies-dexter-fakes-death/.

McGee, M. C. 1990. "Text, Context, and the Fragmentation of Contemporary Culture." *Western Journal of Speech Communication* 54:274–89.

Mittell, Jason. 2015. *Complex TV: The Poetics of Contemporary Television Storytelling*. New York: New York Univ. Press.

Moore, Frazier. 2013. "After 8 Seasons of Vigilante Justice *Dexter* Cuts Its Own Throat in Sappy Series Finish." *Omaha World-Herald*, Sept. 23. At http://www .omaha.com/go/dexter-cuts-its-own-throat-in-sappy-series-end/article_0310 a6a3-7af2-5fa1-8c61-230527b82e23.html.

Peitzman, Louis. 2013. "The *Dexter* Series Finale Was Unbelievably Awful". *Buzz-feed*, Sept. 22. At https://www.buzzfeed.com/louispeitzman/the-dexter-series -finale-was-unbelievably-awful?utm_term=.vvBblNOOW#.poKpom66x.

Pellissier, Jason. 2013. "Final *Dexter* Season Struggles to Live Up to Own Stan-dard." *Technique*, Sept. 5. At http://nique.net/entertainment/2013/09/05/final -dexter-season-struggles-to-live-up-to-own-standard/.

Rys, Richard. 2013. "*Dexter* Series Finale Recap: A Terrible End." *Vulture*, Sept. 23. At http://www.vulture.com/2013/09/dexter-recap-series-finale.html#.

Sethi, Aman. 2015. "The Mystery of India's Deadly Exam Scam." *Guardian*, Dec. 17. At https://www.theguardian.com/world/2015/dec/17/the-mystery-of-indias -deadly-exam-scam.

Shill, Steve, dir. 2013. "Remember the Monsters?" *Dexter*, season 8, episode 12. Written by Scott Buck and Manny Coto. Aired Sept. 22, 2013, Showtime. On *Dexter: The Final Season*. Los Angeles: Showtime. DVD.

Tropiano, Stephen, and Holly Van Buren. 2015. *TV Finales FAQ: All That's Left to Know about the Endings of Your Favorite TV Shows*. Milwaukee: Applause Books.

15

The Dick Van Dyke Show

"The Last Chapter"

MARK DAWIDZIAK

The most iconic of the openings to *The Dick Van Dyke Show* (1961–66) featured its immensely likable star tripping over an ottoman. You remember. We heard the familiar first bars of that wonderfully catchy theme song by Earle Hagen. Comedy writer Rob Petrie (Dick Van Dyke) arrived home, only to have his wife, Laura (Mary Tyler Moore), indicate that they had guests.

The guests, seated on the living room sofa, were Rob's coworkers, Buddy Sorrell (Morey Amsterdam) and Sally Rogers (Rose Marie). Delighted, Rob strode toward his pals, not noticing the ottoman in his path, and over he went.

We fell, too. We fell in love with this adult comedy that split its time between the Petries' home in New Rochelle and the New York City office where Rob, Buddy, and Sally wrote sketches for *The Alan Brady Show*, the fictional show within the show. *The Dick Van Dyke Show*, which CBS premiered on October 3, 1961, ran for five sensational seasons, winning critical acclaim, devoted fans, and fifteen Emmy awards (three for Van Dyke, two for Moore). They actually filmed a few playful versions of that opening, and sometimes Rob fell over the ottoman, and sometimes he didn't. It was a "watch carefully" reminder that here was a whip-smart sitcom designed to keep us on our toes. And that's precisely what it did, all the way to the 158th and final episode. Appropriately titled "The Last Chapter" (Paris and Rich 1966), this finale aired on June 1, 1966. But to fully appreciate how brilliantly the series ended, you need to understand how it began, and we're not talking about Rob tripping over that ottoman. We're talking about how the show's creator and executive producer, Carl Reiner, came up with the idea for a show based on his experience as a TV comedy writer in the 1950s.

That story is told here mostly by Reiner and Van Dyke, both of whom agreed to be interviewed for this chapter. It, too, starts with a bit of a stumble.

The genius behind *The Dick Van Dyke Show*, writer-producer-director-actor-comedian Reiner drew inspiration from his home life as well as from his experiences as a writer and performer for the legendary variety programs *Your Show of Shows* (1950–54) and *Caesar's Hour* (1954–57) (sitting in a writers' room with, among others, Neil Simon, Mel Brooks, and Larry Gelbart).

"We all fed off each other," Reiner said. "We learned from each other. It was a college for all of us. Look how many great writers came out of that writers' room. Everybody confirmed what Doc Simon said, which was that none of us could have gone on to do what we did without that experience."[1]

Determined to create a semiautobiographical sitcom, Reiner piled up a stack of scripts during the summer of 1958, which he spent with his family at a beachfront house on Fire Island. He called his proposed series *Head of the Family*, and he intended to star in it. Indeed, a pilot was filmed in late 1958 with Reiner as Rob Petrie, Barbara Britton as Laura, Morty Gunty as Buddy, Sylvia Miles as Sally, and child actor Gary Morgan as Ritchie. It was pitched to CBS executives, who took a pass. *Head of the Family* might have remained an intriguing footnote to Reiner's career if veteran executive producer Sheldon Leonard hadn't been given the chance to screen it.

"When I did the original pilot, it was almost sold," Reiner said. "It was OK. It was not great. It was OK. It was on the verge of selling, and if it had sold, it probably would have died in a year or so. Then Sheldon Leonard read the thirteen scripts I had written, and I was called in for a meeting. I was starting to do movies at the time, so I was reluctant to revisit this. I told him, 'I don't want to fail with the same stuff twice.'"

Two remarkable things happened. Leonard immediately recognized that the problem with *Head of the Family* was casting, starting with the person playing the character based on Carl Reiner. He just wasn't right for it.

"You won't fail twice," Leonard told him in the thick New York accent that kept him busy as a character actor in films and radio shows in the 1940s and 1950s. "We'll get a better actor to play you."

That cleared the way for Van Dyke, then starring on Broadway in *Bye Bye Birdie*. The second remarkable thing was that Reiner accepted Leonard's

---

1. Carl Reiner, telephone interview by Mark Dawidziak, Sept. 2011; all quotations from Reiner come from this interview.

judgment, putting his ego in check and realizing his place was as a writer and producer (although he made frequent memorable appearances as Rob's tyrannical boss, Alan Brady).

"Sheldon Leonard was absolutely right," Reiner said. "Dick Van Dyke is the best situation-comedy actor who ever lived. I slipped into the role of Alan Brady. I was thinking of getting an actor to play it. But then I started appearing in glimpses, where you'd only see the back of my head. Then the stories started to get more complicated, and it just was getting silly, so I simply turned around and let Alan Brady be seen."

The Dick Van Dyke Show ushered in a new era of television comedy. It was a grown-up comedy about recognizable people who could have been your neighbors or coworkers. It was a smart comedy that embraced the notion that there was intelligent life on the other side of the television screen. And it was the comedy that raised the prime-time standards of quality, leading directly to such celebrated recent series as *Modern Family* (2009–), *The Big Bang Theory* (2007–, with lead characters named Sheldon and Leonard), *Curb Your Enthusiasm* (2000–), and *30 Rock* (2006–13) (the last two about comedy writers). But to argue that *The Dick Van Dyke Show* changed the face of TV comedy is too limiting. In many ways, it was the role model that also led to the great cable *dramas* of the past eighteen years, from *The Sopranos* (1999–2007) and *Mad Men* (2007–15) to *Justified* (2010–15) and *Breaking Bad* (2008–13). Rob Petrie cast as the ancestor of Tony Soprano and Don Draper? This is no laughing matter. (Well, maybe it is.) When Van Dyke tripped over that ottoman, he triggered a tripwire that set into motion most of the quality television that would follow over the next fifty-five years. So here are six degrees of connection that make the case:

1. *The Dick Van Dyke Show* is the traceable headwaters for TV's most direct quality line: Without *The Dick Van Dyke Show*, Mary Tyler Moore doesn't become a star. Without Mary Tyler Moore, there's no *Mary Tyler Moore Show* (1970–77). Without *The Mary Tyler Moore Show*, there's no MTM Enterprises. Without MTM, there's no *Hill Street Blues* (1981–87). And *Hill Street* is the avenue that leads you directly to the great cable dramas, including *The Sopranos*, *Mad Men*, *Justified*, and *Breaking Bad*. "The influence of that show in direct and indirect ways can't be overstated," said Vince Waldron, author of *The Official "Dick Van Dyke Show" Book: The Definitive History of Television's Most Enduring Comedy* (1994). "It rewrote

the book on quality television so profoundly that its DNA has been absorbed by every group show done since."[2]

2. *The Dick Van Dyke Show* was the landmark quality series with regular characters that reflected the creative vision of one innovative writer-producer at the helm. Reiner established the auteur model to be followed by such innovative writer-producers as David Chase (*The Sopranos*), Matthew Weiner (*Mad Men*), Larry David (*Curb Your Enthusiasm*), Aaron Sorkin (*The West Wing* [1999–2006]), Christopher Lloyd and Steve Levitan (*Modern Family*), Tina Fey (*30 Rock*), and Vince Gilligan (*Breaking Bad*), just to name a few. "When I started the *Van Dyke Show*, it was just me," Reiner said. "I was writing about myself, so I wrote thirteen scripts before it even went on the air. I wrote forty of the first sixty by myself. Then I brought in other writers, like [Bill] Persky and [Sam] Denoff and [Jerry] Belson and [Garry] Marshall, and that made my life a little more livable." Waldron believes that "the individual authorial voice of one series creator" is something we take for granted today: "But people like David Chase, Matthew Weiner, and David Simon should doff their hats to Carl Reiner and the legacy he created."

3. In an odd sort of way, *The Dick Van Dyke Show* set the structure for (ready?) *The Sopranos* and so many other shows by making Rob Petrie's work family as important as his actual family—blending and paralleling the two. This is precisely what Chase did with Tony's two families (although, granted, Rob was killing people only with laughter). "Before *The Dick Van Dyke Show*, you occasionally saw sitcom characters at work, but shows focused on either the home life or work," Waldron said. "Breaking the rules, *The Dick Van Dyke Show* made work and home of equal importance."

4. It was the first grown-up comedy, leading to the adult comedy boom of the 1970s: *The Mary Tyler Moore Show*, *The Bob Newhart Show* (1972–78), *M*A*S*H* (1972–83), *The Odd Couple* (1970–75), *All in the Family* (1971–79), and *Barney Miller* (1975–82), among others.

5. The people who worked on *The Dick Van Dyke Show* either went on to create classic comedy shows, as in the case of Garry Marshall

---

2. Vince Waldron, telephone interview by Mark Dawidziak, Sept. 2011; all quotations from Waldron are from this interview, unless otherwise noted.

(*The Odd Couple*, *Happy Days* [1974–84], and *Laverne & Shirley* [1976–83]), or they hired the people who created classic comedies. *The Mary Tyler Moore Show*, for instance, put director-writer-producer James L. Brooks on the map. In the foreword to the revised edition of Waldron's book, the voice of Homer Simpson, Dan Castellaneta, says that without *The Dick Van Dyke Show*, Brooks doesn't hire Matt Groening in the late 1980s to create *The Simpsons*: "If it hadn't been for Dick Van Dyke and the show, that brought him into your living room, there would never have been a Homer Simpson" (Castellaneta 2011, ix). You might also say there would be no *Buffy the Vampire Slayer* (1997–2003). That series was created by Joss Whedon, the son of prolific *Dick Van Dyke Show* writer John Whedon.

6. Many comedy writers of today became comedy writers because they watched *The Dick Van Dyke Show*.

"It's a timeless show, and that's because Carl Reiner is a comedy genius," Van Dyke said. "We knew it was good when we were working on those shows. We were very proud of the work we were doing, and we wanted to keep it good. Everybody worked very hard to keep it at a high level. We were like an improv team. We could read each other's minds. It was the best and happiest working experience of my life. The wonderful thing is we knew at the time it was special."[3]

Although CBS would have renewed *The Dick Van Dyke Show* in 1966, Reiner asked the cast and crew to call it quits while they were still on top of their game. He didn't want a series so special to all of them to get stale and repetitive. Although several wished to go on for a few more seasons, they respected his wishes.

"Would I have gone on if Carl wanted to?" Van Dyke said. "Yes, I certainly would have. Would I have gone on without Carl Reiner? Absolutely not. It was a team effort, but Carl was the team captain, and it wouldn't have been the same show without him."

But how to put a special ending on a special show? Reiner and his team believed they had the answer. Persky and Denoff had penned an episode that struck everyone as the ideal finale. "The Gunslinger" (Paris 1966), aired on May 25, 1966, opens with Rob having a wisdom tooth extracted by his

---

3. Dick Van Dyke, telephone interview by Mark Dawidziak, Sept. 2011; all quotations from Van Dyke are from this interview.

next-door neighbor and dentist Jerry Helper (Jerry Paris, who also directed the episode). Falling asleep under anesthetic, Rob dreams he's a sheriff in a small Wild West town. He can't find his guns, and Big Bad Brady is heading for town.

"We decided 'The Gunslinger' would be the finale because it allowed everyone to be in it," Van Dyke said. "I still think of that as the finale because it was the last one we filmed. We had the party for the cast and the crew after filming that one, so that one felt like the end of this incredible experience."

But for the viewers, it wasn't the end of the trail. Reiner came up with an even more fitting conclusion to the series, so "The Gunslinger," filmed on March 22, 1966, became the show's penultimate episode. "The Last Chapter" (Paris and Rich 1966), filmed on March 15, became the finale for reasons that slyly take us back to the beginning. It opens with Rob telling Laura that he has finished his autobiographical book, *Untitled: A Series of Terribly Important Events in the Fairly Unimportant Life of Robert S. Petrie*. After learning that Rob has sent the manuscript to a publisher, she begins to read the first chapter, setting up scenes from three earlier episodes (one from the first, second, and third seasons). Although the publisher rejects the book, Alan Brady likes it so much, he decides to turn it into a situation comedy based on Rob's life—and Alan will play Rob.

"That brought it full circle, and it also said to the audience this was something that would go on," Reiner said. "It ends, but it doesn't end. There would be an ongoing show that would tell Rob Petrie's story, which was really my story, and it would be a sitcom. Dick Van Dyke played Rob Petrie, a character that came from my life, and now Alan Brady, who I played, was going to play Rob. It came back to the beginning, but it still was about the character of Rob. It begins the cycle all over again, going back to when Dick was hired to play me. When I came up with that, I really patted myself on the back. 'Perfect,' I said, 'perfect.'"

This also was at a time before situation comedies gave much thought to final episodes. There even was a belief that definitive finales could hurt shows repeated through syndication. Reiner got around that by cooking up a finale that embraced both the ending and the beginning. It is so clever, almost surrealistic yet somehow natural, that it tends to get overlooked in discussions of great finales.

"I'm glad you noticed," Reiner said. "I'm very proud of that ending."

That was the end of the series but hardly the end of the story. For Reiner, his story, which became Rob Petrie's story, went on in a rewarding way noted in that sixth and final degree of connection.

"There have been a lot of awards and honors, and I'm grateful for them," Reiner said. "But I'll tell you, the biggest thrill I get, believe it or not, is when successful, brilliant, wonderful writers come up to me and say, 'I'm a writer because I saw *The Dick Van Dyke Show*.' It happens all the time. You see them inspired by what we did, but taking that and breaking down new barriers. That's the biggest thrill of all—the biggest honor."

References

Castellaneta, Dan. 2011. Foreword to Vince Waldron, *The Official "Dick Van Dyke Show" Book: The Definitive History of Television's Most Enduring Comedy*, rev. paperback ed., ix–x. Chicago: Chicago Review Press.

Paris, Jerry, dir. 1966. "The Gunslinger." *The Dick Van Dyke Show*, season 5, episode 31. Written by Bill Persky and Sam Denoff. Aired May 25, CBS. Original broadcast.

Paris, Jerry, and John Rich, dirs. 1966. "The Last Chapter." *The Dick Van Dyke Show*, season 5, episode 32. Written by Carl Reiner, Bill Persky, and Sam Denoff. Aired June 1, CBS. Original broadcast.

Waldron, Vince. 2011. *The Official "Dick Van Dyke Show" Book: The Definitive History of Television's Most Enduring Comedy*. Rev. paperback ed. Chicago: Chicago Review Press.

16

Downton Abbey

"The Finale"

DAVID HINCKLEY

It's tempting to look at the March 2016 finale of PBS's *Downton Abbey* (2011–16) as a fantasy do-over for twentieth-century Great Britain.

Inside the magic bubble created by writer Julian Fellowes and executive producer Gareth Neame, England had survived "the War to End All Wars," struggled to its feet, dusted itself off, and magically frozen time before the country would have to face an economic depression, a second catastrophic war, and the collapse of a way of life embodied in great estates such as Downton Abbey.

If the world could go on indefinite pause as of New Year's Day 1926, as it did in the finale of *Downton Abbey*, both Great Britain and tens of millions of viewers could have the happy ending that would, ironically, contravene most of the warnings woven through all six of *Downton*'s seasons.

Over fifty-two episodes,[1] Fellowes and Neame crafted compelling, sometimes sudsy human dramas that glided from the heiress-and-the-chauffeur story of Lady Sybil Crawley (Jessica Brown Findlay) and Tom Branson (Allen Leech) through the charmingly awkward courtship of butler Charles Carson (Jim Carter) and head housekeeper Elsie Hughes (Phyllis Logan).

But even as ambitious gay footman Thomas Barrow (Rob James-Collier) wended his torturous and sometimes mendacious path toward redemption and acceptance, or Dowager Countess Violet (Maggie Smith) weathered the exposure of her scandalous long-ago affair with a Russian prince, Downton

---

1. All references to *Downton Abbey* come from the originally aired episodes (Fellowes 2011–16).

was tracking the broader ebb of Olde England and the rise of its chastened young successor.

We watched the Labour Party rise on the shoulders of a restless working class. We saw how something as seemingly incidental as the reluctance of Lord Grantham (Hugh Bonneville) to replace Downton's underbutler reflected the increasingly untenable economic model of aristocratic fiefdoms such as Downton Abbey.

The last scene of the final *Downton Abbey* episode suggests that 1926 would likely be a very good year for newlywed Lady Edith Pelham (Laura Carmichael), newlywed and pregnant Lady Mary Crawley Talbot (Michelle Dockery), her husband Henry Talbot (Matthew Goode), newly appointed butler Barrow, kind-hearted cousin Isobel Crawley (Penelope Wilton), her dull but adoring fiancé Lord Merton (Douglas Reith), and pretty much everyone else we liked on the show.

The handful who might suffer, such as Lord Merton's miserable son, Larry (Charlie Anson), and Larry's conniving wife, Amelia (Phoebe Sparrow), would totally deserve it.

But 1926, like all years, was a way station, not an endpoint. It wouldn't be much more than a decade before World War II would explode, perhaps ensnaring young Master George as World War I had pulled in his father.

Downton regularly reminded us that the future is certain, imminent, and inevitable, albeit often in the less lethal context of the great estates.

Within a generation or two, many of those glorious empires would be broken up and sold. Others would be offloaded to the National Trust. The survivors would do whatever was necessary to hang on.

Late in the final season, the Crawley family raised money for the local hospital by hosting an open house, where village residents could pay sixpence to see how the folks in the big house lived.

Carson worried that someone among this unwashed rabble might slip a first edition into an open pocket. Others felt uneasy about the voyeurism. Lord Grantham wondered what the visitors thought they might see: "Lady Mary taking a bath?"

Okay, that would have been worth sixpence.

Money talks, however, in every economic stratum. When the day ended and Branson counted the cash, he floated the idea of holding regular open houses, simply as a revenue stream.

There wasn't much enthusiasm among the Crawleys, who, unlike Branson, were to the manor born. But having someone propose this notion in the mid-1920s will resonate with modern-day tourists, who have visited British estates where the family has retreated to upstairs quarters while the downstairs has been turned over entirely to paying visitors.

When you're trying to keep your great estate afloat, sometimes you have to sacrifice the library.

In a bit of amusing irony, *Downton Abbey* provided a real-life rescue for the estate on which it was filmed, Highclere Castle.

Highclere had been plagued for years by leaks in the massive roof, which had slowly ruined much of what was stored on the top floor. The rental income from the TV show paid for a new roof, presumably among other things.

For all this, neither the finale of *Downton Abbey* nor its prior fifty-one episodes exuded any sense of impending doom. *Downton Abbey* was not set in a world that nurtured pessimism, despite the seemingly ceaseless perils of servants John and Anna Bates (Brendan Coyle and Joanne Froggatt), the long romantic winter for Lady Edith, the perpetual groaning of neurotic footman Joseph Molesley (Kevin Doyle), or the self-inflicted bruises of Mr. Barrow.

All those characters ultimately got much of what they wanted, and while Mr. Barrow's turnaround may have felt abrupt, most *Downton* fans wanted Fellowes and Neame to weave in as many good outcomes as possible.

Ordinarily, audience expectations no more affect the course of a TV show than they affect the course of a baseball game. *Downton Abbey*, however, drew the biggest crowd for any drama in PBS history, and although Fellowes and Neame did not crowdsource story lines, Neame admitted they felt an obligation to produce an ending that would satisfy as many fans as possible.

That required delicate scriptwork for a character such as Lady Mary, whose sharp tongue made it clear early on that she will grow up to become her acerbic grandmother Violet.

Just an episode or two before the finale, Mary had publicly ratted out her sister Edith in a way she knew could ruin the relationship between Edith and Bertie Pelham (Harry Hadden-Paton), a man Edith loved.

Mary didn't have much time to atone for that callous bullying. So instead of having Mary undergo a radical epiphany, Fellowes gave her a sprinkling of remorse and instead worked with the victim, Edith.

Edith became the grown-up, telling Mary that many years from now—there's that pesky future again—"our shared memories will matter more than our mutual dislike."

It was a brilliant parlay that didn't require pretending Edith and Mary had somehow morphed into the mutually adoring sisters Jane and Elizabeth Bennett from *Pride and Prejudice*.

Some skeptics still felt any reconciliation between the Crawley sisters seemed dubious, an arguable assertion countered by little more than an unspoken sense that *Downton* fans had earned a little pixie dust after six seasons strewn with life-changing and lethal obstacles.

In season 3 alone, two well-liked central characters were killed—Sybil in excruciating four-handkerchief detail and Mary's husband, Matthew Crawley (Dan Stevens), with a jolting season ender that did everything but put his head on a pike. Lest anyone doubt *Downton Abbey*'s wry sense of humor, that episode was the show's annual "Christmas special" in the United Kingdom.

Ho, ho, ho.

Matthew's death gave the series a hard midpoint reset in several ways because his romance with Lady Mary had been the show's core melodrama over the first three seasons.

Fans still debate whether having Mary eventually hold tryout camps for suitors was the best way to go. But Matthew's departure did free up screen time for multiple new stories, including the great showers of change that rained on England and—sorry, Violet—mostly made life better, easier, and a little fairer.

Within *Downton Abbey* itself, one of the major changes was a continuing erosion of the strict class lines between masters and staff—an area in which, perhaps because it made for better TV drama, many of the Crawleys had already been notably progressive.

Longtime staffers at Downton, such as Carson and Mary's lady's maid Anna, were regarded as friends and confidantes. When Bates was cleared of a murder we never really know whether he committed, the Crawleys piled downstairs and broke out a bottle of high-end wine for a celebratory toast. They did it again for the engagement of Mr. Carson and Mrs. Hughes.

This solidarity may have peaked in the finale when Anna's water broke in Lady Mary's room.

Mary immediately insisted she help Anna undress—in response to which Anna gasped, "Doesn't seem right," possibly true—and had Anna settle into her own bed.

Let's make the wild guess that wasn't a common occurrence on British estates. While being "in service" was a good job at the turn of the twentieth century, the servant disappeared when the service had been performed.

Interclass familiarity eventually became so commonplace at Downton that it impelled Fellowes to set up several scenes in which Mrs. Hughes reminded her husband that Downton was their job, not their world.

Good-hearted farmer Tim Drewe (Andrew Scarborough) could attest to that. When he tried to help Edith hide the secret of her illegitimate child and Edith got busted, it was Drewe who had to uproot his family and leave the land he had farmed all his life.

That harsh discard felt more true than a later scene in which Lady Mary and others expressed chagrin because they didn't remember luncheon guest Gwen Harding (Rose Leslie), who a decade earlier had spent two years as a Downton housemaid.

Gwen defied Carson by learning to type, became a secretary, and eventually married the kind of man the Crawleys would invite to lunch. Now that's class busting.

Nor did Mary's evolution stop with chagrin. After insisting for years she needed to stay within "our kind," she finished the show by marrying a near commoner. Could it be that titled Brits are subject to the same dictates of the heart that guide the unwashed masses?

Prince William and Kate Middleton or Prince Harry and Meghan Markle notwithstanding, real-life history suggests that might be overstating matters. Although *Downton Abbey* provided a marvelous visual and stylistic re-creation of an era as well as a prescient foreshadowing of a turbulent century, it may have underplayed the rigid and exclusionary nature of the British upper classes.

Lord Grantham turned into a big old teddy bear nicknamed "Donk" who got down on his hands and knees to play with the grandkids. One suspects far more dukes, earls, and lords sent the kids away to school as early as possible, then introduced themselves again once the kids had graduated from Cambridge or Oxford.

But if *Downton Abbey* finessed a few nuances of social history, it was never designed as a socioeconomic documentary. It was mostly a cracking good story, the rare television series that somehow nailed exactly the right mix of heart-wrenching drama and wry wit, personified in Maggie Smith's wonderful Violet.

It all just clicked, right to the end.

A grouchy critic could challenge multiple story points in *Downton Abbey*. It is legitimate to wonder why Carson's supposedly progressive degenerative condition, "the palsy," did not show up until the show's final few minutes.

The best reply may be, "So what?"

We joined our *Downton Abbey* friends the morning after the *Titanic* went down in April 1912, and we left them on the eve of 1926, with all their voices joining to send "Auld Lang Syne" wafting into the dark, cold, and yet somehow reassuringly soft Yorkshire night.

In that sense, the finale of *Downton Abbey* was not a revelation or even an ending. It was a snapshot taken at the end of a long, good day, and if almost everyone was smiling, well, that's what you do at the end of a long, good day.

References

Fellowes, Julian, creator. 2011–16. *Downton Abbey*. Aired Jan. 9, 2011, to Mar. 6, 2016, PBS. Original broadcasts.

17

ER

"And in the End . . ."

STEPHEN SPIGNESI

It is spectacular and wonderfully fitting that John Wells used a Beatles quote to title the 331st and final episode of Michael Crichton's iconic TV series *ER*.

The quote from the *Abbey Road* song "The End"—which, of course, concludes with "the love you take / is equal to the love you make"—is about love and empathy, and if there was ever anything *ER* was about, it was about those things (as well as hematocrit readings, complete CBCs, and saline IVs stat, of course).

The *ER* finale, "And in the End . . . ," which aired on April 2, 2009, was set in the show's present, but it was all about the past as well as the future and was a lovely meditation on how things can come full circle.[1]

The finale mirrored the pilot in many ways, and it also delivered what *ER* fans had always expected from the show: life-and-death scenarios, personal relationships, and flawless illustrations of the power that helping people can have for those who do the helping. "I can't give this up," Mark Greene said with a smile way back in the pilot after being offered a $120,000 per year job in a private practice. He turned down that job to make less than $25,000 a year working in the ER. Why? Because he had to, of course. That's who he was.

In the finale, Mark Greene's twenty-two-year-old daughter Rachel, whom we met in the pilot as a somewhat annoying seven-year-old, applies

---

1. All references to the *ER* finale, "And in the End . . . ," come from Holcomb [2009] 2011.

to medical school and is given a tour of County General by none other than Dr. John Carter, whom we also first met in the pilot. And just as Dr. Benton introduced and addressed Carter as "Dr. Carter" when he was still far away from actually earning and deserving that title, so, too, does Dr. Carter introduce Rachel as "Dr. Greene." Still gives fans chills.

ER debuted on NBC on Monday, September 19, 1994. The cast was impressive and included actors who would go on to become huge names: George Clooney, Julianna Margulies, Anthony Edwards, Noah Wylie, Sherry Stringfield, Eric LaSalle.

The day before, *Chicago Hope* (1994–2000), the other high-profile medical drama of the year, debuted in a rare Sunday broadcast. The debate going on at the time was about which show would triumph.

I bet on *Chicago Hope*, and I was wrong. I even ended up writing a book about the first season of *ER*. Sure, *Chicago Hope* did last for an impressive six seasons and 141 episodes, but it never beat *ER* in the ratings, nor did it even come close to *ER*'s amazing run of 331 episodes.

Cop shows, doc shows, lawyer shows: this is the triumvirate of (almost) fail-safe TV.

Medical shows stand out, however, as the most important of the three because the good ones are often medically accurate, and accuracy serves to bring us into the fictional universe of the show, usually with great vigor.

Cop and lawyer shows, in contrast, although often presenting an acceptable mise-en-scène of legal or law enforcement accuracy, often cut corners for the sake of the story. Medical shows sometimes also do that, but usually their sin is time compression. Medications work faster, patients recover faster, test results are almost immediate, doctors do lab work—all plot elements that are necessary when telling dramatic stories in forty-four minutes. *ER* is one of the greatest TV medical dramas of all time because, narrative compression notwithstanding, the scripts are accurate.

When I was writing *The "ER" Companion* (2016), my goal was to provide detailed medical profiles of every one of the 525 patients in the show's first season.

I bought an emergency-medicine textbook at the Yale School of Medicine bookstore. It was the book Yale med students used at the time, and it was insanely expensive. But it was a gold mine of information, and after getting to know the episodes of *ER* and taking notes, I suspected that the writers of the show (and this is pure speculation) were either using the book as a guide or knew precisely what to do when a patient presented at the ER with a particular problem, and they referred to and embedded this knowledge within the episodes. The show was created by a medical doctor, Michael Crichton, and one of the contributing writers and coproducer was Neal A. Baer, a pediatrician.

I could follow along in the textbook with the regimen of examinations, tests, procedures, medications, and all other steps necessary to result in a patient walking out the door healed.

For example, here's a look at my entry for the sixth patient seen in the first season, as given in *The "ER" Companion*:

1.6. The elderly female

This patient presented with abdominal pain and vomiting of blood. While being examined by Dr. Ross, she experienced a total loss of blood pressure and went into cardiac arrest.

Dr. Benton assisted Doug and ordered the patient's blood typed and cross-matched for 10 units and a hematocrit reading. (It was 23.) Peter also ordered 2 large bore IVs of saline wide open, 4 units of O negative blood, an ampoule of epinephrine, and the administration of 100 milligrams of lidocaine. An IV was started, an NG (nasogastric) tube was inserted, and the patient was defibrillated three times. External heart massage was also performed.

The patient was admitted to the hospital. (Spignesi 2016, 16)

The sequence of actions taken mirror precisely the protocol spelled out in the emergency-medicine textbook for a patient complaining of abdominal pain and vomiting blood.

We rarely saw this kind of intense medical thoroughness on *Marcus Welby, M.D.* (1969–76) or *Dr. Kildare* (1961–66), although they (as well as soap operas such as *General Hospital* [1963–]) were forerunners to both *Chicago Hope* and *ER*.

Michael Crichton initially wrote *ER* in 1974 as a screenplay, thinking he would make it as a feature film. He was clearly "Dr. Mark Greene" in the story, and the script focused on his first-year experiences working in an emergency department after graduating from medical school. The script went nowhere as a movie, so Crichton kept busy by turning to other things, such as adapting his novel *Jurassic Park* as a feature film with director Steven Spielberg. After that successful endeavor, Crichton returned to *ER*, but this time with the idea of doing it as a two-hour pilot for television.

The pilot was shot in an actual out-of-use hospital—Why build sets if the series doesn't survive?—and there were very few changes from the original theatrical script except to shorten it.[2]

The pilot was gritty. And intense. And *fast*. Six years earlier, NBC had seen the end of another medical drama, *St. Elsewhere* (1982–88), and *ER* was, according to legendary TV producer Mark Tinker, "*St. Elsewhere* on methamphetamines" (quoted in Marsi 2006). Long, handheld camera shots were the norm, and the camera—and thus the eyes of the viewer—would travel from room to room, into hallways, sidle up next to gurneys, bump into doctors and nurses, and perhaps finally close in on a wound gushing blood or a gruesome injury to a foot.

The effect was stunning—and disconcerting to some. There wasn't the stability of the tripod-steady shot, the slow tracking shot, the close-up. There was no time to breathe, and if there was ever a technique that captured the frenetic, unpredictable pace of working in an emergency department, *ER*'s long shots embodied it. (Five years later, *The West Wing* [1999–2006] director Thomas Schlamme and writer-creator Aaron Sorkin would use what has become known as the "walk and talk" technique in their show: the camera would follow the actors through hallways and in and out of rooms while they talked. Truth be told, *ER* did it earlier.)

In addition to the "you are there" mojo that dominated so many episodes throughout *ER*'s run, the show also tackled sociocultural issues, including health care, racism, homophobia, corruption, poverty, drug abuse—both by patients *and* medical personnel—and many story lines brought to life scenarios that were, like the verisimilitude the show insisted on for medical procedures, viscerally real.

In the first season, an elderly black man visits the ER complaining of double vision, with no other symptoms. Mark diagnoses it as transient diplopia and tells him to come back if the problem returns. The patient angrily suggests that Mark is dismissing him because he is black. Mark explains that he knows the patient has no medical insurance and that a consultation with a neurologist would cost him an additional $200. (Only $200 to see a specialist? Boy, this series *was* set in the distant past, wasn't it?) The patient then asks Mark if he is Jewish and . . . that's the line. The patient foolishly crosses it, so Mark orders a neuro consult and tells the nurse to bill the patient. But, as is typical of Mark, he does it politely.

2. All references to the *ER* pilot come from Holcomb [1994] 2010.

A situation like this occurs every day in America's emergency rooms. It was happening in the 1990s, and it is still happening now. This scenario illustrates that a badge of honor for *ER* is that the show did not *ever* pull any punches. In an era of toxic political correctness, this approach was and still is commendable.

The finale, as is the case for all finales of much-loved shows, was eagerly anticipated once the announcement that the show was ending had been made. Fifteen seasons was an astonishing record for a TV series, and many fans were hopeful the finale would do the *ER* legacy justice and not tarnish its (mostly) glorious reputation.

Remember the finales of *Seinfeld* (1989–98) and *The Sopranos* (1999–2007)? Even the "it was all a confabulation in an autistic kid's mind" *St. Elsewhere* finale, which seemed stunning at the time, now comes off as a letdown to many fans. (*You mean it was all, like, a dream? Really? Like who shot Bobby Ewing?*) So the *ER* finale was excitedly awaited. *Time* magazine ranked it at number 10 on its list of most anticipated TV finales (Fitzpatrick 2010).

And for serious fans, there was more than a soupçon of anxiety in that anticipation. In the case of the *ER* finale, Thomas Aquinas's belief that anticipation is the greater joy would prove to be false. Fans hoped the powers putting the show together did not screw it up.

If, for example, we learned in the finale that County General was actually an experimental earthling "ant farm" on some alien planet, the collective outrage would have been heard by George Clooney all the way across the Atlantic at his house on Lake Como.

The worry dissipated quickly. The finale delivered. And for many (including me), one of the greatest moments in the history of the series was the final pull-back shot in which we see, for the first and only time, the entire County General Hospital building. Remember what I said about chills?

There are other great moments in the finale, and most of them mirror the pilot. (Writer John Wells and company deserve kudos for this attention to and respect for the show's heritage.)

- In the pilot, a kid swallows a key; in the finale, a kid swallows a set of rosary beads.
- In the pilot, Lydia wakes Mark; in the finale, Lydia wakes Archie. (Are the doctors still using the same room to sleep in? Seems so.)
- In the pilot, Benton teaches Carter how to start an IV; in the finale, Carter teaches Rachel how to start an IV.

· In the pilot, Dr. Greene interviews with a private practice; in the finale, Rachel interviews for a spot at County General.
· The pilot spans twenty-four hours; the finale spans twenty-four hours.

I recently had to spend some time in an emergency department. It was much quieter, and things happened at a much slower pace than on *ER*. Frankly, I was a little disappointed.

References

Fitzpatrick, Laura. 2010. "The *Lost* Finale: Top 10 Most Anticipated TV Endings," *Time*, May 23. At http://content.time.com/time/specials/packages/article/0,28804,1991252_1991263_1991240,00.html.

Holcomb, Rod, dir. [1994] 2010. "24 hours." *ER*, season 1, episode 1. Written by Michael Crichton. Aired Sept. 19, 1994, NBC. *ER: Season 1*. Burbank, CA: Warner Bros. DVD.

———, dir. [2009] 2011. "And in the End. . . ." *ER*, season 15, episode 22. Written by John Wells. Aired Apr. 2, 2009, NBC. *ER: Season 15*. Burbank, CA: Warner Bros. DVD.

Marsi, Steve. 2006. "*St. Elsewhere*: Birth of the Medical Drama." *TV Fanatic*, Dec. 13. At http://www.tvfanatic.com/2006/12/st-elsewhere-birth-of-the-medical-drama.html.

Spignesi, Stephen. 2016. *The "ER" Companion*. Albany, GA: BearManor Books.

18

Family Ties

"Alex Doesn't Live Here Anymore"

ALICE LEPPERT

Paired with its Thursday night lead-in, ratings stalwart *The Cosby Show* (1984–92), *Family Ties* helped usher in an onslaught of long-running family sitcoms in the 1980s, running for seven seasons from 1982 to 1989. NBC Entertainment president Brandon Tartikoff saw sitcoms as the key to turning the last-place network's fortunes around in the early 1980s, and his Thursday night sitcom block was wildly successful (Knight 1982). Ella Taylor notes a shift in the family sitcom genre that was a strategy to combat increasing audience fragmentation in the late network era, claiming, "The format of these series, which develop discrete themes for small children, teenagers, and adults, for women and men as well as for the family as a whole, suggests a demographics in which several markets are identified and laced together to create a new kind of mass audience" (1991, 157). The premise of *Family Ties*, created by Gary David Goldberg, was the generational conflict between aging hippie activist parents Elyse (Meredith Baxter Birney) and Steven Keaton (Michael Gross) and their teenage children, conservative teen dream Alex (Michael J. Fox) and complacent, shallow Mallory (Justine Bateman). Jennifer (Tina Yothers) is precocious and largely shares her parents' values, and a fourth child, Andrew (Brian Bonsall), was added in the third season. Like the majority of sitcom families of the 1980s, the Keatons are white and upper middle class.

The *Family Ties* finale, aired on May 14, 1989, represents a departure from the sitcom's general tone and form—it is heavy on dramatic familial angst, and its original running time was a little longer than an hour.[1]

---

1. All references to the finale come from Weisman [1989] 2013.

As Ken Auletta explains, the running time was at least partially strategic: "Tartikoff burnished his reputation as a scheduling whiz. To attack ABC's conclusion of *War and Remembrance*, for instance, he not only posted the farewell episode of the long-running *Family Ties* against it, but extended the series an extra ten minutes to 9:10 P.M., following it with a popular movie, *Ferris Bueller's Day Off*. These maneuvers allowed NBC to snatch the Sunday ratings lead from ABC" (1992, 549). Alex's impending departure for a job in New York drives the narrative, with the conflict coming from Elyse's resentment of his nonchalance about leaving the family behind in Ohio. The dramatic tone may seem at times overwrought, but *Family Ties* was always sentimental, perhaps best encapsulated in the opening credits, in which a Johnny Mathis and Deniece Williams duet accompanies images of family portraits. This sentimentality is carried through to the extradiegetic ending of the finale episode, when the tearful cast appears for its final curtain call in front of the studio audience. Although the series ends with the removal of its central source of tension, in a fitting conclusion the episode suggests that the series' primary conflict was never as deep as it may have seemed.

A reconstructed Archie Bunker figure for the 1980s, Alex serves as antagonist to virtually every character on the series until he takes Andrew under his wing and attempts to mold the child into a miniature version of himself. Gerard Jones describes Alex as "the jerk-victim . . . made an acceptable target when he is presented as a cartoon of the young Reaganite, by far the least realistic member of the family" (1993, 257). Alex most often clashes with his parents, but his sexist comments even raise the ire of apolitical shopaholic Mallory. However, episodes that highlight conflicting values often end with Alex affirming his parents' ideals. In the season 1 episode "Death of a Grocer" (Mackenzie [1982] 2007a), Alex leaves his job at a mom-and-pop grocery store to work at the big corporate grocery chain Shop-a-Lot. After talking with Elyse about how Steven could work for a network television station but instead chooses to work at PBS, Alex is inspired to return to work for the mom-and-pop store, foregoing corporate greed in favor of the little guy. In the two-part season 7 episode "All in the Neighborhood" (Diamond [1989] 2013a, [1989] 2013b), in which an African American family moves in across the street, Alex has to explain to Andrew the racist block-busting actions of their white neighbors. He begins his explanation by saying, "I want to tell you something in the strictest confidence. Okay, I don't want you telling anybody else I said this. . . . In this situation money's not important," a comment that prompts Andrew to call out to their parents that Alex has a fever. Alex continues, "We have to treat everybody fairly and equally. Whether they're black, they're white, or my personal favorite, Treasury-note green." Although he throws in the comic reference privileging money over people, his insistence that Andrew keep his message of equality secret suggests that it represents his true, inner beliefs rather than the conservative opinions he usually espouses. Although his Reagan-inspired, trickle-down talking points are regularly played for laughs, Alex is repeatedly recuperated into the family, underlining that "family ties" are stronger than economic ones.

The reversal of such a conclusion is exactly what Elyse reacts against in the finale, when Alex secures a job as "the youngest executive in the history of O'Brien, Mathers, and Clark." Alex leaving the family behind for life as a budding yuppie investment banker in Manhattan is prefigured in the season 2 episode, "A Keaton Christmas Carol" (Mackenzie [1983] 2007b). During a sequence depicting "Christmas future," Mallory explains to Alex that the Keaton family has fallen on hard times. When Alex asks, "All of us?" Mallory responds that he lives in New York and is very wealthy. Elyse has resorted to taking in laundry, the only way they can "eke out an existence." Future Alex (an homage to Ebenezer Scrooge) arrives via helicopter looking like one of the capitalist fat-cats from Sergei Eisenstein's *Strike*—bald, overweight, dressed in an elaborate three-piece suit complete with pocket watch, pocket square, and scarf, his fingers adorned with large, gaudy rings. While the family greets him with excitement at the prospect of spending Christmas together, he laughs and instead tosses a large bag of dirty clothes at Elyse, who weeps with joy at the opportunity to do his laundry. However, because this is a dream sequence, the episode concludes with a guilt-ridden Alex dressing as Santa and affirming his love for the family. He also informs them that he's had all of their clothes cleaned and pressed, exclaiming, "I don't want you to ever do laundry again, Mom!"

The series finale includes a subtle reference to this episode when Alex brags about his $75,000 salary. Steven interjects, "Alex, that is a lot of money. It's very impressive. But don't forget to ask this question—Will it bring you fulfillment?" The camera cuts to a reverse shot of Alex, who grins for an extended pause while the studio audience laughs and then replies, "Dad, it'll bring it, it'll clean it, and it'll have it pressed for me in the morning." Whereas Alex's capitalist obsession with money has always been recuperated into the family (as in the Christmas episode), the finale brings this conflict to a head, with Alex's prioritization of profit finally taking him away from the family. However, the conflict is eventually resolved when he and Elyse are revealed as having the tightest familial bond, and the conclusion reiterates Alex's privileging of family values over corporate values.

The finale is structured to gradually build the tension between Elyse and Alex while cementing his bonds with the other family members. Alex has a series of one-on-one conversations with Steven, Jennifer, and Mallory before Elyse blows up at him. He begins with Steven, who sits him down in the living room to continue a "Keaton family tradition" of father–son talks, which comically devolves into clichéd aphorisms such as "A penny saved is a penny earned." Elyse interrupts their conversation with the first hint of antagonism when she discovers Alex has packed a family photo of hers. This seemingly petty disagreement is quickly abandoned in the next scene, which opens comically with Jennifer going around Alex's bedroom with a tape measure, prompting Alex to request that the room be left intact as a shrine to him. Although Jennifer jabs back that she's considering going to law school to become an antitrust attorney so she can send Alex to prison, the two share an emotional hug before she leaves him alone. Mallory then tries to sneak in with a tape measure of her own, which initiates another heart-to-heart conversation. As Mallory and Alex embrace, Steven sneaks in with a tape measure, and the scene fades to black.

After the commercial break, Alex says two more good-byes, one to Mallory's boyfriend, Nick, and next-door neighbor Skippy and another to his girlfriend, Lauren. Both of these conversations are lighthearted (indeed, in his only scene with Lauren, there is no discussion about the future of their relationship—she only congratulates him on his starting salary), and both take place in the living room, a communal space, rather than in the intimate space of Alex's bedroom, underscoring the fact that Alex's closest relationships are with his family. After this brief comedic reprieve, Elyse's simmering resentment crops up in the next scene, when Alex declines to join the family for pizza, and she lashes out at him. Befuddled, Alex exclaims, "Ever since I got this job, you're treating me like I'm not a member of this family." Elyse accuses Alex of acting "like an ungrateful, arrogant, selfish, insufferable little boy, who doesn't have time for his family now that he's become such a big shot," an outburst that inspires Alex to declare that he will leave for New York as soon as possible—the morning after Andrew's school play. Though this move is clearly intended to hurt Elyse, it still manages to display his devotion to family in his dedication to being there for his little brother.

At the play, Steven attempts to smooth things over, asking Alex to apologize to Elyse, but to no avail. This scene serves to highlight the closeness of Elyse and Alex's relationship, as Steven complains to Alex, "This is so frustrating—you're just like your mother." After the play, Elyse returns home alone to a dark house and heads up to Alex's room, where she sits on his bed, turns his bedside portrait of Richard Nixon face down, and lovingly strokes one of his ties. Alex joins her, capping off his series of intimate bedroom discussions. This scene is very long, especially by sitcom standards, and includes Elyse explaining how painful it is for her to say good-bye to him and how she feels as though she's losing part of herself. Alex opens up to Elyse about his fear of failure and the pressure he feels to live up to the image that he has created for himself. At the conclusion of their conversation, Alex assures Elyse that he is going to miss her, and they head downstairs for coffee, but not before Alex sets his Nixon portrait upright, as if to signal that his emotional display was sincere yet "off the record."

The concluding scene resolves the episode-long tension between Alex and Elyse, opening with the two of them arguing over coffee about who Alex's first girlfriend was. When they ask Steven to settle their dispute, the camera pans left to reveal Steven lying face down fast asleep on the kitchen island, thus demonstrating that Alex and Elyse have spent the entire night talking. Further emphasizing the closeness of the mother–son bond, one by one each family member enters the kitchen and promptly falls back asleep at the table. As Alex hears the taxi's horn signaling his imminent departure, he tells the family that he doesn't want any mushy farewell but instead intends to say good-bye "in a manner befitting the youngest executive in the history of O'Brien, Mathers, and Clark," soberly shaking hands with each of them in turn. He walks out the back door and then immediately returns, proclaiming, "I love you guys!" Alex and Elyse hug, and the rest of the family piles on, ending with a freeze-frame on this image of family togetherness. After seven years, Alex's ultimate privileging of the family over the rote performance of corporate culture resolves the conflict at the root of the series one last time.

References

Auletta, Ken. 1992. *Three Blind Mice: How the TV Networks Lost Their Way.* New York: Vintage Books.

Diamond, Matthew, dir. [1989] 2013a. "All in the Neighborhood, Part 1." *Family Ties*, season 7, episode 17. Written by Gary David Goldberg and Ruth Bennett. Aired Mar. 12, 1989, NBC. On *Family Ties: The Seventh and Final Season.* Hollywood, CA: CBS Home Entertainment. DVD.

———, dir. [1989] 2013b. "All in the Neighborhood, Part 2." *Family Ties*, season 7, episode 18. Written by Ruth Bennett. Aired Mar. 19, 1989, NBC. On *Family Ties: The Seventh and Final Season.* Hollywood, CA: CBS Home Entertainment. DVD.

Jones, Gerard. 1993. *Honey, I'm Home! Sitcoms: Selling the American Dream.* New York: St. Martin's Press.

Knight, Bob. 1982. "NBC Sked: It's Tartikoff's Baby." *Variety,* May 5, 1982.

Mackenzie, Will, dir. [1982] 2007a. "Death of a Grocer." *Family Ties,* season 1, episode 9. Written by Gary David Goldberg and Michael J. Weithorn. Aired Dec. 1, 1982, NBC. On *Family Ties: The Complete First Season.* Hollywood, CA: CBS Home Entertainment. DVD.

——, dir. [1983] 2007b. "A Keaton Christmas Carol." *Family Ties,* season 2, episode 9. Written by Rich Reinhart. Aired Dec. 14, 1983, NBC. On *Family Ties: The Second Season.* Hollywood, CA: CBS Home Entertainment. DVD.

Taylor, Ella. 1991. *Prime-Time Families: Television Culture in Postwar America.* Berkeley: Univ. of California Press.

Weisman, Sam, dir. [1989] 2013. "Alex Doesn't Live Here Anymore." *Family Ties,* season 7, episode 25. Written by Susan Borowitz, Katie Ford, Marc Lawrence, and Alan Uger. Aired May 14, 1989, NBC. On *Family Ties: The Seventh and Final Season.* Hollywood, CA: CBS Home Entertainment. DVD.

19

Friends

"The Last One"

SHELLEY COBB AND HANNAH HAMAD

As Joanne Morreale writes, "Sitcoms rarely say good-bye. Most simply disappear at a stroke, the victims of poor ratings that force their cancellation. Increasingly, however, sitcoms call attention to their departure and invite the entire nation to witness their farewell" (2003, 274). Notwithstanding the debt it owed for its national event status to the cultural waves made by the finale of its NBC bedfellow *Seinfeld* (1990–98), no postmillennial American television sitcom finale to date has epitomized this statement more than the final episode of *Friends* (1994–2004), which aired—for the first of what has become countless times—on May 6, 2004.

Alongside *Seinfeld* and quality ensemble medical drama *ER* (1994–2009), *Friends* became the centerpiece of NBC's oft-cited Thursday night line-up of self-declared "Must-See TV" (Lotz 2007; Curtin and Shattuc 2009, 49; Gillan 2011, 181), the slogan that iconically anchored the network's marketing strategy for its flagship shows in the 1990s and early 2000s. Created by Kevin Bright, Marta Kauffman, and David Crane, *Friends*' pilot promised to deliver a show that followed the cultural zeitgeist of Gen X, contemporaneously epitomized in US cinema in films such as *Reality Bites* (Ben Stiller, 1994) and *Empire Records* (Allan Moyle, 1995). Dealing with an "urban family" of precariously employed twentysomethings, each differently resisting or delaying the necessary step to full adult status—the formation of the nuclear family—the show exemplifies the generational truism that "whether or not [this ideal] family model could possibly be realized, Gen Xers knew they would never themselves live it" (Kutulas 2016, 26). However, the series gradually works toward a reversal of this truism, recuperation of the nuclear family, and the idealization of heterosexual coupledom.

For ten seasons that spanned the latter half of the 1990s and early years of the new millennium, *Friends* and its audience followed the Manhattan-based lives and loves of the titular sextet of codependent friends.[1] They include nerdy, academic palaeontologist Ross Geller (David Schwimmer); his clean-freak chef younger sister, Monica Geller (Courteney Cox); her initially naive, rich-girl, ingénue roommate Rachel Green (Jennifer Aniston); and their neighbors: the cerebrally challenged, struggling actor Joey Tribbiani (Matt LeBlanc) and his cynical, wise-cracking, office-worker roommate Chandler Bing (Matthew Perry). Their eccentric neohippy friend, masseuse Phoebe Buffay (Lisa Kudrow), who had previously roomed with Monica, balances the group's gender dynamic and completes its complementary combination of comedic quirks and character idiosyncrasies. Over the course of several seasons, the characters age, couple, reproduce (in some cases), become economically secure, and generally make moves toward settling down, all the while remaining an urban family of friends. By the onset of the tenth and final season, *Friends* is thus on its way to capitulating to the inherent conservatism of the sitcom genre's discourse of family, established in Baby Boom–era shows such as *Leave It to Beaver* (CBS/ABC, 1957–63).

The final season also carefully revisits some of the show's favorite intermittently appearing secondary characters, such as Phoebe's brother, Frank Jr. (Giovanni Ribisi); Chandler's erstwhile former girlfriend Janice (Maggie Wheeler); Joey's chain-smoking theatrical agent, Estelle (June Gable, although Gable does not actually appear because the episode in question deals with this character's death); Rachel's airheaded and comically self-centred sister, Amy (Christina Applegate); and, in the finale, next-generation substitutes for the chick and the duck that Chandler and Joey had previously kept in their apartment as companion animals.

Absent, however, from all of the last three seasons of *Friends*, up to and including the finale, are the show's only regularly recurring gay characters, Carol (Anita Barone/Jane Sibbett) and Susan (Jessica Hecht) (Ross's exwife and her partner), who used to feature in every season.[2] Sidelining Carol and Susan also meant sidelining Ross's son, Ben (for whom Ross has only ever

---

1. All references to the series are from *Friends* 2009.

2. Only Carol appears in episode 16 of the seventh season, "The One with the Truth about London" (aired February 22, 2001). Susan's final appearance is in season 6, episode 16, "The One That Could Have Been Part 2" (aired February 17, 2000).

been a secondary caregiver anyway), enabling his and Rachel's daughter, Emma, to occupy the foreground, ahead of the inevitable reformation of the fated couple. The fact that *Friends* noticeably distanced itself and its central sextet from its only gay characters as its end neared is symptomatic of the compulsory heteronormativity in which the finale revels, as is the final season's expulsion of Ross's palaeontologist girlfriend, Charlie, the show's only recurring African American. This, too, shores up the recidivist tenth-season drive toward idealized unions and heteronormative whiteness reminiscent of the family sitcom of the 1950s.

The last episode is structured around two pieces of story that draw self-conscious attention to its status as the series finale. First, the friends' explicit good-bye to Monica's apartment—"the girls' apartment"—in which she had roomed with Rachel during the early seasons (and previously with Phoebe in the years before the show's diegetic timeframe) and which continued to serve as the anchoring space for the group's friendship as it changed occupancy over time. A significant driving force behind the inevitability of this closure is Monica and Chandler's attempt to become parents through adoption. After an excruciating mix-up joke that has Monica impersonating a reverend so that biological mother, Erica (Anna Faris), will choose them as adoptive parents, Chandler convinces Erica that they are the right couple to adopt her child. In the next episode, the couple decide they don't want to raise their child in the city and must tell their friends they are moving to the suburbs. This sets up many of the finale's jokes about, for example, dismantling the foosball table, replacing the chick and the duck, and Monica and Joey's obsessions with food, all of which construct the groups' good-byes as directly linked to leaving the apartment itself.

The ritualistic destruction of Chandler and Joey's foosball table, in which the new chick and duck have become trapped and which has long served as the symbolic signifier of their decade-long bromance, becomes, in the words of its creators, "a metaphor for the show itself" (Bright, Kauffman, and Crane 2009). The former roommates can't face tearing it apart, so Monica gleefully steps in. The symbolism is overt. Her lack of sentimentality toward the table makes clear her prioritization of her imminent move toward nuclear-family life in the suburbs over her history with their friends. However, among the heavy-handed metaphors of breaking, packing, and moving, new beginnings are also emphasized in the finale through the birth of the twins Chandler and Monica are to adopt, the recent marriage of

Phoebe and Mike (Paul Rudd), and, most importantly, the reformation of Ross and Rachel as a romantic couple.[3]

In a gender, role-reversed echo of the season 1 finale, the climax of the season 10 finale sees Ross and Phoebe chasing Rachel to the airport to stop her from flying to Paris. Saying "I can't do this right now," she boards, leaving Ross weeping in Phoebe's embrace. Arriving home to a voice message from Rachel wishing she had said she loved him and trying to disembark, Ross is acutely frustrated when the message cuts out before he finds whether she did disembark. But then Rachel appears at his door and says, "I got off the plane," setting up a dramatic reunion worthy of a Hollywood rom com. With an extended kiss and one last joke about being "on a break," the romantic and apparently permanent conclusion to Ross and Rachel's relationship rollercoaster signals the series' denouement.

The final scene begins with all six friends standing in the empty apartment while movers take out the last of the furniture. The tone quickly moves between sentimentality and irony as Monica explains that Ross once lived in the apartment with their grandmother during his college days to try to "make it as a dancer." He replies (knowingly), "Do you realize we made it almost ten years without that coming up?" Chandler sentimentally tells the babies that the first place they lived was full of love and laughter, but he quickly shifts the tone to one of ironic humor, pointing out that because of rent control, it was also a "friggin' steal."[4] The friends leave, and the last shot depicts the empty Manhattan apartment (realistically unaffordable to the single twentysomethings of the pilot). It now represents the youthful freedom of lives lived and shared, one day to the next, with friends without children in the midst of an exciting city. As Kutulas writes, "Happily-ever-after for these Gen-Xers is some version of nuclear family even if, as Rachel observes in the series finale, we never get to see Monica and Chandler actually handle twins, two jobs, and a house in the 'burbs" (2016, 27). The final shot makes this happily-ever-after scenario unrepresentable, much like a rom com, but it also means that the abiding cultural image of *Friends* is of a show about life before happily-ever-after.

3. Joey is the only character who remains single at the end of the *Friends* finale, enabling his narrative to continue in the poorly received spin-off *Joey* (2004–6). Of the show's male characters and notwithstanding the contrived homoeroticism of his relationship with Chandler, Joey is also depicted as the most secure in his heterosexuality and with the normativity of his masculinity.

4. See Ewen forthcoming on the economic fantasies of *Friends*.

When *Friends* ended, it opened the floodgates for the emergence of what has become a cycle of what Michael Rennett (2017) terms the "emerging-adult sitcom," epitomized by shows such as *How I Met Your Mother* (2005–14), *The Big Bang Theory* (2007–), and *New Girl* (2011–). As noted earlier, the show's urban family of twentysomethings is historically and culturally representative of Gen X, and, no doubt, members of that cohort are a large part of its syndicated audience. However, Millennials have also, if not more so, become associated with a culture and economy that has diminished the power and possibility of nuclear-family life and are arguably the main demographic that keeps the sitcom on never-ending repeat in the United States and the United Kingdom (Mangan 2016). *Friends* thus may have bid itself and its audience farewell when "The Last One" aired in May 2004, but the cultural afterlife that the show continues to experience demonstrates that even today, we, the audience, are very far from bidding farewell to *Friends*. In 2015, when London-based *Friends* fan Gareth Stranks tweeted his idea for a dark and dismal alternative ending in which the entire story is shown to have been a fantasy imagined by a homeless and drug-addled Phoebe, staring through the window of Central Perk and imagining the life she might lead as a friend of the smug party of five that she habitually watches drink their coffee, it went viral (Denham 2015). Arguably, this alternative struck such a resonant chord owing to its generational appositeness—a bleak and cynical ending befitting the nihilism associated with the Gen X sensibility. But the fact is that the show's Gen X credentials were often more sartorial and discursive than they were ideological or philosophical. And the series was always more at home in the realm of the romantic than the melancholic. Ultimately, then, the finale of *Friends* did not disappoint in the sense that it fulfilled by far the fans' biggest expectation. It brought Ross and Rachel back together once and for all. As Rachel once said, "You know what? Now I got closure."

References

Bright, Kevin, Marta Kauffman, and David Crane. 2009. "Season 10 Commentary." On *Friends: The Complete Series*. Burbank, CA: Warner Bros. Entertainment, distributed by Warner Home Video.

Curtin, Michael, and Jane Shattuc. 2009. *The American Television Industry*. Basingstoke, UK: Palgrave Macmillan.

Denham, Jess. 2015. "'Friends' Fan Comes Up with Horribly Dark Alternative Ending to Sitcom." *Independent*, Aug. 25. At https://www.independent.co.uk/arts

-entertainment/tv/news/friends-fan-comes-up-with-horribly-dark-alternative
-ending-to-sitcom-10470864.html.

Ewen, Neil. Forthcoming. "'If I Don't Input Those Numbers . . . It Doesn't Make
Much of a Difference': Insulated Precarity and Gendered Labour in *Friends*."
Television and New Media.

Friends: The Complete Series. 2009. Burbank, CA: Warner Bros. Entertainment,
distributed by Warner Home Video.

Gillan, Jennifer. 2011. *Television and New Media: Must-Click TV*. New York:
Routledge.

Kutulas, Judy. 2016. "Who Rules the Roost? Sitcom Family Dynamics from the
Cleavers to *Modern Family*." In *The Sitcom Reader: America Re-viewed, Still
Skewed*, edited by Mary M. Dalton and Laura R. Lindner, 17–30. Albany: State
Univ. of New York Press.

Lotz, Amanda. 2007. "Must-See TV: NBC's Dominant Decades." In *NBC: America's Network*, edited by Michele Hilmes, 261–74. Berkeley: Univ. of California
Press.

Mangan, Lucy. 2016. "*Friends* Is Still a Hit after 22 Years and I Think I Know Why."
Guardian, Mar. 30. At https://www.theguardian.com/commentisfree/2016/mar
/30/friends-millennials-gentler-simpler-time.

Morreale, Joanne. 2003. "Sitcoms Say Good-bye: The Cultural Spectacle of *Seinfeld*'s Last Episode." In *Critiquing the Sitcom: A Reader*, edited by Joanne
Morreale, 274–85. Syracuse, NY: Syracuse Univ. Press.

Rennett, Michael. 2017. "How Grown-Ups Are Born: The Emerging Adult Genre
and American Film and Television." PhD diss., Univ. of Texas at Austin.

20

Fringe

"An Enemy of Fate"[1]

STACEY ABBOTT

January 18, 2013, sadly marked the end of *Fringe* (2008–13), the little, much-loved telefantasy show that managed to hold out for five seasons against the odds at Fox, a channel notorious for cancelling cult sci-fi shows in their infancy (for instance, *Firefly* [2002–3], *Wonderfalls* [2004], *Dollhouse* [2009–10]). This was a planned completion rather than a sudden cancellation, however, thus providing the series creators the opportunity to wind up the narrative in a "satisfying" way for them and their fans. Kevin Reilly, president of entertainment at Fox, made the announcement in April 2012 and in particular emphasized the importance of giving the show a suitable end by claiming that "bringing it back for a final 13 allows us to provide the climactic conclusion that its passionate and loyal fans deserve" (quoted in "'Fringe' Renewed" 2012).

It is true that a sudden cancellation is an unsatisfying experience for both creators and fans because it leaves stories left untold and intriguing narrative strands and themes unexplored. I remember the frustration of watching the season 1 finale of *Invasion* (2005–6)—a post-Katrina alien-invasion series that featured an ominous conclusion as the body of the hero's wife, on the verge of death, is being lowered into the alien-infested waters in order to rejuvenate/replace her—just after the announcement that there would be no second season. Just as the show began to show its dark potential and to push to the limit questions of identity and what it means to be human, it was pulled out from under us.

---

1. This chapter first appeared on *CSTonline.tv*, February 15, 2013, and is reprinted with permission of the editors.

The broadcast of a series' finale, however, is an exercise fraught with tension, expectation, and risk of disappointment. The knowledge that this is the last season means that every action in every episode possesses greater significance, as the fans ask, "Where is this going? How will this fit into the end?" There is little room for digression because time is limited and everything must count. This was definitely the case with *Fringe*, and the postfinale discussions I took part in demonstrated a great deal of both satisfaction and frustration. Many people, myself included, expressed disappointment at the far-too-neat conclusion in which "normality" (a topic that is always called into question on *Fringe*) is restored and the dystopian vision posited in the final season is avoided, but they also commented that moments in the finale left them sobbing. This contradictory reaction raises interesting questions about the finale that are worth exploring.

One of the biggest issues with the final season, for me, was also the show's biggest gamble. In the season 4 episode "Letters of Transit" (Chapelle 2012)—a lovely homage to *Casablanca*—the narrative leaps to the year 2036, introducing a dystopian vision of the future in which the human race is now being held hostage by a future, more highly evolved (read unemotional, logical, and therefore in a *Star Trek*-ian sense less-than-human) version of themselves known as the Observers. We are introduced to a new version of the Fringe Division—a government agency originally tasked with investigating crimes caused by fringe science but now largely responsible for policing humanity for the Observers. Some of this new team, however, are members of the resistance movement. Our usual Fringe team is eventually discovered in a form of suspended animation and released to help save the day. The episode ends when it is revealed that one of the Fringe officers in 2036, Etta, is the daughter of the show's main characters, FBI agent Olivia Dunham and Peter Bishop. The remaining episodes of season 4 return to the show's usual timeline, but season 5 once again brings us back to the narrative in 2036, and it is there we remain for the majority of the season. Now my problem is not with the sudden temporal shift, the dystopian vision of the future, or even the at times complicated and illogical narrative surrounding the desire to reset time by traveling into the future to change the past (a nice variation from the usual *Terminator*-style narrative in which someone travels into the past to change the future). These tropes are completely acceptable within a sci-fi series preoccupied with undermining narrative expectations, challenging conceptions of normality and family, and presenting complicated visions of parallel universes and alternate timelines. These are the things we love about *Fringe*.

My problem is with the positioning of a character with whom we have no emotional engagement—namely, Olivia and Peter's daughter, Etta—at the center of the final season's narrative. This is a character who is born and lost to Olivia and Peter in between seasons 4 and 5 (Olivia discovers she is pregnant in season 4), and suddenly we are supposed to share the emotional roller coaster they experience as they find their daughter and then lose her again to the Observers, making Etta the poster child for the resistance and Olivia and Peter's impetus for fighting the Observers (as if saving the world isn't enough). Furthermore, the finale, "An Enemy of Fate,"[2] concludes with the Fringe team successfully resetting time and returning the narrative to the previously glimpsed moment of Olivia, Peter, and the four-year-old Etta playing in the park. This was the moment when the Observers had invaded and the family unit was ripped apart with the disappearance of Etta. Returning to this moment reassures the audience that the normal human timeline has been restored because the Observers do not invade. The sense of normality is presented in the form of the restored nuclear family. On an emotional level, this restoration has no impact—Why should we care, really?—because an emotional response has not been earned. There has been no real engagement with these characters as a family, and therefore there is no emotional catharsis through its restoration. On an ideological level, the manner in which the finale seems to celebrate heteronormativity also sits uncomfortably with our expectations of *Fringe*. The whole notion of reassuring the audience with a return to normality undermines the thematic trajectory of a show that with its images of monstrous bodies, disturbing science, parallel universes, and alternate timelines has never been reassuring.

Family is at the center of *Fringe* from the start, but the series usually celebrates alternative versions of families: Olivia's invitation to her sister, Rachel, and niece to live with her following Rachel's marital separation (season 1); the alternate-timeline narrative in which Olivia is adopted and raised by Nina Sharp (CEO of the multinational science and technology corporation Massive Dynamic) (season 4); the chosen family of the Fringe Division itself, thrown together for professional reasons but bound together as family. Most significant is the show's revelation that Peter is not, in fact, Dr. Walter Bishop's son (who is, in fact, dead) but the son of the Walter Bishop in a parallel universe (a.k.a. the Walternate), stolen by Walter as compensation for the loss of his own Peter. This narrative both raises questions of what

2. All references to the *Fringe* finale come from Wyman 2013.

it means to be family—the Walternate may be Peter's biological father, but there is no emotional bond between them—and positions at the center of the show's narrative an estranged, sometimes fractured relationship between father and son that is gradually restored over the course of the five seasons. This restoration is earned.

This brings us back to the finale. Whereas the restoration of Peter, Olivia, and Etta as a family unit is overly tidy and dissatisfying, the emotional "conclusion" to Walter and Peter's journey together is heartbreaking and yet satisfying. In the finale, Walter must sacrifice himself by traveling into the future to save the past, explaining in a message viewed by Peter before Walter disappears that it is what he has to do as penance for all the pain his blind pursuit of knowledge has caused. Peter's final good-bye to Walter, as he silently mouths, "I love you, Dad," before Walter walks into the wormhole, taking him away from Peter forever, is a moment of earned emotional catharsis as it speaks to the healing of that relationship, the deep love between the two men, and the reversal of traditional family relations, in which the son must let the father go (in a deliberate reversal of season 3, when it is Walter who must learn to let Peter go in order to make a similar sacrifice to save the world). While Walter's sacrifice facilitates the restoration of Peter's own nuclear family with Olivia and Etta, idealized with images of them hugging in the park, the episode does not end on this moment and therefore leaves room to question just how conclusive this "happy ending" is. In fact, the ending is not remotely happy—at least it isn't for me—because the resetting of time means that Peter does not know anything about his father's sacrifice and there is no explanation about Walter's disappearance. The episode ends on Peter's return to his house to find an unexplained envelope from his father, containing the hand-drawn image of a tulip (a symbol Walter once used as a sign that Peter would one day forgive him his failings). The look on Peter's face—he is initially bemused, then quizzical, and finally concerned—expresses all of the questions left unanswered by this ending. The conclusion to *Fringe*, I would therefore argue, may seem too tidy, too heteronormative, and too happy and thus unsatisfying. But that was not my emotional reaction to the finale, which was more akin to heartbreak. The bookending of the "happy ending" with scenes involving Peter and Walter undermines this happiness and infuses it with loss—loss of Walter, loss of family, and loss of *Fringe*.

So do finales work? The tension in this particular example highlights an issue with regard to serial television, pointed out to me by a student on the Cult Film and Television module at the University of Roehampton: television isn't supposed to end. Its pleasure is in the ongoing narrative and the continued disruption to narrative that means that any attempt to construct a "satisfying" finale or "provide the climactic conclusion that its passionate and loyal fans deserve" is futile because doing so undermines the very nature of television itself. So in the spirit of *Fringe*, I can only suggest that perhaps in a parallel universe the show is still on the air as the Fringe unit continues its weekly pursuit of the answers to all of the questions left unresolved.[3]

References

Chapelle, Joe, dir. 2012. "Letters of Transit." *Fringe*, season 4, episode 19. Written by J. J. Abrams, Alex Kurtzman, Roberto Orci, Akiva Goldsman, J. H. Wyman, and Jeff Pinkner. Aired Apr. 20, Fox. Original broadcast.

"'Fringe' Renewed for Final Season by Fox." 2012. *TV by the Numbers*, Apr. 26. At http://tvbythenumbers.zap2it.com/1/fringe-renewed-for-final-season-by-fox/131104/.

Wyman, J. H., dir. 2013. "An Enemy of Fate." *Fringe*, season 5, episode 13. Written by J. H. Wyman. Aired Jan. 18, Fox. Original broadcast.

3. Thanks to my *Facebook* friends, who engaged in avid discussion of the finale; my husband, Simon, with whom I continue to discuss and unpack the final season; and to the students in Roehampton's Cult Film and Television module, who took part in a very dynamic discussion of cult television.

21

The Fugitive

"The Judgment: Parts I and II"

DOUGLAS L. HOWARD

In any book or conversation about television finales, you would be hard-pressed to outrun *The Fugitive*, that brooding Quinn Martin drama that aired on ABC from 1963 to 1967. Arguably inspired by the story of Jean Valjean and Inspector Javert in Victor Hugo's novel *Les misérables* (1862), the bureaucratic paranoia of Franz Kafka's novel *The Trial* (1925), the nomadic narrative of the Western, the Sam Sheppard case,[1] and perhaps even the Book of Job, *The Fugitive* follows the exploits of Richard Kimble (David Janssen), an Indiana doctor wrongly accused and convicted of killing his wife. Escaping from custody after "fate moves its huge hand" and derails the train on which he is being transported to prison, Kimble travels the country in search of the one-armed man (Bill Raisch) who fled the crime scene, only to be doggedly pursued by Lieutenant Philip Gerard (Barry Morse), the fanatical policeman who is, as narrator William Conrad reminds us, "obsessed with his capture."[2] A character study, a noir thriller, and a moral tale about the breakdown of contemporary justice, *The Fugitive* is often more than the sum of its parts. Although Kimble doesn't catch the killer and come to the conclusion of his own hero's journey from episode

---

1. Sam Sheppard was a neurosurgeon tried and convicted of killing his wife in 1954. Although Roy Huggins mentioned both Valjean and the Western in his pitch for the show, he adamantly denied the Sheppard connection. According to Sheppard's attorney, F. Lee Bailey, however, "there was never any doubt [that Richard Kimble's story] was inspired by the Sheppard case" (quoted in Galbraith 1993).

2. All references to episodes of *The Fugitive* come from *The Fugitive* 2007, 2008a, 2008b, 2009a, 2009b, 2009c, 2010, 2011.

to episode,[3] he typically finds himself playing a key role in someone else's narrative and humbly using the burden of his situation to give them some insight into their own lives.

From the beginning, *The Fugitive* was constructed with an ending in mind, but the process of making that happen was almost as much of an ordeal as Kimble's own. In his initial treatment for the series, creator Roy Huggins stressed that it would "be brought to a planned conclusion, that conclusion being of course Richard Kimble's release from his predicament and the ultimate salvation of justice" (quoted in Robertson 1993, 188).[4] After four successful seasons, including a weaker fourth season and a switch to color episodes that diluted the series' noirish appeal, *The Fugitive* could have continued to elude cancellation, but star David Janssen was physically exhausted from the burden of carrying the show and was, according to fellow actor Richard Anderson, "a shell of himself by the time it ended" (quoted in Robertson 1993, 173). (Ironically, this fatigue only added to Janssen's superbly nuanced performance.) Nevertheless, producer Quinn Martin admittedly struggled with the idea of ending Kimble's story for fear that a definitive conclusion would ruin the financial possibilities of syndication.[5] Even after Martin made the decision to go ahead with the finale, network executives were reluctant to give it the green light because, according to producer Leonard Goldberg, they didn't believe that viewers actually "care[d] . . . [about] the character and his story." After Goldberg convinced the advertisers to fund the project, they "begrudgingly" allowed the producers to move forward, but only because he "got it paid for" (Goldberg 2012). Not only did this gamble result in a ratings bonanza, with the last episode's nearly 80 million viewers setting a record that remained unbeaten until the infamous "Who Shot J. R.?" episode of *Dallas* in 1980,[6] but the series also

---

3. Writer David Zurawik has also considered *The Fugitive*'s connection to "Joseph Campbell's ideas of the mythic journey" (cited in Bianculli 1994, 285).

4. Huggins later "played an active creative role in" the big-screen adaptation of *The Fugitive* (Andrew Davis, 1993) with Harrison Ford and was listed as an executive producer in the follow-up film *U.S. Marshals* (Stuart Baird, 1998) as well as in the short-lived TV remake of 2000–2001 (Green 2014, 147–48).

5. "Judgment" writer George Eckstein remembers that Martin "didn't want to end the show" for this very reason (quoted in Etter 2003, 45).

6. Alan Sepinwall and Matt Zoller Seitz put that number at a more exact "78 million" (2016, 79); Mel Proctor refers to the episode's record until *Dallas* in technical terms as a "forty-six rating and a seventy-two percent share" (1995, 32). To put that achievement in perspective, the *Bones* finale in 2017 ended "on a high note" with "a 1.0 rating in the

achieved syndication success many years later on A&E, becoming in the early 1990s "one of the [network's] most highly-rated" daytime broadcasts (Robertson 1993, 173). For all of Martin's concerns, *The Fugitive* proved that a television finale could be big business. In this regard, its finale is the father or grandfather of the contemporary television finale and responsible for the finale's status as a cultural event and spectacle,[7] although, as Alan Sepinwall and Matt Zoller Seitz note, "it took the business another couple of decades to receive the wisdom that audiences like definitive endings" (2016, 320).

This story isn't just about ratings or money or hype, though. To its credit and for its rightful place in television history, *The Fugitive* finale offered (and continues to offer) viewers a good return on their investment, some psychological satisfaction for those four heartbreaking years that they spent with Richard Kimble on the run. If there are flaws or missteps in the script—Robertson refers to the absurdity of the one-armed man's attempt to escape by "climb[ing] *up* the tower" (1993, 174, emphasis in original)—writers George Eckstein and Michael Zagor still crafted a two-part conclusion, "The Judgment," that draws on the series' mythology and answers all of its pressing plot questions, just as it capitalizes on the emotions that the show raised and the drama that it created during Kimble's ordeal.[8] Finally, a beleaguered Lieutenant Gerard is given the chance to question the one-armed man and to ask him—to no avail, of course—what is on everyone else's mind from the beginning: "Did you kill Helen Kimble?" Finally, the truth of what happened that night comes out, as guilt-ridden witness Lloyd Chandler (J. D. Cannon) corroborates what the innocent Kimble had been saying all along.[9] Finally, Kimble gets the showdown that he has been waiting for as he takes out four years of pain and suffering by beating the one-armed man senseless

---

18–49 demographic and an average audience of 4.19 million, its biggest numbers all season" (Schwindt 2017).

7. David Bianculli points to *The Fugitive*'s final episode as a watershed moment in "TV's maturation" (1994, 263).

8. All references to the final episode of *The Fugitive* come from Medford [1967] 2011.

9. Chandler is not, however, the only other person to see the one-armed man on the night of the murder of Kimble's wife. In "Trial by Fire" (3.4), Kimble finds an army captain who admits to seeing the one-armed man flee the crime scene; by the end of the episode, however, the captain is discredited because his admission of a drug problem prevents him from serving as a credible witness.

atop an amusement park attraction.[10] If audiences on August 29, 1967, were looking to have their faith in Kimble and the moral order reaffirmed that night—and, clearly, based on the ratings, they were—then *The Fugitive* gave them exactly what they were running for.[11]

For my money, though, the best part of the finale isn't Gerard's willingness to believe in Kimble or Johnson's death or even Kimble's exoneration. Rather, it is that moment before Kimble walks away from the courthouse with a smile and new girlfriend, Jean Carlisle (Diane Baker), in tow—a new man whose troubles are behind him. Standing on the sidewalk with Jean at his side, Kimble apprehensively eyes the police car that pulls up next to him. The unique mix of fear and dread on his face is unmistakable. These are the emotions he has lived with for the past four years, and this has been his response to the law, a response that has now become reflex. His name may be cleared, and his criminal record may be expunged, but we would be foolish to believe that Kimble, having lived with the threat of an unjust execution for so long, can just dismiss his time on the run like a bad dream and convincingly return to his life as a doctor in the suburbs simply as yet another identity change. We would instead have to expect that Kimble's knee-jerk terror at seeing that police car would be a common occurrence, a kind of post-traumatic stress syndrome, if you will, as would that sad, cigarette-smoking, sleepless night that Jean Carlisle witnesses in part I of the finale. For Richard Kimble, freedom comes with this price; regardless of how forgiving he may be, his psyche will never be the same. Perhaps somewhere in his nightmares, he will always be running—from the system that convicted him, from the police lieutenant who hounded him, from the mysterious "fate" that framed him, just as it allowed him to cheat death on a weekly basis. In setting the example for

10. Although the one-armed man confesses to Kimble at the end of their fight, a fact that Kimble is quick to report to Gerard, he also confesses in "Wife Killer" (3.17) when he nods in response to Kimble's question about his wife's murder. In "The Ivy Maze" (4.21), Professor Fritz Simpson even records Johnson's detailed account of the murder, but Johnson is quick to destroy the tape in a beaker of "sulphuric acid" (!).

11. Robertson effectively debunks the myth that Janssen thought that Kimble was guilty and wanted to end the series "by having [him] remove a prosthetic arm in the final scene" (1993, 175). Not only did several people who worked on the show dismiss the idea as a joke, but Robertson also refers to an interview where Janssen himself admitted that the remark was made "in jest" (quoted in Robertson 1993, 175). Janssen made the same kind of joke on *The Joey Bishop Show* (1961–65), just after the finale was aired, when he quipped, "I killed her" (quoted in Robertson 1993, 179).

television, *The Fugitive* proved not only that a series could end but also that the narrative and its consequences for the characters legitimately could not.

Along these lines, we would also have to believe that Kimble can never look at the country the same way again, having seen so much of it, often the very worst of it, in his pursuit of the one-armed man and his own vindication. For all of the people who are willing to help him in his travels and break the law in doing so—Karen Christian, who is ready to run away with him in "Never Wave Goodbye" (1.4–5); lawyer G. Stanley Lazer, who wants to create a legal defense for him in "Man in a Chariot" (2.1); or that group of fieldworkers who are willing to let Gerard die to save Kimble in "Ill Wind" (3.24)—many others are just as ready to take advantage of his misfortune and use it for their own benefit. Consider, for example, the circus owner in "Last Second of a Big Dream" (2.30), who wants to use Kimble's capture as a way of gaining publicity for his business; faux psychic Sal Mitchell in "Crack in a Crystal Ball" (3.3), who similarly aspires to fame and fortune by trying to orchestrate Kimble's arrest; and discredited deputy Pete Edwards, who tries to cash in on the reward for Kimble's arrest in "Joshua's Kingdom" (4.6). As another character in the series, the American landscape of the 1960s is bleak and cruel, a home to virtually every kind of vice and corruption, a place where someone like Lloyd Chandler can sit in silence to hide his guilt while an innocent man suffers. This is the country that *The Fugitive* shows us.

It also shows us a place where justice is unsympathetic and uncompromising, even and perhaps especially to the innocent, an attitude embodied by the obsessive Gerard.[12] In the series opener, Gerard explains himself (and ultimately his role in this narrative) clearly to his captain: "Others found him guilty. Others were about to execute him. I was just an instrument of the law. And am" (1.1). Compulsively committed to this black-and-white way of thinking, Gerard refuses to consider the impact of Kimble's guilt or innocence on his own role as enforcer. At times, he even suggests that Kimble, in fact, may be innocent. In the season 2 episode "Nemesis," when Gerard's son accidentally winds up in a car with Kimble, Gerard is quick to dismiss the notion that Kimble is a killer, telling a local sheriff instead that "[a] jury

---

12. The flaws in the justice system are often fodder for drama on *The Fugitive* as it shows us various examples of misguided police officers, such as Deputy Steel in "The Last Oasis" (4.1), who considers killing Kimble in cold blood, and misjudged innocents, such as Joe Tucker in "A Taste of Tomorrow" (3.28), who is also convicted of a crime that he did not commit.

said that" (2.5). Even in the finale, after he hears the truth from Chandler's wife and realizes that he has been "[keeping] an innocent man in hell," he is still ready to see Kimble executed without some legal proof to overturn his sentence. Having saved Kimble from certain death at the hands of the one-armed man, he is unmoved when Kimble tells him that Fred Johnson "confessed up there, for what it's worth." "I'm afraid," Gerard coldly responds, "you know what that's worth." Although the show's opening deliberately cuts to a statue of blind justice from the second season on to symbolize Kimble's tragic plight, modern justice on *The Fugitive* is more monster than human, a menace ruining lives and causing chaos, all for the sake of some illusory balance.

In his book *"The Fugitive" in Flight*, Stanley Fish argues that the series, beyond its chronological place in television/cultural history, "is a program, focused not on issues or big political questions but on the struggles of ordinary men and women to find their place . . . in an often hostile and indifferent world" (2011, 15). Indeed, the series largely and at times rather bizarrely ignores current events in its portrayal of Kimble's weekly struggles, events that would no doubt have spoken to the characters in spite of their more immediate concerns. (One wonders, for example, how Kimble would have responded to Oswald's declarations of innocence after the Kennedy assassination.[13]) By the same token, the questions that it asks of viewers in terms of law, order, and morality must have resonated rather deeply with audiences of the 1960s, who lived through Kennedy's death, the civil rights protests, anti-war demonstrations, the counterculture movement,[14] and the US military escalation in Vietnam—which does serve as a plot element in the season 4 episode "The Devil's Disciples" (4.12)—and these questions seem pointedly directed at them. Even if television viewers tuned in to escape from their daily lives, *The Fugitive*'s vision of a hopelessly flawed system out to destroy the individual in search of his own justice was a dark reminder of what they

13. The notion of Janssen's belief in Kimble's guilt, however erroneous—see note 11—was apparently based on his response to the Kennedy assassination. According to the story, which was popularized by television historian Larry Gianakos, Kennedy's death made Janssen "a cynic in real life" (Robertson 1993, 175) and subsequently made him despair about his "hero's" alleged innocence.

14. Ron Simon, curator at the Paley Center for Media, talks about Kimble's appeal to "the counter-culture at the time" as a "man besieged by the establishment" (quoted in Liebenson 2017).

often saw on the nightly news.[15] Regardless of the program's fictional nature, perhaps they needed to see the ending of this particular narrative, to hear "the chimes of freedom" that Bob Dylan so passionately sang about toll for Richard Kimble and others like him, to believe in an America, even if it existed only on television, where the truth would be heard, the guilty would be punished, and the innocent would have their day.

For *The Fugitive*, that day, as William Conrad tells us in the finale, was "Tuesday, August 29th[, 1967]: the day the running stopped."[16] For the television finale, though, the race was just beginning.

References

Bianculli, David. 1994. *Teleliteracy*. New York: Touchstone.

Etter, Jonathan. 2003. *Quinn Martin, Producer: A Behind-the-Scenes History of QM Productions and Its Founder*. Jefferson, NC: McFarland.

Fish, Stanley. 2011. *"The Fugitive" in Flight*. Philadelphia: Univ. of Pennsylvania Press.

The Fugitive: Season 1, Volume 1. 2007. Hollywood, CA: CBS. DVD.

The Fugitive: Season 1, Volume 2. 2008a. Hollywood, CA: CBS. DVD.

The Fugitive: Season 2, Volume 1. 2008b. Hollywood, CA: CBS. DVD.

The Fugitive: Season 2, Volume 2. 2009a. Hollywood, CA: CBS. DVD.

The Fugitive: Season 3, Volume 1. 2009b. Hollywood, CA: CBS. DVD.

The Fugitive: Season 3, Volume 2. 2009c. Hollywood, CA: CBS. DVD.

The Fugitive: The Fourth and Final Season, Volume 1. 2010. Hollywood, CA: CBS. DVD.

The Fugitive: The Fourth and Final Season, Volume 2. 2011. Hollywood, CA: CBS. DVD.

Galbraith, Jane. 1993. "A Look Inside Hollywood and the Movies: 'THE FUGITIVE,' KIND OF: Dr. Richard Kimble, Meet Dr. Sam Sheppard." *Los Angeles Times*, Sept. 12. At http://articles.latimes.com/1993-09-12/entertainment/ca -34167_1_sam-sheppard-case.

15. In his book-length analysis of the series, David Pierson also sees Kimble in context as a counterculture hero through his "affirmation of individualism" (2011, 44).

16. Although the final episode was aired in the United States on August 29, 1967, not everyone saw it on that day or heard William Conrad give that date, "August 29th," in the show's closing moments. Robertson explains that "because of problems encountered in dubbing the episode, other countries had to wait until sometime in September [or October] to see [it]" (1993, 180). *TV Worth Watching* adds that in cities "where the show was pre-empted by regional baseball games," the episode aired a week later, with Conrad announcing the date as "September 5th" ("1967" 2016).

Goldberg, Leonard. 2012. "Leonard Goldberg on 'The Fugitive' Series Finale—EMMYTVLEGENDS.ORG." YouTube video, Aug. 20. At https://www.youtube.com/watch?v=XvhlOCCSDU0.

Green, Paul. 2014. *Roy Huggins: Creator of "Maverick," "77 Sunset Strip," "The Fugitive," and "The Rockford Files."* Jefferson, NC: McFarland.

Liebenson, Donald. 2017. "How *The Fugitive*'s Heart-Pumping Finale Changed TV Forever." *Vanity Fair*, Aug. 29. At https://www.vanityfair.com/hollywood/2017/08/the-fugitive-tv-show-series-finale-judgment-anniversary-kimble-one-armed-man.

Medford, Don, dir. [1967] 2011. "The Judgment: Parts I and II." *The Fugitive*, season 4, episodes 29–30. Written by George Eckstein and Michael Zagor. Aired Aug. 22 and 29, 1967, ABC. On *The Fugitive: The Fourth and Final Season, Volume 2*. Hollywood, CA: CBS. DVD.

"1967: 'Fugitive' Richard Kimble Stops Running." 2016. *TV Worth Watching*, Aug. 29. At http://www.tvworthwatching.com/post/THISDAYINTVHISTORY20160829.aspx.

Pierson, David. 2011. *The Fugitive*. Detroit: Wayne State Univ. Press. EBSCOhost.

Proctor, Mel. 1995. *The Official Fan's Guide to "The Fugitive."* Stamford, CT: Longmeadow Press.

Robertson, Ed. 1993. *"The Fugitive" Recaptured*. Los Angeles: Pomegranate Press.

Schwindt, Oriana. 2017. "'Bones' Series Finale Ratings Crack Season High." *Variety*, Mar. 29. At http://variety.com/2017/tv/news/bones-series-finale-ratings-1202018571/.

Sepinwall, Alan, and Matt Zoller Seitz. 2016. *TV (the Book): Two Experts Pick the Greatest American Shows of All Time*. New York: Grand Central Publishing.

22

Gilmore Girls

"Bon Voyage"

KATHERYN WRIGHT

At the center of the television program *Gilmore Girls* (2000–2007) is the close relationship between Lorelai, portrayed by Lauren Graham, and Rory, Lorelai's daughter and best friend, played by Alexis Bledel. Created by Amy Sherman-Palladino and set in the fictional picturesque town of Stars Hollow, Connecticut, the series ran a total of seven seasons.

The sixth season of *Gilmore Girls* ends with a cliff-hanger in the episode "Partings" (Sherman-Palladino 2006). Lorelai leaves her fiancé, Luke (Scott Patterson), after a season of complications primarily involving his long-lost daughter. The final sequence shows Lorelai pensively lying in bed with her former lover and Rory's father, Christopher (David Sutcliffe), beside her. In the world of Stars Hollow, this ending is as dramatic as President Bartlet (Martin Sheen) relinquishing power when his daughter is abducted at the end of *The West Wing*'s (1999–2006) fourth season. Mirroring Aaron Sorkin's subsequent departure of *The West Wing* in 2003, Sherman-Palladino, along with her husband and fellow writer-director, Daniel Palladino, left the series in the midst of one of its biggest plot twists.

Rumors about why they were leaving circulated before the end of the season, and on April 20, 2006, the couple announced they would not renew their contract. Their reasons focused on the lack of network support for the show. Amy Sherman-Palladino not only guided major plot developments for the show but also wrote and directed a significant portion of the episodes each season. Because of her authorial control over the series, especially in maintaining the fast-talking and pithy tone through the course of six seasons, her absence signaled a major sea change. The final season of *Gilmore Girls* began with concerns by fans and critics about whether her replacement, David Rosenthal, would be able to continue the screwball-comedy-inspired style Sherman-Palladino had cultivated over the run of the show. As the final season developed, the dialogue felt slower, and plotlines (such as Lorelai's abrupt marriage to Christopher) felt rushed. The series ended in speculation, too, with rumors circulating about whether the show would continue in an abbreviated eighth season.

The drama of Sherman-Palladino's departure was heightened by the dissolution of the WB network and the formation of the CW at the start of the 2006–7 season through the merger of the WB with the CBS Corporation (which owned the United Paramount Network, or UPN). On the CW, *Gilmore Girls* continued to occupy its popular Tuesday night time slot at 8:00 p.m. Eastern Standard Time. *Veronica Mars* (2004–7), the critically acclaimed cult series on the former UPN, followed. Even with Sherman-Palladino leaving, anticipation about this line-up signaled the possible beginning of a new era for both shows. The establishment of the CW provided the backdrop for the seventh season and subsequently the airing of the series finale on May 15, 2007.

The plot of the series finale, entitled "Bon Voyage," focuses on Rory leaving Stars Hollow to fulfill her dream of becoming a journalist with an online newspaper.[1] Lorelai also reconciles with Luke and comes to a new understanding with her parents, with whom she has struggled to find common ground for many years. There are no dramatic twists, cliff-hangers, flashbacks, or flash-forwards, nor is the episode longer than any other. The episode provides a feasible ending to the show. "Bon Voyage" begins with Lorelai rushing Rory to the Dragonfly Inn to meet one of its guests and Rory's hero, Christiane Amanpour. Amanpour tells her to "get in there, do what you can, show them what you've got, and the rest can take care of itself." This meeting initiates the transformation of Rory's dream of being a journalist into reality.

Two scenes later Rory is offered a job to follow Senator Barack Obama on the presidential campaign trail. From here, the finale focuses on one of the hardest parts of growing up—saying good-bye. Although Rory's story lines with her friend Paris (Liza Weil) and boyfriend, Logan, conclude in the previous episode when she graduates from Yale University, she now must leave her mother, grandparents, best friend, and hometown. The opening sequence, in which Rory meets her idol, represents the beginning of an actualization process not only for her as a character but also for the series. Rory

---

1. All references to the *Gilmore Girls* final episode come from Chemel 2007.

is now prepared to go out into the professional world as a journalist, a goal she and Lorelai have been working toward for seven seasons.

In terms of narrative continuity, the finale is successful in that it creates a definitive conclusion for the series as a whole. "Bon Voyage," as the title suggests, is all about saying good-bye. To begin, the Gilmore girls say good-bye to each other as they prepare for Rory's departure by completing a to-do list. They banter about Rory sending postcards ("a dying art form") in addition to using email and making phone calls, large versus travel-size shampoo, fanny packs, back supports, and gum. The pain of their separation bleeds through all of their fast-paced dialogue, especially for Lorelai. Her grief culminates in a scene without dialogue, a rarity in *Gilmore Girls*, where linguistic dexterity, clever comebacks, and eclectic cultural references are the norm. Lorelai delicately pulls the covers over Rory's shoulders while her daughter sleeps. The camera zooms in on Lorelai, and she begins to cry while the transitional "la la" musical score plays in the background. At this point, Lorelai seems unable to come to terms with Rory's departure.

For the final sequence of the series, Lorelai makes another attempt to say good-bye. As they stand together in their living room, Lorelai follows her proclamation that "I need more time" by running through reminders and advice. Rory interrupts her: "Mom. You've given me everything I need. Okay?" Lorelai quietly responds, "Okay." *Gilmore Girls* is a television series about conversation and speech, where keeping up with Rory and Lorelai's fast-paced dialogue is a marker for inclusion in the Stars Hollow community. More so, conflicts occur in Lorelai's relationships with Luke, her parents, Rory, and others throughout the series when communication breaks down. Because of the importance of language in the series, the silence in this scene is even more poignant in that it offers a resolution for both characters, who have too much to say but now come to a mutual understanding without the need for words.

Along with Lorelai, the town says good-bye to Rory, just as the audience must say good-bye to Stars Hollow. As such, the finale includes a string of "lasts," such as the town meeting initiated by Luke, who wants to throw Rory a surprise party. Luke's efforts involve several sight gags that provide a final opportunity to see the town working to celebrate the Gilmores as only the quirky residents of Stars Hollow can do. When Lorelai and Rory go to Miss Patty's to collect a "back-support thingy," they find the dance studio strangely locked. As Miss Patty (Liz Torres) peeks her head through the sliding doors, the scene cuts inside the studio, where the entire town lines up along the wall to avoid being seen by Lorelai and Rory. This joke leads into the town meeting, a common comedic affair during the series' run. At the root of these jokes is a celebration of the collection of eccentric characters that made Stars Hollow the place where Lorelai and Rory found a home for themselves.

Apart from Rory's story line, the series finale sees Richard (Edward Herrmann) and Emily (Kelly Bishop) affirming the choice Lorelai made to leave their watch and venture out on her own at seventeen with her baby to Stars Hollow. Standing at the edge of the party, her parents recognize the value in the life Lorelai chose. Completing another story line, Luke's actions during the finale prove the depth of his love for Lorelai, leading to their reunion during this event, capping what has been an on-again, off-again relationship. When Lorelai approaches Luke to thank him, the two embrace outside his diner, with the song "Inside Out" by the Mighty Lemon Drops playing in the background. The camera tracks away from the couple to the continuing celebration in the town square. In this moment, the intimacy between Luke and Lorelai incorporates the communal identity of Stars Hollow.

The last scene of "Bon Voyage" cements the conclusion to the series. Lorelai and Rory get up early so they can go to Luke's together one last time before Rory has to leave. After Rory notices the necklace Luke gave Lorelai the night before, they babble about Rory being the world's greatest reporter. The camera pulls back to the outside of the diner, where the window lined with string lights frames the Gilmore girls with Luke behind the diner counter, mirroring the concluding scene of the pilot episode, which coincidently appears in the series' opening credit sequence. A brief farewell from the CW to *Gilmore Girls* aired after the series finale concluded. The final shot of the Gilmore girls at Luke's bookends the series, providing a nostalgic moment for audiences wherein the beginning of the show comes to terms with the current story line of Rory's impending departure. The past, present, and future collide in this final shot.

Despite the obvious conclusion of the series, fans of *Gilmore Girls* felt the finale was incomplete. Although the finale is one of the better episodes of the seventh season, it still feels too composed and, well, too final. Sherman-Palladino always knew how to tease the emotion out of a scene, but "Bon Voyage" offers an onslaught of tearful good-byes. The neatness of the finale's ending downplays the complex character dynamics at the heart of the series.

The narrative continuity offered by the finale also fails to overcome the memory of Sherman-Palladino's authorial voice. Both before and after her departure, Sherman-Palladino teased fans with the proclamation that she already knew what the "final four words" of *Gilmore Girls* would be, but because she left the show, the finale aired without those words ever being said. Although television critics such as Michael Ausiello (2007) continued to ask her, Sherman-Palladino never revealed them. These final four words became the stuff of legend, at least for those who always wondered what would have happened to their favorite characters had Sherman-Palladino stayed with the series.

Questions about Sherman-Palladino's secret ending challenged the authenticity of the series' conclusion and underpins the contradictory nature of television authorship. Sherman-Palladino's position as the primary creative voice behind *Gilmore Girls* for six seasons counters the reality of televisual narratives as collaborative endeavors. Serialized television series are inevitably shaped by the collective visions of multiple writers, directors, producers, industry executives, and fans. Although Rosenthal's ending endeavored to complement the entire series, "Bon Voyage" would always fall short because it doesn't include the final four words Sherman-Palladino envisioned. The narrative is not complete, but yet it is. This fracture illustrates how the finality of a series finale is not only about what happens in the episode but also about assumptions regarding authorship and authenticity by the myriad audiences who engage with the show.

In the fall of 2015, Rosenthal's series finale was undone. The streaming platform Netflix announced that it would revive *Gilmore Girls*, with Sherman-Palladino returning as showrunner. The new season, tag-lined *A Year in the Life*, includes four 90-minute episodes, each episode focusing on a different season in Stars Hollow over a single year, starting with "Winter." At the beginning of the episode, Rory returns home to Stars Hollow for a quick visit after leaving her apartment in Brooklyn before she heads off to London for work and her exboyfriend, Logan (Matt Czuchry), with whom she still has a romantic attachment even though he is engaged to another woman. Rory's career and personal life are in transition, which drives the character's transformation over the course of the four episodes.

With two notable exceptions, all of the major characters are back. The first exception is Lorelai's father, played by Edward Herrmann, who passed away in 2014. Richard Gilmore's death is written into the revival, with his absence playing a critical role in the story line of Lorelai and her relationship with her mother, Emily. This narrative arc focuses on how Lorelai, Rory, and Emily must figure out how to live their lives without him. Richard's presence looms large over *Gilmore Girls: A Year in the Life*, symbolized by the giant portrait of him hanging in Richard and Emily's Connecticut mansion. By the end of the series, all three women learn how to say good-bye to him.

The second major character not returning in her full capacity is Lorelai's best friend, Sookie, played by Melissa McCarthy. Although Sookie makes a surprise appearance near the conclusion of the final episode, "Fall," part of Lorelai's journey in the Netflix revival involves her coming to terms with Sookie's absence as Lorelai and her longtime work colleague, Michel Gerard (Yanic Truesdale), move into a new phase of their work relationship. Sookie returns to make Lorelai's wedding cake after Lorelai and Luke, who have been living together for many years, finally decide to get married in the updated finale of the series. In this scene, Michel scolds Sookie for leaving Lorelai alone for two years, a "broken shell of a person," to which Lorelai responds that she's "maybe just a little chipped." The conversation ends with Lorelai and Sookie reassuring each other that they're still best friends even after the passage of time.

A large part of this revival involves the revision of characters and stories left unexplored in the seventh season of the original series. Sherman-Palladino suggested she never watched that season except to ensure continuity with the new season nine years later. Perhaps the biggest revelation is that Sherman-Palladino was finally able to write the long-awaited final four words. As Rory and Lorelai sit on the steps of the town gazebo after Lorelai's long-awaited yet magically spontaneous late-night wedding to Luke, Rory begins, "Mom?"

"Yeah?" Lorelai asks, turning her head to face Rory.

Her daughter replies, "I'm pregnant."

This cliff-hanger of an ending leaves many more questions than "Bon Voyage," the first finale, including Rory in career limbo and now single and pregnant. Nevertheless, these final four words represent a mother–daughter relationship coming full circle. The series concludes, again, but with a much more provocative moment of ambiguity, when a close-up on Lorelei's stunned face cuts to the final credit sequence, accompanied by the theme song from the original series, reminding audiences that "all you have to do is call my name / and I'll be there on the next train."

After filming of the new season wrapped but before its release, journalists still asked the actors about the fabled ending. Media coverage of *Gilmore Girls: A Year in the Life* and the creator-sanctioned final four words fed into the incompleteness of "Bon Voyage" as a series finale primarily because Sherman-Palladino did not write the latter. This sense of incompleteness was built up in *Gilmore Girls* lore and circulated across websites such as *Gilmore*

News, in discussions with Sherman-Palladino at events such as the ATX TV Festival, and also in commentary on social media.

The legend of Sherman-Palladino's unwritten ending, finally made known through the revival, calls attention to the nature of endings—the endings of serialized narratives, in particular, where the last episode concludes hundreds of hours of investment over the course of many years. The finale of *Gilmore Girls* mediates a sense of nostalgia built from that long-term investment on behalf of its audiences, but "Bon Voyage" also projects potential futures for its main characters after the show is canceled. Because the series was so closely associated with Sherman-Palladino's authorial voice, the potential futures of Rory, Lorelai, Luke, Emily, and Richard suggested by "Bon Voyage" could never align with their creator's vision for them. Whether the series finale offered an appropriate ending for these characters wasn't the problem. This narrative, like so many, could never be concluded because it wasn't *her* ending. And for those of us who love the series, including me, it wasn't *ours*.

If the last episode of the final season of *Gilmore Girls* no longer qualifies as its finale because of the revival, it nonetheless offers a definitive good-bye to the series as a whole. Netflix has now opted to revisit the potential futures of television series not only for *Gilmore Girls* but also for other programs, including *Arrested Development* (2003–6, 2013–) and *Full House* (1987–95, 2016–). These revivals are nostalgic, revisiting the lives of characters past. Part of this nostalgia comes from a need to understand how the potential futures suggested by the series finale have materialized in a new present tense. Sherman-Palladino's revelation of the final four words remains part of the legacy of this project. "Bon Voyage" was never a conclusion, but a demarcation of time in a story that continued even after the narrative was ostensibly complete.

References

Ausiello, Michael. 2007. "It's Here: Lauren Graham's Final *Gilmore Girls* Interview." *TV Guide.com*, May 7.

Chemel, Lee Shallat. 2007. "Bon Voyage." *Gilmore Girls*, season 7, episode 22. Written by David S. Rosenthal. Aired May 15, 2007, CW. Original broadcast. Also on *Gilmore Girls: The Complete Seventh Season*. Burbank, CA: Warner Home Video. DVD.

Sherman-Palladino, Amy, dir. 2006. "Partings." *Gilmore Girls*, season 6, episode 22. Written by Amy Sherman-Palladino and Daniel Palladino. Aired May 9,

2006, CW. Original broadcast. Also on *Gilmore Girls: The Complete Sixth Season*. Burbank, CA: Warner Home Video. DVD.

Sherman-Palladino, Amy, and Daniel Palladino, dirs. *Gilmore Girls: A Year in the Life*. 2016. Written by Amy Sherman-Palladino and Daniel Palladino. Netflix (streaming). Accessed 2016.

23

Girls

"Latching"

ERIC GOULD

By most measures, the penultimate episode of *Girls* (2012–17), "Goodbye Tour" (Ganatra 2017), offered the standard Hollywood ending to a successful series.

The group of four girls splinter apart in the downbeat portion of the episode, each standing at the real borders of adulthood, early twenties gone. Shoshanna (Zosia Mamet) declares herself done with their chronic self-centeredness and goes off with a newly found fiancé. Adam (Adam Driver) goes back to Jessa (Jemima Kirke) after proposing reconciliation with Hannah (creator and writer Lena Dunham) when he learns she is pregnant.

Then Hannah leaves us with a Mary Tyler Moore–like journey, arriving at Bard College from Brooklyn for an idyllic teaching job, her new life beginning.

She just might make it after all.

Of course, that comparison would have Mary arriving pregnant and unmarried, like Hannah in this millennial version.

Given the *Girls* pedigree of comedy soaked in sour sauce, you knew that Dunham, assisted by cowriters, producers, and mentors Jenni Konner and Judd Apatow, couldn't settle. Her six-season excavation of love, selfishness, and social belly flops on HBO, would, of course, dispense with the happily-ever-after.

And so *Girls* left us appropriately vexed and dissonant. We would have felt cheated otherwise. The last portrait of Hannah in the fade-to-black shot of the finale, "Latching,"[1] is trademark *Girls*—more a tightly cropped indie-style moment of ineffability than a reveal or (shudder) a warm send-off.

1. All references to "Latching" come from Konner 2017.

Finally getting her infant son, Grover, to breastfeed after months of rejection, Hannah wins this first trial of motherhood. But minus the usual repartee of the *Girls* millennial version of Mrs. Parker's Roundtable, there she sits: silent, alone in a darkened room, first smiling at having crossed this threshold, then sober, seemingly apprehensive at all that is ahead.

Earlier in the episode, in frustration over Grover's preference for Marnie's (Allison Williams) attention, Hannah complains to her mother, Loreen (Becky Ann Baker), that his fussiness means the infant hates her.

Loreen scolds Hannah in a moment that *Girls* trolls probably enjoyed, summarizing the recurrent narcissism central to the series' exploration of modern young adults, untied from having to conform as children, free to wallow in the smallest of wants, smallest of fears, smallest of selections on the Starbucks board.

She says, "You want to act like this whole thing was an accident? Like it happened to you? That's fine, Hannah, but it's not honest. You made a choice to have this child, and guess what, it's the first one you can't take back. You can't get your tuition refunded. You can't break the lease. You can't delete his phone number. Your son is not a temp job. He's not Adam, and this is it, honey, this is forever."

Hannah leaves and ends up walking all day, into the night (with Grover left to be cared for by Marnie and Loreen). She encounters a young girl crying, dressed only in a sweatshirt and panties, whom Hannah presumes may be fleeing a sexual encounter gone wrong. Hannah gives the girl her own pants and shoes, trading for and now assuming the girl's original outfit.

But Hannah learns the teen has just run out of her house because she is upset that her mother is forcing her to finish her homework, not allowing her to go to her boyfriend's house.

Hannah then gives the girl more or less a paraphrased version of the scolding Hannah herself had just received—that life isn't supposed to be easy or fun, that you make choices, and that you have people you're responsible to and for. You should be grateful for your parents' sacrifices. "[She] will take care of you forever, even if it means endless, endless pain," Hannah says. "So give me back my jeans!"

In that moment, Hannah and steadfast *Girls* fans of six seasons perhaps got a partial payoff: Hannah's crossover into a semblance of adulthood, her trusty self-absorption is demoted and peeled away; her brand—along with her pants—are reversed. For the moment, she's transformed.

Otherwise, Dunham leaves *Girls* much as she began it, naked (several times this episode), hilarious (Hannah scolding Marnie while wearing a backpack breast pump attached to both nipples—Marnie replies, "O.K., Ghostbuster"), and fiercely critical. Hannah characteristically claws and rants trying to get at the root of her new single-motherhood pain, ugly at times as it often is.

That nakedness, both physical and emotional, has been the better part of *Girls*, much like its preceding male-oriented version, Louis C. K.'s *Louie* (2010–15, FX), which also took no prisoners in pursuit of truth, no matter how harsh the road was to get there. Likewise, Dunham left few of her own, digging down into issues of Hannah's body image, radically shifting gender politics, and a hard-won personal reconciliation—Hannah's career turn into teaching in this final season, acknowledging her original claim in the pilot as maybe not being "*the* voice of my generation" but simply "*a* voice. Of *a* generation" (Dunham 2012).

That's probably the best we can ask for and receive from writers and performers: the willingness to strip themselves, literally and figuratively, in sacrifice for art. The aggressive messiness of *Girls* dispensed with the usual vanity of appearing attractive and smart and spry on TV so that we could go on deeper, authentic dives into misbehavior and triumphs—that is, into lives more like our own. "When your character is a selfish, unformed person—but also a bruised, struggling oddball whose failures are human . . . [t]hat kind of character is unsettling to viewers, because they're forced to feel pangs of identification and judgement, both at once, an unsettling sensation" (Nussbaum 2017).

As *Girls* closes, Hannah's future, her son, now lies on her lap in front her. Instead of one *Girls* lead character, there are now two.

At last, at the last, it isn't about a new boyfriend or a new job or a new apartment . . . or herself.

References

Dunham, Lena, dir. 2012. "Pilot." *Girls*, season 1, episode 1. Written by Lena Dunham. Aired Apr. 15, HBO. Original broadcast.

Ganatra, Nisha, dir. 2017. "Goodbye Tour." *Girls*, season 6, episode 9. Written by Lena Dunham and Jenni Konner. Aired Apr. 9, HBO. Original broadcast.

Konner, Jenni, dir. 2017. "Latching." *Girls*, season 6, episode 10. Written by Judd Apatow, Lena Dunham, and Jenni Konner. Aired Apr. 16, HBO. Original broadcast.

Nussbaum, Emily. 2017. "Goodbye 'Girls': A Fittingly Imperfect Finale." *The New Yorker*, Apr. 18. At https://www.newyorker.com/culture/cultural-comment/good bye-girls-a-fittingly-imperfect-finale.

24

Hill Street Blues

"It Ain't Over Till It's Over"

RONALD WILSON

The opening credits show a police patrol car emerging from a parking garage, lights flashing and siren blasting, as it joins several other patrol cars on the gray, rain-soaked streets of an undisclosed metropolitan city (the patrol cars themselves simply read "Metro Police"). The dull grayness of the cityscape is in stark contrast to the typically bright studio look of a Los Angeles or New York City setting of such cop shows as *Dragnet* (1951–59) and *Police Story* (1974–79). The grittiness of the setting is the perfect look for the series' realistic focus on life in the police precinct known as the Hill Street station, where a shaky verité-style camerawork captures the early-morning roll call that begins each episode by introducing characters and story lines that will be developed within the episode itself and possibly continued into others. *Hill Street Blues* premiered on Thursday nights on NBC in 1981 and, though not overtly popular, developed a fan base attracted to its genre difference from other police television series. That difference is distinguished primarily by characteristics that would be attributed to "quality television": a long-form narrative structure similar to daytime serial formats such as soap operas, a large ensemble cast of characters whose story threads are woven into the series' narrative fabric over several episodes and even several seasons, and a distinct visual style that complements the sense that the viewer is a part of the action.

Hill Street Blues premiered during a period of stylistic innovation in prime-time television programming in the early 1980s. MTM Enterprises' production strategy from 1979 to 1981 was characterized by an emphasis on a series of hour-long episodes marketed to a niche "blue-chip" audience and by a stress on genre hybridization, realism, and the use of an ensemble cast. These strategies were coupled with NBC executive Fred Silverman's wish to

153

create a "down-and-dirty cop show" that would appeal to a more adult constituency than *Starsky & Hutch* (1975–79). The result was *Hill Street Blues*, the creation of writer-producers Steven Bochco and Michael Kozoll, who had previously developed a similar realistic cop dramatic series, *Delvecchio* (1976–77). Silverman wanted them to produce a "cop show that [was] not a standard cops-and-robbers show—a show that [had] more to do with cops' personal lives" (quoted in Gitlin 1983, 279), and so, to this end, Bochco and Kozoll formulated a concept that drew from antiheroic, realistic, urban-crime films such as *Dirty Harry* (Don Siegel, 1971), *The French Connection* (William Friedkin, 1971), and *Electra Glide in Blue* (James William Guercio, 1973). These films present a flawed police system and cops who, as a result of their pessimism about the overly bureaucratic nature of their job, are prepared to operate violently. Yet on the street the police officers in these films display many humanistic qualities that make the films unique to the zeitgeist of the 1970s. In a similar manner, *Hill Street Blues* presented a microcosm of a police environment beleaguered by organizational, social, and personal conflicts and relationships. The series often utilized an "us versus them" narrative wherein a beleaguered police force is embattled by the world both outside and inside its doors. The sense of the Hill as a combat zone was augmented by the visual style of the series, including "quick cuts, a furious pace, a nervous camera made for complexity and congestion, a sense of entanglement and continuous crisis that matched the actual density and convolution of city life, of life in a ghetto police precinct in particular" (Gitlin 1983, 274). The urban environment that constitutes the "Hill" is rife with gang warfare, corruption, and street crime that the police combat on a daily basis.

The mixture of a workplace environment, multiple characters and story arcs, and a visceral, in-your-face photographic style created a different type of cop show that focused more on the day-to-day problems within a police precinct. As the show's title implies, the series is a paean to a collective unit rather than to an individual; there is no Sergeant Friday, Baretta, or Starsky and Hutch to come to the rescue and apprehend criminals in the final minutes of the show's format. Here, resolution may or may not be finalized and story lines are ongoing from one episode to the next. Though the series was popular with critics, it was never as popular with a mass audience, perhaps because of its unconventional approach to both narrative and visual style. When it reached its seventh and final season, it had become even formulaic to its fan base, so that when the final episode aired on May 12, 1987, it was heralded with little fanfare. As one critic stated, the final episode "was a surprise because it contained nothing particularly surprising" (Alleva 1987).

The final episode, appropriately titled "It Ain't Over Till It's Over,"[1] showcases some of the stylistics associated with the critically acclaimed series—its use of a cinema verité visual style (though it is more subdued after seven seasons), its overlapping action and dialogue, and its multiple story lines that interweave through the episode's forty-nine-minute running time. These story threads include an investigation into a series of prostitute murders; the suspension of Lieutenant Norm Buntz (Dennis Franz) while an internal investigation is pending concerning the theft of a suitcase filled with eighty pounds of heroin (a suitcase that made its appearance in episode 1 of the season); the garnishment of Lieutenant Mick Belker's (Bruce Weitz) wages by the IRS; an investigative television reporter's plans to open the concealed wine cellar of a notorious Prohibition-era gangster; and the aftermath of the burning of the Hill Street station itself. Through most of this onscreen mayhem and bustling activity, the finale presents itself as routine as usual, with the unexpected pleasure of seeing the bureaucratic, egotistical chief of police, Fletcher Daniels (Jon Cypher), being hit squarely in the face and knocked down (ironically while television news cameras are rolling in the burned-out shell of the precinct) by Lieutenant Buntz, who, though exonerated of the theft charge, is now about to be fired for threatening to use a firearm while on suspension. The multiple story lines provide the best evidence for the critical success of this television program—they present police as multidimensional human beings rather than as one-dimensional "cops." Steven Bochco once said of the importance of the series, "I think the show really had an impact on the way in which 'civilians' look at cops. We humanized them, made them more understandable and much more accessible in terms of our daily experience. As you begin to do that with any group of professionals, you begin to break down stereotypes, which are really the function of ignorance" (quoted in Terry 1987). This impact is made evident in the series finale, in which the humanity of law enforcement professionals in the Hill Street precinct is highlighted.

The title of the series finale, "It Ain't Over Till It's Over," seems to refer to the quotidian constancy of police work—that no matter what happens, an investigation or a police case is not over until it is over. This idea of continuance over finality pervades the episode and is best represented by the

1. All references to "It Ain't Over Till It's Over" come from Lathan [1987] 2014.

beleaguered character Lieutenant Buntz. It also highlights the narrative difference of *Hill Street Blues* from its network-era cops-and-robbers episodic predecessors.

According to critic Richard Alleva, Norman Buntz has a "refreshingly bad attitude towards life, love, work, citizenship. Buntz hate[s] to be touched, physically or emotionally" (1987). Buntz is a Dirty Harry in a necktie, whose brash, vigilante-style of apprehension belies a somewhat sentimental quality that is exhibited on very few occasions. This is perhaps no more apparent than in his love–hate relationship with his informant, Sid the Snitch (Peter Jurasik). In the final episode, Buntz breaks down and cries, knowing he is about to lose the one thing that he truly loves, "being a cop." The display of vulnerability and loss makes Buntz even more human within the episode.[2]

The first image the viewer sees in the episode is a violent action scene from presumably an old black-and-white gangster film played out on a television screen. Buntz stares blankly at the TV, not really engaging with what is happening onscreen. The opening in essence highlights the disconnection between the fiction and reality of police work. *Hill Street Blues* was atypical of the majority of action-oriented, cops-and-robbers fare on network television at the time. This nuanced comment on the reality versus fiction of police work is further emphasized when Sid the Snitch, who is checking on Buntz, looks at the TV screen and comments, "They ruin these old shows with that colorization stuff." Sid's off-the-cuff critical evaluation notes the attempt to make the old black-and-white films more "realistic" through the then vogueish process of colorization. In a way, the layering of intertextuality of the old-style gangster dramas where law-and-order prevails is also indicative of Buntz's position in the series.

Buntz is a liminal law enforcement officer who is ostracized on the Hill because, in Chief Daniels's words, he is a "throwback." As mentioned earlier, in many respects Buntz is emblematic of the Dirty Harry, "lone wolf" stereotype in that he is constantly battling police bureaucracy as well as the criminals. Daniels also refers to Buntz as "Stormin' Norman" in the episode, thereby stressing Buntz's physical overreactions to tense situations and his combative persona. Buntz, who is accused of the theft of a suitcase of cocaine from the evidence room and is on suspension, faces the growing

2. Interestingly enough, Buntz's exit from the Hill allowed for the production of a short-lived seriocomic spin-off series, *Beverly Hills Buntz* (1987–88), which found him in Los Angeles working as a private detective alongside his compatriot, Sid the Snitch.

reality that he will no longer be a cop, a prospect that visibly upsets him throughout the final episode. If Buntz is indeed a throwback to these earlier characterizations of police detectives as action heroes (which he attempts to resurrect by collaring the real thief within the precinct—Internal Affairs Department lieutenant Jim Shipman [Arthur Taxier]), his psychological plight is uncharacteristic of earlier action-oriented police television dramas. That emotional plight showcases the human quality of the innovative police series by focusing on real problems encountered by real individuals.

The concluding scene of the episode and the series provides a fitting anti-climax to the program's emphasis on the collective known simply as "the Hill." The fire marshal has given his blessing to the building's structure, referring to it on a personal level: "It came through like a champ. They don't build 'em like this anymore." The remarks are addressed to a minor character, Desk Sergeant Jenkins (Lawrence Tierney), who has appeared in only a few episodes of the sixth and seventh seasons. Lieutenant Buntz—or, to be exact, the former Lieutenant Buntz—is seen leaving with a small bag (most likely containing his personal possessions), and as he departs, the phone rings. Jenkins answers with the final words of the series, "Hill Street," before the shot fades to black. The final words reflect a sense of continuance that life will go on at the precinct, if only in the collective imagination of its viewers. Only a relatively minor character who represents the collective unity of the precinct itself could provide this sense of normalcy; had these words been uttered by one of the regular cast of characters, they would not have the same emotional effect. The utterance of the two words, "Hill Street," suggests that the police station is still in running order no matter what happens and brings closure to this innovative series.

References

Alleva, Richard. 1987. "On Screen: Goodby [*sic*] to *Hill Street Blues*." *Crisis Magazine*, July 1. At http://www.crisismagazine.com/1987/on-screen-goodby-to-hill-street-blues.

Gitlin, Todd. 1983. *Inside Prime Time*. New York: Pantheon Books.

Lathan, Stan, dir. [1987] 2014. "It Ain't Over Till It's Over." *Hill Street Blues*, season 7, episode 22. Written by Jeffrey Lewis, David Milch, and John Romano. Aired May 12, 1987, NBC. On *Hill Street Blues: The Complete Series*. Los Angeles: Shout! Factory. DVD.

Terry, Clifford. 1987. "*Hill Street* Finale: It's Time to Go." *Chicago Tribune*, May 12. At http://www.articles.chicagotribune.com/1987-05-12/features/8702050132.

25

Homicide

Homicide: The Movie

JONATHAN NICHOLS-PETHICK

Homicide lasted seven seasons on NBC, from 1993 to 1999, ending for good in 2000 when NBC aired *Homicide: The Movie* as the series finale. That it lasted so long is surprising because it was almost canceled at least three different times during its first four years of existence. Following a relatively solid performance in its debut after Super Bowl XXVII, the series from then on languished in the ratings and lived perpetually on the network bubble, saved only, it seems, by the critical praise it received regularly (see Shales 1993), the fierce loyalty of its stalwart fan base, and the network executives' desire to be able to point to their support of a quality drama despite challenging ratings. As then NBC president of entertainment Warren Littlefield told *Entertainment Weekly* after renewing the show for a seventh season, "Each season we felt that it would be a mistake to extinguish it—there was just too much there that was too good" (quoted in Fretts 1998). In short, the series lived in a state of perpetual uncertainty.

Uncertainty may in fact be the guiding principle for understanding *Homicide*. The story lines themselves were built on no small amount of uncertainty, with the writers willing to leave narrative—and moral—conclusions hanging within and across episodes. Bringing this thread together with its precarious place on the network schedule, we can see that the uncertainty that defined *Homicide* was a matter of both aesthetics and business. Although every product of the commercial culture industry exists at the intersection of art and commerce, the *Homicide* finales illustrate this tension more clearly than most. The series' status as an uncertain television commodity forced its creators to produce an equally uncertain initial ending; meanwhile, its status as a significant artistic creation encouraged the network nine months later to use it as part of a confounding economic strategy.

When executive producer Tom Fontana set about writing the final episode of *Homicide*'s seventh season, he had not heard whether the series would be back on the NBC schedule the following year. Under normal circumstances, network leadership would likely have informed the cast and crew of the series' status well in advance of the May announcements of the next year's schedule. But circumstances were far from normal at NBC in the late 1990s, and uncertainty at the top translated to uncertainty for the series and resulted in a finale that, in the words of Tom Fontana, was "neither fish nor fowl" (quoted in Deggans 2000).

The network uncertainty began in late 1997, when Jerry Seinfeld announced that *Seinfeld* (1989–98) would not be back following the 1997–98 season. In addition, NBC was forced to pay out an enormous sum of $13 million per episode to keep *ER* on the schedule. Finally, the network also lost its contract with the NFL. This triple blow is often cited as the only reason that *Homicide* was renewed for its seventh season. Having failed to meet the condition that it beat the CBS series *Nash Bridges* (1996–2001) in the ratings during its sixth season, *Homicide* seemed a likely candidate for cancellation in 1998. But with so much uncertainty in the schedule and with waning network revenues, *Homicide* seemed—in 1998 at least—to be a safe bet (Kalat 1999, 266).

By the end of the year, however, a different kind of uncertainty reared its head and shifted the fortunes of the series again. First, Warren Littlefield, one of its biggest champions at the network, was replaced as NBC president of entertainment by Scott Sassa in October 1998. Sassa came from the business side of the network, having recently headed the station division, and was named the heir apparent to Don Ohlmeyer, the head of NBC West Coast, who was slated to step down in 1999 (Perren 2004, 111). Sassa took over for Ohlmeyer in February 1999 and hired Garth Ancier in May as his president of entertainment. This ferment at the top of the network coincided with development season at a time when Sassa wanted to move the network toward more family-oriented shows (Carter 1999b). According to *Variety* in March 1999, "If NBC finds the right family-friendly companion to 'Providence,' the web will probably pull the plug on 'Homicide'" (Adalian 1999). Thus, the uncertainty at the network—about money, about the schedule, about the network's direction—loomed large over the production of the *Homicide* season 7 finale.

The season 7 finale bears the marks of network uncertainty in the text itself: a narrative that has to function as both a possible series finale and a possible season finale. These two types of texts, of course, function differently for commercial serial television. For television serials, season fina-les are designed to provide a provocation—to bring a season arc to a close but also suggest several possible paths forward. In other words, a season finale paradoxically opens the text. By contrast, a series finale is designed to do the opposite. The primary function of the series finale, especially those of long-running serial dramas, is to stop the narrative flow. The series needs no further momentum, and the finale functions instead to offer writers and producers a chance to close their story worlds for good and to offer audi-ences who have invested in the program a way to close off their ongoing relationship with the characters in a meaningful way. The season 7 finale accomplished neither of these things.

The central narrative of the episode, "Forgive Us Our Trespasses,"[1] focuses on Detective Tim Bayliss's (Kyle Secor) growing frustration with the Baltimore court system's inability to try Luke Ryland, a suspect apprehended in an earlier episode ("Homicide.com"), in a timely manner, resulting in his eventual acquittal on a technicality. Bayliss eventually confronts Ryland, who displays no remorse and, in fact, suggests to Bayliss that he will con-tinue his webcasting of murder from New Orleans, effectively escaping fur-ther scrutiny in Baltimore. Not much later in the episode, Ryland turns up dead, executed in the street. The audience has every reason to suspect that Bayliss has taken justice into his own hands, a possibility underscored by two cryptic conversations he has with fellow detective John Munch (Richard Belzer) and state's attorney Ed Danvers (Zeljko Ivanek). Despite the hints, though, the audience is never granted any certainty. This open-endedness suggests that the episode was operating as a season finale, opening up new possibilities for a potential season 8 during which Bayliss might become the prime suspect in a murder investigation.

At the same time, the penultimate sequence of the episode suggests a dif-ferent kind of closure. Bayliss is putting items from his desk into a box, the same kind of box he arrived with in the first episode. Lieutenant Al Giardello (Yaphet Kotto) approaches him:

GIARDELLO: Spring cleaning?
BAYLISS: Yeah, just getting rid of a few things here I don't need anymore.
GIARDELLO: Good. It's good in May to sweep things clean.

1. All references to "Forgive Us Our Trespasses" come from Taylor [1999] 2006.

Once Giardello moves on, Bayliss picks up his box and walks through the squad room and out the door (pausing for a forty-five-second rapid-fire montage covering the entire series). Bayliss doesn't say he's leaving, but the sequence suggests otherwise by mirroring the introduction of Bayliss in the first episode, wandering aimlessly through the squad room with his box, looking for a desk. The sequence suggests that Bayliss has come full circle. And the final scene suggests that the series itself has come full circle as Detectives Meldrick Lewis (Clark Johnson) and Rene Sheppard (Michael Michele) reenact a shortened version of the opening scene of the series, replicating key lines of dialogue and ending on the line that ended that scene in the pilot episode: "That's the problem with this job—it's got nothin' to do with life." Clearly, the series is setting up the possibility that this will be the end at the very same time that it is opening up possibilities for another season. Left without a clear path forward, the producers and writers opted for a dual structure that satisfied the impulse for neither a season finale nor a series finale. The frustration of that situation can be heard echoing through Giardello's last line about sweeping things clean in May: a snarky sideways glance at the network that had strung the series along, only to likely cancel it in May.

When in May 1999, NBC did finally announce that it would be replacing *Homicide* with a new series (a romantic comedy called *Cold Feet* [September–October 1999]), Scott Sassa and Garth Ancier assured Tom Fontana that the reason was purely economic. *Homicide* had already completed 122 episodes, more than enough to make it at least relatively valuable in the syndication market. (The off-network rights in fact had already been sold to CourtTV.) NBC owned the series, so it made sense to capitalize on its after-market value at a time when revenues were falling. Furthermore, the series would cost approximately $200,000 more per episode to produce than a new series (Carter 1999a). For these reasons and the fact that *Homicide* had been falling in the ratings for the previous two seasons, it was all the more confounding that NBC turned around and pitched a two-hour movie event for *Homicide* to run during sweeps week the following February. As Tom Fontana told reporter Eric Deggans in 2000, "I was stunned. I think it's ironic that we're a sweeps movie for NBC, when they usually put on ice skating or something instead of us. There's so many ironies connected to this, I've lost count."

Irony aside, it is tempting to think that NBC made this decision as a way of offering esteemed producers such as Tom Fontana and Barry Levinson an olive branch and giving the audience a chance to get the closure they so desired. But television networks don't typically operate on altruism. Economics is the more likely answer again. First, *Cold Feet* was a ratings failure, averaging only a 4.9/9 rating/share across four episodes before it was canceled by the network (Adalian 1999). (In another bit of irony, it was replaced by reruns of another police procedural, *Law & Order* [1990–2010].) Second, in July 1999 the NAACP publicly threatened to sue the networks if they didn't address the dearth of minority representation in their programming (Haynes 1999). *Homicide* was perhaps the most racially integrated series on the network schedule in its time. As early as 1993, after *Homicide*'s first season, the NAACP had written to NBC informing the network of its dismay that the series was under threat of cancellation and urging NBC to keep the series on the air (Zurawik 1993). The movie acted perhaps as a gesture of good faith in the hopes of staving off the threat of an advertiser boycott by the NAACP (Jubera 1995).[2] Third, NBC (along with the other networks) was suffering a great deal of uncertainty about the future status of its revenue. During the February 2000 sweeps, NBC finished a distant second, with audience numbers down by 8 percent; of the four broadcast networks, only ABC gained ground on the strength of multiple nights of *Who Wants to Be a Millionaire?* (2002–), which was hardly a measure of the network's standard offering (Lowry 2000).

The *Homicide* movie was built around a "red ball," indicating a case of the highest priority. The case involved the shooting of Giardello during a campaign rally in support of his run for mayor of Baltimore, which had left him in critical condition. In addition to serving its economic function as a sufficiently "special" event, marketed as such by the network to garner sweeps week ratings, the movie also served its intended aesthetic functions: to provide a clear end to the narrative flow of the series.[3] First, though a logistic puzzle, the movie featured every regular character from the entire run of the series, even those who had been killed off earlier, giving viewers a final opportunity to get answers about what became of them. Second, it effectively resolved the primary relationship of the series, between Bayliss and Frank Pembleton (Andre Braugher), with Bayliss forcing Pembleton to

2. For an excellent discussion of the conditions that led the networks to this dearth of minority representation, see the chapter "Where Have All the Black Shows Gone?" in Herman Gray's book *Cultural Moves: African American and the Politics of Representation* (2005), 77–88.

3. All references to *Homicide: The Movie* come from de Segonzac [2000] 2006.

hear his confession about killing Luke Ryland and closing the case (marked by Ryland's name on "the board" being written in blue—the color depicting a case from the previous year finally being closed). But not before engaging in a discussion about the balance of good and evil.

> PEMBLETON: There's a line between right and wrong. . . .
> . . . BAYLISS: Sometimes you can lose your bearings. Sometimes the line isn't so clear.
> PEMBLETON: Of course the line is clear. There's good, there's evil.
> BAYLISS: You never shot anyone, did you?
> PEMBLETON: No.
> BAYLISS: No. And you never would.
> PEMBLETON: I never had to. I've been lucky.
> BAYLISS: Yeah, the righteous cop. The line's always been clear to you.
> PEMBLETON: Not always.
> BAYLISS: Time for one more confession, Frank.

The uncertainty about Bayliss's actions is thus resolved, but the uncertainty about the distinction between right and wrong, good and evil, is renewed. It's worth noting that this moral ambivalence became one of the hallmarks of the surge of what has become a renaissance in television drama driven by cable and premium channels such as AMC and HBO and manifested in series such as *Breaking Bad* (2008–13), *The Walking Dead* (2010–), *Justified* (2010–15), and *The Wire* (2002–8), all led, of course, by the HBO series *The Sopranos* (1999–2007).

At the conclusion of the movie, it is revealed that Giardello has, in fact, died from his injuries. The final scene depicts him returning to the squad room surrounded by the dead. He eventually comes upon deceased detectives Steve Crosetti (John Polito) and Beau Felton (Daniel Baldwin), who invite him to play a game of cards in what appears to be a kind of purgatory. Felton informs him that the "best thing about this place" is that "all the worries and cares you had in life, they don't matter anymore. Rest in peace means what it says." Giardello—in some ways the anchor of the series—becomes its most fitting metaphor: gone in one sense, still present in another—in the perpetually uncertain afterlife. And finally at peace.

Although many critics expressed disappointment in the quality of the movie, as a finale it works in ways that the ending of season 7 did (or could) not. The narrative flow is halted, its primary questions are answered, and its textual possibilities are mostly foreclosed except in the series' afterlife in the ancillary marketplace (see Nichols-Pethick 2001). The movie's melo-dramatic overtures—depicting the biggest of all "red balls"—threaten the integrity of a series that prided itself initially on its desire to explicitly avoid such ostentatious trappings. At the same time, the resolution of Giardello's murder is positioned as so simple that it allows the "mysteries" of the story to reside in the character interactions and the moral complexities of their jobs. As an example of a true series finale, serving both a narrative function (closing threads without sacrificing the moral complexity that is so central to the series as a whole) and an audience function (providing final glimpses of—and closure for—all its characters, again, in all their moral complexity), the movie is particularly successful.

The finales of *Homicide* are instructive not only as narrative examples but also with regard to the structure and function of the entire series—its artistic ambitions and its status as a television commodity. The uncertainty surrounding the fate of the series epitomized the tension between art and commerce that animates all commercial culture. Not knowing their fate, forced to hedge their bets for the ending of season 7, the producers were forced to leave just enough ambiguity to continue if necessary and just enough closure to satisfy the series' loyal fans should the season 7 finale be the end. The movie emerged from a condition of economic uncertainty to provide (ironically) some stability for the network while offering the produc-ers an opportunity to craft a conclusion that would be central to the series in a way that made sense—even if that sense was ultimately contested, pro-visional, uncertain.

References

Adalian, Josef. 1999. "NBC Ices 'Cold Feet.'" *Variety*, Nov. 1. At http://variety .com/1999/tv/news/nbc-ices-cold-feet-1117757615/.

Carter, Bill. 1999a. "'Homicide' Is Cancelled; NBC Cites Economics." *New York Times*, May 14. At http://www.nytimes.com/1999/05/14/movies/homicide-is -canceled-nbc-cites-economics.html?_r=0.

———. 1999b. "The Media Business; NBC Names a New President for Its Enter-tainment Division." *New York Times*, Mar. 16. At http://www.nytimes.com /1999/03/16/business/the-media-business-nbc-names-a-new-president-for-its -entertainment-division.html.

Deggans, Eric. 2000. "NBC Hopes Death Becomes 'Homicide.'" *St. Petersburg Times*, Feb. 11. At http://www.sptimes.com/News/021100/Floridian/NBC _hopes_death_becom.shtml.

de Segonzac, Jean, dir. [2000] 2006. *Homicide: The Movie*. Written by Tom Fontana, James Yoshimura, and Eric Overmyer. Aired Feb. 13, 2000, NBC. New York: A&E Home Video. DVD.

Fretts, Bruce. 1998. "'Homidice [*sic*]: Life on the Street' Lives On." *Entertainment Weekly*, May 1. At http://ew.com/article/1998/05/01/homidice-life-street-lives/.

Gray, Herman. 2005. *Cultural Moves: African Americans and the Politics of Representation*. Berkeley: Univ. of California Press.

Haynes, V. Dion. 1999. "Bashing TV Whitewash, NAACP Threatens to Sue." *Chicago Tribune*, July 13. At http://articles.chicagotribune.com/1999-07-13 /news/9907130059_1_display-by-network-executives-naacp-president-kweisi -mfume-minorities.

Jubera, Drew. 1995. "One of a Kind 'Homicide' Sets New Standard for Depictions of African-Americans." *Chicago Tribune*, June 9. At http://articles.chicago tribune.com/1995-06-09/features/9506090006_1_frank-pembleton-african -american-homicide.

Kalat, David. 1999. *"Homicide: Life on the Street": The Unofficial Companion*. Los Angeles: Renaissance Books.

Lowry, Brian. 2000. "ABC Claims Its Second Sweeps Win." *Los Angeles Times*, Mar. 3. At http://articles.latimes.com/2000/mar/03/entertainment/ca-4799.

Nichols-Pethick, Jonathan. 2001. "Lifetime on the Street: Textual Strategies of Syndication." *Velvet Light Trap* 47:62–73.

Perren, Alisa. 2004. "Garth Ancier." In *Encyclopedia of Television*, edited by Horace Newcomb, 111–12. New York: Fitzroy Dearborn.

"Renewal Outlook Bleak for 'Homicide.'" 1999. *Lubbock Avalanche-Journal*, Apr. 17. At http://lubbockonline.com/stories/041899/index.shtml#.V9hXo9JTGAg.

Shales, Tom. 1993. "'Homicide': NBC's Next Victim?" *Washington Post*, Apr. 27. At https://www.washingtonpost.com/archive/lifestyle/1993/04/27/homicide-nbcs -next-victim/4eb8c4d3-3616-48ee-9b72-c4a4ab4b6e57/.

Taylor, Alan, dir. [1999] 2006. "Forgive Us Our Trespasses." *Homicide: Life on the Street*, season 7, episode 22. Written by Tom Fontana. Aired May 21, 1999, NBC. On *Homicide: Life on the Street: The Complete Season 7*. New York: A&E Home Video. DVD.

Zurawik, David. 1993. "NAACP Urges NBC to Renew 'Homicide.'" *Baltimore Sun*, Apr. 22. At http://articles.baltimoresun.com/1993-04-22/features/1993112183 _1_homicide-renew-nbc.

26

House, M.D.

"Everybody Dies"

DOUGLAS SNAUFFER

House, M.D. (2004–12) was just what the doctor had ordered for the Fox network in 2004. Indeed, Fox needed *House*. It had a couple of dramatic hits: *24* (2001–10, 2014) and *The O.C.* (2003–7), as well as the animated programs *The Simpsons* (1989–) and *King of the Hill* (1997–2010). But none was a big ratings winner. As a matter of fact, during the 2003–4 TV season, Fox didn't have a single dramatic program in the Nielsen top thirty. What it had was *American Idol*, the hit music competition that had premiered in 2002 and continued to dominate time slots on both Tuesday and Wednesday evenings (ranking number 2 and number 3, respectively). There was also the highly rated (number 14) but scathingly reviewed reality show *My Big Fat Obnoxious Fiancé* (2004), which the network chose not to renew. Those two reality shows were the highlights of Fox's season (Brooks and Marsh 2007). Fox stuck with its usual strategies when putting together its fall 2004 schedule. Along with the *American Idol* juggernaut, it rolled out such new titles as *Renovate My Family*, *Trading Spouses: Meet Your New Mommy*, and *My Big Fat Obnoxious Boss*. On Tuesdays at 9:00 p.m., it introduced the Oscar de la Hoya reality boxing series *The Next Great Champ*, which was canceled after only four telecasts. Only then, after the demise of the most noted failure of the season, did *House, M.D.* inherit its time slot and make its debut, becoming an immediate hit with both fans and critics (Brooks and Marsh 2007).

House takes place primarily within the walls of fictional Princeton Plainsboro Teaching Hospital in New Jersey. Unlike most hospital dramas (such as *ER* [1994–2009], *Grey's Anatomy* [2005–], *Chicago Med* [2015–]), *House* is more of a weekly medical mystery. When Gail Berman, Fox Broadcasting's president of entertainment, first heard a pitch for the series, she was agreeable but stated: "I want a medical show, but I don't want to see white coats going down the hallway" (quoted in DeVries 2008). So *House* became a rather unique medical drama, both in concept and execution.

Dr. Gregory House (Hugh Laurie) is the head of the Department of Diagnostic Medicine at Princeton Plainsboro. He is a board-certified diagnostician with a double specialty in infectious disease and nephrology, a brilliant doctor but an extremely flawed human being. In 2000, he experienced an infarction in his right leg while playing golf. It was misdiagnosed by a doctor and went untreated for three days until House himself recognized the symptoms. By then it was too late, and the muscle was dead, leaving him facing a lifetime of chronic pain and narcotic addiction.

House is fascinated by disease and sees each new case as a puzzle. The press often compared him to Sherlock Holmes, of whom series' creator David Shore was a fan. "Holmes" and "House" share similarities: their arrogance, methodology for solving mysteries (Holmes, crimes; House, medical ailments), drug addiction (Holmes, cocaine; House, Vicodin), musical inclinations (Holmes, violin; House, piano and guitar), addresses (Holmes, 221B Baker Street; House, apartment 221B), and even best friends (Holmes, Dr. Watson; House, Dr. Wilson) (McNab 2012).

Dr. James Wilson (Robert Sean Leonard) is head of oncology at Princeton Plainsboro. He and House have been friends for twenty years. Wilson was originally to have played more of a Mr. Watson–type of role to House's Sherlock Holmes. But with Princeton Plainsboro being a teaching hospital, it was decided House should have a team of young specialists to serve in that capacity.

The team would change over the years, but the initial group consists of Eric Foreman (Omar Epps), an African American neurologist; Robert Chase (Jesse Spencer), an Australian surgeon; and Allison Cameron (Jennifer Morrison), an immunologist. House reports to Lisa Cuddy (Lisa Edelstein), the hospital's dean of medicine. She and House were once romantically involved, and there is still a great deal of sexual tension between them.

The series was rolled out on November 16, 2004, amid a flurry of positive reviews, many singling out Laurie's performance. "House is a rarity for TV: a true antihero, someone who's hard to embrace but easy to accept," opined Charlie McCollum in the *San Jose Mercury News/Contra Costa Times* (2004). Aaron Barnhart of the *Kansas City Star* remarked, "Want to see a terrific performance by a comedic actor who may singlehandedly save the medical drama? Here's your guy" (2004). Yet even with glowing reviews, there were still doubts as to whether *House* would survive. Since hitting it big with *American Idol*, Fox had developed a large stable of reality-TV projects, along with a quick trigger finger when it came to cancelling nonreality programs that weren't immediate hits. In critiquing the pilot for *House*, Andrew Ryan of the *Globe and Mail* remarked: "The outstanding pilot is the good news. The bad news is that Fox has an atrocious track record of supporting dramas, which means *House* will likely be DOA by Thanksgiving" (2004).

TV viewers were likewise impressed; *House, M.D.* finished its first year ranked number 24, and by the end of its sophomore season it had broken into the top ten (Brooks and Marsh 2007). House may be a drug addict and misanthropist, but he is also a genius who ignores the rules, hates authority, and gets things done, and people were drawn to that side of him. They might have felt differently had he been their doctor.

House may find championing an illness rewarding, but he isn't as fond of the patients themselves. As a matter of fact, he avoids them altogether whenever possible, leaving direct contact with the sick to his fellows. "[House] is arrogant, rude and considers all patients lying idiots. He will do anything, illegal or otherwise, to ensure that his patients—passive objects of his expert attentions—get the investigations and treatments he knows they need" (Fogoros 2009).

Not that the medicine practiced on *House* is always medically sound. The writers typically began each episode with a specific disease and worked backward in creating symptoms and situations to lead the doctors to a conclusion. They often stretched accuracy and credibility for the sake of dramatic impact. Princeton Plainsboro also seems to allow a patient to receive the complete attentions of a team of top doctors without anyone ever asking about the patient's ability to pay.

The series remained popular, eventually airing in nearly seventy countries to an audience of more than 80 million viewers each week. Hugh Laurie received six Emmy nominations as lead actor but never took one home, although he did win two Golden Globes for best actor. The series did become somewhat formulaic as the years passed, and the story lines became a bit repetitive. But viewers continued to tune in. It wasn't until the season 7 finale that many felt the show went too far when House, hurt, angry, and jealous that a romantic reconciliation with Cuddy hadn't worked out, drives his car through the front of her house. He avoids jail time but lands in rehab for his drug use and anger issues.

The decision was made that *House*'s eighth season would be its last. The question on everyone's mind was how David Shore would choose to end the story, and, for Shore, the pressure was certainly on. *House* had a considerable audience whose members tended to be well educated, tech savvy, passionate, and unforgiving. They would congregate on the Internet and carefully dissect each new episode of the program, proffering praise and criticism as they saw fit. No doubt Shore and his staff were feeling the heat.

In the new episodes starting in October 2011, House is completing his stint in rehab and is released on probation. Complicating his return to Princeton Plainsboro is Cuddy's resignation to start a new life with her adopted daughter, a development used to explain Lisa Edelstein's departure from the program owing to a contract dispute.

About halfway through the season, in early 2012, the public was tipped off to the title of the series' final script—"Everybody Dies"—a nod to the show's first episode, which had been dubbed "Everybody Lies." The revelation set off a wave of possible scenarios among *House* aficionados. The general consensus reached by fans was that a major player would meet his or her demise.

Then in the final moments of the episode titled "Body and Soul" (aired April 23, 2012), Wilson reveals to House that he has been diagnosed with a stage II thymoma.[1] With intensive chemotherapy, he might live another one to three years, but without it perhaps six months. Wilson opts for treatment, but after the first round of chemo produces no substantial results, he decides to accept his fate and forgo any further therapy.

Wilson's decision is understandable. As a top oncologist who has treated thousands of patients, he is more than qualified to judge his own odds. And he has seen firsthand what the procedures he is considering can do to a person's mind and body. Based on his own experiences, Wilson makes a personal choice he feels is best for himself, and that is to live whatever time he has left to the fullest, not laying in the cancer suite of a hospital suffering the debilitating effects of radiation therapy.

But House cannot let go so easily. He tries to pressure Wilson into continuing with his course of treatment for whatever time it will afford him, oblivious to or perhaps regardless of the consequences Wilson might face in terms of personal comfort or dignity. The question naturally arises as to whether House has Wilson's best interests or his own in mind. As codependent as House has grown on his best friend, one might say his only "real" friend, his true intentions can easily be called suspect.

---

1. All references to "Body and Soul" come from Schwartz 2012.

House finally implodes in the next-to-last episode, "Holding On" (aired May 14, 2012).[2] Foreman presents House with season hockey tickets and suggests they go together. Foreman hopes to show House that he will continue to have people who care for him after Wilson is gone, but House rebukes his efforts and proceeds to tear up the tickets and flush them down a toilet at the hospital, where they back up the plumbing and cause a ceiling to collapse in the MRI chamber, nearly killing a patient. Then House nearly strangles a patient who has attempted suicide for not wanting to live when Wilson is so desperate to.

These events unsettle even House, who finally makes peace with Wilson's decision to let go. The two friends then decide to take a road trip by motorcycle and spend the five months Wilson has left traveling together. But then House is charged with felony vandalism for causing the destruction of the hospital's MRI machine. His probation is revoked, and he has to face returning to jail to serve out the remainder of his six-month sentence, one month longer than Wilson has to live.

In the series finale, "Everybody Dies" (aired May 21, 2012),[3] House is devastated and feels he has nothing to live for. Desperate to feel happy, he chooses to follow the lead of Oliver (James LeGros), a patient he met while working in the hospital's clinic, a hard-core heroin addict with no intention of getting sober and facing reality. House follows Oliver home to an abandoned warehouse to get high. At some point, House passes out, and Oliver dies from an overdose with a lit cigarette in his mouth, which ignites a fire in the old structure. Rather than making his way to safety, House surrenders to the approaching fire.

Then, as he awaits his fate, he begins to hallucinate and is confronted by "ghosts" from his past. First (and perhaps most fitting) is Dr. Lawrence Kutner (Kal Penn), a former member of House's team who committed suicide in the season 5 episode "Simple Explanation" (aired April 6, 2009). Kutner asks House why he isn't heading for an exit. "I'm going to jail, losing my job, losing my best friend," House retorts. "You think that's the sum total of who you are? A doctor? A friend to Wilson?" Kutner shoots back.

The Kutner apparition is followed by those of Stacy Warner (Sela Ward), a woman whom House came very close to marrying; Dominika Patrova (Karolina Wydra), an immigrant who did marry House to get a green card;

2. All references to "Holding On" come from Sapochnik 2012.
3. All references to "Everybody Dies" come from Shore 2012.

and Allison Cameron, who was always the member of House's team with the most sympathy for others. All were women whom House had loved and been loved by.

These people had the greatest impact on House's life, whether he realized it or not. Each made an attempt to reach House and get him to take an honest look at his life. Ideally, Cuddy would have been there, too; without a doubt, she had been the most compelling and dynamic force in his life. Lisa Edelstein's presence was sorely missed in the finale.

House eventually realizes that his current predicament is the result of his own choice to accept Wilson's decision to die. House respects Wilson, so if Wilson chooses to die rather than to live with pain, then why shouldn't House make the same choice? Through the intervention of the figments from his past, House eventually comes to understand that he *is* more than simply a doctor or Wilson's best friend—that he has other reasons to live and that if he was once happy, then he could be happy again. He suddenly wants to live, but by then it appears to be too late as the floor of the warehouse literally drops out from beneath him (Kotsko 2009).

At House's funeral, only Wilson has the courage to stand up amid a sea of false praise and call House out for what he truly was, an uncompassionate, "arrogant ass." Just then Wilson is interrupted by a series of incoming text messages that read, "SHUT UP, YOU IDIOT!" It is House, who survived the fire, only to fake his own death (yet another nod to Sherlock Holmes) to avoid prison. Wilson just smiles knowingly.

The last scene features House and Wilson together. "You're destroying your entire life," Wilson admonishes. "You can never go back from this. You'll go to jail for years. You can never be a doctor again." House just smirks. "I'm dead, Wilson. How do you want to spend your last five months?" And off they ride.

The *House* finale was a very satisfying conclusion to the series, particularly after the often disappointing story lines of that crowning season. The general consensus among fans had been that House would die, so the decision by producers to have Wilson face his mortality instead was not only unexpected but emotionally compelling to viewers.

The dire impact was also felt on-screen. Dealing with Wilson's fate is even more disturbing to House than his own terminal diagnosis would have been. It forces him to finally reevaluate his life (with the aid of drug-fueled hallucinations); the previous eight seasons had demonstrated that nothing short of his love for his best friend and his distress at losing the only true human contact he has left in the world would compel him to do so.

So after eight years and 176 episodes, House finds the elusive truth he has been chasing all his life and does so on his own terms.

References

Barnhart, Aaron. 2004. Review of *House, M.D. Kansas City Star*, Nov. 16.

Brooks, Tim, and Earle Marsh. 2007. *The Complete Directory to Prime Time Network and Cable TV Shows, 1946–2007*. New York: Ballantine Books.

DeVries, Lynn. 2008. "Interview with *House* Executive Producer, Katie Jacobs." *TV Drama Watch*, Nov. 16. At http://tvdramawatch.com/2008/11/16/interview-with-house-executive-producer-katie-jacobs/.

Fogoros, Dr. Richard. 2009. "Ethics Essay: Why Does America Love Dr. House?" *Better Health Network*, Apr. 15. At http://getbetterhealth.com/ethics-essay-why-does-america-love-dr-house/2009.04.15.

Kotsko, Adam. 2009. "The Ethics of Dr. Gregory House." *Popmatters*, Apr. 22. At http://www.popmatters.com/feature/the-ethics-of-dr.-gregory-house/.

McCollum, Charlie. 2004. Review of *House, M.D. San Jose Mercury News/Contra Costa Times*, Nov. 15.

McNab, Peter. 2012. "'House, M.D.': An Appreciation and Analysis by Mario Sikora." *Nine Points Magazine*, July 1. At http://www.ninepointsmagazine.org/house-m-d-an-appreciation-and-analysis-by-mario-sikora/.

Ryan, Andrew. 2004. "The New Fall Season." *Globe and Mail*, Nov. 14. At http://www.theglobeandmail.com/arts/the-new-fall-season/article1003865/?page=all.

Sapochnik, Miguel, dir. 2012. "Holding On." *House, M.D.*, season 8, episode 21. Written by Russel Friend, Garrett Lerner, and David Foster. Aired May 14, Fox. Original broadcast.

Schwartz, Stefan, dir. 2012. "Body and Soul." *House, M.D.*, season 8, episode 18. Written by Dustin Paddoek. Aired Apr. 23, Fox. Original broadcast.

Shore, David, dir. 2012. "Everybody Dies." *House, M.D.*, season 8, episode 22. Written by Peter Blake, David Shore, and Eli Attie. Aired May 21, Fox. Original broadcast.

27

How I Met Your Mother

"Last Forever"

CLINTON BRYANT AND KATHERYN WRIGHT

The final scene of the series finale of CBS's *How I Met Your Mother* (2005–14) parallels the last scene in the pilot episode. Ted Mosby (Josh Radnor) stands outside Robin Scherbatsky's (Cobie Smulders) window in the rain, holding up the blue French horn they stole from a restaurant during their first date. Robin looks down at him from her apartment, a modern-day Juliet. The music swells, the song lyrics "remember, remember" rising as the shot cuts to a title screen that reads "How I Met Your Mother." So concludes the romance story of Ted and Robin.

How I Met Your Mother is a sitcom created by Carter Bays and Craig Thomas. The narrative frame involves Ted telling his two children in the year 2030 the story of how he met their mother. Each episode takes place in the past, with the first episode beginning when Ted meets Robin in 2005. As Ted's girlfriend, she joins his group of friends, which includes Lily Aldrin (Alyson Hannigan) and Marshall Eriksen (Jason Segel), a couple in a long-term relationship at the start of the series, and Barney Stinson (Neil Patrick Harris), a playboy with a strong commitment to what he calls "the bro code." Ted, Barney, and Robin are caught in a love triangle for seven seasons that ends with Robin choosing to marry Barney in the final season even though Ted is still in love with her. Lily becomes Robin's best friend and confidant, while Marshall is Ted's closest ally. This "gang" of five friends are at the core of the series, a chronicle of their late twenties and early thirties hanging out at MacLaren's in New York.

From the outset of the series, the audience knows that Robin is not Ted's children's mother. The mystery behind who the mother is provides a running through-line to the series as a whole. Throughout each season, there are clues to the identity of Ted's wife, all of which indicate that he will meet her at what is revealed to be a train station after Barney and Robin's wedding. Each season but the last covers about a year in Ted's story, and the last season is broken up over the course of the weekend leading up to the ceremony. Some of the plotlines in this final season involve Robin having doubts about her choice and Ted deciding to leave New York rather than see her marry someone else. Several episodes include flash-forwards rather than flashbacks, detailing some of what happens after Ted meets his future wife. In the next-to-last episode, Robin and Barney finally get married.

For the two-part finale entitled "Last Forever," the temporal structure of *How I Met Your Mother* dramatically shifts.[1] The finale discards the narrative frame of Ted telling the story to his children until the end of the second part. The narrative compresses almost two decades into less than an hour of screen time, leading up to the time when Ted finishes telling his teenage children the story of how he met their mother. The two episodes that make up the finale jump ahead multiple times over the course of many years. Audiences are pushed through time, showing the breakup of Barney and Robin's relationship, Lily and Marshall's personal and professional triumphs, and Ted's subsequent meeting with the titular mother. In so doing, the finale inverts the timeline that has defined the entire premise of the series as a whole.

The inversion of this temporal structure in the finale is part of a larger fracturing that occurs in the narrative in terms of both its form and its content. The finale details the fractured relationship among the five friends after the wedding. The initial indication of this fracturing comes with a jettisoning of the first-person narrative. Most of the episodes in the series are narrated by Ted in 2030 through a voiceover by Bob Saget. The voiceover contextualizes the particular episode, offering information about things that occur in the future that are affected by what is happening in the present. The voiceover also informs audiences of things the characters aren't aware of, while drawing connections between the past, present, and future. This contextualization by future Ted structures the story, moving the narrative arc toward the inevitable conclusion of Ted meeting the mother of his children. In the first part of the finale, however, the voiceover disappears. The absence of future Ted's voiceover reorients the sitcom to a third-person perspective. The finale is not a typical episode; it is the summary of the years after Ted

---

1. All references to the two-part finale of *How I Met Your Mother* come from Fryman 2014a, 2014b.

meets the mother of his children and of how Robin separates herself from the group. Audiences are no longer remembering with future Ted but looking forward into the characters' futures without his guidance or insight. Ted, similarly, is no longer remembering the past as a narrative but becomes swept up in his future life.

Along with the shift in the timeframe and absence of a voiceover comes a splintering of the group of friends. The finale suddenly is less about how Ted finally meets the mother and more about what happens after they meet and how Robin's relationships with the other main characters fracture. This fracturing begins with the breakup of Robin and Barney's marriage in the first part of "Last Forever." The couple's quick breakup occurs in less than twenty minutes after their marriage on-screen, but in chronological time it takes place three years later. The group is assembled in Ted's home when Barney and Robin inform them they have split up. There is a flashback to Barney and Robin in a hotel room in Argentina; she is on assignment, and he is trying to maintain his lifestyle blog. After an argument, Robin asks Barney whether he would take an "exit ramp" from their relationship if she were to offer it. Deferring the question for booze and sex, the scene comes back a few moments later with Barney saying, "I love you, Robin. And when we got married, I made a vow that I would always tell you the truth." The flashback ends, coming back to Robin announcing to the group, "We got a divorce." Even as the scene ends with the announcement that Lily and Marshall are going to be parents for a third time and a promise that "we won't stop hanging out," Barney notes, "We hardly see one another as it is."

Robin's place in the group further fractures when Lily and Marshall hold a "Happy Halloween, Farewell to the Apartment" party. This party alludes to other Halloween parties from past episodes, such as the one where Ted wore the "hanging chad" costume. Now, however, Ted no longer is waiting for someone, as the mother of his children walks up in a complimentary "Gore–Lieberman" sweatshirt. Her presence further alienates Robin, who leaves the party early. As she leaves, Lily begs her to stay because this is one of the "big moments." Robin responds, "It's never going to be how it was." Lily wears a "white whale" costume because she feels like one owing to her pregnancy, but the symbolism borrowed from *Moby-Dick* offers a reminder that Robin is no longer the object of Ted's desire. Robin's divorce and separation from her husband and the entire gang fracture the relational dynamics at the core of the series.

The second part of the finale begins a gradual reconstruction of those broken relationships, shifting the narrative's focus away from how Ted meets

the mother of his children to how Robin returns to the gang. The first indication of this reconstruction is Barney becoming a father. When he leaves
Robin, Barney tells Ted, as justification for his continued philandering,
that if he can't commit to Robin, then he can't commit to anyone. In 2019,
an unnamed woman, a parallel to the "mother" of Ted's children, who is
unnamed until the conclusion of the series, gets pregnant and gives birth to
Barney's daughter, Ellie. When he meets his daughter for the first time, he
tells her that she is the love of his life. After that point, he chases girls in bars
only to tell them to return home. He becomes more responsible, which gives
space in the group for Robin to return without his promiscuity threatening
her emotional integrity.

Ellie's birth signals the beginning of a healing process for this group of
friends. There are several chance meetings with Robin over the years, culminating with the "mother" inviting her to attend Ted's long-awaited wedding,
which occurs seven years after he and the mother meet. Ted's previous long-
term girlfriends didn't want Robin to be a part of Ted's life because of Robin
and Ted's former relationship. The mother, who remains unnamed at this
point, welcomes Robin back as a best friend, however. She realigns rather
than tears apart the group, making her integral to its reconstruction. At their
wedding ceremony, the voiceover returns but with Radnor rather than Saget
voicing the narrative. The shift in who narrates is significant because it is
the moment when the future becomes the present tense of the series. Ted no
longer is remembering the past but crafting a new future for himself from
the wedding to the eventual death of his wife only a few years later in the
series' timeline.

In the final five minutes of the series, which Ted narrates, many questions
are answered. We learn that Ted's wife passed away, which is part of the reason why he's telling this story. The children, however, reveal the truth that
Ted is in love with their aunt Robin, and he wants their approval to reconnect with her after all of these years. We also learn that the mother's name
is Tracy McConnell, a detail that is finally revealed in the next-to-last scene
of the episode during the long-awaited flashback to the initial conversation
between her and Ted at the train station. *How I Met Your Mother* had been
building up to this meeting for the entire run of the series, with clues about
the encounter (such as the yellow umbrella) hidden in previous seasons. This
moment, however, is not the final scene of the series. Instead, it is Ted's
reunion with Robin, as he holds the blue French horn from their first date,
that concludes everything. Ted and Robin finally reunite, answering Barney's

constant call throughout the series to "wait for it" before the punchline of the story is given.

As much as the finale breaks with the show's established organization, the refrain of remembrance pulls it back together. The call to "remember, remember" is about reestablishing the group's cohesion, which becomes the story of *How I Met Your Mother*. This fracturing and reassembling cast the entire series in a new light, which perhaps explains some of the frustrations voiced by critics and fans about the finale. When the two-part episode aired, many were angry about the breakup of Robin and Barney, whose relationship was the focal point of the show for the final season. Others were unhappy about the death of Ted's wife, feeling her presence in the show was too fleeting given the nine-year buildup to her introduction. Because of these factors, a group of fans started a petition to have the creators write and shoot a new finale. The essence of what these disgruntled viewers expressed by signing the petition perhaps is best voiced in Todd VanDerWeff's review of the finale. VanDerWerff writes, "The story the series ultimately settled on was that of not just how Ted met Tracy (and told his kids all about not just that but also several seemingly unconnected adventures) but also how his kids told him to get out of his own head and start fucking Robin again after his wife had been dead for a socially acceptable period of time." Although VanDerWerff summarizes the show's general outline somewhat crassly, his actual objection is about how the shift in the temporal structure of the narrative upsets the series' status quo. The shift realigns a story told in retrospect to a story told in the present tense, in which Ted and presumably the gang reconnect with Robin. That's not what the show *was* about, but it's what the show *is* about. The fracturing and healing of the group rewrites the narrative tension that had been built over the course of nine seasons, putting audiences in Ted's position as they wait for an uncertain future.

So, what to do with a finale titled "Last Forever"? In keeping with the tone of the series, it is a pun that suggests both a definitive ending of Ted's story—this is the last forever episode—and a question about whether its fairy-tale ending between Ted and Robin will last forever. Ted lifting the blue French horn toward Robin, flanked by her pack of dogs, is both an emblem of their past relationships and a symbol of their, and our, unknown future. Ted is an unreliable narrator who doesn't fully understand the purpose in telling his own story, a fact revealed at the series' conclusion. Audiences who bought into the reliability of Ted's narrative, however, felt cheated. The alternate ending circulated online after the conclusion of the show offered them an easier finish, where the series closes with him meeting Tracy for the first time after a brief flashback sequence of key moments across its nine seasons. She doesn't die, and the series was always about Ted meeting the mother of his children. This alternate ending robs the show of its complexity. The actual conclusion offers a sense of both certainty and uncertainty, both the fairy-tale ending and the chance that the fairy-tale ending could be fleeting. By the end of the show, viewers left very much like Ted began *How I Met Your Mother*, narrating their own stories as they work to remember the people and places that continue to make them who they are in the present tense.

References

Booth, Paul. 2011. "Memories, Temporalities, Fictions: Temporal Displacement in Contemporary Television." *Television & New Media* 12, no. 4: 370–88.

Fryman, Pamela, dir. 2014a. "Last Forever: Part One." 2014. *How I Met Your Mother*, season 9, episode 23. Written by Carter Bays and Craig Thomas. Aired Mar. 31, CBS. Original broadcast.

———, dir. 2014b. "Last Forever: Part Two." 2014. *How I Met Your Mother*, season 9, episode 24. Written by Carter Bays and Craig Thomas. Aired Mar. 31, CBS. Original broadcast.

"'How I Met Your Mother' Official Alternate Ending." 2014. YouTube video, 4:16. Posted by flavi_us, Sept. 6. At https://www.youtube.com/watch?v=RoHUs8J7x94.

VanDerWerff, Todd. 2014. "Does *How I Met Your Mother*'s Finale Ruin It for All Time?" *A.V. Club*, Apr. 1. At http://www.avclub.com/review/does-how-i-met-your-mothers-finale-ruin-it-all-tim-202906.

28

Howdy Doody

"Clarabell's Big Surprise"

MICHAEL DONOVAN

There have been a wide variety of final episodes: funny (*Bob Newhart* [1982–90]), touching (*The Mary Tyler Moore Show* [1970–77]), and controversial (*St. Elsewhere* [1982–88], *The Sopranos* [1999–2007]). But if you're old enough to remember, there was none more final and traumatic than the finale of *The Howdy Doody Show*.

The Howdy Doody Show was a staple of kids' viewing from late 1947 (when for a short time it was called *The Puppet Playhouse*) to 1960. It ran on NBC five days a week until 1954, when the competition of *The Mickey Mouse Club* (1955–58) forced Howdy's move to Saturday mornings. Howdy and Milton Berle's *Texaco Star Theater* (1948–56) are generally credited with the spike in television sales in the late 1940s, as the "17 million sets in America [in] 1951 [was dramatically] up from just 5,000 at the end of World War II" (Hayes 2008, 87). *The Howdy Doody Show* is also credited with being the first show to produce "more than one thousand continuous episodes and, later, the first show in color on television" (Dircks 2004, 247). Howdy Doody was a friendly, happy marionette who lived in Doodyville. Along with Howdy, Doodyville was inhabited by a group of puppets, such as Doodyville mayor Phineas T. Bluster and Flub-A-Dub, as well as several characters without strings. Among the human residents of Doodyville were Chief Thunderthud and Princess Summerfall Winterspring, all led by Buffalo Bob Smith. Each show featured the Peanut Gallery, a live studio audience of squirming little kids hyped up on sugar who, when Buffalo Bob asked, "Hey, kids, what time is it?" screamed, "IT'S HOWDY DOODY TIME!" Then they would all burst into the opening theme song, which to this day people of a certain age can still sing word for word:

It's Howdy Doody time.
It's Howdy Doody time.
Bob Smith and Howdy, too,
Say, "Howdy do" to you.
Let's give a rousing cheer,
'cause Howdy Doody's here.
It's time to start the show,
So, kids, let's go!

Buffalo Bob helped Howdy and his friends through a number of slapstick "adventures," including Howdy's run for president. Howdy's campaign demonstrated the show's popularity as well as TV's marketing potential when Buffalo Bob received more than sixty thousand requests for "Howdy Doody for President" buttons.

Buffalo Bob's constant companion and kid favorite was Clarabell the Clown, originally played by future kids' star Bob Keeshan, who became Captain Kangaroo. With his big red nose and zebra-striped pajamas, Clarabell was a funny, happy clown (in the days before TV clowns were either serial killers or members of a sex club). But Clarabell couldn't speak. He communicated only with hand signals and by honking the horn he wore around his waist. Clarabell honked his way through every "adventure," to the delight of thousands of kids in the studio and at home.

But in 1960 after more than 2,300 shows, a decision was made that *The Howdy Doody Show* had run its course, and it was time to end it. However, there was one last surprise "plot" line for the final episode, "Clarabell's Big Surprise" (Hultgren 1960), aired on September 24 that year. Clarabell (now played by Lew Anderson) let it be known that he could actually speak! Everyone in and outside of Doodyville was astounded. And so it was that as we came to the final moments of the final episode, and the camera slowly and dramatically moved in to an extreme close-up of Clarabell's face, his lips began moving like a stuttering guppy, and we heard his first and last words: "Good-bye, kids."

Only God knows how many young Baby Boomers spent part of their adult lives on a shrink's couch as a result.

References

Dircks, Phyllis T. 2004. "Howdy Doody in the Courtroom." In *American Puppetry: Collections, History and Performance*, edited by Phyllis T. Dircks, 245–57. Jefferson, NC: McFarland.

Hayes, Dade. 2008. *Anytime Playdate: Inside the Preschool Entertainment Boom, or How Television Became My Baby's Best Friend*. New York: Simon and Schuster.

Hultgren, Bob, dir. 1960. "Clarabell's Big Surprise." *The Howdy Doody Show*. Written by Jack Weinstock and Willie Gilbert. Aired Sept. 24, NBC. YouTube video, 5:49, posted Jan. 30, 2013. At https://www.youtube.com/watch?v=IJ6ybvlsb4s.

29

Jericho

"Patriots and Tyrants"

JEFFREY BUSSOLINI

Jericho is a postapocalyptic political thriller that ran for two seasons (one entire season of twenty-two episodes and one additional compacted season of seven episodes) on CBS between 2006 and 2008. The show opens with the return of prodigal son Jake Green (Skeet Ulrich) to the small, idyllic town of Jericho, Kansas, and the destruction of nearby Denver in a nuclear attack. Cut off from the outside world, residents in the town don't know the extent of the damage, and they slowly learn more about the political effects and causes of the nuclear detonations (finding out from a phone message, for instance, that Atlanta was destroyed). Although the show's title would seem to reference the West Bank town of Jericho, one of the oldest permanently inhabited cities on earth and the place to which the Israelites returned from bondage in Egypt, the program recalls other television shows and films, such as *The Day After* (Nicholas Meyer, 1983) and *Red Dawn* (John Milius, 1984; Don Bradley, 2012). *The Day After* is also set in Kansas, the geographic "center of the nation," and it refutes the notion that Kansas would be safe and insulated in the event of nuclear exchange (John Lithgow's memorable speech in the barbershop). *Jericho*, like *Red Dawn*, seems to offer a picture of survival and resistance in the American countryside. Nonetheless, it does portray destruction and vulnerability (specifically of the United States) to a level unprecedented among major television programs. That the show ran at all in the last years of the George W. Bush administration is noteworthy given its explicitly critical stance toward federal and corporate corruption—Ravenwood, a clear analogue to the private military company Blackwater, and its parent Jennings and Rall, a Halliburton-like entity, are major villains.

The finale of *Jericho* is noteworthy for several reasons. First, as noted, the show is about the end of the United States: as the show closes, the country is split into three parts: the Allied States of America, centered in Cheyenne, Wyoming; the Eastern United States, centered in Columbus, Ohio; and the Republic of Texas, run from San Antonio. One of the last lines speaks of the "next American civil war." Second, the program was canceled after the first season but was brought back by a successful support campaign. Fans mailed some twenty tons of nuts to the CBS offices in reference to a comment made by Jake's grandfather regarding the Battle of the Bulge ("nuts" was an expression of defiant resistance for the US Army troops outgunned by more numerous Nazi forces) and engaged in an overwhelming electronic correspondence campaign to sway network executives. The second season served as a coda after the original cancellation. Like a musical coda, the second season is a compact revisiting and extension of main themes from the first season. This also means that, in effect, the show has two finales because the first was thought to be the end to the show when it aired, while the second brings the "piece" of the show to a dramatic conclusion.

By the final episode of the first season, "Why We Fight" (1.22, aired May 9, 2007),[1] *Jericho* is quickly falling into hostile relations with the neighboring town of New Bern as the latter's residents try to seize resources (mainly food and salt) from Jericho. The episode ends with New Bern making an all-out attack on Jericho. As in the ambiguity about survival in *The Day After*, viewers were left to wonder whether the protagonists would survive the onslaught and whether Jericho would be subject to the authoritarian style of government adopted in New Bern after the nuclear attacks. Despite the organization and fighting spirit of Jericho's residents, things look bad for them because they are outnumbered and outgunned by New Bern's fighters. Jake's father, Johnston Green (played by Gerald McRaney), a former Jericho mayor and one-time army Ranger, is killed during the battle, a visible symbol of the toll to Jericho. The ambiguity of this end may, in fact, tend toward the pessimistic, like the conclusion of *The Day After*, where survival is possible but doubtful (in some ways also parallel to the outlook of the nuclear cinema classic *On the Beach* [Stanley Kramer, 1959]). Regardless of the outcome of the battle, this "first finale" poses a pessimistic response about the aftermath of disaster in America. Rather than finding common cause, neighboring communities take up arms against one another. Although *Jericho* is undoubtedly an instance of post–September 11 television—Can we

1. All references to episodes in *Jericho* come from Steinberg, Schaer, and Chbosky 2006–8.

imagine the show having been conceived or produced otherwise?—it also first appeared a year after the fiasco of Hurricane Katrina, in which major damage was caused to New Orleans and the Gulf Coast and the lackluster federal response immeasurably worsened the toll. (Perhaps it is salutary in this respect that the most hysterical stories of violence and disorder among residents after the hurricane have now been diagnosed as sensational, racist accounts—which led to a murderous police response—and replaced by myriad other tales of cooperation and mutual aid.)

The major altercation ending the first season of *Jericho* opened the way to a reframing of the show in the second season. The initial episode of season 2 features the assertion of much more visible and powerful federal authority in the form of troops under Major Edward Beck (Esai Morales) of the Allied States of America (ASA) Army. This sudden uptick of government control is a deus ex machina enabling the quick cessation of the dire hostilities between New Bern and Jericho, though mistrust and hatred continue between the towns. But the arrival of the army also allows an important evolution in the show. We learn from Chavez, a former colleague of CIA officer Robert Hawkins (played by the inestimable Lennie James), that the country has been split in three. It also quickly becomes evident that the multinational corporation Jennings and Rall is heavily involved with the new ASA government in Cheyenne. The show shifts from Jericho as a town of isolated survivalists trying to endure and find out what they can about the outside world to a political thriller and tale of corporate corruption. The residents of the town shift from the immediate tasks of survival—finding enough food, medical supplies, and fuel, avoiding deadly factional conflicts within and outside the town—to dealing with a new authority in the seemingly benign and humanitarian Jennings and Rall corporation, which administers much of the business of the Cheyenne government.

Soon enough Jake and the other residents of Jericho learn that Jennings and Rall is not all that it appears. The company not only provides relief but also functions as an authoritarian entity that takes responsibility for security in a broad sense, even carrying out summary executions without trial (through mercenary subsidiary Ravenwood). The ASA military, operating under direction of the Cheyenne/Jennings and Rall government, designates entire areas of the new country as "insurgent zones," against which deadly force is to be used.

As the seven episodes of season 2 unfold, action and intrigue move along briskly, such that an "entire" season's worth of plot development is contained in an abbreviated season of one-third the normal season size (seven episodes versus twenty-two). Although the producers had to deal with changes and limitations (a new director of photography and line producer as well as a shooting schedule per episode compressed from eight days to seven), they decided to follow a story arc that would encompass the larger scope of a full season. For viewers, this results in a swift crackle of dramatic intensity as the season unfolds, each episode covering the ground of three "normal" episodes. Through Jennings and Rall, power-hungry and debased partnerships between business and government become a major focus. Ultimately, it is revealed that the Cheyenne ASA government is little more than a front for the Jennings and Rall corporation; that the nuclear attacks were carried out by an individual, "John Smith" (Xander Berkeley), in an attempt to destroy the dangerous scourge of Jennings and Rall; and that the ASA government subsequently used the attacks as a pretense to launch counterattacks against North Korea and Iran—even though the plutonium signature of the bombs that hit America indicates that the plutonium was milled at Seversk, making them former Soviet nukes rather than Iranian or North Korean.[2]

All of this is fairly deep dramatic territory, primarily because it is not *too* far removed from actual events in the news, though ostensibly fiction. For viewers living through the unfolding accounts of Blackwater operations and Halliburton extortion of money from the federal government, coupled with spectacular developments in repression such as the USA PATRIOT Act of 2001 and the notorious National Security Agency and AT&T monitoring of domestic communications, *Jericho* hit close to home. The fact that Wyoming, adopted home of Dick Cheney, and Texas, home base of the Bush regime, figure so prominently in the narrative can't help but stand out. The series was a story, to be sure, but one so heavily affected by real events that watching it could prove either therapeutic or unsettling depending on one's disposition.

"Patriots and Tyrants," the last season 2 episode and the ultimate finale of the show, aired on March 25, 2008, ends on a dramatic high note (and could have set the stage for further development of the story—indeed, another major turn—in a third season).[3] Robert Hawkins and Jake, having discovered that the Cheyenne government's story of the attacks is false and having recovered the last of the bombs, which was originally held by

2. The remake of *Red Dawn* in 2012 also recast the invader as North Korea, changed from China in postproduction, rather than the Soviet and Cuban forces of the original film (1984).

3. I have not taken into account the season 3 comics here.

Hawkins, follow the only remaining option: to take the bomb to the Republic of Texas to expose the cover up and prevent Texas from joining the ASA (which, according to Chavez, "would be the ball game"—the end of the "old" United States, which is now centered in Columbus, Ohio). As Hawkins (seriously wounded) and Jake are about to be downed by the ASA Air Force as they make their way to Texas, fighters from the Texas Air National Guard intercept and destroy the Cheyenne patrols, clearing the way for the protagonists to reach Texas but starting civil war. Although as a viewer I would have welcomed a third and subsequent seasons to explore the political geography of the show's universe, I also found the coda of the second season to be a significant extension of the story and a more satisfying end than the season 1 finale. *Jericho*'s creators took full advantage of the unexpected opportunity to make another season and wisely, adventurously decided to cover an entire season's ground in the episodes allotted. Suffice it to say that the viewer's understanding of the dynamics and universe of the show was significantly deepened and transformed in the second season.

The show's (double) cancellation was the object of much discussion among fans and TV insiders. First and foremost, the show struggled with ratings. It was popular and had a devoted following, but *Jericho* never attracted the kind of audience that would have assured it an easy renewal. Perhaps the subject matter itself and the show's gritty nature limited the audience—only so many people want to watch a show about the aftermath of a nuclear war! The show also suffered from timing and competition issues that affected the number of viewers. For some of its run, it was aired at the same time as *Bones* (2005–17), a popular show drawing a large audience. In addition, the second season of *Jericho* was aired as a midseason replacement during ongoing disruptions after the writers' strike in the spring of 2008, which meant that more than nine months had elapsed since the end of season 1, and viewers had to wait through several announced and then delayed dates for the show's resumption. The second season never attained the viewership levels of the first one. So both pure viewer numbers and contributing factors such as scheduling afflicted *Jericho*'s longevity.

In addition, fans and critics speculated that the show's political and social commentary contributed to its demise. Although the series *24* (2001–10, 2014) also portrayed the vulnerability of the United States, even depicting a nuclear detonation in the country (albeit over a sparsely populated desert), its ideological message was much clearer: Jack Bauer is still acting as an "American hero" who is dedicated to the safety and integrity of the nation. He deals with government corruption and subterfuge, but these issues are cosmetic compared to the deep systemic corruption portrayed in *Jericho*, where ideological messages are much less certain. Though some viewers responded that the political content was likely insignificant compared to the ratings in motivating the show's cancellation, the mood of *Jericho*'s story, it seems, can't be ruled out in accounting for the finale—at least in terms of how it drew in or turned away viewers.

References

Steinberg, Jonathan, Josh Schaer, and Stephen Chbosky, creators. 2006–8. *Jericho*. Aired Sept. 20, 2006, to Mar. 25, 2008, CBS. iTunes. Accessed May–Nov. 2016.

30

Justified

"The Promise"

STEPHANIE GRAVES

To fully appreciate the finale of *Justified* (2010–15), one must to go back to the beginning.

Premiering in the spring of 2010, *Justified* functioned as FX's heir apparent to the critically respected crime drama *The Shield* (2001–8). Developed by Graham Yost—whose previous writing credits included *Speed* (Jan de Bont, 1994), *Broken Arrow* (John Woo, 1996), and the Nickelodeon children's contemporary Western series *Hey Dude* (1989–91)—it is based on the short story "Fire in the Hole" ([2001] 2011) and earlier novels *Pronto* (1993) and *Riding the Rap* (1995) by renowned crime writer Elmore Leonard, who also served as an executive producer of *Justified* up until his death in 2013. Set in and around Harlan County, Kentucky, the show centers around Deputy US Marshal Raylan Givens (Timothy Olyphant) and his complex and often fraught relationship with outlaw Boyd Crowder (Walton Goggins), a sometime ally but more often adversary with whom Raylan shares a great deal of history. Imbued with the trademark stylized dialogue of an Elmore Leonard work, the series ran for six seasons, concluding in 2015 with "The Promise" (episode 13), directed by Adam Arkin. *Justified*'s logical inclusion in the body of television that comprises the much-touted current Golden Age is reflected in its enthusiastic reception by critics; the 97 percent rating on the criticism-aggregating website Rotten Tomatoes attests to its critical appeal ("*Justified*" 2015). Nonetheless, as Adam Epstein points out in the *Atlantic*, its consistent quality went largely unrewarded: "*Justified* was a critical darling, but that acclaim failed to translate to awards glory, even as shows that weren't as consistently praised racked up nomination after nomination" (2015). It garnered only a few Emmy nominations for performances (winning two for supporting actors Margo Martindale and Jeremy Davies), but never for Best Drama, and it never exceeded a rather middling popularity among viewers, with FX's motorcycle-gang drama *Sons of Anarchy* (2008–14) often having more than double the viewers (Epstein 2015).

Yet from pilot to finale *Justified* consistently delivers top-notch performances by the entire cast, while the remarkable writing cleverly blends genres to craft a show that is smart, dark, and funny. *Justified* walks a line between modern Western, police procedural, and what scholar Gary Hoppenstand terms "Kentucky noir," a hard-boiled detective story that replaces the traditional high-contrast urban setting with the shadowy dive bars and verdant hollers of the American South (2011, 193). Compulsively clad in a white Stetson hat, Raylan is the badge-wearing, gun-slinging hero of classic Western fare transposed into a modern Southern setting and yoked—at least somewhat—by the constrictions of the modern-day legal system. This genre hybridity allows complex and often contrasting ideologies to be explored, and the show stands out among its contemporaries for the unabashed regionality of its setting. *Justified* embraces the specificity of eastern Kentucky, narratively tackling regional concerns, in particular those tied to regional poverty and disenfranchisement, such as rural drug trafficking, mountaintop-removal mining, racial tensions, religious fundamentalism, and domestic violence. Further, it is worth noting that although often featuring ridiculous or grotesque characters, *Justified* never stoops to treating the South as a punchline; the show generally complicates rather than simplifies, thus avoiding one-dimensional caricatures. Similarly distinctive is its use of the Southern Gothic, a mode not often portrayed on television. The region's labyrinthine topography stands in for the obfuscated landscapes and shadowy castles of the gothic, whose traditional interest in investigating madness, decay, and despair often shapes the show's narrative. The obsessive relationships with family, history, and place that circumscribe the Southern Gothic are common concerns in *Justified*; the people of Harlan are inextricably linked by their shared history, pathologically revisiting the sins of the past (Marshall 2013, 4–7). This is particularly true of Raylan and Boyd; from the outset, their conflicted, contentious relationship is not only informed by their own shared history but also complicated by the complex relationship between their fathers.

The Southern Gothic functions in *Justified* as a means of addressing anxieties about identity; Raylan's forced return to Kentucky after killing gangster Tommy Bucks in episode 1 of season 1 highlights his anxieties about his identity in relation to the past he has tried so hard to escape—a past completely bound up in location. The people of Harlan know Raylan, know his family, and he is bounded by that familiarity even as he struggles against it. Place is an inextricable component of identity; perhaps this, as media scholar Laura Crossley posits, is why Raylan chooses to inhabit impermanent, "transitory dwelling place[s]" such as dilapidated motels and a spartan room above a bar (2014, 63–64). His refusal to put down roots is indicative of his resistance to being known, to having identity assigned to him. Where notions of home and place function as a means of establishing identity, and in a region where the present is often merely a palimpsest overlaying the past, identity becomes fixed and inescapable. Raylan struggles against this cultural construction, and this apprehension about inescapability and inevitability foregrounds one of the fundamental concerns of *Justified*: To what degree are people capable of change?

If this is the central question posed by the series, then the finale, "The Promise," is the answer to that question.[1] Yet the finale should not be considered outside the context provided by the pilot episode, "Fire in the Hole."[2] The pilot and the finale are a duet, a call-and-response echoing across six seasons. Based closely on Leonard's story "Fire in the Hole," the first episode opens with a classic Western showdown incongruously set across a poolside table in Miami. The twenty-four-hour ultimatum Raylan gave Bucks to leave town has expired. Raylan pushes the situation to force Bucks to draw on him, and when Bucks does, Raylan has *justification* to kill. After Raylan is sent back to Kentucky, he is dispatched by the Marshals Service to investigate his old friend Boyd Crowder, who in the twenty or so years since Raylan left Harlan has quit paying taxes and become the evangelical neo-Nazi leader of a ragtag group of white supremacists. Raylan listens amusedly to Boyd's philosophy but eventually cuts through the bluster and rhetoric, telling Boyd, "You like to get money and blow shit up." This essentialist assessment of Boyd is dead on; although Boyd undergoes volatile transformations throughout the course of the show, these two traits remain. His outlaw enterprises are threatened by Raylan's presence, but he is further inconvenienced because of his intentions toward Ava Crowder (Joelle Carter). Ava, the long-suffering wife of Boyd's brother, Bowman, has recently over dinner dispatched the abusive Bowman with his own deer rifle; rather than launching the expected vendetta, Boyd has romantic inclinations toward Ava—yet Ava's interest is

1. All references to "The Promise" are from Arkin 2015.
2. All references to "Fire in the Hole" are from Dinner [2010] 2011.

in Raylan. These compounded circumstances inspire Boyd to issue the same twenty-four-hour ultimatum to Raylan. Boyd, like Raylan, forces the inevitable showdown, coercing Raylan into sitting across from him at Ava's dinner table, questioning him about how the other shooting occurred. When Boyd goes for the gun sitting on the table, Raylan does indeed shoot him; as Boyd lies on the floor bleeding, Raylan leans over him and apologizes: "I'm sorry . . . but you called it." Ava asks why he apologized, and Raylan only offers the explanation, "Boyd and I dug coal together."

Originally, this shooting was slated to be the end of Boyd Crowder; in Leonard's story, he dies, and Raylan offers the same line about their relationship: "Boyd and I dug coal together" (Leonard [2001] 2011, 112). However, the strength of Goggins's performance and his chemistry with Olyphant inspired Yost to rework the ending to keep Boyd around as Raylan's foil (Mittell 2015, 67; Sepinwall 2015). Which brings us, six years later, to "The Promise," wherein even the title is a callback to "Fire in the Hole." In television scholar Jason Mittell's taxonomy, "The Promise" is what he terms a proper finale, a "conclusion with a going away party" (2015, 322). It was announced in the *Hollywood Reporter* in January 2014 that season 6 would be the last, thus the season was deliberately aiming for a narrative end (Goldberg 2014). Written by Graham Yost, Fred Golan, Dave Andron, and Benjamin Cavell—all staff writers since season 1—the finale acts as a reinscription of the narrative concerns put into motion at the outset. Raylan is still pursuing Boyd and trying to save Ava. Even small details from the pilot resurface seventy-eight episodes later: Dewey Crowe's (Damon Herriman) gator-tooth necklace, Winona's (Natalie Zea) remarks about Raylan's anger, and Boyd's "mud people" diatribe and penchant for "blowing shit up" are referenced, each a small gift to the perceptive viewer. Fittingly, a showdown between Boyd and Raylan with Ava as witness bookends the narrative—this time orchestrated by Raylan, who has been straying farther afield from the righteous center in his quest to take Boyd down. In the pilot, he tells Boyd, "You make me pull, I'll put you down," and that "promise" is revisited here in the finale; with Boyd poised to surrender, Raylan instead suggests another way. When Boyd asks, "I pull, you put me down?," Raylan, nodding, offers, "Either way, I am gonna put you down." Raylan is so desperate for Boyd to give him the excuse he requires to finally kill him that when Boyd explains he is out of bullets, Raylan kicks a gun over. When Boyd still refuses to pull—refuses to grant the circular closure for which Raylan so desperately longs—we see Raylan contemplate killing Boyd anyway, the tremble in his face and body as he hangs on the precipice of the decision to end what he began in the pilot. This thematic concern over the titular dilemma is a recurring touchstone, but here it becomes the primary tension: Will Raylan kill Boyd, and will the killing be justified? Alasdair Wilkins of the *A.V. Club* observes, "Boyd providing Raylan with justification to shoot wouldn't tell us anything about Boyd that we don't already know, and such an action would forever obscure the one thing we really need to know about Raylan" (2015). The scene cuts away; we see Boyd being led off in handcuffs, thwarting what Raylan considers an inescapable resolution but allowing him to remain "justified."

Structurally, all this has occurred within the first twenty minutes of the narrative, and as Raylan drives away and the melancholy refrain of the song "You'll Never Leave Harlan Alive" begins to play, our expectations of the reliable structure of televisual narrative are frustrated by the subversion of form. Yet both Raylan and the viewers get what feels like the inevitable violent climax when gun-slinging psychopath Boon (Jonathan Tucker) forces a Western-style showdown in the middle of the road. Raylan kills Boon, yet his white hat gets shot—a visual puncture through the metaphoric binary of the good guy/bad guy trope. When Raylan dons Boon's black hat in the denouement, it can be read as Raylan's rejection of the simplistic dichotomy of good versus evil and as an acknowledgment instead of the spectrum in between. The coda, which then moves forward four years, offers some closure about the main characters' fates; Raylan is back in Miami, though he and Winona's relationship has again failed; Ava is much unchanged, though relocated and hiding out in California with her four-year-old son; and Boyd is once again preaching while incarcerated. "You know you're repeating yourself, right?" Raylan asks while visiting Boyd to deliver fabricated news of Ava's demise. This repetition underscores the aforementioned anxiety regarding inevitability and inescapability; the return to the beginning and the obsessive reinscription of the past reiterate that in this world and especially on this time scale people do not fundamentally change but instead play out the same pathologies over and over. Boyd inquires why Raylan elected to deliver this news in person, but Boyd, knowing Raylan as well as if not more than himself, answers his own question: "We dug coal together," the perfect final line that embodies the complexities of what these men will always be to one another. "The Promise" makes good on the events set in motion six seasons earlier, not only acting as a reward to the longtime viewer but also crafting a fitting narrative end that both surprises and satisfies.

References

Arkin, Adam, dir. 2015. "The Promise." *Justified*, season 6, episode 13. Written by Graham Yost, Fred Golan, Dave Andron, and Benjamin Cavell. Aired Apr. 14, 2015, FX. On *Justified: Season Six*. Culver City, CA: Sony. DVD.

Crossley, Laura. 2014. "Gangstagrass: Hybridity and Popular Culture in *Justified*." *Journal of Popular Television* 2, no. 1: 57–75.

Dinner, Michael, dir. [2010] 2011. "Fire in the Hole." *Justified*, season 1, episode 1. Written by Graham Yost. Aired Mar. 16, 2010, FX. On *Justified: Season One*. Culver City, CA: Sony Pictures. DVD.

Epstein, Adam. 2015. "*Justified*: A Neglected Rebel amid Television's Golden Age." *Atlantic*, Apr. 14. At http://www.theatlantic.com/entertainment/archive/2015 /04/justified-a-rebel-of-golden-age-television/390486/.

Goldberg, Lesley. 2014. "It's Official: *Justified* to End after Season 6." *Hollywood Reporter*, Jan. 14. At http://www.hollywoodreporter.com/live-feed/official -justified-end-season-6-670791.

Hoppenstand, Gary. 2011. "Editorial: Kentucky Noir." *Journal of Popular Culture* 44, no. 2: 193–94.

"*Justified*." 2016. Rotten Tomatoes. At https://www.rottentomatoes.com/tv/justified/.

Leonard, Elmore. 1993. *Pronto*. New York: Delacorte Press.

———. 1995. *Riding the Rap*. New York: Delacorte Press.

———. [2001] 2011. "Fire in the Hole." In *Fire in the Hole and Other Stories*, 57–112. New York: William Morrow.

Marshall, Bridget M. 2013. "Defining Southern Gothic." In *Critical Insights: Southern Gothic Literature*, edited by Jay Ellis, 3–18. Ipswich, MA: Salem Press.

Mittell, Jason. 2015. *Complex TV: The Poetics of Contemporary Television Story-telling*. New York: New York Univ. Press.

"The Promise." 2016. Internet Movie DataBase. At http://www.imdb.com/title /tt4217814/?ref_=ttep_ep13.

Sepinwall, Alan. 2015. "Goodbye to *Justified*, a Sharp-Tongued, Quick-Drawing Pleasure to the End." *Hitfix*, Apr. 13. At http://www.hitfix.com/whats-alan -watching/goodbye-to-justified-a-sharp-tongued-quick-drawing-pleasure-to -the-end.

Wilkins, Alasdair. 2015. "*Justified*: 'The Promise.'" *A.V. Club*, Apr. 14. At http:// www.avclub.com/tvclub/justified-promise-218067.

31

The L Word

"Last Word"

TERESA FORDE

The L Word is a glossy, soaplike drama that ran for six seasons on Showtime in the United States from 2004 to 2009, in fifteen other countries across Europe, as well as in Canada and Brazil. It depicts the lives of a group of lesbians living in West Hollywood, Los Angeles, as part of a lesbian community. In addition to lesbian relationships, the show includes stories about transgender, bisexual, and straight characters. Ilene Chaiken, cowriter on *The L Word*, wanted to make the show appealing to a more mainstream audience, and by developing it from the perspective of a group of lesbians, Chaiken and the show's creators shifted the "norm" so viewers could identify with the main characters and their world. *The L Word* was also groundbreaking in its depiction of characters' sex lives, which are a significant part of the show. Chaiken hoped that *The L Word* would be a catalyst for future shows involving lesbian, gay, bisexual, transgender, and queer (LGBTQ) representations on television. A great deal is often invested in such representations, and although the show deals with many issues, from trans experiences to lesbian marriage, in this regard it concerns itself primarily with personal relationships, love, and sex.

Throughout its six seasons, *The L Word* focuses on Bette Porter (Jennifer Beals) and Tina Kennard (Laurel Holloman), the main couple of the show.[1] Their relationship fuels many of the story lines, including infidelity, domestic life, and pregnancy. Another key character, Alice Pieszecki (Leisha Hailey), a journalist, comments on relationships and the gossip that draws the characters together. One of the most enigmatic characters is the promiscuous Shane

1. All references to episodes of *The L Word* come from *The L Word* 2010.

McCutcheon (Katherine Moennig), a popular character who is also vulnerable. Bette's sister, Kit Porter (Pam Grier), is straight and a recovering alcoholic, and Max Sweeney (Daniela Sea) is a trans character who is pregnant at the end of the show. The subplot of the Moira/Max transition is particularly poignant, if fleetingly prioritized, and expands the scope of the series. Max's story could have been given more time to develop in the show to cover the complexity of his experience, such as the use of illegal hormones, because the pace of his transition is not realistic. The depiction of Max's trans identity is seen as educational and liberal in tone, emphasizing marginalization even within the lesbian community (Reed 2009, 170). Also, Max becomes a more grounded character, which shifts the emphasis from his experiences as being the problem in order to criticize other characters' reactions to him. Other examples of the many relationships on the show include those of Bette and Jodi Lerner (Marlee Matlin), the deaf artist; Alice and Dana Fairbanks (Erin Daniels), who controversially dies of cancer early in the series; Alice and Tasha Williams (Rose Rollins), who is initially serving in the military; Shane and Carmen Morales (Sarah Shahi), whom Shane jilted at the altar; Shane and Molly Kroll (Clementine Ford) and their thwarted romance; and Shane and Jenny Schecter (Mia Kirshnir), who somewhat surprisingly reemerge as a couple in the final season.

Early on in the series, Alice compiles a wallchart as a record of "who slept with whom." Alice's chart represents the interconnectedness of the characters on *The L Word* through their sexual relationships. Friends and lovers crisscross and link, which is an important element of the show (Secomb 2007, 136–37). The chart also emphasizes something more complicated, both "who slept with whom" and "who loved whom" in its widest sense, and celebrates both character relationships as well as the reliance on a small group for all of one's needs. *The L Word* is set in sunny California and features attractive and largely affluent characters who enjoy socializing and clubbing as part of a lesbian community. The title emphasizes the potentially shocking and titillating nature of the show; the use of just the letter *L* suggests an illicit, unspoken, or transgressive word and implies "lipstick lesbians," a term that describes lesbians who visually conform to gender-normative tropes. The show acknowledges its relationship to its fans and a certain responsibility to consider relevant themes within its story lines. However, in many ways it also depicts a kind of Hollywood fantasy world of class and privilege. The show established fan interest in the look of the characters and influenced fans' dress and style. For example, Shane, as the predatory Lotharia, has a much copied "look." Fanfiction focuses on particular relationships, such as the Tina and Bette, "TiBette," relationship (Walker 2010). Many fan sites both official (*The L Word*'s online Fanisode) and unofficial (*The L Word* Fan Site and the_L-Word_Fan_Fiction_Group) produce fanfiction to modify and expand on the story lines, character arcs, and lives beyond the series as fans take a particular stance on issues depicted within the show (Walker 2010). Its sensational approach has led to awards, such as Bravo's A-List TV's Sexiest Moment (2009) for a notable sex scene between Tina and Bette.

The show also traces the character arc of Jenny, from her initial hetero-sexual relationship with Tim Haspel (Eric Mabius) to her subsequent recognition of her lesbian identity as well as her interest in creative writing and her career success as a novelist and screenwriter. Jenny functions largely as the outsider who is introduced into the community. She bases her exploitative and successful novel *Lez Girls* on the people around her, providing a thinly veiled account of the community she knows. She then adapts the novel to make a film; the film studio co-opts the film and, against the women's wishes, changes the ending to make the lesbian lead go back to "her man." Jenny's manipulation of other people's lives, in her writing and elsewhere, is seen as exploitative and contemptible by some of the characters within the drama and enables the viewer to feel antagonistic toward her. By the end of season 6, she has made a number of potential enemies who figuratively "could have killed her." All eight episodes of the final season leading up to the finale were intended to function as a murder mystery. The season begins with Jenny's death from drowning in the pool at Bette and Tina's house. In true Hollywood style, the whole season provides flashbacks leading up to her death and, to this end, serves as an extended finale; the last scenes of the final episode, "Last Word,"[2] take us back to the start of season 6 as the characters are interviewed about their lives and the police arrive on the scene and take everyone down to the station.

After the expansion of story lines in seasons 3 and 4, the show returned to its original form in season 5. There was a great deal of anticipation regarding the last season and in particular the finale. Although *The L Word* finale initially appears to be the culmination of the murder mystery, it turns into an interrogation of the characters and their relationships within the show. Apparently, even the other cast members did not know until the lead-up to the finale that Jenny has died. In a telling moment at one point during her interrogation, Alice wonders why the police are asking her so many questions

2. All references to "Last Word" come from Chaiken [2009] 2010.

and what these questions have to do with who killed Jenny. Viewer responses to the finale ranged from intrigue to frustration and mourning for the end of the show. However, the final sequences where the characters come together as actors are ultimately very satisfying. The detective who arrives to investigate Jenny's death, Sergeant Duffy, is played by Lucy Lawless, famous for her titular role in *Xena: Warrior Princess* (1995–2001), which had its own substantial lesbian fan base. At the start of season 6, Sergeant Duffy begins her introduction to the crime scene with "what a lovely family you have," which appears to be directed to Bette, Tina, and their daughter, Angelica (Olivia Windbiel), although Duffy could be referring to all of the characters in the room as an extended family or "family," as Max calls them. The group help Sergeant Duffy by suggesting what should happen next and volunteer to go to the station for questioning. They seem to be collectively creating the scene, being complicit and playing along.

The finale also implies but does not provide any closure. It does not give some fans the hoped for yet unlikely fairy-tale reunion of Carmen with Shane or even the more realistic possibility for Shane and Molly after Shane discovers that Molly had written her a letter that Jenny hid. Neither does the finale shed any real light on what happened to Jenny. The "who killed Jenny" teaser was used to promote the lead-up to the final episode, but the revelation of the assumed and accused killer, Alice, was planned for a spin-off series about a women's prison called *The Farm* (2009). Written by Chaiken, the pilot of *The Farm* was filmed and broadcast, depicting Alice as an inmate, but Showtime decided not to pick up the full series. The network did, however, pick up the reality series created by Chaiken and inspired by the drama, *The Real L Word* (2010–12), which was based in Los Angeles and Brooklyn. Chaiken was also executive producer for the documentary *L Word Mississippi: Hate the Sin* (Lauren Lazin, 2014), exploring prejudice against lesbians in the American South.

The motivation for *The L Word*'s finale challenges the purpose of series finales: Should *The L Word* have ended, as some suggest, like *The Sopranos* (1999–2007), in media res, or opted for a big finish? In becoming a potential murder mystery, Jenny's death forms a catalyst. In response to the sergeant's questioning, each character discusses her relationships and motivation and gives us a chance to reevaluate them. After the show ended, the "Interrogation Tapes," released on Showtime's US website, revealed additional information about the characters with new interview footage. However, these tapes are sometimes contradictory in relation to what is revealed in the show, fueling frustration with this drawn-out "whodunit."

The L Word finale could be seen as problematic as an ending not only because it does not offer any real closure in terms of the stories within the show but also because it turns the focus on issues of trust and forgiveness. When questioned, the characters recall moments from their pasts as a form of eulogy to the show. Jenny's death is a foil to retrace their stories and how they shifted from a close-knit group of women to individuals experiencing tension and distrust in their relationships but still feeling an underlying bond (Warn 2009). Jenny's video for Bette and Tina's going-away party also brings together many of the characters in the finale. The set-up of Jenny lying dead in the pool and the extended flashback sequence echo the film noir classic *Sunset Boulevard* (Billy Wilder, 1950), which is also the name of the drag queen who becomes Kit's lover in the final season.

The contribution by Rose Troche, director of *Go Fish* (1994), as director and a member of the production team of *The L Word* arguably places the latter in a continuum of queer and feminist representations on screen (Aaron 2006, 38). In the final scene, as the characters walk toward the police station, holding hands, the background opens out over Los Angeles, and they begin to smile knowingly and self-consciously as Jenny joins them. As a drama, "*The L Word*, from its very first episode has drawn us into the world of lesbian and bisexual life beyond coming out and giving birth, as it explores the ups and downs of the[ir] personal and professional lives" (Warn 2006, 5). The final images also depict a community of actors celebrating their work, their colleagues, and a "moment of community," which brings its own utopian and aspirational feelings (Dyer 1992, 158). Through its provocative story lines and in its LGBTQ representations, *The L Word* challenged both television and social conventions, just as the finale challenged viewers and put this lesbian drama under the spotlight one last time. Since *The L Word* completed its run, and as we continue to consider its legacy, trans issues have become more prominent, as seen in the award-winning drama *Transparent* (2014–) and even in the well-documented journey of Caitlyn Jenner, and other shows such as *Orange Is the New Black* (2013–) have broadened their representations of class, race, and sexuality.

References

Aaron, Michelle. 2006. "New Queer Cable? *The L Word*, the Small Picture, and the Big Picture." In *Reading "The L Word": Outing Contemporary Television*, edited by Kim Akass and Janet McCabe, 33–39. London: I. B. Taurus.

Chaiken, Ilene, dir. [2009] 2010. "Last Word." *The L Word*, season 6, episode 8. Written by Ilene Chaiken. Aired Mar. 8, 2009, Showtime. On *The L Word: The Complete Series*. Hollywood, CA: Twentieth Century Fox. DVD.

Dyer, Richard. 1992. "In Defence of Disco." In *Only Entertainment*, edited by Richard Dyer, 151–60. London: Routledge.

The L Word: The Complete Series. 2010. Hollywood, CA: Twentieth Century Fox. DVD.

Reed, Jennifer. 2010. "Reading Gender Politics on *The L Word*: The Moira/Max Transitions." *Journal of Popular Film and Television* 37, no. 4: 169–78.

Secomb, Linnell. 2007. *Philosophy and Love: From Plato to Popular Culture*. Edinburgh: Edinburgh Univ. Press.

Walker, B. 2010. "*The L Word* Fan Fiction Reimagining Intimate Partner Violence." *Participations* 7, no. 2: 380–95.

Warn, Sarah. 2006. Introduction to *Reading the L Word: Outing Contemporary Television*, edited by Kim Akass and Janet McCabe, 1–8. London: I. B. Taurus.

———. 2009. "'Last Word' of 'The L Word': Lame, Lacking, Legacy-Tarnishing." Afterellen: The Pop Culture Site That Plays for Your Team, Mar. 9. At http://www.afterellen.com/TV/2009/3/lword-finale?page=0,1.

32

The Larry Sanders Show

"Flip"

DEAN DEFINO

Over the closing credits of the finale of HBO's series *The Larry Sanders Show* (1992–98), Shawn Colvin sings words penned four decades earlier by Carole King: "Tonight the light of love is in your eyes. / But will you love me tomorrow?" It is hard to imagine words—tender, raw, and not a little cynical—that more perfectly illustrate the unlikely pathos that underlies this comedy set in the vacuous world of a late-night talk show. The finale, titled "Flip," focuses on the very last episode of the fictional show-within-a-show, also called *The Larry Sanders Show*, which has been canceled after a decade-long network run.[1] *The Larry Sanders Show* covers the last five years of that run as the talk show struggles to survive in the post–Johnny Carson late-night world (Johnny retired only three months before the HBO series began). In this new landscape, Jay Leno and David Letterman battle for dominance, Arsenio Hall looks (briefly) like the wave of the future, and Larry seems doomed to the role of also-ran. The series is driven by the existential anxieties and dark, self-effacing humor of the series' cocreator and star, Garry Shandling, who plays the titular talk-show host as a version of himself. Adding to the hall-of-mirrors effect, *Sanders* features real-life celebrities—more than one hundred of them over its six seasons—playing typically unflattering versions of themselves in stories framed by the circumstances and scandals of their real lives. But rather than simply presenting a broad satire on Hollywood, *Sanders* reflects on the crisis of existing in the virtual world of celebrity, where one's professional and, indeed, personal validation is tied up in finding, cultivating, and maintaining an audience. Sure,

---

1. All references to the series come from *The Larry Sanders Show* 2010.

you love me now, but will you when the next shiny thing comes along? "Will you still love me tomorrow?"

Sanders is often praised for its pervasive influence on form (walk-and-talk tracking shots; single-camera docurealism; humor punctuated by long pauses and silences) and for blurring the line between reality and fiction. It would be difficult to imagine the mock-doc framing and humor of discomfort in *The Office* (US, 2005–13), *Parks and Recreation* (2009–15), or *Modern Family* (2009–) without *Sanders*, to say nothing of the skewering of celebrity pretense in *Curb Your Enthusiasm* (2000–), *Extras* (2005–7), *30 Rock* (2006–13), and *Veep* (2012–). The series pokes fun at the debased culture of Hollywood through the hollow rituals of the late-night talk show. Night after night, Larry reads bland, instantly dated jokes off of cue cards to an audience whose laughter is triggered by his avuncular producer, Artie (Rip Torn), waving his hands in the air and through the preshow warm-up by his dim-witted, bitter sidekick, Hank (Jeffrey Tambor), who places the burden of success on the audience: "The better you are, the better Larry is." Night after night, Larry and his guests offer a pantomime of exaggerated praise for each other's talents in incestuous acts of self-promotion. But when the cameras are off, their true feelings come out. The ultimate example of this is Jim Carrey's appearance in the finale, when he serenades Larry with a hilarious version of "And I'm Telling You I'm Not Going" but during the commercial turns furiously on Larry, who had refused to support him early in his career. "I'm here for three good reasons: last show, big ratings, movie coming out," he says, giving Larry the middle finger. "Otherwise I'd be home watching *Nightline*, as usual."

Behind the scenes, things are still more twisted. For the bulk of the last season of *Sanders*, Larry's agent (Bob Odenkirk) has been scheming to kill Larry's show by pitching another of his clients, Jon Stewart, to the network. In the finale, former staff members (all of whom Larry has mistreated) line up backstage at the final taping of *The Larry Sanders Show* to gloat at Larry's misfortune, or, as one former writer (Jeremy Piven) puts it, "to see if after you fired me and fucked up my life, whether you'd stand there like we were old buddies." "Well, now you know," Larry responds, grinning miserably. During the final broadcast, Tom Petty and Clint Black argue in the green room over who will get to sing to Larry. When Artie tries to break up the argument, Petty rages, "I thought I was your Bette Midler"—in reference to the final Carson show—then physically attacks both Black and Greg Kinnear. And shortly after the taping, Hank lets his bottled-up feelings toward Larry burst in a rage-filled rant (which, ever the sycophant, he repents almost immediately).

In one way, these comic dramas serve to highlight the absurd idea of saying good-bye to something as insubstantial as a late-night talk show. A genre designed to ease viewers toward the oblivion of sleep, it is necessarily weightless and perishable. When Jerry Seinfeld appears on the last broadcast of *The Larry Sanders Show*, he jokes that whereas *Seinfeld* will run in syndication (seemingly forever), Larry's show will simply fade away. When another ultra-successful sitcom star, Tim Allen, attempts to summarize Larry's legacy, he can only repeat the phrase "Ten years!" over and over, as though the ultimate measure of Larry's success has been that he somehow managed to stay on the air this long. Off-air, Larry's agent is blunter: "Larry's a thing of the past," he tells Jon Stewart, who is suddenly overcome with guilt for taking Larry's job. "This is Darwinism. Don't fight it; you'll fuckin' lose." But as the HBO series shows, fleeting and insubstantial are not the same as inconsequential. There are reasons why David Letterman remains one of the most famous people in the world and why the final episodes of *The Tonight Show Starring Johnny Carson* in 1992 remain among the highest-rated late-night programs of all time. Clearly, we develop attachments to our Sandmen. And they for us. In Larry's series finale closing monologue, he acknowledges the existential bond by admitting, "I don't know exactly what I'm going to do without you."

But *Sanders* rarely turns its cameras on the audience, focusing instead on backstage dramas and the existential toll of existing in a mediated reality. The series is less about the larger cultural phenomena of TV than about what TV does to human beings, be they emotionally damaged narcissists such as Hank, weathered workaholics such as Artie, or deeply insecure egomaniacs such as Larry, fed a diet of paranoia and empty affirmation and needing to be *seen* in order to feel fully present and alive. This theme explains in part the needy tone of Larry's commercial-break catchphrase, "No flipping," punctuated by his jerky pantomime of clicking an invisible remote control, and why he watches his own show every night while lying in bed, often with a woman, his TV image serving as an aphrodisiac (in one episode, he beds Sharon Stone but suffers erectile dysfunction right up to the moment the show's theme music begins to play).

No one is more aware of the tenuous nature of the audience/celebrity bond than Larry, which is why he worries so much over the details of his final show and whatever legacy he may leave. The finale of *Sanders* opens with him studying Jack Paar's *Tonight Show* farewell in 1962. According to Shandling, he chose Paar over Johnny Carson because he felt that viewers would have too personal a connection to Carson and did not want his character, Larry, to suffer comparisons to Johnny. Larry studies the Paar footage like a puzzle, a code that, once cracked, will direct him to the "right" thing to say and the "right" way to say it. Rather than looking inwardly for some profound personal insight, he looks for corollaries, models, cues, thus illustrating the moral crisis at the center of his character: in effect, he is trying to figure out how to fake sincerity, to script profundity. "Should I mention God?" he asks Artie. "Well, hell, you've plugged everyone else on the planet," Artie responds. "Why not give the Deity his due?"

Larry does end up saying "God bless you" near the end of his mono-logue, following a simple, moving thanks to his staff and his audience. But his final words are another sort of benediction: "You may now flip." With these words, Larry releases his ten-year grip on his audience, on his show, and on his televised self. Though not a voluntary choice (his show was can-celed), the good-bye is a powerful moment and one of the few times we feel actual sympathy for Larry. The feeling is amplified a moment later when Artie comes out to hug Larry, but it is almost immediately undercut when we realize that Larry's outpouring of feeling isn't love but fear: he is frozen to his seat, unable to move, to physically remove himself from the fading spot-light. Without it, he is impotent. Artie eventually pulls him up, and as they make their way down the hallway to a smattering of applause, Larry tosses one more joke to the gallery: "I hope we beat Leno!"

Shandling often claimed that *Sanders* is a show about love and about how people, however damaged and grotesque, need affirmation. Measured by that standard, the series is as conventional as any sitcom or Lifetime movie—except that it refuses to resolve or even fully develop the emotions it calls up. At their most basic affective level, conventional narratives operate as catharsis machines: comedies make us laugh, and dramas make us cry, most often out of sympathy, empathy, or love for characters. But *Sanders*, which is both comedy *and* drama, is more interested in the limitations of feeling and the awkward conventions surrounding them. The series finale, "Flip," is a perfect case in point. Here dry humor is cut with messy moments of emotional outburst that come and go too quickly to allow for sympa-thy, such as Artie cursing away tears while hiding in the costume room at the beginning of the episode or Clint Black singing a heartbreak ballad to Larry from the couch midprogram while Larry tries to hide his discomfort with being sung to by a man or Hank's blow-up in the final scene, which is peppered with false bravado ("There was lots of money and lots of pussy") and banal clichés ("There is a book called Hank Kingsley, but there is a new chapter, and you, sir, are not in it!"). In each case, characters seem caught between pantomiming emotions and *feeling* them, perhaps because they are unable to tell the difference.

In the closing scene of the finale, after Hank blows up and returns apologetically after backing his car into a dumpster, Artie offers an olive branch: "Come on, Lawrence, let's help a brother out here. He's all hooked up on a dumpster." The dumpster wreck is some sort of metaphor for the state of Hank's life now that *The Larry Sanders Show* is over, but mostly it is just another joke at his expense. The three men walk out of the studio, and Hank asks if they want to get together the next day. Larry begs off, claiming he has a date, and so Artie suggests they go to their usual postshow restaurant to "think this over." His remark harkens back to an earlier moment in the finale, when actor Bruno Kirby complains about being bumped from the show again; Artie promises to book him in the future but then briefly bursts into tears as he realizes that can never happen. Their rituals, their lives together are coming to an end. As Artie, Hank, and Larry exit the soundstage, Larry takes one last look, and the voice of Shawn Colvin rises over the closing titles. In many ways, it is a typical end to a long-form television narrative: the lights go down on the primary set, freezing it in memory as it evokes countless scenes played upon it. But the question—"Will you still love me tomorrow?"—cuts through any easy sentiment, demanding we ask what it all means. Is it a story about how media debases or one about how human nature endures? Is it a story about love and loss or one about transference and fear? These are profound questions to ask regarding a television comedy, made more so by the series' unwillingness to offer simple catharsis or easy resolutions, even when saying good-night and good-bye.

References

The Larry Sanders Show: The Complete Series. 2010. Los Angeles: Shout! Factory. DVD.

33

Life on Mars (UK)

Season 2, Episode 8

TRISHA DUNLEAVY

"My name is Sam Tyler. I had an accident and woke up in 1973. Am I mad, in a coma, or back in time? Whatever's happened, it's like I've landed on a different planet. Now maybe if I can work out the reason, I can get home."[1] As the monologue that opens each episode, these lines introduce the inventive concept for the British drama *Life on Mars* (2006–7). Following a car accident in 2006, Detective Chief Inspector Sam Tyler (John Simm) regains consciousness in a Manchester cityscape, whose buildings, streets, cars, and people not only seem to belong to some past era but are also eerily reminiscent of his own childhood in the 1970s. As he dazedly takes in his new surroundings, clothes, car, and police identity card and enters an archaic version of his workplace in 2006, Tyler is stunned to realize that he has somehow shifted thirty-three years back in time. The year is 1973, and he is Detective Inspector Sam Tyler, newly arrived on official transfer from nearby Hyde.

Created by Matthew Graham, Ashley Pharoah, and Tony Jordan, *Life on Mars* (*LoM*) was produced by British drama "indie" company Kudos Film and Television, commissioned by BBC Wales, and filmed in Manchester. Complemented by a handful of police regulars and succession of episode guests, the key characters flanking Tyler are his unorthodox senior officer Gene Hunt (Philip Glenister) and police colleague Annie Cartwright (Liz White). Debuting in January 2006 on BBC1 and comprising two seasons of eight episodes each, *LoM* proved unusually successful, the 7 million or so viewers it regularly delivered (Chapman 2006, 7) being an outstanding

---

1. All references to the British series come from *Life on Mars* 2006, 2007.

achievement in British TV's competitive digital era. *LoM* was then adapted for the American network ABC, but this essay focuses on the BBC original, a drama created first and foremost to appeal to Britons.

Although *LoM* has been celebrated "as a significant historical moment in the evolution of the [British] police series" (Chapman 2006, 7), its distinctiveness begins with its conceptual blending of the "police procedural" with science-fiction fantasy. The context for such significant risk taking—aside from the creative opportunities afforded by the Public Service Broadcasting remit and noncommercial schedule for which *LoM* was commissioned—was the commitment by Kudos (as producer) and by Graham, Pharoah, and Jordan (as creators) to produce "fast-paced, stylish and modern" British TV drama that could provide a British response to the innovations and influence of American "quality drama" (Chapman 2006, 7).

"Quality" acquired its own conventions in British TV drama between the 1970s and 1990s (see, for example, Cooke 2003 and Nelson 2007). By 2000, however, the possibilities for "quality drama" were being revisited and reshaped as the British TV industry adapted to a multichannel digital environment. An important influence on this transition was the popularity of a category called "American quality drama" (AQD), whose features were first examined by Robert Thompson (1996). Developing through the 1980s and 1990s and exemplified by such widely exported shows as *Hill Street Blues* (NBC, 1981–87), *NYPD Blue* (ABC, 1993–2005), and *House M.D.* (Fox, 2004–12), AQD extended its influence to non-American TV industries, a process involving the integration of key AQD strategies into existing national TV drama paradigms.[2] The resulting programming, here labeled "contemporary quality drama" (CQD), entails the pursuit of high production values, increased narrative density and complexity, and the accentuation of style through mise-en-scène. But intrinsic to the form of "quality" that has resonated in leading instances of AQD and CQD is the commitment to "taking an existing genre and transforming it" (Thompson 1996, 13). Underlining how this ambition influenced *LoM* was its creators' determination to "do something different" (Chapman 2006, 7), specifically to avoid turning out what Graham called "another bloody cop show" (quoted in Chapman 2006, 7). As a landmark British series whose reenvisioning of

2. Examples include Britain's series *Spooks* (2002–11), *Hustle* (2004–12), and *Skins* (2007–12); France's series *The Spiral* (2005–); Australia's series *Blue Heelers* (1994–2006); and New Zealand's series *Outrageous Fortune* (2005–10).

the British police drama extends to its self-reflexive awareness of this genre's history, *LoM* is emblematic of CQD in three notable ways.

First, *LoM* achieves a novelty of concept and narrative perspective through its blending of a "police procedural" formula with the kind of "time-travel" trope that has been a characteristic of science fiction. This is an instance of "generic mixing" (Mittell 2004, 154), a strategy that, although not always used, has vastly extended the conceptual possibilities for AQD and CQD programs. Although *LoM*'s crime stories do deploy the perennial crime formula of "transgression, pursuit, capture [and] retribution" (Sparks 1993, 86), its time-travel trope facilitates *LoM*'s predominant setting in urban (Mancunian) Britain of the early 1970s, a setting that is responsible for the complex narrative perspective that distinguishes the series. *LoM*'s stylish approach to the construction of this historical world imbues it with nostalgic appeal, but the twenty-first-century gaze through which Sam Tyler regards and assesses the world of 1973 allows for a revisionist perspective on the stories and characters involved. With Sam Tyler as its primary vehicle, *LoM* trains a post–political correctness lens on Britain of the 1970s, a society in which male chauvinism and machismo, institutional racism, the subordination of women, casual violence, and police corruption are all seen to exist as rarely challenged features of the period. The social repercussions are exemplified by Tyler's "Gov," Gene Hunt, a character whose behavior is tolerated by his police colleagues but violates the twenty-first-century standards against which Tyler is uniquely positioned to judge it. Operating through Tyler's twenty-first-century perspective, *LoM* delivers an ambivalent assessment of Britain of the 1970s, even as it lovingly reconstructs the era by way of painstaking attention to verisimilitude, chic representations of fashion, and a soundtrack packed with solid-gold "Britpop" from that decade. These elements imbue the series with nostalgic appeal, but the critical perspective *LoM* achieves through the "generic mix" that forms its concept allows it to challenge the very notion of nostalgia for a past era by highlighting some key ways in which British society has changed for the better.

Second, *LoM* deploys self-reflexivity, another of AQD's "signature" features (Thompson 1996, 15). Self-reflexive references are used in *LoM* to acknowledge the program's own textuality, to celebrate British popular culture of the 1970s, and to imbue the show with an additional layer of intrigue for media-literate viewers, in particular those who remember Britain in this decade. *LoM* episodes reference *Starsky & Hutch* (ABC, 1975–79) and *The Wizard of Oz* (Victor Fleming, 1939) among other texts, but the most significant reference—the text to which *LoM* pays its most deferential self-reflexive homage—is *The Sweeney* (ITV, 1975–78), an unusually popular British police drama (Cooke 2003, 115).[3] *LoM* is littered with allusions to *The Sweeney*. These allusions are especially overt in the series' characterization of Gene Hunt, whose language, attire, and "no holds barred" approach to chasing criminals make him a comic caricature of *The Sweeney*'s lead character, Jack Regan (John Thaw). Of course, it is only to those who watched *The Sweeney* that this self-reflexive dimension is available. As Robin Nelson explains, "The intertextual play works fully only if viewers saw *The Sweeney* in the seventies and feel the resonances, which is why the fifty-somethings in my audience survey locate *Life on Mars* in traditions of both British television and British cultural life. For those who recall the earlier police series and its popularity, a '*Sweeney* awareness' heightens the pleasure in Hunt's more elaborately forced expostulations. He even outdoes Regan, with phrases such as 'She's as nervous as a very small nun at a penguin shoot'" (2012, 22–23).

LoM's self-reflexive acknowledgments of British culture of the 1970s are considerably more diverse than just homage to *The Sweeney*. Arguing that the series "is replete with references to popular culture," James Chapman (2006, 15) finds other examples. A recurring reference is the test-pattern girl, who horrifies Tyler by escaping the confines of his black-and-white TV set, but *LoM* also alludes to specific programs shown in the 1970s, including episodes of the BBC children's series *The Basil Brush Show* (1968–80) and *Camberwick Green* (1966).

Third, a feature that has been significantly developed by more recent instances of AQD and CQD, is "narrative complexity" (Mittell 2006), or complexities in the use of form and modality and the deployment of contributing strategies. Although *LoM*'s stories unfold in the kind of linear pattern that is sometimes rejected by narratively complex dramas, its complexity flows from its sophisticated intermingling of episodic and serial modes, the former emphasizing "crimes of the week" and the latter Tyler's central predicament as a displaced time traveler. *LoM*'s 1970s-styled "cop shop," its regular characters, and the successive criminal acts that dominate most episodes utilize what John Ellis terms a "problematic," or perpetual dilemma, whose purpose is to generate a flow of episodic stories, but to do so within a

---

3. Although this referencing of *The Sweeney* is considered important to the success of BBC's *LoM*, there was no obvious attempt to replicate it (perhaps by referencing an American TV drama of proximate cultural status from the 1970s) in ABC's adaptation of the series for an American audience.

familiar, repeated framework (1989, 154; see also Dunleavy 2009, 54). But even if its episodes are focused on developing and resolving these "crimes of the week," the serial thread that is integral to *LoM*—the exploration of the repercussions of Sam's arrival in an alien world, the understandings of the future that he brings to 1973, and the lingering question of whether he will be able to return to the world from which he came—forms the "overarching story" that is characteristic of high-end serials (Dunleavy 2009, 54). As the thread whose trajectory ties together *LoM*'s two seasons, this serialized story of time shift and dislocation informs the successive conflicts generated by *LoM*'s policing problematic. *LoM*'s narrative is further complicated by the ways in which Tyler's two worlds, that of 2006 and that of 1973, are sometimes juxtaposed, the movements between them being psychologically motivated by his alienation and his desire to "get home." Tyler hears voices from 2006, which come to him mainly through phone calls and direct addresses through his TV set, suggesting that he survived his accident and is now in a hospital as an unconscious patient wired to a life-support machine. Accordingly, Tyler's dilemma is not only that he is a "fish out of water" in 1973 but also that because his life continues in 2006, he inhabits connected but irreconcilable worlds. It is the ongoing juxtaposition of these different dimensions, facilitated by the episodic and serial modes through which these stories unfold, that imbues *LoM* with narrative complexity.

Together these CQD elements combine to progress, complicate, and finally resolve the dilemma of Tyler's struggle to comprehend how and why he has arrived in 1973 and to adapt to life in an alien world. Given the inexplicable nature of this predicament, the question that pervades *LoM* is whether the world into which Tyler has been hurtled is real or the imaginative product of his comatose state and damaged brain.

With previous episodes taken up with "crimes of the week," the *LoM* finale is given unusual significance by directly confronting the question of whether Tyler's experience in the 1970s is real or imagined. The penultimate episode introduces Frank Morgan (Ralph Brown), a senior officer from Hyde, who, as the only character who knows how Tyler might get home, seems willing to help him. However, as a revelation exclusive to the finale, Morgan is seen to inhabit both of the worlds that Tyler occupies, which points to the probability of a coma scenario. In 1973, Morgan is a senior police officer from Hyde who, as part of a top-level undercover operation gathering "evidence" about Hunt, has "planted" Tyler in Hunt's unit. The notion that Tyler's journey is entirely imagined is suggested by Morgan's narratively juxtaposed dual role as a police officer working undercover in 1973 and the surgeon who, in a "medical" operation in 2006, finally manages to remove the tumor lodged in Tyler's brain.

It is through Morgan's alternative personas that *LoM*'s finale offers two explanations for Tyler's situation that viewers are left to reconcile for themselves. One is that his injured yet active subconscious has cleverly constructed the world in 2006 as an imagined future, simultaneously erasing his memory of being a rising detective and Morgan's talented protégé in the 1970s. The other explanation, an alternative that the closing moments of the series dangle as the "pay-off" for those immersed in *LoM*'s serial story, is that Tyler really has time-shifted from 2006 back to 1973 by partially "dying" in the modern world and being somehow fully recalibrated thirty-three years in the past. Referencing Tyler's abortive attempt to escape from 1973 in *LoM*'s first episode by jumping off the nearest tall building, the finale's payoff sees him leap, smilingly, to his "death" from the top floor of a skyscraper in 2006 in a successful bid to return to 1973.

By taking this step, Tyler chooses which of the two worlds he prefers to live in. His leap back to 1973 is also *LoM*'s most audacious act of self-reflexive awareness. It acknowledges not only the enduring popularity of the police procedural as genre but also the specific appeals of *The Sweeney* and its characters. *LoM*'s closing narrative twist is that, having returned to the technology-steeped, politically correct world of 2006 from which he came, Sam Tyler finally deems the twenty-first-century world the most alien and least real.

Postscript: The Finale of ABC's *Life on Mars*

LoM reached American audiences in two main forms. The first was its run on BBC America (2006–7), and the second was its adaptation for ABC (2008–9).[4] Providing a telling example of the creative challenges of format adaptation in TV drama, the American version, whose ratings began strongly but declined as the season progressed, did not perform well enough to continue. However, the seventeen episodes of the American version (the BBC original has sixteen episodes in total, structured into two eight-episode seasons) allow a comparison of the two *LoMs* in their development and probing of the central mystery of how and why Sam Tyler traveled in time. In resolving this question, the American *LoM* provides a notably different answer to the

4. All references to the American series come from *Life on Mars* 2009.

British original by concluding with the revelation that Tyler is not a police officer but an astronaut from 2035 on a NASA mission to discover whether there is life on the planet Mars. Accordingly, Tyler's presence in the 1970s is explained as a fantasy generated by the spaceship computer to occupy his mind during the two-year journey. The American *LoM*'s unequivocal assertion that Tyler's experience is "all a dream" is underscored by the presence of all of the series' core characters on this same mission. Among them, Gene Hunt is renamed "Major Tom" after the lost space traveler in David Bowie's song "Space Oddity" and unmasked as Tyler's father. It is because of its revelation that Tyler's experience in the 1970s has no basis in diegetic reality that the ABC finale evoked frustration and disappointment in viewers (Sepinwall 2009) in contrast to viewers' perceptions of the original *LoM* finale as a "perfect" ending (Wilde 2007).

References

Chapman, James. 2006. "Not 'Another Bloody Cop Show': *Life on Mars* and British Television Drama." *Film International* 38:6–19.

Cooke, Lez. 2003. *British Television Drama: A History*. London: British Film Institute.

Dunleavy, Trisha. 2009. *Television Drama: Form, Agency, Innovation*. Basingstoke, UK: Palgrave Macmillan.

Ellis, John. 1989. *Visible Fictions: Cinema, Television, Video*. London: Routledge.

Life on Mars: The Complete Series. 2009. Burbank, CA: Buena Vista Home Entertainment. DVD.

Life on Mars: The Complete Series One. 2006. London: Kudos Film and Television. DVD.

Life on Mars: The Complete Series Two. 2007. London: Kudos Film and Television. DVD.

Mittell, Jason. 2004. *Genre and Television: From Cop Shows to Cartoons in American Culture*. New York: Routledge.

———. 2006. "Narrative Complexity in Contemporary American Television." *Velvet Light Trap* 58:29–40.

Nelson, Robin. 2007. *State of Play: Contemporary "High-End" TV Drama*. Manchester: Manchester Univ. Press.

———. 2012. "Hybridity and Innovation in a British Television Context." In *"Life on Mars": From Manchester to New York*, edited by Stephen Lacey and Ruth McElroy, 19–30. Cardiff: Univ. of Wales Press.

Sepinwall, Alan. 2009. "*Life on Mars*, 'Life Is a Rock': The Series Ends Badly." *Star-Ledger*, Apr. 2. At http://www.nj.com/entertainment/tvindex/ssf/2009/04.

Sparks, Richard. 1993. "*Inspector Morse*: 'The Last Enemy' (Peter Buckman)." In *British Television Drama in the 1980s*, edited by George Brandt, 86–102. Cambridge: Cambridge Univ. Press.

Thompson, Robert J. 1996. *From "Hill Street Blues" to "ER": Television's Second Golden Age*. Syracuse, NY: Syracuse Univ. Press.

Wilde, Jon. 2007. "*Life on Mars*: The Perfect Finale." *Guardian*, Apr. 1. At https://www.theguardian.com/culture.tvandradioblog/2007.

34

Lost

"The End"

NIKKI STAFFORD

On May 23, 2010, a wounded man stumbled through a jungle and collapsed on the ground. Viewers watching at home sat forward in anticipation as he stared at the sky with a serene look on his face. His eyes closed, the screen went white, and a violin plucked one last mournful string.

After six seasons, *Lost* (2004–10) was over.[1] The most anticipated finale of the decade had concluded and left in its wake a firestorm of debate, praise, and condemnation. Some naysayers argued that the series finale was the biggest disappointment in television history. In fact, however, it is a perfect example of how a complex show can be developed and successfully conclude the character arcs of a story as well as tie together all of the themes it has explored for so many years.

On the surface, *Lost* is a show about survivors of a plane crash who suddenly find themselves on a not-so-deserted island and are forced to deal with the island's inhabitants, its supernatural complexities, and their own psychological baggage from the past. On a deeper level, *Lost* explores the tension and harmony between faith and science by looking at them through the themes of black versus white, self versus other, and solitude versus togetherness. It is a show about love, hate, family, friends, relationships, revenge, birth, death, faith, healing, and, above all, hope. In other words, it is a show about all of us.

Lost's showrunners, Damon Lindelof and Carlton Cuse—or "Darlton," as they came to be known among fans—were avowed television geeks and knew the canon of television finales within which they were writing. They

---

1. All references to *Lost* are from Lieber, Abrams, and Lindelof 2004–10.

had maintained a close level of contact with fans from the beginning of the series and built up the show in its six seasons as a gradual crescendo of questions: What is the island? Why is Walt special? Where did the polar bears come from? What is the Dharma Initiative? How did the Others get there? Who built the statue on the beach? From the moment Charlie asks in the show's pilot episode, "Guys, where are we?" the focus had always been on those questions. In the show's sixth season, a character cuts off another's series of questions by saying, "Every question I answer will simply lead to another question," which was easily the best description of *Lost*'s most talked-about quality. So in the lead-up to the finale, it stood to reason that for a show so focused on questions, the emphasis in the final hours would be on the answers.

Except . . . it wasn't. All of the questions appeared to be unanswered when the final credits rolled. There was no definitive explanation of what the island really was or what had caused the supernatural elements there. Many of the mysteries that fans had been discussing and arguing about for years were still up for debate. But those who thought the lack of answers reflected little more than lazy writing (forcing the audience to come up with the answers) had completely missed the point of the show, which is that life isn't about the finish line—it's about the process of getting there.

Lost is a unique series for several reasons, not least of which is its interactive nature. Owing to a very well-read writing staff, the show explores philosophy, history, literature, psychology, physics, and religion. Characters are cleverly named after philosophers, not as a joke but because each name reflects something about that character's philosophy. Books are shown sitting on shelves or being read by characters or lying on tables. At the beginning of the show's second season, Darlton indicated to fans that the books were important and that if they read them, they might get a richer, deeper understanding of the show. Suddenly more avid fans of the series were being exposed to works such as Flann O'Brien's *The Third Policeman* (1967), Philip K. Dick's *VALIS* (1981), and Salman Rushdie's *Haroun and the Sea of Stories* (1990). When characters are seen holding copies of Stephen Hawking's *A Brief History of Time* (1988) in the show's third season, fans rushed out to find a copy and attempted to make their way through the heady tome, trying to wrap their heads around the scientific theories of time travel. They were rewarded (as was anyone who paid enough attention also to read Kurt Vonnegut's *Slaughterhouse-Five* [1969]) when the characters began time and consciousness traveling in the show's fourth season.

The two key characters through which the series explores the central theme of science versus faith are Jack Shephard (Matthew Fox) and John Locke (Terry O'Quinn), and by looking at their story arc one can begin to understand what *Lost*'s finale is really all about. Locke, the man of faith, believes the island is important and that he is special. He boards the plane a paraplegic, but when he crash-lands on the island, he stands on his own two feet. The island has given him a miracle and makes him an instant disciple. For the duration of the show, he believes that everyone who survived the plane crash has been brought there for a reason. They have a destiny, and that destiny can be fulfilled only by staying on the island.

Jack, in contrast, believes only in what he can see with his eyes. Throughout the series, the strain between Jack and Locke builds to a breaking point— while Locke insists the island is special and they must stay, Jack insists they return home and leave the island behind. Locke believes the island is a place where miracles happen, where they landed because they were destined to; Jack doesn't believe in miracles or destiny.

But over the series' six seasons, Jack's resolve begins to falter, and when forces even he doesn't understand draw him back to the island after Locke's death, he is a changed man. After having Locke's words eat away at him for three years, he suddenly becomes a man of faith. In the finale, we discover the island is harboring "the Source" of all life and death, and when it becomes compromised, Jack, the man of science, sacrifices himself to save the island and, by extension, the world.

Just as Jack and Locke—and all of the characters on the show—are constantly asking questions to try to find themselves and their purpose in the world, the writers expected the viewers to ask questions, too. The interactive nature of *Lost* wasn't just a gimmick—it was the key to understanding the show. It prompted the more avid viewers to do their homework; to read all of the literature that was referenced on the show; to reacquaint themselves with what they knew about philosophy, physics, and psychology; and to ask questions and discuss with groups of *Lost* fans what the possible answers could be. On the show, Jacob, the island's guardian (Mark Pellegrino), isn't just toying with the survivors; he needs to let them find the answers by themselves. The survivors have to struggle with their own emotional baggage, pinpoint what their problems are, and come to terms with them in order to move on peacefully. Answers do not come easily to the survivors, whether they are on the island or off, and it is through asking constant questions that they are able to realize their purpose. Locke receives a miracle and becomes an instant believer, but his faith wavers in critical moments. Jack, in contrast, has to find faith after suffering through a long series of obstacles, and once he finds it, he has more conviction than any other character on the show.

Aside from concluding the six-season overarching arc, the *Lost* series finale had to resolve a second story line that was rather new to the show. At the beginning of season 6 (the show's final season), the *Lost* writers introduced an alternate universe where all of the same characters exist, but their lives are slightly different. Unhappy lives are suddenly happy; relationships have changed. Audiences wondered if the "sideways world," as it came to be known, was a "what-if" universe where we could see what would have happened to the characters if the island hadn't meddled in their lives. In the finale, it is revealed that the sideways world is actually a Buddhist *bardo*, a plane that exists between death and the afterlife, and that each of the survivors at some point died and is now continuing to work through his or her emotional problems in this world where their consciousness exists and has created scenarios in which to resolve their issues. The questions that dogged them in life are still with them after death, and they have to keep asking those questions if they are ever to find the answers. Once they do, they have a flash of realization that they are actually dead, and they know where they have to go. In the final moments of the series, they all come together and their "shepherd," Jack's father, Christian, opens a door that allows them to move into the next life.

In "The End," the appropriately titled finale episode, the emphasis is on the importance of the questions one must ask along the way if one can ever hope to find the answers. If *Lost* is a show where characters are not spoon-fed the answers, isn't it appropriate that the show should demand the same of its viewers? The answers to all of the questions on *Lost* are out there, despite what the finale might have led some to believe, but it's up to the viewers to find them. Many fans, including me, still believe some of those answers can be found in the show, and if you do all the extracurricular reading and research, you can easily find them (the solution to why the polar bears are on the island is answered in season 2, for example). But for many of the questions, there simply aren't clear-cut answers. In those more personal cases, the writers couldn't solve the puzzle for viewers because each viewer has a different perspective of the show and thus has to bring his or her own experience to answering those questions for himself or herself. In other words, my answer to one question may be different than yours. The show's message is that the world isn't made up of dichotomies—there is no good or evil, just varying mixtures of both; the world isn't black and white, but rather various shades of gray. Therefore, the answers to life's mysteries aren't easy to come by, and no one else can answer them for you. The answer to whether there is such a thing as destiny is unique to each person watching that show. It's up to you to find out for yourself.

Among the many literary allusions on *Lost*, the two recurring ones are to *Alice's Adventures in Wonderland* and *The Wizard of Oz*.[2] Just as Alice disappears down a rabbit hole into a strange world that doesn't make much sense, so, too, do the survivors find themselves in a weird Wonderland of their own, chasing their personal demons like white rabbits through the jungle. Ben Linus (Michael Emerson) is the man behind the curtain, seemingly controlling the smoke monster and terrifying everyone, when, in fact, he is absolutely powerless. But in light of the series finale, the two references take on a different resonance. When Alice leaves Wonderland, she assumes it was all a dream, and although she doesn't definitively know what purpose any of the characters served or why those strange things happened to her, she has come to a different understanding of herself. In *The Wizard of Oz*, Dorothy is on a quest to return home. Despite the weird and wonderful nature of Oz, all she wants is to be with the people she loves and to find a way back to them. At the end of the film, Dorothy discovers she had the power to return home the whole time; she just had to click her heels together. Similarly, *Lost* was simply a six-year life lesson that aimed to guide viewers to find answers by looking inside themselves . . . to find out they had the power to answer the questions the whole time.

In *Lost*'s first season, John Locke teaches Walt how to play backgammon and introduces the game as "two players, two sides. One is light, and one is dark." These ominous words set forth the main thrust of *Lost* as a parable of good versus evil. Jack, however, famously tells the survivors that if they don't live together, they will die alone. His words set up the other side of the story—the one that focuses on love and sacrifice and connection. These two characters encapsulate the two sides of *Lost*, a TV show that is a mystery wrapped in an enigma but also a story about people who are lost and trying to find their way. In the finale, both of these threads resolve beautifully, with gorgeous writing, acting, and direction.

2. Here I am referring to the Lewis Carroll book *Alice's Adventures in Wonderland* (1865) and to the MGM movie musical *The Wizard of Oz* from 1939 that starred Judy Garland and was directed by Victor Fleming. *Lost* relied on direct quotations from that film more so than on the book *The Wonderful Wizard of Oz* (1900) by L. Frank Baum.

Perhaps a few years from now, the *Lost* finale will be regarded as one of the most perfect series culminations of all time. Until then, fans can continue to debate the intricacies of this fascinating show and interpret it for themselves—the way the writers always intended them to.

References

Lieber, Jeffrey, J. J. Abrams, and Damon Lindelof, creators. 2004–10. *Lost*. Executive producers Carlton Cuse and Damon Lindelof. Aired Sept. 22, 2004, to May 23, 2010, ABC. Original broadcasts.

35

Mad Men

"Person to Person"

DOUGLAS L. HOWARD

So, here we are, about three years later or more, and I am still struggling with the ending of the *Mad Men* (2007–15) finale and Don Draper's meditation on the universal benefits of Coca-Cola, struggling perhaps as much with what I thought I saw as with what I was supposed to see. I felt ready for almost anything leading up to that episode—even Don's sudden transformation into the notorious D. B. Cooper[1]—especially after all of those impulsive, life-changing decisions on the part of the show's characters through its seven seasons and its penchant for unpredictability. (After all, where else on television would you see a secretary run over a man's foot with a riding lawn mower in an office?) And, in this regard, the finale did not disappoint.[2] It is as final as a show about people in advertising moving through the 1960s, history, and American culture could be. (We know that Watergate, Mark Spitz, Archie Bunker, and inflation are waiting for them around the corner.) Peggy realizes that she has been in love with Stan all along, Joan lets Richard go to start her own business, and Roger goes off to smoke and drink with Megan's mother, whom he now introduces as his own. Facing death from an untreatable cancer, Betty decides to use the time that she has left in school. And Pete reconciles with his wife and goes on to the good life as an executive for Learjet in Kansas. (Really? A happy ending for Pete? Now

---

1. The theory that Don Draper is D. B. Cooper was first suggested by Lindsey Green in 2013—"Draper will be gone without a trace," she predicted—and picked up steam in the show's final weeks.
2. All references to the *Mad Men* finale, "Person to Person," come from Weiner 2015.

that's a surprise.[3]) But the central story on *Mad Men* is always Don's. After cutting out on work yet again and driving across the country, Don literally "finds himself" in a commune by the sea. Crying and hugging it out with Leonard, a poor stranger in a group-therapy circle, Don appears to let go of his feelings of alienation and isolation and in the show's closing moments is dreaming up one of the most famous ads of all, McCann Erickson's hilltop Coke campaign of 1971. Or at least that is the pitch. And this is where I find myself still thinking about that ending, Leonard, Don, and that chorus that wants to teach me "to sing in perfect harmony."

In many ways, in the final season Don is taken down or apart by degrees as the various elements of the identity or persona that he has so meticulously crafted are stripped away and removed to get him to that point and to the "Leonard" that is underneath and looking to be acknowledged.[4] In a matter of episodes, he loses his model-actress wife, Megan (7.7), his swanky New York apartment (7.10), and the ad agency with his name (7.11). He gives away a significant portion of the money that he received from McCann Erickson to Megan as a settlement (7.9). He also appears to lose his ability to sway people with his rhetoric and optimism and to sell his coworkers on the idea that the McCann takeover is "the beginning of something," with no one paying attention to him at the end of the episode "Time and Life" (7.11). He walks away from his job (7.12). He confesses to his part in the death of his commanding officer in Korea (7.13). Seeing some of himself in the fledging motel con-man Andy, he even gives his Cadillac away (7.13), and if that car exemplifies the persona of Don Draper—a car salesman in season 2 describes him, in fact, as "a walking Cadillac" (2.7)—we could make a big deal out of the symbolism there, that he is giving away or abandoning what he is and getting down to the truth about himself. In his final conversation with Peggy Olson in the series, in that "person-to-person" phone call, he is brutally honest about who he is and what he has done: "I broke all my vows. I scandalized my child. I took another man's name and made nothing of it."

Through this physical as well as psychological journey, through this soul searching, we could credibly believe that Don, in being broken down and in breaking himself down, comes to some recognition of himself as someone who feels unloved or undeserving of love or who simply doesn't know what

3. In an interview with David Bianculli, Weiner even called Pete Campbell "the villain" of the show (Bianculli 2016, 476).

4. All references to the series in general come from Weiner 2007–15.

love is. (Cue that Foreigner song.) As a result, he has sabotaged virtually every relationship in his life and pushed away anyone who has tried to get close to him, from his wife and family to his coworkers, as part of a self-fulfilling prophecy, to legitimize and reaffirm the way that he subconsciously feels about himself. Writer-director Matthew Weiner revealed in his first talk after the final episode aired that Leonard, the man whom Don meets in the group-therapy room, "probably [has] the most important role on the series" and that Don in that scene "[is] embracing a part of himself" (Egner 2015). Regardless of how nicely Don dresses or how confidently he presents himself, he has seen himself as Leonard, the unappreciated office worker, all along. In his painful revelation to the group, Leonard pours Don's heart out and explains him in ways that Don himself had not realized until that moment. For Don, then, this hug with Leonard, this gesture—again, person to person—is nothing short of finally forgiving and accepting himself.

Weiner, however, also wanted "the audience [to] feel that [Don] was embracing . . . them [as well] and that they were heard" (Egner 2015). Essentially, in that moment, Don is acknowledging the Leonard in all of us, the consumers he had pitched and sold to over the years. "I just know how people work," Don confidently tells Stephanie at the commune, and in this advice that he has given others through the course of the show, Peggy among them, we see, yet again, how Don has been able to manipulate and convince his public and get them to do what he wants. In this reaching out with Leonard, though, Don is not socioeconomically and physically above that public (and us) in some Madison Avenue skyscraper, but on common ground, flawed, human, needy, and crying. Much has been made of Don's "Dick Whitman" identity and its connection to Walt Whitman, the poet, as Melanie Hernandez and David Thomas Holmberg remind us, "whose *Leaves of Grass* sets forth as its task the creation and articulation of a new America and a new type of American," just as Don creates a new America through the "poetry" of his advertising (2011, 26). Along these lines, *Mad Men* could be the "Song of Don's Self," and we could conceive of this embrace as Don's way of saying, "I contain multitudes" (Whitman 1986, 1326). Or, perhaps, in a "Crossing Brooklyn Ferry" sense, we could see it as being a case of "I am with you, you men and women of a generation, or ever so many generations hence" (Whitman 1986, 21)—in your offices, your hotel rooms, your martini business lunches, and even your hippie communes, baring your souls and meditating. Or as Anna Draper, the wife of the man whose identity Don assumed, puts it to Don in her transcendental tarot card reading of his future, "Every living thing is connected to you. . . . [T]he only thing keeping you from being happy is the belief that you are alone." Where Don's insight into people is the key to his success in advertising, it might also, in the end, have been his key to being one of them; in hugging it out with Leonard, he finally listens to the music of humanity and sees himself as part of it. Don's smile, then, could be the fulfillment of Anna's reading/prophecy, and the Coke ad—the only way, of course, that Don can express himself—would be the literal manifestation of that unity, a chorus of singers lifting their voices in harmony, all in the name of selling soda.

For all of the products hawked over the years on *Mad Men*—and there were quite a few—I still have a hard time buying this one, and I don't just mean the Coke. And I say this not solely because I'm cynical or jaded or because years of watching enigmatic sociopaths and morally challenged murderers on television have finally taken their toll, although that certainly is a context for the series and my viewing. I know that Weiner, in serving up the Kool-Aid (or Coke), wanted us to believe in the reality of Don's conversion. Why shouldn't we come to it, as the "professor" advises before Roger Sterling's LSD trip, "with a spirit of optimism" (5.5)? Why shouldn't we accept that someone does get out of Madison Avenue alive and honestly is renewed? Like Fox Mulder, I want to believe, but I can't. For starters, and I hate to sound like Roger or Pete Campbell about this, we have seen Don do this same thing previously in the show's story line.[5] In many ways, the last episode recalls the episode "The Mountain King" in season 2, when Don goes out to California and visits Anna Draper. As their conversation turns to Don's marriage, he opens up to Anna, just as he does later on with Peggy. "I ruined everything," he confesses, "my family, my wife, my kids. . . . My brother came to find me; I told him to go away" (2.12). As Don walks out into the ocean at the end of the episode, with his eyes closed and his face turned toward the sun, the waves wash over him baptismally. Singing of redemption and "a new life to begin," George Jones plays out to the credits, and these signs suggest that Don might be starting over. In the final episode of the season, he begs Betty to take him back, and they seem united in dealing with the untimely news of her pregnancy. But as Don himself tells Anna rather coldly in "The Mountain King," "People don't change"[6]—this is a

---

5. Psychologist Stephanie Newman, an expert whose opinion Don would, of course, dismiss, similarly doubts his ability to sustain long-term change; rather, in *"Mad Men" on the Couch* she describes these "moments of insight" as "fleeting" and "transient" (2012, 36).

6. Weiner actually said this in a Rotten Tomatoes interview: "I always want to say, people don't change. The issues of your everyday life don't change" (Ricard 2015).

central issue for both the series and the finale—and, not long into season 3, he is back to his old tricks, posing as an accountant on a business trip, seducing a stewardess, and telling Sally that the airline pin in his luggage was for her all along (3.1). (Maybe Willie Nelson's "To All The Girls I've Loved Before" would have been a more appropriate song for Don's ocean baptism.) When Don finally comes "clean" about his identity in "The Gypsy and the Hobo" (3.11), moreover, it is not because out in the surf he has washed away his fear of being honest with Betty, but because she has found the key to his desk drawer in the laundry and uncovered the truth about Dick Whitman while he is away at work. John Teti talks about the ending as part of "a cycle of renewal" (2015), and a cycle or a pattern of behavior could be what we are looking at. It may be all sunshine and smiles in the last scene because it looks like another new start for Don—after all, he likes beginnings—but from what the series has showed us of the advertising lifestyle, it is inevitably going to wheel—or perhaps "carousel"?—him back to this place of existential angst and conflicted desire.

And then there's the matter of the Coca-Cola ad campaign. Don's transformation might be easier to swallow if we didn't have to wash it down with a bottle of Coke. If he honestly has changed and does feel a connection to people that he did not before, then why does he feel the need to commodify and exploit that breakthrough by using it to sell soda? How legitimate can that connection be if, in the end, it only serves as the center of a product endorsement? If you've seen *Justified* (2010–15), then you'll know what I mean when I say that there is just something so "Boyd Crowder" about it.[7] It demeans the sincerity of the experience. Having bonded with Leonard in the therapy seminar, Don is not thinking about how he can be a better father or a better husband to the next Mrs. Draper du jour or what his next step should be toward some kind of self-actualization. He is thinking about how he can repackage his "coming to Jesus" moment as a sales pitch, one that will substantially increase Coke's profit margin—and be a major win for seedy, scummy McCann Erickson—all under the guise of social harmony. Why struggle to find inner peace when you can get it out of a vending machine for a dollar (or a quarter back then)? That certainly runs contrary to what Bert Cooper tells him in that vision in season 7: "The best things in life are free" (7.7).

---

7. Boyd is the white supremacist who ultimately uses his religious conversion as a front for his criminal activities. For more on *Justified*, see chapter 30.

Perhaps the most disturbing thing about the Coke ad, as far as Don is concerned, is how it celebrates the product as "the real thing," a bizarre endorsement given how much he wrestles with the real over the course of the show. For Don, whether it is cigarettes, hotels, luggage, or laxatives, the image or surface always takes precedence over the substance. It doesn't matter if the product itself is any good; it only matters that people want it. And this is never more true than when it comes to who and what Don is or, better yet, who he appears to be. Playing off of his name, Hernandez and Holmberg have commented on how Don "drapes the American social corpus" through his ads (2011, 26), but the most effective blank space that he drapes or covers is always himself. That *Ad Age* reporter who describes him as "a handsome cypher" in episode 1 of season 4 may not be far from the truth, and the series largely works as Don's attempt to define just what that space is. If people won't accept Dick Whitman, the bastard son of a prostitute—and "people" include Don most of all—then maybe they will buy Don Draper, that "idealized version of self," as Gary Edgerton tells us in a *CST* column, "that Dick . . . [has] constructed from all the images he's internalized from the many books and magazines we see him reading, the movies and television we see him watching, and the advertising he absorbs and creates" (2016). Like Bret Easton Ellis's character Patrick Bateman in *American Psycho*, "there is an idea of a [Don Draper], some kind of abstraction, but there is no real [Don], only an entity, something illusory" (1991, 376).[8] Whether he ever existed in the first place, he becomes what Jean Baudrillard calls "the hyperreal," living out "the play of reality" (1988, 146) through this identity that he has literally and figuratively manufactured. If Don discovers himself in the end, if, in reaching out to Leonard, he touches something psychologically real or what he thinks is real about himself, then why does he connect that real to Coke? Why does he use that word, *real*, to describe a product when the other, more personal "real," if that's what it is, is something that he has gained only through a lifetime of sacrifice and loss? In season 6, Don is quick to complain when someone on his staff uses the word *love* in an ad for Dow Oven Cleaner: "Let's leave it where we want it," he admonishes. "We want that electric jolt to the body" (6.1). If a word such as *love*, something

8. Don's imaginary act of murder in the episode "Mystery Date" (5.3) certainly compares to how Bateman commits murders in his head in response to a similar lifestyle. In the same way that Bateman is confused for other businessmen because they all are part of a type, Don becomes anxious during a meeting at McCann Erickson in part because all of the ad men in the room seem to be the same (7.12).

that is especially difficult for Don and is the focus of Leonard's speech, is off-limits for a kitchen ad, then you would think that celebrating the "real-ness" of Coke would be equally blasphemous, particularly at that stage of Don's story. But it isn't. In the end, does Jim Hobart sell Don on his future or essentially sentence him with that grave pronouncement in the episode "Time and Life": "Coca-Cola" (7.11)?

In some ways, from his engagement with and perpetuation of the hyper-real, the ending still seems more like an ad for happiness that Don might pitch than the ending of a narrative arc. Seeing him smile in that final scene, you can almost hear the tagline: "Happiness: when you've found it, you'll know." (Or is it "Happiness: the cure for the common existence"?)

I don't doubt the intention here. Matt Zoller Seitz has said that Weiner "is not a cynical artist" and wasn't working with the same dark edge that David Chase used for *The Sopranos* (2015). I think that Weiner and maybe some of us, maybe all of us, want to believe in the reality of Don Draper or at least in the realistic possibilities of the Dick Whitman/Don Draper character, just like the other characters on the show want to believe in the best of him. In their final phone call, Peggy simply cannot believe in Don's attempt to cast himself as a bad person: "What did you ever do that was so bad?" she wonders. Maybe from some moral-physiognomic place we want our good-looking cultural representatives to reflect and demonstrate posi-tive moral values. Of course, Captain America must be both handsome and decent, and, of course, Don Draper is capable of more than just ads and adul-tery. In a *CST* post in 2012 (Howard 2012), I took issue with *Slate* writer Tom Scocca for bashing how *Mad Men* and Don, in particular, had found their way into the public discourse as well as how audiences were accepting the show as a matter of historical record. "It is time for someone to tell you this," Scocca wrote, "Don Draper *is not a real person*" (2012, emphasis in original). I stand by what I said then. We know that Don Draper is not real, but we want to entertain the likelihood that there is some truth to and within his character and to believe that there is something real and knowable and genuinely good in there. As Don himself says at one point, "We want [peo-ple] to be who we want them to be," and he is no exception. Weiner wanted to believe that he, too, knew Don; if Leonard is Don, Ellen Horne points out that he "looks a little like Matt Weiner" (2015). In the finale, Weiner's great trick may have been in daring us to consider and to debate or, more appro-priately, to sell us on the honesty of Don's catharsis. (As the creator of the show, Weiner, too, must be implicated in the very process of advertising and sales that he was commenting on.) In the same way that Don tells a client in the pilot that advertising is "a billboard on the side of the road that screams with reassurance that whatever you're doing is okay," Weiner wanted us to believe that for all that Don has done in seven seasons of television, for all of the indiscretions and improprieties he is guilty of, where Don is and who he is at the end of the series are okay. Weiner may have been trying to tap into that optimism that still drives us as consumers of media as well as of manufacturing. We want to believe that Windows 10 is better than Windows 9, that the new flatscreen has inkier blacks than the old one (even if our eyes can't detect the difference), and that the six-pack of Coke that we buy is something that we actually need as opposed to something that we are talked into by a flashy ad or a famous spokesperson. But with those things as well as with enlightenment and salvation, we would still do well to exercise a little "caveat emptor."

References

Baudrillard, Jean. 1988. *Selected Writings*. Edited by Mark Poster. Stanford, CA: Stanford Univ. Press.

Bianculli, David. 2016. *The Platinum Age of Television: From "I Love Lucy" to "The Walking Dead": How TV Became Terrific*. New York: Doubleday.

Edgerton, Gary. 2016. "A *Mad Men* Potpourri." *CSTonline*, Mar. 17. At https://cstonline.net/a-mad-men-potpourri-by-gary-edgerton/.

Egner, Jeremy. 2015. "Matthew Weiner on the Coke Ad and the Meaning of *Mad Men*." *New York Times*, May 20. At http://artsbeat.blogs.nytimes.com/2015/05/20/matthew-weiner-discusses-the-coke-ad-and-don-draper-mad-men/?_r=0.

Ellis, Bret Easton. 1991. *American Psycho*. New York: Vintage.

Green, Lindsey. 2013. "Where Don Draper Ends, D. B. Cooper Begins." *Medium*, June 23. At https://medium.com/thelist/where-don-draper-ends-d-b-cooper-begins-e96804523838#.u7xh67x6o.

Hernandez, Melanie, and David Thomas Holmberg. 2011. "'We'll Start Over Like Adam and Eve': The Subversion of Classic American Mythology." In *Analyzing "Mad Men": Critical Essays on the Television Series*, edited by Scott F. Stoddart, 15–44. Jefferson, NC: McFarland.

Horne, Ellen. 2015. "The *Mad Men* Finale We Needed, but Didn't Deserve." WNYC, May 22. At http://www.wnyc.org/story/mad-men-finale-we-needed-didnt-deserve/.

Howard, Douglas L. 2012. "Real Mad: Don Draper and Television Reality." *CSTonline*, July 17. At https://cstonline.net/real-mad-don-draper-and-television-reality-by-douglas-howard/.

Newman, Stephanie. 2012. *"Mad Men" on the Couch*. New York: Thomas Dunne.

Ricard, Sarah. 2015. "Matthew Weiner Interview: 'People Don't Change.'" Rotten Tomatoes, May 13. At https://editorial.rottentomatoes.com/article/matthew-weiner-interview-people-dont-change/.

Scocca, Tom. 2012. "Don Draper's Shocking Secret: He Doesn't Exist." *Slate*, June 8. At http://www.slate.com/articles/arts/scocca/2012/06/mad_men_season_5_why_do_obsessive_fans_and_the_new_york_times_mistake_the_show_for_reality_.html.

Seitz, Matt Zoller. 2015. "*Mad Men* Series Finale Recap: I'm Okay, You're Okay." *Vulture*, May 18. At http://www.vulture.com/2015/05/mad-men-recap-season-7-episode-14.html.

Teti, John. 2015. "*Mad Men*: 'Person to Person.'" *A.V. Club*, May 18. At http://www.avclub.com/tvclub/mad-men-person-person-219567.

Weiner, Matthew, creator. 2007–15. *Mad Men*. Aired July 19, 2007, to May 17, 2015, AMC. Netflix. Streamed Aug.–Nov. 2016.

———, dir. 2015. "Person to Person." *Mad Men*, season 7, episode 14. Written by Matthew Weiner. Aired May 17, 2015, AMC. Netflix. Streamed Nov. 2016.

Whitman, Walt. 1986. *The Complete Poems*. Edited by Francis Murphy. New York: Penguin.

36

The Mary Tyler Moore Show

"The Last Show"

DANA HELLER

Mary Tyler Moore was having the time of her life. The last thing she wanted was for her award-winning situation comedy to end. However, by 1976 the show's creators, James L. Brooks and Alan Burns, were running out of fresh story ideas for Mary Richards and her crew of close-knit coworkers at WJM-TV in Minneapolis. They were eager to move on to new projects. After consulting with the show's producers and her then husband and business partner, Grant Tinker, Moore realized that the best course of action would be to end the series on a high note, while it was still performing well in the ratings, even though it pained her. The seventh and final season of the groundbreaking CBS sitcom that bore Moore's name—and, quite arguably, the very concept of a situation-comedy finale—was a product of this conflict, involving writers' career ambitions, producers' recognition of industrial risks, and Moore's deep emotional attachment to a cast and crew who had over the course of seven years come to feel like family.

Mary Tyler Moore (accredited as *The Mary Tyler Moore Show*, although the latter never appeared in the opening title sequence) premiered on September 19, 1970. At that time, nobody could have predicted that this sitcom would win a record twenty-nine Primetime Emmys (the NBC sitcom *Frasier* [1993–2004] topped that with thirty in 2002) plus a Peabody Award (1977), spur three spin-offs (*Rhoda* [1974–78], *Phyllis* [1975–77], and *Lou Grant* [1977–82]), and nearly half a century later remain a staple of television "best of" lists, including the Writers Guild of America's "101 Best Written TV Series of All Time," where it ranks sixth (Writers Guild of America–West 2013). The show was an unlikely success story, an opportunity handed to Moore at a transitional point in her career. Nationally adored as Laura Petrie, Rob Petrie's ebullient young wife on *The Dick Van Dyke Show* (CBS,

1961–66), Moore's subsequent effort to establish a Hollywood film career fell flat at the box office. Hoping to lend his friend a hand, Van Dyke asked her to reunite with him for a CBS variety special. The special garnered such high ratings that CBS immediately offered Moore a half-hour slot with a commitment of twenty-four episodes, no pilot required.

The creative team hired for the project, led by Brooks and Burns, initially envisioned Mary Richards as a thirty-year-old divorcée who moves to the city to establish an independent life. CBS executives balked at the idea. Not only were they certain that mainstream audiences would reject a divorced woman as a lead character, but they also feared that audiences would think she had divorced Van Dyke, which could kill the series. So the premise was tweaked: Mary Richards would move to Minneapolis seeking work as a secretary in a small television station after her fiancé, a medical student whom she had supported through school, broke off their engagement. The network accepted this compromise. With casting under way, Moore and Tinker established their own company to produce the series, MTM Enterprises. The company's logo featured a meowing orange cat encircled by a gold ribbon—a playful riff on the MGM lion.[1]

When MTM delivered the first episode to CBS for pre-air audience testing, *The Mary Tyler Moore Show* achieved another distinction, albeit an inauspicious one: "the lowest ranked [first] television episode ever viewed in the history of CBS" (Werts 1997). Focus groups "hated everything": they saw Mary Richards as a loser and questioned why she was still single. They disliked Rhoda Morgenstern (Valerie Harper) because she was mean to Mary. Lou Grant (Ed Asner) seemed very Jewish. The network took notice of the episode's poor performance and buried the show in a dreaded time slot—Saturday night, known within the industry as "date night." When Bob Wood became president of CBS, he recognized the show's originality and moved it to an earlier slot with hopes of building a wider audience. Gradually, the show caught on. However, it's worth noting that *The Mary Tyler Moore Show*'s contemporary standing as a television milestone did not occur overnight. Even when the show began garnering critical praise and industry awards—in fact, throughout the entire span of its run—it never occupied a top spot in the ratings but tended to hover more modestly within the 16–20 range.

---

1. For a comprehensive study of MTM production history, including *The Mary Tyler Moore Show*, see Feuer, Kerr, and Vahimagi 1984.

Indeed, in 1970 (one year before Norman Lear's series *All in the Family* [1971–79] premiered on CBS), *The Mary Tyler Moore Show* was likely to confuse viewers. It broke decisively with the conventions of the sitcom, a genre then widely regarded as intrinsically superficial, built on implausible premises, reliant upon predictable resolutions and insipid gags, and stocked with one-dimensional characters and relationships that never changed. *The Mary Tyler Moore Show*, in contrast, was marked by a sophisticated comedic writing style that appealed to adult sensibilities. Story lines were realistic and reflective of broader social and cultural shifts that were reshaping ideas about marriage and family, sex and sexuality, gender and race, work and the economy. Writers deftly touched upon controversial issues, such as equal pay for women, premarital sex, homosexuality, marital infidelity, prostitution, and violent death, often within the context of classic sitcom setups (e.g., Mary's fit of uncontrollable laughter during the funeral eulogy for Chuckles the Clown). The ensemble cast was composed of fully realized characters whom audiences could find lovable while still recognizing their human flaws—Lou's perpetual grumpiness, Phyllis Lindstrom's (Cloris Leachman) calculated snobbishness, Rhoda's unrelenting self-mockery. The series was unique in its commitment to allowing these characters to develop depth over time, thus enabling the writers to draw comedy from the characters themselves rather than from standard gag lines. And by placing a cohort of strong women—and strong female friendships—at the forefront of the series, the show opened up new comedic perspectives and possibilities that transformed the situation comedy, clearing the way for future shows such as *The Golden Girls* (NBC, 1985–92), *Designing Women* (CBS, 1986–93), *Sex and The City* (HBO, 1998–2004), and *Girls* (HBO, 2012–17).

The final season of *The Mary Tyler Moore Show* was both an organic outgrowth of these aesthetic innovations and a significant formal innovation in itself. Never before had a finale for a situation comedy been planned, let alone crafted as a reflexive meditation on what it means to experience an ending, to let go of people you have worked and grown with. The season was built on plot points designed to give closure to the main characters' story lines and to resolve conflicts that had long simmered, such as the ongoing rivalry between news writer Murray Slaughter (Gavin MacLeod) and the buffoonish anchorman Ted Baxter (Ted Knight) as well as Mary's legal limbo after being held in contempt of court for refusing to name a source. And it satisfied audience curiosity about possibilities only hinted at, as when in the penultimate episode Lou and Mary finally go on a date, only to mutually realize their romantic incompatibility.

Aptly titled "The Last Show,"[2] the series finale aired in the United States on March 19, 1977. The script, a collaborative effort, invited participation from every writer who had contributed more than one episode. The premise sets the stage for characters to say good-bye to one another within the context of the mise-en-scène: WJM-TV is sold to new management, which initiates a rash of firings in response to low ratings. With the numbers for the *Six O'Clock News* in decline, Lou, Mary, and Murray apprehensively anticipate the inevitable firing of the notoriously incompetent Ted. However, in an ironic reversal, Ted is the only one who is not handed a pink slip. Mary is devastated by this turn of events. To cheer her up, Lou uses the last of the newsroom's discretionary funds to bring Rhoda and Phyllis to town for a surprise reunion (Harper and Leachman had left the show in 1974 and 1975, respectively, for their own spin-offs).

After Ted delivers an awkward on-air tribute to his departing colleagues, inexplicably sending them off to the lyrics of the World War I song "It's a Long Way to Tipperary," the cast—including Ted's wife, Georgette (Georgia Engel), and the Happy Homemaker, Sue Ann Nivens (Betty White)—bid their farewells. Unabashedly sentimental, Mary's speech is a perfect television instance of art imitating life: "I just wanted you to know that sometimes I get concerned about being a career woman. I get to thinking my job is too important to me, and I tell myself that the people I work with are just the people I work with. And not my family. And last night, I thought, 'What is a family, anyway?' They're just people who make you feel less alone . . . and really loved. And that's what you've done for me. Thank you for being my family." These words and the nuclear-family dynamic that developed among the WJM-TV news team produced a new critical term, the *television work family*, a now-pervasive trope that refers to the re-creation of conventional Oedipal relations and hierarchies within the narrative space of a television work environment (Taylor 1989, 139).

Mary's farewell speech and Lou's uncharacteristic confession, "I treasure you people," spark a tearful, tenacious group hug. Georgette observes that they need tissues. A box of Kleenex sits on a desk a few feet away. "How will we get to it?" asks Sue Ann. Refusing to let go of one another, the group spontaneously begins shuffling, en masse, toward the tissues. Unscripted and improvised, this moment would become the most memorable image of "The Last Show," one that would be parodied in future series finales. Finally, the

---

2. All references to "The Last Show" come from Sandrich 1977.

cast break their hold and exit the newsroom, all singing "It's a Long Way to Tipperary." Mary is the last to walk through the door, where she pauses, takes a final look around, and—with a gratified smile—shuts off the light.

One cannot overstate the poignancy—and the lasting influence—of this television event. Henceforward, any sitcom (or dramatic series, for that matter) that wrote its own ending would do so in the shadow of the MTM model. Describing preparations for the series finale of *Friends* (NBC, 1994–2004), executive producer David Crane recalled that writers screened numerous sitcom finales, but none more painstakingly than "The Last Show," which, he said, represents the "gold standard" (quoted in Hartlaub 2004). When planning the final season of *30 Rock* (NBC, 2006–13), staff writers didn't simply review the final season of *The Mary Tyler Moore Show* but appropriated it as a template for resolving their own characters' story lines (VanDerWerff 2013).

However, the brilliance of the "The Last Show" is not what it resolves but what it leaves unsettled. Unlike Rachel Green (Jennifer Aniston) in *Friends*, who aborts plans to move to Paris for her dream job when Ross intercepts her at the airport to proclaim his love, or Liz Lemon (Tina Fey) in *30 Rock*, who loses her job but gains a new adopted family, Mary Richards remains throughout the duration of her story a self-sufficient, comfortably single, childless career woman. Indeed, if anything marks *The Mary Tyler Moore Show* as a television milestone, it's that the series architects never yielded to the pressures of the "marriage plot," the narrative device that conventionally signals a happy ending for female protagonists. As Mary exits the newsroom for the last time, her future is uncertain. She has no job and nobody waiting for her at home. We don't know what she'll do. But we do know that she'll make it because she's already proven that she can.

References

Feuer, Jane, Paul Kerr, and Tess Vahimagi, eds. 1984. *MTM "Quality Television."* London: British Film Institute.

Hartlaub, Peter. 2004. "*Friends*' Challenge—Finding Right Words to Say Goodbye." *SF Gate*, Jan. 15. At http://www.sfgate.com/entertainment/article/Friends-challenge-finding-right-words-to-say-2830232.php.

Sandrich, Jay, dir. 1977. "The Last Show." *The Mary Tyler Moore Show*, season 7, episode 24. Written by James Brooks, Allan Burns, Stan Daniels, Bob Ellison, David Lloyd, and Ed Weinberger. Aired Mar. 19, CBS. iTunes. Accessed June 4, 2016.

Taylor, Ella. 1989. *Prime Time Families: Television Culture in Postwar America.* Berkeley and Los Angeles: Univ. of California Press.

VanDerWerff, Todd. 2013. "How *30 Rock*'s Well-Plotted Final Season Echoes *The Mary Tyler Moore Show.*" *A.V. Club*, Jan. 31. At http://www.avclub.com /article/how-i30-rockis-well-plotted-final-season-echoes-it-91814.

Werts, Diane. 1997. "Mary Tyler Moore Interview." Archive of American Television, Oct. 23. At http://www.emmytvlegends.org/interviews/people/mary-tyler -moore.

Writers Guild of America–West. 2013. "101 Best Written TV Series of All Time." At http://www.wga.org/content/default.aspx?id=4925.

37

M*A*S*H

"Goodbye, Farewell, and Amen"

DAVID SCOTT DIFFRIENT

At one point in "Kidney Now!," an episode of *30 Rock* (NBC, 2006–13), Milton Greene (Jack Donaghy's [Alec Baldwin] father, played by Alan Alda) remarks, "A guy crying about a chicken and a baby? I thought this was a comedy show!" Fans of the Emmy Award–winning medical sitcom *M*A*S*H* (CBS, 1972–83) will likely get the reference embedded in that line of dialogue in an episode of a more recent but equally beloved comedy series celebrated for its intertextual density and sophisticated wordplay. Spoken by an actor who had first gained fame for playing a hard-drinking, fast-talking, womanizing surgeon drafted into service during the Korean War, this otherwise nonsensical remark about someone brought to tears by the sight of "a chicken and a baby" will not be lost on audiences who have seen the final episode of *M*A*S*H*. Entitled "Goodbye, Farewell, and Amen," that legendary episode, like the 250 that preceded it over the series' eleven-year broadcast history, revolves around the exploits of the many men and women populating Mobile Army Surgical Hospital 4077.[1] Yet it focuses primarily on the inner demons plaguing one person in particular: Alan Alda's character, Captain Benjamin "Hawkeye" Pierce.

Throughout the first half of this two-hour-plus episode, Hawkeye is shown undergoing psychiatric evaluations at a mental health facility, with his own soft-spoken doctor—Major Sidney Freedman (Allan Arbus)—administering a "talking cure" for the visibly agitated patient. What Freedman, after several attempts, finally manages to pull from the recesses of Hawkeye's repressed memories is a traumatic moment from his recent past, one

---

1. All references to "Goodbye, Farewell, and Amen" come from Alda [1983] 2008.

involving a Korean baby whose audible crying aboard a bus full of medical personnel and war refugees threatened to draw enemy fire. Because he asked the mother of the baby (seated at the back of the bus) to silence it, Hawkeye feels partly responsible for the woman's decision to stifle the child's crying so strongly and for so long that the infant passed away in her arms. It seems that the trauma resulting from that nighttime incident can be assuaged only through an act of tactical misremembrance—through Hawkeye's convenient yet necessary replacement of the crying baby with a clucking chicken in his mind. Thus, Alda's winking allusion to "a chicken and a baby" in *30 Rock* serves to remind audiences that the satirical tone and observational humor with which *M*A*S*H* is often associated was largely missing from its famous finale—a relatively downbeat, tear-filled episode (directed by Alda) that to this day remains the most-watched nonsporting event in US prime-time television history.[2]

Although Super Bowl XLIV, which aired on February 7, 2010, dethroned "Goodbye, Farewell, and Amen" from its top spot (in terms of the total number of television households tuned in to each program), *M*A*S*H*'s finale still holds the record for highest-rated broadcast, according to A. C. Nielsen figures. With a Nielsen rating of 60.2 (the percentage of the entire population of TV-equipped homes tuned in to the finale), the airing of "Goodbye, Farewell, and Amen" on February 28, 1983, far surpasses the football game's 45.0 rating and will likely remain unbeaten as the TV industry continues to fragment with the rise of additional niche markets, targeted programming, and new consumption patterns in an age of media convergence (Bianculli 2016, 486). Many of the nearly 106 million viewers who tuned in to CBS stations on that historic night noted the program's tonal shift, its gravitation into the dark corridors of the male protagonist's damaged psyche (visually expressed by way of Hawkeye's new surroundings, the drab-green walls of a sanatorium cell and the ceiling fan would later draw comparisons to the beginning of Francis Ford Coppola's film *Apocalypse Now* [1979]). Indeed, TV audiences were primed to experience the emotional "pain, conflict and obstacles" that producer Gene Reynolds believed were such an intrinsic part

---

2. Alan Alda, who directed "Goodbye, Farewell, and Amen," was one of the eight credited writers on this final episode of *M*A*S*H* (see Alda [1983] 2008). The downbeat tone of the script in general and Alda's performance in particular prove the lie to the comment made by Abed Nadir (Danny Pudi) in the NBC comedy *Community* (2009–15), "You're like Hawkeye on *M*A*S*H*. He kept his upbeat humor and charm, even in the eleventh year of the Korean War" (Russo 2010).

of the final episode's success (quoted in Wittebols 2003, 140), with advance publicity hinting at the many potentially upsetting plot developments involving not only Hawkeye but also Father Francis Mulcahy (William Christopher) and Major Charles Winchester III (David Ogden Stiers)—two of the major characters who undergo similarly disturbing setbacks over the course of the narrative. Through an aggressive promotional campaign on the network's part, supplemented with tabloid "scoops" and script "reveals" that only whetted the audience's appetite for more *M*A*S*H*-related discourse in the culture at large, "Goodbye, Farewell, and Amen" became a must-see media event unlike any before it, one whose length and initially gloomy, melancholic tone set it apart from other famous TV finales, such as *The Odd Couple*'s "Felix Remarries" (March 7, 1975) and *The Mary Tyler Moore Show*'s "The Last Show" (March 19, 1977).

Significantly, the extradiegetic discourses surrounding the *M*A*S*H* finale, many of which provided advance "buzz" and "spoilers" about its narrative resolutions, are paralleled in the diegetic buildup toward the signing of an armistice agreement that will bring the fighting in Korea to an end. News of the imminent truce, communicated to the camp via Armed Forces Radio broadcasts and delivered by Robert Pierpoint (a former journalist playing himself, whose voice can be heard on the loudspeakers), offers fleeting glimmers of hope to the men and women of the 4077, which is inundated with incoming wounded after a particularly bloody conflict in nearby Kumsong. While Hawkeye is away being treated for the psychological ordeal that he has been enduring since the bus incident, his friends back at the 4077 struggle to stitch up the many bodies being brought in by MedEvac helicopter and Jeep. Their struggles are compounded by the large number of refugees, children, and Chinese prisoners of war amassing outside the operating tent. The prospect of going home helps to alleviate the strain, however, making it possible for the doctors and nurses to maintain a positive outlook despite the unrelenting influx of wounded soldiers and the persistent shelling that threatens to turn this functional yet makeshift hospital into a full-fledged war zone.

Significantly, Hawkeye's "Swamp mate,"—Captain B. J. Hunnicutt (Mike Farrell)—a fourth-season replacement for Hawkeye's earlier partner in crime, "Trapper John" McIntyre (Wayne Rogers)—is given an opportunity to leave the camp early once his discharge papers arrive. Overjoyed to learn that he might be back in his home in Mill Valley, California, in time to celebrate his daughter's second birthday, B. J. rushes to board a helicopter heading toward Kimpo airport. However, this leaves him little time to compose a thoughtful farewell message for Hawkeye. Like his predecessor, Trapper, who was last seen in the final episode of season 3, "Abyssinia, Henry," B. J. not only leaves the operating-room staff shorthanded but also upsets his already addled friend by departing without telling him good-bye. His failure to effectively communicate his emotions to Hawkeye by way of pen and paper means that B. J.'s time in Korea is not yet over. Indeed, several scenes later, the doctor, saddened not to be on a plane bound for San Francisco owing to the cancellation of all flights departing from Guam, returns to the camp, setting the stage for a more "appropriate" (emotionally expressive) send-off of this and other characters in the episode's final minutes.

In several of the scenes that precede that send-off, viewers are reminded of the things that make *M*A*S*H* such an unusual program, a show that distinguished itself from earlier military sitcoms (such as *McHale's Navy* [ABC, 1962–66] and *Hogan's Heroes* [CBS, 1965–71]) by mixing comedy and drama, momentous events and mundane nonevents. If not exactly representative of the series as a whole, "Goodbye, Farewell, and Amen" nevertheless contains elements that exemplify *M*A*S*H*'s stylistic tendencies and thematic preoccupations, thus summing up some of the reasons why so many fans had stuck with the program since its debut in 1972 (the year when Gene Reynolds and Larry Gelbart initiated this small-screen adaptation of Robert Altman's film of the same title, released in 1970). Dedicated viewers of *M*A*S*H* know that several episodes of the series spill over with intertextual references to studio-era Hollywood films, and this episode is no different, featuring allusions to such classic melodramas as *Gaslight* (George Cukor, 1944) and *The Snake Pit* (Anatole Litvak, 1948), both of which Hawkeye mentions during his stay at the "wacketeria." While recovering from his nervous breakdown in Ward D, Hawkeye writes a missive to his father that explains his condition. The letter, which begins "Dear Dad," recalls the nearly dozen epistolary narratives produced throughout the run of *M*A*S*H* (including "Dear Dad" from season 1 and "Dear Uncle Abdul" from season 8).

In addition, by the time "Goodbye, Farewell, and Amen" aired, fans had grown accustomed to witnessing scenes in which outdoor activities such as badminton, basketball, baseball, soccer, and even lawn bowling transpire amid other, less family-friendly pastimes such as gambling and consuming alcohol. This is true, for instance, of "Dear Dad . . . Three," an episode in season 2 that opens with a volleyball game being played by a group of men and women, while inside the Swamp Major Frank Burns (Larry Linville) and Trapper play five-card stud. This habitual foregrounding of gameplay is referenced in the second scene of the series finale, a flashback presented from Hawkeye's perspective that shows the doctors and nurses of the 4077 taking a much-needed Fourth of July break near a cove located north of the port city of Inchon. Sun shines down on the beach as the group plays a variety of sports, including volleyball and baseball, while the cooking of barbeque completes this picture of temporary contentment and collective merriment. Ironically, Hawkeye describes the act of leaving this beach-party setting and returning to the 4077 as "going home," an expression that anticipates the characters' actual departure for the United States in the final moments, following a wedding celebration that subtly connotes the ritualistic dimensions of televisual narrative.

Weddings between American military personnel and Korean women had been depicted on the program since the season 2 episode "L.I.P." (an acronym for "local indigenous personnel"), usually as a means of highlighting the racial bigotry and bureaucratic obstacles faced by individuals who prepared for a new life together back in the United States (where cultural barriers and more insidious forms of institutionalized discrimination inevitably awaited fresh-faced war brides). In the penultimate scene leading up to the finale's lengthy farewell sequence, Sergeant Maxwell Klinger (Jamie Farr) marries a Korean woman named Soon-Lee (Rosalind Chao), their bond not only assuaging any lingering anxieties that audiences might have felt about the company clerk's earlier cross-dressing pursuit of a Section 8 (psychiatric discharge) but also allegorically cementing the asymmetrical power dynamic between the US government and the First Republic of Korea (whose ineffectual leader, President Syngman Rhee, is mentioned by name in this and several other episodes). What is perhaps most surprising about this blissful union between the Lebanese American from Toledo and the local Korean woman who has been searching for her missing family members in Chorwon—besides the fact that Klinger is willing to stay behind and continue the search after his friends from the 4077 have left—is the quickness with which the couple's relationship has developed over a single week. Introduced in "As Time Goes By,"[3] the episode that immediately preceded the series finale, Soon-Lee has an initially combative relationship with Klinger, who receives an order from headquarters to lock up a suspected female sniper in preparation for her interrogation. But during the Fourth of July flashback

3. All references to "As Time Goes By" come from Metcalfe [1983] 2008.

that transpires in the opening minutes of "Goodbye, Farewell, and Amen," the two walk along the beach collecting seashells and laying the seeds for a speedy flowering of romance in the scenes that follow.

Significantly, "As Time Goes By," aired one week prior to the finale and directed by Burt Metcalfe, was actually shot last[4] and thus had special meaning for the many creative personnel involved in its production. Besides featuring a subplot about Soon-Lee's initial incarceration and eventual exoneration (once Klinger has shown that the bullet extracted from a downed pilot is too big to have come from the rifle she had been carrying), it hinges on the attempt made by Major Margaret Houlihan (Loretta Swit) to cobble together a time capsule holding various cultural artifacts or material objects that might commemorate the 4077 personnel's professional experiences and give future generations of Koreans a glimpse into their private lives. Culminating with a touching scene in which the former "Hot Lips" (who is now respected by her male peers in the camp) prepares to bury said objects— including the teddy bear once cherished by Corporal "Radar" O'Reilly (Gary Burghoff) and a fishing lure that once belonged to the ill-fated commanding officer Henry Blake (McLean Stevenson)—in the ground, "As Time Goes By" might have served as a compelling end to the series, giving audiences the opportunity to reflect one last time on the costs of war and the power of cultural productions to keep the memories of friends alive. However, the series decision makers' deemed the tellingly titled episode "Goodbye, Farewell, and Amen" more effective, more *instructive*, as a means of wrapping up the program while gradually reorienting its narrative compass away from the past and toward the future by episode's end. It thus fulfilled the producers' desire not only to memorialize the contributions of medical staff during the so-called Forgotten War (which, strictly speaking, lacked an official "end") but also to enact a series of narratively motivated farewells that might serve as a model for spectatorial relinquishment, literally *showing* the audience *how to let go.*

With the possible exception of the lengthy toast scene, in which the entire camp gathers together for a final party in the mess tent (featuring a series of spoken comments about the characters' future plans for their lives back in the States that might remind audiences of the tearful celebration that brings

---

4. According to the Associated Press, the penultimate episode was the last one shot, with production wrapping up for good on January 14, 1983 (Buck 1983).

the final wedding-themed episode of *Happy Days* ["Passages," May 8, 1984] to an end),[5] the true heart and soul of *M*A*S*H*'s finale can be found in its final minutes, maudlin though they might seem to some contemporary viewers. Indeed, when fans of the series think back to this episode, memories of the main characters' individual departures are what likely spring to mind. One by one, the gang disperses, first when a nearly deaf Father Mulcahy (who lost most of his hearing while trying to help a group of Chinese prisoners of war flee mortar fire) leaves for Sister Theresa's orphanage and then when Margaret expresses her feelings for Hawkeye through a prolonged kiss. Like B. J. earlier, who had struggled to express in words what he was feeling about his fellow chest cutter, the suddenly speechless head nurse finds a different way to say good-bye, through a physical action that, with the exception of a few episodes, would have been unthinkable seasons earlier, when she and the skirt-chasing Hawkeye remained combatively aligned against one another. Following Margaret's departure, Charles (who had given her his book of Elizabeth Barrett Browning poems and continues to grieve the loss of a group of Mozart-playing Chinese musicians, who have been killed) descends from his proverbial high horse and leaves the camp on a garbage truck driven by Staff Sergeant Luther Rizzo (G. W. Bailey). It is an incongruous means of transport for someone about to become head of thoracic surgery at Boston Mercy Hospital. Conversely, Colonel Sherman Potter (Harry Morgan) mounts an actual horse, Sophie, and receives a military salute from Hawkeye and B. J. before riding off into the sunset like a noble Western sheriff.

With only themselves to say good-bye to now, Hawkeye and B. J. share a tender moment of camaraderie in the closing minutes, the latter character finally making up for his earlier missed opportunity to do so. However, with spoken words once again failing to denote the immensity of emotions displayed on their faces, the two simply embrace. B. J. tells his friend that he has left him a "note" and then rumbles away on his freshly painted motorcycle. Hawkeye, the last major character to leave the camp, ascends into the sky via helicopter, casting his gaze down on the patch of earth that has been his "home" for the past three years and seeing the word *GOOD-BYE*

5. James H. Wittebols states that the final party scene "serves as a microcosm of the show—illustrating the different backgrounds of each person, expressing the affection the members of the 4077 have had for each other, hinting about where their lives will take them after the war and revealing how some of them have been changed by their experiences" (2003, 139).

spelled out in large stones. With the land of Korea serving as a metaphorical medium for his message (a stand-in for the pen and paper that failed him earlier), B. J. bids adieu to both Hawkeye and the televiewing audience, who by this point have gained an apprenticeship in the fine art of wishing farewell. This might be *M*A*S*H*'s most significant contribution to TV history, its rhetorical solicitation to an imagined community of viewers who in the closing minutes learn how to say good-bye to a much-loved series. Although the series was swiftly followed by a critically panned sequel, *AfterMASH* (CBS, 1983–85) and has been rerun endlessly thanks to off-network and cable syndication, it has never been able to reach the heights that it achieved on that February night in 1983, when the eyes of the nation were focused for a short time on a singularly unique finale. To quote Robert Pierpoint, the radio announcer who roughly thirty years earlier, on July 27, 1953, spread the good news of the cease-fire against an oddly reassuring sonic backdrop of silence: "There it is. . . . That's the sound of peace."

References

Alda, Alan, dir. [1983] 2008. "Goodbye, Farewell, and Amen." *M*A*S*H*, season 11, episode 16. Written by Alan Alda, Burt Metcalf, John Rappaport, Dan Wilcox, Thad Mumford, Elias Davis, David Pollock, and Karen Hall. Aired Feb. 28, 1983, CBS. On *M*A*S*H: Season 11 DVD Collector's Edition*. Beverly Hills, CA: 20th Century Fox Home Entertainment. DVD.

Bianculli, David. 2016. *The Platinum Age of Television: From "I Love Lucy" to "The Walking Dead."* New York: Doubleday.

Buck, Jerry. 1983. "Tears, Autographs, and Hugs during Final Day of *M*A*S*H* Filming." Associated Press, Jan. 15.

Metcalfe, Burt, dir. [1983] 2008. "As Time Goes By." *M*A*S*H*, season 11, episode 15. Written by Dan Wilcox and Thad Mumford. Aired Feb. 21, 1983, CBS. On *M*A*S*H: Season 11 DVD Collector's Edition*. Beverly Hills, CA: 20th Century Fox Home Entertainment. DVD.

Russo, Joe, dir. 2010. "Investigative Journalism." *Community*, season 1, episode 13. Written by Jon Pollack and Tim Hobert. Aired Jan. 14, NBC. Original broadcast.

Wittebols, James H. 2003. *Watching "M*A*S*H," Watching America: A Social History of the 1972–1983 Television Series.* Jefferson, NC: McFarland Press.

38

Moonlighting

"Lunar Eclipse"

KARIN BEELER

Moonlighting (1985–89), an innovative American dramedy that starred Bruce Willis and Cybill Shepherd as private detectives David Addison and Maddie Hayes in a love–hate relationship, captivated television viewers and the television industry. Winner of three Golden Globe awards for television drama and nominated for many other awards, *Moonlighting* was created by Glenn Gordon Caron, whose earlier success with a detective duo in *Remington Steele* (1982–87) paved the way for this series (Wilcox 1996, 26). With its leading funnyman and straight woman who thrive on animated conversations reminiscent of romantic and screwball comedy, *Moonlighting* represented a key turning point in the history of television programming. Not only did this "dramedy" highlight a male–female detective duo format in the rather offbeat, dysfunctional office setting of Blue Moon Investigations, but it also incorporated a number of innovative features, such as characters speaking in verse; postmodern, self-reflexive techniques; and dream sequences (Burkhead 2013, 75)—techniques that have been used by subsequent series, from telefantasy (*Buffy the Vampire Slayer* [1997–2003]) to situation comedy (*Malcolm in the Middle* [2000–6]) and office comedy (*Ugly Betty* [2006–10]).

The show's final episode, "Lunar Eclipse" (5.13), aired on May 14, 1989.[1] The story revolves around David's breakup with his girlfriend, Annie (Maddie's cousin) (Virginia Madsen), and the wedding preparations of Herbert Viola (Curtis Armstrong) and Agnes DiPesto (Allyce Beasley), the

---

1. All references to the series, including its finale, come from *Moonlighting* 2005, 2006a, 2006b, 2007.

242

sidekicks at the Blue Moon detective agency. The finale incorporates much of what made *Moonlighting* an example of experimental, "quality" television, including its hybrid form as a television dramedy consisting of serious, comic, detective, and postmodern elements. Innovative use of music, rhyme, and tense dialogue between Maddie and David, along with slapstick moments and breaking the fourth wall, are key characteristics of this episode and the series in general. Themes of love, deception, and marriage as well as sight gags punctuate the finale. The alternating moments of humor, conflict, and nostalgia that infuse this final episode are representative of the ambivalence that characterized not only the relationship between David and Maddie but also the relationship between the show's producers, television fans, and the television actors who played the main characters.

Moonlighting's success was based largely on the quirky yet captivating relationship between the leading characters, David Addison and Maddie Hayes. In her autobiography, Shepherd indicates that, partway through the script for the pilot, creator Glenn Gordon Caron "realized he was writing the character Maddie Hayes as Cybill Shepherd" (2000, 229). The actress had already established herself as a successful model and as an actress in films such as *The Last Picture Show* (Peter Bogdanovich, 1971) and *The Heartbreak Kid* (Elaine May, 1972). But Bruce Willis—now known for his huge box-office success in the *Die Hard* films, *Twelve Monkeys* (Terry Gilliam, 1995), *The Fifth Element* (Luc Besson, 1997), and *The Sixth Sense* (M. Night Shyamalan, 1999)—was a relatively unknown actor at the time. Caron's show centered around Maddie, a former model in financial straits who decides to run the detective agency that had previously served as a tax shelter for her, and this is where she meets David, her future employee-partner.

Moonlighting capitalized on the sexual tension between Maddie and David, who were engaged in an ongoing love–hate relationship. The "Will they or won't they?" (Thompson 1997, 112) question of when or whether these two characters were going to consummate their relationship (Thompson 1997, 115) became the single most important issue for the show as fans and the media eagerly anticipated this television event. More than 60 million viewers watched the long-awaited episode "I am Curious . . . Maddie" (Klauss 2003–4). However, not too long after the grand event took place in season 3, this sense of "closure" ironically became the explanation that fans and television critics offered for the show's demise. As the finale, "Lunar Eclipse" (5.13), suggests, though, another contributing factor to the fans' declining interest in the show could have been the loss of romance in the Maddie–David relationship. Fans and critics also claimed that *Moonlighting* "jumped the shark" through Maddie's sudden marriage to Walter Bishop, a stranger she meets on a train (Williams 1998, 98). Off-camera conflicts between the show's stars, challenging production schedules, strained relations between Shepherd and Caron, Shepherd's pregnancy (she gave birth to twins on October 6, 1987), and Caron's decision to leave the show after the end of the third season undoubtedly influenced *Moonlighting*'s ratings as well.

Moonlighting belongs to the period in television history that has been called television's "second Golden Age" (Thompson 1997, 12). By the 1980s, television had established itself as a familiar medium in the North American household. And so it is perhaps not surprising that shows such as *Moonlighting* and *St. Elsewhere* (1982–88), for example, began to take a more self-conscious look at the interesting "contract" between the medium and the savvy audiences who had become comfortable with a medium that had entered households in the 1950s. As Jane Feuer has pointed out, the conservative politics of US president Ronald Reagan (1981–89) were offset by artistic risk taking in television that had a "postmodern concern with images as images" (1995, 1).

"Lunar Eclipse," written by Ron Clark, is memorable because of the way the "artistic risk taking" infused the show with the genre hybridity (drama, romantic comedy, detective story) that was characteristic of the show's heyday. However, the finale also highlights how far *Moonlighting* had departed from its own television past. Most fans and critics agree that *Moonlighting*'s brightest hour occurred in the first three seasons. These seasons were under the creative control of creator and showrunner Caron, who indicates that he rewrote most of the first forty-four episodes.[2] Even though Caron was not part of the production team for the final episode, the finale tried to recapture some of the creativity, experimentation, and self-awareness that the series had demonstrated when he was part of the team. Jay Daniel, the finale's executive producer, had worked closely with Caron during the show's early years as coproducer and director and had remained involved during the show's last two seasons. Dennis Dugan, who directed "Lunar Eclipse," also has an acting role as a fictional producer called Cy, thus reinforcing *Moonlighting*'s self-conscious knowledge of itself as television.

"Lunar Eclipse," as the episode title suggests, is all about overlap and doubling and includes the plot device of deception. A significant part of the

2. Caron makes this claim in the DVD commentary on the season 3 episode "Atomic Shakespeare" (Caron 2006). See Hodgdon 1992 for further discussion of this episode.

plot involves David's romantic relationship with Maddie's married cousin Annie, thus reinforcing his image as a ladies' man. The marriage of Agnes and Herbert ("Bert") make up the other story line, while Maddie and David share most of their screen time near the end of the episode in scenes of postmodern uncertainty. The shift from union to chaos occurs during the interaction of various "couples." The Bert–Agnes and David–Annie story lines overlap when Bert is mistaken for David by the private detective that Annie's husband has hired to track down her lover. Much of the urgency in the early part of the episode is facilitated through the editing technique of cross-cutting as David, with Bert's help, tries to keep Annie away from her husband, who has just arrived in Los Angeles.

Parallel editing also allows the viewer to watch Agnes and Maddie holding a conversation about Agnes's wedding jitters in one room, while in another room David serves as confidant to Bert, who has had reservations about getting married ever since Agnes "popped the question." These gendered conversations are reminiscent of the exchanges Maddie and David sometimes had with Agnes and Bert in earlier episodes, but it is interesting that Maddie and David, rather than Agnes and Bert, are placed in the role of confidants. This is probably because the episode focuses more on the farcical relationship of this secondary couple than on the main characters, Maddie and David, who are no longer romantically involved. In fact, what is noticeably absent in the finale is any extended sequence with Maddie and David; the viewer sees the two characters together near the end of the episode and in a final musical montage, but much of the earlier sequences involve David and Annie or Bert and Agnes. The latter pair generate most of the comedy, and the fact that the New Age minister who presides over their wedding is played by 1960s guru Timothy Leary only enhances the quirkiness of this union between Bert, a junior detective, and Agnes, Blue Moon's rhyming receptionist.

The comedy clearly pervades the episode and even includes a parody of the detective genre to create the effect of postmodern bricolage. For example, a detective follows Bert as the latter accompanies Agnes into a lingerie shop. Allusions to the classic television series *Perry Mason* (1957–66) are also incorporated through the use of that series' famous theme song, but the seriousness of the music is juxtaposed to the image of the detective licking a giant lollipop while Bert anxiously holds onto women's lingerie and crashes into racks of undergarments. This parody of the detective element is a fitting tribute to Caron, who repeatedly incorporated detective genre features only to subvert them.

In addition to mixing genres, *Moonlighting* broke the fourth wall through "self-reflexive strategies" (Joyrich 1996, 109), or self-conscious references to the "constructed" nature of television. For example, in the finale of season 2, which stars Judd Nelson and Whoopi Goldberg, the set is dismantled much to these characters' bewilderment. The series finale evokes the existential angst of this earlier episode through the use of similar music as well as by once again dismantling the set and highlighting the imminent artistic "death" of the two leading characters (a network executive informs David that he and Maddie have been canceled). Their termination also affects the life of the supporting character Agnes, who loses the ability to rhyme, a quirky character trait that is one of *Moonlighting*'s signature features.

For much of the series' run, Cybill Shepherd and Bruce Willis carried the show, and even though the relationship of their characters faltered during the last two seasons, in the series finale Maddie and David briefly reunite to consider marriage in a church as part of a desperate attempt to avoid their fictional demise. A high-angle shot presents them in a vulnerable position and suggests a godlike presence looking down on them. With this shot, the view of the director and the view of the spectator are conflated, and the audience is made to feel complicit in the removal of the characters. (Ratings were, after all, one of the factors that hastened the cancellation of *Moonlighting*.) The show ends with television clips from previous episodes, and because these clips constitute the final images of Maddie and David, the viewer may be led to believe that Maddie and David have been subverted by the artistic medium that gave them life.

Yet even as the episode highlights the death of these characters, it never allows the spectator to forget how television also preserves the images of its fictional constructs, thus drawing the spectator back into a voyeuristic gaze at these characters. In other words, the finale appears to cast aside some of its cynicism by returning to a closed form that validates the nostalgia of times or episodes gone by. The last words between Maddie and David include Maddie saying she can't imagine not seeing him the next day. It is worth noting that David does not reply directly; rather, the camera shot provides an eye-line match, with David looking back at Maddie and Maddie in turn gazing in his direction, followed by a series of flashbacks from previous episodes accompanied by the nondiegetic music of Ray Charles and Betty Carter's duet "We'll Be Together Again." Thus, during its final moments, *Moonlighting* emphasizes the act of communication through an exchange of looks that reaffirms the visual element of this television scene. Furthermore, the words of the song speak for David and Maddie because their voices are not audible during the flashback montage. They have effectively been rendered silent. This silencing may also suggest that these characters are simply not able to return to the romance of the early years because they have "outgrown" one another; many viewers would probably have concurred because it was difficult to ignore the alienating effects of the final season's first episode, "A Womb with a View," and its bizarre presentation of Maddie's miscarriage, with a "baby David" cast as the fetus. One could argue that the "romance" of David and Maddie's relationship is perhaps best preserved through depictions of these characters in earlier episodes, as suggested in the short flashback montage at the end of the finale. Ultimately, their unique relationship is defined by romantic desire and deferral rather than by fulfillment. At the end of "Lunar Eclipse," the audience is informed through textual commentary that Blue Moon Investigations "ceased operations on May 14th, 1989," the finale's airdate. This sign of closure is, however, disrupted once more, perhaps as a way of expressing what Linda Hutcheon has called postmodernism's suspicion of final answers (1988, x). We are informed that the Anselmo case, a running gag about a case that the *Moonlighting* characters mention in several episodes, is never solved.

As a dramedy of the 1980s, *Moonlighting* made a distinctive contribution to the history of television by breaking the fourth wall and pushing the boundaries of the medium. As the show's finale, "Lunar Eclipse," demonstrates, *Moonlighting* was a detective show that was so much more than a detective show. It was experimental and creative for its time, even though it still used familiar forms or genres from television and film to entertain the viewers of the 1980s. In this sense, it fits Jason Mittell's notion of parody, which can "make fun of a genre" without being "subsumed by the parody" (2004, 160). In a *Rolling Stone* interview in February 1986, Caron called *Moonlighting* the television show that "*knows* a little bit that it's on TV" (quoted in Klauss and Hopkins 2003–4). However, although Caron's creation was a product of the 1980s, its self-consciousness and its hybridity have the potential to engage a whole new generation of viewers, who may be introduced to the series through DVDs, fan sites, and television studies courses.

References

Burkhead, Cynthia. 2013. *Dreams in American Television Narratives: From "Dallas" to "Buffy."* London: Bloomsbury.

Caron, Glenn Gordon. 2006. "Commentary on 'Atomic Shakespeare.'" *Moonlighting*, season 3, episode 7. Written by Ron Osborn and Jeff Reno. Directed by

Will Mackenzie. Aired Nov. 25, 1986, ABC. On *Moonlighting: Season Three*. Santa Monica, CA: Lions Gate Entertainment. DVD.

Feuer, Jane. 1995. *Seeing through the Eighties: Television and Reaganism*. Durham, NC: Duke Univ. Press.

Hodgdon, Barbara. 1992. "Katherina Bound; or, Play(K)ating the Strictures of Everyday Life." *PMLA* 107, no. 3: 538–53.

Hutcheon, Linda. 1988. *The Canadian Postmodern: A Study of Contemporary English-Canadian Fiction*. Toronto: Oxford Univ. Press.

Joyrich, Lynne. 1996. *Re-viewing Reception: Television, Gender, and Postmodern Culture*. Bloomington: Indiana Univ. Press.

Klauss, Cindy. 2003–4. "Act IV, Episode #86314: Maddie & David 'Do It.'" At http://www.davidandmaddie.com/doit.htm.

Klauss, Cindy, and Diane Hopkins. 2003–4. "*Moonlighting*: Glenn Gordon Caron." At http://www.davidandmaddie.com/ggcaron.htm.

Mittell, Jason. 2004. *Genre and Television: From Cop Shows to Cartoons in American Culture*. London: Routledge.

Moonlighting: Seasons One and Two. 2005. Santa Monica, CA: Lions Gate Entertainment. DVD.

Moonlighting: Season Three. 2006a. Santa Monica, CA: Lions Gate Entertainment. DVD.

Moonlighting: Season Four. 2006b. Santa Monica, CA: Lions Gate Entertainment. DVD.

Moonlighting: Season Five. 2007. Santa Monica, CA: Lions Gate Entertainment. DVD.

Shepherd, Cybill. 2000. *Cybill Disobedience*. New York: Avon Books/HarperCollins.

Thompson, Robert J. 1997. *Television's Second Golden Age: From "Hill Street Blues" to "ER."* New York: Continuum.

Wilcox, Rhonda V. 1996. "Dominant Female, Superior Male Control Schemata in *Lois and Clark*, *Moonlighting*, and *Remington Steele*." *Journal of Popular Film and Television* 24 (Spring): 26–33.

Williams, J. P. 1988. "The Mystique of *Moonlighting*: 'When You Care Enough to Watch the Very Best.'" *Journal of Popular Film and Television* 16, no. 3: 90–99.

39

Newhart

"The Last Newhart"

CYNTHIA BURKHEAD

MTM Enterprises concluded the 1980s with two of the most talked about finales in television history. On May 25, 1988, *St. Elsewhere* (1982–88) ended with a variation of the "it was all just a dream" trope, a narrative device sure to prompt either appreciation or anger from television audiences. On May 21, 1990, almost two years to the day after Tommy Westphall stared into his snow globe and Mimsie the cat flatlined, "The Last Newhart" (8.24), the finale of *Newhart* (1982–90) aired,[1] giving MTM and the 1980s not one but two of television's best oneiric finales. Whereas *St. Elsewhere*'s finale, "The Last One," produced its closure through a heavily intratextual narrative, "The Last Newhart" took full advantage of its already established playful intertextuality to produce what C. W. Marshall and Tiffany Potter call "one of the most sophisticated narrative gestures in a comedy" (2012, 192).

The episode setup for "The Last Newhart" provides no hints of the finale surprise. Indeed, the story leading to the last scene works to draw the audience's attention to a more conventional narrative ending, where all the series conflicts are resolved and viewers are left imagining a peaceful future for the main characters. Throughout *Newhart*, Dick Loudon, the big-city author turned small-town innkeeper, encounters one annoyance after the other, typically in the form of the townspeople and his own employees. These irritants are the basis for the deadpan jokes delivered by Bob Newhart, always the straight man, as Dick Loudon. The final episode travels five years into the future, when all the townspeople and Stratford Inn staff have left with their

---

1. All references to "The Last Newhart" come from Martin 1990.

payouts from the Japanese company that has built a golf resort in the never-named Vermont town—all except Dick Loudon. But the madcap group of townies and employees returns to the Stratford Inn for a visit, driving Dick to the edge. He yells, "You're all crazy!" and steps outside to escape their chaos. This moment so close to the thirty-minute mark suggests a permanent escape for Dick; after all, his antagonists will be leaving the inn, and he can settle in to the peaceful life for which he came to Vermont in the first place. This step outside the door is sure to lead to a happily-ever-after moment—except he is hit in the head with a golf ball.

Lights out. Cut to a familiar-looking bed in a familiar-looking Chicago apartment. Dick/Bob wakes up and nudges the lump in the bed next to him, who turns out to be Emily (Suzanne Pleshette), schoolteacher and wife of Dr. Robert "Bob" Hartley, the lead character in Bob Newhart's earlier sitcom, *The Bob Newhart Show* (1972–78). The laughs from the studio audience come as soon as Bob turns on the bedside lamp, and they see the trademark plaid bedding so famous that Suzanne Pleshette created her own line of linens around it. The laughs escalate once the actress appears from under the covers, and they continue to the credits.

This finale scene merits the surprise and laughter it elicits, but the surprise is mitigated somewhat by considering the groundwork *Newhart* began laying in season 1 for an ultimate crossover to *The Bob Newhart Show*. This happened in *Newhart* both through forging textual connections to other series and through bringing characters from and references to *The Bob Newhart Show* into the Vermont innkeeper's story. An example of general television intertextuality is found in the season 5 episode, "Much to Do without Muffin" (5.24) (Baldwin 1987), in which Michael (Peter Scolari) is watching *Gilligan's Island* (1964–67) with some Beaver Lodge members. When Michael asks them to leave before the episode is over, the character played by Russell Johnson, the Professor on *Gilligan's Island*, protests that he wants to stay and see how the episode ends. This type of narrative fun places *Newhart* in the larger family of television sitcoms, but, more importantly, it establishes *Newhart* as a program willing to create more intricate narratives than most situation comedies of the 1980s. Yet although these general story crossovers are amusing and cognitively challenging for viewers, it is the self-reflective intertextuality occurring in various internal and external narrative moments beginning early in *Newhart*'s run that lays the path to "The Last Newhart."

The first of these moments happens through an "inside joke" in the season 1 episode "No Tigers at the Circus" (1.6 [Mackenzie 1982]). After the

Stratford Inn is denied Historic Landmark status, a despondent Dick Loudon sits in his dark study watching television. Viewers see only the back of the TV, and Dick is wearing headphones, so we don't hear what he hears. His wife, Joanna (Mary Frann), comes in to rouse Dick out of his misery, and she removes his headphones. We then hear the title song to *The Bob Newhart Show*, which Dick refers to as his favorite program. This scene plays as a tip of the hat to Bob Newhart's loyal viewers but also serves as the foundation for the intricate narrative thread building to *Newhart*'s finale episode.

Development of this thread continues in the season 5 episode "Harris Ankles PIV for Web Post" (5.22 [Wyman 1987]). Dick and Michael are discussing television shows of the 1970s, and Michael mentions "that show with the shrink who stuttered." Dick quickly tells him the shrink didn't stutter; he "stammered." For a moment in this defensive response, we see not Dick Loudon the character, but Bob Newhart the comedian, who vocally attributed his success to the trademark stammer (Gostin 2005).

Another layer of this development occurs almost three years after "No Tigers at the Circus" aired, but it does not take place in the *Newhart* narrative. Instead, it is part of the deeply intertextual story of MTM's other hit, *St. Elsewhere*. In the *St. Elsewhere* episode "Close Encounters" (4.7 [Laneuville 1985]), *The Bob Newhart Show*'s obnoxious and highly neurotic character Elliot Carlin (Jack Riley), Dr. Bob Hartley's nemesis patient, ends up in the St. Eligius psychiatric ward displaying the same paranoid behaviors that made Carlin one of the most popular characters of *The Bob Newhart Show*. At this point, the crossing over of Mr. Carlin only connects the stories of *St. Elsewhere* and Bob Newhart's earlier comedy. But then the season 8 episode of *Newhart*, "Good Neighbor Sam" (8.14 [Shallat 1990]), makes another connection to Newhart's earlier sitcom. Bill Daily, who played Howard Borden, Emily and Bob Hartley's next-door neighbor on *The Bob Newhart Show*, guest stars as a guest at the inn who purchases the house next door.

Unlike most shows using intertextuality as a type of narrative shortcut to meaning, *Newhart* uses the technique in a much more incestuous manner. Most references aren't made to stories outside Bob Newhart's creative world; they are made to a specific sitcom separated from *Newhart* by only four years, a different supporting cast, and a different setting for a very similar comedic situation. Both Bob Hartley and Dick Loudon are frowning (and stammering) straight men playing to the comedy antics of their neighbors and coworkers. Both Emily Hartley and Joanna Loudon are level-headed working wives whose optimism functions to balance their husbands' cynicism.

There are enough changes in scenery and customs to make the Vermont countryside seem very unlike urban Chicago, but these differences are only surface alterations concealing parallel worlds. The connections *Newhart* makes to its ancestor story slowly pull the concealing fabric away until all is made clear in the final moments of the series.

Before that happens, however, *Newhart* offers the penultimate reference to its earlier self. Almost three years to the day after "Close Encounters" finds Mr. Carlin at St. Eligius Hospital in MTM's drama series, in the episode "I Married Dick" (7.4 [Shallat 1988]) of *Newhart* Dick Loudon agrees to attend couples' therapy with Joanna, who believes their marriage is getting stale. Interestingly, this same situation occurs in *The Bob Newhart Show* episode "I'm Okay, You're Okay, so What's Wrong?" (2.10 [Laneuville 1973]). In *Newhart*'s version, Dick and Joanna are in the counselor's waiting room, and a patient exits the doctor's office. The patient is unnamed, but he is played by Jack Riley. His belligerent conversation with Dick makes it clear the patient is Elliot Carlin. Dick comments on the patient's vague familiarity, and the patient answers, "I'd love to stay around and listen to you stutter, but I have a life to live . . . psycho." Confirming the audience's suspicions, the counselor asks Dick and Joanna to excuse the patient: "It's taken me years to undo the damage that was done to him by some quack in Chicago."

Again, fans of *The Bob Newhart Show* are the insiders for this joke, the audience being directly addressed, but they are also the viewers being prepared for what Jason Mittell labels a "trick ending" (2015, 234). After all, audiences unfamiliar with Bob Newhart's earlier program are surely left disoriented in the final moments of the *Newhart* finale. They may be familiar with Bob's description to Emily of the "crazy little town in Vermont" where "nothing made sense," but they have no context in which to place Suzanne Pleshette. They are familiar with the people Bob describes—"The maid was an heiress. Her husband talked in alliteration. The handyman kept missing the point of things. And then there were these three woodsmen, but only one of 'em talked"—but who is the woman he is talking to, the one making a television "curtain call," to use Mittell's expression (2015, 325), whom Bob suggests should wear sweaters more often? While the majority of viewers were celebrating the *Newhart* finale from their insider status, these others were left with more questions than answers, creating an experience much like the one felt by viewers of *The Sopranos* (1999–2007) finale.

Whether insiders or not, then, viewers are subject to the "narrative pyrotechnics" (Mittell 2006, 35) of the *Newhart* finale, an effect shaped largely by the narrative complexity established through the story's self-reflexive reminiscence of a parallel story world. It doesn't matter that the show's writers didn't imagine the ending, according to Newhart himself, until sometime during season 6, when his wife, Ginny, suggested ending the show with a dream sequence, telling him he should wake up next to Suzanne Pleshette (Stransky 2010). It doesn't matter that as late as 1988 *Newhart* producer Stephen Grossman claimed, "There are no real surprises on the show, nor should there be" (quoted in Mayerle 1989, 100). The entire eight-season run of *Newhart* is essentially rewritten in its final scene, so what really matters is how well "the most inconspicuous hit on television" (Pollan 1985, 66) handled those last minutes. By all accounts, *Newhart* handled them very well. In 2005, *TV Guide* and TV Land produced a "100 Most Unexpected TV Moments" countdown, and *Newhart*'s finale was selected to end it, establishing the show in the number 1 position ("*TV Guide* and TV Land" 2005). After twenty-six years, this finale is still one of the most remembered and celebrated moments in TV history. Not a bad legacy for a quiet little situation comedy (or two).

References

Baldwin, Peter, dir. 1987. "Much to Do without Muffin." 1987. *Newhart*, season 5, episode 24. Written by Norm Gunzenhauser, David Tyron King, and Tom Seeley. Aired Apr. 13, CBS. YouTube video, 21:58, posted July 25, 2012. At https://www.youtube.com/watch?v=od3UerdSMCU.

Gostin, Nicki. 2005. "The Stammering Standup." Interview of Bob Newhart. *Newsweek*, Apr. 14. At http://www.newsweek.com/stammering-stand-116585.

Laneuville, Eric, dir. 1973. "I'm Okay, You're Okay, so What's Wrong?" *The Bob Newhart Show*, season 2, episode 10. Written by Earl Barret. Aired Nov. 17, CBS. YouTube video, 20:29, posted November 16, 2016. At https://www.youtube.com/watch?v=iVM3WHG0WY0.

———, dir. 1985. "Close Encounters." *St. Elsewhere*, season 4, episode 7. Written by Norma Safford Vela, John Masius, and Tom Fontana. Aired Nov. 20, NBC. YouTube video, 54:41, posted November 4, 2016. At https://www.youtube.com/watch?v=Rz9lGRrc45Q.

Mackenzie, Will, dir. 1982. "No Tigers at the Circus." *Newhart*, season 1, episode 6. Written by Earl Pomerantz. Aired Nov. 29, CBS. YouTube video, 24:59, posted Mar. 31, 2012. At https://www.youtube.com/watch?v=13RkJ2UdKtA.

Marshall, C. W., and Tiffany Potter. 2012. "Thinking Inside the Box: A Short View of the Immorality and Profaneness of Television Studies." In *From Text to Txting: New Media in the Classroom*, edited by Paul Budra and Clint Burnham, 182–213. Bloomington: Indiana Univ. Press.

Martin, Dick, dir. 1990. "The Last Newhart." *Newhart*, season 8, episode 24. Written by Mark Egan, Mark Solomon, and Bob Bendetson. Aired May 21, CBS. YouTube video, 22:25, posted July 27, 2012. At https://www.youtube.com/watch?v=_l84cBsVtK4.

Mayerle, Judine. 1989. "The Most Inconspicuous Hit on Television." *Journal of Popular Film & Television* 17, no. 3: 100–112.

Mittell, Jason. 2006. "Narrative Complexity in Contemporary American Television." *Velvet Light Trap* 58:29–40.

———. 2015. *Complex TV: The Poetics of Contemporary Television Storytelling*. New York: New York Univ. Press.

Pollan, Michael. 1985. "Bob Newhart: Prime Time's Bland Eminence." *Channels of Communication* 5 (Sept. 3): 66–67.

Shallat, Lee, dir. 1988. "I Married Dick." *Newhart*, season 7, episode 4. Written by Shelley Zellman. Aired Nov. 21, CBS. YouTube video, 23:59, posted July 26, 2012. At https://www.youtube.com/watch?v=GekKDEpx-KA.

———, dir. 1990. "Good Neighbor Sam." *Newhart*, season 8, episode 14. Written by Nell Scovell. Aired Jan. 29, CBS. YouTube video, 22:24, posted July 27, 2012. At https://www.youtube.com/watch?v=adCH0DqlkcE.

Stransky, Tanner. 2010. "20 Years Ago: 'Newhart' Ends with a Shock." *Entertainment Weekly*, June 17. At http://ew.com/article/2010/06/17/20-years-ago-newhart-ends-with-a-shock/.

"*TV Guide* and TV Land Join Forces to Count Down the 100 Most Unexpected TV Moments." 2005. PR Newswire, Dec. 5. At http://www.prnewswire.com/news-releases/tv-guide-and-tv-land-join-forces-to-count-down-the-100-most-unexpected-tv-moments-55122557.html.

Wyman, Douglas, dir. 1987. "Harris Ankles PIV for Web Post." *Newhart*, season 5, episode 22. Written by Douglas Wyman. Aired Mar. 16, CBS. YouTube video, 21:58, posted July 25, 2012. At https://www.youtube.com/watch?v=zm0PirwtK00.

40

Nichols

"All in the Family"

DAVID BIANCULLI

Nichols was an offbeat Western that lasted only one season on NBC in 1971–72, but it was a very good one—and one with a very memorable finale. *Nichols* starred James Garner in a show that, in effect, was television's missing link between Garner's two NBC hits: his star-making turn as cowardly cowboy Bret Maverick in *Maverick* (1957–60) and his subsequent six-year run as private eye Jim Rockford in *The Rockford Files* (1974–80). As in those two long-cherished genre series, *Nichols* featured Garner as a man who, unlike many of his colleagues and adversaries, is averse to drawing his weapon and to violence in general.[1] Even as sheriff of the town that bears his name, Nichols carries out his duties without carrying a gun—until the final episode, when he borrows and handles a firearm only for a moment and for the very last time.

Garner's return to TV after leaving *Maverick* was created and produced by Frank R. Pierson, whose TV production credits range from the stylish Richard Boone Western *Have Gun—Will Travel* (1957–63) to such modern series as *Mad Men* (2007–15) and *The Good Wife* (2009–16). For the movies, Pierson wrote the screenplays for *Cat Ballou* (Elliot Silverstein, 1965), *Cool Hand Luke* (Stuart Rosenberg, 1967), and *Dog Day Afternoon* (Sidney Lumet, 1975)—all films about mavericks and rebels. In *Nichols*, Garner's title character (no first name is given) is introduced as an eighteen-year veteran of the US Army, serving in the Seventh Cavalry in Arizona in 1914, who gives notice and resigns after his commanding officer begins using a new type of weapon: a rapid-fire machine gun. Nichols returns to the small,

---

1. All references to the series come from *Nichols* 2013.

remote Arizona town founded by and named after his family, only to find that his mother is dead and her farm sold. Nichols stays on in Nichols, reluctantly accepting the vacant job of sheriff—but only after refusing to carry a gun. As in *Maverick*, Garner's laid-back protagonist in *Nichols* is more interested in poker and women than in showdowns at high noon.

"That's one of my favorites," Garner said about *Nichols* in an interview for the Archive of American Television in 1999. "I loved that series." Garner's costars included Stuart Margolin (who later would reteam with Garner by portraying Angel on *The Rockford Files*) as deputy Mitch Mitchell, Neva Patterson as the town matriarch known as "Ma," and Margot Kidder (before her star-making role as Lois Lane in the *Superman* movie [Richard Donner, 1978]) as sexy barmaid Ruth. Featured players included M. Emmet Walsh, John Beck, and a pre-*M*A*S*H* William Christopher. Behind the scenes, the *Nichols* team included executive producers Meta Rosenberg and writer Juanita Bartlett (both of whom would continue on to *Rockford*) as well as such directors as John Badham, Paul Bogart, Robert Butler, Ivan Dixon, and series creator Pierson. Throughout its first and only season, the less than conventionally heroic hero of *Nichols* would carry on a playful flirtation with Ruth, uphold the law when absolutely necessary, play a lot of card games at the local hotel or saloon, and saddle up to ride the dusty streets of the town named after him—not on a horse but on a Harley-Davidson motorcycle, which by that time had been in production for a decade.

"*Nichols* was anti-violence, pro–civil rights, and pro–women's rights," Garner observes proudly in *The Garner Files: A Memoir*. "The critics liked us," he adds, "and our ratings were better than a lot of shows that got picked up by the networks in those days. But the network canceled us anyway" (Garner and Winokur 2011, 192).

One reason for the cancellation was the unconventionality of its central character in the early 1970s. On TV, the Korean War army surgeon Hawkeye Pierce (Alan Alda) on the CBS series *M*A*S*H* (1972–83), a similarly peace-loving, conflict-avoiding hero, wouldn't appear until the following season, so Garner—even after pioneering the maverick, quite literally, in *Maverick*—was swimming against the established TV tide. Another reason was purely political. The year 1972, during which many installments of *Nichols* were presented, included the presidential campaign in which Richard M. Nixon ran for reelection against Democratic challenger George McGovern. Eight of the twenty-four episodes of *Nichols*, fully one-third, were pre-empted by political campaigns and coverage, so viewing patterns were all but impossible to establish. NBC instituted a name change for the series early on, pushing the show's star power by retitling it *James Garner as Nichols*, but that was all the help the network offered. Near the end of the season, Garner was informed that NBC was not planning to renew *Nichols* for a second season. Garner, who not only starred in the show and believed in it strongly but also coproduced it with Warner Bros. via his company Cherokee Productions, was furious.

"I was so angry and disappointed," Garner admits in his memoirs, "I decided to kill Nichols off in the last episode" (Garner and Winokur 2011, 192). In his Archive of American Television interview, Garner elaborated, "That was my idea. Because they'd canceled it. I said, 'Okay, I'll fix them. They want to cancel it? We'll just kill him'" (Garner 1999).

The last first-run episode of *Nichols* to be televised was in May 1972, but it was an out-of-sequence, previously pre-empted episode titled "Bertha," pulled off the shelf and presented by NBC months after *Nichols* had ended its narrative with what it intended as a very final sendoff. That finale episode, televised on March 14, 1972, was named "All in the Family," a nod to the TV season's most popular program, as well as a hint that this last episode of *Nichols* was about to introduce a new character: another member of the Nichols family. The episode itself was a *Nichols* family affair as well: Garner suggested the initial outrageous idea; series creator Pierson was credited with the story; and staff writer Juanita Bartlett wrote the teleplay. Along with director Jeremy Paul Kagan, they collaborated, or conspired, on a final *Nichols* that, in saying good-bye to its character and its place on the network schedule, was indeed a finale for the ages.

"All in the Family" begins with a familiar Western staple, the barroom brawl, where a tough town visitor named Quinn, played by guest star Anthony Zerbe, and his two menacing sidekicks are trashing the local saloon and several of its unfortunate patrons. Across the street, Nichols is at the town hotel, engaged in a game of poker and clearly on a winning streak. We see him win the next hand as well, but with a two-pair combination that, to anyone familiar with Western lore, doesn't bode well: the point is understated and presented almost subliminally, but the last hand Nichols draws is aces and eights, the same so-called dead man's hand held by Wild Bill Hickok just as he was shot and killed while playing poker in Deadwood (a pulled-from-history event eventually dramatized in HBO's series *Deadwood* [2004–6]). Nichols's deputy, Mitch, runs from saloon to poker game to warn Nichols of Quinn's massive misbehavior, and Nichols reluctantly but casually leaves his card game to stop the mischief, or what he says is only a temporary interruption. "You're under arrest," Nichols tells Quinn, who laughs at the idea of an unarmed sheriff. "You know I don't carry a gun," Nichols tells Quinn wearily but then, just to make things official, asks to borrow one from a bystander. The instant Nichols's hand makes contact with the gun, before he even gets a chance to grip it, Quinn fires his weapon with a shot so fierce it blows Nichols off his feet and lays him out on the dirt street, an event so unexpected that the townspeople just stand and stare. Deputy Mitch is the first to approach and lean over Nichols, who doesn't respond as Mitch examines him. "He's dead," Mitch tells the crowd and repeats himself three times. Then come the opening credits, promising James Garner as *Nichols*—even though, by that time, our hero is gone for good.

But there's another Nichols to come, which is part of the finale's twisted charm. No sooner do we return from the opening credits and commercial break than there's a new visitor to Nichols: the slain lawman's twin brother, Jim Nichols, who has come to town to pay respects and seek justice. This Nichols has a big droopy mustache and wears a black hat that's an obvious echo of the one worn by Garner as Bret Maverick on *Maverick*. "He may look like his brother," observes one townsperson, "but he's different." The residents of the town named Nichols warm to him immediately, offering him the job of sheriff and, in Ruth's case, her attentions and affections as well—all of which he turns down because he's so appalled that his brother's killer, Quinn, is still walking around as a free man. Everyone warns him against standing up to Quinn, but this new Nichols is determined and defiant. "I've got more chances than my brother had," he tells them coldly. "I know I'm alone."

Like his brother, though, this new Nichols is a pacifist, or at least reluctant to carry or draw a weapon. So when he confronts Quinn, he does so with logic (protecting himself by arguing that killing two different Nichols brothers surely would draw the attention of lawmen in nearby towns) and with a threat of socialized vengeance. "This town's gonna hang you," Nichols informs Quinn. "I'm just gonna wait." And wait is exactly what he does, until the town tires of ignoring and accepting the violent and bullying behavior of Quinn and his cronies. Nichols, without pinning on a sheriff's badge, eventually tells Quinn he's making a citizen's arrest, standing alone against the outlaw and his gang, and when Quinn laughs, the citizens of Nichols surround them, guns drawn, to stand with and defend their new champion. "This town just got its spine back," the matriarch announces after the gang has been vanquished and Quinn, rather than hung, has been incarcerated for trial. Once again, she offers Nichols the job of sheriff, and Ruth offers herself to him to sweeten the pot. Nichols kisses Ruth, but it's a good-bye kiss as he prepares to leave town for good. "Nothing here for me, Ma," he tells the matriarch, climbing onto his saddle and riding past the city limits.

Even here, though, *Nichols* has some final twists to hand out. The saddle on which Nichols climbs isn't on a horse but on his late brother's Harley, which he rides loudly and proudly out of town—past the Bank of Nichols, past the Nichols Cafe, and finally past a sign that says, "You are now leaving Nichols." The TV series ends with a freeze frame of that sign and its ultradefiant message to the NBC network. In the final episode of *Nichols*, James Garner and company not only killed the central character but introduced a twin brother and had the brother leave the town and the show at the end of the finale. Many accounts of the demise of *Nichols* have asserted that this last episode, with its introduction of a slightly more heroic twin brother, was Garner's way of hoping to appease the network and earn a second-season renewal, but Garner insists that wasn't the case. *Nichols* the TV series was dead, he says, so he figured he may as well go out with the character suffering the same fate—and then some. "You're gonna cancel it, we're gonna kill him," Garner said with a smile during his Archive of American Television interview (Garner 1999). And Garner had the power to make that happen, providing an essentially unhappy ending involving the dead hero's twin brother—in one final sweeping gesture saying good-bye for good to the character, the sibling, the town, and the series called *Nichols*.

Garner, assessing his approach to the *Nichols* finale and alluding to the famous Mel Brooks line, added for emphasis: "It's good to be the king" (Garner 1999).

References

Garner, James. 1999. "James Garner Interview Part 3 of 6—EMMY TV LEGENDS.ORG." Interviewed by Morrie Gelman. Archive of American Television, Mar. 17. At http://www.emmytvlegends.org/interviews/people/james-garner#.

Garner, James, and Jon Winokur. 2011. *The Garner Files: A Memoir*. New York: Simon & Schuster.

Nichols: The Complete Series. 2013. Burbank, CA: Warner Archive Collection. DVD.

41

Nurse Jackie

"I Say a Little Prayer"

JOANNE MORREALE

The medical dramedy *Nurse Jackie* aired on Showtime from 2009 to 2015. Although the show's ratings were acceptable but not outstanding for a pay cable program, it helped Showtime carve out its brand identity and compete with HBO as a source of prestige programming. During the course of its run, *Nurse Jackie* was nominated for twenty-three Primetime Emmy Awards. Edie Falco won the Emmy for Outstanding Lead Actress in a Comedy in 2010, and Merritt Wever won the award for Outstanding Supporting Actress in 2013. Notably, in her acceptance speech Falco proclaimed, "I'm not funny," a remark she later explained by telling the press that her performance was more dramatic than comedic. Indeed, although the show had light moments, its depiction of addiction and addiction's effects on personal and professional relations was not typical fare for comedy. For its first four seasons, the show was written and produced by Liz Brixius, Linda Wallem, and Evan Dunsky. Brixius and Wallem quit the show in 2012 when their relationship dissolved, and Clyde Phillips, known for his work as showrunner on *Dexter* (2006–13), ran the final three seasons and was responsible for the series finale.

Nurse Jackie was initially part of Showtime's signature lineup of half-hour shows that featured strong, complicated, deeply flawed women. Liz Brixius recounted the impetus for the show: "Guys' stories tend to be about conquests—getting the job, winning the Olympics, whatever. Women['s] stories aren't as immediately climactic so they need to play out over the course of three months. . . . And every medical show out there has been about doctors. Doctors are unable to do what they do without nurses. We want to tell those stories" (quoted in Kinon 2009). *Nurse Jackie* tells the story of Jackie Peyton, a dedicated, highly competent New York City emergency-room nurse who copes with the stresses of her job and her life by taking painkillers.[1] The series both begins and ends with Jackie on her back—in the opening scene of the pilot, Jackie has slipped and is on the floor; in a voiceover, she expresses her fear of the repercussions of her injury, "What do you call a nurse with a bad back? Unemployed." The opening lays out the premises and illustrates the show's visual style, where narrative realism is punctuated by fantasy sequences. There is a slow-motion close-up of pill capsules floating downward, while on the soundtrack k. d. lang sings the theme to *Valley of the Dolls*, a well-known book (Jacqueline Susann, 1966) and cult film (Mark Robson, 1967) about three young women in the entertainment industry who succumb to drug addiction. Jackie's voice then claims that she has control over her drug use, even as the cascading pills continue to fill the screen: "Sixteen grains, no more, no less. Just a little bump to get me through the day." But for seven seasons, Jackie's life spins further and further out of control as her drug dependency escalates. The show alternates between Jackie's complicated home and work life. At the beginning of the series, she is a married mother with two young daughters, while at work she claims to be unmarried and begins an affair with the hospital pharmacist, Eddie (Paul Schulze), who supplies her with drugs. In the first few seasons, she manages to keep her addiction and duplicitous behavior hidden, but her husband (Dominic Fumusa) eventually learns of her deceptions, and they divorce in season 4. By season 5, her coworkers are also aware that she has a problem, and she is caught lying to her most supportive allies. Every season ends with Jackie in a predicament from which it seems it will be impossible to extricate herself, and, though she always finds a way, the situations become more extreme as she spirals more deeply into addiction.

In a television landscape dominated by male antiheroes—most notably in Edie Falco's previous television vehicle, *The Sopranos* (1999–2007), and Phillips's previous show, *Dexter*—Nurse Jackie was the premiere female antihero. I use Margrethe Bruun Vaage's definition of the antihero as "a clearly—even severely—morally flawed main character whom the spectator is nonetheless encouraged to feel with, like, and root for." She adds, "The antihero series typically encourages sympathy for the antihero initially, but increasingly also questions this positive orientation with the antihero. So the spectator is intended to feel conflicted at the end of the antihero series"

1. All references to episodes of *Nurse Jackie*, including the finale, come from Brixius, Dunsky, and Wallem 2009–15.

(2016, 14). Like her male counterparts, Jackie is a complex character who operates according to a moral code, albeit self-defined, but is morally transgressive by any conventional standards. Jackie routinely lies, cheats, and steals, whether to assist patients she deems deserving or, more critically, to support her drug habit. The show's setting, the fictional All Saints Hospital in New York City, both sets up the show's religious themes and comments ironically on Jackie's character. For example, in the pilot episode, a new nurse, Zoey (Merritt Wever), who becomes Jackie's friend, protégé, and eventually supervisor, notices Jackie's dedication and tells her that she is a saint, a point visually underscored when Jackie kisses the forehead of one of her patients. As is typical in the antihero series, the episode works to elicit sympathy for Jackie despite her morally questionable behavior. Her bad back initially offers an excuse for her drug use, while her equanimity in the midst of multiple emergency-room crises demonstrates her skilled professionalism. In the course of the day, she becomes frustrated when a disengaged doctor dismisses her expertise, with the result that they lose the patient, a bike messenger who has been struck by a car. But at the same time, during the same episode, Jackie forges the bike messenger's signature onto an organ donor card and then steals money from a sadistic Libyan diplomat and gives it to the bike messenger's bereft girlfriend. She also flushes the diplomat's severed ear down the toilet so that it cannot be resutured. At the end of the pilot episode, she tells another bike messenger to be careful. When he responds by cursing at her, she slashes his tires.

The pilot sets the tone for the show's exploration of an antihero who is simultaneously moral and immoral. Jackie articulates the show's central tension when she quotes one of the nuns who taught her at school: "Those with the greatest capacity for good are the ones with the greatest capacity for evil"—and then adds, "Smart nun." Jackie is aware of her own contradictory nature, of the split between her public self—the honest, capable, caring nurse who is "good"—and her self-serving, deceptive inner self who operates according to her own moral code. At the end of the pilot episode, Eddie gives her drugs and tells her he loves her. "Love you too," she replies. Then there is an abrupt cut. Jackie slips on a wedding ring as she arrives home and is greeted by her husband and daughters, who are seen by viewers for the first time. In voiceover, Jackie repeats St. Augustine's famous line, "Make me good, God . . . but not yet," as she steps into the shadows. The final reveal, typical of the series' narrative structure as a whole, surprises viewers and challenges their sympathies—Jackie's previous actions have had some moral justification, but here her deception is entirely immoral. As Bruun Vaage writes in regard to the female-antihero series, "As the seasons progress our sympathy for the antihero is repeatedly put to the test, and the negative consequences for the antihero's family are emphasized" (2016, 192).

Throughout the series, Jackie struggles to be "good," though it is never clear to what extent she desires to be perceived as "good" just so that she can continue to indulge her habit. Like all addicts, she convinces those around her of her sincerity in wanting to get clean—she convinces her family, her lovers, her coworkers, and often even the show's viewers that she is in recovery. For example, after her addiction is discovered in season 4, she enters rehab and is drug free for the entirety of season 5, but in the last shot of that season's final episode, she celebrates her one-year anniversary by popping a pill. In season 6, she initiates an at-home detox, supported by her exlover, Eddie; her new lover, Frank; and her female AA sponsor. By the end of the season, Jackie has dispensed with her sponsor, ended her relationship with Frank, destroyed her relationship with her daughters and exhusband, and lost the trust of her coworkers. The season ends when Zoey, who had been one of Jackie's most loyal supporters, confides in their boss, Dr. Gloria Akalitus (Anna Deveare Smith), that she thinks Jackie is using drugs again. Akalitus demands that Jackie take a drug test, which prompts Jackie to flee in a car laden with drugs supplied by Eddie. But her "good" side prevails as she stops to help the victims of a car accident. When she attempts to leave, she crashes into an ambulance, which leads to the discovery of the drugs in her car. For the first time in the series, Jackie's behavior is criminalized, and the final season opens with her release from jail and impending court trial. As she awaits her trial, she is reinstated at All Saints only on the conditions that she have no contact with patients and submits to regular urine tests administered by Zoey, who is now her supervisor. Throughout the series, Zoey's relationship with Jackie has followed the same trajectory as the viewers'— from initial admiration in the pilot to friendship and respect and then to eventual disillusionment and feelings of betrayal. As Edie Falco commented, viewers' perceptions of Jackie changed over the years: "You start out rooting for her and then you understand why it gets harder to do so as her behavior gets more despicable" (quoted in Goldberg 2015).

Showtime renewed a seventh season of *Nurse Jackie* in March 2014 but announced that season 7 would be its last. Producers Clyde Phillips and Richie Jackson were thus able to plan both the season arc and final episode in a manner that brought the show to a conclusion. Series finales are always challenging endeavors, but even more so for shows that feature antiheroes—Should the antiheroes be punished for their misdeeds, or can they be redeemed? Shows that end ambiguously, as occurred most famously in *The Sopranos*, often incur the wrath of viewers, who desire the certitude of closure. Clyde Phillips, who said he would have ended his former series *Dexter* differently (see chapter 14), promised that *Nurse Jackie* would have an "authentic" ending that would leave viewers satisfied (Goldberg 2015).

The final episode, "I Say a Little Prayer," circles back to the pilot and reiterates the show's concern with the nature of good and evil while staying true to its portrayal of addiction. The episode begins with Jackie in the hospital chapel where her daughter is about to be confirmed. As in the pilot, she asks God to "make me good." Later in the episode, she even repeats her "saintly" behavior by washing the feet of one of her patients, who is bathed in light. Again, we see her under pressure, though this time it is not owing to the hectic pace of a hospital emergency room. Rather, her crisis is more existential: the hospital is closing; her old friend, Dr. Eleanor O'Hara (Eve Best), has returned to say good-bye but immediately spots that Jackie is using drugs again; her one ally at the hospital, Dr. Bernard Prince (Tony Shalhoub), is dying of a brain tumor; and Zoey turns down Jackie's offer to work together at Bellevue. Although both Jackie and Eddie were selling drugs to pay for her legal bills after her arrest the previous season, Eddie offers to take the rap alone and will go to prison. The staff have a final good-bye party before the hospital closes, but Jackie, who has only recently been reinstated as a nurse, is now a marginal member of the group that she had once anchored. She stands alone in the corner, apart from the celebration. Then there is a cut to the bathroom, and Jackie snorts a line from a bag of heroin that she has stolen from the drug-addicted patient whose feet she washed.

Everything moves in slow motion as Jackie leaves the bathroom. She removes her stethoscope, watch, and ID card and puts them on the counter—she is no longer "Nurse Jackie." She walks down the crowded New York City street amid an anonymous crowd. She wears only her scrubs, while the people around her are bundled in winter clothes. A boy with green hair runs by—he is the boy she met in rehab during season 4, who later died of a drug overdose. Another boy on a bicycle rides by, evoking the bike messenger who died in the pilot. Again we hear the theme song from *Valley of the Dolls*, with the line "gotta get off of this merry-go-round." Jackie walks through Times Square, where a group of people on mats are doing yoga. Jackie joins them as they adopt the "corpse" pose, while k. d. lang's voice belts out the song's refrain, "Is this a dream?"

There is an abrupt cut, and Jackie is on her back on the floor of the hospital. Presumably her trip through Times Square has been a dream. The series ends as it began, though this time Jackie has clearly lost the control she asserted in the opening scene. Zoey rushes to her side and seemingly answers Jackie's earlier prayer, "Let me be good," by reassuring her, "You're good Jackie, you're good." While Zoey's comment means to reassure Jackie that she is alive, it simultaneously works to define the character. Jackie's lips make a slight movement, but it is unclear whether she is responding to Zoey or dying. What is clear is that Nurse Jackie will be the final person treated at the hospital before it closes down. Clyde Phillips said that the producers originally planned an ending in which there is a fire in the hospital, and though it appears that Jackie has perished in the flames, in fact she escapes and is free to start over. But they decided on an ending that would stay true to the character and the nature of addiction, though it would be open to interpretation (Littleton 2015). Either way, the ending complicates what it means to root for the antihero—either she dies, or she once again loses everything. Redemption—represented by Jackie's plea to "let me be good"— can happen only once Jackie gets off of the metaphorical merry-go-round. The cycle—of the show and of Jackie's life—is broken.

References

Brixius, Liz, Evan Dunsky, and Linda Wallem, creators. 2009–15. *Nurse Jackie*. Aired June 8, 2009, to June 28, 2015, Showtime. Showtime On Demand. Accessed Sept. 2015.

Bruun Vaage, Margrethe. 2016. *The Antihero in American Television*. New York: Routledge.

Goldberg, Lesley. 2015. "*Nurse Jackie* Final Episode Will Have 'Authentic' Ending—Plus Watch the Trailer." *Hollywood Reporter*, Jan. 12. At http://www.hollywoodreporter.com/live-feed/nurse-jackie-final-season-will-763157.

Kinon, Cristina. 2009. "*Nurse Jackie* Star Edie Falco, Mary-Louise Parker, More Strong Women Lift Showtime." *New York Daily News*, Feb. 15. At http://www.nydailynews.com/entertainment/tv-movies/real-life-nurses-pull-plug-jackie-article-1.376199.

Littleton, Cynthia. 2015. "'Nurse Jackie' Finale: Showrunner Reveals Alternate Ending for Edie Falco Series." *Variety*, June 28. At http://variety.com/2015/tv/news/nurse-jackie-finale-edie-falco-alternate-ending-1201530273/.

42

The Office (UK)

"Christmas Special, Parts 1 and 2"

ASOKAN NIRMALARAJAH

In 2003, at a DVD recording of his stand-up special *Animals*, Ricky Gervais paused during a parodic recital of the Bible to muse, "Chapter 3: his difficult third [season]. . . . He's gonna get criticized whatever, innit? After all the good he did in one and two. He should just leave it there" (Brigstocke 2003, with ellipses indicating a pause). The witty aside struck a chord with a British audience eagerly anticipating another season[1] of the comic's claim to fame, the cult BBC Two sitcom *The Office* (2001–3).[2] But coming off the surprise success of the first two seasons, Gervais and cocreator Stephen Merchant decided to put an end to the show and opted for a two-part finale. Airing on two consecutive nights in late 2003 on BBC One, "Christmas Special" wrapped up the show's story lines and thus preempted a possibly "difficult third season." It also serves as a textbook example of the kind of artistic control a show's creator demands over his "creation," particularly over its ending (as implicit in Gervais's sly equation of himself to God). But, despite the series' critical acclaim and several awards, *The Office* finale also drew criticism for concluding a bleak, open-ended serial narrative with a rather neat, "cinematic" happy ending. Critics wondered how a show that delighted in comically stressing the tedium of everyday office life and that once chose to leave its sad-faced, self-delusional characters in a state of personal and professional limbo could close with such a redemptive coda.[3]

1. To minimize confusion, I use the American term *season* throughout instead of the British term *series*.

2. All references to episodes of *The Office* come from *The Office: Special Edition* 2011.

3. Travis Hoover, one of the more critical voices, argues that the finale "forces a closure that violates everything the series stood for" and that "its movement towards climactic

In his study *The End: Narration and Closure in the Cinema* (1995), Richard Neupert notes that the end of a film "allows for, or even demands, the viewer's reconsideration of prior motifs or events" (31). The "cinematic" closure to *The Office*, then, could be read in two ways: either as a superfluous, tacked-on ending to a serial narrative that relies on the inspired repetition of stock sitcom situations and has already closed on a fitting note of emotional despair for its characters or, as suggested by Emma Tinker, "as a framing device" that "radically problematize[s]" the show's docusoap form (2009, 765), retrospectively rewriting the previous two seasons as part of a larger, conventionally "filmic" three-act structure. Hence, the difficulty Gervais spoke of in his stand-up derives from the notion that as a fairly classical narrative with a beginning, middle, and end, *The Office* had no room left for a third season. If the first season established the characters and their environment in a state of equilibrium, and the second introduced internal changes and new characters who challenged the status quo, then the finale could only resolve the conflicts and stage a return to equilibrium.

In the fictional universe of the sitcom, this last act takes the form of a follow-up special to the earlier fly-on-the-wall TV docusoap about the daily grind at the Slough branch of paper merchant Wernham-Hogg, catching up with its cast not only three years *down* but also three years *on* the road. The first shot of the finale departs from a basic convention of *The Office* by showing one of its protagonists, former regional manager David Brent (Gervais), driving instead of sitting behind his desk. Over this shot, we hear Brent's criticism of the original BBC docusoap program as a "stitch-up" that made him out to be a "plonker" (British slang for "fool"). The conceit of turning the finale into a reunion show for a fictional reality program thus adds the self-reflexive novelty of reencountering characters who have viewed earlier episodes of the reality program. Accordingly, the finale starts with Brent relating derogatory comments made by strangers regarding his awkward behavior on the program and sales clerk Tim Canterbury (Martin Freeman) dryly recalling the discomfiture of having to reexperience his unfulfilled yearning for worker Dawn Tinsley (Lucy Davis) on national television.

---

release is incongruous after the two years of droning sameness that went on—hilariously—with no end in sight" (2003). And on the *British Comedy Guide* website, amid the usual praise for the show, the ending is criticized as being "sickly-sweet" and the comedy as being not "quite as sharp" as before ("*The Office*" 2010).

Continuing on from major events of the season 2 finale, "Christmas Special" features at its center both Brent's and Tim's failed aspirations for recognition and love, switching between Brent's humiliating life as a minor TV celebrity after his redundancy and the unresolved romantic tensions between Tim and former receptionist Dawn following her departure to the United States with her fiancé, Lee. These emotionally resonant, soapish story lines, however, become apparent only gradually in the first two seasons, for *The Office*, as a show about the boredom of work, initially relied on a "sitcom formula based on familiarity, repetition, and unchanging characters and locations" (Morreale 2000, 111), if taking the conventions to imaginative extremes. The story arc of the first season, for example, deals with the threat of downsizing, introduced in the pilot episode and resolved in the finale. The episodes in between, however, are fairly self-contained and relate only marginally to the main plot. Like the episodes of the second season, they rely instead on quirky characters engaging in schoolyard behavior, socially awkward situations, and minor events such as management classes, appraisals, fire drills, birthday parties, quizzes, charities, and so on—all of which are set indoors with everyone wearing business suits. The episodes also often end abruptly and feature a short scene during the credits as a comic afterthought, suggesting that life goes on despite any cut to black.

Without a laugh track and shot in a mockumentary style featuring talking-heads commentary by the principals, *The Office* was initially perceived as a parody of popular BBC workplace docusoaps such as *Airport* (1996–2008), *A Life of Grime* (1999–2004), and *Traffic Cops* (2003–). But the show does not spoof the genre. It uses it for comic and melodramatic storytelling. The two-camera crew is constantly engaged in constructing little soapish narratives around its "real-life" characters, snatching moments of privacy through frames (doors, windows, blinds) and past office stock or bodies blocking the view. These visuals, enhanced by a muted color palette, conjure a stifling atmosphere of entrapment.[4] But the "prisoners" are not

---

4. The eponymous office is very much a prison the viewer visits every time the show's tired, melancholy theme song "Handbags and Gladrags" starts over the opening credits sequence. This opening's short survey of Slough—as the camera recedes slowly right to left, over the vertical, horizontal lines of gray, drab high-rise offices and parking garages, moves on to a roundabout during morning traffic, and eventually settles on the facade of the office building—is a rare glimpse of the outside world. The show takes place entirely within the enclosure of an office that sustains itself by making, selling, and using paper. It therefore "becomes less a workplace than a living environment characterized by an odd circularity

just trapped by the nondescript office microcosm, the drab surroundings of Slough, their clothes (see Brent's bland suit, shirt, tie, goatee, and slumped posture), and the camera frame. They are also stunted personalities with little backstory and no future. Tim is singled out to be the audience surrogate whose laid-back self-deprecation masks a need for connection and an inability to move on. He may be one of the few to possess some self-awareness and is, according to Merchant, therefore "the one who's trapped in hell" (Gervais and Merchant 2010). But his cynical remarks also make him a smug commentator on his own life. While Brent and his assistant, Gareth Keenan (Mackenzie Crook), pursue their imaginary selves as an entertainer and a soldier within the office, most employees are bored individuals clinging to steady jobs and mourning their "pipe dreams" (Brent) as musicians (Keith [Ewen MacIntosh]), illustrators (Dawn), or academics (Tim). Both the first and second seasons move toward a moment of escape from the office/prison for some, if only to have them end up staying because of personal fears, rejection, and better payment, choosing to "move up," "grow up," and "just leave the dice alone" (Tim).

The final episodes find Tim still fastened to his desk, playing pranks on former desk neighbor Gareth and enduring the self-centered talk of a new coworker, an obnoxious pregnant woman. During one of her monologues about the insufferably confining finance department she left, the camera zooms in on his weary face, trapping it in the frame and asking us to read the desperation written on it. This is one of many overt instances in the finale when the manipulation on the part of the documentary crew becomes noticeable. Through deliberate misdirections, a montage that links Tim and Dawn repeatedly in a single narrative thread, the interviewer's voice being heard for the first time, and the manipulation of crucial plot turns (such as paying for Dawn's Christmas trip to Slough), the presence of the filming crew is felt more keenly. Dawn's return, something that Tim both dreads and desires, also prompts the question whether we have misread her previous behavior as much as Tim has; in earlier episodes, he was conflicted about confronting her solely on the assumption that their feelings are mutual. Both characters deny it, but their relationship has all the hallmarks of a classic Victorian melodrama (see Merchant 2004). Building romantic tension with awkward touches, meaningful silences, and the framing of

---

because consumption and production, the means and the purpose for its existence, literally cancel each other out" (Tinker 2009, 759).

Tim and Dawn together, the show creates both hindrances and avenues for their love. Although Tim is no match for her virile fiancé, Lee, their coworker Gareth is used as a copula figure they mock to enjoy each other's company guilt free.

Meanwhile, Brent seems to have fulfilled his character destiny and become an unsuccessful and lonely traveling salesman, regularly returning to his former workplace in a desperate need for acceptance. Everyone is introduced as a certain type in the pilot, and Dawn singles Brent out as a "wanker" and "a sad little man." He lives down to the first insult during the first season by eventually agreeing to downsize his branch to net himself a promotion. But the second season turns him into a British take on Willy Loman of *Death of a Salesman*, who yearns for respect yet lacks the intellectual means and social graces to merit it. A frequent situation of the first season has Brent reacting to the arrival of a new character: from recruits (Ricky, Donna, and Karen), whom he delights in showing around the office, to an outside facilitator he demoralizes during staff training and his obnoxious friend Chris Finch (Ralph Ineson), whom he openly admires. As a fairly conventional sitcom, then, *The Office*'s "narrative structure was based on an inside/outside dichotomy. The disruptions that provided the motor for individual plots came mainly from intrusions from the 'outside,' intrusions that were rejected" (Morreale 2000, 112). The second season, however, introduces intrusions that cannot be rejected. When Slough incorporates another branch from Swindon, new regulars join the office, confronting the existing ones with better versions of their personae. Hence, Brent feels overshadowed by his more competent, attractive, and well-liked superior, Neil Godwin (Patrick Baladi), and Dawn is temporarily replaced in Tim's affections by the more vivacious Rachel (Stacey Roca). In short, the sitcom becomes, in Gervais's words, "a soap with laughs" (Gervais and Merchant 2010).

The first part of "Christmas Special" ends with both Tim and Brent at their lowest in their respective fates, effectively setting up the unexpected redemption at the end of the finale. After trying to impress both Neil and Finch with a blind date he brings to the office Christmas party, Brent undergoes a change in attitude by finally telling his role model Finch to "fuck off" after Finch insults Brent's date. Meanwhile, Tim muses that he does not believe in happy endings, only to experience one when he is saved from his fate as a lonely office clerk by Dawn's surprise return and admission of love. Both endings are fairly stock ones for a television show, yet, given the amount of pain and suffering that preceded them, these last-minute reversals feel somehow "earned." These satisfying cinematic closures for an open-ended serial narrative could be described as happy and quite organic endings, for they conform to certain "canons of construction" (Bordwell 1982, 2)—that is, to the sentimental tales of redemption Gervais and Merchant set out to tell. As a generic hybrid between a workplace sitcom and an ongoing-relationship drama, *The Office* always had two possible avenues it could take: either to extend the narrative indefinitely, as many of its foreign adaptations did, in particular the popular American one that ran for nine seasons (2005–13), or limit itself to two seasons of six half-hour episodes each and two forty-five-minute specials—a narrative brevity typical for British shows, from sitcoms such as *Fawlty Towers* (1975–79), *Blackadder* (1982–83), and *Spaced* (1999–2001) to crime dramas such as *Life on Mars* (2006–7). If the ending to the second season implied that nothing would ever change for these characters imprisoned by their work and their personae, the finale imparts the hope that there may still be a better life outside of the new melodramatic space of *The Office*.[5]

References

Bordwell, David. 1982. "Happily Ever After, Part Two." *Velvet Light Trap* 19:2–7.

Brigstocke, Dominic, dir. 2003. *Ricky Gervais Live: Animals*. Written by Ricky Gervais. Universal City, CA: Universal Pictures. DVD.

Gervais, Ricky, and Stephen Merchant. 2010. Interviewed by Bruce Dessau. *BFI*, July 24. At http://www.bfi.org.uk/features/interviews/gervaismerchant.htm.

Hoover, Travis. 2003. Review of *The Office Special*. *FilmFreakCentral*, Dec. 23. At http://filmfreakcentral.net/dvdreviews/officespecial.htm.

Merchant, Stephen. 2004. Interview on *The Office: Closed for Business*. Supplementary documentary. London: BBC.

5. In 2013, Ricky Gervais revisited the character David Brent in the short *The Return of Brent*, a ten-minute film produced for charity and released on Red Nose Day, March 15, on BBC One. It chronicles Brent's futile and hilariously misguided attempts to break into the music business with the song "Equality Street" and its accompanying music video, including a rap part performed by Doc Brown. Brent's musical ambitions were also the subject of a YouTube web series, "Learn Guitar with David Brent," and eventually a motion picture, *David Brent: Life on the Road* (Ricky Gervais, 2016). All of these titles do not figure as a continuation of *The Office* as much as an extension of the media presence of the comic persona of David Brent. Hence, the motion picture imitates none of the show's narrative dynamics and focuses on mockumentary humor derived from the awkward relationship between the musician Brent and his documentary crew, recalling Gervais's great inspiration for *The Office*: *This Is Spinal Tap* (Rob Reiner, 1984).

Morreale, Joanne. 2000. "Sitcoms Say Goodbye: The Cultural Spectacle of *Seinfeld*'s Last Episode." *Journal of Popular Film and Television* 28, no. 3: 108–15.

Neupert, Richard. 1995. *The End: Narration and Closure in the Cinema*. Detroit: Wayne State Univ. Press.

"The Office." 2010. *British Comedy Guide*, June 20. At http://www.sitcom.co.uk/the_office/about.shtml.

The Office: Closed for Business. 2004. Supplementary documentary. London: BBC.

The Office: Special Edition. 2011. London: BBC. DVD.

Tinker, Emma. 2009. "Talking Cookie Jars and Tongue-Tied Bodies: Posthumanism and *The Office*." *Journal of Popular Culture* 42, no. 4: 756–72.

43

The Office (US)

"Finale"

J. JEREMY WISNEWSKI

Take a paper company, three–four romances, a couple of incompetent bosses, a documentary. Combine ingredients with a helping of comedy and great writing. Bake for two years if trying the dry-but-delicious UK version; bake for nine if you're interested in the high-fat American version. That's how you make *The Office*.

If *The Office* is a meal, the finale must be the dessert.

If you haven't tasted the end of the US version of *The Office*, you'll be pleased to know that, much like the show it concludes, it manages to surprise us even while trafficking in some well-worn tropes (love triangles, rivalries, paper sales). In fact, the show's *finale* (or dessert, if you haven't tired of the metaphor) manages to stretch out over several episodes, oxymoronic as that may sound. The result is a delight both fitting the show's many story arcs and making a rather delicious point: the finale isn't actually *final*. Even after dessert, you'll eat again.

But enough with the food metaphors. We're talking about a laugh-track-less sitcom purporting to be a documentary; we're talking about paper and paper people. You'll recall the origin of the show: Ricky Gervais brought us David Brent, the brutally inappropriate regional manager of Wernham-Hogg Paper Company, based out of Slough, England. We had two marvelous seasons (2001–3) of funny yet difficult-to-watch British wit.

And then the show migrated to the United States. The US version stumbled a bit those first few episodes—which were near exact copies of the British original—but eventually it found its stride, and it kept walking for nearly a decade. Along the way, stories came and went: Jim (John Krasinski) and Pam (Jenna Fischer) sort out their love lives amid stacks of A4 double-bond, all the while working for a good-natured but incompetent boss, Michael

Scott (Steve Carell), and with coworker Dwight K. Schrute (Rainn Wilson), who is as bizarre as they come in the Schrute family, and that's saying something. The rest of the office crew presents a case study of characters: from the accountants to human resources, from the interns to upper management, we watch lives lived out in documentary form.

The Office made a premise of breaking the fourth wall—a show knowing it has an audience. We watch footage for a documentary made about life at a midsize American paper company. The characters talk directly to the documentary makers, who peek into the private and professional lives of the employees at Dunder-Mifflin. How do you end a show that purports to be a documentary about real life and its drudgery? It isn't by asking rhetorical questions, clearly. It's by having the characters watch the show they've been making. The finale finds our beloved characters one year later, reflecting on what they have seen when the documentary, secret footage and all, finally airs.[1]

Each of the last episodes—the antepenultimate, penultimate, and ultimate—is twice as a long as a normal episode, and each winds up a major story line while priming us for the end: the airing of the documentary and the filming of the subsequent DVD bonus material. Each episode *feels* as if it concludes something (which it does), providing the normal satisfaction of narrative closure, wrapping things up for the viewer (unlike the last episode of, say, The Sopranos [1999–2007]). In the literal finale, when the office has an open forum about the documentary they are in, story lines close up like liquor stores in a newly dry county and sometimes at a comic pace. As we gets hints of what's to come in the finale through promotional advertisements for the debut of the documentary during the show, we find love triangles settled (Angela [Angela Kinsey] marries Dwight), crises resolved (Jim and Pam decide to leave Scranton for Philly), and people moving on (Stanley [Leslie David Baker] retires; Kevin [Brian Baumgartner] gets fired; Andy Bernard [Ed Helms] pursues his luck in entertainment; Toby [Paul Lieberstein] moves to New York; Erin [Ellie Kemper] finds her biological mom, then her dad). The characters are invited to reflect on the ending that they, as characters, have created and even to answer questions about their lives in an open panel discussion. The DVD needs bonus features, after all!

Self-aware characters ponder the end of their stories, their own self-deception, and their past mistakes. But they do it with bittersweet smiles. *The*

---

1. All references to "Finale" are from Kwapis 2013.

Office finale may sound like Kafka or Dostoevsky watching the Kings of Comedy stand-up tour, but it is, I think, more interesting than that.

The Office extended finale is an homage to the ability to intertwine the interesting and the mundane—something that may well be the central requirement of a happy life. Even as all the characters know their story is ending (when the documentary airs), the structure of the end of the series reveals that endings are commonplace (double-length finale-like episodes, one after the other, closing up loopholes and suggesting resolutions) and that they even entail new beginnings. In this respect, the show's end confirms something I have thought for a while: endings, by their very nature, are *suspicious*. The world keeps going, after all.

As the show builds to its end, the staff on the documentary are horrified that they have been filmed partially in secret, acknowledging that they have done things in the show that no one would do if he knew he were being watched (except, of course, beet farmer and [spoiler!] eventual Dunder-Mifflin manager Dwight K. Shrute). The finale makes us think about that abyss between who we are and who we pretend to be. This theme anchored the show over the years as it drifted into new territory, new cast members, new plotlines. Michael Scott, regional manager, begins the decade-long journey sure that he is loved by his employees, sure that he is the greatest boss ever—a feat accomplished only through chronic self-deception. Just outside his office door, we find Jim and Pam, stupidly in love from the get-go but unable to see the nature of their own feelings for each other. For, like, years.

The show made concessions to believability, as we all must. The series wrapped up the main Jim-and-Pam story line seasons before the final one but replaced its intrigues with new ones: Dwight and Angela, Andy and Erin, Oscar [Oscar Nuñez] and the senator. In the end, we see Erin, the new receptionist, dating a new salesman, Pete (a.k.a "Plop" [Jack Lacy]) just as Jim and Pam decide at long last to leave the paper company where they met and lazily wooed each other over several seasons.

And that's what we see in the finale: it is over, and yet it isn't. Jim and Pam move on, but a new budding relationship plays out the same tropes. Michael Scott is long gone—seasons gone—but another quirky manager emerges, along with another assistant to the regional manager. Everyone is different, but everything's the same—a kind of archetypal eternal return, to shamelessly twist an idea from Nietzsche (from the Stoics, really). In the finale, we see that intimate link between repetition and difference: the relationships and tensions of the office are *essential to it*—once one issue is solved, another will take its place; once one tension is relieved, another will emerge.

Daily life really is like that, and perhaps that is the true genius of *The Office* finale. It purports to be a faux documentary of daily life, one that shows us drudgeries and trials with a close look at one venue. Despite the fact that we all know it's fiction, it delivers what it promises: an accurate picture of much of work life, which is to say much of daily life. No matter what successes we have or what goals we achieve, there will always be more obstacles. And there will always be difficult people. No matter who occupies particular social and professional roles, certain tensions will emerge and irritate us. The finale shows us our fate, as a society and as persons. It shows us what Camus told us so long ago: we are like Sisyphus and his rock—condemned to repeat the same pattern of action again and again, with no end in sight.

But the note *The Office* ends on is not a sour one. After all, even though the same scripts will be acted out again and again all over the world—office romance, incompetent boss, irritating coworker—we still find Jim and Pam happy. Hell, even Michael Scott and Dwight wind up happy. Here, perhaps, is not so much the wistful dream of the happy ending but rather a little piece of hope in the sometimes barren landscape of professional life. We have to go through the drudgery—we have to push the rock, sell the paper—but we might find someone who'll do it with us, who'll keep us company. Classic stuff, truly.

Admittedly, the self-reflection occasioned by the finale—by the characters seeing the very show we viewers have been watching—isn't some kind of cure-all to their bad habits or self-deception. Most of them are no wiser. But perhaps *we* are a little wiser, viewers and documentarians of our own lives, getting entertained on our couches while we watch fictional people sell fictional paper and perhaps now seeing our own lives play out before us.

And if no self-reflection is to be had, laughter will at least be a soothing substitute.

References

Kwapis, Ken, dir. 2013. "Finale." *The Office*, season 9, episode 23. Written by Greg Daniels. Aired May 16, NBC. Netflix. Accessed June–July 2016.

44

Oz

"Exeunt Omnes"

BILL YOUSMAN

In 1997, the US prison and jail population had reached a previously unimagined high of 1.7 million people, an increase of more than 5 percent from the previous year. Every week 1,177 new prisoners were being added to federal and state institutions (Gilliard and Beck 1998). The United States was in the midst of a decades-long boom in incarceration that would make it the number one nation on the planet with respect to incarcerating its own people (Lee 2015). Furthermore, most of those sentenced to prison were people of color, with the prison population explosion disproportionately affecting black and Latino communities that were heavily policed but poorly represented in court (Alexander 2012).

The year 1997 was also the year that *Oz* (1997–2003) debuted on HBO. Set inside a fictional maximum-security prison, the series quickly became a signature program for HBO, running for six seasons. *Oz* still has the distinction of being one of a small number of dramatic programs that feature characters *after* they have been imprisoned. Despite television's obsession with law and order, *Oz* represents something unique, a program in which the crimes that the characters committed are merely background, and the main focus is on their lives after they have arrived at the fictional Oswald State Penitentiary.

Debuting at a politically and culturally critical moment in US history, *Oz* was not only reflective of larger trends in American society, particularly in terms of social responses to crime and issues of justice and race, but also representative of a transformation that was under way in the television industry.

Appearing in 1972, HBO was the first pay-television service to emerge with the advent of cable. During its formative years, HBO featured mostly second-run films and live sporting events. In the 1980s, it began producing original films and television programs, in particular shows aimed at children. Beginning in the 1990s, however, it expanded its original programming, and *Oz* became its first hour-long dramatic series in 1997, arguably kicking off a new era in risky and innovative television aimed at adult audiences (DeFino 2014, 201). Kim Akass and Janet McCabe explain that HBO deliberately marketed itself as a different type of network. Within this context, we can see that early programs such as *Oz* played a key role in allowing HBO to brand itself as the television home of quality, innovation, and artistry: "Latitude to tell stories differently, creative personnel given the autonomy to work with minimal interference and without having to compromise, has [*sic*] become the trademark of HBO—how they endlessly speak about and sell themselves, how the media talks about them and how their customers have come to understand what they are paying for" (2007, 297).

Oz exemplified HBO's strategy of offering controversial content that advertiser-funded television couldn't risk owing to concerns about alienating viewers or the companies that try to reach them. Programs like *Oz* that featured profanity, nudity, explicit sex, violence, and other adult content were thought to be attractive to subscribers because they offered material not available on broadcast television. In addition, during the 1990s HBO built up a reputation among television critics for quality programs that pushed the boundaries of conventional television artistically. *Oz* was thus one of a series of programs that established HBO as a serious player in the field of original television production. As Catherine Johnson puts it,

> The most commented upon aspect of HBO's shift towards constructing its brand as the home of quality television was its development of prestige original dramas. . . . Series such as *The Sopranos* (1999–2007), *Six Feet Under* (2001–5), *Oz* (1997–2003) and *Sex and the City* (1998–2004) all tackled adult themes, such as sex, violence, morality and death in an explicit manner that would be difficult to achieve within the FCC [Federal Communication Commission] guidelines for the national networks. Yet, in each case, such representations were not simply additional titillation for the viewer, but rather interwoven into the dramatic fabric of each series in order to allow the drama to explore its themes in a rich, textured and believable manner. (2012, 29–30)

Although *Oz* was not the most critically acclaimed or most watched of the new breed of HBO original dramas, it was the first, and it established many of the conventions of the programs that followed in its wake, including a focus on ethically complicated antiheroes and unflinchingly graphic violence and sex. It was also one of the first television programs to portray gay sexual relationships explicitly. Much of the sex on *Oz* involves men only, sometimes in consensual relationships, sometimes raping and being raped, and sometimes in scenes that seem to revel in blurring the distinction.

Al Auster points out that in the 1990s *Oz* would never have had a chance at being greenlighted by a more traditional network. He identifies *Oz* as a "template for future HBO programs" and notes, "[*Oz*] showed that the maverick network would not hesitate to produce even the most risky of creative conceptions" (2005, 239).

Thus, *Oz* might be considered not only a groundbreaking television program in some ways but also one that is rife with ideological complexities and troubling, often stereotypical representations of the incarcerated. *Oz*'s creator, Tom Fontana, made a point of telling interviewers that to represent prison life in as real a manner as possible, he had visited several maximum-security prisons. However, a textual analysis of the six-year run shows that images of extreme and bizarre episodes of violence are at the heart of Fontana's attempt to make a "realistic" prison drama (Yousman 2013, 213). As I have argued elsewhere, *Oz* offers viewers a terrifying glimpse into a hidden aspect of American life, presenting a vision of a prison inhabited by sadistic, dangerous, brutal criminals that any sane society would rightly lock away forever: "Constant scenes of savage inmates attacking each other and the guards, and even visitors to the prison, reinforce the notion that these men and this place must be feared. Even the opening credits—scenes of riots and brawls and stabbings and rapes played in quick succession, underscored by eerie, percussive, dangerous sounding music—convey a message of fear. The most graphic violent scenes are not displayed once but are shown over and over again in flashbacks" (Yousman 2009, 275).

The final episode of *Oz* continues the show's pattern of unrelenting violence, including assaults, brawls, and murders, as multiple vignettes and overlapping plotlines are introduced in an attempt to provide closure to the stories of most of the key characters from previous seasons. In a promotional spot, actor Terry Kinney, who plays the flawed but goodhearted prison official Tim McManus, described the finale as "anarchy, madness, tragedy, catastrophe, joy and revelation all at the same time."

Entitled "Exeunt Omnes," a stage direction in Latin meaning "they all go out," episode 8 of season 6 is consistent with the series' grim tone.[1]

---

1. All references to "Exeunt Omnes" come from Zakrzewski [2003] 2006.

At the end of this final episode, many of the characters to whom viewers had been introduced during the program's run are dead; others have their dreams of parole and a better life crushed; and the prison itself is evacuated after a lethal Anthrax-like powder is released into the air when a suspicious package is opened in the mail room. It is a final act of revenge committed by Keller (Christopher Meloni), one of *Oz*'s most vile characters, just before his own suicide.

The penultimate scenes of the finale are of prisoners and staff being taken away in buses and workers in hazmat suits attempting to cleanse the empty cells and common areas of the toxic substance. Concluding the series with an act of biological terrorism serves as a powerful metaphor for the toxicity of prison life itself because no one, prisoners and staff alike, is immune to the poisonous effects.

Oz's grim finale reflects the grand ambitions of the series and both HBO's and Tom Fontana's desire for the program to be taken seriously as important and groundbreaking. After all, this is the network that adopted the slogan "It's not TV. It's HBO" to brand programs such as *Oz* as something more culturally significant than mere entertainment. (As Toby Miller quips, HBO might have just as well flattered its subscribers with the tagline "You're Not a Viewer. You're a Connoisseur" [2008, xi].) In *Oz*'s final episode, the appeal to viewers' cultural capital is marked through allusions to both Greek and Shakespearean drama. The entire episode is a series of vignettes featuring key characters attempting to find peace and love but usually being thwarted, if not destroyed, in their attempts. All of these painful and traumatic stories occur while the prisoners are rehearsing for a performance of *Macbeth*, a somewhat heavy-handed way of painting prison life as a modern-day tragedy worthy of the attention of poets and playwrights. Similarly, the vignettes are also framed by a narrative device meant to invoke the tragic dramas of ancient Greece, such as Sophocles's Oedipus cycle and Aeschylus's Oresteia.

The episode opens with a chorus of prisoners chanting, "I'm innocent," until the wheelchair-bound narrator, Augustus Hill (Harold Perrineau), proclaims: "You go to any prison, you ask any guy who's serving time, and he'll tell you he's innocent. 'I got a bum rap, I had a lousy lawyer, I was in Toledo visiting my mamma.' Yeah, you'll hear a whole pack of lies. But what about that one brother who's telling the truth, the one who really is innocent? His voice is buried so damn deep beneath the others he's gonna grow hoarse just trying to be heard."

This opening statement seems to reify the integrity of the US penal system, suggesting that it is rare indeed for an innocent person to be unjustly sentenced to prison. Yet there is the hint of doubt, representing the ambiguous take on the US criminal justice system that was a hallmark of *Oz* throughout its entire run.

Augustus returns several times throughout the final-episode, telling supposedly true but bizarre tales of real prisoners who are killed while trying to escape, who sneak out of prison just to buy beer and then sneak back in, who molest young visitors. This referencing of true stories seems to suggest to viewers (and critics of the show) that, yes, the stories of *Oz* have been strange and implausible, but that is only because prison life itself is strange and implausible.

Augustus's interruptions disrupt the narrative flow as he tells several other stories that critique not prisoners but the system. These stories exemplify the often contradictory ideological complexity of *Oz*: a judge indicted for sexual misconduct; a prison that bans all sexually explicit magazines because they "impede rehabilitation"; prisoners being charged for room and board and medical care so that they end up leaving prison in debt to the state; and Supreme Court justice Antonin Scalia's infamous statement that judges who don't support the death penalty should resign.

Augustus also offers the closing words of the final episode, a statement that seems an attempt to tie up all of the chaos and death of the previous six seasons in a neat little package but finally offers no real resolution or clear position:

> So what have we learned? What's the lesson for today? For all the never-ending days and restless nights in Oz? That morality is transient? That virtue cannot exist without violence? That to be honest is to be flawed? That the giving and taking of love both debases and elevates us? That God or Allah or Yahweh has answers to questions we dare not even ask? The story is simple. A man lives in prison and dies. How he dies, that's easy. The who and the why is the complex part. The human part. The only part worth knowing.

Augustus kisses his fingers. He is framed in an extreme close-up: "Peace." The screen grows dark, the percussive theme music blares, and the final credits roll.

Oz ends as it began, unrelenting in its bleak sense of human nature, rife with violence, contradictory in its impulses, unclear about its stance on crime and punishment, filled simultaneously with both empathy for its characters and a reliance on harmful stereotypes, a somewhat noble, somewhat cynical, terribly flawed attempt to take viewers behind the walls of a real American tragedy.

References

Akass, Kim, and Janet McCabe. 2007. "Analysing Fictional Television Genres." In *Media Studies: Key Issues and Debates*, edited by Eoin Devereux, 283–301. London: Sage.

Alexander, Michelle. 2012. *The New Jim Crow: Mass Incarceration in the Age of Colorblindness*. New York: New Press.

Auster, Al. 2005. "HBO's Approach to Generic Transformation." In *Thinking outside the Box: A Contemporary Television Genre Reader*, edited by Gary R. Edgerton and Brian Geoffrey Rose, 226–46. Lexington: Univ. Press of Kentucky.

DeFino, Dean J. 2014. *The HBO Effect*. New York: Bloomsbury.

Gilliard, Darrell K., and Allen J. Beck. 1998. "Prisoners in 1997." US Bureau of Justice Statistics. At http://www.bjs.gov/content/pub/pdf/p97.pdf.

Johnson, Catherine. 2012. *Branding Television*. New York: Routledge.

Lee, Michelle Ye Hee. 2015. "Yes, U.S. Locks People Up at a Higher Rate Than Any Other Country." *Washington Post*, July 7. At https://www.washingtonpost.com/news/fact-checker/wp/2015/07/07/yes-u-s-locks-people-up-at-a-higher-rate-than-any-other-country/.

Miller, Toby. 2008. "Foreword: It's Television." In *It's HBO. It's not TV: Watching HBO in the Post-television era*, edited by Marc Leverette, Brian L. Ott, and Cara Louise Buckley, ix–xii. New York: Routledge.

Yousman, Bill. 2009. "Inside *Oz*: Hyperviolence, Race and Class Nightmares, and the Engrossing Spectacle of Terror." *Communication and Critical/Cultural Studies* 6, no. 3: 265–84.

———. 2013. "Revisiting Hall's Encoding/Decoding Model: Ex-prisoners Respond to Television Representations of Incarceration." *Review of Education, Pedagogy, and Cultural Studies* 35, no. 3: 197–216.

Zakrzewski, Alex, dir. [2003] 2006. "Exeunt Omnes." *Oz*, season 6, episode 8. Written by Tom Fontana. Aired Feb. 23, 2003, HBO. On *Oz: The Complete Sixth Season*. New York: HBO Video. DVD.

45

Prime Suspect

"The Final Act"[1]

DEBORAH JERMYN

Since the earliest days of television drama, the cop show has maintained a regular presence in international television schedules, enjoying the status of a "banker" genre among programmers eager to secure a loyal and sizeable audience. Although it has sometimes seemed to drift into predictability and to trade in stereotypes as a result—the cop show format is littered ad infinitum with hard-living but devoted maverick cops who take on the bureaucratic might of their bosses—it has also nevertheless been regularly reinvented and reinvigorated. Despite the genre's well-worn character types and settings, then, this process of renewal has ensured that certain landmark cop series have managed to retain the police show's reputation for timeliness, aesthetic creativity, and, at its very best, provocative social comment.

When the ITV miniseries *Prime Suspect* (1991–2006) was first broadcast on British television in April 1991, it swiftly became apparent that it was a new instance of the genre "at its very best" and was met by extraordinary levels of critical and public debate. Audiences were captivated as its protagonist, the resilient, career-driven Detective Chief Inspector Jane Tennison (Helen Mirren), sought a serial killer who rapes and tortures his female victims, all the while fighting for her own survival in the chauvinistic world of the police. The press applauded this "belter of a suspense thriller" for bringing an inventive twist to the cop show by conceiving a female detective who is "a masterpiece of observation and subtlety" (Paterson 1991, 136).

1. Parts of this essay were previously featured in my book *Prime Suspect* (London: BFI Palgrave Macmillan, 2010) and have been reproduced with permission of Palgrave Macmillan.

Female cops were not a new feature in the genre by the 1990s, of course, with series such as *Police Woman* (NBC, 1974–78) and *Cagney & Lacey* (CBS, 1981–88) in the United States and *Juliet Bravo* (BBC, 1980–85) in the United Kingdom constituting important precursors in this respect. But the sheer originality of a female cop as driven and yet as nuanced as Tennison took audiences and critics used to the predominantly male heroes of police drama by surprise.

Tennison's personal story line vividly exposed the everyday misogyny and opposition women faced in working in an enduringly masculine institution, while detailing how the demands of the profession slowly bring about the breakdown of personal relationships, a narrative that perfectly tapped into a zeitgeist absorbed by the issue of the "glass ceiling" facing professional women.[2] All this was memorably threaded through a police procedural that featured unprecedented levels of forensic detail and graphic imagery in the genre. The series' forays into the police labs and morgues set new aesthetic benchmarks and thematic preoccupations for the genre, which were subsequently enthusiastically and controversially embraced by series such as *Silent Witness* (BBC, 1996–) and *CSI: Crime Scene Investigation* (CBS, 2000–2015) (see Jermyn 2010). Overnight, *Prime Suspect* became one of the most talked-about British TV programs in recent memory, giving rise, as Philip Purser noted in the *Daily Telegraph*, to a nation "united, divided, mesmerized, offended and generally caught up in a television whodunit" (1991) and in the process securing series creator Lynda La Plante's status as one of the leading television dramatists in UK history (Hallam 2005).

Following the first season's worldwide distribution and its success on US public television as part of PBS's prestigious program *Mystery!*, *Prime Suspect* was subsequently produced by Granada in association with WGBH, the Boston-based, noncommercial TV and radio broadcast service and leading producer of PBS prime-time programming. It would go on to number seven seasons over a fifteen-year period and continue to tackle other equally disquieting themes and "taboo" social issues, from police racism to war crime, with the tenacious and scrupulous but flawed Tennison at the helm. By the time *Prime Suspect* reached its finale with "The Final Act" in 2006 (directed by Philip Martin and written by Frank Deasy), it had amassed a plethora of awards, including three Emmys for Outstanding Miniseries and endless accolades for Mirren in one of TV drama's most celebrated performances.

2. All references to *Prime Suspect* come from *Prime Suspect* 2006.

Over the course of the series' lifetime, as critics and fans argued over whether Tennison should or shouldn't attain a work–life balance, should or shouldn't make it to the top brass, should or shouldn't slip steadily into alcoholism, she would refuse to be bullied out of her profession. She would instead achieve the senior rank of detective superintendent and continue to investigate a series of harrowing cases while fighting her own demons, losing lovers and family in the process, and, somewhere along the way, entering the annals of television history as a TV cop who broke the mold. Described in this way, *Prime Suspect*'s landmark accomplishments and the esteem it enjoyed seem incontestable. Why was it, then, that the series finale was widely received as so painfully disappointing, so unsatisfying, so dismally conservative by so many people, ensuring that *Prime Suspect* went out on a wave of controversy rather than jubilation?

Throughout the series, Tennison has always unwound with a drink after a tough day, just like generations of tough-guy cops before her, and her growing reliance on booze is hinted at earlier in the series. But the immediacy and extent of her decline into full-blown alcoholism as "The Final Act" opens still comes as a jolt, especially because it was not particularly signaled in season 6. As the drama commences, she is seen waking up on the sofa, looking disheveled in the cold morning light. A whisky bottle on the table confirms that she is coming round with a hangover, while bleak, foreboding music connotes that we find her in dark times. Looking at her watch, she curses out loud as she realizes she's overslept and looks confusedly at the phone next to her, its receiver lying off the hook. Later at her office, it will emerge that Tennison had taken an important call the night before about a missing teenage girl, Sallie Sturdy, but she has no recollection of it. Soon enough, Sallie's dead body will be found on the local heath, and this murder will constitute Tennison's last case. Now, as Tennison wakes and tries to piece together the previous evening, her confusion is dramatically intercut with scenes of the missing girl's mother running through the streets frantically looking for her daughter. Tennison looks in the mirror, perplexed to find a bruise on her head, then notices that the toilet seat in the bathroom has oddly been left up. Going to her bedroom, she pulls back her duvet and stands looking at her bed, as we and she start to surmise that she may well have had a one-night stand she can't remember.

Alarm bells ring loud in this startling opening sequence and not merely because the previous night's binge drinking (and indeed years of bad habits) have left Tennison looking so suddenly weary and aged. Rather, what is equally disconcerting is how Tennison's professionalism has apparently deserted her. Her drinking has caused a blackout so encompassing that she can't remember Sallie's case being called in, and her hangover has made her late for work—lapses that the Tennison of old would not have tolerated. On the eve of retirement, she is coerced by her boss into attending Alcoholics Anonymous meetings on the threat of being signed off "on leave" forthwith. "Old school, that's Tennison," he rails against her after their meeting: "Battered, burnt out. Dinosaurs." For Tennison, drinking now signifies debility, not attitude—not the winding down of a maverick cop but rather the weakness of a loose cannon who can't be relied on.

For all its polish and tension, "The Final Act" makes for difficult viewing as it chips away at Tennison's dignity and ability to do the job she loves. Her once-trusted instinct seems lost to her as she misses clues, lets her suspect slip through her fingers, and fails to see till the last juncture that Sallie's killer, her classmate Penny, has been there in front of her all along. As the case progresses, the two strike up an unlikely friendship, and Tennison can't help falling for this bright, spirited girl as she admits to Penny—and to herself at last—that she is lonely. Penny stands symbolically both for Tennison's own lost youth, that moment of teenage promise when the world was still hers for the taking, and for the child she never had. It is telling that this last season focuses both on the murder of a teenage girl and on the development of Tennison's warm and unexpected relationship with another, as if to remind the single, child-free Tennison of what might have been, the family and daughter she might have had. After her father dies and she is left truly without a single close, loving relationship, Tennison visits her parents' home. As she drunkenly dons her old police cap and dances alone in her old bedroom to the faded LPs of her youth, she cuts a tragic figure. What would her teenage self, who first donned a police cap when she was just seventeen years old, make of the woman she has become? In season 3, Tennison expresses no regrets to her former lover Jake that she didn't choose a life and family with him over her career years ago, observing, "I got what I wanted. I got my job." Later, in season 5, her boss tells her that a junior female colleague has specifically asked to work under her when she relocates to Manchester, commenting, "You're a role model, Jane, an icon in the force." Yet "The Final Act" does little to celebrate Tennison's life and career or to recall what she has achieved. It is instead preoccupied with ghosts from the past, lost hopes, unfulfilled possibilities.

In the last minutes of the finale, Tennison solves Sallie's murder, as she swore she would, but it is a hollow victory indeed. In contrast to the ending of the first *Prime Suspect*, which sees her crack the case and jubilantly celebrating with her team, at the end of "The Final Act" Tennison leaves the office and walks out into the streets of London for the final time, alone, so estranged from everyone that she chooses to skip her own retirement party. For all these reasons, "The Final Act" proved highly divisive among audiences and critics, giving rise to some animated debate. Writing in the *Guardian*, for example, Libby Brooks bemoaned how Tennison had been written out with "vodka for breakfast, poisoned relationships and an empty future. . . . [I]t was a depressing ending for a character who was emblematic of women's struggle to succeed in the workplace" (2006). But didn't this bleak conclusion simply remain true to the program's original realist, "gritty" aspirations? It would have seemed trite and unfaithful to the preceding decade and a half of *Prime Suspect* for Tennison to get the happy ending on all fronts that had always eluded her—bagging her killer, falling in love, and smashing the glass ceiling on her way out. Or had the series betrayed the conviction of the early Tennison for a sadly reactionary and all too predictable portrayal of her demise, constituting a dire warning for women everywhere that a lonely retirement is the price to be paid for devoting oneself single-mindedly to one's work? Far from celebrating Tennison's achievements, the finale overwhelmingly positioned her working life as one marked by loss and sacrifice, and it provided a melancholy exit for one of television drama's most memorable women.

"The Final Act" was perhaps always destined to be contentious, given the heightened burden of representation that Tennison came to embody for women in the genre. Rather than trying only to reconcile the irresolvable tensions she figured, however, we might do well instead to reflect on her legacy. Tennison's impact on the cop show was undeniable; *Prime Suspect* opened the door to a whole slew of skillful, complex, senior female investigators made possible in her wake. She proved that female protagonists could more than ably lead an investigation and lead the genre, bagging audiences, accolades, and awards in the process—a final act arguably more satisfying than any retirement party could ever have been.

References

Brooks, Libby. 2006. "Past Her Prime." *Guardian*, Oct. 23. At http://commentis free.guardian.co.uk/libby_brooks/2006/10/post_536.html.

Hallam, Julia. 2005. *Lynda La Plante*. Manchester, UK: Manchester Univ. Press.

Jermyn, Deborah. 2010. *Prime Suspect*. London: BFI Palgrave Macmillan.
Paterson, Elaine. 1991. "Gritty Woman." *Time Out*, Apr. 10.
Prime Suspect: Complete Collection. 2006. London: Granada Ventures. DVD.
Purser, Philip. 1991. "Prejudice? It's a Fair Cop." *Daily Telegraph*, Apr. 10.

46

The Prisoner

"Fall Out"

JOANNE MORREALE

One of the most famous closing episodes of a television series is the finale of the classic British series *The Prisoner*, which originally aired on ITV in 1967–68. *The Prisoner* was a seventeen-episode dramatic television series produced and created by its star, Patrick McGoohan, along with George Markstein. It was seemingly a spy series that played on the popularity of the secret-agent genre during the Cold War. The opening credits tell the story: a government agent resigns, then is immediately abducted and brought to an isolated island resort community known as "The Village."[1] In every episode, the Prisoner, identified only as "Number 6," attempts to escape and learn the identity of his captor, Number 1, and viewers try to solve the puzzle alongside him. Every week a different Number 2 tries to break the Prisoner, and the only recurring character is a dwarf who plays the Butler in service to Number 2. Up until the final episode, there is no narrative progression or resolution, and every episode ends with the Prisoner returning to the initial situation of entrapment.

For McGoohan, who had formed his own production company, Everyman Films, in 1960, the series offered the opportunity to use the medium of television to challenge viewers. In an interview in 1977, he stated, "I wanted to have controversy, argument, fights, discussions, people in anger waving fists in my face saying, 'How dare you? Why don't you make more *Secret Agents* that we can understand?' I was delighted with that reaction. . . . That was the intention of the exercise" (Troyer 1977). There are parallels between McGoohan's experiences with the series *Secret Agent* (1964–67)—known as

1. All references to the series come from *The Prisoner* 2009.

Danger Man in the United Kingdom—and the plot of *The Prisoner*. Two episodes into the new season of what was then a hit show, McGoohan abruptly resigned from *Danger Man* to pursue production of *The Prisoner*. In his words, "I'd made 54 of those [*Danger Man* episodes] and I thought that was an adequate amount" (Troyer 1977). In effect, both McGoohan and the Prisoner leave successful careers and rebel from the constricting social-industrial forces that induce conformity and complacency. As Chris Gregory comments, "*The Prisoner* not only symbolizes the struggle of the Individual against society, but dramatizes the immense difficulties involved in getting one strong creative voice to be heard against the corporate clamor that is the television industry. When the Prisoner declares . . . I am not a number, I am a free man . . . he is rebelling not only against 'society' but against the medium of television itself" (1997, 32).

Because McGoohan was a proven bankable star, ITV financier Lew Grade agreed to produce the new show, despite admitting that he didn't fully understand it (Carrazé and Oswald [1989] 1990, 210). ITV was the commercial competitor to the centrally funded BBC, and its economics worked by selling programs with mainstream appeal to the United States. As a spy series, *The Prisoner* could be exported to the United States, but by also marketing it as McGoohan's artistic vision, ITV was able to stave off criticism that the company was abandoning Britain's public-service mission by catering to popular tastes. Catherine Johnson writes that by appealing to both popular and highbrow audiences, *The Prisoner* answered the British government's call for programs that were challenging and controversial in form and content. As an unconventional genre text, it simultaneously entertained and provoked viewers. Johnson asserts that *The Prisoner*'s balance of the "serious" and "popular" was its most radical and creative element (2005, 63).

The resultant series was a mixture of spy, science fiction, fantasy, and political allegory, whose formal experimentation also disrupted conventional modes of viewing. In the course of the seventeen-episode series, *The Prisoner* took aim at politics, art, religion, science, education, psychology, government, and media, while its visual style combined narrative realism, theatrically staged artificiality, and surrealist fantasy (see Gregory 1997, 35–55). The result defamiliarized viewers and forced them to decipher meaning, which was unusual in an era that predated the complex narratives common today. *The Prisoner* has been referred to as "one of the most enigmatic series ever on television" (Buxton 1990, 93) and is an example of what M. Keith Booker refers to as "strange" television: "certain television programs that produce a kind of cognitive estrangement that encourages viewers to look at the world in a new and different way, rather than merely act as passive consumers of the television signal and the consumerist messages it inevitably carries" (2002, 2).

The Prisoner aired in the United States on CBS in 1968 and has been rebroadcast intermittently through the years. It has also been released on DVD and has recently regained recognition because of the "reimagining" of the original series coproduced by ITV and AMC. Although original viewers may have watched to ultimately learn who Number 1 is and whether the Prisoner will eventually escape, over the years *The Prisoner* has maintained a cult following as contemporary viewers puzzle over what it all means, especially the provocative final episode. *The Prisoner* is perhaps best known for its famous conclusion, "Fall Out" (written and directed by McGoohan).

The Prisoner's finale was the first time that a narrative television program refused conventional closure. In a typical narrative, the ending would reveal the identity of Number 1, and the Prisoner would finally escape. "Fall Out" begins by setting up these expectations, though it quickly shifts to the level of allegory as it addresses questions such as the meaning of the individual, identity, and the possibility of revolutionary action. It opens as a continuation of the preceding episode, "Once Upon a Time," in which Number 2 is defeated and the Prisoner demands that the Supervisor and the Butler take him to see Number 1. They walk through a subterranean corridor beneath the Village and emerge into a room where they see a cardboard mannequin of the Prisoner. The mannequin wears the suit the Prisoner wore at the beginning of the pilot episode, "Arrival," before he is forced to adopt the uniform of Number 6. A voice declares, "We thought you'd feel happier as yourself," and the Prisoner dons his old clothing. As the three men continue down the corridor, jukeboxes play the Beatles song "All You Need Is Love." According to Tony Williams, "At the time this [song] was the anthem of the hippie nonconformist revolt against establishment values, a revolt which was to collapse into futility after 'inoculation' by bourgeois ideology" (1990, 71).

As the Prisoner emerges into a cavelike structure, various representatives of society greet him: a court magistrate, a troop of soldiers marching in step, and three tiers of joined desks where "delegates" sit. The latter are clad in white hoods and robes as well as the classical mask of Greek tragicomedy. They are distinguishable from one another by placards titled "Pacifists," "Activists," "Anarchists," "Reactionaries," "Defectors," "Therapy," "Entertainment," and so on, naming various social forms and movements. The Supervisor dons a robe and sits behind a placard titled "Identification." The President of the court then opens the proceedings. He makes explicit *The*

Prisoner's narrative premise and says, "This session is called in a matter of democratic crisis. And we are gathered here to resolve the question of revolt." As the jury applauds, he continues, "The community is at stake and we have the means to protect it." The Prisoner appears to have won the battle: the President declares that the Prisoner has "gloriously vindicated the right of the individual to be individual." He then asks the Prisoner to observe the ceremonies from the chair of honor, a throne that sits above the proceedings, and the Prisoner complies. Tony Williams suggests that in this scene the Prisoner's position as a passive viewer of the proceedings who thinks that he is in control mimics that of the television viewer: "Both Number 6 and the viewer are presumably individuals in full control of their destiny. But Number 6's enthronement in the viewer's chair presumes a royal control that is illusory. As we shall learn, Number 6 is not a coherent individual but a divided self. The same is not less true of the average viewer" (1990, 72).

Ultimately, the show reveals the Prisoner as a divided subject, both within himself and from other people. The conclusion of *The Prisoner* asserts the illusion of individual identity and the impossibility of any subjectivity that can exist outside of the control of the society in which it is created. As the Prisoner sits on his throne, the President tells the jury that he will consider three instances of revolt. The first is Number 48, a youthful hippie; the second is Number 2 from the episode "Once Upon a Time"; and the third is the Prisoner. The President announces: "We have just witnessed two forms of revolt. The first, uncoordinated youth rebelling against nothing it can define. The second, an established, secure member of the Establishment turning upon and biting the hand that feeds him. Well, these attitudes are dangerous. They contribute nothing to our culture, and they must be stamped out."

He then claims that the third kind of revolt, the Prisoner's, is that of "a revolutionary of different caliber. He has revolted, resisted, fought . . . [and] maintained the right to be an individual." The President tells the Prisoner that he is free to go because he is the "only individual" and asks him to make a speech. But when the Prisoner begins, the word *I* is lost in a cacophony of voices that echo "aye" (sounding like "I"). The President then takes him to meet Number 1, who is wearing the same white robe and tragicomic mask as the jury. Number 1's back is to the Prisoner, and he watches a screen that replays a scene from the pilot episode, "Arrival," in which the Prisoner asserts his individuality. But the word *I* reverberates, and the closing image of every episode—a still of the Prisoner's face behind bars—flashes repeatedly onscreen. Number 1 turns to face the Prisoner with arms outstretched. The Prisoner then tears off Number 1's mask and finds the face of a monkey beneath it. He rips off the monkey face and finds his own face. The Prisoner is his own captor, a point that affirms his divided identity and the impossibility of escape or revolution.

As the episode continues, the Prisoner (accompanied by the Butler) then appears to defeat the controllers, escape from the Village, and return to his apartment in London. Yet as the Butler takes the Prisoner to his car, a black hearse from the series' opening credit sequence pulls up alongside them. When the Prisoner drives off, the Butler walks up the stairs to his apartment, which has a number 1 on the door. The door opens and closes automatically, just as it did in the Village. The series concludes with the same clap of thunder and shot of the Prisoner driving his sports car on the open road that began the series.

The circular ending confounds viewers' conventional expectations of narrative closure and denies them the pleasure of resolution. In fact, hordes of angry viewers jammed the ITV switchboard in England for days after the initial airing of the series finale. The shot of the Prisoner's own face behind the mask of Number 1 was only fifty-two frames long, and in the days before VCRs many viewers were unsure of what they had seen or what it meant. According to McGoohan, "In fact, when the last episode came out in England, it had one of the largest viewing audiences, they tell me, ever over there, because everyone wanted to know who No. 1 was, because they thought it would be a 'James Bond' type of No. 1. When they did finally see it, there was a near-riot and I was going to be lynched. And I had to go into hiding in the mountains for two weeks, until things calmed down" (Troyer 1997). In 1967, viewers expected that the central enigma would be solved in a logically coherent manner. Even though *The Prisoner* had always oscillated between the realistic and fantastic, in the end there was still the expectation that the rational order of narrative—and the world—would be reaffirmed.

Over the years, *The Prisoner* has maintained its cult following, with numerous websites, more than twenty-five books, and even college courses devoted to it. It remains a remarkable text that defied conventional expectations and used television as a means of social critique long before it was commonplace to do so. Although some fans may have been frustrated by its ending, the finale was a daring and important work that was true to McGoohan's vision. "Fall Out" challenged assumptions of coherent identity, the individual, and the ability to revolt against an oppressive society, and in so doing it enabled *The Prisoner*'s social commentary to remain relevant today. *The Prisoner*'s finale continues to be the definitive mark of a complex narrative whose form and content were ahead of their time.

References

Booker, M. Keith. 2002. *Strange TV: Innovative Television Series from "The Twilight Zone" to "The X-Files."* Westport, CT: Greenwood Press.

Buxton, David. 1990. *From "The Avengers" to "Miami Vice": Form and Ideology in Television Series.* Manchester: Manchester Univ. Press.

Carrazé, Alain, and Hélène Oswald. [1989] 1990. *The Prisoner.* Translated by Christine Donougher. New York: W. H. Allen.

Gregory, Chris. 1997. *Be Seeing You: Decoding "The Prisoner."* Luton, UK: Univ. of Luton Press.

Johnson, Catherine. 2005. *Telefantasy.* London: British Film Industry.

The Prisoner: The Complete Series. 2009. Santa Monica, CA: Lionsgate Films. DVD.

Troyer, Warner. 1977. Interview with Patrick McGoohan for the Ontario Educational Communications Authority, Mar. At http://www.cult-tv.co.uk/mcgoohan.htm.

Williams, Tony. 1990. "Authorship Conflict in *The Prisoner.*" In *Making Television: Authorship and the Production Process*, edited by Robert Thompson and Gary Burns, 71–85. New York: Praeger.

47

Quantum Leap

"Mirror Image"

LINCOLN GERAGHTY

The success of *Star Trek: The Next Generation* (TNG, 1987–94), which reenergized the franchise in 1987, reminded networks and television audiences that science fiction was still a marketable genre on the small screen. It led to what M. Keith Booker describes as an "Age of Plenty" (2004, 111). The 1990s saw a proliferation of new science-fiction series hot on the heels of *TNG*'s last season in 1994. As well as concurrent series such as *Star Trek*'s own *Deep Space Nine* (1993–99) and *Voyager* (1995–2001), there followed *The X-Files* (1993–2002), *Babylon 5* (1994–98), *Sliders* (1995–2000), *Space: Above and Beyond* (1995–96), *Stargate SG-1* (1997–2007), *Lexx* (1997–2002), Gene Roddenberry's *Earth: Final Conflict* (1997–2002), and a new version of *The Outer Limits* (1995–2002). However, alongside all of these examples came a series that not only reflected the networks' desire to cater to an increasingly large share of the viewing audience but also showed just how intelligent and thought provoking science fiction on television could be. That series was *Quantum Leap* (1989–93).

The impact of *Quantum Leap* meant that the concept of prime-time "quality television" was firmly established by the mid-1990s, and its episodic format also encouraged cable networks such as the Sci-Fi Channel (founded in 1992) to continue investing because long-running series attracted a loyal and relatively affluent audience that could afford to buy into the ever-growing merchandising market. For Derek Kompare, cable networks "function as television *boutiques*: venues offering a limited array of products for specialized audiences" (2005, 172). Series that started on the major networks—*Quantum Leap* on NBC, for example—ended up on cable through syndication, adding to the pleasure of the rerun marathon that had become a staple cable marketing tool to attract fans. John Ellis describes the entire industry at the start of the new millennium as "rushing towards an emerging era of plenty" (2002, 162) in that it offered new technologies for and new challenges to the way we watch television. In many ways, *Quantum Leap* started that trend and laid the foundation for what science fiction would become in the new millennium.

On its own, the story of Dr. Sam Beckett's (Scott Bakula) whimsical time-traveling tour of the twentieth century was one of the more warm-hearted series of the decade, focusing on the individual's potential to enact change that, however small, could improve other people's lives forever. The series stood in marked contrast to the epic space operas mentioned earlier yet still garnered a devoted fan base that showed science fiction's continuing capacity to attract a family audience in this period of change. After the series' cancellation due to poor ratings, the genre would witness a bleak turn in which such positivism would give way to deep-seated national paranoia and pessimism about the future and about where the country was going politically and socially, exemplified in series such as *The X-Files* on Fox (Geraghty 2009, 98).

Donald P. Bellisario created *Quantum Leap* as an attempt to bring a science fiction anthology series to mainstream audiences and pitched it to NBC not as action adventure but as something more multilayered: "It was more of an anthology show. We weren't locked into an action-adventure format. I wanted warm, humanistic stories, sometimes as a comedy, sometimes fantasy drama, sometimes as an action-adventure and sometimes as a romantic story" (quoted in Garcia and Phillips 2009, 190). Certainly, over the course of five seasons and ninety-five episodes, we do see a range of stories that flirt with all manner of genres and story lines. Sam, accompanied by his long-standing yet holographic companion Al Calavicci (Dean Stockwell), enters the bodies of a multitude of characters who are clearly drawn from the archive of television archetypes: disaffected teens, single mothers, deadbeat dads, and so on. Being a time-travel show, *Quantum Leap* is able to play with famous moments in American history such as the Vietnam War, Watergate, the civil rights movement, and John Kennedy's assassination while at the same time remaining decidedly grounded within the more humdrum lives of the main protagonists Sam becomes in each season's episodes. Bellisario said, "I wanted stories about real people, not historical figures" (quoted in Garcia and Phillips 2009, 190).

Each episode sees Sam "leap" into the body of a stranger from history, usually a nonfamous person (except on the rare occasions, when he leaps into the body of a well-known person—Lee Harvey Oswald and Elvis Presley, for example) who lived within the span of Sam's own timeline. Bellisario established this "rule" to keep Sam from leaping around history from ancient Egypt to medieval England and to keep the series focused on the little guy, "so the show had some sense of reality to it" (quoted in Phillips and Garcia 1996, 280). This decision to keep Sam within the latter half of the twentieth century brought its own challenges but did not curtail story or character development. This was in part because both Sam and Al are actors who revel in their close-knit relationship. The show is driven by their buddy–buddy dynamic: Sam the altruistic scientist who wants to make a difference and Al the loyal companion whose moral code informs the actions of both when trying to help those in need. Indeed, for Kayla Wiggins (1993), *Quantum Leap* pairs a hero with an antihero in a battle against the wrongs of history—albeit a battle that Sam brings upon himself by stepping into the Quantum Leap Accelerator before it is fully tested. Yet this sort of action characterizes him as a selfless hero, willing to put his scientific knowledge and intellect to the test in order to help people: "Sam is truly a man of the 1990s, sensitive and caring. He has high moral standards and beliefs, coupled with the questioning nature of the scientist" (Wiggins 1993, 111). Al's more chauvinistic and dated representation of masculinity, according to Wiggins, can "be overlooked in part because [it is] excused by the difficult life he has led, and in part because of his unswerving dedication to the project and to Sam" (112).

As mentioned earlier, *Quantum Leap* focuses on the intimate moments of history, personal stories that do not have immense epoch-changing significance but are relatable to audiences who can share in some of the emotions evoked: for example, saying good-bye to a loved one before he dies or getting another chance to marry your childhood sweetheart. Coexecutive producer Deborah Pratt described the big moments, the celebrity moments—where Sam gets to meet Marilyn Monroe before she dies or to tell Buddy Holly that "Peggy Sue" is a better title for his new song than "Piggy Sue"—as "kisses with history" (quoted in Phillips and Garcia 1996, 280). On a narrative level, *Quantum Leap* involves a determined sense of duty—"to put right what once went wrong" and to "change history for the better," as its opening credits stirringly eulogize. Nevertheless, its attempts at showing how history can be changed for the better are channeled through the very idealistic and strong-headed lead, who will stop at nothing to change history to facilitate his return home. For David Simmons, the fact that personal experiences are depicted as just as important to history as major events and historical figures means the series "undermines any sense of history as monolithic. . . . [T]he show offers a distinctly post-modern sense of the micro-narratives of individual histories, promoting the idea that there are hidden stories within the historical narratives that we think we know" (2016, 155). Time-travel narratives within the genre of science fiction are common and multifaceted; *Quantum Leap*'s use of time travel and temporal paradoxes to drive the story of Sam's journey home is in many ways framed not only by a sense of duty for those he helps but also by nostalgia.

This nostalgia for times past, filtered through moments in American history that mean something deeply personal to the characters who experienced them, serves to underscore the significance of the television medium itself. Television, for Robert Hanke, is "a site of struggle over the meanings of historical experiences, in the shape of popular memory. . . . [A]s a vehicle of popular memory [television] becomes an important site within which to examine the formation of contemporary historical consciousness and/or subjectivity" (2000, 42). *Quantum Leap* therefore uses nostalgia for times past, moments of popular memory, and as a backdrop for character development and individual change. Sam is most often affected by this use of nostalgia because he is the one who directly engages with real people and real lives throughout history. Such experiences over the course of the series regularly push Sam to question who is making him leap into other people's bodies and whether he will ever get back to his own time. In the final episode, "Mirror Image," these questions come to the fore.[1]

Leaping into a bar in a coal-mining town on his birth date in 1953, Sam realizes he has leaped into his own body, and people can see him as the audience sees him (looking slightly older than he did when he first started leaping). Faces and names appear familiar to him, and, despite there being a need for Sam to help prevent two people from dying in a mining accident, he feels that this is not a typical mission. Al is initially unable to find him in this timeline, so Sam takes advice from the bartender (also called Al). Their conversations become increasingly philosophical in tone, and it is revealed that bartender Al knows about Sam's leaping—Sam even thinks it is the bartender (God in disguise) who has been making him leap around time. Ambiguities abound throughout the episode, in part because the story was not originally intended to be the final episode but rather the season 5 finale. However, because the show was canceled, questions about who is really controlling Sam's movements through time are not answered—they are asked

---

1. All references to "Mirror Image" come from Whitmore [1993] 2006.

but left up to audience members to make up their own minds. One thing that is confirmed is that Sam never returns home—an outcome made all the more stark by a voiceover and the use of a black screen.

For many fans, this lack of closure to the series and the depressing revelation that Sam never gets back to his own time make "Mirror Image" both a unique and a disappointing episode. Indeed, I would argue that this ending (hurriedly reedited when NBC pulled the series) turns *Quantum Leap* into something a little different from how I described it earlier. The bleak turn in science-fiction television, which many would argue occurs with *The X-Files*, in fact starts with "Mirror Image" and its almost despairing coda that Sam Beckett is still leaping through time. Booker describes the series as the "warmest and fuzziest" (2004, 112), but if we take Sam's narrative journey as incomplete, then *Quantum Leap* is itself left without its main character. He is lost, and Al will seemingly never be able to find him again: the friends are split up, Sam is alone. Quite a depressing thought when you think back to how the series espouses companionship through some of the toughest personal moments in history. Indeed, for me, there is an emotional component to this unexpected ending that almost dissuades me from ever going back to watch any episodes again—even some of the classic, light-hearted ones. To remember that Sam never returns home makes his efforts over the course of the series seem worthless, a literal waste of "time" both for fans watching and him leaping. I would compare this response to the feelings expressed by fans about the *Lost* (2004–10) finale, which many saw as a let-down because of the lack of resolution and what they considered the meaningless sacrifices made by characters throughout the series.

The ironic paradox of *Quantum Leap* is that the incomprehensibility of unending time wins over the individual's power to control his or her destiny—something that Sam has been trying to help people do in every episode. Bellisario tried to assuage fans' disappointment by saying that "it was Sam choosing his own fate. The kind of person that he was, he kept going from place to place to help people. Scott [Bakula] and I decided that's what it was" (quoted in Phillips and Garcia 1996, 286). Yet this revisioning of the story goes only some way in reclaiming the positivity of the series as a whole. Sam as hero, continuing to be a hero through time, is a strong element of the series' appeal, but if the show is about nostalgia for times past and personal histories revisited, then the return home (the crucial part of what nostalgia means) is denied to the series' and science-fiction television's most nostalgic of all protagonists.

References

Booker, M. Keith. 2004. *Science Fiction Television*. Westport, CT: Praeger.

Ellis, John. 2002. *Seeing Things: Television in the Age of Uncertainty*. London: I. B. Tauris.

Garcia, Frank, and Mark Phillips. 2009. *Science Fiction Television Series, 1990–2004: Histories, Casts, and Credits for 58 Shows*. Jefferson, NC: McFarland.

Geraghty, Lincoln. 2009. *American Science Fiction Film and Television*. Oxford: Berg.

Hanke, Robert. 2000. "*Quantum Leap*: The Postmodern Challenge of Television as History." *Film & History* 30, no. 2: 41–49.

Kompare, Derek. 2005. *Rerun Nation: How Repeats Invented American Television*. New York: Routledge.

Phillips, Mark, and Frank Garcia. 1996. *Science Fiction Television Series: Episode Guides, Histories, and Casts and Credits for 62 Prime Time Shows, 1959 through 1989*. Vol. 1. Jefferson, NC: McFarland.

Simmons, David. 2016. "'*Bonanza* Was Never Like This': *Quantum Leap* and Interrogating Nostalgia." In *Time on TV: Narrative Time, Time Travel, and Time Travellers in Popular Television Culture*, edited by Lorna Jowett, Kevin Lee Robinson, and David Simmons, 145–56. London: I. B. Tauris.

Whitmore, James, Jr., dir. [1993] 2006. "Mirror Image." *Quantum Leap*, season 5, episode 22. Written by Donald P. Bellisario. Aired May 5, 1993, NBC. On *Quantum Leap: The Complete Fifth Season*. Burbank: Universal Television, 2006. DVD.

Wiggins, Kayla McKinney. 1993. "Epic Heroes, Ethical Issues, and Time Paradoxes in *Quantum Leap*." *Journal of Popular Film and Television* 21, no. 3: 111–20.

48

Rectify

"All I'm Sayin'"[1]

ERIC GOULD

Small dramas usually mean even smaller audiences, but in the case of *Rectify* (2013–16), which finished its final season in December 2016 on SundanceTV, the "little show that could" proved that there remains a market for stories in which nothing explodes, a psychopath isn't lurking around the next corner, and life moves at a pace that is credible. Life in *Rectify* mirrored our own.

Rectify's farewell, "All I'm Sayin',"[2] was notably upbeat for a show that made its hay in the everyday downbeat of melancholy.

With the series' trademark immersion in scenes that hold quietly onto the stillness of ordinary life, the finale does give us a glimpse of what might lie ahead for wrongly accused Daniel Holden (Aden Young), who at the beginning of the series is released from nineteen years on death row when new DNA evidence leads to his death sentence being vacated.

Released back to his family as a grown man, Daniel, often vacuous and minus a sense of self after almost two decades isolated in a cell for the murder of his high school girlfriend, Hanna Dean, finally sees that life dissolving away from him. With a new investigation now being opened into the murder of Hanna and the likelihood of being cleared, he begins to see himself as a survivor, not an excon, and can envision a new future.

He has accepted the possibility of hope.

The fourth and final *Rectify* season follows Daniel's exile from his fictional hometown of Paulie, Georgia, to a halfway house for excons in

1. An earlier, shorter version of this essay appeared at tvworthwatching.com, Dec. 17, 2016.

2. All references to "All I'm Sayin'" come from McKinnon 2016.

Nashville, where he has agreed to relocate to satisfy the Georgia prosecutors weighing whether to return him to prison for supposed parole violations.

Now, in the stirring "All I'm Sayin'" final scene, we see the soft-spoken Daniel on his bed, eyes open, daydreaming of his future (or is it a jump cut forward?) in a field walking toward his love interest of the final season, the bohemian artist Chloe (Caitlin FitzGerald), holding her newborn child. (Chloe's pregnancy is the result of a prior broken relationship.)

Earlier in the episode, the message of *Rectify* and the series title come from Daniel's sister Amantha (Abigail Spencer), thinking on twenty years of fighting for his release and the possibility of his conviction finally being legally overturned. "It doesn't matter what happens at this point. I mean, it matters. Of course, it matters. But nothing will rectify what's happened. Or what would bring back Hanna, or my dad, or my eighteen-year-old brother."

Amantha and the other characters of *Rectify* seem steeped and steadied in that idea, too—carrying the wreckage of life after the damage has been done, carrying loss but not being defined by it.

Daniel's mother, Janet (J. Cameron Smith), has decided to sell the long-time family tire store, and her marriage to Ted Talbot Sr. (Bruce McKinnon) has survived a shaky patch resulting from Daniel's return. The Talbots, Daniel's stepfamily, including Teddy Jr. (Clayne Crawford), have had to adjust to Daniel, whom they thought would never be freed, having come to the Holden family after the crime and after Daniel was imprisoned.

Indeed, the entire Holden–Talbot family have come through intact, even Teddy Jr.'s estranged wife, Tawney (Adelaide Clemmons). Although in the final season Teddy Jr. and Tawney's separation has become a decision to divorce and Tawney is often in the margins as Daniel's unrequited desire, she is still accepted by the family and is there at a family dinner to take the phone and add a fond good-bye to him as he vaguely mentions an upcoming trip, the one we learn is to Ohio to find Chloe, who has left Nashville without saying good-bye.

Daniel's epiphany seems likewise to ripple through the family, helping them all move past the two decades that he was incarcerated.

Perhaps more importantly, apart from being a tale of injustice, the exquisitely constructed series, which regularly made critics top-ten lists since its premiere in 2013 (winning a Peabody in 2014), is memorable for its compelling tone.

Aided by an often moody, percussive soundtrack by Gabriel Mann that washes upon us along with the emotional tides of the series, *Rectify* regularly plunges us into small-town life, free of the usual TV car wrecks and mayhem. It feels less like a television show and more often like a literary dive into a southern lyricism reminiscent of Carson McCullers or Cormac McCarthy.

Indeed, *Rectify*'s tone and twang, for viewers, are perhaps its most grounded and most attractive gateway—like the embodiment of the late Elmore Leonard's world in *Justified* (2010–15). *Rectify* fans were treated to homespun clarity each week, deceptively simple in its terseness and its dialect but obviously no less deep in its psychological excavation.

Leonard, who once wrote, "if it sounds like writing, I rewrite it" (2001), is perhaps a relevant precedent for discussing *Rectify* creator and writer Ray McKinnon. Also an actor, McKinnon starred as Reverend Smith in the David Milch HBO series *Deadwood* (2004–6), playing a character whose moral and psychological plight worsened among the relentless cheating and murdering of the gold prospectors and thieves around him. As he mentally unravels, Reverend Smith grows increasingly obtuse in his religious references, more senseless, yet seemingly more rapt and divine in his visions.

Much of the world McKinnon created for *Rectify* evokes this naturalism, aided by conspicuous long pauses and spaces. Likewise, much of *Rectify*'s tone lives in Daniel's stilted manner of speaking and his awkward inability to make small talk after nineteen years in isolation.

These intentional pauses in *Rectify* give the audience the poetry and the dramatic beats for pondering the ambiguities inherent in the character's predicaments. The unspoken moment—a device unnatural for television screenplays, which, by nature, want to compress and concentrate time—is both a regular visitor and virtually a character in *Rectify*.

Those empty spaces speak volumes about *Rectify*'s essential themes, apart from the major plot thread of Daniel's guilt or innocence in the murder of Hanna Dean: the power of forgiveness, perseverance, and reconciliation. McKinnon commented, "You see it time and again where the human condition can be tragic and unjustifiable and inexplicable, and yet human beings continue to endure" (quoted in Potts 2016).

Although the question of Hanna's murder is wrapped (a future trial will reveal that the murderer was one of Daniel's high school pals, Chris or Trey, during a drug party gone wrong down by the river that night), *Rectify* is not simply a murder mystery. Unlike the story line of the first two seasons of *The Killing* (2011–12), AMC's interminable parade of red herrings around the murder of a young woman, the plot of *Rectify* unpeels slowly, credibly, tying up some plot threads while leaving others, such as Daniel's destiny with Chloe, suggested but ambiguous.

Although closing the series' main story line, the finale suggests new openings, leaves doors slightly ajar, its sense of closure and time well invested and well mixed with the invisible footprints of characters' steps yet ahead. It feels as if there is much more to learn, and audiences who remained faithful to niche cable or streaming dramas felt that the expansive television industry could reward them in the future with more of the same.

That's perhaps the significance of *Rectify* and other little shows like it, such as the HBO series *Enlightened* (2011–13) and the FX show *Terriers* (2010). Aside from its commercial arc, *Rectify* is more about the interpersonal stakes of the situation it explores and what we might do if we were in these character's shoes—within the series and without.

McKinnon's world and the tightly knit *Rectify* ensemble were that deep and that compelling to return to each week.

The series was compelling for McKinnon, too. He joked that writing and directing the series as well as understanding its characters' empathy and his own were "a very expensive form of therapy" (quoted in Seitz 2016).

And although we may not often be able to render our innermost, nuanced feelings as easily or as poetically as McKinnon's characters, we are certainly better for having watched.

References

Leonard, Elmore. 2001. "Writers on Writing: Easy on the Adverbs, Exclamation Points, and Especially Hooptedoodle." *New York Times*, July 16. At http://www.nytimes.com/2001/07/16/arts/writers-writing-easy-adverbs-exclamation-points-especially-hooptedoodle.html.

McKinnon, Ray, dir. 2016. "All I'm Sayin'." *Rectify*, season 4, episode 8. Written by Ray McKinnon. Aired Dec. 14, SundanceTV. Original broadcast.

Potts, Kimberly. 2016. "'Rectify' Series Finale Postmortem: Creator Ray McKinnon Talks About Planning That Satisfying Ending, Returning Cast, Romance, and Reunion Possibilities." *YahooTV*, Dec. 15. At https://www.yahoo.com/tv/rectify-series-finale-postmortem-creator-ray-mckinnon-talks-about-planning-that-satisfying-ending-returning-cast-romance-and-reunion-possibilities-182314758.html.

Seitz, Matt Zoller. 2016. "Ray McKinnon on the End of 'Rectify': 'There Is No Definitive Interpretation.'" *Vulture*, Dec. 14. At http://www.vulture.com/2016/12/ray-mckinnon-rectify-series-finale-interview.html.

49

Roseanne

"Into That Good Night, Parts 1 and 2"

MICHELE BYERS

The first time I wrote about *Roseanne* (1988–97) was not long after the series had been put to rest for good.[1] Looking back on that work, like looking back on the show itself through a lens of almost two decades, is to consider televisual history, personal history, and theoretical history. Consider: *Roseanne* ENDED before the premieres of *Sex and the City*, *Dawson's Creek*, and *Will & Grace* in 1998, of *The Sopranos* and *SpongeBob* in 1999, and of *Survivor* and *Queer as Folk* (US version) in 2000; before Netflix, Hulu, and Amazon Prime; before streaming video, on demand, and iTunes. In 1997, most of us had VHS players, and being able to buy used cassettes was a novelty and a thrill. It was rare to be able to buy cassettes of TV shows; for that, you had to rely on syndication and your own recorder and box of tapes. In 1997, David Lavery had published only two books about TV series, and they were two of only a very small number of books that delved into the study of television text in a rigorous but also deeply appreciative way. And, well, in 1997 I was a twenty-six-year-old graduate student trying to figure out what to write my thesis about.[2]

I'm here, of course, to write about the end of *Roseanne*, the finale, but it's impossible to do that without situating the show itself. *Roseanne*, for anyone

---

1. This essay was written before the reboot of *Roseanne* aired in 2018. I do not discuss the reboot, Roseanne Barr's public support for Donald Trump, or the racist tweets that led to the cancellation of the new series the week the last series of edits of this chapter were due. Though all these things are important, especially in relation to questions of intersectionality and the work of white femininity in the maintenance of systems of oppression, they are beyond the scope of this essay.

2. It was on *Buffy the Vampire Slayer* (1997–2003).

who doesn't know, was a sitcom developed by and for stand-up comic Rose-anne Barr in the mid-1980s by producers Marcy Carsey and Tom Werner, who were also behind *The Cosby Show* (1984–92) and many other hit sit-coms. The show was offered as that decade's version of the blue-collar sitcom of earlier decades but had a darker edge rooted in the brash, cynical stylings of its titular character: a smart, working wife and mother of three. The show was extremely popular, ranking in the Nielsen top five for its first six seasons and top twenty for its first eight. In fact, it only really faltered in its final (ninth) season, when it slipped to thirty-fifth ("*Roseanne*" 2016).

The drop wasn't surprising. The final season departed significantly from what was seen as the series' authentic, feminist, blue-collar (white) tropes, focusing instead on the foibles of the Conner family after they win $108 mil-lion in the state lottery. The final season was full of weak satire and unprec-edented melodrama, punctuated by an unusually long list of cameos. Still, in my reviewing of that final season for this chapter, the nostalgia I feel for the characters, for the setting, and even, in a strange way, for the 1990s and the sociopolitics of that time disrupts, somewhat, my memory of how annoyed I was by the final season in 1996–97. That sense of disappointment came to a magnificent climax at the end of the two-part series finale, when the charac-ter Roseanne admitted that not only had the whole final season been a fan-tasy she created for herself to survive the death of her husband but also that, in fact, many of the things we thought we knew about the characters were lies wrought by her creative, artistic meddling. The characters we had loved for almost a decade, she informed us, were not who we thought they were.

At the time, I thought this admission was unforgiveable. But I'll come back to that in a bit.

Most writing on *Roseanne* addresses the actor/titular character, in par-ticular her role, which offered a feminist, working-class critique of the notion of wife and mother as "domestic goddess." This work focuses on Roseanne Barr and the transgressively gendered image of white femininity she tried to bring from the comedy stage to the sitcom screen. A key aspect of the transgression is located in Roseanne's highly visible body, the fat woman's body being a particular anathema to television. Kathleen Rowe describes Roseanne as enacting a "semiotics of the unruly" in which she refuses to be made an object of someone else's admonishing gaze (1994, 203). By making a willing spectacle of herself, Roseanne created "a space to act out the dilem-mas of femininity" (205). She was a woman who strained against the "ide-ology of the 'perfect wife and mother'" (210) and, in so doing, also pushed the boundaries of what was representable in the sitcom culture of the time.

To understand the finale of *Roseanne*, you need to situate the last episodes in the context of a number of highly contrived things that happen starting in season 8: Darlene (Sara Gilbert) gets pregnant and decides to marry David (Johnny Galecki), and Dan (John Goodman) has a heart attack at their wedding. In the season 9 opener, the Conners and Harrises win the state lottery. Dan has a dalliance with his mother's nurse in California, while Roseanne spends much of the season living a parodic rich-and-famous lifestyle (almost a commentary on her own life off-screen [see Caldwell 1995, 262]). The shock of almost losing Darlene and David's premature baby, Harris Conner Healy, brings the matriarch home to the bosom of her sitcom clan. On a variety of levels, these narrative choices are unsettling, almost a form of treason against the established way of knowing the series and its core characters.

The first part of the finale, "Into That Good Night,"[3] finds Dan and Roseanne reconciled, planning the refurbishment of son DJ's room to make way for Darlene, David, and baby Harris. The banter between Roseanne and Dan is familiar and leads into the opening credit sequence featuring framed photographs of each character morphing through their seasonal transitions into the present. This has a suturing effect because it reminds us of our temporal investment in the show and of the affective relationships we have built with characters who have grown and changed over almost a decade. With the return to the show, however, the sutures begin to rip. The rest of the two-part episode is built on a series of reversals as the narrative races between the series' familiar, lovingly sarcastic world and an uncanny, saccharine version of itself. For example, Roseanne offers familiar quips: telling Darlene that the best part of having children is "when you mold their tiny egos to fit your every whim" and DJ (Michael Fishman) that "we love the new baby more than you." At the same time, we find her saying earnestly, "We need to pray like we fight: out loud and in public." Darlene, suddenly softened by motherhood, admits: "I need to learn stuff from you," and later, "I feel safe being near my mom right now."

In part 2, the Conners stage a party for Harris's two-month birthday. The episode opens with the filing in of many primary and secondary characters. One by one, they go up to the baby's room and talk to her in ways that (re)establish them within known conventions. Then the scene breaks,

---

3. All references to "Into That Good Night, Parts 1 and 2" come from Halvorson [1997] 2013.

and we see the familiar exterior of the Conner house. Back inside, all are at the (new, postlottery) dining table eating Chinese take-out. The camera pans around the table, an echo of the original opening credit sequence, and we hear them all arguing good-naturedly. It is a very familiar scene. But then we hear Roseanne in voiceover; one by one, she goes through the characters we know and makes them creatures of her own invention. She tells us that Becky (Sarah Chalke) brought David—not Mark—home, but she thought that David fit better with Darlene and that Mark (Glenn Quinn) fit better with Becky. She tells us: "I still think they would be better the other way around. So, in my writing, I did what any good mother would do . . . I fixed it." This gives the end of the episode the feeling of a *mise-en-abîme*, a story within a story or a character within a character within a character. This feeling only intensifies a few minutes later when Roseanne reveals that the last season—and maybe the whole series—is just a story she wrote for herself.

The set behind Roseanne goes black and disappears. "I lost Dan," she begins, and she is revealed to be sitting at a desk in her basement.

> Dan and I always felt that it was our responsibility as parents to improve the lives of our children by 50 percent over our own. And we did. . . . As a modern wife, I walked a tightrope between tradition and progress, and, usually, I failed, by one outsider's standards or another's. But I figured out that neither winning nor losing count for women like they do for men. . . . When you're a blue-collar woman and your husband dies, it takes away your whole sense of security. So I began writing about having all the money in the world . . . just like the people on TV, where nobody has any real problems and everything's solved within thirty minutes.

Maybe this is essentialist and not terribly intersectional, but *Roseanne*'s version of feminism, as familiar and worn as that original living-room set, is essentialist and nonintersectional. The series, and Roseanne Barr as its representative, here offer a critique of middle-class (white) femininity as standard (in television anyway) by speaking in a collective voice ("we"), but without delving into the complex ways that intersectional social locations differently impact women, including working-class women.

In the second half of the monologue, the voice shifts:

> For a while, I lost myself in food and a depression so deep that I couldn't even get out of bed till I saw that my family needed me. . . . As I wrote about my life, I relived it, and whatever I didn't like, I rearranged. . . . But

the more I wrote, the more I understood myself and why I had made the choices I made, and that was the real jackpot. I learned that dreams don't work without action; I learned that no one could stop me but me. I learned that love is stronger than hate. And most important, I learned that God does exist. He and/or She is right inside you, underneath the pain, the sorrow, and the shame.

This voice doesn't invoke a collective presence or action. It represents only "I."

This is what, I think, many of the harsh critics of the finale reacted to. The problem was not that the finale wasn't funny, but that it took away from the things that were most transgressive about the series and its heroine and replaced them with something much more domestic (both in the sense of being homey and being tame). It was a letdown. The authenticity that formed the bedrock of *Roseanne*'s popularity was pulled from under the audience. The finale's premise felt less like a dream and more like a trick.

For me, however, the finale has grown more deeply affective. With time, I have become less invested in narrative coherence. My own identification has shifted: at twenty-six, I identified more with Darlene (the old Darlene anyway) as wayward daughter; at forty-five, I identify more with Roseanne as mother. Returning to the finale of *Roseanne* was, for me, to ride very different affective rails than I had the first time. This time I felt a deep sense of compassion for the lesson Roseanne was trying to impart about loss, longing, and the way that writing through these things, in fantasy, can be cathartic and liberating.

In her rumination on the "art of television's endings," Jane Feuer states that "the funniest shows always had [*sic*] the most elegiac finales" (2005). The *Roseanne* finale does not have the moxie of the *Seinfeld* (1989–98) finale, the artistry of the *Six Feet Under* (2001–5) finale, or the irony of *The Sopranos* (1999–2007) finale. But what would a "better" ending have looked like? Would Becky have gone to medical school while Mark (David?) stayed home and minded the kids? Would Darlene have become a successful writer, David a successful artist? Would DJ have gone to film school, and little Jerry have ended up a linebacker for the Maroons? Would Dan and Roseanne have continued on in the house on Third and Delaware, living happily ever after? In the end, the refusal of this fantasy is as problematic as Roseanne's trick. The last five minutes of the finale rob us of our established relationship to the characters and the series but also of the "happily ever after" we imagine for them. As Feuer points out, unlike soaps and other texts that "lack that sense of an ending that leads to a final truth and knowledge," *Roseanne* explicitly offers this form of closure: that form just isn't the truth or knowledge the audience was anticipating or desired (2005).

Joanne Morreale asserts that "sitcoms rarely say good-bye." Those that do, she continues, are increasingly self-referential, offering "a final nod to viewers before the series leaves the air" and an ever "greater emphasis upon the discursive relationship set up between text and viewer" (2003, 274, 276). In the first part of the *Roseanne* finale, Dan says to Roseanne: "What you want used to be the right thing to do. Has that changed?" Maybe it's a hint about what's to follow: a reminder that *Roseanne* was always more about her voice and vision than about a social contract (as if Roseanne would have kept that contract anyway). The scene reminds us that, although it feels as if everything has changed, nothing really has. In refusing to acquiesce to our expectations and our desires, in the end Roseanne is actually behaving in much the same way she always had.

References

Caldwell, John T. 1995. *Televisuality: Style, Crisis, and Authority in American Television*. New Brunswick, NJ: Rutgers Univ. Press.

Feuer, Jane. 2005. "Discovering the Art of Television's Endings." *Flow* 2, no. 7. At http://www.flowjournal.org/2005/06/mash-desperate-housewives-er-huff-judging -amy-mary-tyler-moore-genre-televisuality-season-finale/.

Halvorson, Gary, dir. [1997] 2013. "Into That Good Night, Parts 1 and 2." *Roseanne*, season 9, episode 23. Teleplay by Jessica Pentland and Jennifer Pentland (part 1). Written by Roseanne Barr and Allan Stephan (part 2). Aired May 20, 1997, ABC. On *Roseanne: The Complete Ninth Season*. Minneapolis: Mill Creek Entertainment. DVD.

Morreale, Joanne. 2003. "Sitcoms Say Good-Bye: The Cultural Spectacle of *Seinfeld*'s Last Episode." In *Critiquing the Sitcom*, edited by Joanne Morreale, 274–85. Syracuse, NY: Syracuse Univ. Press.

"*Roseanne*." 2016. *Wikipedia*, last modified Sept. 12. At https://en.wikipedia.org /w/index.php?title=Roseanne&oldid=739124346.

Rowe, Kathleen K. 1994. "Roseanne: Unruly Woman as Domestic Goddess." In *Television: The Critical View*, 5th ed., edited by Horace Newcomb, 202–11. Oxford: Oxford Univ. Press.

Further Reading

Douglas, Susan. 1995. "Sitcom Women: We've Come a Long Way, Maybe." *Ms.*, Nov.–Dec.

Dow, Bonnie. 1996. *Prime-Time Feminism: Television, Media Culture, and the Women's Movement since 1970*. Philadelphia: Univ. of Pennsylvania Press.

Gross, Larry. 2001. *Up From Invisibility: Lesbians, Gay Men, and the Media in America*. New York: Columbia Univ. Press.

Johnson, Victoria. 2008. *Heartland TV: Prime Time Television and the Struggle for U.S. Identity*. New York: New York Univ. Press.

Lee, Janet. 1992. "Subversive Sitcoms." *Women's Studies* 21, no. 1: 87–101.

50

Seinfeld

"The Finale, Parts 1 and 2"

ZEKE JARVIS

Seinfeld ran from 1989 to 1998, with Jerry Seinfeld, Julia Louis-Dreyfus, Michael Richards, and Jason Alexander in the principal roles as Jerry, Elaine, Kramer, and George. The show was originally developed by Jerry Seinfeld and Larry David (who would go on to develop *Curb Your Enthusiasm* [2000–]) after the success of Seinfeld's stand-up comedy and David's work on the sketch-comedy show *Fridays* (1980–82). Although David was involved mainly in the writing of the show, he did make a number of cameos. *Seinfeld* is set in New York City, and it focuses largely on personal anxieties, comical and petty struggles, and attempts at dating, job hunting, and other mundane tasks. Its story lines could range from Kramer (Jerry's goofball neighbor) trying to sue a coffee shop after he spills hot coffee on himself while sneaking his drink into a movie theater to Jerry trying to dump his current girlfriend in order to pursue his girlfriend's roommate. And its premise is different from that of many sitcoms in that a central familial or workplace setting doesn't ground the characters' experiences.

Many viewers seem to remember the show as having likeable characters who interact in an entertaining way, but in interviews and on DVD commentaries Jerry and the writing staff regularly point out that the characters are shallow and selfish and often enjoy other people's suffering. That sort of shallowness is also often heightened by the characters' childishness, with George and Jerry regularly debating childish topics such as Superman, baseball heroes, and the game "ink a dink," which relied on childhood rhymes to make major decisions. Like the male characters' superficial nature, this focus on childhood and childish topics and practices give many of the characters a decided lack of emotional depth. A number of episodes revolve around either George or Jerry receiving criticism after failing to demonstrate a proper level of empathy, such as when Jerry is unable to express sympathy for a girlfriend and George pushes an elderly woman out of the way to flee what he believes to be a burning building. Although these actions might not sound humorous on the surface, the show regularly received positive reactions from both critics and fans when it was aired.

In addition to this lack of emotional connection between the characters, the show is unique in its lack of consistent content. As stated earlier, although "situation comedies" often have consistent conceits or situations from which the comedy comes (Lucy's constant attempt to break into show business in *I Love Lucy* [1951–57], for instance, or the central and distinctive location of the bar in *Cheers* [1982–93]), *Seinfeld* is known for being "a show about nothing," where the characters could take on a variety of odd tasks or desires from week to week. In fact, the notion that the show is "about nothing" became part of a string of episodes in which Jerry and his friend George pitch a sitcom to NBC within the world of the show. This situation leads to a great deal of metacommentary upon the show, with events such as the casting of actors to play the different characters and the actress playing Elaine pointing out that George and Jerry are not including female characters in meaningful roles on the show. While some animated television shows—*The Simpsons* (1989–), for instance—had employed self-reflexive humor before *Seinfeld* was aired, *Seinfeld* was the first live-action show to have a string of such episodes, and they are very much in keeping with the series' pushing of the envelope.

Although NBC network executives were not immediately sold on *Seinfeld*, it quickly became a major critical and commercial success. In its last four seasons, the show held the number 1 or number 2 ratings spot every year, and the finale of the series came in at number 1 in the Nielsen ratings. The series also won many awards, including Golden Globes and Emmys, and it was consistently nominated in the years that it did not win. It also consistently received positive reviews by a variety of critics. In addition to these critical successes, the show had a more diffuse and, arguably, unprecedented type of success. Much of its basic language became a sort of shorthand in American speech, whether it was the dismissive terms that the characters would use for side characters, such as *close talker* for people who would lean in while talking or *vegetable lasagna* for a man that Elaine could not be bothered to talk to in a meaningful way, or the euphemisms used, such as "master of my domain" for someone who did not masturbate (a topic that many shows would not even be able to get to air) and thus a way to discuss the character's self-control. In an era before memes and social media,

Seinfeld was able to change the American lexicon in a way that few other shows had before or have since.

With all of this excitement and critical success, there is little surprise that viewers would have very high expectations for the two-part finale.[1] The plot revolves around the Good Samaritan Law, an actual law that can make ignoring a person being victimized a criminal offense. The group of core friends, Jerry, George, Elaine, and Kramer, embark on a trip to celebrate the successful deal for the series cowritten by Jerry and George and airing on NBC. After some of Kramer's foolishness, the plane crashes, though the friends are uninjured. As they wait for assistance, they go around the small town in Massachusetts that is nearest the site of the crash. While there, the friends witness an overweight man being robbed, and instead of going to his aid, they laugh and ridicule him. The victim then approaches a police officer and reports the four friends. They are brought up on charges for not helping, and they contact Jackie Chiles, an attorney who appeared in earlier episodes.

Because the trial will set precedent for the Good Samaritan Law, it garners national focus, and the prosecuting attorney brings in a number of figures from the four friends' past. The second part of the finale consists of a parade of people who have been alienated or hurt by one or more of them. The friends are found guilty and sentenced to jail time. The episode ends with them being led to a cell, where George and Jerry engage in the same trivial argument they had in the first episode of the series, showing that they have not grown at all.

The finale was a major cultural event recognized in a variety of ways. TV Land, for instance, did not air any programming against it. Despite the high expectations and the major commercial success of the final episodes, the audience reception of them was generally negative. Many critics panned the finale for highlighting the negative traits of the characters, and others felt that it was simply rehashing old jokes, not giving sufficient new plotting and material or a clear sense of resolution to the series. Nevertheless, some critics and comedians praised the episodes, stating that the crime of "doing nothing" is very much in line with the vision of a show "about nothing" and that the spirit of the shallow, disaffected characters is consistent with the setting and world of the show's best episodes.

Members of the cast and crew have generally been apologetic about the episodes since their airing. Not long after the show's broadcast, Jerry Seinfeld

---

1. All references to "The Finale, Parts 1 and 2," come from Ackerman [1998] 2007.

hosted *Saturday Night Live*. One of the first sketches was a mash-up of *Seinfeld* and *Oz* (1997–2003), the HBO series set in a harsh prison environment. During the sketch, Jerry talks to the other prisoners, admitting that perhaps he and Elaine should have gotten married in the finale. When Larry David had the cast back on a follow-up show in *Curb Your Enthusiasm*, many commentators claimed that he was attempting a "do-over" of the botched *Seinfeld* finale, with him and Jerry actually referring to the complaints about the finale in the *Curb* episode.

Other commentators and observers simply claimed that expectations were so high for the series' finale that any episode would be fundamentally disappointing, so the reaction was not necessarily to the quality of the final episodes but rather to the quality of the final episodes relative to the best episodes in the total run of the show. Giving some credence to this theory, enthusiasm for the show has not dampened since its original run. It has run regularly in syndication, and sales of DVDs and other merchandise have been strong. There has been some speculation regarding a *Seinfeld* curse related to the poor finale, some claiming that none of the cast has achieved the success that he or she had in the series. Certain incidents have given a sense that the cast has struggled (Jason Alexander's failed shows, for instance, and Michael Richards's meltdown involving the repeated use of a racial slur in his stand-up work), but Julia Louis-Dreyfus has won Emmys for her work on *The New Adventures of Old Christine* (2006–10) and *Veep* (2012–). Seinfeld himself has also had successful ventures. These and other strong performances by some of the cast members have led most observers to conclude that the "curse" is more a matter of the cast reaching a high point with *Seinfeld* rather than having any real drop-off stemming from a poor end to the series.

As a viewer, I tend to sympathize with the writers of the show. It is easy to see that they were trying to give a gift to the fans, letting them remember their favorite characters and moments from the show. The parade of odd side characters was a good reminder of the show's quirky and funny atmosphere. While I understand the feeling that this parade made the finale not quite a clip show and not quite a new episode (or episodes), I think the problem with the finale was less the episodes themselves and more that the series was very well executed, which made it impossible for the writers to both give closure and live up to the best episodes of the middle years of the series. Having Jerry and Elaine marry each other would have been too sentimental and would have been unrealistic for these particular characters. Having the characters drift apart would have been unsatisfying. The other core problem for the writers was that unlike a dramatic series, which has clearly defined story arcs, *Seinfeld* was very episodic in nature, making it hard to have a resolution that tied things together in a logical way. In a sense, the mishmash of characters from different episodes was in line with the nature of the series; it just did not make the final episodes feel like a conclusion. That said, leaving the characters in a jail cell but largely unchanged by being told that they are shallow and self-involved seems appropriate and logical. After all, a show "about nothing" would have a hard time making any clear statement without betraying its own vision.

References

Ackerman, Andy, dir. [1998] 2007. "The Finale, Parts 1 and 2." *Seinfeld*, season 9, episodes 23–24. Written by Larry David. Aired May 14, 1998, NBC. On *Seinfeld: Season 9*. Culver City, CA: Sony Pictures Home Entertainment. DVD.

51

Sex and the City

The Finales

KIM AKASS

The ending of *Sex and the City* (HBO, 1998–2004) came at a time of peak popularity for the series. Our girls—Carrie Bradshaw (Sarah Jessica Parker), Charlotte York (Kristin Davis), Miranda Hobbes (Cynthia Nixon), and Samantha Jones (Kim Cattrall)—got the endings they deserved. Carrie found love with Mr. Big (Chris Noth); Miranda and Steve Brady (David Eigenberg) moved to Brooklyn; Charlotte and Harry Goldenblatt (Evan Handler) were finally approved to adopt; and Sam rediscovered her orgasm after treatment for breast cancer. Whether fans liked the finale or not (and many didn't), these characters' stories were over, and the loose ends had been tied up ("*Sex and the City* [End of Season 6]" 2004). Two years later, however, amid rumors of a film, three alternative endings appeared on YouTube. Ostensibly filmed to forestall leaks in the lead-up to the finale, each plays out a different scenario: in one, Carrie marries the Russian ("*Sex and the City*—Alternative Ending (2)" 2006); in another, she breaks up with Big ("*Sex and the City*—Alternative Ending (3)" 2006); and, in a third, she announces that she and Big are staying together in unwedded bliss ("*Sex and the City*—Alternative Ending (1)" 2006). Two years later, the first of the *Sex and the City* films was released (King 2008), and then a second, *Sex and the City 2* (King 2010), two years after that. In the space of six years, *Sex and the City* enjoyed six finales. How then can we talk about the ending of a television series that has never truly ended? And how can we consider a finale that continues to resist full closure?

When *Sex and the City* first appeared on our television screens, it met mixed reviews. Charlotte Raven famously declared that she "couldn't bear the idea of anyone believing (or affecting to believe) that this worthless pile of swill was in any sense culturally relevant" (1999). And yet the series went on to hit a cultural nerve. Representative of a certain time and place (New York's Manhattan, the turn-of-the-millennium years), aired during a particular ideological shift (pre- to post–September 11, 2001), and privileging a certain class of women (white, liberal, single, and mostly heterosexual), the show seemed to speak only to a limited audience. By the end of its six-year run, however, the series was considered one of US TV's highest-rated sitcoms, was listed as one of *Time*'s "all-TIME 100 TV shows" (Poniewozik 2007), and was nominated for more than fifty Emmy Awards and twenty-four Golden Globes (winning seven and eight, respectively)—not so shabby for a series that was, for Lee Siegel at least, "the biggest hoax perpetrated on straight single women in the history of entertainment" (2002, 32).

Central to critical and scholarly responses was the question of whether the series was feminist or not. For many, our *Sex and the City* women could never be considered feminist. They were obsessed with shoes, sex, and shopping, and by the beginning of season 2 even Miranda remarked: "All we talk about anymore is Big, or balls, or small dicks. How does it happen that four such smart women have nothing to talk about but boyfriends? It's like seventh grade with bank accounts" ("Take Me Out to the Ball Game," 2.1).[1] And despite regularly failing the Bechdel test, the friends spent a large part of every episode gathered round a table, kvetching about their lives in a show of solidarity not seen since *The Golden Girls* (1985–92). Although the *Sex and the City* women were never overtly feminist, and the series was often criticized for its lack of black or working-class representation, the characters and plots showed just how fun female friendships are, with or without a man.

Sex and the City fits into a tradition of television series characterized by their long, open-ended, circular narratives. Like the soap opera, the sitcom emerges from a radio, then TV, tradition. Defined by their need for a continually evolving narrative, long-arc series are designed to keep stories alive and endings at bay, and they thrive on deferred gratification. *Sex and the City*, at the same time, owes a debt to its filmic forebear—the romantic comedy—a genre dependent on delayed consummation. This need to delay the final union, however, should not be taken literally here because the twenty-first-century television narrative had to work overtime to keep the lovers apart. With Carrie and Big signposted as "the right couple" from the very

---

1. All references to episodes of *Sex and the City* come from *Sex and the City* 2000, 2001, 2003a, 2003b, and 2004.

beginning ("Sex and the City," 1.1), their relationship proved unworkable for many reasons; Big's commitment phobia, his marriage to Natasha ("Ex and the City," 2.18), and his move to Napa ("I Heart NY," 4.18) all worked against their eventual union. This on–off relationship allowed Carrie to enjoy other romantic relationships, but, lost in the romantic-fiction narrative, our heroine was enthralled by the idea of her "big love," always longing for the unobtainable Mr. Big.

Little wonder, then, that when the finale, "An American Girl in Paris, Parts Une and Deux," aired on February 15 and 22, 2004, it got such mixed reactions.[2] Played over a montage of vignettes of her friends, Carrie's final voiceover tells us that the most "significant relationship of all is the one you have with yourself." She takes a call; revealed, at last, as "John," Big has put his house in California up for sale and is coming back to New York. Carrie tells us: "If you can find someone to love the 'you' you love, well, that's just fabulous." For many, after six long years of tumultuous ups and downs, Carrie and Big's ending seemed a little too pat, too trite, too perfect, and the fans couldn't help but wonder—Had Carrie and her friends "sold out"?

Rumors of a follow-up film began almost immediately, and after various delays, *Sex and the City* began filming in September 2007 and premiered in London's Leicester Square in May 2008. Although still riding the success of the television series, which by now had been syndicated globally, the movie was met with lukewarm critical responses. The transition from small to big screen was never going to be easy, particularly for the fans who had lived with the series' women weekly. For some, a running time of 145 minutes was too long: "a vulgar, shrill, deeply shallow [and] overlong . . . addendum to a show that had, over the years, evolved and expanded in surprising ways" (Dargis 2008). Nevertheless, the box-office success was considerable, with the film recording the biggest opening for an R-rated comedy, a romantic comedy (Friedman 2008), and a film starring women (Setoodeh 2008), grossing $415.2 million globally ("Box Office" 2010). There seemed no reason not to make a second sequel, and so filming started in September 2009.

If critical responses to the first film had been muted, the media response to *Sex and the City 2* (King 2010) was unprecedented. Of the first film *Newsweek* had asked whether "it's not a case of 'Sexism in the City.' Men hated the movie before it even opened [and] . . . gave it such a nasty tongue lashing

2. All references to "An American Girl in Paris, Parts Une and Deux," come from Van Patten 2004.

you would have thought they were talking about an ex-girlfriend" (Setoodeh 2008). By the time *Sex and the City 2* was released, the knives were well and truly out, and before the film even premiered, it had received savage reviews.

Central to the criticism was the setting of the film in the Middle East. Although the *Sex and the City* women were never avowedly feminist, placing them in an intensely patriarchal world where women have little freedom was provocative, to say the least. Added to the overconsumption of designer labels and the sumptuous luxury of an all-expenses paid trip to Abu Dhabi, the film seemed ostentatious and at odds with the recession-hit culture of 2008. Critics certainly hated the film. And this time it was not just male reporters and journalists who savaged it. For Lindy West, *Sex and the City 2* "takes everything that I hold dear as a woman and as a human—working hard, contributing to society, not being an entitled cunt like it's my job—and rapes it to death with a stiletto that costs more than my car" (2010).

But the worst criticism was saved for the main female characters. For Sukhdev Sandhu, the women's crime was "getting older," and he aimed his most vitriolic attack on Sarah Jessica Parker for "looking, if you happen to go for human pipe-cleaners, absolutely fabulous . . . like a cross between Wurzel Gummidge [*sic*] and Bride of Chucky" (2010). Andrew O'Hagan went one further in the *London Evening Standard* by describing the women as "greedy, faithless, spoiled, patronizing . . . morons" and by calling Samantha a "blond slut" whose inner life "stops at her labia" and who possesses "the desperate mentality of the School Bike" (2010). It seemed that we had gone full circle and were again back in 1998, reading the reviews of the first few episodes of the television series, only this time the criticism was overtly and savagely misogynist. Bidisha, writing in the *Guardian*, wondered whether the critics used the film as an excuse to "spew out a sexist torrent completely out of proportion to what they were reviewing," which may have had something to do with "the spectacle of a lot of grown women together" that "apparently fills [these critics], bafflingly, with contempt" (2010).

Part of the problem for this *Sex and the City* film was in how it revealed the truth behind that happy-ever-after narrative. Whereas the first film focused entirely on Carrie and Big's wedding, the second had no such romantic notions. Sam's sexual adventures had again been curtailed, this time through menopause; Carrie's big romance had settled into nights in front of the TV; and motherhood was not at all what Charlotte had imagined. The truth behind the fiction had never been laid so bare, and the uncomfortable revelations contained in this perhaps final *Sex in the City* film were almost too much for reviewers who had already been faced with the not-so-happy ending lurking beneath the series finale. But the second film still did well, despite the critical mauling, grossing a worldwide total of nearly $300 million and being the highest-grossing romantic comedy of 2010 ("*Sex and the City 2* (2010)" n.d.).

For me, *Sex and the City*'s latest finale spoke directly to the series' legions of loyal fans. The series had always been famed for its honest, forthright depiction of women, sex, and the single girl, and *Sex and the City 2*, although flawed, delivered on the series' original promise. For the *Hollywood Reporter*, the women had never seemed so "profoundly feminist" as they were in *Sex and the City 2* (Farber 2010), and even if for many they were also "blatantly anti-Muslim," the sheer chutzpah of their last outing was in the open criticism of a patriarchal ideology that oppresses women. In this film, Carrie, Miranda, Charlotte, and Samantha offered an antidote to the neat, closed ending of the television series and spoke to and of women's lives, but they were critically denigrated for doing so.

The original series finale, with its traditional happy ending, could only ever be unpicked by the film versions. Women's journeys, through friendships, boyfriends, marriage, children, and menopause, are so rarely celebrated that *Sex and the City*, the television series and the films, should go down in history as an ever so brief moment that allowed women a voice. If, as Laura Mulvey tells us, "the strength of the melodramatic form lies in the amount of dust the story raises along the road" (1977–78, 54), the *Sex and the City* films gave us a chance to see how the "over-determined irreconcilables" (Mulvey 1977–78, 54) played out for our girls. And despite what critics would have us believe, *Sex and the City* delivered on its initial promise back in 1998, even if it "put up a resistance to being neatly settled in the last five minutes" (Mulvey 1977–78, 54).

In the end, I can't help but wonder whether we have seen the last of *Sex and the City*. Rumors regularly surface about a third film, and legions of fans patiently wait for the final installment of the story. Sarah Jessica Parker has confirmed that another outing (either season 7 or film number three) could be on the cards; even the show's creator, Darren Star, is on record as saying that the finale "ultimately betrayed" the group's stories by undermining the fact that "women don't ultimately find happiness from marriage" (quoted in Shepherd 2016) and as suggesting there could be another chapter. Maybe our girls will be back: older and wiser, still friends, and embracing the resolution of their stories. We can only wait and hope for that final finale.

References

Bidisha. 2010. "Why the *Sex and the City* 2 Reviews Were Misogynistic." *Guardian*, June 4. At https://www.theguardian.com/lifeandstyle/2010/jun/04/sex-and-city-critics-misogynists.

"Box Office: 'Sex and the City 2' Nabs $3 Million at Midnight." 2010. *Hitflix*, May 27. At http://www.hitfix.com/articles/box-office-sex-and-the-city-2-nabs-3-million-at-midnight?m=g.

Dargis, Manohla. 2008. "The Girls Are Back in Town." *New York Times*, May 30. At http://www.nytimes.com/2008/05/30/movies/30sex.html?_r=0.

Farber, Stephen. 2010. "*Sex and the City 2*: Film Review." *Hollywood Reporter*, Oct. 24. At http://www.hollywoodreporter.com/review/sex-city-2-film-review-29657.

Friedman, Josh. 2008. "'Sex' Is a Big Hit among Women." *Los Angeles Times*, June 2. At http://articles.latimes.com/2008/jun/02/business/fi-boxoffice2.

King, Michael Patrick, dir. 2008. *Sex and the City*. Burbank, CA: Warner Home Video. DVD.

——, dir. 2010. *Sex and the City 2*. Burbank, CA: Warner Home Video. DVD.

Mulvey, Laura. 1977–78. "Notes on Sirk and Melodrama." *Movie* 25:53–56.

O'Hagan, Andrew. 2010. "*Sex and the City 2* Is Ugly on the Inside." *London Evening Standard*, May 28. At http://www.standard.co.uk/goingout/film/sex-and-the-city-2-is-ugly-on-the-inside-7420066.html.

Poniewozik, James. 2007. "All-TIME 100 TV Shows." *Time*, Sept. 6. At http://time.com/collection/all-time-100-tv-shows/.

Raven, Charlotte. 1999. "All Men Are Bastards. Discuss . . ." *Guardian*, Feb. 9. At https://www.theguardian.com/Columnists/Column/0,,238284,00.html.

Sandhu, Sukhdev. 2010. "*Sex and the City 2*, a Review." *Telegraph*, May 28. At http://www.telegraph.co.uk/culture/film/filmreviews/7764817/Sex-and-the-City-2-review.html.

Setoodeh, Ramin. 2008. "Criticism of 'Sex and the City' Is Mostly Sexist." *Newsweek*, June 2.

"*Sex and the City*—Alternative Ending (1)." 2006. YouTube video, 0:47, posted Dec. 18. At https://www.youtube.com/watch?v=IN0pGZtbco4&feature=youtu.be.

"*Sex and the City*—Alternative Ending (2)." 2006. YouTube video, 1:09, posted Dec. 18. At https://www.youtube.com/watch?v=VQ1NhPlAyM4&feature=youtu.be.

"*Sex and the City*—Alternative Ending (3)." 2006. YouTube video, 1:20, posted Dec. 18. At https://www.youtube.com/watch?v=dSdpLb22sqo&feature=youtu.be.

Sex and the City: The Complete First Season. 2000. Universal City, CA: HBO Video. DVD.

Sex and the City: The Complete Second Season. 2001. Universal City, CA: HBO Video. DVD.

Sex and the City: The Complete Third Season. 2002. Universal City, CA: HBO Video. DVD.

Sex and the City: The Complete Fourth Season. 2003a. Universal City, CA: HBO Video. DVD.

Sex and the City: The Complete Fifth Season. 2003b. Universal City, CA: HBO Video. DVD.

Sex and the City: The Complete Sixth Season. 2004. Universal City, CA: HBO Video. DVD.

"*Sex and the City* (End of Season 6)." 2008. YouTube video, 1:52, posted Mar. 22. At https://www.youtube.com/watch?v=oKAXcnhGMIE.

"*Sex and the City 2* (2010)." n.d. *Box Office Mojo.* At http://www.boxofficemojo .com/movies/?id=sexandthecity2.htm. Accessed July 13, 2016.

Shepherd, Jack. 2016. "*Sex and the City* Reunion: Sarah Jessica Parker All but Confirms Film 3/Season 7." *Independent*, Sept. 26. At http://www.independent .co.uk/arts-entertainment/films/news/sex-and-the-city-reunion-sarah-jessica -parker-film-3-season-7-a7330096.html.

Siegel, Lee. 2002. "Relationshipism: Who Is Carrie Bradshaw Really Dating?" *New Republic*, Nov. 18.

Van Patten, Timothy, dir. 2004. "An American Girl in Paris, Parts Une and Deux." *Sex and the City*, season 6, episodes 19–20. Written by Michael Patrick King. Aired Feb. 15 and 22, 2004, HBO. On *Sex and the City: The Complete Sixth Season*. Universal City, CA: HBO Video. DVD.

West, Lindy. 2010. "Burkas and Bikinis." *Stranger*, May 27. At http://www.the stranger.com/seattle/burkas-and-birkins/Content?oid=4132715.

52

The Shield

"Family Meeting"

DOUGLAS L. HOWARD

As television endings go, the last episode of *The Shield* (2001–8) received just about all of the critical accolades that a writers' room could ever want: "breathtaking" (Flynn 2008), "emotionally overpowering" (Hyden 2008), and the "holy mother of all finales" (Havrilesky 2008a). But in the weeks and months leading up to its end in 2008, viewers were probably thinking as much about creator David Chase and Tony Soprano as they were about creator Shawn Ryan and Vic Mackey.[1] Just as Chase had helped to launch a new era in television programming with *The Sopranos* (1999–2007), he also set the standard for the "quality television" finale nearly a year and a half before *The Shield* finale with his (in)famous "cut to black" following that final scene in the restaurant with Tony (James Gandolfini) and his family. Like Chase, Ryan, with *The Shield*, had also crafted a compelling drama around a morally complex figure, Vic Mackey (Michael Chiklis), an intense, self-serving cop who, along with the like-minded members of his ultraviolent Strike Team, breaks the law just as much as he breaks suspects during interrogation or breaks bones and fights crime out in Farmington. So there might well have been reason to believe that Ryan, too, would somehow leave audiences fumbling in the dark in the show's final moments, as Mackey, after seven seasons of corruption, extortion, infidelity, theft, and murder, tries to see justice done while avoiding its application to himself. In bringing his characters together one last time for a "family meeting," however, *The Shield*'s creator had more in mind than just onion rings and music by

1. Acknowledging his debt to the HBO series, Ryan also believed that people simply could not "write [about *The Shield*] without referencing *The Sopranos*" (Sepinwall 2008).

Journey, something more definitive and darker, perhaps, than a blank television screen.

For all that it may have owed to *The Sopranos* or, for that matter, to tense cop dramas such as *NYPD Blue* (1993–2005) and *Homicide: Life on the Street* (1993–99), *The Shield* was, from the beginning, clearly something different, a show that in its gritty, brutal, blood-stained portrayal of Farmington's mean streets and meaner police officers constantly forced viewers to rethink and redefine their notions of justice and morality. If the police cars were still black and white, the answers on *The Shield* rarely were. This kind of complexity is established early on in the pilot when the "Barn's" detectives struggle to interrogate Dr. Grady, a remorseless "domination-control pedophile" who is holding a young girl captive.[2] "I'm a different kind of cop" (1.1), Mackey tells the doctor, and though that might sound cliché in the world of television police procedurals, he quickly gives those words new meaning as he mercilessly begins to beat the information out of his suspect. Although he called Mackey in precisely for this purpose, to break the doctor, even David Aceveda (Benito Martinez), Mackey's captain, has to turn off the closed-circuit television in the observation room and turn his back on Grady's torture. But moments later Vic walks out with an address, and in the girl's rescue we might be inclined to see some endorsement of police brutality or yet another example of how the ends justify the means.[3] In this seedy world of drug dealers, rapists, serial killers, and gang warfare, Vic and his Strike Team might seem like a necessary evil, a close-knit group of Dirty Harrys for the new millennium gone wild.

But any public daring to give such power and authority to law enforcement in exchange for its own protection is ultimately responsible for the abuses that must ensue. As Claudette Wyms (C. C. H. Pounder) explains the problem to Aceveda in a speech that continues to refer to the nationwide debate on race, policing, and public safety, "What people want these days is to make it to their cars without getting mugged, come home from work, see their stereo still there. Hear about some murder in the barrio, find out the

2. All references to episodes in *The Shield* come from *The Shield* 2002, 2003, 2004, 2005, 2007, 2008, 2009.

3. Discussing the development of plotlines and the moral justification for Vic's behavior in the writers' room, consulting producer James Manos Jr. explained, "The rule of thumb on *The Shield* was Vic Mackey could throw anybody off the roof; he could do whatever he wanted as long as the person he was throwing off the roof did something worse than he did" ("An Interview" 2010, 17).

next day the police caught the guy. If having all that means some cop roughs up some nigger or spic in the ghetto, as far as most people are concerned, it's 'don't ask, don't tell'" (1.1).[4] For Ryan and his writers, this self-interest and complacency were issues they wanted to question and explore in more detail by playing them out to the extreme. Although Vic and his team often abandon Miranda rights to bust a drug dealer or find a rapist or killer, this infraction is, to be sure, the least of their offenses. From planting evidence to coercing and blackmailing others, committing conspiracy, and frying a gang leader's face on a stove top, the Strike Team consistently set a new low for police behavior on television. At the end of the pilot, Vic even kills a Strike Team member who is investigating him for his criminal activities, an unforgivable sin that sets the stage for the rest of the series.

By *The Shield*'s "Final Act," the team's sordid string of illegal activities begins to catch up with them and their solidarity unwinds. Following their robbery of the Armenian Money Train in season 2, they become more suspicious and mistrustful of one another, to the point where Vic's second in command, Shane Vendrell (Walton Goggins), misguidedly kills fellow team member Curtis Lemansky (Kenny Johnson) on his own in season 5 in order to protect his partners and keep Lem from talking. In contrast to his interrogation of Grady in season 1, Vic, in his search for Lem's killer, savagely tortures and kills the wrong man in season 6. When Shane finally comes clean, he and Vic, at odds throughout the series, become irreparably estranged, to the point in season 7 where they even conspire to kill one other. After the shooter "Two Man" confesses to Shane's role in the botched attempt on Ronnie Gardocki's (David Rees Snell) life, Shane is forced to go on the run with his pregnant wife and son, while Vic negotiates an immunity deal for himself with Olivia Murray (Laurie Holden) and Immigration and Customs Enforcement (ICE). Falling for the fake arrest of his wife, Vic, however, fails to include his loyal partner Ronnie in his deal; in one of the show's most shocking moments, he confesses to all of his crimes before promising a stunned Olivia that he will "string Ronnie along" to take the fall for the bulk of them.

As Vic prepared to bring down the drug kingpin Beltran (Francesco Quinn) and provide ICE with a major drug bust in exchange for immunity,

4. Along these lines, Mike Chopra-Gant believes that by repeatedly placing the power of "'natural' justice" in the hands of a "middle-aged white man," the series "conveys a compelling sense that a successfully integrated multicultural society is inevitably dependent on the continuing power of the white patriarch" (2012, 132–33).

fans and critics of the show, in looking ahead, were forced to deal with their ambivalence toward him and what would be the most appropriate conclusion to his story, in the same way that they had to when the end came for Tony Soprano.[5] Heather Havrilesky perfectly expressed this conflict in her *Salon* piece prior to the last episode: "I want Vic Mackey to live happily ever after [but] I'm preparing myself—like most loyal viewers—to see [him] go down, big time" (2008b).[6]

As a finale, "Family Meeting" (7.13) does touch, in some way, upon most of the major characters in the series, from Dutch's (Jay Karnes) interrogation of the manipulative teen killer Lloyd to the end of Steve Billings's (David Marciano) laughable lawsuit against the city and Aceveda's encounter with outspoken mayoral candidate Robert Huggins (André Benjamin).[7] But, like all of the other episodes that came before it, this one does not necessarily offer an easy resolution for those involved or deteriorate into a sentimental good-bye to Vic and his cronies. Rather, in "interrogating" them one last time, the finale, like Vic himself, pulls no punches. Wyms is dying from lupus. Though Julien Lowe (Michael Jace) has made a commitment to suppressing his homosexual inclinations and now enjoys married life with his wife and children, he still looks longingly at a gay couple out on the street. For all of their mutual animosity, the ambitious Aceveda continues to work with Vic to get his own face out in front of the Beltran bust. And then there is the central drama of the Strike Team, or what is left of it.

From his run-in with the gang leader Antwon Mitchell to the murder of Lem to his dealings with the Armenian mob, Shane consistently tries to emulate Vic's ability to maneuver outside of the law and at times to outmaneuver Vic himself; each move serves only to illustrate Shane's shortsightedness. In the finale, his bad judgment finally catches up with him. As he scrambles to cut a deal for his injured wife, Mara, and keep his children out of foster care, Shane finds himself with no choice but to turn to Vic and

---

5. During the lead-up to the last episode of *The Sopranos*, blogger Mark McGuire, for example, reconciled his "love" for Tony with his desire for justice and his need to see our adherence to societal standards "validated": "No matter how we much we root for the villain, he has to get it in the end. Crime doesn't—can't—pay" (2001).

6. Havrilesky, incidentally, also mentioned the last episode of *The Sopranos* in her essay. In thinking about *The Shield* finale, she predicted, "This bad man's entire life is about to explode right in his face, and you can bet there won't be '80s pop playing when it does" (2008b).

7. All references to "Family Meeting" come from Johnson [2008] 2009.

to use his knowledge of their crimes to pressure him into helping them. He is horrified to learn the truth about Vic's immunity deal, however, in his final phone conversation with his mentor turned nemesis—the final contact, in fact, that they will ever have. "Now I'm walking away clean," Vic smirks, "and you're the pathetic asshole headed for Antwon Mitchell-ville." When Shane takes one last stab at Vic with the knowledge that Vic's wife, Corrine (Cathy Cahlin Ryan), has been working with the police against him and that "the mother of [his] children has been playing [him]," Vic is merciless in his retaliation and his vision of the future for Shane and his family: "When you and queen bitch are serving your mandatory life sentences apart, I'm gonna check in on Jackson and this other kid once a year on their birthdays. I'm gonna tell them some good old stories about Ma and Pa, muss their hair, take them out for an ice cream." Distraught, out of options, out of time, and clearly facing the justice-system scenario that Vic has so painfully painted for him, Shane returns home to call a "family meeting," a rather innocent name for such gruesome intentions (and for an episode with such shocking scenes and high drama). The police break through the door just as he shoots himself, and they find the bodies of his poisoned son and pregnant wife arranged peacefully on the bed in the next room. Shane pays then, pays completely for his reckless ways, but in the horror of this murder–suicide we have to wonder if this is justice or just a bloody tragedy.

Moreover, for all of the importance that both Vic and Shane place on family—in their phone conversation, it is the topic that they choose to deal each other the greatest injury—family, ironically, that they ultimately sacrifice as a result of their crimes. While Shane takes some comfort, perhaps, from the knowledge that he and his family die together, Vic is denied the solace of togetherness as Corrine and his children go into witness protection in the wake of his immunity deal. (Olivia Murray agrees to relocate them as yet another way of getting back at Mackey.) And if the Strike Team is another family of sorts, built on trust and brotherhood, Vic loses them, too, loses them all in the end—Lem, Shane, and finally Ronnie. Though he mistakenly believes that he shares Vic's immunity (because Vic, as part of his deal, cannot tell him the truth), a betrayed and enraged Ronnie is arrested for all of the team's crimes (or, as Dutch tells him, "[t]he last three years") shortly after he and Vic singlehandedly bring down Beltran.

Inasmuch as Claudette is consistently the voice of moral conviction on the series, she, as the Barn's conscience, is appropriately also the one who puts Mackey's career in perspective in one of the final scenes in the interrogation room.[8] "All those busts, all those confessions you got in this room, illegal or otherwise, all the drugs you got off the street tonight for ICE," she charges as she lays out the grisly crime-scene photos of Shane and his family and as Vic sits pensively, uncomfortably on the other side of the table. "You must be very proud of yourself. This is what the 'hero' left on his way out the door." Looking down at the photographs, at what he has done, he appears shaken and remorseful, just as shaken and remorseful as he is in the show's final moments, slumped in his cubicle at ICE, where he will spend the next three years off the streets, laboriously analyzing reports and writing memos. As Wyms points out, Vic has done a great deal of good in his time at the Barn, so, perhaps, there is some justice in the fact that he is the only Strike Team member who does not die or go to jail, who walks away scot-free. But he has also done a great deal of bad, so if he must, as Corrine maintained in a previous episode, "pay some kind of price," just as Shane does, then there is equally some kind of justice in Vic's fate: the loss of everything and everyone he has ever held dear. Alone in the office at the end, he can only stare at photos of his children and of Lem and think about what his actions, his crimes, have cost him, a private hell (or purgatory, at least) for Mackey, the renegade cop.

Of course, Vic's silence only leaves us with questions. Does he genuinely feel bad?[9] What is he really feeling through all of this? If remorse is a real possibility for Vic, would he have been able to do all that he does in the end, or is he, like Tony Soprano, more sociopathic than he would ever dare admit? (When Corrine asks Vic in an earlier episode of the last season if he feels guilty about all of the things that he has done with the Strike Team, he says that he does not "think about it" [7.8].) As onerous as his desk duty may be, Vic still walks out of the office with gun in hand. He is still out there. Who knows where he will be in three years and what new deals he will have created for himself?

8. In an essay on *The Shield*, I talk about "the interrogation room as a place of confession" and "a place of truth" (Howard 2012, 106), for the interrogators as well as their suspects. Where Vic's violent interrogation of Grady proves that the doctor is a criminal and shows how far Vic will go to get what he wants, Wyms's interrogation of Mackey amounts to a final accounting of his character.

9. Again, inasmuch as the interrogation room is a place of truth, Vic may reveal some sense of guilt and responsibility for what he has done. As Ryan explains Vic's violent response to the camera in the room, "[He] realizes he probably let someone see something he didn't want to be seen, and he compartmentalizes again and turns it off" (Sepinwall 2008).

Like *The Sopranos, Dexter* (2006–13), *Mad Men* (2007–15), and so many other series covered in this book, *The Shield*, as a serial narrative, ends with some open-ended closure, and we are certainly left to speculate as to what happens next. (Even Shawn Ryan considered the possibilities: "I envision Ronnie with a shaved head, probably having to sidle up to some of the white supremacist crowd [in prison] to stay alive, so that might be interesting to see" [Sepinwall 2008].[10]) Given the kinds of criminals that have come through the Barn's doors and the kinds of personal/moral problems that the other officers have faced from season to season, we have to wonder if the Barn will be able to survive without someone like Vic or if more restrained, less-violent, "by the book" police officers will be able to keep the peace or stem the tide of criminality out on the streets of Farmington. As Colonel Jessep justifies himself to Daniel Kaffee in that iconic speech in *A Few Good Men*, "My existence, while grotesque and incomprehensible to you, saves lives. You don't want the truth because deep down, in places you don't talk about at parties, you want me on that wall; you need me on that wall" (Reiner [1992] 2001). As grotesque as Vic's existence is, does Farmington—or, for that matter, do we—need him or some version of him to survive?[11] And if we give the Jesseps and Mackeys of the world free reign in exchange for our personal safety, can we live with the consequences of our silent complicity? Maybe we can't handle the truth. On a larger level, Vic's freedom, as restricted as it might be, is in many ways appropriate because there are no easy answers to the moral questions that the show asks. Like Mackey, they are still out there, too, as policy makers and pundits continue to debate and define police powers, as racial tensions between the police and the public continue to escalate, and as controversial police shootings are reviewed by authorities and tried in the court of public opinion.[12] In this very real and troubling sense, *The Shield* is still with us.

Chase's ending for *The Sopranos* may well have referred to the inherent difficulty in any definitive ending for characters as complex as Tony and

10. Although Ryan was curious to know "what Vic Mackey is doing now," he also said in an interview by *Entertainment Weekly*'s Derek Lawrence in 2017 that he had mixed feelings about reviving the show.

11. In my essay on *The Shield*, I wonder if, "in his absence, . . . another [Mackey would] be forced to rise up, created [and necessitated] by the streets themselves" (Howard 2012, 123).

12. Considering these issues in detail, German Lopez bluntly concludes, "Policing in America is broken" (2017).

Vic, a difficulty that showrunners have addressed in various ways in this era of quality television. Audiences, after all, alternately support and despise these antiheroes, so any ending that dares to finish their story runs the risk of moralizing about them as well as about the audience itself. (Chase has openly rejected such aesthetic visions of moral accountability, in part because they run counter to his realistic sensibilities.[13]) If these protagonists are punished, then our support of them should also be condemned and denied. (I am reminded of Mark McGuire's suggestion that Tony Soprano has "to pay for *our* sins" [2001, my emphasis].) If they go free and are rewarded, then these shows could stand as endorsements of such bad behavior. Viewers in search of a resolution to the moral dilemmas that these characters pose might well be better off finding themselves in a "cut to black" and in the darkness of an existential void on their television screens. But, with *The Shield*, Shawn Ryan demonstrated another way in which such stories could be told and be both resolved and unresolved, in which the needle of conscience could be threaded (and unthreaded) for all involved, and in which the thematic possibilities of reward, crime, and punishment could be explored while still being true to the characters, the story lines, and the edgy intensity that had been a staple of the series from the beginning. For all of the comparisons that were made to that other series and that other ending, *The Shield*, then, in the end and in its ending left this example for television on its way out the door.

References

Chopra-Gant, Mike. 2012. "'You Want Me to Lick Your Balls, Daddy?' Masculinity, Race, and Power in *The Shield*." In *Interrogating "The Shield,"* edited by Nicholas Ray, 124–44. Syracuse, NY: Syracuse Univ. Press.

Flynn, Gillian. 2008. "*The Shield*." *Entertainment Weekly*, Nov. 19. At http://www.ew.com/article/2008/11/19/.

Havrilesky, Heather. 2008a. "Damned for All Time." *Salon*, Nov. 25. At http://www.salon.com/2008/11/26/shield/.

———. 2008b. "Rebel without a Badge." *Salon*, Nov. 11. At http://www.salon.com/2008/11/11/the_shield/.

13. In discussing the "Employee of the Month" episode of *The Sopranos* with Brett Martin, Chase explained exactly why he never had Dr. Jennifer Melfi's (Lorraine Bracco) attacker brought to "justice" by Tony or provided viewers with some morally satisfying resolution: "That's not the way the world works" (quoted in Martin 2007, 181).

Howard, Douglas L. 2012. "Scenes from the Interrogation Room: Power, Character, Truth, and Justice in *The Shield*." In *Interrogating "The Shield,"* edited by Nicholas Ray, 105–23. Syracuse, NY: Syracuse Univ. Press.

Hyden, Steven. 2008. "*The Shield*: 'Family Meeting.'" *A.V. Club*, Nov. 25. At http://www.avclub.com/tvclub/the-shield-family-meeting-13394.

"An Interview with *Dexter* Writer and Developer James Manos, Jr." 2010. In *"Dexter": Investigating Cutting Edge Television*, edited by Douglas L. Howard, 14–24. London: I. B. Tauris.

Johnson, Clark, dir. [2008] 2009. "Family Meeting." *The Shield*, season 7, episode 13. Written by Shawn Ryan. Aired Nov. 25, 2008, FX. On *The Shield, Season 7: The Final Act*. Culver City, CA: Sony Home Entertainment. DVD.

Lawrence, Derek. 2017. "*The Shield*: Creator Shawn Ryan on the Possibility of a Revival." *Entertainment Weekly*, Mar. 14. At http://ew.com/tv/2017/03/14/the-shield-shawn-ryan-15th-anniversary/.

Lopez, German. 2017. "American Policing Is Broken: Here's How to Fix It." *Vox*, Sept. 1. At https://www.vox.com/policy-and-politics/2016/11/29/12989428/police-shooting-race-crime.

Martin, Brett. 2007. *"The Sopranos": The Complete Book*. New York: HBO.

McGuire, Mark. 2001. "Tony Soprano Must Die." *Times Union*, Mar. 2. Reprinted in "Tony Soprano Must Die . . . or Not." *Times Union*, June 7, 2007. At http://blog.timesunion.com/television/simple-question/416/.

Reiner, Rob, dir. [1992] 2001. *A Few Good Men*. Culver City, CA: Columbia Tristar Home Video. DVD.

Sepinwall, Alan. 2008. "*The Shield*: Shawn Ryan Post-final Q&A." *What's Alan Watching*, Nov. 25. At http://sepinwall.blogspot.com/2008/11/shield-shawn-ryan-post-finale-q.html.

The Shield: The Complete First Season. 2002. Beverly Hills, CA: 20th Century Fox Home Entertainment. DVD.

The Shield: The Complete Second Season. 2003. Beverly Hills, CA: 20th Century Fox Home Entertainment. DVD.

The Shield: Season 3. 2004. Beverly Hills, CA: 20th Century Fox Home Entertainment. DVD.

The Shield: Season 4. 2005. Beverly Hills, CA: 20th Century Fox Home Entertainment. DVD.

The Shield: Season 5. 2007. Beverly Hills, CA: 20th Century Fox Home Entertainment. DVD.

The Shield: Season 6. 2008. Culver City, CA: Sony Home Entertainment. DVD.

The Shield: Season 7: The Final Act. 2009. Culver City, CA: Sony Home Entertainment. DVD.

53

Six Feet Under

"Everyone's Waiting"

ERIC GOULD

Leave it to a show about our least favorite subject to leave behind a finale that lives on long after its broadcast, like a revered ancestor in his spectral authority, as one of the most remembered of all.

And this ghost endures against its backdrop—the neurotic goings-on of Fisher & Sons Funeral Home and its resident proprietors, the privileged, middle-class owners who plod their way through their love–hate of the place.

Such is the nature of things—a TV show and its alchemic recipe, sometimes a success, often not.

Who knew?

Of all the many things that HBO's *Six Feet Under* accomplished after five seasons (2001–5), the two most notable might be its humanism, literally, in all its courage over daily demise and, in the circumstance of the Fisher clan—off duty, off the job—the other narrative foot remarkably mucked in the mud of astonishingly chronic, almost Olympian dysfunction.

In other words, the show steeped in death is often at its core a tale of polarities—a long list of things to be grateful for and our ingenious ability to be quite the opposite.

As *Six Feet Under* swings wildly between those poles, it gyrates, hurly-burly, between others: oldest son Nate (Peter Krause), finally surrendering to his life as an adult and coproprietor of Fisher & Sons but chronically dissatisfied, as voiced by his father's mocking ghost; brother David (Michael C. Hall), straight-laced, uptight, caught between his self-recrimination and self-acceptance as a gay man finally out of the closet; mother Ruth (Frances Conroy), widowed by Nate Sr.'s death in a car accident, her view of herself as a self-sacrificing nurturer vexed by the alienated family around her; and young daughter Claire (Lauren Ambrose), experiencing the turmoil of youth and artistic impulse, lurching, flourishing, yet surrounded by the dead and grieving in the mortuary where she lives.

These are tantalizing, illuminating balancing acts that are set upon a remarkably sturdy dramatic foundation. That is owed, in part, to the series' long-form poetic technique, the anaphora of allowing its long arc to progress in each episode only after the introduction of the latest Fisher & Sons occupant by showing his or her often unsavory demise, followed by a ghostly white title card giving his or her birth and death dates (O'Sullivan 2010).

That episodic conceit of the *Six Feet Under* deaths celebrates life's absurd pageant.[1] These deaths come in every variant, swinging from the horrific to the comic. Episode 302 sees a suicide victim arrive after his murder spree at work claims three others. In episode 402, a religious woman runs into traffic chasing what she thinks is a flock of souls ascending to heaven because she believes the Rapture has begun. She is killed, never knowing they are really blow-up sex dolls that have escaped the netting of a delivery truck driven by a couple of frat boys.

Perhaps no one was more qualified about his subject than creator and writer Alan Ball. His older sister was killed in a car accident in which he, a thirteen-year-old at the time, also was a passenger (Waxman 2002). Over the next years, there were a series of deaths in Ball's family, culminating in the loss of his father while Ball was in college. He said later, "When you're 13 years old and one of the persons most close to you dies right in front of you, death is a constant companion" (Ball 2012). Like character Claire Fisher, Ball was the baby of the family, eight years younger than his sister and almost two decades younger than his oldest brother.

Given the often downbeat nature of *Six Feet Under*, it's a surprise to learn that Ball's initial jobs in Hollywood were on sitcoms, first as a writer on ABC's *Grace under Fire* (1993–98), then moving to CBS's *Cybill* (1995–98). Both shows hardened him to the hazards of being a writer in the commercial network system and the vanities of leading stars (Brett Butler and Cybill Shepherd, respectively) unwilling to be portrayed in unfavorable comic situations.

While in his third and last year on *Cybill*, Ball wrote the screenplay for *American Beauty* (Sam Mendes, 1999). That movie won five Academy Awards, including for him the Outstanding Original Screenplay Award. He

---

1. All references to the episodes of *Six Feet Under* come from Ball 2001–5.

began work on *Six Feet Under* for HBO immediately after that, saying his work in formulaic comedy was the "best, worst experience" a writer could have; because it required him to persevere through something so difficult, he would readily recognize and avoid the pitfalls and flourish in the next good opportunity (Ball 2012).

Six Feet Under ran for five seasons at the start of the new century, totaling more than sixty episodes. It received more than 150 television award nominations and won many, including a directing award Emmy for Ball in 2002. The series' wide popularity stood upon its fearlessness in excavating the Fisher family's neuroticism, self-inflicted failures, casual cruelty—and enduring loyalty to each other.

Through those harrowing dives, the series is perhaps one of the more sober and truthful explorations of love and commitment done on television.

Ball's examination of what it is to suffer and sustain is at the root of his *Six Feet Under* narrative and is its legacy. About this approach, he said, "You look for that humanity, that glimmer of something that makes you feel compassionate, no matter what they do." He added, "People can behave really badly. We can still see the pain in them that's causing them to behave that way but not everybody has to be nice . . . it doesn't mean you approve of it" (Ball 2012).

Also essential to fully understanding the series is Ball's interest in Buddhist philosophy. It informed one of his most discussed sequences in *American Beauty*, an extended shot of a plastic bag mundanely carried along by the wind, seeming to dance in choreographed movement. He said, "Life is suffering. We have desires and expectations and egos and we compare the reality we have, which is miraculous and wondrous, with this reality we desire. That somehow distances us from actually taking part fully with the reality we do have and that creates suffering. For me, the thing that I love is that it's all about the present moment" (quoted in Molitorisz 2011a).

Life as something vaporous and elusive and our inability to recognize that truth are reprised in the *Six Feet Under* finale, "Everyone's Waiting."[2] Having to decide whether to sell the funeral home after Nate's death, David asks Ruth, "We've been clutching so desperately to the past, and for what?" (He doesn't sell, after a visitation from Nate's ghost, with the noncorporeal Nate now assuming their late father's role.)

---

2. All references to "Everyone's Waiting" come from Ball 2005.

Claire, leaving home for her drive to New York to become an assistant in a stock photography company, turns to take a picture of her family as they are gathered on the front porch to say good-bye to her. As she raises the camera, Nate's ghost behind her whispers, "You can't take a picture of this. It's already gone."

It is no accident that the succeeding final sequence, of Claire's drive from California to New York, also begins a metaphysical shift for the audience and again mirrors Ball's interest. She moves literally from west to east in her journey, starting out in tears, Nate chasing her in the side-view mirror, and grows more at peace as she crosses the American desert.

These subversions of Western thinking and the idea of death as the end dive deeper as the time sequence becomes unraveled in flash-forwards superimposed over Claire's trip. The future begins to be revealed as she drives, and our linear view of time as past, present, and future is undone. Events are happening in simultaneity, in totality, with time now a great wheel where all points are omniscient, transcendent, and each is able to see the others. The center is everywhere that Claire is. As passengers in that car, we are asked to witness time and death outside of our usual context.

Claire's six-minute drive to the soundtrack of Sia's song "Breathe Me" has, of course, become one of the most remembered and beloved television farewells. With Claire at the wheel, *Six Feet Under* gives us an exquisite demise, a montage of jump cuts super-fast-forwarding to the deaths, in turn, of each of its main characters. In the end of this series about endings, those who spent their lives ushering others through the final exit meet their own ultimate fates.

They include Brenda (Rachel Griffiths), Nate's on-again, off-again partner, who has finally righted her sexual compulsions. She goes on to adopt Nate's daughter, Maya, from another relationship and raises her with Willa, their daughter who is born after Nate's death ("The Silence," episode 507). Intensely scrutinized as a child by her psychotherapist parents, Brenda has become a therapist. Ball said, "From day one Brenda was a person who had herself explained to her. She was conditioned to be a narcissist. . . . [H]er sexual compulsion during those early seasons was about feeling, not thinking" (Ball 2012). And, of course, she passes away while listening to still-narcissist brother Billy (Jeremy Sisto) talking about his favorite subject: himself. In the one comic moment of the finale, he literally talks her to death.

Ruth, surrounded by family at her hospital bed, sees Nate Sr.'s ghost waiting, uncharacteristically smiling, and then Nate's, just outside the door. Both are welcoming her to the other side.

David, having taught his adoptive son, Durrell, the funeral business and passing it down to him (as it was passed down to him by his father), sees his now-deceased partner Keith (Matthew St. Patrick), vibrant and young, coming to meet him just as David collapses at a family picnic at the old age of seventy-five.

In the penultimate scene, as Claire continues east, we flash to her lying frail, at the age of 101, having outlived her family, a solitary nurse nearby. She is surrounded by her photos of them throughout their lives, seen as the camera swings quickly through her Manhattan apartment and ends in a close-up of her on her own death bed in 2085.

It was always Ball's intent to confront death as a recurrent, natural part of life, something to be accepted, not feared. Nate's death, four episodes prior to the finale, allows all of the *Six Feet Under* characters to release themselves from their bonds to the past. Ball said, "Death is a companion for all of us, whether we acknowledge it or not, whether we're aware of it or not, and it's not necessarily a terrible thing" (quoted in Molitorisz 2011b).

In a great circle, the series closes as the main title sequence always has: unclasped hands tear apart forever, time-lapsed flowers wilt in a quick second. There is a macabre clattering, recalling skeletons and embalming-room pots and pans. And here, last, the camera pans away from Claire's car, still driving east, its perspective and image zooming skyward. The series ends, yet Claire's early journey has just begun.

All fades to white.

References

Ball, Alan, creator. 2001–5. *Six Feet Under.* Aired June 3, 2001, to Aug. 21, 2005, HBO. HBO On Demand. Accessed Jan.–Feb. 2017.

———, dir. 2005. "Everyone's Waiting." *Six Feet Under*, episode 12, season 5. Written by Alan Ball. Aired Aug. 21, HBO. HBO On Demand. Accessed Jan.–Feb. 2017.

———. 2012. Interview. Archive of American Television, Mar. 29. At http://www.emmytvlegends.org/interviews/people/alan-ball#.

Molitorisz, Sacha. 2011a. "Alan Ball." *Sydney Morning Herald*, Oct. 2. At http://www.smh.com.au/entertainment/tv-and-radio/alan-ball-20110929-1kzvv.html.

———. 2011b. "Fangtastic." *Sydney Morning Herald*, Aug. 27. At http://www.smh.com.au/entertainment/tv-and-radio/fangtastic-20110824-1janq.html.

O'Sullivan, Sean. 2010. "Broken on Purpose: Poetry, Serial Television, and the Season." *Storyworlds* 2. At http://www.jstor.org/stable/10.5250/storyworlds.2 .1.59.

Waxman, Sharon. 2002. "Alan Ball's Life after Death." *Washington Post*, May 26. At https://www.washingtonpost.com/archive/lifestyle/style/2002/05/26/alan -balls-life-after-death/47492a0b-169b-4e13-8663-6d8747fc6a20/?utm_term =.8254d785d9f8.

54

Smallville

"Finale"

STAN BEELER

Smallville, the extremely popular addition to DC Comics' Superman franchise—first under the aegis of the WB network, then, after a merger, under the CW—was originally broadcast in 2001, and its finale was shown in 2011. The show was developed by the writing team of Alfred Gough and Miles Millar, who served as its showrunners and executive producers until 2008,[1] and it chronicled the teen years of Clark Kent (Tom Welling), an alien orphan who develops the alter ego Superman. Although it may seem that the show was based on the Superboy comics, which also focused upon the early life of Clark Kent, in fact for copyright reasons *Smallville* avoided the name "Superboy" (McNary 2006; Kroll 2013), and for aesthetic reasons the young Clark Kent in the TV series never wears the iconic Superman costume or employs the power of flight. The creators of the show referred to the latter decision as the "no flights, no tights" policy (Denison 2011, 65), and it remained in effect until "it ultimately fell by the wayside in [the] two-hour May 13 series finale" (Goldberg 2011).

One of the more interesting institutional aspects of *Smallville* is that the traditionally male-centered Superman mythos was embraced by the CW network, a cable venue that was noted for its success with female viewers. Dawn Ostroff, president of Entertainment for the CW during *Smallville*'s run, stated that the show was part of a strategy to expand into the male demographic, while not abandoning the network's core audience, "18- [to] 34[-year-old] women." "Women," she added, "love to watch action-adventure franchise

---

1. Along with Millar and Gough, the showrunners for *Smallville* included Todd Slavkin, Darren Swimmer, Kelly Souders, and Brian Peterson.

shows" (Hibberd 2010). *Smallville* is a Superman story that incorporates elements that marketing executives perceived as attractive to a female audience (e.g., the importance of women in the superhero's life and the emotional relationships between the characters) while attracting a male audience to a female-targeted network environment (Stevens 2010). Moreover, the intense focus on the love–hate relationship between Lex Luthor (Michael Rosenbaum) and Clark Kent indicates that the network attempted to include the lucrative gay demographic in its version of the Superman story (Davis 2004, 136).

Smallville is a prime example of the modern television narrative's move toward increased serialization (Mittell 2006). Although the first two seasons were more or less episodic examples of the monster-of-the-week genre, from the third season until its conclusion, *Smallville* employed the technique of long story arcs, often with a villain or problem that is not resolved until the season finale. The movement away from an episodic format enabled a novelistic structure with a concomitant increase in the use of character development as a narrative strategy. This is especially interesting because the show began as a study of the "teenage" superhero and his friends but ended ten years later, well past its protagonists' teen years. After this much time, not even the skillful use of cinematography and costuming could convince the audience that the central figures of the series were still attending high school. The creative staff of *Smallville* overcame the inherent "best before date" limitation of actors portraying teens by embracing the march of time. The diegetic reality of *Smallville* is not static; it follows the characters as they age and progress from their teen years into their early twenties. *Smallville* also tends to incorporate trends in music and fashion of the mundane world outside of the show's diegesis (Beeler 2011, 13–14). Moreover, the central figures of the show move from the eponymous small-town venue to the big city (aptly named Metropolis) and take up adult careers. Indeed, as is common with maturing youth, members of the *Smallville* core cast find new friends, become estranged from old companions, and develop new love interests outside their high school environment.

Serialized television maintains audience interest through the use of central problems or questions that usually remain unanswered during the course of the show. If a question is resolved, then a new question must take its place. For example, the questions concerning the future of Lana Lang's (Kristin Kreuk) relationship with Clark end and are replaced with similar questions concerning Clark's relationship with Lois Lane (Erica Durance). The finale episode of *Smallville* was designed to resolve most of the open questions at the heart of this continuing narrative.[2] For the core *Smallville* audience during its original broadcasts, these burning questions included: Will Clark finally marry Lois? Will Chloe Sullivan (Allison Mack) marry Oliver Queen (Justin Hartley)? And, for the more action-oriented types, when will Clark put on the suit and fly?

The opening of the final episode implies a resolution to the Chloe question while employing a direct reference to the comic-book heritage of the franchise. Chloe—who is, incidentally, one of the few primary characters in the TV series who has no precedent in the comic universe—is reading a bedtime story from a DC comic to a boy who appears to be her son. Significantly, the comic is entitled *Smallville*, not *Superboy*. This *Princess Bride*-like frame story then cuts to an ominous rogue planet crashing through the solar system on its way to destroy Earth. (The story in the comic is the enclosed narrative of the episode.) This apocalyptic vision is the setup for the conclusion of the final season's story arc, in which the mysterious villain Darkseid is vanquished. The banner title "Seven Years Earlier" fixes the time of the enclosed narrative.

The narrative then moves to Lois and Clark arguing over her intention to cancel their wedding. It is clear that the emotional thread of Clark and Lois's indefinitely postponed love affair takes precedence in the multiple plotlines of this concluding episode. However, the macrocosm of world-ending danger is firmly linked to this romantic problem because it is the current reason that Lois and Clark cannot have a "normal," happy life together. In a particularly revealing scene, Lois argues that she must cancel her wedding to Clark, and Chloe assures her that Clark "needs to rest; to love; to laugh. And when he finally decides to take to the skies, he's going to need you to ground him." Lois responds, "That's what I am afraid of. I'm grounding him; keeping him from soaring to new heights." Despite much soul-searching on the part of both bride and groom, the much-anticipated wedding almost takes place. However, it cannot be completed because Chloe must save Clark from losing his powers forever by preventing him from putting on a wedding ring of gold kryptonite, which brings the proceedings to a grinding halt. (One presumes that the symbolic reference is to Chloe's long-standing yet fruitless crush on Clark.) In keeping with the softer side of the Superman tenor of the show, a large proportion of the scenes in the enclosed narrative are concerned with emotional relationships involving the major female characters: Chloe, Tess

2. All references to "Finale" are from Beeman and Fair 2011.

(Cassidy Freeman), and Martha Kent (Annette O'Toole), Clark's adoptive mother.

This theme of emotional maturation carries over to Clark's need to become his own (super)man. He must forgo his dependence on his mentors and make his own choices. Indeed, while discussing the future with the shade of Jor-El (Terence Stamp), his dead father, Clark says that he realizes that he can't keep leaning on (the spirits of) his biological father, Jor-El, and his adoptive father, Jonathan Kent (John Schneider); he has to reject the influence of both father figures in an attempt to gain control over his life. The final episode of *Smallville* is the culmination of ten years of Clark's development from orphan prodigy to world-saving hero. He must deal with confusing and conflicting advice from his fiancé, his mother, and his friends, and, perhaps most significantly, he must reconcile with the template of himself that he has built up throughout his teenage years. "I need to go beyond where either of you [the two father figures] can guide me anymore; to be the hero that the world needs me to be. . . . I need to make my own path." In a traditional superhero story, the tendency is to make the realization of the hero's powers the most important part of the narrative. However, in *Smallville* it is the emotional maturity to wield those powers that is of greatest importance. In this more female-friendly version of the Superman mythos, the reversed precedence of emotional elements is appropriate. Although the male coming-of-age story and the full realization of the hero's destiny are still central elements of the narrative, it is his feelings about those powers and his new role in life that are of central significance.

In keeping with the twin themes of emotional development and interpersonal relationships, Lex Luthor returns after a long absence from the show to complain that Clark has always been a reluctant "chosen one" and that Clark's greatness was fostered by the negative counterbalance Lex himself provided. The narrative significance of their love–hate relationship is highlighted when Lex's sister poisons him with a drug that erases his memory, and he murders her. As his memory disappears, the screen is filled with short excerpts of the high points of his relationship with Clark over the years.

This flashback technique is repeated during Clark's final struggle with the archvillain of the tenth season, who has appropriated the body of Lionel Luther (John Glover). Vignettes of high points of the entire run of the show play as a backdrop to Clark's struggle with his destiny. During the climax of this process of self-realization, Clark goes to the Fortress of Solitude and receives his costume and blessing from Jor-El, his Kryptonian father, as well as from the shade of Jonathan Kent. As soon as he dons the suit, the camera angle changes, the lighting shifts, and the boyish good looks of Clark Kent are transformed to something very close to the steely-eyed, hard-jawed Superman portrayed in the comic books. The resolution of the threats to humankind are almost an anticlimax, and the narrative quickly returns to the frame story. We are assured that Lois and Clark will be married soon (after a seven-year hiatus), the boy listening to the bedtime story is identified as Oliver Queen's son, and the process of resolving unanswered questions is complete.

Smallville's finale is one of the more effective examples of serial resolution that can be found in contemporary television. Because it rests upon three-quarters of a century of mythology concerning the adult phase of Superman's life, the show does not have to deal with audience concerns regarding the hero's subsequent life. Instead, it neatly ties up the emotional threads that provide the heart of this more gender-balanced telling of the old tale.

References

Beeler, Stan. 2011. "From Comic Book to Bildungsroman: *Smallville*, Narrative, and the Education of a Young Hero." In *The "Smallville" Chronicles: Critical Essays on the Television Series*, edited by Lincoln Geraghty, 3–24. Lanham, MD: Scarecrow.

Beeman, Greg, and Kevin Fair, dirs. 2011. "Finale." *Smallville*, season 10, episodes 21–22. Written by Al Septian and Turi Meyer (part 1), Kelly Souders and Brian Peterson (part 2). Aired May 13, CW. Original broadcast.

Davis, Glyn. 2004. "'Saying It Out Loud': Revealing Television's Queer Teens." In *Teen TV: Genre, Consumption, and Identity*, edited by Glyn Davis and Kay Dickinson, 127–40. London: British Film Institute.

Denison, Rayna. 2011. "No Flights, No Tights: *Smallville* and the Roles of Special Effects in Television." In *The "Smallville" Chronicles: Critical Essays on the Television Series*, edited by Lincoln Geraghty, 65–86. Lanham, MD: Scarecrow.

Goldberg, Lesley. 2011. "'Smallville': Why We Didn't See Tom Welling in the Suit." *Hollywood Reporter*, May 27. At http://www.hollywoodreporter.com/live-feed/smallville-why-we-didn-t-192811.

Hibberd, James. 2010. "Q&A: CW's Ostroff Talks Pilots, 'Vampire Diaries' and More." *Hollywood Reporter*, Mar. 4. At http://livefeed.hollywoodreporter.com/2010/03/qa-the-cws-dawn-ostroff.html.

Kroll, Justin. 2013. "Warner Bros. Wins Final Element of 'Superman' Copyright Case." *Variety*, Nov. 21. At http://variety.com/2013/film/news/warner-bros-wins-final-element-of-superman-copyright-case-1200865554/.

McNary, Dave. 2006. "Super Snit in 'Smallville.'" *Variety*, Apr. 4. At http://variety
.com/2006/biz/markets-festivals/super-snit-in-smallville-1117941008/.

Mittell, Jason. 2006. "Narrative Complexity in Contemporary American Television." *Velvet Light Trap* 58:29–40.

Stevens, Michael. 2010. "*Smallville* Returning for Tenth Season." *Hollywood North Report*, Mar. 5. At http://www.imdb.com/news/ni1710647/.

55

Sons of Anarchy

"Papa's Goods"

AMANDA POTTER

After seven seasons of motorcycles and mayhem on *Sons of Anarchy* (2008–14), a series described as "*Hamlet* on Harleys" (see, for example, Carpenter 2008 and Donahue 2014), the series protagonist, Jax Teller (Charlie Hunnam), meets death head on in the series finale, "Papa's Goods." Jax leaves his sons in the hands of his exwife and says good-bye to his "brothers"—members of the Sons of Anarchy Motorcycle Club Redwood Original (SAMCRO), which Jax has led as president since he took over from Clay Morrow (Ron Perlman) at the end of season 4. Jax then takes to the highway on his father's old motorcycle and, chased by a series of police cars, rides into a truck near the place where his father crashed years earlier.[1]

The extended end sequence, which cuts between Jax's final ride, SAMCRO members at home and at the clubhouse, and the car taking his sons away to a new life, is accompanied by a song cowritten by series creator Kurt Sutter, "Come Join the Murder." The song highlights the ambiguous and ultimately fatal nature of life as a member of SAMCRO, where murder is both the metaphorical brotherhood offered by the collective, or "murder," of crows and the real murder that is expected from club members, who are rewarded with a "men of mayhem" patch when they spill blood for the club. The series ends with Jax, arms outstretched on a collision course, both a rebel outlaw and a Christ-like figure hoping to achieve redemption for his children (see Robinson 2014). The series ends as it began, with two crows eating a piece of bread in the middle of the road, but instead of Jax riding his motorcycle along the road, the image that follows the crows in the pilot

---

1. All references to episodes of *Sons of Anarchy* come from Sutter 2008–14.

episode, we see Jax's blood seeping onto the road. In the pilot episode, Jax and his mother Gemma (Katey Sagal) discuss how "Tellers don't die easy," Gemma referring to Jax's father, who had taken two days to die after his motorcycle crash, but Jax's words, "we just die bloody," become a prophecy of his own death.

Sons of Anarchy was created by Kurt Sutter, who had previously worked on the Los Angeles–based police drama *The Shield* (2001–8), and aired from 2008 to 2014 on the US cable network FX and from 2008 to 2012 on the UK minor channel 5USA, with the final two seasons not being broadcast. Although it did not garner many awards (no Emmy awards and a single Golden Globe for Katey Sagal as best actress in 2011), the series was popular among many critics as well as fans and achieved a major ratings success in the United States for FX ("*Sons of Anarchy* Rides to Ratings" 2014). The series was sometimes difficult to watch, with scenes of extreme violence in every episode, including torture and rape. However, the ultimate message, emphasized by the series finale, is that crime does not pay, as the characters ultimately give their lives for their violent lifestyle.

Sutter's inspirations were *Hamlet* and the idea that although motorcycle clubs were set up with good intentions, they ended up becoming criminal organizations. In an interview for *New York Magazine* in 2013, Sutter explained: "I envisioned the first guy that put on that leather jacket and said, 'Let's get on our bikes and have a few beers.' How does that guy feel about his guys becoming outlaws? That guy for me became John Teller, the founder of the club. Then I thought, What if that guy is the father in *Hamlet*? What if that guy is the ghost of John Teller? That archetype enabled me to establish the prince, our lead guy, Jax Teller. I loosely based all my characters on ones from *Hamlet*" (Seitz 2013).

The series starts with Jax's mother, Gemma, married to his father's best friend, Clay, following his father's death, like Gertrude and Claudius, as their names suggest. Jax suspects and later confirms that Clay had a hand in John Teller's death by tampering with his motorcycle. Gemma chose Clay over John, and in the pilot episode she tells Clay, "I don't want the ghost of John Teller poisoning [Jax]." However, Gemma's relationship with Jax, even more than Hamlet's with Gertrude, can be read as an Oedipal one (see Zanin 2013). Gemma and Jax may joke about his "mommy issues"—for example, when he embarks on a relationship with an older woman, brothel madam Colette—but Gemma really does want to be the "queen" of the club to Jax's "king." She stands behind Jax as he sits at the club table at the end of season 5, when his wife, Tara (Maggie Siff), has been taken into custody.

Tara had stood behind Jax in the same place at the end of season 4, where Gemma had originally stood behind Jax's father, as shown in an old photograph. Gemma is literally the power behind the throne.

When Gemma tells Nero (Jimmy Smits), her lover and Jax's friend and business partner, "I was a good mother" ("Suits of Woe," 7.11) she truly believes it, but her duty to her son is tied to her duty as matriarch of the motorcycle club, an unofficial position that is much more important than the title "Old Lady" suggests. Fiercely loyal to the club, Gemma kills Tara brutally at the end of season 6 when she thinks Tara has made a deal with the authorities. Gemma and club member Juice conspire throughout the final season to keep this murder a secret, pinning the blame on a Chinese gang. It is the unraveling of this secret that leads to Jax shooting his mother, an act that "had to be done" as revenge for Tara but also because of the harm the murder has done to the club from the gang warfare that ensues after retribution is taken against the Chinese for an act they did not commit.

Jax wants his sons to grow up in a different world but fails at a number of attempts throughout the series to leave the club with Tara, even almost leaving his kidnapped son Abel with adoptive parents in Ireland because he thinks his son might have a better life there. Before he rides to his death, his final words to his dead father at the place marking John Teller's fatal "accident" are: "It was too late for me, I was already inside it, and, Gemma, she had plans. It's not too late for my boys. I promise they'll never know this life of chaos." But, unbeknownst to Jax, Gemma has plans for Abel and has already put them into action by passing to him John Teller's gold ring spelling out the word *son* at the fence of his school playground,[2] telling him: "This was your Grandpa John's, and I gave it to your daddy when he patched into the club. This one's for you, so you have it when you become a member" (7.11). Abel plays with the ring in the back of his mother's car as they leave with Nero for their new life, suggesting that it may be too late for Abel, too, a child already traumatized by the death of his stepmother, whom he had believed to be his birth mother, and the realization that she was killed by his grandmother.

Jax is identified with the prince of Denmark when he is called "the prince" by Clay in the episode "Fa Guan" (2.9) and by Alcohol, Tobacco, and Firearms agent June Stahl, who tries to turn Jax from "the prince" into a

---

2. Jax wears two separate rings, featuring the letters SO and NS, respectively. The narrative doesn't explain why Gemma now has the ring she gave to Jax after John Teller died.

"rat" prince who informs on his club ("NS," 3.13).[3] Although *Sons of Anarchy* does not slavishly follow the plot of *Hamlet*, and we cannot easily map all the characters onto their Shakespearean counterparts,[4] as in *Hamlet* the cycle of manipulation and revenge backfires on all those who are involved and ends in a bloodbath. The revenger was and continues to be an ambiguous character who is rarely allowed to survive.[5]

In an interview for arts show *The Treatment* on Los Angeles–based radio station KCRW in 2013, Kurt Sutter prefigured the series ending when he said, "These are guys that are making very dangerous and deadly decisions, and ultimately I believe that violence begets violence, and, at the end of the day, there just can't be a happy ending no matter how noble the cause when you make those kind of violent choices. . . . There is a come-uppance that has to happen and there is a tragedy and a tragic sense of 'Can Jax get out whole? Can anybody get out whole? Can they get out alive?'" (Sutter 2013). However much the viewer can sympathize with the character of Jax, Jax has caused the deaths of many people, both directly and indirectly. Although none of his victims was entirely innocent, some were undeserving, such as former sheriff Wayne Unser (Dayton Callie), who spends the series helping Jax's family and is killed by Jax when he tries to protect Gemma from murder at the hands of her son ("Red Rose," 7.12). It is difficult to forgive Hamlet for his lack of remorse for killing Polonius, who he says was "a foolish prating knave" (*Hamlet*, 3.4.2221), and it is Jax's murder of Unser as much as the revenge killing of his mother—an act that Nero says is a "wound that's too deep to heal" (7.11)—that finally seals his fate.

In act 5 of *Hamlet*, as the prince of Denmark accepts the challenge to a duel that will ultimately end in his death, he tells his friend Horatio:

> If it be now, 'tis not to come. If it be not to come, it will be now. If it be not now, yet it will come. The readiness is all. Since man, of aught he leaves, knows aught, what is't to leave betimes? Let be. (5.2.234–38)

Like Hamlet, at the end of the series Jax has accepted his fate, having come to the realization that he will never be able to reconcile his roles as club member and revenger with his role as a father; "a good father and a good outlaw can't

---

3. The reference to "the prince" also invokes Machiavelli; see Dale and Foy 2013.

4. For a potential mapping, see "*Sons of Anarchy*—the *Hamlet* Conclusion" 2014.

5. For a discussion of revenge tragedy and the role of the avenger, see Watson 1990. For a discussion of *Sons of Anarchy* as revenge tragedy, see Harris 2012.

settle inside the same man." Jax asks Nero to take the role of Horatio, to tell Jax's story after he is gone. Nero is given instructions to tell "everything" to Jax's exwife, Wendy (Drea de Matteo), so that she can share it with Jax's sons when they are ready to hear it and "grow up hating the thought" of their criminal father, so that the future generation will learn from the past. Nero is also to help Jax by settling his affairs, as Horatio is asked to pass on the crown of Denmark to Fortinbras. Nero is to ensure that Jax's property is sold for Wendy and his sons so that they can move away to their new life, and the shares he has in businesses are to go to the club. Jax himself takes on the more violent settling of affairs, telling the district attorney that she must wait until the end of the day when "the bad guys lose" and members of the Real IRA (Real Irish Republican Army, a paramilitary organization in the series), a corrupt former cop, and black gangster August Marks are shot dead.

Chibs (Tommy Flanagan), the vice president of SAMCRO, is given his instructions to go ahead with a "mayhem vote"—the vote on whether Jax must be killed, and Jax tells Chibs to "trust that what I want is the best thing for me and my family, for our club." Chibs must now take the role of "leader," and under his guidance the club members reluctantly and unanimously vote for Jax to "meet Mr. Mayhem" for crimes against the club, including Jax's murder of Jury White, president of the Indian Hills charter, which led to the presidents of the Sons of Anarchy charters requiring the mayhem vote. Jax tells Chibs, "I'm ready," when the vote has taken place and he must die, but the club members have conspired with Jax to allow him to choose his own death rather than be killed at the hands of his "brothers." Jax "would never put the burden on you guys," so as Chibs picks up the gun, seemingly to shoot Jax, he shoots Happy in the arm, as if Jax has shot him trying to escape. Jax therefore has a kinder end than Clay, who is shot by Jax with the club members watching after Clay's own mayhem vote led by Jax at the end of season 6.

The afterword of *Sons of Anarchy* is not Hamlet's words of acceptance, to "let be," but rather another quotation from *Hamlet*:

> Doubt thou the stars are fire;
> Doubt that the sun doth move;
> Doubt truth to be a liar;
> But never doubt I love. (2.2.124–27)

These are words Hamlet has written to Ophelia, read out by Polonius to Gertrude and Claudius. Hamlet does not have the opportunity to reconcile with Ophelia before her death, and his "good-bye" to her in her grave consists of fighting with Laertes over her body (5.1). Jax, however, is given the whole final episode to say good-bye to his friends and family as well as to tie up all loose ends and make changes for the Sons of Anarchy, abolishing the unwritten rule that forbids black members and finally getting SAMCRO out of the gun trade with the Real IRA. When Jax says, "I've got this," he really has. At the beginning of the episode, he visits the graves of his best friend, Opie, and his wife, Tara, leaving his club rings and his wedding ring on their respective graves. He then visits all his friends and family members in turn and tells them that he loves them and kisses them, starting with former porn star and Opie's girlfriend, Lyla; his exwife, Wendy; and both his sons. Over seven seasons, Wendy has grown from the junkie who almost killed her unborn child with an overdose to, in Jax's words in this scene, "a good mum." Jax's final farewell is to his "brothers" in the club. He tells them, "I love you all," and hugs them one by one before he leaves for his final motorbike ride. Before he kills Gemma in the preceding episode, he tells Nero that, despite everything, "I still love her, you know; she's my mom" (7.11). For a self-confessed "bad guy," Jax's final defining characteristic is his propensity to love. Under other circumstances, he, like Hamlet, could have "proved most royally" (*Hamlet*, 5.2.444), but as a murderer he has to die.

The *Sons of Anarchy* series finale is satisfying, and although the conclusion is inevitable, viewers are still offered some surprises along the way. Jax, the modern-day Hamlet, is never going to be able to "get out alive," and the whole of the last season has built up to Jax finding out his mother's guilty secret, leading to matricide. Jax has been at the heart of the series from the beginning, and the finale ends, as it began, with Jax on a motorcycle, but only after he has been allowed to say good-bye, to viewers as well as to the other characters. The finale offers potential hope for the future through Jax's sons, and for the Sons (of Anarchy), thanks to the plans and changes Jax has made. But the finale also offers the alternative possibility that the club and the cycle of violence might continue into the next generation, embodied by the club ring in the hands of Abel and also hinted at by the enigmatic crows in the road. It is fitting that a series that has made us care about ambiguous characters in ambiguous situations ends on a note that is both final and ambiguous.

References

Carpenter, Susan. 2008. "Think *Hamlet* on Harleys." *Los Angeles Times*, Oct. 26. At http://articles.latimes.com/2008/oct/26/entertainment/ca-sonsofanarchy26.

Dale, Timothy M., and Joseph J Foy. 2013. "'The Rat Prince' and *The Prince*: The Machiavellian Politics of the MC." In *"Sons of Anarchy" and Philosophy: Brains before Bullets*, edited by George A. Dunn and Jason T. Eberl, 65–72. Malden MA: Wiley Blackwell.

Donahue, Anne T. 2014. "*Sons of Anarchy*: Shakespeare on Motorcycle Wheels." *Guardian*, Dec. 11. At http://www.theguardian.com/tv-and-radio/tvandradio blog/2014/dec/10/sons-of-anarchy-shakespeare-on-wheels.

Harris, Geraldine. 2012. "A Return to Form? Postmasculinist Television Drama and Tragic Heroes in the Wake of *The Sopranos*." *New Review of Film and Television Studies* 10, no. 4: 443–62.

Robinson, Joanna. 2014. "*Sons of Anarchy* Series Finale Rides Off into the Sunset on a Worn Out Metaphor." *Vanity Fair*, Dec. 10. At http://www.vanityfair.com /hollywood/2014/12/sons-of-anarchy-series-finale-jax-dies.

Seitz, Matt Zoller. 2013. "Sutter Explains His Cultural Influences." *New York Magazine*, Sept. 16. At http://www.vulture.com/2013/09/kurt-sutter-explains-his -cultural-influences.html.

"*Sons of Anarchy*—the *Hamlet* Conclusion: Finalized." 2014. *Influx Magazine*, Sept. 10. At http://influxmagazine.com/sons-of-anarchy-the-hamlet-conclusion/.

"*Sons of Anarchy* Rides to Ratings Records at FX." 2014. TV by the Numbers, Dec. 15. At http://tvbythenumbers.zap2it.com/2014/12/15/sons-of-anarchy-rides-to -ratings-records-at-fx/.

Sutter, Kurt, creator. 2008–14. *Sons of Anarchy*. Aired Sept. 3, 2008, to Dec. 9, 2014, FX. Sky Box Sets (streaming). Accessed Jan.–July 2016.

———. 2013. Interviewed by Elvis Mitchell. *The Treatment*, KCRW, Nov. 6. At http://www.kcrw.com/news-culture/shows/the-treatment/kurt-sutter-sons-of -anarchy.

Watson, Robert N. "Tragedy." 1990. In *The Cambridge Companion to English Renaissance Drama*, edited by A. R. Braunmuller and Michael Hattaway, 301– 51. Cambridge: Cambridge Univ. Press.

Zanin, Andrea. 2013. "Sometimes a Motorcycle Is Just a Motorcycle: Freud and Hamlet Come to Charming." In *"Sons of Anarchy" and Philosophy: Brains before Bullets*, edited by George A. Dunn and Jason T. Eberl, 153–64. Malden, MA: Wiley Blackwell.

56

The Sopranos

"Made in America"

GARY R. EDGERTON

The Museum of Modern Art in New York sponsored an early retrospective of *The Sopranos* (1999–2007, HBO) during the first two weeks of February 2001. Scheduled one month before the premiere of the third season, seasons 1 and 2 were screened in their entirety at the museum's Titus Theatre, culminating in an interview of David Chase on February 12 by media critic Ken Auletta. Asked by Auletta how he planned to finish the fourth and what at the time was planned to be the final season of *The Sopranos*, Chase was purposefully vague, saying that he hoped to "avoid predictability" but added almost as an aside, "I don't think [Tony Soprano] should die" (quoted in Seitz 2001).

Three years later, on March 2, 2004, or less than a week before the debut of the fifth season, David Chase told Terry Gross of *Fresh Air* that he had decided how he would end the series because "I do need to know that to proceed now" (Chase 2004). What occurred on June 10, 2007, after three contractual reprieves that extended *The Sopranos* into a fifth and sixth season and then a nine-episode part 2 of the sixth season, was one of the most controversial finales in television history. Many audience members felt confused, even cheated by the open-endedness of the last scene. It frustrated their need for closure. Journalists and bloggers had a field day trying to decipher whether Tony Soprano (James Gandolfini) had survived or not. The ensuing uproar remained a cultural flashpoint for weeks.

For his part, David Chase refused to explain his intentions, other than to say that "there was a clean trend on view—a definite sense of what Tony and Carmela's future looks like" (quoted in Martin 2007, 184). Suffice it to say, Chase had made up his mind long before writing and directing the eighty-sixth and last episode that his epic domestic-gangster drama would end with

352

Tony glancing up toward the camera like a deer in the headlights and then an abrupt smash cut to black.

David Chase's thorough awareness of the gangster's long-standing tradition in film and television is clearly evident in the series finale. A half-century before the debut of *The Sopranos*, Robert Warshow had mapped out the terrain of "the gangster as tragic hero" in his seminal article for the *Partisan Review* in 1948. Warshow zeroed in on the general audience's ambivalence toward the gangster-hero when he described him as "a creature of the imagination. The real city produces only criminals; the imaginary city produces the gangster: he is what we want to be and what we are afraid we may become" (243). This sort of personal identification is at the heart of Tony Soprano's widespread appeal. It is also the kind of ambivalence that David Chase and his writing team struggled with throughout the six-plus seasons of *The Sopranos*.

At times, Tony's situation does verge on tragedy; just as often, though, he is depicted as just another common criminal, especially during part 2 of the series' sixth and final season (specifically episodes 78 through 86). As the series wound down, Chase and his writers gave viewers fewer reasons to like Tony as he grows increasingly narcissistic and sociopathic, a direction that is not preordained in the way *The Sopranos*' narrative evolves. Warshow recognized that "when we come upon [the gangster,] he has already made his choice or the choice has already been made for him . . . [and] we are not permitted to ask whether at some point he could have chosen to be something else than what he is" (1948, 243).

This classical brand of narrative determinism gives way to a far more complicated fictional world in *The Sopranos*. As the son of "Johnny Boy" Soprano and the nephew of "Junior" Soprano, Tony was indeed born into the family business. As early as "Down Neck" (1.7 [Senna Ferrara 1999]), however, he reveals to Dr. Jennifer Melfi (Lorraine Bracco) that "sometimes I think about what life would have been like if my father hadn't gotten mixed up in the things he got mixed up in." Half-jokingly he muses, "Maybe I'd be selling patio furniture in San Diego or whatever."

More seriously, viewers literally see him in "Join the Club" (6.2 [Nutter 2006]) and "Mayhem" (6.3 [Bender 2006]) as a different person, Kevin Finnerty, a solar-heating-systems salesman from Arizona, after Tony is shot in the stomach by a confused and demented Uncle Junior (Dominic Chianese) toward the end of "Members Only" (6.1 [Van Patten 2006]). This severe trauma plunges Tony into a deep coma, where he appears several times as Finnerty in his own dreams. Kevin Finnerty is a gentler, far more self-reflective version of Tony, even asking at one point, "I'm forty-six years old. Who am I? Where am I going?" When Tony finally comes out of his coma, he temporarily adopts a new attitude toward life, telling Carmela (Edie Falco), his sister, Janice (Aida Turturro), and later Dr. Melfi that "from now on, every day is a gift."

Slowly but surely, though, the ruthless, cold-hearted, and self-absorbed Tony reemerges with a vengeance—even snuffing the life out of his nephew, Christopher (Michael Imperioli), and then flying off to Las Vegas to sleep with his nephew's mistress in "Kennedy and Heidi" (6.18 [Taylor 2007b]). In a highly manipulative gesture, Dr. Kupferberg (Peter Bogdanovich) tells Dr. Melfi in "The Second Coming" (6.19 [Van Patten 2007]) that the psychological research suggests that talk therapy is useless with sociopaths. He warns her that "they sharpen their skills as con men on their therapists." Despite her justified annoyance with Kupferberg, Melfi checks out his claims in the clinical literature and learns he's right on target.

Soon afterward, Melfi terminates her relationship with Tony Soprano in an emotionally turbulent scene in "The Blue Comet" (6.20 [Taylor 2007a]). Tony pleads, "We're making progress . . . after seven years." Melfi nonetheless sees his appeal as just more duplicity, telling him that "since you are in crisis, I don't want to waste your time." Considering the centrality of therapy to the entire eighty-six-hour narrative flow of *The Sopranos*, Dr. Melfi's act of closing her office door in Tony's face in the penultimate episode is a kind of psychological and spiritual death sentence for him because, in essence, she is writing him off for good as incurable and irredeemable.

Tony Soprano is never more diminished than in the opening and closing scenes of *The Sopranos'* finale, "Made in America" (6.21).[1] In the first scene, he is shown from a bird's-eye view holed up in a second-floor bedroom of a safe house cradling the AR-10 machine gun that his brother-in-law, Bobby "Bacala" (Steve Schirripa), gave him on his forty-seventh birthday. In "The Blue Comet," Bobby was assassinated by the rival Brooklyn mob, and Tony's best friend and consigliere, Silvio Dante (Steven Van Zandt), was wounded and rendered comatose. Tony momentarily flashes back to Bobby's prescient remark that "you probably don't even hear it when it happens," reconfirming his brother-in-law's own abrupt demise in a model-train store and foreshadowing what probably lies ahead for Tony in "Made in America."

1. All references to "Made in America" come from Chase 2007.

Like *The Sopranos* as a whole, the final episode is far more preoccupied with family matters than with mob business. A great deal of closure actually occurs in "Made in America": Carmela continues to build and sell houses on speculation with Tony's blood money as her way of coping with a future that's precarious at best; their daughter, Meadow (Jamie-Lynn Sigler), appears destined for a career in law through her budding relationship with lawyer Patrick Parisi; their son, A. J. (Robert Iler), after spiralling into depression in season 6 (mirroring his dad), seems on the upswing when Tony finally finds him a starter position in the movie business; and Tony's longtime blood nemesis, Uncle Junior, is now confined to a nursing home, lost in senile dementia.

Even Tony Soprano's work situation has somewhat improved in the war between the North Jersey and Brooklyn mobs because his chief antagonist and rival crime boss, Phil Leotardo (Frank Vincent), has been shot dead in front of his wife and grandchildren following a fragile truce that is brokered between the DiMeo and Lupertazzi crime families earlier in the finale. Nevertheless, many people still have a reason to kill Tony. In addition, Tony's lawyer, Neil Mink (David Margulies), has just informed him that his captain, Carlo Gervasi (Arthur Nascarella), "has flipped" (become an informant for the FBI) and that his "hunch is there is an 80 to 90 percent chance you'll be indicted." The FBI has been hot on Tony Soprano's trail ever since the beginning of the series, slowly building a case against him.

The momentum of the nearly eighty-six-hour serial narrative is, therefore, ginned up to a fevered pitch as Tony enters Holsten's family restaurant in the final scene, choosing a booth to wait for his family and selecting Journey's power ballad "Don't Stop Believing" on the jukebox (which adds a slowly building intensity to the subsequent action). Tony sits alone in Holsten's, an impending indictment looming over his head like the sword of Damocles, until Carmela arrives first to join him and then their son, A. J., shows up. All of the stylistics of this final scene—the ever-quickening montage editing accompanied by Journey's hard-driving melodramatic anthem—belie a seemingly ordinary family outing. Director of photography Alik Sakharov admitted that the entire scene was "shot listed" and that "we deliberately jumped the line when certain characters entered the diner [a trucker sporting a USA cap, a suspicious-looking stranger in a Members Only jacket, and a pair of young African American males] to bring a little edge to it" (Sakharov 2007).

Furthermore, Sakharov revealed that he and David Chase intentionally incorporated references to *The Godfather* (Francis Ford Coppola, 1972) ("when the guy went into the bathroom [like Michael Corleone] to build suspense") and to the end of *2001: A Space Odyssey* (Stanley Kubrick, 1968) ("where it looks like something is happening but the audience is left wondering") (Sakharov 2007). Finally, the bell on the entrance door jingles, Tony looks up ostensibly to see Meadow come in, the picture famously cuts to black, and there is a complete cessation of sound. Time has abruptly run out for the series as Tony is left staring forlornly at the camera, anxiously waiting for the next shoe to drop.

Colin McArthur has written in *Underworld U.S.A.* "that the gangster [lying] dead in the street [is] perhaps the most rigid convention of the genre, repeated through successive phases of its development" (1972, 35). "Success is evil and dangerous," wrote Robert Warshow; thus, this "dilemma" is embodied "in the person of the gangster" and alleviated "by his death. The dilemma is resolved because it is his death, not ours. We are safe for the moment" (1948, 244).

In this way, although viewers vicariously participated in Tony's numerous transgressions for six-plus seasons, being simultaneously thrilled and appalled, they also, in turn, counted on eventually being purged of any connection with him when he ultimately receives what he has coming to him in the end. "The way I see it is that Tony Soprano had been people's alter ego," contended David Chase. "They had gleefully watched him rob, kill, pillage, lie and cheat. They had cheered him on. And then, all of a sudden, they wanted to see him punished for all that. They wanted 'justice'" (quoted in Martin 2007, 184). Chase, however, was reluctant to oblige.

In the final analysis, David Chase refused to let either Tony Soprano or the audience off the hook. He defied generic convention by delivering an open-ended conclusion that closed with a whimper not a bang, dooming Tony to nervously live out whatever time he has left, looking over his shoulder for either the FBI (which is closing in on him fast) or one of the many underworld enemies he has made over the years. Right up to the last shot, Chase preserved the rigorous fidelity of the fictional world he had created. Put another way, "it was a question of loyalty to viewer expectations, as against loyalty to the internal coherence of the materials," delineated David Milch, creator of *NYPD Blue* (1993–2005, ABC, with Steven Bochco) and *Deadwood* (2004–6, HBO). "Mr. Chase's position was loyalty to the internal dynamics of the materials and the characters" (quoted in Carter 2007).

Unlike the "gangster as tragic hero," Tony Soprano doesn't go out in a mythic blaze of glory, which Warshow described as an "astonishingly complete presentation of the modern sense of tragedy" (1948, 241). Tony instead remains frozen in time as merely a common criminal and dysfunctional family man. Audience members, moreover, were not allowed to pull away from the gangster visually, emotionally, or psychologically but were instead left to ruminate on the meaning of the final shot and the inconclusiveness of Tony's fate. David Chase gave *The Sopranos*' viewers a criminal of unheroic proportions, less tragic than ordinary, and someone they were fully complicit with from start to finish. As the last shot cuts to black, Tony Soprano fades into memory, just another banal reflection of America caught in millennial decline.

All told, *The Sopranos*' finale is much like the series itself: operatic, unconventional, audacious, often incisive, occasionally enigmatic. The culminating smash cut to black underscores the lack of options left for Tony. As Chase explained, "All I wanted to do was present the idea of how short life is and how precious it is. The only way I felt I could do that was rip it away" (quoted in Seitz 2014). The audience's final impression of Tony Soprano is intentionally one in which he is emotionally vulnerable, with his mortality on full display. His fate has long been sealed by the choices he has made and the actions he has taken over the previous eighty-five hours of the series. The last shot of "Made in America" is yet another one of those quotidian moments that set *The Sopranos* apart. This lifelike quality is thus what made the series original and the finale so affecting and memorable.

References

Bender, Jack, dir. 2006. "Mayhem." *The Sopranos*, season 6, episode 3. Written by Matthew Weiner. Aired Mar. 26, HBO. Original broadcast.

Carter, Bill. 2007. "TV Writers Were Also Watching *Sopranos*." *New York Times*, June 12. At http://www.nytimes.com/2007/06/12/arts/television/12sopr.html.

Chase, David. 2004. Interviewed by Terry Gross. *Fresh Air*, NPR, Mar. 2.

———, dir. 2007. "Made in America." *The Sopranos*, season 6, episode 21. Written by David Chase. Aired June 10, HBO. Original broadcast.

Martin, Brett. 2007. *"The Sopranos": The Complete Book*. New York: Time Home Entertainment.

McArthur, Colin. 1972. *Underworld U.S.A.* New York: Viking.

Nutter, David, dir. 2006. "Join the Club." *The Sopranos*, season 6, episode 2. Written by David Chase. Aired Mar. 19, HBO. Original broadcast.

Sakharov, Alik. 2007. Interviewed by Stephen Pizzello in "*The Sopranos*, Part 1." *American Cinematographer*, podcast, June 20. At http://www.theasc.com/ac_magazine/podcasts.php.

Seitz, Matt Zoller. 2001. "Leaving the Family." *Newark Star-Ledger*, Feb. 14.

———. 2014. "David Chase Offers Response to 'Tony Soprano Didn't Die' Article." *Vulture*, Aug. 27. At http://www.vulture.com/2014/08/david-chase-statement -response-to-tony-soprano-didnt-die.html.

Senna Ferrara, Lorraine, dir. 1999. "Down Neck." *The Sopranos*, season 1, episode 7. Written by Robin Green and Mitchell Burgess. Aired Feb. 21, HBO. Original broadcast.

Taylor, Alan, dir. 2007a. "The Blue Comet." *The Sopranos*, season 6, episode 20. Written by David Chase and Matthew Weiner. Aired June 3, HBO. Original broadcast.

———, dir. 2007b. "Kennedy and Heidi." *The Sopranos*, season 6, episode 18. Written by Matthew Weiner and David Chase. Aired May 13, HBO. Original broadcast.

Van Patten, Tim, dir. 2006. "Members Only." *The Sopranos*, season 6, episode 1. Written by Terence Winter. Aired Mar. 12, HBO. Original broadcast.

———, dir. 2007. "The Second Coming." *The Sopranos*, season 6, episode 19. Written by Terence Winter. Aired May 20, HBO. Original broadcast.

Warshow, Robert. 1948. "The Gangster as Tragic Hero." *Partisan Review* 15, no. 2: 240–44.

57

Spaced

"Leaves"

LYNNE HIBBERD

The end of the series *Spaced* (1999–2001) didn't compromise the future of UK Channel 4, signal the death of the British sitcom, or leave millions of viewers speculating over what the future would hold for its characters or actors. It's most likely to be remembered some years from now in a celebrity talking-heads program—"I remember *Spaced*! I liked the bit when . . ."—warranting it a further few minutes in the spotlight of nostalgia before disappearing from view once again. *Spaced* is no more or less than a *good* program—funny to an audience who found humor in its knowing intertextual references, the warmth of its characters, the surreal stories, and mundane outcomes. Why then does it warrant a place in a book that examines the endings of such television greats as *Sex and the City* (HBO, 1998–2004), *The Sopranos* (HBO, 1999–2007), and *Lost* (ABC, 2004–10)—series that rightly belong in a television canon or can be credited with changing the institution and practices of TV? Precisely because of its ordinariness. It's a TV series consumed much like any other: watched devotedly by some, sporadically by others, not at all by many. It's not HBO; it's just TV.

Spaced was written by and starred Simon Pegg and Jessica Hynes as the main characters Tim and Daisy, who share a normal, albeit very affordable, London flat. Quirky landlady Marsha (Julia Deakin) occupies the top-floor flat of the house with her errant and never-seen teenage daughter, while artist Brian (Mark Heap) lives downstairs. Tim's best mate, Mike (Nick Frost), and Daisy's friend Twist (Katy Carmichael) make frequent visits.[1]

---

1. All references to episodes of *Spaced* come from *Spaced* 2006.

As a production, *Spaced* was very much a collaboration of friends who had met on the acting and comedy circuit. Hynes brought in Katy Carmichael, a friend from a previous stage performance, to play Twist; Pegg convinced director Edgar Wright to cast his best mate, Nick Frost, as Mike. (In the DVD extra "Skip to the End" [2006], both actors express their delight and disbelief at Frost being taken on board despite having no previous acting experience.) The first season went out on Channel 4 at 9:30 p.m. on Friday nights, where it was well placed in the TV flow of the early 2000s alongside two other comedies that relied on making the mundane extraordinary. *The Royle Family* (1998–2000, Granada) brought hilarity to the routine existence of a Manchester family who rarely moved off the furniture surrounding their TV set. *The League of Gentlemen* (1999–2002, BBC) portrayed small-town life in Royston Vasey through multiple intertextual references to create a mixture of comedy and horror that reached a macabre peak in the Christmas special of 2000 and went well beyond its best in the feature film *The League of Gentlemen's Apocalypse* (Steve Bendelack, 2005). Channel 4 was reportedly so happy with the first season of *Spaced* that it commissioned a second before the first had been shown, though both Pegg and Hynes claim that it was always going to be a short-lived affair. Like many recent acclaimed UK television comedies, including *The Office* (BBC, 2001–3), *Extras* (BBC, 2005–7), *Gavin and Stacey* (BBC, 2007–10), and *The Thick of It* (BBC, 2005–9), *Spaced* finished at its peak at the end of the second season.

A key feature of *Spaced* is the intertextual references that pepper the series. Intertextuality has become a mainstay of many quality US series and a defining feature of HBO's original programming, but it rarely denotes "quality" in UK texts in the same way. Much of the joy of *Spaced* comes from its allusions to cinema, as its producers, self-confessed "movie geeks," parody, lampoon, and pay homage to Hollywood blockbusters, European art cinema, and Hong Kong action flicks. These moments are often fleeting, lasting a fraction of a second and making up a single shot or memorable phrase. They allow the audience a brief instance of speculation—"Hey, wasn't that . . . ?"—before the action proceeds. Sometimes they form the basis of a joke, as when Tim, left alone in charge of a comic book shop, launches a diatribe against the evils posed by the disappointing episodes 1–3 of George Lucas's *Star Wars* series, and a reverse shot reveals the bewildered expression of an eight-year-old boy wanting a Jar Jar Binks toy. Sometimes the narrative drive of an episode owes a great deal to a specific film or genre, as when a bid to recover errant dog Colin from a local animal experiment center is carried out with the precision of a military operation in *Where Eagles Dare*

(Brian G. Hutton, 1968). But the pervasive intertextual references must have proved something of a problem for the show's finale: How does one dramatically conclude a show that has mocked the hyperbole of the big screen so effectively?

As a structuring device, movie references present a limited number of strategic possibilities: include more of them, make them in relation to specific films, make them more aesthetically demanding, or don't make them at all. Each of these possibilities poses its own problems. Making multitudinous references can be tedious, diverting viewers from the main feature, a colossal game of spot-the-Hitchcock. Intertextual references are a natural, spontaneous part of Daisy and Tim's existence, something that grounds them as characters whose lives are so governed by popular culture that they can consider their own existence only in those terms ("Skip to the End" 2006). As a consequence, film references appropriate a film style to express the moment, and all of the references are made to specific films or genres that are part of Daisy and Tim's world. (Here is a wonderful chance to engage in audience identification with the characters: *of course*, audience members would have seen *The Shining* [Stanley Kubrick, 1980] and would have ruthlessly mocked *Titanic* [James Cameron, 1997]. And although I'm convinced they would also have seen *The Terminator* [James Cameron, 1984], re-creating the blockbuster effects aesthetically would be well beyond the budget of even the most lavish UK TV drama.) *Spaced*'s take on intertextuality is resolutely low budget, as in the season 2 episode "Gone," when Daisy and Tim are involved in a fracas that is resolved in a slow-motion shoot-out. In a mash-up of *Butch Cassidy and the Sundance Kid* (George Roy Hill, 1969), *Bad Boys* (Michael Bay, 1995), and *The Matrix* (Lana Wachowski and Lilly Wachowski, 1999), pistols are replaced with fingers and *kbsh* sounds, and the shooting is enacted, rather than filmed, in slow motion. In a demonstrative display of acting excellence, every child's dream is replayed: the chance to live in the movies for a moment without the need for a special-effects budget. The final option, foregoing references altogether, would have robbed the audience. (Hitchcock might have eventually conceded to having to appear in the first scene of his movies, but he was there nevertheless.) No references would have been so out of kilter with the regular experience of the characters as to be unfeasible.

At least in part because of its multitude of references, *Spaced* commanded a loyal and committed following when it was aired, many of whom contributed to the online chat of the web forum Spaced Out (http://www.Spaced -out.org.uk/). The website, launched by fan Nick Lee, was so successful in generating buzz about the program that Channel 4 eventually withdrew the "official" *Spaced* site in acknowledgment that the fan-created forum was superior, effectively validating the audience's reception of the series over and above that of its producers. The pop-culture references in *Spaced* formed the basis of lively web discussions, allowing its audience to show that they "got it." The collector's edition DVD includes an Homage-o-Meter for viewers to check whether they get a full score for correctly identifying the reference sources.

The finale of *Spaced* says something about the end of a television series. Daisy's last-episode voiceover begins, "They say that the real family of the twenty-first century is made up of friends." Although a camera tilts to reveal a scene that then leads her to conclude, "But that's bollocks," in the case of *Spaced* it is true; the series lives on in homage at the website, and the devotion of its audience is explicitly acknowledged in the collector's edition of the DVD box set. "Thank you for purchasing this special three disc presentation of the quirky, award-winning sitcom, *Spaced*," reads the cover blurb. "Particular thanks if you have already purchased the existing versions of the quirky, award-winning sitcom *Spaced*, and you're buying it all over again for the new bits. That's exactly the sort of thing a *Spaced* fan would do."

The end of *Spaced* also suggests a little about the end of television. In the United Kingdom, the public-service ethos that has underpinned television struggles in the face of a digital marketplace. *Spaced*'s ability to exist as a lone TV series, despite its obvious amenability to spin-offs, suggests that there is still much value in this. The pictures may have gotten smaller, but they're no less popular.

Instead of aiming for a grand finale, the last episode of *Spaced* eases its viewers into something more familiar, every day, and nostalgic by toning down the Hollywood hyperbole that has infiltrated the show's two seasons and by providing opening credits that would be familiar to any viewer of the bittersweet British comedy *The Royle Family* as well as indicative of the level of pathos to follow. Daisy, Tim, and the rest of the cast are filmed in blue and white, united in front of a flickering TV set, while Oasis's song "Half the World Away" plays over the time-lapsed credit sequence. This is not the first episode to refer to TV series as well as to film; references—albeit fleeting—are made to *The A-Team* (1983–87), *Roobarb and Custard* (1974), *Charlie's Angels* (1976–81), *Thunderbirds* (1965–66), *Why Don't You?* (1973–95), *Blue Peter* (1958–2010), and *Scooby Doo* (1969–72), programs reflecting the age and experiences of the *Spaced* audience. Twist's absence from the final show, explained as her having "gone to Manchester," is a familiar excuse for nonappearance to any viewer of British soaps: the character has emigrated "up north" or "down south," respectively. This divide is indicated by the Oasis track: geographical proximity often fails to bridge cultural chasms.

The end of *Spaced* effectively crystallizes a moment in time, ensuring that Daisy and Tim will never move out of a very late adolescence (they are in their mid- to late twenties) and into the adulthood of mortgages, jobs, love interests—in other words, into their thirties. It ensures that the pop-culture references maintain relevance. This developmental stage, which presumably many in the series' audience are either in or at least able to readily identify with, stops *Spaced* from entering into fully fledged adulthood. This crystallizing is important in relieving Daisy and Tim of any pressure to be romantically united, a possibility hinted at on occasions through the series, though left mercifully unrealized. Ending *Spaced* with a neat resolution would have sealed the fate of the characters in a way that is quite at odds with their small-scale filmic lives. The hyperbolic references to Hollywood work in *Spaced* because its world is little, familiar, warm, comfortable, and domestic, able to comfortably contain the exuberant hyperreality of cinema on a microscale. The end of *Spaced* shows a TV series stopping in its prime. It didn't burn out or conclude; it stopped. "Everyone leaves," sighs Daisy in the last episode. "Everybody doesn't leave," cajoles Tim, but on learning that his new girlfriend has accepted a job in America, he quickly amends his optimism: "You know I said everyone didn't leave? Well, they do. Everyone leaves." The end of the show, though, gives little indication that anyone has left. Regular characters remain in situ on sofas, with only the audience feeling that life has gone on without them. But this is the British sitcom. Seemingly with a cultural commitment to producing comedy that can never just be funny but has to contain at least the possibility of tears, the *Spaced* finale is as close to a happy Hollywood resolution as its audience could hope for.

References

"Skip to the End." 2006. DVD extra. On *Spaced: 3 Disc Collectors' Edition*. London: Channel 4 DVD. DVD.

Spaced: 3 Disc Collectors' Edition. 2006. London: Channel 4 DVD. DVD.

58

Star Trek: The Next Generation

"All Good Things . . ."

JASON P. VEST

"You just don't get it, do you, Jean-Luc? The trial never ends," says Q (John de Lancie), the powerful extraterrestrial being who has bedevilled Captain Jean-Luc Picard (Patrick Stewart) for seven seasons of *Star Trek: The Next Generation* (*TNG*, 1987–94), near the conclusion of the series finale, "All Good Things. . . ."[1] Q's comment, along with the ellipsis included in the episode's title by writers Ronald D. Moore and Brannon Braga, slyly acknowledges that *Star Trek* never truly ends but keeps growing, just as Q hopes Picard and humanity will when he places them on trial to account for their actions while exploring the final frontier.

Even more fitting are Picard's last words when he joins his command crew's regular poker game in *TNG*'s closing scene: "So, five card stud. Nothing wild. And the sky's the limit." Dennis McCarthy's majestic score takes the audience from an overhead shot of Picard and company to an outside view of the USS *Enterprise-D* as it sails through space, onto new adventures for these intrepid voyagers. This conclusion is as terrific a finale as any in American television history, and had this scene been the last on-camera glimpse of these characters, it would indeed be the perfect ending that filmmaker Roger Lay Jr. proclaims in his audio commentary for the episode's single-issue Blu-ray disc (Lay 2014). Yet everyone reading these words knows (as everyone watching "All Good Things . . ." knew during the finale's original broadcast on May 23, 1994) that this outing was not the end for *TNG*'s cast. A film franchise beckoned, making "All Good Things . . ." an honored resident of that venerable television subgenre, the nonfinale finale.

---

1. All references to "All Good Things . . ." come from Kobe [1994] 2014.

Continuing a successful television series after its network- or studio-mandated cancellation was once an impossible prospect. Even so, reunion movies became a staple of network schedules in the 1970s and 1980s, while other series begat what Hollywood producers, in their tireless ransacking of the English language, now call "remakes," "reboots," or "reimaginings." Ronald D. Moore's sleek update (2003–9) of Glen Larson's kitschy *Battlestar Galactica* (1978–79) may be the best-known twenty-first-century example of this phenomenon, although *Dragnet* (1951–59), *The Fugitive* (1963–67), *Hawaii Five-O* (1968–80), and *Kojak* (1973–78) have all appeared in newer versions, whether on the big screen or on television.

Sequel and *spinoff* are yet other terms describing television series that pick up story lines, settings, and themes established by earlier programs. The sequel—of which *TNG* is a prime example—allows its parent series (in this case, Gene Roddenberry's *Star Trek* [1966–69], the program known by fans as "the Original Series") to become narrative backdrop for its characters, events, and developments. Spinoffs, by contrast, take place in the same time period as sequels but in different geographical locales to examine previously underutilized aspects of their forerunners. *Star Trek: Deep Space Nine* (1993–99) and *Star Trek: Voyager* (1995–2001) expanded Roddenberry's franchise by becoming *TNG* spinoffs as much as Original Series sequels. *Star Trek: Enterprise* (2001–5)—set one century before the events of the Original Series—serves as a straight prequel. The Original Series even received its own animated continuation, *Star Trek: The Animated Series*, running in 1973–74 on NBC and seeing all principal cast members, save Walter Koenig, return to voice their characters. *Star Trek*, as this brief production history attests, is among Hollywood's most popular and profitable franchises, crossing many media formats but best flourishing on television. As if to confirm this notion, CBS began presenting *Star Trek: Discovery*, the sixth live-action series, on its All Access streaming service in September 2017.

Few industry observers predicted this longevity after the Original Series' tepidly reviewed first episode, "The Man Trap," premiered on September 8, 1966. Roddenberry's first *Star Trek* did not even get a proper finale, if by this term we mean an episode designed to tie up a program's narrative loose ends. "Turnabout Intruder," the final *Star Trek* episode broadcast (on June 3, 1969, only six weeks before the first manned moon landing), is not only a standard adventure for Captain James T. Kirk (William Shatner) and his crew but also a robustly sexist story that has one of Kirk's former lovers, the mentally unstable Dr. Janice Lester (Sandra Smith), switching bodies with him so that she can take command of the starship *Enterprise*. The episode concludes moments after this body switch is reversed, with the restored Kirk, First Officer Spock (Leonard Nimoy), and Chief Engineer Montgomery Scott (James Doohan) regretting Lester's mental hysteria before walking into a turbolift, whose closing doors signal not so much the end of the series as they do the producers' decision not to develop a fitting conclusion for *Star Trek*.

"All Good Things . . . ," therefore, becomes the first true *Trek* finale. Indeed, it bookends *TNG* by resurrecting not only Q but also the humanity-on-trial premise that Roddenberry added to the pilot, "Encounter at Farpoint," to meet Paramount Television's desire for the *TNG* premiere to be two hours long. This favorite Roddenberry concept, of seemingly omnipotent extraterrestrials examining humanity's flaws, appears in numerous Original Series episodes but had never been so artfully explored as in Moore and Braga's story of Picard shuttling between past, present, and future in an effort to prevent humanity's destruction.

This tripartite structure recalls Billy Pilgrim's time slipping in Kurt Vonnegut's novel *Slaughterhouse-Five* (1969) and Ebenezer Scrooge's ghostly travels in Charles Dickens's novella *A Christmas Carol* (1843), but these literary connections obscure just how well "All Good Things . . ." ties together *TNG*'s themes, characters, and narrative conventions. Moore and Braga reveal in their Blu-ray audio commentary that they explicitly conceived the episode, discussed intermittently by *TNG*'s writing staff during the series' final two years, to parallel "Farpoint." They also expected executive producer Michael Piller—the man generally credited with saving the show by taking control of the writers' room at the start of season 3 and by authoring that year's indelible, Picard-abducted-by-the-Borg cliff-hanger, "The Best of Both Worlds"—to write the last script. Moore and Braga's assignment, which added to an already heavy workload that included an entire year spent preparing the screenplay for the *Star Trek* film franchise's seventh movie (*Star Trek: Generations* [David Carson, 1994]) while fulfilling their daily duties as writers-producers for *TNG*'s final season, meant that they had one month, in Braga's words, "to bang out the script" (Moore and Braga 2014), which seems an impossibly short time for so significant a task.

Moore and Braga succeed on almost every level, particularly in constructing the "valentine to the show" that Moore mentions in his commentary remarks (Moore and Braga 2014). To my mind, "All Good Things . . ." is *the* textbook example of what a series finale should be: tightly scripted, beautifully produced, superbly acted, and, when finished, unforgettable. It features a marvelous performance by Patrick Stewart as Picard, which is high praise indeed considering the actor's terrific work throughout *TNG*. Stewart as Picard is indomitable, driving the narrative forward and backward in time so skillfully that viewers (or, at least, this viewer) sometimes forget that the captain is a fictional character, not a living person. When Picard's consciousness jumps twenty-five years into the future, to find himself an old man suffering from dementia produced by an Alzheimer's-like condition, Stewart makes even short lines such as "Tea? Earl Grey, hot!" and "Engage" both funny and heartrending as the cantankerous Picard struggles to piece together the mystery of his time traveling without the help of the powerful intellect that *TNG*'s audience has admired for seven seasons.

Nearly every scene offers delights for longtime viewers. Miles O'Brien's (Colm Meaney) first encounter with Data (Brent Spiner), the *Enterprise*'s android second-in-command, emblematizes how "All Good Things . . ." strikes a nearly perfect balance among unabashed nostalgia, mature characterization, and *TNG*'s inventive use of time travel. When O'Brien utters the expression "burning the midnight oil," Data interrogates the perplexed O'Brien about "the etymology of that idiom" in words that perfectly recall Data's less-sophisticated understanding of human language and personal interaction in "Encounter at Farpoint." Indeed, the fact that this scene is set just before the events of "Farpoint," showing us a vignette that might have been—but was not—included in the pilot episode, demonstrates how canny Moore and Braga are in crosscutting three distinct time periods to examine *TNG*'s many strengths (and occasional weaknesses). Spiner masterfully captures the quizzical expressions, earnest inflections, and general befuddlement that characterize Data during *TNG*'s first season, making it yet another Emmy-worthy performance from a *Trek* actor who never received an award (a regrettably common oversight in the franchise's history).

The Academy of Television Arts & Sciences, however, nominated *TNG* for the Outstanding Drama Series Emmy in 1994, largely on the strength of "All Good Things . . . ," so admirers cannot say that the entertainment industry never acknowledged *TNG*'s creative quality. *Star Trek: The Next Generation* is the only syndicated, scripted weekly series ever to receive such a nomination, although Moore and Braga's crackerjack teleplay was unjustifiably shut out of the Outstanding Writing in a Drama Series category by *NYPD Blue* (1993–2005), which even among its many terrific scripts included nothing that achieves the poetry of "All Good Things. . . ."

This response may sound like fawning admiration more than critical analysis, but my enthusiasm for "All Good Things . . ." remains undiminished decades later. This episode revolves around a mind-tripping predestination paradox—in which Picard's efforts to repair an anomaly that propagates backward through time in fact create that very anomaly—to marry the clever time-travel plots that Moore and Braga honed during their years on *TNG*. Moore, after all, cowrote the season 3 episode "Yesterday's Enterprise," in which another temporal rift brings the *Enterprise-D*'s predecessor forward in time, triggering an alternate history in which Starfleet fights a losing war with the Klingons, and Braga authored the season 5 episode "Cause and Effect," perhaps the finest time-loop narrative ever committed to film. "All Good Things . . ." seamlessly melds these concepts into a charming story in which Q sends Picard through time to give the captain one last chance to preserve human history. Picard does so only by destroying his ship in the past, present, and future to solve the paradox, prompting Q to note, in the episode's most poignant dialogue, "*That* is the exploration that awaits you. Not mapping stars and studying nebulae, but charting the unknown possibilities of existence." John de Lancie's lovely performance communicates Q's regard for Picard's accomplishment, vexation at the man's intellectual limitations, and pride in his potential.

"All Good Things . . . ," therefore, is as close to a perfect television series finale as I know and certainly the best nonfinale finale ever broadcast in America. It set the bar so high for all later *Trek* series that Ira Steven Behr and Hans Beimler had to pull out all the stops when writing *Deep Space Nine*'s impressive finale, "What You Leave Behind," by deifying protagonist Benjamin Sisko (Avery Brooks). *Voyager*'s producers imported so many elements from "All Good Things . . ." into its excellent finale, "Endgame" (chief among them, the captain traveling through time and one crewmember suffering a degenerative brain disease), that it qualifies as both affectionate homage and outright rip-off. *Enterprise*'s roundly panned finale, "These Are the Voyages . . . ," comes nowhere close to these earlier episodes' quality despite its cast's good work, its title's invocation of *Star Trek*'s founding credo, and the ellipsis meant to remind careful viewers of "All Good Things. . . ."

We can only hope that *Star Trek: Discovery* will achieve the same dramatic heights as "All Good Things . . ." when reaching its inevitable end. Everyone associated with *TNG*'s concluding episode should be proud of this terrific, even paradigmatic series finale. Although "All Good Things . . ." was not the end for *TNG*'s characters, it remains a fitting conclusion for their televised adventures and a moving work of art in its own right.

References

Kobe, Winrich, dir. [1994] 2014. "All Good Things. . . ." *Star Trek: The Next Generation*, season 7, episodes 25–26. Written by Ronald D. Moore and Brannon Braga. Aired May 23, 1994, in syndication. On *Star Trek: The Next Generation. Season Seven*. Studio City, CA: CBS Home Entertainment. Blu-ray DVD.

Lay, Roger, Jr. 2014. "Audio commentary on 'All Good Things. . . .'" On *Star Trek: The Next Generation. Season Seven*. Studio City, CA: CBS Home Entertainment. Blu-ray DVD.

Moore, Ronald D., and Brannon Braga. 2014. "Audio commentary on 'All Good Things. . . .'" On *Star Trek: The Next Generation. Season Seven*. Studio City, CA: CBS Home Entertainment. Blu-ray DVD.

59

St. Elsewhere

"The Last One"

ROBERT J. THOMPSON

In the pilot episode of *The Sopranos* (1999–2007, HBO), as Tony Soprano collapses from the panic attack that serves as the etiological foundation of the entire series, an aria from Puccini's *La Rondine*—"Chi il bel sogno di Doretta"—plays in the background. It's sung by a soprano, if not a Soprano, and it takes a little bit of an interpretive stretch to justify why the lyrics of this song fit the emerging narrative of Tony's crisis. It's tempting to think that it is there for another reason. It turns out that eleven years earlier that same aria played as an introduction to the final scene of the final episode of the medical drama *St. Elsewhere* (1982–88, NBC).

Many television critics and historians see *The Sopranos* as the most conspicuous commencement of the third Golden Age of television. The first Golden Age is generally perceived as the period that brought us the live theatrical broadcasts of the late 1940s and early 1950s, and the second as the flowering of "quality TV" that started in the early 1980s with shows such as *Hill Street Blues* (1981–87, NBC) and *St. Elsewhere*. The pilot of *The Sopranos* serves up links to both of these earlier eras. Nancy Marchand, who played Livia Soprano, also played the female lead in "Marty" (1953), an installment of *The Philco-Goodyear TV Playhouse* (1948–55), which is commonly cited as the magnum opus of the first Golden Age of television. And the presence of that Puccini aria in the first *Sopranos* episode ties the show to the final episode of a masterpiece of the second Golden Age.

It takes no critical creativity to see why this song belonged in the *St. Elsewhere* finale.[1] We learn in the last scene that *St. Elsewhere* is such stuff as

1. All references to the *St. Elsewhere* final episode, "The Last One," come from Tinker 1988. In preparation for this essay, I relied on a complete collection of *St. Elsewhere* that I

dreams are made on . . . literally. As a tempest rages outside, we go on to find that the entire series—all 137 episodes, save this very last scene—has existed only in the imagination of Tommy Westphall, an autistic adolescent boy. Just before this alarming information is revealed, "Chi il bel sogno di Doretta" (Doretta's beautiful dream) plays in the background. And just as Tommy enters the room, the climatic lyrics swell in volume: "Ah! mio sogno!" (Oh, my dream!). Then the series ends in a way that is at least as surprising as the way *The Sopranos* ends nearly two decades later.[2]

St. Elsewhere, a series about a struggling hospital in a struggling Boston neighborhood, debuted on NBC in the autumn of 1982. The final episode aired on May, 25, 1988, and it exhibited all of the usual characteristics for which the show had come to be known. There were multiple interlocking stories. There were the literate dialogue of high drama and, as had become compulsory after the first season, the puns and buffoonery of low comedy. There were gracefully lyrical shots wherein the camera would flowingly follow the action from scene to scene without a cut. And there were, of course, the slyly sprinkled word games and cultural references that were catnip to careful viewers in a time when this kind of comic high jinks was still rare on television. Among the many examples:

There were patients with naughty names: Mr. Skank and Mr. Merkin.

There were bad puns: a doctor, momentarily stepping away from a patient dressed as a Viking, warns, "Don't leif, Erikson"; an orderly in a hurry shouts, "Elly, hold that 'vator."[3]

There were references to pop-music lyrics: one doctor, reflecting on the fact that his three-year internship is over, muses, "It's the end of the world as we know it, and I feel fine"; another, upon reacting to the crashing of a plane into the hospital, exclaims, "Jumpin' Jack, what was that flash?"

---

taped on a big top-loading Betamax as they originally aired on NBC from 1982 through 1988 (see Brand and Falsey 1982–88).

2. In 1998, New Video released eight episodes on four VHS tapes entitled *The Very Best of St. Elsewhere*. I selected the episodes and wrote the box copy, but I was unaware at the time that much of the original music would be replaced. Sadly, the aria under discussion is not heard in this home-video release. We hear instead some sentimental synthesized strings and piano.

3. Elevator jokes, like the announcements over the hospital intercom, had become standard operating procedure in the show. My favorite: "Nurse Redding, hold that Otis!" As obvious as these jokes seem in print, they were buried in the ambient sound and complex shots and were very easy to miss as the series aired in the 1980s, especially for an audience that had not yet gotten used to watching and listening to TV carefully.

And there were many, many references to other television shows. Some were obscure: a shout in the hallway to "move that gurney, Hal!" required you to know that Hal Gurnee was at the time directing the groundbreaking show *Late Night with David Letterman* (1982–93) on NBC. Others were more transparent. In one scene, a patient is being given a haircut by a barber who looks exactly like Floyd, the Mayberry barber in *The Andy Griffith Show* (1960–68, CBS) and its spinoff *Mayberry R.F.D.* (1968–71, CBS). This barber's name is also "Floyd," as we learn when a doctor points out that "Floyd has been the barber at St. Eligius for years . . . he may bury us all." In terms of tonsorial jokes on TV, it doesn't get much better than that.

The final episode did differ from the rest in one important way, however. Denzel Washington, who had appeared in all six seasons as Dr. Philip Chandler (though perhaps never quite used to his full potential), is nowhere to be seen. By the time the episode was filmed, Washington was crossing his own personal Delaware to glory as a movie star.

What most people remember about the final episode, though, is the ontologically challenging final scene. Many viewers and many of the show's cast felt that the scene was a betrayal of both the characters and the audience. If you didn't like the actual ending, however, the episode provided a number of alternatives.

Dramaturgically, the final episode of *St. Elsewhere* has not one ending scene but six. Like two lovers who can't decide who should hang up the phone first, the show delivers a string of scenes, any one of which would have been certainly serviceable as a curtain closer. Starting early in the third act, final-adjacent scenes start to stack up like flights over Logan International on the Wednesday before Thanksgiving. Before the episode finally and actually ends, there are four candidate scenes that might have acted as endings. Then there's the actual ending, followed by a coda ending.

The Origins Ending

The final episode of *St. Elsewhere* is a nod, an ode, to its own origins. Tribute is paid to the founding of the first television network, the medical-show genre, the source of the idea of a "series finale," and the program from which sprung both *St. Elsewhere* and the production company that made it.

This all starts even before the opening credits play. In a theatrical flourish, Dr. Wayne Fiscus (Howie Mandel) pulls open the curtain in a hospital examination room to reveal his patient, who looks for all the world like central casting's idea of a typical network executive. The very first words of the episode belong to Fiscus, who tells his patient, "So you see, General Sarnoff, it's quite a network, and optic nerves need their rest. So do your eyes a favor and cut down on the time you spend in front of the television." The final episode thus aptly begins with a shout-out to General David Sarnoff, the executive who more than sixty years earlier had started NBC, the network on which *St. Elsewhere* aired. Throughout the series, the producers took several veiled jabs at the network management, especially after NBC was acquired by General Electric in 1986. This reference was no different. "General Sarnoff" may have a fancy suit and a $200 haircut, but he gets no speaking lines, and he seems like kind of a doofus. After he departs, Dr. Fiscus complains to a colleague, "I've helped hundreds of people in this room. I've reattached limbs, patched up bullet wounds, brought lives back from the brink . . . and my last patient at St. Eligius shouldn't be someone who spent his entire existence in front of the tube."[4]

Having acknowledged the establishment of the first broadcast network, the episode goes on to recognize the first great series finale. In the early decades of American television, it was highly unusual to end a series with definitive narrative closure. The final episode was just like the episodes that had preceded it. Gilligan dresses as a woman in the final episode of *Gilligan's Island* (1964–67, CBS), but, other than that, nothing notable happens—no rescue from the island, no wedding, nothing special.[5] In that same year, however, there was a significant exception to this rule. *The Fugitive* (1963–67, ABC) made series finale history in 1967 by actually bringing its story to an Aristotelean conclusion that was watched by more people than any TV series episode up until that time. (For more on *The Fugitive* finale, see chapter 21.) In the first episode of *The Fugitive*, Dr. Richard Kimble (David Janssen) is sentenced to die for killing his wife. He escapes from the law and spends four seasons looking for the one-armed man (Bill Raisch) who did kill her. In the final episode, Kimble's innocence is proven after he finds the one-armed man, who ultimately plunges to his death from a tower.

4. This episode may also contain an allusion to another NBC executive, Brandon Tartikoff, who had been a supporter of the show throughout its run. One of the final patients treated at St. Eligius is suffering from Hodgkin's lymphoma, and he talks about his time in New Haven. Tartikoff had gone to Yale and also suffered from Hodgkin's, to which he would succumb in 1997 at the age of forty-eight.

5. It would be more than ten years before the castaways are rescued in a NBC reunion special in 1978.

Although *The Fugitive* may not have been the first series to provide a tidy finale, its finale was by far the most remarkable, even if the practice wouldn't catch on for another decade. And so the season finale of *St. Elsewhere* gives it its due. A patient has gone missing. A nurse announces that he's "an amputee, Dr. Kimble's patient . . . he's a fugitive." Orderly Warren Coolidge (Byron Stewart, reprising a role he played on *The White Shadow* [1978–81, CBS])[6] ends up chasing this one-armed man throughout the hospital, allowing for a final tour of what was one of the most extensive studio sets in television at the time. We later learn that they have finally caught the "fugitive," appropriately atop the water tower on the roof of the hospital. What he was running from is never made clear and, of course, doesn't matter. Unlike the homage to the founding of NBC, the nod to *The Fugitive* is more than a passing reference. The story of the missing amputee is told over several scenes throughout the episode.

Acknowledgment is also paid to the generic origins of *St. Elsewhere*. Two references are made to old medical-theme TV shows. One is obscure: in an argument between two nurses, a throwaway line is delivered that mentions the title (*The Nurses*) and star (Zina Bethune) of a forgotten CBS series that ran from 1962 to 1965. The other is more obvious: a doctor in the morgue refers to "Patient 4077. Blake, Henry. Cause of death thought to be injuries sustained in a helicopter crash." Colonel Henry Blake (McLean Stevenson) of the 4077th Mobile Army Surgical Hospital was, of course, killed in like manner on a much-celebrated episode of *M*A*S*H* (1972–83, CBS) in 1975.

These paeans to TV originals, though, are just the lead-up to yet another one, more overt and probably more recognizable to an audience in 1988. *St. Elsewhere* was made by MTM Enterprises, the independent production company that had launched the "quality TV" revolution in 1981 with *Hill Street Blues*. (For more on MTM, see Feuer, Kerr, and Vahimagi 1984 and Thompson 1996, 46–58.) Before that, the company had been gathering critically acclaimed credentials with series on CBS such as *The Bob Newhart Show* (1972–78), *WKRP in Cincinnati* (1972–78), *Lou Grant* (1977–82),

---

6. In this episode and others, Coolidge wears a "Carver High School" T-shirt, the school Coolidge attended in *The White Shadow*. Stewart's presence in *St. Elsewhere* in the same role he played in *The White Shadow* made for some comic dissonance on occasion. In one episode, Timothy Van Patten, who starred as Coolidge's Carver classmate in *The White Shadow*, shows up, to Coolidge's confusion, in a different role in *St. Elsewhere*. In another episode, a patient watches *The White Shadow* in his room, suggesting that Coolidge exists as a fictional TV character who is also working at St. Eligius.

and *The White Shadow*. MTM was founded in 1969 as an entity to produce its first and most successful series, *The Mary Tyler Moore Show* (1970–77, CBS) (see chapter 36). Ten years after the end of *The Fugitive*, it was this program that finally established the series finale as a thing. In that last episode, a new station manager decides to fire the entire WJM news team (except for the incompetent Ted Baxter). In the final scene of this final episode, as the entire cast is preparing to leave the set for the last time, in art and in life, they all huddle together in a group hug, then shuffle across the room as one organism to get some tissue from Mary's desk to staunch their weeping. Mary recites a moving monologue that nicely sums up the nature of the workplace-family genre that characterized so much of the work of MTM Enterprises; they all join in a non sequitur singing of "It's a Long Way to Tipperary"; and the lights go out on an instant classic of the just-emerging tradition of the series finale. (For more on this finale, see chapter 36.)

In July 1988, MTM Enterprises would be sold to the UK broadcasting company TVS Entertainment. In May of that year, *St. Elsewhere*'s final episode offered its obeisance to the final episode of the show that started it all with respect to finales. The title of the last episode of *The Mary Tyler Moore Show* is "The Last Show"; the title of the *St. Elsewhere* finale is "The Last One." In a direct restaging, Doctors Jackie Wade (Sagan Lewis) and Carol Novino (Cindy Pickett) arrive bearing gifts to see off the departing residents (and original cast members) Wayne Fiscus and Jack Morrison (David Morse). There's a group hug, a shuffle to the tissues, and when Jack asks, "What do we do now?" Wayne responds, "Maybe we should sing 'It's a Long Way to Tipperary.'" Jack even delivers a characteristically inarticulate version of Mary's more eloquent "workplace-family" monologue. Like the original, this scene is sweet, sentimental, and funny. For those who hated the way this episode *actually* ended, they might want to just stop the VHS tape here and call it a day.[7]

But there were more endings coming up.

The Tragic Ending

The homage to *The Mary Tyler Moore Show* plays out in the *St. Elsewhere* finale's third act. After three intervening scenes, the act ends with the death

---

7. *St. Elsewhere* had in its fourth season already done an extraordinary tribute to *The Mary Tyler Moore Show* ("Close Encounters," November 20, 1985), in which a character becomes convinced that he is Mary Richards. See an extensive discussion of this episode in Thompson 1996, 86–89.

of Dr. Daniel Auschlander. Auschlander (played by Norman Lloyd, who had worked with Charlie Chaplin, Alfred Hitchcock, and Orson Welles) is the soul and anchor of the show. He had been at the hospital forever, and he served with a steady and sober kindness. His presence is also a metaphor for the show itself. We learn in the pilot episode that he has terminal liver cancer and that he is expected to die soon. Yet, miraculously, he survives six seasons (three years[8]) right into the last episode. From the start, the diagnosis for *St. Elsewhere* itself was as dismal as Daniel's. Chronic low ratings suggested imminent cancellation at several points during its run, especially in the early years. Auschlander's unlikely survival mirrored the long run of the series itself. And, in the end, both the man and the show succumbed in unexpected ways. Auschlander was battling cancer, but he dies of a stroke. *St. Elsewhere* battled cancellation, but it wasn't canceled; it ended because of production costs that were too high for MTM to keep making the show for NBC (Mahoney and Paskowski 1988; Auletta 1991, 449).

The death of Dr. Auschlander makes perfect sense for the final episode, and the fourth-act scene in which he is eulogized by his lifelong friend and colleague has all the trappings of a final scene of a series finale. The cast of the show—a big crowd—is gathered in the hospital cafeteria as Dr. Donald Westphall (Ed Flanders) recites his funereal oratory: "We have to say good-bye to Daniel Auschlander, who I've known for forty-three years. With Daniel's death we've lost some of the spirit of this place, some of the compassion. But I think most importantly we've lost his experience. But ends mean beginnings, don't they? There was a time when Daniel didn't exist. And that time has come again. And I think we should be glad that we lived in the time he did." These tear-jerking words, accompanied by high-melodramatic variations on the show's theme song, are followed by a lingering pan shot of the cast. A perfect way to end the show. But it still isn't over. In the very next scene, we get . . .

---

8. The show aired for six seasons, but its story line covers only three years. The chronology of each two-year period is complicated. One holiday might be celebrated in one season, but another in the next. It is as though each half-year is going through an entire year. The writers on the show referred to this passage of time as "Fontana time," named for Tom Fontana, who joined the show as producer and writer in 1983 and became central to shaping its identity starting in the second season (Mark Tinker, telephone interview by Robert J. Thompson, Apr. 18, 1993).

The Snarky Ending

Even with only ten minutes left in this series, the writers were apparently compelled to introduce a brand-new character. He's a very young-looking first-year resident at St. Eligius, a symbol of the generation that will take the place of those we have been farewelling for the past three-quarters of an hour. But he's also a symbol of something old.

St. Elsewhere was created by Joshua Brand and John Falsey, both of whom had written for *The White Shadow*, the MTM show from *St. Elsewhere*'s executive producer Bruce Paltrow. Following in the footsteps of *Hill Street Blues*, Brand and Falsey attempted to take a tired old genre and make it more "realistic." Rejecting the godlike TV doctors such as Ben Casey, Marcus Welby, and Trapper John, M.D. (the one played by Pernell Roberts, that is), they wanted to present the medical establishment warts and all. But they may have overdone it. During the first season of *St. Elsewhere*, they became known by their colleagues as "Dr. Death and Mr. Depression." They left after the first season (in tense circumstances, it seems) as the rest of the creative staff attempted to lighten the tone of the show (Turow 1989, 242–44).

And so, of course, Brand and Falsey get dissed in the final episode. In treating a patient's pain, the young new intern prescribes ten times the normal dose of medication—enough to kill the patient. The intern's name? Brandon Falsey. It's a deeply embedded inside joke, a bone tossed to the most ardent of fans.[9]

The Superobvious, "I Saw That Coming" Comic Ending

After his quick treatment of General Sarnoff in the very first scene of the final episode, Dr. Fiscus is introduced to another patient. She's a fully costumed opera singer, her body bedecked in the trappings of a zaftig Valkyrie, her head behelmeted with horns. In transit to the hospital, she somehow still hasn't surrendered her seven-foot spear. Her ailment? She's got laryngitis. The problem? She's the star of the show, and tonight's the final dress rehearsal! It's an old-school sitcom set-up, but it's used to elegant effect here.

---

9. In preparation for writing the pilot, Brand and Falsey had done research at the Cleveland Clinic. In an even more obscure origins reference in the final episode, Dr. Mark Craig (William Daniels) announces that he is resigning from his long career at St. Eligius and following his wife to a hospital in Cleveland.

Fiscus orders her to let her vocal cords rest; she's not to talk or even whisper. This treatment allows Fiscus to deliver to her an uninterrupted monologue about his three years at St. Eligius, reminding us all of the show's overall narrative and of characters who have come and gone and died. Fiscus is the perfect character to offer this nostalgic look back. If Dr. Auschlander is the patriarchal soul of the hospital, Fiscus is the soul of the institution's new generation. He has some pretty serious spiritual credentials, too. In a season 5 episode based loosely on Dante's *Commedia*, he dies and rises from the dead.

In a masterful display of comic timing, the story of the opera singer is dropped in the first third of the show and doesn't return until seven minutes before the end, leaving viewers plenty of time to forget the obvious comic set-up so they can be surprised by its inevitable resolution. Throughout the episode, Dr. Fiscus has been reluctant to take his final leave of the hospital. His residency is over. Everyone has said good-bye. But he keeps hanging around, finding one patient here, another there, who might need his help.

While Fiscus is waiting for potential customers in the ER, Dr. John Gideon (Ronny Cox), the head of the hospital, approaches him from behind. "What are you still doing here?" he asks. "Dr. Fiscus, go home. It's finished. The year's over. Your residency's over." "No sir," Fiscus replies. "It ain't over 'til the fat lady sings." And then, of course, we hear the warm-up arpeggios of the opera singer we haven't seen in two acts. The idiom isn't very polite, and the joke is about as fusty as jokes get, but the "fat lady" singing is enough to get Fiscus to finally exit the hospital, the theatrical sliding doors of the ER mirroring the opening of the exam-room cubicle curtains that started the episode.

As Fiscus departs, the camera zooms into an extreme close-up of the opera singer's tonsils. Her high note hits the emergency room and then blends into the recording of an actual opera performance, which brings us to . . .

The (Un)Real Ending

Dr. Donald Westphall sits in the office of his best friend, Dr. Daniel Auschlander, who has died just hours earlier. The Puccini aria plays in the background, which is appropriate because Donald and Daniel had many times before sat in this office listening to opera and talking about medicine, the past, and life. Now Donald is alone. Outside, the Lear-like lightning has been superseded by a surprising spring snowstorm. Westphall's life is far removed from Pangloss's best-of-all-possible-worlds Westphalia. Everything seems hopeless: his wife died long ago in a car accident when she went out to get ice cream; his autistic son, Tommy, is getting older and harder to manage; his daughter has left the nest; his dearest friend has died—and it's snowing in springtime. Just as the aria reaches the lyric "Oh, my dream!" Tommy barges into the office, runs to the window, and stares out onto the falling snow. This is the final shot of the show as we have known it for six seasons. In the very next shot, only five seconds long and with the last note of the "beautiful dream" aria still lingering, all former diegesis is blown to smithereens.

This short shot is from Tommy's point of view, but he's no longer looking out at the snow; he's now looking in upon it. What he sees is the exterior of St. Eligius in a blizzard, and then the whole image begins to shake. It shakes, we learn in the next shot, because Tommy is shaking it. He's sitting on the floor of a dimly lit, well-worn apartment shaking and staring into a snow globe. Above him sits a man whose face is covered by the newspaper he is reading. In walks a man who looks like Donald Westphall—but he's not a doctor; he's a construction worker. He says, "Hi Pop" to the man in the chair, who, in another theatrical "curtain" trick so typical of this episode, brings down his newspaper to reveal that he's Daniel Auschlander. Only he can't be Daniel because Daniel is dead; Daniel is not Donald's "pop," and this guy also appears not to be a doctor.

When Daniel (?) asks his son, Donald (?), about his day up on the building, Donald responds, "Well, we finally topped off the twenty-second story." As did most dramatic series at the time, that season of *St. Elsewhere* consisted of twenty-two episodes. If the twenty-second story has already been topped off, we can infer that *St. Elsewhere* is already over, and whatever it is we're watching now is something else entirely.

"Daniel" and "Donald"—or whoever they are now—have left the narrative confines of *St. Elsewhere*. Only Tommy continues in his original role as an autistic child. As "Donald" prepares to take Tommy to bed, he says: "I don't understand this autism thing, Pop. But he is my son. I talk to him; I don't even know if he can hear me. He sits there all day long in his own world staring at that toy. What's he thinkin' about?" He then helps Tommy to his feet, and as he leaves the room, he sets the snow globe onto the top of a television set. As a lushly orchestrated version of the *St. Elsewhere* theme song builds, the camera moves in to a close-up of the snow globe, inside of which (as we should already know if we have been paying really close attention) is a model of a building that looks exactly like St. Eligius Hospital—left, in the end, where it had always been: *on TV.*

What was Tommy "thinkin' about"? Apparently, six seasons of Emmy Award–winning television.

But now it's over, bringing to mind Fiscus's sly quote from that R.E.M. song in the first scene of the episode: "It's the end of the world as we know it." Some of the producers of the show said that they had felt the need to provide a permanent close to the show, to eliminate the possibility of remakes or reunions (Haithman 1988). This ending doesn't really achieve that permanence, however. Nothing happens here that precludes Tommy from getting up the next morning and thinking up season 7.

There was a precedent for *St. Elsewhere*'s provocative exit strategy. Less than two years earlier, the first episode of the tenth season of *Dallas* (1978–91, CBS) revealed that the entire ninth season had been just a dream of one of the principal characters. And two years later, in 1990, the final episode of the MTM series *Newhart* (1982–90, CBS) would reveal that the entire series had been a dream of the lead character of an earlier MTM series, *The Bob Newhart Show* (see chapter 39). The *Dallas* dream, however, was devised merely as a way to bring back a character who had already died, and the *Newhart* dream was just a hilarious punchline. *St. Elsewhere*'s final scene seems to aspire to something a little more ambitious.

This scene lasts just two minutes, but there's a great deal going on in it. Besides the Puccini aria, yet another opera is evoked, if not actually heard: The Who's *Tommy*, about another unresponsive boy who lives in his imagination and looks into glass (in his case a mirror; in Tommy Westphall's case a snow globe; in our case a television screen). The worry Tommy Westphall's father has—"I don't even know if he can hear me"—nicely echoes the song "Tommy, Can You Hear Me?" on the album *Tommy*.

Most notably, however, the producers of *St. Elsewhere* used these last two minutes to link themselves with what many critics have called the greatest film in the history of the American cinema. One can't see a snow globe without thinking of *Citizen Kane* (Orson Welles, 1941). At the beginning of that film, we see a building that is then revealed to be only a toy; at the end of *St. Elsewhere* we see the same. In both cases, the snow globe is central to the meaning of the story. Charles Foster Kane stares into his globe, nostalgically thinking of a life that he has lost; Tommy's stares create a world that never existed.

Of the many ideas for ending the series that were considered, one, recounted by producer-writer Tom Fontana, is especially interesting. The final scene would have played out exactly as it did until the very end. As the snow globe is set down, there would be a whole collection of other globes already on the TV set: one containing the newsroom from *The Mary Tyler Moore Show*, another the gymnasium from *The White Shadow*, another Bob's office from *The Bob Newhart Show*, and so on. Tommy, in this version, has dreamed up MTM's entire corpus.[10]

The Coda

But, for all that, the episode still isn't over. The writers and producers had one more trick up their sleeves. The series *really* ends with the death of a cat.

Besides bearing the initials of Mary Tyler Moore, the name "MTM Enterprises" was also a variant of the legendary studio giant MGM. In the television company's logo, which played after the end credits of every episode of the series it produced, MGM's roaring lion was replaced with a mewing kitten. As the years went on, the company began to play with this two-second-long logo. At the end of episodes of *The White Shadow*, a series about a high school basketball coach, the cat dribbled a basketball in its paw. For cop show *Hill Street Blues*, it wore the hat of a police officer, and on detective show *Remington Steele* (1982–87, NBC) it sported Sherlock's deerstalker hat and briar pipe. Kitty caught a fly ball at the end of every episode of baseball drama *Bay City Blues* (1983, NBC) and quacked after each installment of *The Duck Factory* (1963–67, NBC), a comedy about an animation studio. The word *meow*, as spoken by Bob Newhart, came out of the cat's mouth at the end of the credits on *Newhart*, and on the MTM Home Video logo, the cat, holding a remote-control device in its paw, meows, rewinds itself, and meows again.

Predictably, every episode of *St. Elsewhere* ended with the cat performing the obligatory meow while outfitted in a standard-issue green surgical mask and gown. Except for the last episode. This time, the cat was shown during the entire roll of the final credits, not just at the very end. But kitty was unconscious, sprawled out on a hospital bed, attached to an intravenous tube and a cardiograph machine. As the credits played, the *beep-beep-beep* of the heart monitor could be heard, and the sine waves of kitty's heartbeat could be seen on the monitor's screen. At the end, however, we heard a steady *beeeeeeep* and saw a flat line on the monitor.

Lots of important things happened in 1988, but for our purposes here I'll name just three. *St. Elsewhere* ended, MTM Enterprises was sold, and

10. Tom Fontana, telephone interview by Robert J. Thompson, Apr. 19, 1993.

Mimsie, the MTM company cat—an actual cat, upon whom the MTM logo was based—died at the age of twenty, just about the same age as MTM itself. Verily, it was the end of an era.

References

Auletta, Ken. 1991. *Three Blind Mice: How the TV Networks Lost Their Way.* New York: Random House.

Brand, Joshua, and John Falsey, creators. 1982–88. *St. Elsewhere.* Aired Oct. 26, 1982, to May 25, 1988, NBC. Original broadcasts.

Feuer, Jane, Paul Kerr, and Tise Vahimagi, eds. 1984. *MTM—Quality Television.* London: British Film Institute.

Haithman, Diane. 1988. "On Television, There's More Than One Way to Say Goodby [*sic*]: 'St. Elsewhere' as Seen through a Glass Darkly." *Los Angeles Times*, May 26.

Mahoney, William, and Marianne Paskowski. 1988. "MTM Breaks 'St. Elsewhere' Silence." *Electronic Media*, Mar. 7.

Thompson, Robert J. 1996. *Television's Second Golden Age.* New York: Continuum.

Tinker, Mark, dir. 1988. "The Last One." 1988. *St. Elsewhere*, season 6, episode 22. Teleplay by Bruce Paltrow and Mark Tinker. Story by Tom Fontana, John Tinker, and Channing Gibson. Aired May 25, NBC. Original broadcast.

Turow, Joseph. 1989. *Playing Doctor: Television, Storytelling, and Medical Power.* New York: Oxford Univ. Press.

60

That Was the Week That Was

"May 4, 1965"

DAVID BIANCULLI

Of all the television series finales ever presented, the finale for the US version of *That Was the Week That Was*, a topical comedy show aired in 1964–65 on NBC, may be the boldest of them all.[1] This show was defiantly liberal, outspoken, and political at a time when television entertainment programs, at least on American TV, were none of those things. It was so controversial and to its philosophical opponents so abrasive that it didn't last long and was pre-empted often, especially during the presidential election year of 1964. But because it was a live show, its producers and cast members and writers were aware, weeks in advance, that it was coming to a rather abrupt end— and because it was a live show, they were able to go out swinging, singing, lambasting targets, and slaughtering sacred cows to the very end, without a safety net, knowing that whatever they presented on the final episode of *That Was the Week That Was* would indeed be their last word on the subject, on whatever subject they chose. And that's why and how they went out not with a whimper but with a very big bang.

TW3, as *That Was the Week That Was* is commonly and conveniently abbreviated, was an Americanized version of a show that began in the United Kingdom (as *All in the Family* [1971–79] would be a handful of years later). The British *TW3* didn't live long, either: it lasted only from 1962 to 1963 on BBC-TV and had been canceled long before the NBC series incarnation was launched in the United States in 1964. But both shows were unusually, excitingly ambitious. Like HBO's *Last Week Tonight with John Oliver*

---

1. All references to the final episode of *That Was the Week That Was* come from "May 4, 1965" 1965.

383

(2014–), the *TW3* news summaries were pointedly opinionated dissections of the week's headlines, coupled with looks at longer-running and more complex issues. Like HBO's *Real Time with Bill Maher* (2003–) and NBC's *Saturday Night Live* (1975–), *TW3* was televised live. Also like *Saturday Night Live*, *TW3* had a comedian pretending to be a TV news anchor, relaying the headlines and stories of the day and the week. Like Comedy Central's *The Daily Show* (1996–), *TW3* presented fake news reporters who delivered "reports" while standing in front of green-screen images that seemingly placed them in harm's way or at least at the site of breaking news. And like the late, great *Smothers Brothers Comedy Hour* (1967–69), *TW3* often softened its most pointed satirical barbs by accompanying them with music. All that in mid-1960s, when most scripted TV entertainment was intentionally, insultingly banal.

And NBC's *TW3* crew, in its final installment, would be so bold and so indecorous as to point that out. "Big deal, this show, we're really not important at all," sang Phyllis Newman in one number, commenting dryly on both the cancellation of *TW3* and the new programs about to take its place. "Tonight, we'll go, but look what you've got to look forward to for fall." And then she added, quite tellingly: *"Run for Your Life* and *My Mother the Car* / Sometimes you don't know how lucky you are."

On the original BBC series, *TW3* was hosted by a smirking David Frost, featured Millicent Martin as a singer of topical songs, and included, among its writing staff, future *Monty Python's Flying Circus* (1969–74) star John Cleese and future *The Singing Detective* (1986) creator Dennis Potter. For the NBC version, journeyman actor Elliott Reid began as host, but Frost soon crossed the pond to replace him in the United States, and it was Frost who was on hand for the final American hour of *That Was the Week That Was*. Also along for that last proudly bumpy ride were cast regulars and singers Nancy Ames and Phyllis Newman; comedy cast member and writer Buck Henry; brilliant topical and satirical songwriter Tom Lehrer; puppeteer Burr Tillstrom; and writers Herb Sargent (later an early shaper of *Saturday Night Live*) and Gloria Steinem. Yes, that Gloria Steinem.

On the day NBC's *TW3* finale was broadcast live, May 4, 1965, among the recent headlines to which the show reacted was President Lyndon B. Johnson's decision, less than a week earlier, to send twenty-two thousand US troops into the Dominican Republic, purportedly to protect the island of Santo Domingo from falling under control of a Communist dictatorship, as Cuba had a few years earlier. This executive decision allowed Buck Henry to portray war correspondent "John Canceler" (a playful pun on then prominent NBC reporter John Chancellor) and to run frantically from one global hot spot to another, merely by changing the projected image shown behind him. In his frenetic report, he went from Washington, DC, to the Israeli/Syrian border, then from Saigon in Vietnam to NBC's 30 Rock headquarters in New York, "where war has waged between NBC and *That Was the Week That Was*"—and where, Henry's fake news reporter John Canceler continued, "Buck Henry, whoever he is, will be publically tried on *Hullabaloo* for war crimes."

The Santo Domingo invasion also was covered in song, with Newman's performance of Tom Lehrer's new composition "Send the Marines." (Sample lyrics: "For might makes right / and till they've seen the light / they've got to be protected / and all their rights respected / till somebody we like can be elected.") Also, for the show's final outing, *TW3* proudly invited cast member Tillstrom to perform a live reprise of his stark and touching piece "Berlin Wall," which had recently won a prestigious Peabody Award after its initial appearance in *TW3*. Tillstrom, accompanied by solo piano and without resorting to puppets, used his own forearms, wrists, and hands to portray the recently erected Berlin Wall, separating East and West Germany, as well as loving and anguished residents on both sides. After concluding the performance, Tillstrom—never seen as the puppeteer on the famous children's TV show *Kukla, Fran & Ollie* (1947–57)—emerged to take one final, poignant bow.

The other blows landed in this last *TW3*, except for a few topical "Weekend Update"–style punchlines by Frost at his "news desk," were memorably musical.

In front of giant blowups of the CBS, NBC, and ABC logos (back then, those networks were not only the Big Three but also the Only Three), Newman, in a number mentioned earlier, sang derisively of the shows that had just been renewed or announced for the networks' coming fall schedules, while *TW3* had been ignominiously canceled. "After all, if you want entertainment intellectual style," she sang sarcastically, "there's always *Lawrence Welk*, *Donna Reed*, *Patty Duke*, and *Gomer Pyle*."

On a finale in which the advertisers included Johnson Wax, Bufferin pain reliever, Score deodorant, Revlon Moon Drops "Wet" lipstick, Colorsilk hair coloring, and Glade air freshener—but not a single cigarette advertiser—Buck Henry noted the current, controversial congressional hearings about placing health warnings on cigarette packets. "Let's have a cheerful little song," he said, at which time Nancy Ames stepped up to sing that old classic "Smoke Gets in Your Eyes." As the TV image shifted to close-ups of X-rays of diseased lungs, Ames sang the lyrics "Something deep inside / cannot be denied"—and the studio audience laughed nervously. Scenes of smokers and cigarette ads were intercut with scenes of patients being wheeled into operating rooms. Talk about bold.

Nancy Ames also got to lead the entire company on the show's closing number—an appropriately apocalyptic ditty, given the occasion. Written by Tom Lehrer, "We Will All Go Together When We Go" was an ode to the threat of global nuclear annihilation. In this context, though, its message also served as a perfect tongue-in-cheek sign-off and warning from the troublemaking troubadours at *TW3*: "You will all go directly to your respective Valhallas," Ames sang. "Go directly, do not pass go, do not collect two hundred dollahs."

And then Ames, to put a final capper on the finale, sang, "That was *That Was the Week That Was*," and added with a wry smile, "It's over, so bye-bye."

More than fifty years later, in prime time on broadcast television, we have never quite seen the show's like again.

References

"May 4, 1965." 1965. *That Was the Week That Was.* Aired May 4, 1965, NBC. Paley Center for Media Catalog ID: T78:0131.

61

30 Rock

"Hogcock/Last Lunch"

AMY M. DAMICO

In season 1, episode 3 of *30 Rock* (Bernstein 2006), NBC executive Jack Donaghy is perplexed that enthusiastic and seemingly unsophisticated NBC page Kenneth has beaten him at poker when no one else can. Jack reviews Kenneth's personnel file and discovers that the Myers Briggs assessment determined that Kenneth is extroverted, intuitive, and aggressive. Jack says to writer Liz Lemon: "It's the same as mine. Could be trouble down the line." Later in the episode, Kenneth eventually loses in poker to Jack and with the loss goes his job. When Liz compliments Jack on not ultimately requiring that Kenneth leave NBC, Jack responds in what viewers have come to recognize as his brilliantly written vernacular style, "The Italians have a saying, Lemon. Keep your friends close and your enemies closer, and although they've never won a war or mass-produced a decent car, in this area they are correct. In five years, we will either be working for him or be dead by his hand." Seven seasons later, Jack's intuition about Kenneth is realized; though they are not enemies, Kenneth becomes the president of NBC, and the final scene of the *30 Rock* finale indicates that Kenneth will be president for a long, long time.

Created by Tina Fey and loosely based on her time as a head writer at *Saturday Night Live* (1975–), *30 Rock* (2006–13) is a situation comedy that tells the story of a team of NBC employees working on the weekly live comedy show called *The Girlie Show*, or *TGS*.[1] The group includes the protagonist

1. In the first episode, *The Girlie Show* is renamed *The Girlie Show with Tracy Jordan*. However, during the show's run, it is referred to mainly by its original title or the acronym *TGS*.

head writer, Liz Lemon (Tina Fey); NBC executive Jack Donaghy (Alec Baldwin); self-absorbed actors Tracy Jordan and Jenna Maroney (Tracy Morgan and Jane Krakowski); producer Pete Hornberger (Scott Adsit); NBC page Kenneth Parcell (Jack McBrayer); and a group of writers, support staff, and friends. Fey enlisted her former *SNL* colleague Robert Carlock to join her as a cohead writer and executive producer of the show, and together they assembled a writing team (Jack Burditt, Kay Cannon, Dave Finkel, Brett Baer, Matt Hubbard, Daisy Gardner, John Riggi, and Donald Glover) from a variety of comedic backgrounds (Fey 2011, 171–75).

Shot on film primarily in single camera style, *30 Rock* is a workplace sitcom set in the NBC studios. The comedy of *30 Rock* is a blend of smart jokes, social commentary, popular-culture references, and creative pronunciation. Made-up words and phrases punctuate the dialogue and become part of the fabric of the show. At the time of *30 Rock*'s debut in 2006, streaming series, cable, premium cable, and Internet programming were competing for viewers, and as a result, traditional television networks were seeing a decline in viewership. The *30 Rock* plotline takes place during this time period and inherently addresses this shift by integrating elements of the corporate structure of network TV in its narratives. Over the years, the show pokes fun at NBC, its then-parent company General Electric, and the various strategies used to generate needed capital. At the same time, the moderate success of *30 Rock* itself implies that quality network television can be a player in this changing landscape.

One noteworthy stylistic feature of *30 Rock* is the use of flash cuts, or short flashbacks, that provide a quick view of the past or a glimpse of scene-related material. *Sitcom* author Saul Austerlitz suggests, "These jolts of comic punctuation are *30 Rock*'s most recognizable stylistic feature, and they give the series, mostly enclosed within cramped writers' rooms and offices, the feel of a much more varied show" (2014, 363). These flashbacks are usually just seconds long and often include intertextual references. They are central to the show's humor and fast pacing. One analysis of *30 Rock*'s use of flashbacks suggests that intertextuality is performed in a particular way:

> With numerous jokes and gags that reference other filmic and televisual texts, *30 Rock* assumes its viewers are steeped in knowledge of these texts and rewards them for this knowledge. But this alone isn't what distinguishes *30 Rock*'s particular take on the intertextual flashback. Rather than only referencing other texts and rewarding viewers, it points to the inadequacy,

the exhaustion, of such tropes and conventions and, instead, mines that exhaustion for humor. (Dickey 2013, 69–70)

Though the sitcom was not exceedingly popular among viewers, it was praised by critics, and its producers, cast, and writers won multiple high-profile awards. Perhaps one of the reasons for this disconnect has to do with the steady stream of nods to popular culture. Although some of the show's intertextual references clearly connect to mainstream culture, others are less obvious but no doubt recognized by culture critics and television writers, who are immersed in such material. When reflecting on her show's reception, Fey pointed out, "We weren't trying to make a low-rated critical darling that snarled in the face of conventionality," and explained that her team attempted to "course correct the show to make it more accessible" (Fey 2011, 190), but to little avail. The show cultivated a dedicated following, however, and lasted seven seasons. Its terrific finale provides closure with humor and emotion.

The final two-part episode of *30 Rock*, "Hogcock/Last Lunch," finds the *TGS* team having to produce one more episode of the show before it is off the air for good.[2] Members of the *TGS* team struggle in their own ways as they embark on this final good-bye: Jack and Liz argue, the writers fight, Tracy tries to sabotage the show, Pete plans to fake his own death, and Jenna resists admitting she is upset. At the same time, viewers see other personal struggles via the show's trademark comic storytelling—new mom Liz comes to terms with her preference to work while her husband stays home; Jack tries to find out what is meaningful outside work; Tracy confronts his fear of being abandoned; and Jenna wrestles with her next career move. The end of *TGS* allows the characters to get to a place where they can say good-bye to one another and, by extension, to *30 Rock*'s audience. The finale reminds viewers that television continues and that the *TGS* staff may see one another in different roles, just as *30 Rock* audiences will likely engage with new art constructed by former *30 Rock* writers, actors, and producers.

Many of the finale scenes encapsulate what the sitcom had done all along—simultaneously utilize and poke fun at elements of the television industry. For example, in one scene, when Liz is looking for Tracy, network graphics for *Grizz & Hers*, a show based on Jordan sidekick Grizz's new job, slide across the screen in the foreground of the scene taking place. Liz

2. All references to "Hogcock/Last Lunch" come from McCarthy-Miller 2013.

acts as if she sees these graphics, joking about just this type of ubiquitous TV show promotion. In a previous episode, the twist that Kenneth has been appointed the new president of NBC is both fitting because of his love of NBC and of the most banal television and perplexing because of his lack of experience. And yet his intuition about television, alluded to in season 1, is on display when Liz pitches a new show to him as she searches for a new job in the wake of *TGS*'s end. Kenneth turns her down because her pitch includes words on his "TV writer no-no list"—"*women, writer*, and *quality*"—which suggests that Liz's show might simply not be entertaining, in Kenneth's view, and perhaps not profitable, underscoring the observation that "*30 Rock* consistently points out that television is simultaneously the best and the worst" (Greenwald 2013).

Most of the finale is funny and emotional in ways that adhere to the show's style. In a *New York Times* interview, Robert Carlock reflected that his favorite parts of the show were when it was "perversely sweet . . . when there'd be these sweet moments for the characters, our version of emotion, I guess, that were a little off" (Shattuck 2013). This description captures many of the final scenes, in which the characters articulate declarations of platonic love. For example, Liz convinces Tracy to return to the studio after he runs away because he is worried about saying good-bye and not seeing anyone ever again. After an honest exchange that results in Liz agreeing they may not stay in touch, she says emotionally: "Because the human heart is not properly connected to the human brain, I love you, and I'm going to miss you . . . but tonight might be it." This sentiment is delivered in a strip club, where Liz is seen visually trying not to gag in response to her surroundings. In a touching exchange between Liz and Jack, expressed feelings are punctuated by bits of humor. Jack says: "There is a word. A once special word that has been tragically co-opted by the romance industrial complex, and I would hate to use it here and have you think I was suggesting any kind of romantic sentiment." He continues but is eventually interrupted by Liz, who says, "I love you too, Jack." This scene is one of the most memorable of the finale given the deep friendship Liz and Jack develop over the series. As critic James Poniewozik points out, "Their work-love—more unlikely than most odd-couple romantic pairings—has always been one of the most important parts of the show: a love that's about respect, mutual concern and high regard" (2013). Finally, when Kenneth appears to take Jenna's mirror away, a silly montage of clips set to music shows Jenna looking at herself in the mirror again and again. When the montage ends, Jenna is in tears. Later in the episode, a more traditional montage is used to capture brief clips of main characters as the finale nears its end. However, this montage is set to Jenna singing the song "Rural Juror," a mostly intelligible song that refers back to a season 1 plot element in which Jenna stars in an independent film of the same title. The difficulty of pronouncing the title became a joke throughout the series, and it is fitting that this song is paired with an otherwise touching montage.

When signing off from *TGS*, Tracy articulates a sentiment that applies to *30 Rock* itself: "Thank you, America. That's our show. Not a lot of people watched it, but the joke's on you. Because we got paid anyway." The finale also includes an epilogue that provides glimpses of what characters are doing a year later. This final note keeps the characters alive in viewers' imaginations, as they are free to consider what might be next for *TGS* alum. The last scene, featuring Liz's great-granddaughter pitching a show to a seemingly immortal Kenneth,[3] takes place in a future where spaceships can be seen outside his NBC window, suggesting that although individual shows end, NBC, and television itself, survives.

References

Austerlitz, Saul. 2014. *Sitcom: A History in 24 Episodes from "I Love Lucy" to "Community."* Chicago: Chicago Review Press.

Bernstein, Adam, dir. 2006. "Blind Date." *30 Rock*, season 1, episode 3. Written by Tina Fey and John Riggi. Aired Oct. 25, NBC. Netflix. Accessed May–June 2016.

Dickey, Selena. 2013. "Intertextuality and the Common Places: *30 Rock* and the New Sitcom." Master's thesis, Univ. of Colorado. At http://digital.auraria.edu /content/AA/00/00/01/15/00001/AA00000115_00001.pdf.

Fey, Tina. 2011. *Bossypants*. New York, Little Brown.

Greenwald, Andy. 2013. "The *30 Rock* Finale: An Essentially Perfect End to One of the Funniest Comedies of All Time." *Grantland*, Feb. 1. At http://grantland .com/hollywood-prospectus/the-30-rock-finale-an-essentially-perfect-end-to -one-of-the-funniest-comedies-of-all-time/.

McCarthy-Miller, Beth, dir. 2013. "Hogcock/Last Lunch." *30 Rock*, season 7, episode 12. Written by Tina Fey, Jack Burditt, Robert Carlock, and Tracey Wigfield. Aired Jan. 13, NBC. Netflix. Accessed May–June 2016.

3. Over the years, fans have theorized that Kenneth is immortal and have viewed the last scene in the finale as confirmation.

Poniewozik, James. 2013. "*30 Rock* Finale: I Lizzed, I Cried." *Time*, Jan. 31. At http://entertainment.time.com/2013/01/31/30-rock-finale-i-lizzed-i-cried/.

Shattuck, Kathryn. 2013. "Emmys Watch: Robert Carlock on *30 Rock*." *Artsbeat* (blog), *New York Times*, Sept. 20. At http://artsbeat.blogs.nytimes.com/2013 /09/20/emmys-watch-robert-carlock-on-30-rock/?_r=0.

62

The Tonight Show Starring Johnny Carson

May 21–22, 1992

BILL BRIOUX

It was New Year's Eve, 1974, and, for this seventeen-year-old, my girlfriend's parents' house was the late-night place to be.

We were cozy on the couch, watching TV. Her mom and dad had left earlier in the evening and would not be home until way past midnight. It wasn't long before I started fumbling with the hooks on the back of her bra. She pitched in, or we'd still be there.

While this was going on, Johnny Carson was bantering with his amiable sidekick, Ed McMahon. Back before every network had a *New Year's Rockin' Eve*–style special, NBC used to have Johnny and Ed ring in the New Year with a special edition of *The Tonight Show*.

Getting to stay up to see *Tonight* was an important passage into adulthood. For a teenager back then, it was like going to your first adult party. You could almost smell the cigarettes and taste the booze. There was a sense that this was strictly for grown-ups.

Same with my girlfriend's breasts. There they were, live and in color, right smack in front of me. But just beyond them, there on the boob tube, were Johnny and Ed. They weren't as lovely as the girls, but they were almost as hypnotizing. As Mighty Carson Arts Player and movie matinee host Art Fern would have said, I was at "a fork in the road."

In the end, I did what Johnny and Ed would have wanted me to do—and have kept abreast of late-night TV ever since.

How big was Johnny? During his incredible thirty-year run as host of *The Tonight Show* (1962–92), Johnny Carson was the undisputed king of late night. He drew more late-night viewers then than a prime-time hit would draw today. No one came close to putting a dent in NBC's late-night ratings, not Joey Bishop, Merv Griffin, or Dick Cavett—combined.

Yet for all those thousands of mimed golf swings, hit-and-miss mono-logue jokes, and "Hi-yos," Boomers will still stop and view a YouTube clip of Dean Martin sneaking his cigarette ashes into George Gobel's drink or Ed Ames's tomahawk toss into TV history. Most of these Boomers grew to iden-tify, however, with David Letterman, a new kind of smartass who brought late night into the age of irony.

To a generation of Millennials weaned on *The Daily Show* (1996–), Car-son is even more last century. My son was born in 1993, the year after Car-son ended his thirty-year run on *The Tonight Show*. To him and many of his peers, Carson is a punchline on *The Simpsons* (1989–) (in an early episode, Carson is seen doing a Carnac gag, goofing on the B-sharps).

Carson's relatively fast fade into comedy obscurity is further proof that, for all his fame and for all that time slot's intimacy, late night is television at its most ephemeral.

Which is the way Carson wanted it. In one of his rare interviews, he explained how he saw *Tonight* as "the last arena of television that the medium originally was supposed to be—live, immediate entertainment." Never get bogged down in planning, he said: "It all boils down to just going out there and being my natural self and seeing what would happen" (Haley 1967). Carson understood that late-night television was TV at its most immediate and intimate—as well as at its most live and dangerous.

His legacy, therefore, has to be considered in context. Sneaking a ciga-rette at his desk, flirting with Angie Dickinson and Morgan Fairchild, spar-ring with Rodney Dangerfield and Don Rickles, he was as cool as TV got back in the age of Don Draper.

Carson didn't start out that way. A shy kid from the Midwest, he served in the navy before dabbling in radio in Omaha, Nebraska. In 1949, he hosted an early-afternoon TV series out of Omaha called *The Squirrel's Nest*. He learned his craft from being thrown into the deep end of early TV, hosting *Carson's Coffee Break* (1953), *Carson's Cellar* (1953), and game shows such as *Earn Your Vacation* (1954) and *Who Do You Trust?* (1957–62). Along the way, he gained the respect of some of his comedy heroes, writing for Red Skelton and performing with one of his biggest influences, Jack Benny.

There was no such thing as late-night TV when Carson began his career. Late night and Carson began finding their way along separate tracks throughout the 1950s, seemingly fated to someday intersect.

Bill Maher has said that "everybody who ever has done a talk show should pay a royalty to Steve Allen" (Alba 2005, back cover). The witty Chicago native, Allen, who died in October 2000, hosted *The Tonight Show* from 1953 (when it began as a local New York series, going national in 1954) until 1957. During those years, he established virtually every late-night talk show convention still being worked today. The desk, the band, the opening monologue, the banter with guests, man-in-the-street bits, viewer mail—Allen did it first.

The giddy spontaneity of these shows made them stand out from the usual TV fare. "[Allen's] early work," Letterman once said, "is really the foundation for what late-night shows have become" (quoted in Alba 2005, 15).

In the late 1950s and early 1960s, people watched Carson's *Tonight* predecessor, Jack Paar, as much for the meltdowns as for the monologues. Richard Corliss of *Time* magazine wrote on Paar's passing in 2004 that "the show was his couch, the camera his shrink" (2004). Paar hosted *Tonight* from 1957 to 1962 and ushered in an era of sophistication in late night. Political leaders such as John F. Kennedy, Richard Nixon, and even Fidel Castro were featured, along with singers, authors, and comedians.

Yet Paar, who at forty-seven walked away from *The Tonight Show* after five years, is largely forgotten. As is Steve Allen.

Using a series of temporary hosts—including Groucho Marx—NBC waited for Carson to escape his CBS contract. His debut, on October 1, 1962, is lost to posterity along with most of the Paar shows and much of Carson's first decade when the original master tapes were deemed to be taking up too much room in storage and so were junked in the early 1970s.

Carson wasn't an instant hit but soon caught on. The twinkle-eyed host was a good conversationalist and always seemed to make the guest shine. Carson had a knack for getting bigger laughs with the bad jokes than with the good ones, mugging his way through every bomb.

What audiences recognized was that the nimble-witted Nebraskan was brattier than Paar. His blend of silliness and sophistication made him the perfect late-night host during the ever-more permissive 1960s and 1970s. He was the sly and sanitized Hugh Hefner of the airwaves.

Carson's hold on the popular imagination of the day is probably best demonstrated by the many rumors and myths that sprang up as a result of the lost decade of *Tonight*. Some of the things that supposedly happened would have had him suspended from television for life, such as his response to Arnold Palmer's story about his wife kissing his balls before each tournament—"I bet that made his putter stick out"—or his snappy rejoinder to Zsa Zsa Gabor, sitting with a cat, who asked if he'd like to pet her pussy—"Yeah, but the damn cat's in the way."

In reality, as *TV Guide* observed in 1968, for all his reputation as an envelope pusher, "Johnny's television manners [were] usually as impeccable as a parson's" (quoted in Brioux 2008, 3).

Even Carson's famous crack to Dolly Parton in the late 1970s that he would give "about a year's pay to peek under there," referring to her blouse, seems tame by today's standards.

When I spoke with Ed McMahon in 2006, he confirmed the boss liked to keep things live and dangerous. He seldom bantered with guests before the show or during commercial breaks because "he wanted all the best stories to happen on the show." If he and Carson had a skit to rehearse—for instance, when the host dressed up as "Aunt Blabby"—they would do a quick run-through in Carson's office.[1]

One desk bit that was never rehearsed was "Carnac the Magnificent." Carson would stumble out in an oversize turban and divine answers to questions McMahon announced were "hermetically sealed and kept in a mayonnaise jar on Funk and Wagnall's porch since noon that day."

A typical exchange: "Sis Boom Bah." Question: "Describe the sound of an exploding sheep."

Friends with Carson dating back to his daytime game-show days, McMahon confirmed Carson was an intensely private man. "He never wanted to air his dirty laundry in public."[2]

Carson's off-screen elusiveness only added to his legend. He was rarely spotted in prime time or in other media and all but vanished upon retiring in 1992.

Carl Reiner says he found Carson "standoffish" and "aloof" at times (Jones and Catalena 2012). Doc Severinsen, his long-time bandleader, admitted he was intimidated by the boss (Jones and Catalena 2012).

A profile in *Life* magazine done around 1970 described Carson as a man "burdened by layers of shyness . . . of insecurity and suspicion built up over years of feeling deserted by agents, let down by associates, taken for granted by NBC, surrounded by yes men, and misled by bad advice" (quoted in Bushkin 2013, 57).

All that was likely true, but Carson may have simply been savvy enough to sense that turning down interviews and shunning the Hollywood scene

---

1. Ed McMahon, telephone interview by Bill Brioux, Oct. 2006.
2. McMahon interview, Oct. 2006.

just made him and his show all the more intriguing. Or maybe he just saved it all for the show. His personal life, especially his three failed marriages, was often fodder for his monologues. Carson may have single-handedly liberalized perceptions of divorce in society.

As he did with wives, Carson was able to move with the times. Taking his show from New York to "beautiful downtown Burbank" in the early 1970s was symbolic of a general power shift in the entertainment industry to the West Coast. He was a barometer of style and taste and profited with a line of sporty men's wear.

I attended a taping of Carson's *Tonight Show* in Burbank in the late 1980s and was fascinated to see how he completely ignored his guest throughout the commercial break, turning away to draw puffs on a cigarette or have his makeup retouched. (I'll never forget, too, seeing the band assemble seconds before the show started—slipping on jackets and picking up instruments—and still hitting their cue pitch perfect with that Paul Anka–penned theme).

As a young reporter based in Los Angeles, I tried to set up an interview with Carson. This greatly amused his press agent, Bill Barron, one of the veterans at the Hollywood public-relations firm Mahoney-Wasserman. Barron was kind enough to meet me at his Wilshire Boulevard office and gently explain that I had a better chance of interviewing the pope.

I did, however, attend three live tapings of *The Tonight Show* during the Carson years in Burbank. By the mid-1980s, Carson had whittled his schedule down to the point that he often wasn't hosting his own show. I saw guest hosts Garry Shandling and Joan Rivers before finally catching the master.

Hearing McMahon boom, "Heeere's Johnny!," and seeing Carson split NBC's rainbow-colored curtain was an unforgettable moment of sheer electricity.

Instead of the army of writers later found on *The Daily Show* (1996–) and *Conan* (2010–), Carson's staff usually numbered only about five. Al Jean, the long-time showrunner on *The Simpsons*, got his first writing job on Carson's *Tonight Show* and calls him the "Citizen Kane of comedy." "In some ways it was a one-of-a-kind thrill—like meeting JFK or something," he says (Jones and Catalena 2012).

Jean says he met Carson three or four times over his tenure. "He was very polite, but he was a very private guy." "I would meet other writers who worked for him in different eras, and it was always the same story. He was private, he was . . . I still think the best who ever did it, but there was a barrier there where you never really knew what the real him was like. People never even knew how he voted, for example. He was pretty good at not letting on" (Jones and Catalena 2012).

Dolly Parton, whose curvaceous figure was a favorite *Tonight Show* target, felt the host had a hard time with fame. "From the first," she told *TV Guide*, "I noticed he has that nervousness that people with charisma all seem to have—something born of a discomfort with the limelight, but a confidence of knowing who you are. He is an uncomfortable person that you are comfortable being with" (quoted in Cox and Corkery 1992).

From the start, Carson was most comfortable with his fellow comedians. He was, to them, the most powerful man in show business, the guy who could make them stars.

"Warhol said that everyone gets their 15 minutes of fame," wrote Sid Caesar in *TV Guide* a few weeks before Carson's *Tonight* exit. "Johnny's the one who gave it to them" (quoted in Cox and Corkery 1992).

Being called over to the couch by Johnny Carson on *Tonight* was, as Carl Reiner once said, like being blessed by "the Pope" (quoted in Fox 2012). Jay Leno, Jerry Seinfeld, Ray Romano, Joan Rivers, Garry Shandling, Roseanne Barr, Ellen DeGeneres, Bill Maher, and Drew Carey have acknowledged their debt to Carson.

Carey even dreamed about his *Tonight Show* appearance and was astounded when everything turned out the way it had in his dream. Carson genuinely laughed at Carey's routine, called him over to the couch, and gave him that unforgettable wink. Yet once the show was over, Carey says, backstage at NBC Studios he had to wait behind a velvet rope to say good-bye to the host. "When Carson would leave for the day," as I noted in an article in 2012, "he would pass by the roped-off area, shake hands, grant a last-minute 'thanks,' and be off" (Brioux 2012a).

There is evidence, however, that Carson could be as charming off the air as he was on TV. Former *SCTV* funnyman Dave Thomas, then working on Brett Butler's sitcom *Grace under Fire* (1993–98), says he got a call out of the blue from a just-retired Carson inviting him to lunch. "The meeting gave me the goosebumps," says Thomas, who found Carson "bright, curious, witty, engaging—just like on TV" (quoted in Brioux 2005).

Another Canadian, David Steinberg, talked about how he hated the "preinterview"—the first step all late-night talk shows use to line up stories that their guests will tell on the show.

"When I started out with Carson in '68," Steinberg said, "I wanted to improvise." He felt his Second City training was all he needed to prepare for *Tonight* or any other live-to-tape television: "Carson said to me, 'This is a formula, and it's not for people like you, but it's for dull people. When they're not working, and they don't know whether they're funny or not, I have to know what the outline is. I have to know where they're going to help the story and all of that'" (quoted in Brioux 2012b).

Steinberg said it took him four years as a guest to get Carson to trust him enough to ditch the preinterview. He was finally allowed to provide just bullet points—"Lakers, daughters, courtship," he would say by way of examples. He told Carson, "You can interrupt me whenever you want, and I will find an out, and you will know when I'm finished" (quoted in Brioux 2012b).

Steinberg said only a select few got this carte-blanche guest-segment treatment from Carson, singling out Bob Newhart as another guest nimble enough to just vamp with Johnny. Don Rickles, you'd have to guess, was also on that list.

Carson announced his retirement in 1991 and took a season-long victory lap. His second-to-last episode, which aired May 21, 1992, saw him welcome two can't-miss guests: Robin Williams and Bette Midler.[3] Williams opened with a prop gag, pushing a rocking chair for Johnny through the famous rainbow-colored curtains. He goofed on the comedy target of the day, Vice President Dan Quayle's attack on TV single mom Murphy Brown. He demonstrated—to Carson's delight—a new way to imitate President George H. W. Bush.

"Basically what you do is you take John Wayne," said Williams, standing to demonstrate, "and you tighten up his ass"—except the word *ass* was bleeped out with what sounded like an antique car horn; it was, after all, still 1992.

"We're out of here tomorrow night," quipped Carson as Williams kept pushing the envelope, "what do I care?"

Williams was followed by Midler. To the tune "You Made Me Love You," she paid tribute to the host:

You made me watch you.
I didn't want to do it.
Jack Paar had put me through it.
You made me watch you.
I love the jokes you're floggin'.
When you are monologue-in.

3. All references to this penultimate episode come from "Season 30, Episode 119" 1992.

She finished the bit sitting on Carson's desk, telling the host, "You're the greatest straight man who ever walked the earth—and I knew my share of straight men."

Midler was never more divine, returning to the couch and segueing into an impromptu, tender duet with Carson on his favorite song, "Here Comes That Rainy Day."

After the break, Midler sat on a stool midstage, next to her piano player. She called herself "the last fool Mr. Carson will have to suffer gladly."

She then serenaded the talk-show host with the melancholy saloon standard "One for My Baby (and One More for the Road)." *The Tonight Show* cameraman swung wide, catching Carson in semidarkness, hand on cheek, gazing at Midler from behind the desk. By song's end, Carson and half of America had to wipe away a tear.

It was a moment frozen in time, leaving viewers feeling as if they were saying good-bye more to a friend than to a legend. Midler won an Emmy for her performance.

There was one more episode, but it was a clip show without any guests.[4] Carson came through the curtains one last time to thunderous applause. Sitting on a stool on his usual monologue spot, he referred to his thirty-year run and told his audience that if he could "magically, somehow, make it run backwards, I would like to do the whole thing all over again."

Carson repeated that notion at the very end of the broadcast. "I am one of the lucky people in the world," he told his audience. "I found something I always wanted to do, and I have enjoyed every single minute of it." He thanked Ed and Doc.

Carson's last words were to viewers. He bid them "a heartfelt goodnight" and told them he hoped they would welcome him back when he found something else to do on television. But aside from a couple of brief appearances on David Letterman's new show on CBS the following year, he never gave them the chance.

His death at seventy-nine in January 2005 was like a death in the family. The news rocked the semiannual Television Critics Association winter press tour in Los Angeles. As word quickly spread, reporters scrambled back to their rooms to write, ditching sessions featuring ABC stars such as Oprah Winfrey and the actors in *Desperate Housewives* (2004–12). It was Carson's last gift to NBC.

4. All references to the last episode come from "Season 30, Episode 120" 1992.

I had this to say after Johnny's death in 2005: "Carson once joked that he wanted [the sentence] 'I'll be right back' on his tombstone. He seemed to know, however, that fame [is] fickle; life happens quickly, and when it's over, it's over. Maybe it was the [Carnac] in him" (Brioux 2005).

References

Alba, Ben. 2005. *Inventing Late Night: Steve Allen and the Original Tonight Show.* Amherst, NY: Prometheus Books.

Brioux, Bill. 2005. "Good Night, Johnny." *Esksfans*, Jan. 24. At http://www.esks fans.com/forum/showthread.php?3500-Late-Night-King-Dies&s=c4294c23 1f3bd48af0b01b512c485c44.

———. 2008. *Truth and Rumors: The Reality behind TV's Most Famous Myths.* Westport, CT: Praeger.

———. 2012a. "PBS Special Probes Life of Late-Night King." *Trail Daily Times*, May 11.

———. 2012b. "Twenty Years Ago Today: Johnny Carson's Farewell." *Brioux.TV*, May 22. At https://brioux.tv/2012/05/twenty-years-ago-today-johnny-carsons -farewell/.

Bushkin, Henry. 2013. *Johnny Carson.* New York: Houghton Mifflin Harcourt.

Corliss, Richard. 2004. "That Old Feeling: Paar Excellence." *Time*, Jan. 30. At http://content.time.com/time/arts/article/0,8599,585397,00.html.

Cox, Stephen, and Paul Corkery. 1992. "End of an Era." *TV Guide*, May 9.

Fox, Jesse David. 2012. "Can You Guess Whom Johnny Carson Asked to 'the Couch'?" *Vulture*, May 15. At http://www.vulture.com/2012/05/can-you-guess -whom-johnny-carson-asked-to-the-couch.html.

Haley, Alex. 1967. "*Playboy* Interview: Johnny Carson." *Playboy*, Dec. 1967.

Jones, Peter, and Mark Catalena. 2012. "Johnny Carson: King of Late Night." *American Masters*, May 14, PBS. Original broadcast.

"Season 30, Episode 119." 1992. *The Tonight Show Starring Johnny Carson.* Aired May 21, NBC. Original broadcast.

"Season 30, Episode 120." 1992. *The Tonight Show Starring Johnny Carson.* Aired May 22, NBC. Original broadcast.

63

Torchwood

"Exit Wounds," Children of Earth, Miracle Day

LYNNETTE PORTER

At the end of the second season of *Torchwood* (2006–11), Captain Jack Harkness (John Barrowman) quotes T. S. Eliot: "The end is where we start from" ("Exit Wounds," 2.13).[1] At the time, Captain Jack could never have known just how prophetic his choice of quotations would become. Between season 2 and 3, 3 and 4, and even 4 and possibly a future 5, *Torchwood*, like its lead character, the immortal Jack Harkness, died in its current form, only to be reborn for new adventures. It may be the only television series to date that has had two "faux finales" before the likely real one.

The original premise involves intergalactic space–time traveler Captain Jack—a spinoff character from long-running science fiction series *Doctor Who* (1963–89, 2005–)—becoming stuck on Earth without transportation. He eventually becomes the leader of Torchwood, a secret organization working outside the British government to deal with both nonhumanoid life forms, everyone from visiting aliens (some from Captain Jack's past) to malevolent pixies and human time travelers. Torchwood is literally an underground organization; its base, the Hub, sits beneath the city plaza in Cardiff, Wales. All kinds of supernatural and extraterrestrial activity take place along the Cardiff Rift, a fictitious wormhole that drops life forms or artifacts near the Hub. In addition to at-least-bisexual leader Captain Jack (whose sexual orientation is often emphasized within episodes), Torchwood employs tech specialist Toshiko Sato (Naoko Mori), Dr. Owen Harper (Burn Gorman), field agent/second-in-command Gwen Cooper (Eve Myles), and office clerk turned agent (and Jack's romantic partner during seasons 2 and 3) Ianto Jones (Gareth David-Lloyd).

1. All references to "Exit Wounds" come from Way [2008] 2012.

From the beginning, cocreator and frequent scriptwriter Russell T. Davies admitted that *Torchwood* is "an unusual show. I mean it's got a great big bisexual lead character. It's got barmy sequences. It's got two gay men. . . . It's got the Welsh, frankly. Which is by no means normal for British drama! . . . [A]ll those unusual qualities made it distinctive, made it original, and made it stand out" (Jensen 2009). Its resurrection after each perceived "finale" is only one more unique element of this resilient series.

Three Television Finales

During seasons 1 and 2 (thirteen episodes each, aired 2006–8 on BBC Three), *Torchwood* developed a reputation as a guilty-viewing pleasure because of its often outlandish plots, many involving aliens who visit Earth for sex. During season 2, the stories become more serious in tone and topic. Tosh and Owen, for example, die in the line of duty. By the episode "Exit Wounds," the first "faux finale," the Torchwood team is down to three members. Such a devastating emotional loss, for Torchwood and fans, leads to Captain Jack's memorable "finale"-styled words that "the end is where we start from"—the end of *Torchwood* as presented during its first twenty-six episodes could be the beginning of something new.

The five-part miniseries *Children of Earth* (also known as "season 3" and broadcast on five consecutive nights in July 2009) reinvented the series as a sociopolitical thriller.[2] Because it had been filmed in Cardiff in late 2008 but not announced on the BBC's schedule during the first half of 2009, fans began to despair that it would ever be broadcast. Then when it was finally on prime-time BBC One's July schedule, fans worried that the BBC was using *Torchwood* as "burn-off" summer programming when few viewers would be home to watch. However, *Children of Earth* became a critical success. Favorably compared with *Quatermass* (1979) (Turberville 2011), *Children of Earth* hooked new fans with its intriguing plot and character development. Davies and Barrowman's appearance at the San Diego Comic-Con in 2009 received plenty of media attention (Wilkes 2009), and at the BAFTA Cymru Awards in 2010 *Children of Earth* won for Best Drama ("BAFTA Cymru Success" 2010). Critics praised the writing and acting as well as the tightness of the five-hour, five-night TV event (Blair 2012).

---

2. All references to *Children of Earth* come from *Torchwood: Children of Earth* 2009.

Critics commented that *Torchwood* improved significantly after the regular-series "finale," which allowed Davies to erase problem areas and develop new characters and a large-scale dramatic plot, and new viewers generally liked the dark side of *Torchwood* evident in *Children of Earth*. Longtime fans, however, took to the Internet to denounce the miniseries as the final destruction of *Torchwood*. Not only does fan favorite Ianto Jones die in Captain Jack's arms, but Jack also ends up sacrificing his grandson to save Earth from yet another alien incursion. At the end of the miniseries, a grim-faced Captain Jack abandons the planet he has long defended. By then, the Hub has been obliterated, and only Gwen Cooper remains behind in the wreckage of what was Torchwood. As Davies later explained to fans, "Powerful drama isn't just there to make you smile. . . . Drama should make people uncomfortable. I've always happily done that" (Jensen 2009).

The miniseries' global critical acclaim seemed to indicate that, despite the dire plot and its ramifications for longtime *Torchwood* fans, the BBC would quickly commission season 4. A series of events, however, increasingly made that fourth season seem less likely and the last episode of *Children of Earth* a true finale: showrunner Davies moved to the United States, series cocreator Julie Gardner began a new job in Los Angeles with BBC Worldwide, and the BBC faced widely publicized possible restructuring and budget cutbacks. *Torchwood* remained in limbo until 2011, when it was learned that *Children of Earth* could be relegated to "faux finale" status.

In early January that year, the BBC announced the production of *Miracle Day* as a joint UK-US project commissioned by controller of BBC drama Ben Stephenson and Starz president and CEO Chris Albrecht.[3] The press release described the premise: "The plot of *Miracle Day* is the most explosive *Torchwood* storyline yet. . . . All across the world, nobody dies. . . . The result: a population boom, overnight. . . . It's said that in four months' time, the human race will cease to be viable. But this can't be a natural event—someone's got to be behind it. It's a race against time as C.I.A. agent Rex Matheson [American actor Mekhi Phifer] investigates a global conspiracy. The answers lie within an old, secret British institute[, Torchwood]" ("*Torchwood* Cast Led" 2011). Davies helmed a contingent of US and UK writers meeting in Los Angeles to forge a less Welsh series in favor of new American characters who could develop an international Torchwood organization. Although the series was filmed primarily in Los Angeles, *Torchwood* was expanded to

3. All references to *Miracle Day* come from *Torchwood: Miracle Day* 2011.

global locations, including but not limited to Cardiff (Ausiello 2010). When Barrowman agreed to work in the United States ("Barrowman" 2010), fans realized that although the BBC was involved and would broadcast episodes, the series would no longer retain the British (or specifically Welsh) elements that first attracted them.

The ten-episode season 4 miniseries further cemented *Torchwood*'s reputation as, in Davies's words, "a digital weapon" that could become whatever its corporate producers (who footed the bill) and he decided it should (more lucratively) become next.[4] Yet despite the international hype and the promising production partnership between the BBC and Starz, *Miracle Day* was hardly the miracle that *Torchwood* needed to continue as a television series. The plot often confused viewers with its changing weekly focus on new characters, many of whom are quickly killed off. In an *io9* article asking whether ratings had drifted into "apocalyptic territory," one critic noted a drop from 1.5 million Starz viewers for the first episode to around 900,000 for later episodes (Anders 2011). *Digital Spy*, after balancing *Miracle Day*'s strengths (e.g., new cast, larger scale) against its weaknesses (e.g., culture clash, dangling plot threads), concluded that this latest season "might not have been perfect, but we're hoping that there's life in *Torchwood* yet. The show has performed relatively well ratings-wise in the U.K., but ultimately it's success in the U.S. that matters, given the financial stake that Starz now has in the show" (Jeffery 2011).

Although Captain Jack ends up saving Earth (again), the miniseries seems to push him aside so that former CIA agent Rex Matheson can take over. The third (and likely real) television finale, "The Blood Line," sets up the likelihood of a new, American Torchwood—and a new American *Torchwood*. However, neither the BBC nor Starz has hinted at additional television episodes. The digital weapon seems to have misfired.

In early 2012, Myles told the media that *Torchwood* fans should have closure, but "everything's still very much on hold. . . . Every [season] we've changed our format [and] we've always had a gap in between." She hoped *Torchwood* would be revived in 2013, preferably in Wales. "That's where it was born and maybe it'd be nice to end there" (quoted in Jeffery 2012). At the end of 2012, Davies explained that *Torchwood* had not been officially

---

4. Expanding on the idea of "a digital weapon," Davies described the show as a "kind of a multi-purpose, multi-adaptable, shape-shifting weapon that can become anything" (quoted in Ausiello 2009).

canceled by the BBC or Starz. "It's in a nice limbo. . . . [and] can come back in ten, twenty years' time" (quoted in Connelly 2012), perhaps like parent *Doctor Who*, which had an original run from 1963 to 1989, a long hiatus before a US television movie in 1996, and another long hiatus before the current run beginning in 2005.

Wanted: A New Definition of "Finale"

Since its inglorious third and likely final television "finale" in 2011, *Torchwood* has continued to entertain fans with new audio CDs (e.g., *Mr. Invincible* and *Red Skies* [2012]) and a Captain Jack novel, *Exodus Code* (2013), penned by John Barrowman and Carole Barrowman. In 2015, Big Finish Audio began production on a series of six *Torchwood* dramas featuring original cast members, including David-Lloyd as the ever-popular Ianto Jones. Jason Haigh-Ellery, an executive producer of the latest *Torchwood* audiobooks, enthused that there are "many new *Torchwood* tales to be told, and I can't wait for Jack and his team to defend the Earth once again" ("*Torchwood*" 2015). The first series of audiobooks proved so popular in pre-release sales that only a few months after the announcement of the first series a second went into production (Nissim 2015). Although *Torchwood* has pushed the boundaries of how far fans will continue to follow a series that periodically (and brutally) morphs into something completely different or seems to end entirely but then is resurrected months or years later, many die-hard fans (including those at Big Finish) still believe that *Torchwood* is viable entertainment, especially if it returns to its Welsh roots.

Torchwood helps illustrate a problem in defining "finale." The television series *Torchwood* may have ended, but its characters—played (or written) by the roles' originating actors—continue to star in adventures published or broadcast in other media under the *Torchwood* name and with the BBC's copyright blessing. Big Finish Audio dramas are the latest in a long line of comic books, radio dramas, and tie-in novels keeping fans invested in the series during the very long hiatus between season 4 and a possible season 5. *Torchwood* is the television anomaly that defies a convenient definition of "finale."

Perhaps more significantly within media studies, *Torchwood*'s television production history and its expansion into multiple media with new stories featuring television cast members raise questions about the definition of "finale" or even "series." After all, how far can one television series be reimagined before viewers perceive it as an entirely new show? Would an

American series, should one go into production, still be considered *Torch-wood*, or would it be perceived as a new series only loosely affiliated with its parent and more closely resembling *CSI* (2000–2015)? In addition, is *finale* applicable only as a term in television? Is a single originating medium, in this case television, the measure of a series' lifespan, with new stories in other media deemed of lesser (or no) importance? Or does, as Captain Jack suggests during *Torchwood*'s first "faux finale," one ending only become a starting point for a television series' afterlife in multimedia heaven?

References

Anders, Charlie Jane. 2011. "*Torchwood: Miracle Day* Ratings Drifting into Apocalyptic Territory?" *io9*, Aug. 25. At http://io9.com/5834427/torchwood-miracle-day-ratings-drifting-into-apocalyptic-territory.

Ausiello, Michael. 2009. "*Torchwood* Boss to Angry Fans: Go Watch *Supernatural*." *Entertainment Weekly*, July 24. At http://ausiellofiles.ew.com/2009/07/24/backlash-shmacklash-thats-torchwood-creator-russell-t-davies-reaction-to-the-outcry-over-the-death-of-gareth-david-lloyds/.

———. 2010. "Breaking: Starz Acquires *Torchwood*." *Entertainment Weekly*, June 7. At http://ausiellofiles.ew.com/2010/06/07/starz-acquires-torchwood/.

"BAFTA Cymru Success for Welsh TV at Awards Ceremony." 2010. *BBC News*, May 24. At http://www.bbc.co.uk/news/10145580.

"Barrowman: Eva Longoria Groped Me." 2010. Press Association, June 15. At http://www.google.com/hostednews/ukpress/article/ALeqM5jJ1ZwGJdpC3ri9ZYyEiwGhkSz-UQ.

Blair, Andrew. 2012. "Revisiting *Torchwood*: *Children of Earth*." *Den of Geek*, Dec. 20. At http://www.denofgeek.com/tv/torchwood/23900/revisiting-torchwood-children-of-earth.

Connelly, Brendon. 2012. "Davies Says *Torchwood* 'in Limbo,' Could Be Back in 'Ten or Twenty Years.'" *Bleeding Cool*, Oct. 30. At http://www.bleedingcool.com/2012/10/30/davies-says-torchwood-in-limbo-could-be-back-in-ten-or-twenty-years/.

Jeffery, Morgan. 2011. "*Torchwood: Miracle Day*: Success or Failure?" *Digital Spy*, Sept. 16. At http://www.digitalspy.com/tv/s8/torchwood/tubetalk/a340582/torchwood-miracle-day-success-or-failure.html#~pnTwnTKCPxBDYo.

———. 2012. "*Torchwood* Star Eve Myles: 'The Fans Deserve Closure.'" *Digital Spy*, Jan. 26. At http://www.digitalspy.com/british-tv/s8/torchwood/news/a362247/torchwood-star-eve-myles-the-fans-deserve-closure.html #ixzz3kh8ZBF4n.

Jensen, Michael. 2009. "*Torchwood*'s Russell T. Davies Makes No Apologies—for Anything." *AfterElton*, July 30. At http://www.afterelton.com/TV/2009/7/russeltdavies?page=0%2C3.

Nissim, Mayer. 2015. "*Torchwood* Is Getting a Second Audio Series with Six Brand-New Episodes." *Digital Spy*, Sept. 11. At http://www.digitalspy.com/british-tv /s8/torchwood/news/a668052/torchwood-is-getting-a-second-audio-series-with -six-brand-new-episodes.html#~po7EbDiuheGADi.

"*Torchwood*." 2015. *Big Finish*, May 3. At http://www.bigfinish.com/news/v/torch wood.

"*Torchwood* Cast Led by *Independence Day* and *ER* Stars." 2011. BBC Worldwide Press Releases, Jan. 8. At http://www.bbc.co.uk/pressoffice/bbcworldwide/world widestories/pressreleases/2011/01_january/torchwood_cast.shtml.

Torchwood: Children of Earth. 2009. *Torchwood*, season 3. London: BBC Home Entertainment, 2009. DVD.

Torchwood: Miracle Day. 2011. *Torchwood*, season 4. London: BBC Home Entertainment, 2011. DVD.

Turberville, Huw. 2011. "*Torchwood*, 'Miracle Day,' Episode One, Review." *Telegraph*, July 13. At http://www.telegraph.co.uk/culture/tvandradio/doctor-who /8635562/Torchwood-Miracle-Day-episode-one-BBC-One-review.html.

Way, Ashley, dir. [2008] 2012. "Exit Wounds." *Torchwood*, season 2, episode 13. Written by Chris Chibnall. Aired Apr. 4, 2008, BBC. On *Torchwood: The Complete Second Season*. London: BBC Home Entertainment. DVD.

Wilkes, Neil. 2009. "Live: *Torchwood* Panel at Comic-Con." *Digital Spy*, July 26. At http://www.digitalspy.com/british-tv/s8/torchwood/tubetalk/a167433/live -torchwood-panel-at-comic-con.html#~po5FLkaXnXXd96.

64

True Blood

"Thank You"

TERESA FORDE

True Blood ran for seven seasons on HBO, from 2008 to 2014. Based on the Southern Vampire Mysteries series of novels by Charlaine Harris, it tells the story of Sookie Stackhouse (Anna Paquin), a bar waitress in Bon Temps, a Louisiana town inhabited by werewolves, shapeshifters, witches, and, of course, vampires. Sookie is part fairy and can hear other people's thoughts; her blood is also highly desired by vampires. She is portrayed as an innocent and, particularly in the novels, as an active sunbather, which contrasts greatly with her attraction to the ghostly vampire Bill Compton (Stephen Moyer), whom she saves in the first episode after he is bound by silver chains. The initial seasons of the show center on Sookie and Bill's relationship and the issues they face as a vampire–human couple. The fact that the actors, Anna Paquin and Stephen Moyer, became a couple in real life compounded the interest among fans in their relationship on screen.

True Blood's showrunner Alan Ball is also the creator of the influential HBO series *Six Feet Under* (2001–5), as well as of the Cinemax series *Banshee* (2013–16), the latter illustrating the same type of dynamic, rapid montage opening credits used in *True Blood*. *Six Feet Under*, in contrast, set the tone for quirky characters and challenging subject matter. Ball's work for television often considers the ways in which gay identities are positioned in relation to traditional masculine and feminine tropes and the extent to which gay individuals negotiate aggression, victimization, and self-expression. The vampires on *True Blood* are hetero, homo, bicurious, or bisexual and emulate human desires, but just in an often hyperrealized manner owing to their enhanced physical prowess.

Although the vampires in *True Blood* are already an international phenomenon in the story because of the "Great Revelation" that has allowed them to mainstream (that is, live as vampires out in the open), the series, like *Banshee*, makes much of its location and portrays its small town as a pocket of violence, passion, and morality, where warring factions claim a "stake" on their territory. Vampire Bill was once a soldier, and this reference to his past reinforces the historic nature of Louisiana; at one point, he even delivers a lecture on the Old South based on his firsthand experiences. The show's use of the supernatural also draws upon the mystical nature of Southern Gothic. As Caroline Ruddell and Brigid Cherry argue, "The parodying of excess in *True Blood* is central to understanding its remediation of the gothic. . . . Comedy, excess and heated scenes, both violent and sexual, combine to create an ironic tone in keeping with the HBO brand" (2012, 53), a brand built on providing subscribers with challenging subject matter that will not necessarily pass network censors.

In the unlawful world of Bon Temps, the police are either absent or corrupt, with vigilante forces fighting for control. The American Vampire League aims to establish the same political representation and rights for vampires that human Americans have and espouses a belief in assimilation, although vampires themselves are split into those who sympathize with humans and purists who essentially see them as food. (The invention of a synthetic alternative to snacking on humans, Tru Blood, could transform power relationships but unfortunately is a less-tasty alternative to the real thing for the vampires.) *True Blood* is violent and also sexually transgressive, as portrayed in the relationships between vampires and humans; sadistic and masochistic tendencies are brought to the fore, although the show's wry humor diffuses many of those situations. Sookie stands out as different in this regard, from her clothes—she favors shorts and tops—to her innocence and general lack of guile, possibly the result of her gift of telepathy, which, conversely, often makes her difficult for others to "read."

The large ensemble of characters in *True Blood* represent an array of perspectives on vampires, including whether to accept them or not because they are enigmatic yet dangerous superhuman figures. Sookie is more open to accepting those who are deemed different in society because she has felt like an outsider for much of her life owing to her telepathic abilities and the strain of being able to hear people's thoughts and attitudes. As Tia Gaynor argues, "*True Blood*'s political commentary provides an ideal canvas on which to draw parallels between other narratives in the show and in contemporary American society" (2014, 359). Characters such as Lafayette Reynolds (Nelsan Ellis), a friend and workmate of Sookie's, depict other forms of difference in the series. An African American gay man living in the South who also experiences isolation and discrimination, Lafayette finds love with Jesus Velasquez (Kevin Alejandro), who helps him to communicate with the dead. Tara Thornton (Rutina Wesley), Lafayette's cousin, is another African American character who is Sookie's closest friend from childhood. Tara, fiercely defensive and strong, was raised by an alcoholic mother, is bisexual, and eventually is made into a vampire without her permission. Tara also possesses a capacity for magic or spirituality in the show.

Bill Compton and Eric Northman (Alexander Skarsgård), another prominent vampire, become rivals over Sookie; she also has a relationship with the werewolf Alcide Hervaux (Joe Manganiello) and a close friendship with her boss at Merlotte's Bar and Grill, the shape-shifter Sam Merlotte (Sam Trammell), whom Harris controversially makes into Sookie's husband at the end of the novels. During the show's run, Vampire Bill transforms from a polite, southern gentleman suitor into a vampire god and back again. Initially, Bill is forced under duress to "make" Jessica Hamby (Deborah Ann Woll) into a vampire and feels guilty about his new protégée. Breaking up with Sookie, he decides to mainstream and then work with the Authority and finally to drink the ancient blood of Lilith and seek ultimate power. Eric runs the vampire bar Fangtasia in Shreveport with Pam de Beaufort (Kristin Bauer van Straten), who is Eric's "turned" progeny, and their bar is the place where humans go to "fang-bang" with the ever enticing vampires. Eric also seeks control over his own destiny in the hierarchical vampire world. For critics Patricia Brace and Robert Arp, the series plays out an analogy between vampires and gay people, and coming out of the coffin correlates to coming out of the closet: "Or consider the play on the Fred Phelpsian slogan 'God hates fags' found in the lit-up sign in the opening credits of *True Blood* that displays the message 'God hates fangs'" (2010, 93). These tensions fuel much of the action within the show.

The cult popularity of the show led to a graphic-novel series, character blogs, *A Drop of True Blood* web "minisodes," a "coming-out-of-the-coffin" website supporting vampires, a viral ad poster campaign, and a documentary. For the final season, as Salli Jokinen recognizes, "HBO . . . shifted focus and put the existing fan base truly to the epicentre of *True Blood*'s final marketing campaign. In fact, the overarching core message communicated throughout the whole campaign—that of being sad that the show is close to its own 'true death'—could've easily been a brainchild of a devoted fan" (2014). The finale title, "Thank You," clearly identifies the show's relationship to its devoted fans.[1]

After a dip in the number of viewers and further criticism of the show's direction when Ball left after season 5, HBO announced that the seventh season would be the last for the series. The final season was anticipated with taglines such as "Goodbyes suck," "Take one last bite," and "#TrueToTheEnd." The finale, aired on August 24, 2014, depicts Sookie in the aftermath of a crescendo of supernatural events, culminating in H-Vamps—that is, vampires infected with Hepatitis V—descending on Bon Temps in a killing spree. When Bill is weakened by Hepatitis V, he refuses to be cured because he seeks the true death and wants to be reunited with his wife and children. He wants Sookie to kill him with her fairy light, but, wishing to keep her fairy side, she decides to stake him instead. In a scene that is somewhat reminiscent of a macabre sexual death ritual, she sits on top of him, kisses him, and then stakes his heart; kneeling in his coffin, she becomes covered in his blood.

Drawing together the stories of so many characters is never easy. Nevertheless, the finale has been heavily criticized for various reasons. Although Bill refers to Sookie's desire to be pregnant as a reason for not remaining with her, he wants her to give up her fairy light so that other vampires will not seek her out and she will become fully human (i.e., lose her telepathy). However, he encourages Jessica and Hoyt Fortenberry (Jim Parrack) to marry, presumably because Jessica is a vampire and cannot become pregnant anyway, regardless of Hoyt's situation. Fans have even renamed the finale "No Thank You" (Sparks 2014) and "Unhappily Ever After" (Ocasio 2014) in their reviews because of Bill's sacrifice and Sookie's part in his death.

The limited focus on Tara and Lafayette's narratives in the finale was also a source of criticism. Lafayette and Lettie Mae Thornton, Tara's mother (Adina Porter), call Tara from the dead after she is unceremoniously killed by H-Vamps in the previous episode. Tara and her mother forgive each other, but there is little other mourning for Tara in the episode, aside from Sookie's childhood memory of her gran's request to Tara to remind Sookie that she has the right to be whoever she wants to be. Both Tara and Lafayette are sharp and witty characters, so viewers mourned their absence.

Characters who fare better in the finale include Eric and Pam, who produce a New Blood based on the antidote to Hep V present within the blood of Sarah Newlin (Anna Camp), who was responsible for so many vampire

---

1. All references to "Thank You" come from Winant 2014.

deaths through the disease. A few years after Bill's death, Eric is shown in a television infomercial talking about how the blood was synthesized and promoting its qualities. However, Eric fails to tell viewers that Sarah is still alive, tied up in a basement, and hired out to vampires, who feed on her blood in what may be a somewhat fitting yet gruesome finale to her character's plotline. In this parody sequence, Eric and Pam achieve the success they always sought and are now rich and famous. Their ambivalence is exemplified in the character Ginger (Tara Buck), who works as a waitress at Fangtasia. In many ways, Ginger performs the typical trope of horror "scream queen." Pam took Ginger's idea for Fangtasia, and both Pam and Eric often "glamor" Ginger so that she forgets things that have happened and comes under their control, although she would probably stay with them anyway. Eric and Pam have relationships with humans and are often benevolent to Ginger, and Eric finally rewards Ginger for her loyalty by agreeing to have sex with her, but they have also tortured humans and treated them as slaves.

Finally, at the end of the episode, Sookie is shown in the future, several years after Bill's demise. She is hosting a Thanksgiving Day meal for a group of guests from Bon Temps who are friends, including humans and vamps in relationships with each other. Sookie is heavily pregnant, and we see a glimpse of the back of someone whom we assume is her husband. As the show's producer, Brian Buckner, explains, they did not want to reveal his identity: "What we wanted to know was that she was happy and living the life that she wanted to lead, and to introduce some other stranger in the last five minutes of the finale wouldn't have made a lot of sense. So we made a choice it's everyman, it doesn't matter" (Bierly 2014). In a way, Sookie has a double finale: one ending in which she gives up her life with Bill and the second ending in which she is living a "normal" life. This double ending is reminiscent of Ada in *The Piano* (Jane Campion, 1993), who contemplates death but decides to live "happily ever after." Ball's departure left the series adrift, and it may have seen one season too many. The finale has been viewed as "simply too little, too late" (Lowry 2014), but it does encapsulate Sookie's original tenacity and determination as she becomes the "True Blood" equivalent of the "final girl," but on her own terms.

References

Bierly, Mandi. 2014. "'True Blood' producer Brian Buckner Answers Burning Finale Questions." *Entertainment Weekly*, Aug. 25. At http://www.ew.com/article/2014/08/25/true-blood-series-finale-sookie-husband.

Brace, Patricia, and Robert Arp. 2010. "Coming Out of the Coffin and Coming Out of the Closet." In *"True Blood" Philosophy: We Wanna Think Bad Things with You*, edited by George A. Dunn and Rebecca Housel, 93–108. Hoboken, NJ: Wiley.

Gaynor, Tia Sherèe. 2014. "Vampires Suck: Parallel Narratives in the Marginalization of the Other." *Administrative Theory and Praxis* 36, no. 3: 348–72.

Jokinen, Salli. 2014. "Online Marketing Done Right—the Case of HBO's *True Blood*." *[Yoke]*, June 17. At http://yokedesign.com.au/blog/online-marketing -done-right-the-case-of-hbo-true-blood/.

Lowry, Brian. 2014. "'True Blood' Finale: TV's True Death Can't Redeem HBO Drama." *Variety*, Aug. 24. At http://variety.com/2014/tv/columns/true-blood -finale-tvs-true-death-cant-redeem-hbo-drama-spoilers-1201288635/.

Ocasio, Anthony. 2014. "'True Blood' Series Finale Review—Unhappily Ever After." *ScreenRant*, Aug. 25. At http://screenrant.com/true-blood-series-finale -review-spoilers-bill-dead/.

Ruddell, Caroline, and Brigid Cherry. 2012. "More Than Cold and Heartless: The Southern Gothic Milieu of *True Blood*." In *"True Blood": Investigating Vampires and Southern Gothic*, edited by Brigid Cherry, 39–55. London: I. B. Taurus.

Sparks, Lily. 2014. "*True Blood* Series Finale Review: No Thank You." *TV.com*, Aug. 25. At http://www.tv.com/shows/true-blood/community/post/true-blood -ending-season-7-episode-10-thank-you-review-140860942455/.

Winant, Scott, dir. 2014. "Thank You." *True Blood*, season 7, episode 10. Written by Brian Buckner. Aired Aug. 24, 2014, HBO. On *True Blood: The Complete Series*. Burbank, CA: Warner Home Video. DVD.

65

Twin Peaks

"Episode 2.22" and Beyond

ADAM OCHONICKY

In recent years, fans of cult television series have often sounded a common refrain: "*x* seasons and a movie." Such hopes demonstrate how revivals across mediums, networks, and distribution platforms have increasingly destabilized notions of closure in the television finale. One especially important example of this phenomenon is *Twin Peaks* (ABC, 1990–91; Showtime, 2017), a serial narrative cocreated by writer Mark Frost and writer-director David Lynch.[1] The series debuted on ABC to critical acclaim and massive viewership in the spring of 1990. From the feature-length pilot episode through the first season's seven episodes, audiences responded strongly to the mystery of local homecoming queen Laura Palmer's (Sheryl Lee) brutal murder. Filtered through the analytic but cheerful perspective of outsider FBI special agent Dale Cooper (Kyle MacLachlan), viewers were introduced to numerous eccentric locals, from the good-hearted straight man Sheriff Harry S. Truman (Michael Ontkean) to the enigmatic Log Lady (Catherine E. Coulson), who always carries a wood log to which she attributes sentience.[2]

Notably, Frost and Lynch had not intended ever to reveal who killed Laura Palmer (or at least to delay the revelation as long as possible).[3] Under

---

1. Episodes of *Twin Peaks* were not given titles by David Lynch and Mark Frost, and no titles are listed in the packaging or on the menu screens of the region 1 DVD box sets. According to the *Twin Peaks* Online website, episode titles were added to the series "[w]hen [it was] broadcast in Germany" ("*Twin Peaks* FAQ" n.d.). Translated versions of those titles have since been used to identify episodes on streaming services such as Netflix. The unofficial title of episode 2.22 is "Beyond Life and Death."

2. All references to the original series come from *Twin Peaks* 2007.

3. In "Secrets from Another Place: Creating *Twin Peaks*" (de Lauzirika 2007a), a feature on *Twin Peaks: Definitive Gold Box Edition*, Frost states that they planned to eventually

pressure from ABC, however, they were compelled to wrap up the central murder mystery only a third of the way through season 2. Shockingly, Laura's father Leland Palmer (Ray Wise)—who is possessed by a malicious super-natural entity known as Bob (Frank Silva)—is identified as her murderer and incestuous abuser. Although the Leland-as-killer twist actually opened up the series to new mysteries, audience indifference to these ensuing narrative threads led to declining viewership, multiple hiatuses, schedule shuffling, and, eventually, cancellation by ABC.

Twin Peaks initially found its surprising popular success through jarring tonal shifts and a unique blend of genres. Stephen Lacey identifies within the series traces of the "soap opera, sitcom, detective story, horror movie, 1950s-style juvenile delinquent film, TV commercial ('damn fine coffee'), and film noir, among others" (2016, 127). In addition, Lynch brought his distinctive filmic style and narrative sensibilities to the production—dream-like imagery, usage of spotlights and strobe effects, and ominous ambient rumblings in the sound design, to list just a few. Over the first two seasons, he directed multiple episodes, including the pilot, both season premieres, the intense season 2 episode that exposes Bob's possession of Leland, and the singularly bizarre, infamously open-ended final episode of the series. Together, *Twin Peaks*' mixture of high production values, heavily serial-ized narrative, genre mashing, quirky characters, and elusive mysteries has exerted a major influence on numerous subsequent programs that belies its relatively short life on ABC. For instance, popular series such as *The X-Files* (Fox, 1993–2002, 2016–18) and *Lost* (ABC, 2004–10), the quickly canceled *American Gothic* (CBS, 1995–96) and *Happy Town* (ABC, 2010), and the current *Wayward Pines* (Fox, 2015–) and *Stranger Things* (Netflix, 2016–) have, to varying degrees, borrowed (or attempted to borrow) qualities that yielded *Twin Peaks*' simultaneously mainstream and cultish appeal.

A little more than a year after *Twin Peaks*' final two episodes aired on June 10, 1991, the titular town reappeared in American theaters in the form of *Twin Peaks: Fire Walk with Me* (1992).[4] Lynch's poorly received film—a

---

resolve the murder but sought to continue deferring it. By contrast, in "A Slice of Lynch" (de Lauzirika 2007b), also a feature in this edition, Lynch contradicts Frost and asserts, "The thing that kills me is that the murder of Laura Palmer was never supposed to be solved. . . . There was room for so many other, you know, mysteries, but that mystery was sacred, and it held the other ones."

4. All references to *Twin Peaks: Fire Walk with Me* come from Lynch [1992] 2002.

prequel that also references the last scene of the series finale—details a prior FBI investigation into the related murder of Teresa Banks (Pamela Gidley) as well as the horrific final days of Laura Palmer. In the introduction to an early scholarly anthology on *Twin Peaks*, David Lavery notes that the status of *Twin Peaks: Fire Walk with Me* as "a commercial and critical dud" seemed to be the final nail in the coffin for the once-acclaimed series (1995, 3).[5] More than two decades after the release of *Twin Peaks: Fire Walk with Me*, though, Frost, Lynch, and much of the original cast once again revisited the secret-laden Pacific Northwest town—and significantly broadened the mythos of *Twin Peaks*—in a limited series produced by the American premium cable network Showtime in 2017. The revival's eighteen episodes aired on Sunday evenings and were simultaneously available online via Showtime's streaming services.[6]

The fitful production history of *Twin Peaks* lends the series a sense of enduring inconclusiveness. While addressing the "ends" of television programs, Jason Mittell remarks, "Every television series begins, but not all of them end—or at least not all series conclude" (2015, 319). Mittell then proceeds to identify a "spectrum of closure" that ranges from meticulously plotted finales to series that stop production without a proper narrative, thematic, and/or emotional resolution for audiences (319–21). Of particular note are what Mittell configures as two opposing categories: "a *cessation*, which is a stoppage or wrap-up without a definite finality that it will be the end of the series," and "a *resurrection*, when an already concluded series returns, either on television or in another medium" (321–22, emphasis in original). One peculiar result of cessations and resurrections across mediums, networks, or other exhibition platforms—as with *Twin Peaks* and

---

5. *Twin Peaks: Fire Walk with Me* has, however, received a critical reassessment for a variety of reasons, including its status as a harrowing, albeit abstract, depiction of sexual abuse. For spirited defenses of the film, see Pappademas 2012 and Marsh 2013.

6. All references to the revival come from *Twin Peaks* 2017. In the interim between *Twin Peaks: Fire Walk with Me* and the series' return on Showtime, other cult shows, such as *Firefly* (2002–3) and *Veronica Mars* (2004–7), also returned as full-length movies. Following cancellation by traditional networks, new seasons of *Arrested Development* (2003–6, 2013–) and *Community* (2009–15) arrived via online sources of distribution, Netflix and Yahoo!, respectively. Finally, *The X-Files* (1993–2002) received two feature films, the second of which appeared six years after the series was canceled, as well as a belated tenth season in 2016 and an eleventh season in 2018. (*Editors' note*: For more on the *Veronica Mars* and *The X-Files* finales, see chapters 66 and 71 in this collection.)

other shows—is what I describe as "the uncanceled series finale." Episodes that once served, regardless of how briefly, as the de facto last word on a particular show become reframed as marking the start of a mere interlude before the televisual narrative resumes. Accordingly, the designation *uncanceled series finale* complements Mittell's terms by drawing attention to ways in which a revival essentially recasts what had been the finale of a series as simply a placeholder for "more to come," to adapt a traditional proclamation of television bumpers.

Interestingly, the original series finale of *Twin Peaks* has taken on self-reflexive connotations in light of the program's multiple rebirths over the past twenty-five years. With cancellation imminent, Lynch returned to direct the season 2 finale—the twenty-ninth episode of the series—which was his first time behind the camera for the show since episode 14, or the seventh episode of the second season (although he had made recurring guest appearances on-screen as Regional Bureau Chief Gordon Cole during the interim). Instead of attempting to neatly wrap up the series, Lynch memorably deviated from the finale's original script and delivered a still astonishingly surreal episode of network television; such experimental aesthetics would become the norm for all subsequent incarnations of *Twin Peaks*, which were exclusively directed by Lynch. In this original series finale, Lynch alternates between dutifully advancing lingering subplots in an almost uniformly bleak fashion and further expanding the show's mysteries via an extended excursion into an extradimensional space known as the Black Lodge.[7] The iconic imagery and sound design of the Black Lodge first appeared during a dream sequence in the Lynch-directed second episode of *Twin Peaks* and includes "walls" made of long red curtains; a repeating chevron pattern across the floor; strobe lights; white marble statuary; a seating area with three worn chairs;

---

7. Without delving too deeply into the complexities of these subplots, scenes in the final episode depict the emotional fallout of genealogical revelations in the Hayward household; a mutually unsatisfying outcome for the romantic entanglements of Nadine Hurley (Wendy Robie), Big Ed Hurley (Everett McGill), Norma Jennings (Peggy Lipton), and Mike Nelson (Gary Hershberger); a bomb exploding at the local bank that potentially kills regular characters Audrey Horne (Sherilyn Fenn), Pete Martell (Jack Nance), and Andrew Packard (Dan O'Herlihy), although the revival indicates that Audrey survived; a tender scene between Deputy Andy Brennan (Harry Goaz) and Police Department receptionist Lucy Moran (Kimmy Robertson) in which they discuss Lucy's anxieties about pregnancy; and a light-hearted encounter between Bobby Briggs (Dana Ashbrook), Shelly Johnson (Mädchen Amick), and Heidi (Andrea Hays), a German waitress at the Double R Diner, that duplicates a scene from the pilot episode.

the presence of the Man from Another Place (Michael J. Anderson), a cryptic dwarf who wears a red suit and sometimes dances alone; and, of course, dialogue that actors recorded phonetically backward but that was played in reverse so as to be aurally comprehensible. (Such dialogue was automatically subtitled for viewers during the original broadcast.) Given that Dale Cooper's dream was a much-discussed element of *Twin Peaks'* early popularity, the final episode's scenes in the Black Lodge function as an extended celebration and amplification of what viewers had once found so compelling about the series—a victory lap of sorts on the precipice of cancellation.

Among the many digressive plot threads of season 2, the mystery of the Black Lodge—home to Bob and the Man from Another Place, among other entities—becomes increasingly foregrounded because of its status as a connection between the supernatural elements of *Twin Peaks* and the emerging threat of Dale's deranged former partner, Windom Earle (Kenneth Welsh). Over the second half of season 2, Windom seeks to access the Black Lodge in order to harness its mystical powers. In the finale, Windom kidnaps Dale's love interest, Annie Blackburn (Heather Graham), a former nun with a dark past, and brings her into the Black Lodge. After Dale tracks them into this strange realm, the Man from Another Place greets him and explains that the area with chairs is the "waiting room." As the Black Lodge sequence continues, Lynch accentuates the series-long theme of duality with various white-eyed doppelgängers who menace Dale, including doubles of Laura Palmer, Leland, the Man from Another Place, and, most unsettling, Dale himself.[8] While wandering through the mazelike rooms and corridors of the Black Lodge—which, like the doppelgängers, also double and repeat—Dale eventually locates Windom, who requests Dale's soul in exchange for Annie. Dale agrees, but Bob intervenes, claims Windom's soul, and instructs Dale to leave. Upon retreating, Dale is pursued by his own doppelgänger, which overtakes him just before he exits the Black Lodge. An unconscious Dale and Annie then reappear in the forest outside of the Black Lodge's entrance.

The final scene of the episode depicts what seems to be Dale waking up in his room at the Great Northern Hotel under the watch of Sheriff Truman and Dr. Will Hayward (Warren Frost). "Dale" announces that he must

8. Throughout the series, numerous characters are shown to have layered, often duplicitous aspects of their identities. In addition, Maddy Ferguson (also played by Sheryl Lee) appears midway through season 1 as Laura Palmer's nearly identical cousin, and she also is brutally murdered by Leland later in the series.

brush his teeth and so enters the bathroom, where he smashes his face into a mirror that reflects Bob's visage. Having apparently escaped from the Black Lodge with assistance from Bob, Dale's evil doppelgänger laughs maniacally and repeats, "How's Annie?" The scene fades to black, and thus *Twin Peaks'* life as an ABC series came to a resolutely unresolved endpoint.[9] Rather than proceeding from this cliff-hanger, *Twin Peaks: Fire Walk with Me* simply reaffirms Dale's tragic fate. Midway through the film, a bloodied Annie manifests in Laura's bed and states, "My name is Annie. I've been with Dale and Laura. The Good Dale is in the Lodge, and he can't leave. Write it in your diary." At the film's conclusion, Dale stands beside the just-murdered Laura Palmer in the Black Lodge, and an angel floats above them.[10] Much of the limited series broadcast in 2017 is a direct continuation of the second season's final episode, as Lynch and Frost show Dale's efforts to leave the Black Lodge and be restored to his previous state; however, the protracted reawakening of Dale's consciousness does not culminate until the sixteenth installment, and the revival's intriguingly ambiguous conclusion suggests that Dale may be jumping across alternate timelines and dimensions or, even more grimly, is still confined in the Black Lodge.

What, then, is the true "ending" of *Twin Peaks*? Dale's doppelgänger laughing to himself in the mirror? The oddly peaceful final shot of *Twin Peaks: Fire Walk with Me*? Does the revival provide a sense of definitive closure with its implication that the series' inaugural mystery—the murder of Laura Palmer—no longer occurred as a result of Dale's willful alteration of the past and accompanying generation of multiple timelines? Or are those on-screen events merely an imprisoned Dale's dreams? An early unofficial stopping point was certainly identified by viewers who abandoned the show after the revelation of Laura's killer in the first half of season 2. Conversely, Marc Dolan notes that the second season's "hybrid narrative form" consists of "five clearly divided, smaller episodic serials," which firmly situates the program's ongoing endings and beginnings within the soap opera storytelling tradition (1995, 41).

For a program that prominently features the atemporal, multidimensional space of the Black Lodge, perhaps uncertainty regarding the parameters of

---

9. Alex Pappademas describes the original series finale as "still the strangest hour of prime-time television ever broadcast" (2012).

10. In Laura's bedroom, there is a painting of an angel serving food to children; on the night that Laura is killed, the angel vanishes from the painting.

Twin Peaks is appropriate.[11] In hindsight, even with its many cliff-hangers, *Twin Peaks*' uncanceled-series finale offers viewers potential ways of processing the show's looping themes and flickering existence. During the episode, Laura appears to Dale in the Black Lodge and states, "I'll see you again in twenty-five years. Meanwhile." She poses as if holding an invisible object and then disappears. A few moments later Laura's twitching doppelgänger mimics this gesture, snarls, "Meanwhile," and begins screaming loudly. Within the original context of the episode, Laura's first comment seems to reference Dale's earlier dream in which he is depicted as significantly aged inside the Black Lodge. Now, as fans and critics alike have noted, this statement acquires extratextual resonance because of the revival's appearance roughly twenty-five years after ABC first canceled *Twin Peaks*.[12] In fact, the Showtime limited series commences by replaying footage of this encounter between Dale and Laura from episode 2.22.

Beyond this coincidence, however, Laura's final bit of dialogue in season 2—"meanwhile"—further reflects on the nature of the series. *Twin Peaks* began with the end of a life, concluded with the start of a new major narrative thread, continued as a prequel film that acknowledged events from the finale, and sat dormant for more than two-and-a-half decades until a revival on a premium television network depicted events that may have undone the death of Laura Palmer, which had anchored the series since its first scene. In terms of the series' production history, a feature-length pilot and twenty-eight episodes preceded the original series finale; from *Twin Peaks: Fire Walk with Me* through the limited series in 2017, roughly twenty hours of *Twin Peaks* content followed that finale, thereby reconfiguring episode 2.22 as a dramatic hinge just past the middle of the overarching narrative of the

---

11. Lavery discusses how early "tie-in books" such as *The Secret Diary of Laura Palmer* (1990) and *The Autobiography of F.B.I. Special Agent Dale Cooper* (1991) first expanded the series' narrative boundaries beyond that of a standard televisual text (1995, 7–11). Mark Frost would continue this tradition with two fictional books—*The Secret History of Twin Peaks* (2016) and *Twin Peaks: The Final Dossier* (2017)—detailing supposedly canonical information, much of which is not depicted in television or film incarnations of the series.

12. Prior to the announcement of the revival, fans of *Twin Peaks* experienced what Rebecca Williams describes as "interim fandom . . . a period in which audiences assume that their beloved object is dormant, but it becomes active again. This usually refers to periods in which fan texts are neither officially canceled nor assured of a return" (2016, 146). Oddly, the lengthy waiting period experienced by fans of *Twin Peaks* corresponds to the interval of Dale's stasis within the Black Lodge in the series' diegesis.

franchise rather than the unresolved stopping point that it once was. More-over, *Twin Peaks*' subsequent incarnations are consistently oriented around this episode's primary setting and events. The three shots during the end credits of the original series finale, the film, and the revival's final episode all return to the same location: the waiting room in the Black Lodge. In episode 2.22, the credit sequence is a static shot of a coffee cup set against the chevron floor of the Black Lodge, and the focus shifts to reveal a reflection of Laura's upside-down face in the black liquid; in *Twin Peaks: Fire Walk with Me*, the end credits play over a freeze-frame close-up of Laura's face from the aforementioned concluding scene with Dale and Laura beneath an angel; finally, the end credits of the revival's last installment scroll across a close-up of Laura whispering in Dale's ear that plays in extreme slow motion. The latter shot repeats moments from the second and eighteenth episodes of the limited series and also visually references the original dream sequence shown in the second episode of the first season. Because *Twin Peaks*' major plot points regularly turn upon knowledge of precise spatiotemporal coordinates, the recurrent setting shared by these three final shots assumes greater significance than might otherwise be the case. Even as *Twin Peaks* has evolved into alternate forms—much like the Man from Another Place in the revival—the franchise persistently circles back to these meetings between Dale Cooper and Laura Palmer in the Black Lodge, which double as reaffirmations of Dale's continual entrapment.[13] Given the repetitions that follow episode 2.22, this uncanceled-series finale should be recognized as a simultaneous ending *and* starting point in the looping temporality that orders the *Twin Peaks* universe.

As becomes more pronounced with each version of the series, *Twin Peaks* has always been fundamentally in media res through its incessant resistance to conclusions and consistent emphasis on parallel themes, actions, and characters. Events have happened, will happen, and happen again, to paraphrase one of the series' most famous lines—yet these ostensibly disparate temporalities somehow seem to be concurrent. This irregular sense of time is made overt throughout the revival. In the second and final installments of the limited series, Philip Gerard/the One-Armed Man (Al Strobel)—a traveling salesman who had been possessed by a supernatural entity named "Mike" and was a former partner of Bob but later renounced evil—and Dale

---

13. In *Twin Peaks: Fire Walk with Me*, the Man from Another Place is revealed to be the severed arm of Philip Gerard/the One-Armed Man/Mike. In the revival, the Man from Another Place/the Arm has "evolved" into the form of a talking tree.

are seated together in the Black Lodge; in both episodes, Philip asks, "Is it future, or is it past?"[14] During the revival's final scene, Dale returns to the Palmer house with someone whom he believes to be Laura Palmer but who claims to be Carrie Page (both characters are played by Sheryl Lee). There, they meet the current owner, Alice Tremond (Mary Reber), who denies having knowledge of the Palmer family and states that she purchased the home from a Mrs. Chalfont.[15] Deflated by this information, Dale and Carrie retreat to the street, where the former bewilderingly ponders, "What year is this?" Off-screen, the voice of Laura's mother, Sarah Palmer (Grace Zabriskie), abruptly calls out, "Laura"; Carrie (or is it Laura?) shrieks as the lights of the Palmer house blink out, and the screen fades to black. The simple, perplexing answer to both Philip Gerard's and Dale Cooper's questions was actually provided by Laura Palmer and her doppelgänger in the second season's uncanceled-series finale: in *Twin Peaks*, the answer is always "meanwhile." Mirroring the "good" Dale's indefinite purgatorial confinement, *Twin Peaks* exists as a perpetual "meanwhile" or, rather, as a constant elsewhere that is forever out of time but somehow still present, like the haunted existence of the Black Lodge's eternal denizens.

References

De Lauzirika, Charles, dir. 2007a. "Secrets from Another Place: Creating *Twin Peaks*." On *Twin Peaks: Definitive Gold Box Edition*. Los Angeles: CBS. DVD.
———, dir. 2007b. "A Slice of Lynch." On *Twin Peaks: Definitive Gold Box Edition*. Los Angeles: CBS. DVD.

14. This mysterious question also twice repeats in *The Missing Pieces* (Lynch 2014), which is a feature-length collection of extra footage shot during the production of *Twin Peaks: Fire Walk with Me*. Lynch first edited this material together for the Blu-ray box set *Twin Peaks: The Entire Mystery* (2014). In an extended version of a scene from the film, Dale encounters the Man from Another Place/the Arm in the Black Lodge; the latter asks, "Is it future, or is it past?" As with the exchange between Philip Gerard and Dale in the revival, a second version of this scene appears near the end of *The Missing Pieces*, during which the question is restated. When Dale then inquires about his present location and how to leave, the Man from Another Place/the Arm tauntingly replies, "You are here. Now there is no place to go BUT HOME!"

15. "Mrs. Tremond" and "Mrs. Chalfont" are the names of a known Black Lodge entity (Frances Bay) featured in both the original series and the film. Further adding to the mystery of this scene is the fact that Lynch cast Mary Reber, the real-life owner of the home used as the Palmers', as Alice Tremond.

Dolan, Marc. 1995. "The Peaks and Valleys of Serial Creativity: What Happened to/on *Twin Peaks*." In *Full of Secrets: Critical Approaches to "Twin Peaks,"* edited by David Lavery, 30–50. Detroit: Wayne State Univ. Press.

Frost, Mark, and David Lynch, creators. 2017. *Twin Peaks*. Showtime Networks. Showtime streaming on Amazon Channels. Accessed May–Sept., Oct. 2017.

Lacey, Stephen. 2016. "Just Plain *Odd*: Some Thoughts on Performance Styles in *Twin Peaks*." *Cinema Journal* 55, no. 3: 126–31.

Lavery, David. 1995. "Introduction: The Semiotics of Cobbler: *Twin Peaks*' Interpretive Community." In *Full of Secrets: Critical Approaches to "Twin Peaks,"* edited by David Lavery, 1–21. Detroit: Wayne State Univ. Press.

Lynch, David, dir. [1992] 2002. *Twin Peaks: Fire Walk with Me*. Los Angeles: New Line Home Entertainment. DVD.

———, dir. 2014. *The Missing Pieces*. On *Twin Peaks: Fire Walk with Me*. Los Angeles: Criterion Collection. Blu-ray DVD.

Marsh, Calum. 2013. "*Twin Peaks: Fire Walk with Me* Is David Lynch's Masterpiece." *Village Voice*, May 17. At http://www.villagevoice.com/2013/05/17/twin -peaks-fire-walk-with-me-is-david-lynchs-masterpiece/.

Mittell, Jason. 2015. *Complex TV: The Poetics of Contemporary Television Storytelling*. New York: New York Univ. Press.

Pappademas, Alex. 2012. "Anatomy of a Fascinating Disaster: *Fire Walk with Me*." *Grantland*, Aug. 29. At http://grantland.com/features/twenty-things-david-lynch -fire-walk-its-20th-anniversary/.

Twin Peaks: Definitive Gold Box Edition. 2007. Los Angeles: CBS. DVD.

Twin Peaks: The Entire Mystery. 2014. Hollywood, CA: Paramount Pictures.

"*Twin Peaks* FAQ: TV Episode Questions." n.d. *Twin Peaks Online*. At http://www .twinpeaks.org/faqeps.htm#e3. Accessed Oct. 15, 2016.

Williams, Rebecca. 2016. "Ontological Security, Authorship, and Resurrection: Exploring *Twin Peaks*' Social Media Afterlife." *Cinema Journal* 55, no. 3: 143–47.

66

Veronica Mars

"The Bitch Is Back"

JOSEPH S. WALKER

Like *Buffy the Vampire Slayer* creator Joss Whedon, novelist and writer Rob Thomas has created a number of television shows—*Cupid* (1998–99), *Veronica Mars* (2004–7), *Party Down* (2009–10)—that have earned great critical praise and extreme devotion from a body of fans while failing to find general ratings success and ultimately ending prematurely. Like Whedon, too, Thomas's most enduring creation is a high school blonde who becomes an assertive heroine in a genre where girls have more typically been victims. It would be unfair, however, to see Veronica Mars as simply an imitation of Buffy; she is very much a successful independent creation. Veronica is a complex, engaging character: determined, loyal, funny, and always the smartest person in the room but flawed by the suspicious, cynical, and sometimes vindictive nature her experiences have bred in her. Although the original TV show about her came to a highly unsatisfying end, we are fortunate that its creators and fans sought innovative ways to continue her story.

Veronica Mars aired a total of sixty-four episodes, from September 2004 to May 2007, in three seasons, the first two on UPN and the third on the CW, the network created when the UPN and WB networks merged. Where *Buffy* was a reimagining of the horror genre, *Veronica Mars* reworked the hard-boiled detective story. Kristen Bell starred as the title character, a high school junior as the series opened who also assists her private-eye father, Keith Mars (Enrico Colantoni), with his business while using the skills she has acquired from him to solve cases on her own. Early reviews of the series, like the one by Gillian Flynn in *Entertainment Weekly*, invariably noted that this premise was reminiscent of Nancy Drew, popular culture's only familiar previous example of a girl detective, but concluded that the series was "far more than Drew redux" (2004). The series itself winked at the comparison;

425

in one season 3 episode ("There's Got to Be a Morning-After Pill," 3.12 [Block 2007]), Keith, while working undercover, introduces himself and Veronica as "Carson Drew and my daughter, Nancy." However, *Veronica Mars* deals with far darker and more disturbing crimes than any incarnation of the sunny, essentially innocent Nancy could comfortably encompass—murder, child abuse, date rape, identity theft, school violence, and so on.

One of the show's most explicit themes, unusually for an American television series aimed at young viewers, is class conflict. The fictional setting of Neptune, California, is a beach town near the Mexican border divided sharply between the ultrarich (most notably software mogul Jake Kane [Kyle Secor] and his family) and their employees and servants, with little evidence of a significant middle class. The children of both groups attend Neptune High, where sharp lines of privilege divide the well-off "09ers" (so named for their exclusive zip code) from their less-fortunate classmates, creating tensions that frequently mark the cases Veronica takes on for her classmates. For example, the season 1 episode "Return of the Kane" (Anderson 2004) revolves around attempts to rig a student council election to ensure the continuation of controversial policies favoring the 09ers.

In the pilot episode (Piznarski 2004), Veronica tells us (via voiceover, a device borrowed from film noir detective stories that will continue to be used throughout the series) that she, despite her family's relative poverty, had once been accepted among the exclusive 09er clique, in part because her father was at that time the sheriff and in part because she was dating Jake Kane's son, Duncan. Her status changed, however, when Lilly Kane (Amanda Seyfried), Duncan's sister and Veronica's best friend, was murdered, a case that became a national media sensation. Keith believed at the time that a member of the Kane family was involved in the murder and persisted in this belief, even after a disgruntled Kane employee (falsely) confessed to the crime. Because of this persistence, he has been driven from office and socially ostracized, with even his wife, Lianne (Corinne Bohrer), abandoning him. Only Veronica remains loyal, which has caused her in turn to become an outcast among her peers. Although these events are surely traumatic enough, we also learn during the pilot episode that Veronica was drugged and raped at a party, though she has no idea who did it.

The pilot episode thus establishes the goals that will carry Veronica through the first season: she is determined to learn who raped her, to expose Lilly's real killer, to rescue her father's reputation, and to find her missing mother and restore her family. Although individual episodes usually focus on the smaller cases Veronica takes on, either on her own or to assist her father, these larger goals are always present and provide a tight narrative structure to the entire season. Again, there is a similarity here to *Buffy*, where each season is built around the gradual escalation to a showdown with the "big bad." However, the frequently dark and gritty tone that dominates *Mars* extends to these quests as well, and, despite her determination and considerable abilities, Veronica is only partially successful. Although she does find her mother, Lianne has become a hopeless alcoholic who steals Veronica's carefully hoarded college fund and flees the family again. Veronica learns who killed Lilly, but in the second season the killer succeeds in tainting the evidence against him and is acquitted of the crime. She learns only in the final episode of the second season that she had incorrectly identified her rapist at the end of the first season. Ultimately, the only one of her initial goals that she unambiguously fulfills is restoring her father's reputation.

The latter is significant for a number of reasons. First, the emotional heart of the series is the relationship between Keith and Veronica. This is one important way in which Veronica differs from Buffy Summers, whose series revolves around the tightly knit "Scooby gang." Although Veronica does find reliable allies among her classmates—athletic Wallace (Percy Daggs III), budding hacker Mac (Tina Majorino), and motorcycle gang leader Weevil (Francis Capra)—they never cohere into a unified group and never challenge the primacy of her loyalty to her father. The two occasionally clash, usually when Keith feels that Veronica is taking unnecessary risks, which leads Veronica to frequently mislead her father about what she is doing. For the most part, however, their relationship is founded on deep mutual understanding and respect, to a degree that is highly unusual for parent–child relationships as depicted on American television. Keith and Veronica are fiercely loyal to and proud of each other from the beginning of the show to its end.

Second, although class conflict is the most explicit theme of *Veronica Mars*, a concern for the imperiled patriarchy is the deepest and most persistent. Despite being built around a strong, smart, female protagonist, the show repeatedly traces disruptions of the social order to the failure, disappearance, or corruption of the father, suggesting that stability can be found only if the father can be restored or replaced. For example, Logan Echolls (Jason Dohring), a classmate of Veronica who had been Lilly's boyfriend, is established in the pilot episode as being the most self-centered, cruel, and destructive of the 09ers. In later episodes, however, these traits are revealed to have been the result of the physical and emotional abuse Logan has suffered at the hands of his philandering movie-star father. Logan's efforts to overcome this abuse and become a better man than his father provide his character arc and ultimately make him, with enormous fan approval, Veronica's main romantic partner. Another instructive example can be found in "Meet John Smith" (Winer 2004), the third episode of the series. Here, a classmate asks Veronica to find the father he had believed dead. She ultimately learns that the man—John Smith, a name that suggests that the character stands in for American masculinity generally—has become a postoperative transsexual, a literal feminization of the patriarch. Against a backdrop of such stories and patterns, Keith Mars stands out as virtually the only character in the series to function as a dependable, capable, and successful conventional father. Significantly, his only momentary failure on this score comes in the third season, when Veronica learns that he is having an affair with a married woman, and he can only offer explanations and rationalizations that are all too reminiscent of the many straying husbands the two of them have caught in their work. Veronica flees their apartment, tearfully telling Keith he had been her "one shining example"; Keith, unable to continue disappointing her, breaks off the affair ("Of Vice and Men," 3.7 [Winer 2006]).

Stylistically, *Veronica Mars* is a hybrid that draws upon the iconography and tropes of both film noir and more traditional high school narratives. The California settings are mostly sunny and bright, but many significant sequences are set at night and feature moody, threatening lighting and cinematography. Veronica's sense of isolation and distance from her peers is frequently, especially at the high school, emphasized by scenes where she is motionless in the foreground while others zip around and behind her in sped-up motion. Her voiceovers, like her dialogue, are marked by witty wordplay and a bantering flair. Although the show's style was consistent throughout its three seasons, the narrative structure changed significantly; as in many series structured around an initial mystery, the show never quite recaptured the same sense of momentum and focus once the question of who killed Lilly Kane was answered. The second season centered on Veronica's investigation of the bombing of a school bus she was supposed to have been on, though this task never preoccupies her or the audience as Lilly's murder had, and more time was given over to continuing subplots such as her relationship with Logan. In the third season, Veronica and several of her classmates move from high school to the local college, and the idea of a season-long mystery was abandoned in an effort to draw in more new viewers. The initial intention was to use shorter cases, each of which would take up several episodes, but this structure also didn't last, and the last several episodes of the series are essentially self-contained.

Although *Veronica Mars* generated real devotion among both fans and critics, it never drew strong ratings, and a fourth season was always unlikely. Despite this, the producers were confident enough to end the third season on a cliff-hanger. In the final episode, "The Bitch Is Back" (Fields 2007), Veronica seeks revenge against a Skull-and-Bones-like organization that releases a video of her having sex with her new boyfriend, Stosh "Piz" Piznarski (Chris Lowell) (Veronica has, by this point, broken up with Logan because of his continuing anger issues). In the course of her investigation, she is videotaped breaking into an 09er house and faces possible prosecution. Keith, who has been restored to the position of acting sheriff and is now running for election to the position, destroys the evidence against his daughter, but this act is discovered and reported in the newspaper on the day of the election. The episode—and the series—ends with Veronica, knowing that she has probably caused Keith to return to a state of public disgrace, casting her own vote for him and then walking down the streets of Neptune in the rain. The downbeat ending is very much in tune with the dark tone of much of the series but also highly unsatisfying, leaving Veronica in a place of guilt and isolation.[1]

That she does not remain there speaks to the show's position in a modern mediascape where neither fans nor producers must accept any ending as "the" ending. Efforts to continue Veronica's story in some way began almost immediately. The DVD set of the third season includes a fifteen-minute film, labeled *Season 4 Presentation*, in which we see Veronica now working as a rookie FBI agent with an entirely new supporting cast. In accompanying material, Thomas explains that this film was presented to the CW as a proposal for a new direction in season 4 of the series but was rejected. Including the film on the DVD set blurs the lines between fans and producers; the producers are shown indulging in the kind of scenario that would normally be the province of fan fiction, whereas fans are allowed to see how the narrative on the screen necessarily echoes the circumstances of production. Nothing ultimately came of the Veronica-in-the-FBI possibility, but in the following years Thomas and Kristen Bell continued to speak publicly of their desire to continue *Veronica Mars*, probably as a movie, with Bell in particular suggesting that continuing fan demand would help this to happen.

---

1. Enlightening treatments of the original run of the series, including the themes of class and patriarchy, can be found in *Investigating "Veronica Mars": Essays on the Teen Detective Series* (Wilcox and Turnbull 2011).

It was six years before these hopes came to fruition in a way nobody in 2007 could have foreseen. In March 2013, Thomas and Bell launched a *Veronica Mars* movie fund-raising campaign on the crowdfunding website Kickstarter, which allows individuals to pledge money to proposed creative projects in exchange for special merchandise and other benefits. Kickstarter had, to this point, been used mostly by amateur artists, musicians, and inventers; by turning to the site to fund what would have previously been a studio-funded venture, Thomas and Bell were breaking new ground. They promised that if they raised $2 million within thirty days, they would make the first of a proposed series of *Veronica Mars* films, which would be given limited theatrical release. The appeal posted to the website was remarkably warm and open, with Bell repeatedly addressing fans as "marshmallows" and promising high levels of access to the various stages of production.

The campaign was phenomenally successful; the required funds were raised within twenty-four hours, and the final tally was more than $5.7 million, enough to substantially increase the film's production values. *Veronica Mars* thus modeled a new way in which fans and creators could collaborate to sidestep the traditional channels of production and distribution. In an increasingly fragmented media universe, the loyalty of a relatively small group of devoted fans can be enough to ensure that almost any "finale" must now be regarded as possibly temporary; it's a truth that has now also been demonstrated by, among other series, *Arrested Development* (2003–6, 2013–), *Gilmore Girls* (2000–2007, 2016), and *Mystery Science Theater 3000* (1988–99, 2017–). For many years, fan fiction was the only way for shows to live on after leaving the airwaves. Today, *Veronica Mars*, entirely aside from its considerable merits as a series, is historic for helping to make the very concept of the finale seem obsolete.

Ultimately released in 2014, *Veronica Mars* the movie explicitly takes as its central task undoing the downbeat season 3 finale.[2] At the start of the movie, it has been nine years since Veronica has worked as a detective or spoken to Logan. Still dating Piz, she is now a freshly minted graduate of Columbia Law School, interviewing for a job with a high-powered New York law firm. Her plans are disrupted by an event that makes national news: Logan's new girlfriend, another former classmate turned pop star,

---

2. All references to the film *Veronica Mars* come from Thomas 2014.

has been murdered, and Logan is the prime suspect. When he calls Veronica for help, she returns to Neptune—conveniently, the trip also coincides with her ten-year high school reunion—initially intending only to help him find a lawyer, but she is inevitably drawn into the investigation and returns to her PI roots.

The central mystery is well structured, if somewhat conventional. Ultimately, the film is far more invested in celebrating and restoring the world of Neptune, as seen in the original series. Every significant character from the show makes at least a cameo appearance. There are also a number of metatextual winks to the fans, some of whom, as a result of large donations, appear as extras: a New York street musician performs the show's theme song ("We Used to Be Friends" by the Dandy Warhols); Piz makes disparaging comments about artists who rely on Kickstarter; a character says he heard Veronica was in the FBI; Bell's real-life husband, the actor Dax Shepard, hits on Veronica in a bar.

The film's central appeal is the restoration of the Veronica the fans loved in the first place. She is initially reluctant to involve herself in the investigation, telling both the law firm she hopes to join and Logan that she "doesn't really do that anymore." At several points, she speaks of detective work as an addiction she has successfully broken. As the film goes on, however, her resistance quickly breaks down; in a scene that is the equivalent of Bruce Wayne going to the Batcave, she opens a box in her old room to retrieve her stun gun and hidden microphones. By the end of the film, she has solved the mystery, broken up with Piz to reconcile with Logan, and rejected the idea of working as a lawyer. The film even anticipates future installments by providing a new, long-term case for her in the form of a corrupt police department that has hospitalized Keith and framed Weevil for attempted murder. The film's final scene finds her with her feet up on the desk at Mars Investigations, telling us in voiceover that this is where she belongs, in the fight: "My name is Veronica, and I'm an addict. Hello, Veronica."

It is appropriate for the film to end on this note of greeting. Although Veronica's further adventures have, to this point, been confined to a pair of paperback novels cowritten by Thomas and, interestingly, officially licensed fan fiction available as Amazon e-texts, both the creators' and the fans' continuing enthusiasm means that she could easily appear on film again. Ultimately, *Veronica Mars* lacks anything that could be called a definitive finale. It is a creation of the contemporary age, where closure is a state of mind always open to renegotiation.

References

Anderson, Sarah Pia, dir. 2004. "Return of the Kane." *Veronica Mars*, season 1, episode 6. Written by Phil Klemmer (teleplay) and Rob Thomas (story). Aired Nov. 2, UPN. Amazon Prime (streaming). Accessed May–Nov. 2016.

Block, Tricia, dir. 2007. "There's Got to Be a Morning-After Pill." *Veronica Mars*, season 3, episode 12. Written by Jonathan Moskin, Phil Klemmer, and John Enbom (teleplay) and Jonathan Moskin and David Mulei (story). Aired Feb. 6, UPN. Amazon Prime (streaming). Accessed May–Nov. 2016.

Fields, Michael, dir. 2007. "The Bitch Is Back." 2007. *Veronica Mars*, season 3, episode 20. Written by Rob Thomas and Diane Ruggiero. Aired May 22, CW. Amazon Prime (streaming). Accessed May–Nov. 2016.

Flynn, Gillian. 2004. Review of *Veronica Mars. Entertainment Weekly*, Oct. 29. At http://www.ew.com/article/2004/10/29/veronica-mars.

Piznarski, Mark, dir. 2004. "Pilot." *Veronica Mars*, season 1, episode 1. Written by Rob Thomas. Aired Sept. 22, CW. Amazon Prime (streaming). Accessed May–Nov. 2016.

Thomas, Rob, dir. 2014. *Veronica Mars*. Written by Rob Thomas and Diane Ruggiero. Amazon Prime (streaming). Accessed May–Nov. 2016.

Wilcox, Rhonda V., and Sue Turnbull, eds. 2011. *Investigating "Veronica Mars": Essays on the Teen Detective Series*. Jefferson, NC: McFarland.

Winer, Harry, dir. 2004. "Meet John Smith." *Veronica Mars*, season 1, episode 3. Written by Jed Seidel. Aired Oct. 12, UPN. Amazon Prime (streaming). Accessed May–Nov. 2016.

———, dir. 2006. "Of Vice and Men." *Veronica Mars*, season 3, episode 7. Written by Phil Klemmer. Aired Nov. 14, CW. Amazon Prime (streaming). Accessed May–Nov. 2016.

67

The West Wing

"Tomorrow"

GARY GRAVELY

Following the conclusion of its subpar fifth season, NBC's political hit *The West Wing* (1999–2006) found itself needing an infusion of energy to recapture the former success it had achieved just a few seasons earlier. The critically acclaimed series, focusing on President Josiah Bartlet (Martin Sheen) and his entourage of brilliant White House staffers, had swept awards shows from the Emmys and Golden Globes to the Peabodys while under the direction of series creator Aaron Sorkin. However, both Sorkin and Thomas Schlamme left the show after the fourth season, putting it in the hands of John Wells, a producer best known for his work with another NBC hit, *ER* (1994–2009). The show floundered, however, as it moved from a narrative filled with fast-paced dialogue and liberal idealism to just another ratings-seeking series. A show that had once treated its viewership to intricate plots worthy of its subject matter became a generic television drama composed of ripped-from-the-headlines plots and popcorn movie teasers.

At the pinnacle of its creativity, *The West Wing* could realistically depict political situations with deft clarity, allowing plotlines to develop naturally, moving from plot to subplot and back to plot. Such a fluctuation of priorities worked just as it would within the actual West Wing, as exemplified by the multiepisode depiction of the selection and confirmation process of Roberto Mendoza (Edward James Olmos) as a Supreme Court justice during the first season. The prominence of this task rose and fell in priority on the president's agenda much as one would expect for such a complex political process in the perpetually shifting landscape of actual White House business. In contrast, the fifth season treated a Supreme Court vacancy and an even more complicated confirmation process within the confines of one episode featuring a guest appearance by Glenn Close.

However, the appeal of less-complex and therefore potentially more viewer-friendly story arcs did not result in the ratings increase NBC was seeking in the show's post-Sorkin era, and so the network searched for an alternative. It found such an alternative in the possibility of rendering the Bartlet administration in a lame-duck state while the remaining two seasons of the show would focus on the search for his successor. To fill the roles of candidates for this job, *The West Wing* turned to two veteran television actors quite accustomed to playing the lead male role in a popular television series. Alan Alda claimed the role of Arnold Vinick, a moderate California senator, whose gravitas could compete with Sheen's Bartlet but who could also serve as a Republican even the traditional liberal viewership of the show would find appealing. On the Democratic side, a younger heir apparent to Bartlet was sought who could also command a presidential presence. The network executives believed they found this person in Jimmy Smits, who had demonstrated himself capable of performing as a leading dramatic actor in both *L.A. Law* (1986–94) and *NYPD Blue* (1993–2005).

The final two seasons of *The West Wing* switch the focus back and forth between both the final days of the Bartlet administration and the campaign trail fight between Vinick and Matt Santos (Smits). Josh Lyman (Bradley Whitford), Bartlet's deputy chief of staff, enters center stage, finding in Santos the outsider candidate who might wrench the Democratic nomination away from ill-qualified Vice President Bob Russell (Gary Cole). Much like Dr. John Carter (Noah Wylie) in *ER*, Lyman had been a central figure in *The West Wing* from the beginning, even among several more well-known cast members. The show's pilot focuses on his nearly being fired, much as the pilot of *ER* centers on Carter's first day at County General. But whereas Wylie took the spotlight in *ER* simply owing to a gradual matriculation of the remaining original cast members to other endeavors, Whitford's character became the focus of *The West Wing* when his role is enlarged because of his interactions with the newly inserted character Santos.

Mirroring his mentor Leo McGarry's (John Spencer) molding of Bartlet from a fringe candidate to the presidency, Lyman finds in Santos an unknown but principled and talented politician he can assist in continuing the Bartlet legacy. Early in the primary election season, the politically savvy Lyman looks around and finds all the establishment candidates unworthy of the office or incapable of defeating Vinick. The sixth season follows the rise of Santos as Lyman works to help him win the Democratic nomination in a contest against Bartlet's current and former vice presidents, Bob Russell and John Hoynes (Tim Matheson). Santos wins the Democratic nomination in a brokered convention, while the formidable Vinick wins the Republican nomination easily, setting up the general election as the main story line for the seventh and final season.

The plans for the seventh season hit a major obstacle, though, when veteran member of the cast John Spencer passed away midway through filming the final season. Spencer's role had diminished since his character Leo McGarry had suffered a heart attack and been forced to give up his position as Bartlet's chief of staff at the beginning of the sixth season. McGarry's heart attack served as an eerie coincidence, considering Spencer's own death occurred as the result of one, forcing the writers to have McGarry die off-screen just as he is beginning to take a larger role as Santos's running mate. The death occurs on election night, when Santos upsets Vinick, an election whose outcome the writers changed following Spencer's passing (Steinberg 2006). The rest of the season then focuses on the fallout from McGarry's death and the transition from the Bartlet to the Santos administration.

The last few episodes provide both closure and a new beginning as the series moves onward to its finale, appropriately titled "Tomorrow."[1] Old cast members return, including Rob Lowe as Josh's best friend and former White House speechwriter Sam Seaborn and Mary-Louise Parker as Josh's former girlfriend and rival Amy Gardner. Communications director Toby Ziegler (Richard Schiff) undergoes a felony charge for revealing the existence of a top-secret military space shuttle. Romances bloom, including the culmination of Lyman's flirtatious interactions with his assistant, Donna Moss (Janel Maloney). The show is concluding but simultaneously hinting at the future.

"Tomorrow" provides the show an opportunity to give Bartlet a proper send-off while also previewing what is to come. By doing this, *The West Wing* is allowed to end as the show it had always been: a story about both a great president and his dynamic staff. In ending with an inauguration episode, *The West Wing* is able to demonstrate that it is time to move onward and forward. Although one remains constantly aware that Santos will soon be occupying the Oval Office with Josh, Sam, and company at his side, the finale focuses primarily on Bartlet as he completes his final day in office. Reminiscences and final tasks dominate the show as the viewer watches Bartlet and the remaining members of his staff take their last rounds of the

---

1. All references to "Tomorrow" come from Misiano 2006.

offices they have feverishly occupied and worked in for the past eight years (or seven seasons).

As the lone remaining member of Bartlet's initial staff, C. J. Cregg (Allison Janney), the former press secretary who has replaced McGarry as chief of staff, has the largest role in the finale outside of the outgoing and incoming presidents. The camera finds her reflectively watching over the transition. With the viewers, she watches and wonders whether Bartlet will sign Toby's pardon, and, along with Mrs. Bartlet (Stockard Channing) and Barlet's personal secretary, Deborah Federer (Lily Tomlin), she works to make sure Bartlet accomplishes his final acts before abdicating the office. Her poignant visit to the briefing room reminds everyone just how much she has grown and the show has changed since it first entered the national conscience with its snappy, smart dialogue written by Sorkin. When she leaves the White House gate and answers a tourist's question by replying that she does not work at the White House, the viewer is reminded of the reality that the show is coming to an end.

In addition to C. J.'s exit, we also see President Bartlet giving his former personal aide, Charlie (Dulé Hill), his personal copy of the Constitution. This near-melodramatic scene parallels a previous father–son scene between the two when Bartlet gives Charlie a carving knife that is both a family heirloom and crafted by Paul Revere. Charlie is finally leaving the scene where he received Bartlet's wisdom and forging ahead into the new world his experience and talent have afforded him. He greets one of the new Santos staffers and suddenly becomes aware of his own departure from the setting that had come to dominate his life. When we see him join Will Bailey (Joshua Malina) and Kate Harper (Mary McCormack) on their way out the door, the fact that we soon will be losing our own vantage point becomes distinctly clear. We watch the three of them wonder what lies outside the hallways they have frantically chatted in for the past several seasons. The Santos administration is beginning its term in the White House, but neither Charlie and friends, nor we, will witness it.

The future accomplishments of the Santos administration will have to be left to our imaginations, but "tomorrow" looks very bright as longtime fans of the show speculate just what the next few years will hold for Josh and Sam and how they will help Santos fulfill his promise as Bartlet's successor. The most notable example of such speculation can be found in the Twitter accounts fans have created for multiple characters—in particular Josh, Sam, and now (according to Twitter) Congresswoman Donna—which frequently comment on real-world events. Unsurprisingly, these Twitter accounts have been quite busy since the election of Donald Trump as president, echoing reactions similar to Sorkin's own ("Read the Letter Aaron Sorkin Wrote" 2016). In fact, having Twitter's most infamous user elected to the same office once occupied by the fictional ideal of Josiah Bartlet has resulted in a rise in the show's viewership (Stolworthy 2017). The bleakness and divisiveness of our current political landscape have sent many distressed liberals back to Sorkin's fantasy world of liberal idealism and high-minded rhetoric (I just finished my own rewatching of the series with my wife, who had never seen it). Even more than a decade later, the show still affects how its viewers perceive the political landscape.

In fact, a few years after the show ended, some writers for *The West Wing* would admit to a relationship with Obama adviser David Axelrod, which they utilized in helping to create the character of Santos (Mittell 2008). They wanted a young, vibrant leader whom Josh could guide as a worthy successor to the wise fatherlike figure of Bartlet. After Obama's Democratic Convention keynote speech in 2004, the new senator from Illinois seemed to fit the bill as a prototype for the *West Wing* writers' fictional outsider candidate. Little could they have imagined that Obama would be undertaking his own outsider campaign for the presidency just a couple of years later, but the parallels proved eerie to the point that many *West Wing* fans began to notice the similarity. The fact that Santos is first introduced as a proponent of a patients' medical rights bill makes the connection even more ironic.

However, *The West Wing*'s ending belongs to Bartlet, and the conclusion of the wise statesman's time in office claims the primary focus of the series finale. We watch as he reflects on his accomplishments in office and ponders what his legacy will achieve. He pardons Toby while regretting the trouble it will cause the new Santos administration. A much younger and healthier man takes Bartlet's job, but his wife reminds him that he "made it," referring to the fact that he accomplished a great deal despite the difficulties presented by his multiple sclerosis. His health is intact, and the job has been completed.

"Tomorrow" serves as an appropriate conclusion for *The West Wing*. Although many fans who continued through the post-Sorkin years may long for the lost opportunity to see what the Santos administration will hold for Josh, Donna, Sam, and company, the series finale demonstrates that *The West Wing* was the Bartlet administration. This fact resonates in the final scene, with a fitting tribute reminding fans of the show at its zenith. On his way home, Bartlet opens the gift McGarry's daughter left for him earlier that day. As if a gift from the heavens, it's the napkin Leo wrote on that started it all: "Bartlet for America."

References

Misiano, Christopher, dir. 2006. "Tomorrow." *The West Wing*, season 7, episode 22. Written by John Wells. Aired May 14, NBC. Original broadcast.

Mittell, Jason. 2008. "Obama & Santos, Together Again." *Just TV*, Feb. 27. At https://justtv.wordpress.com/2008/02/27/obama-santos-together-again/.

"Read the Letter Aaron Sorkin Wrote His Daughter After Donald Trump Was Elected President." 2016. *Vanity Fair*, Nov. 9. At https://www.vanityfair.com /hollywood/2016/11/aaron-sorkin-donald-trump-president-letter-daughter.

Steinberg, Jacques. 2006. "'West Wing' Writers' Novel Way of Picking the President." *New York Times*, Apr. 10. At http://www.nytimes.com/2006/04/10/arts /television/10wing.html?_r=0.

Stolworthy, Jacob. 2017. "Donald Trump Presidency Sparks Rise in *The West Wing* Viewership." *The Independent*, Feb. 16. At http://www.independent.co.uk/arts -entertainment/tv/news/donald-trump-the-west-wing-where-to-watch-aaron -sorkin-a7583516.html.

68

Will & Grace

"The Finale"

BRETT MILLS

The final episode of *Will & Grace* (1998–2006) aired on NBC on May 18, 2006.[1] Simply titled "The Finale," it strove to depict happy endings for its four main characters and did so by extending its narrative far into the future. We saw the four main characters—the eponymous Will and Grace plus their friends Jack and Karen (played by Eric McCormack, Debra Messing, Sean Hayes, and Megan Mullally)—up to twenty years on from the hitherto contemporaneous setting of the program, as the narrative explores the ways in which friendships wax and wane over time. In particular, it depicts the previously rock-solid and almost claustrophobic friendship of Will and Grace as vulnerable to the changing circumstances wrought by finding partners and having children. That achieving this narrative conclusion requires a dream sequence, a musical interlude, and multiple time jumps demonstrates the problems long-running episodic series encounter when trying to reach satisfying narrative conclusions. After all, given that the production logic of much television is one determined to delay endings as much as possible in order to produce more and more episodes, such series have a built-in anathema to endings. That a program is ending has to be announced—hence, the titling of the episode "The Finale."

The difficulties the series encountered in finding narrative conclusions for its characters are a result of the particularities of what made the program a success in the first place. After all, *Will & Grace* is a significant piece of popular culture because of its status as a successful program in which leading characters are homosexual. In the series, Will and Grace share a flat and

1. All references to "The Finale" come from *Will & Grace* 2011.

439

have been friends since meeting at college. Will is gay, and Grace is straight. Will is a successful lawyer, and Grace runs her own interior design company. Flashbacks show that when they first met, Grace was attracted to Will, but this frisson of romance is predominantly absent for much of the series. Instead, the program is interested primarily in how friendship functions over time and how such bonds respond to and are affected by changing personal circumstances. In doing so, it aligns itself with series such as *Friends* (NBC, 1994–2004) that similarly mine twentysomethings' altering circumstances as they progress through adulthood. As such, throughout its run *Will & Grace* depicts its eponymous characters engaging in a wide range of romantic relationships with varying degrees of success, but their friendship a constant that can be returned to when such relationships fail. This means that the program's dynamic is dependent on the characters not finding true happiness outside of their friendship. Such relationships are merely narrative points that enable the friendship upon which the program rests to be tested and reasserted. In that sense, the series functions as an ongoing critique of traditional, monogamous, lifelong pairings (whether heterosexual, homosexual, or something else) and posits friendship as the true constant that enables security and happiness.

This is evident in the program's two other main characters, Jack and Karen. Jack is Will's friend from school and helped Will accept his sexuality; Jack, too, is gay. Karen is ostensibly Grace's assistant at her interior design company, but this work is merely a distraction from her wealthy, socialite lifestyle and extensive consumption of alcohol and pills. Like Will and Grace, Jack engages in many romantic liaisons throughout the series but never finds a lifelong soulmate. Although Karen is married to Stan, she is shown to engage in sexual activity with a wide range of partners, and her sexuality is consistently fluid and "cannot be contained within a heterosexual framework or a normalized gay discourse" (Mitchell 2006, 90). Karen and Jack form a close friendship, often uniting in their mockery of the program's eponymous characters. But the friendships of all four are the key relationships within the program, with notions of settling down merely passing events seeming to trouble the more important aspects of kinship. Where the program does depict marriage—that of Karen's to Stan—it does so in an ambiguous manner. Karen consistently refers to her love of her husband while at the same time acknowledging the sexual activities she must undertake in order to maintain access to his fortune. Where the series does depict a traditional relationship, then, it does so in a manner that foregrounds its contractual aspects and therefore positions marriage as more of a chore rather than a supportive, nurturing, fun friendship. As such, it is "the question of marriage . . . that fuels the primary anxiety or problem that this show attempts to negotiate" (Quimby 2005, 713).

More important than this, though, is *Will & Grace*'s position as a successful, long-running series on a major network that features homosexual characters in recurring lead roles. Its groundbreaking nature and the influence it had can be attested to by two things: it was the first program on American television with a gay male lead; three years later, more than twenty series had recurring gay or lesbian characters (Battles and Hilton-Morrow 2002, 87). *Will & Grace* debuted in 1998, a year after the lead character in the sitcom *Ellen* (ABC, 1994–98) came out in an episode that was groundbreaking and highly controversial. Yet although the "general positive response to the coming-out episodes [in *Ellen*] . . . seemed to indicate that previously censored forms of sexuality were gliding rather easily out of the closet and into prime-time" (Dow 2001, 124), *Ellen* was canceled within a year. Its difficulty in maintaining itself can be attributed to its focus on the narrative of coming out; once this goal was achieved, there was narratively little for the main character to do. For Will and Jack in *Will & Grace*, however, coming out is an event that occurred in their lives prior to the program's main narratives, and thus they are not defined primarily by this significant moment. Furthermore, whereas sitcoms featuring underrepresented identities such as homosexuality commonly show them as "fish out of water" in a heteronormative world, *Will & Grace* instead normalizes a "gay world" within which heterosexuality is marked as aberrant (Cooper 2003, 517). It is thus straight characters who are depicted as "fish out of water" required to justify and explain their "deviant" behavior in a homosexual world. *Will & Grace* can, then, be placed in a lineage of sitcoms such as *All in the Family* (CBS, 1971–79) and *Maude* (CBS, 1972–78) that "validated strategies of non-normative interpretation that are a hallmark of subculture" (Castiglia and Reed 2004, 160).

But what effect might such representations have on the real world outside of television? Trying to ascertain whether popular-culture depictions in various media alter how audiences see the world is hard to do. Rather than seeing this process as straightforward cause and effect, it is instead more fruitful to place television within the realm of "parasocial interaction," "the phenomenon [in which] viewers form beliefs and attitudes about people they know only through television, regardless of whether such people are fictional characters or real people" (Schiappa, Gregg, and Hewes 2006, 20). Ascertaining whether this process takes place is hard enough, but deciding whether the depictions of a range of sexual identities on *Will & Grace* represent a progressive or realistic engagement with real-world politics remains moot. So although acknowledging that "in 2012, Vice President Joe Biden cited *Will & Grace* as a touchstone for his views on marriage equality" (Hayes 2013, 58) might point toward the series' progressive impact, it has also been argued that the program "broke as many barriers as it inadvertently reinforced" (Hayes 2013, 58). This reinforcement means it has been criticized for "the liberal façade created by its discourse of humor and apolitical rhetorical stance" (Mitchell 2005, 1052), whereby depictions of homosexuality are rendered acceptable for mainstream audiences simply because of their comic nature, and the program studiously avoids "representing same-sex physical intimacy and overtly political storylines" (Becker 2006, 172). Furthermore, "content analysis shows that *Will & Grace* reaffirms the close relationship between femininity and gay masculinity" (Linneman 2008, 599), which suggests that the characters function as stereotypes rather than as radical and progressive alternative forms of depiction.

These contradictions are brought to the fore in "The Finale," in which the characters' sexual fluidity and reliance on friendship come into conflict with the need of an ending. What kind of happy ending can be wrought from characters so studiously opposed to traditional notions of coupledom, when it is precisely the act of settling down that typically renders a denouement satisfying and irreversible? A program must give a logic as to *why* it is ending because it is premised on the long-running endlessness of seriality. In a flash-forward two decades on from the program's setting, Will's son and Grace's daughter accidentally meet one another when moving into their dorm rooms at college. Clearly attracted to one another, they go for a coffee. In a further flash-forward, it is revealed they are to marry. Earlier in the episode and years earlier in the story line, Will and Grace had drifted apart, in part because of an argument but also because of their difficulty in arranging times to meet in their busy schedules. It is thus their children's heterosexuality that brings them back into alignment with one another, reestablishing their friendship. But it is this heterosexuality that also offers the happy ending every series apparently needs. Although this plotline could be seen as the program reneging on the oppositional stance it has taken throughout its run, it is clear that the series actually has little interest in this heteronormative event. We are not shown the wedding, and the couple involved appear only in a single scene. Their narrative function is little more than as catalysts to the reestablishment of the friendships that have motivated the program's comic energy throughout.

In the episode's final scene, Will, Grace, Jack, and Karen meet in a bar twenty years in the future, the ravages of time showing on their faces (except for on Karen's, which has remained unchanged thanks to masses of plastic surgery). They share a drink, but as they toast, the scene suddenly shifts: they are in the same bar again, but now in the time setting of the series (the early 2000s) and its viewing audience, wrinkle free and smiling and laughing as an intimate group of friends, just as they have for the previous 193 episodes. The narrative that represents an end is elsewhere, at an off-screen wedding. Instead, the viewer is left with a reaffirmation of the importance of friendship and community over family, heterosexuality and marriage. The four are depicted as without baggage, responsibility, and goals, as they are in the very first episode. So, despite the multiple complex relationships they have been through, despite their children, despite their wealth of responsibilities, they remain defined by the friendships they maintained throughout the eight years the series broadcast. That a program can so blithely throw a wedding into its mix but then move on from it with little care for its significance reiterates the series' disinterest in those kinds of conventions that typically constitute a television finale. It is an episode that powerfully highlights the reactionary nature of television finales and the limited nature of the stories that can constitute them. As such, it feels more like an antifinale, straining at the heterosexual norms that constrain what counts as a happy ending. Given this, it is unsurprising that the episode has to be called "The Finale" in order to remind viewers of its intended purpose, but it is also unsurprising that the episode has such an unflamboyant, uninteresting, uninventive title as "The Finale," for its very ending critiques what it means to come to an end.[2]

References

Battles, Kathleen, and Wendy Hilton-Morrow. 2002. "Gay Characters in Conventional Spaces: *Will & Grace* and the Situation Comedy Genre." *Critical Studies in Media Communication* 19, no. 1: 87–105.

Becker, Ron. 2006. *Gay TV and Straight America*. New Brunswick, NJ: Rutgers Univ. Press.

2. *Editors' note*: As with *Roseanne*, the series further undermined this idea of finale and undid the finale itself when it returned in 2017, as it largely dismissed the previous ending as Karen's dream.

Castiglia, Christopher, and Christopher Reed. 2004. "'Ah, Yes, I Remember It Well': Memory and Queer Culture in *Will & Grace.*" *Cultural Critique* 56, no. 1: 158–88.

Cooper, Evan. 2003. "Decoding *Will & Grace*: Mass Audience Reception of a Popular Network Situation Comedy." *Sociological Perspectives* 46, no. 4: 513–33.

Dow, Bonnie J. 2001. "*Ellen*, Television, and the Politics of Gay and Lesbian Visibility." *Critical Studies in Media Communication* 18, no. 2: 123–40.

Hayes, Dade. 2013. "When Will Met Grace, It Changed Not Just Television but Society Too." *Broadcasting & Cable*, Sept. 30, 58.

Linneman, Thomas J. 2008. "How Do You Solve a Problem Like Will Truman? The Feminization of Masculinities on *Will & Grace.*" *Men and Masculinities* 10, no. 5: 583–603.

Mitchell, Danielle. 2005. "Producing Containment: The Rhetorical Construction of Difference in *Will & Grace.*" *Journal of Popular Culture* 38, no. 6: 1050–68.

———. 2006. "Straight and Crazy? Bisexual and Easy? Or Drunken Floozy? The Queer Politics of Karen Walker." In *The New Queer Aesthetic on Television*, edited by James R. Keller and Leslie Stratyner, 85–98. Jefferson, NC: McFarland.

Quimby, Karin. 2005. "*Will & Grace*: Negotiating (Gay) Marriage on Prime-Time Television." *Journal of Popular Culture* 38, no. 4: 713–31.

Schiappa, Edward, Peter B. Gregg, and Dean E. Hewes. 2006. "Can One TV Show Make a Difference? *Will & Grace* and the Parasocial Contact Hypothesis." *Journal of Homosexuality* 51, no. 4: 15–37.

Will & Grace: Series Finale. 2011. London: Universal Pictures UK. DVD.

69

The Wire

"-30-"

PAUL R. WRIGHT

David Simon and Ed Burns's much-lauded, oft-discussed, yet not always actually watched masterpiece *The Wire* (HBO, 2002–8) routinely makes the list of the television medium's greatest achievements—and often enough tops all such lists.[1] Masquerading as a police procedural tackling the war on drugs in Baltimore, the show evolved over five seasons to treat subjects ranging from the tortuous death of labor unions to the political rhetoric of reform and the political realities of urban electoral machinery, the school-to-prison pipeline, and the contemporary media's journalistic failure to document the decay of the American city. In becoming television's most sustained exploration of the modern American city-state, which was at the end of the day the show's one true protagonist, *The Wire* also emerged as the first American drama with a fully historiographical consciousness and, arguably, a corresponding class consciousness that is more symptomatically Howard Zinn than genetically Karl Marx.[2]

The patterning of American urban history as an imprint of systemic poverty and racism—its "rhyming"—is a major theme to help reassess *The Wire* as a series and its structurally daring finale, "-30-."[3] Since the airing of the series finale in 2008, countless critics, viewers, and interpreters have talked

---

1. In *TV (the Book)* (2016), for example, Alan Sepinwall and Matt Zoller Seitz rank *The Wire* as television's third-greatest show of all time: by "grant[ing] abundant humanity" to all its characters, "the world of *The Wire* is not a clichéd or stylized TV world. It strives to approximate this one" (38).

2. As Simon has made clear, "I'm not a Marxist. I am often mistaken for a Marxist" (Pearson and Andrews 2009).

3. All references to "-30-" come from Johnson [2008] 2011.

and written about it as a kind of object lesson in "history repeating itself"—a narrative example of one generation of compromised Baltimoreans replacing the other in the drug trade, the police force, city hall, and other dysfunctional institutions under raw capitalism. The idea that "nothing changes" is the driving theme behind these accounts of the finale, whose title, "-30-," is jargon for the end of a news story, borrowed from David Simon's former world, journalism, itself a major target of the final season of *The Wire*. The term is used in traditional print journalism as a typographic signal of story's end, but its roots go deeper into the use of the telegraph during the Civil War, when "-30-" signaled the end of a vital military transmission. To the extent that *The Wire* depicts an undeclared yet bloody civil war among petty bureaucracies and institutions that degrade rather than serve the poor, the finale title has fitting roots in our bloody and racially charged history.

This "nothing changes" account of the *Wire* finale has always troubled me, in part because it does not adequately capture the full achievement of the series and its coda. One might understandably be tempted to see this "nothing changes" interpretation manifest in a schematic discussion of the characters at series' end. We were told by fans and critics alike that Detective Jimmy McNulty (Dominic West) as maverick cop is replaced by Detective Leander Sydnor (Corey Parker Robinson), who is depicted in the finale courting the favor of the same hack judge and the same sort of disastrous outcome as McNulty in the first episode. We were told that the renegade drug dealer cum stick-up artist Omar (Michael Kenneth Williams) is replaced in turn by season 4 protagonist and high-school dropout Michael Lee (Tristan Mack Wilds); that recovering heroin addict Bubbles (Andre Royo) is supplanted by the new addict Dukie (Jermaine Crawford); that Cedric Daniels (Lance Reddick), the cop who at last refuses to sell his integrity to be commissioner, would be followed by his de facto protégé Ellis Carver (Seth Gilliam); that corrupt former commissioner Burrell (Frankie Faison) would be succeeded by the equally corrupt Stan Valchek (Al Brown); that Machiavellian mayor Thomas Carcetti (Aidan Gillen) would become governor and be succeeded in Baltimore by the manipulative Nerese Campbell (Marlyne Barrett); that the old Barksdale and Stanfield drug cartels would be successors who would continue to buy from international drug wholesalers such as the elusive "Greek" (Bill Raymond); that Avon Barksdale's (Wood Harris) most heartless killer, Wee-Bey Price (Hassan Johnson), would be joined in prison for life by Chris Partlow (Gbenga Akinnagbe), who plays the same role with respect to Marlo Stanfield (Jamie Hector). And in Marlo himself there seems at series' end to be held in suspension two conflicting impulses and two possible fates—one to be the successor to Stringer Bell (Idris Elba) as drug dealer turned real-estate entrepreneur, the other to be the next Avon as king of the violent Baltimore streets. These are just a few examples of generational turnover in the series finale and in the arc of the show as a whole.

Many of these developments are signaled visually and musically in the concluding montage that is the hallmark of the final episode of each season of *The Wire*. The closing song of the series that accompanies images of a dying Baltimore is the one with which the show began—the Blind Boys of Alabama covering Tom Waits's original tune "Way Down in the Hole." That song also accompanies the show's inventive, evolving, and now much studied credit sequences.[4] The credit sequences, different for each season and scored with a different artist's version of the Waits song,[5] reflect and expound on each season's thematic agenda. The images that bombard us in the credit and series finale sequences include not only the miseries of the drug trade and the violent consequences of the misguided war on it but also images of anxiety and rebellion in an age of surveillance.[6] Waits's song is a wilfully discordant, tortured modern gospel tune in the voice of a soul hostage to his own depravity. The song, a hymn self-consciously out of sync with itself, not only evokes the addictions and personal demons of the various characters on all sides of "the game" but also shows more broadly our vulnerability in the face of what Simon calls our postmodern gods—namely, our institutions (Talbot 2007). The "song" in *The Wire* does indeed seem to stay the same, and it has all the agony and prophetic power of the "sorrow songs" studied so poetically by W. E. B. Du Bois in *The Souls of Black Folk* ([1903] 1999).

Certainly, I will not deny that in fundamental ways the finale does indeed ask careful viewers to see continuities in Baltimore's and America's history

4. See, for example, Andrew Dignan, Kevin Lee, and Matt Zoller Seitz's (2008) video essays on the credit sequences, a masterclass in the critical assessment of such sequences in the current wave of "golden age" dramas.

5. The song is performed in season 1 by the Blind Boys of Alabama; in season 2 by Tom Waits; in season 3 by the Neville Brothers; in season 4 by Domaje; and in season 5 by Steve Earle.

6. That the show first aired in the year after the attacks on September 11, 2001, and the USA PATRIOT Act gives the credit sequence a special resonance—this connection is captured in the iconic video camera that is smashed by apprentice drug dealers toward the end of each season's credit sequence.

of systemic decay in the face of institutional racism, class discrimination, and unfettered capitalism. And yet these simple narrative equivalences risk becoming a reductive and needlessly cynical take on *The Wire*—which is ultimately much less a bleak exercise in "urban naturalism" than it is often assumed to be.

In his DVD commentary on the series finale, Simon stressed that he never intended the series or finale to be read so schematically as one character merely being transposed into another with respect to moral outcome, social position, or structural role under a broken social contract (Simon 2011). Simon instead suggested that to view the characters and stories of *The Wire* as trapped in a kind of purgatorial nightmare is to potentially dehumanize them precisely as a Hobbesian market economy does already. If anything, the finale is asking something else and something higher of its viewers. It is not only asking us to see the resemblances and to hear the echoes from one generation of institutional oppression to the next but also calling on us to respect the humanity of the individuals who live out that tortured history as well as their potential to be other than mere objects of a malevolent system.

It is in this sense that the finale is more about history rhyming than repeating—and therefore is not some humorless and numbing exercise in showing the horrors of the modern city-state as a kind of ghetto tourism or poverty porn. Alternatively, *The Wire* is to be understood more provocatively and progressively as a brutally honest depiction of repetitions of injustice that we have collectively foisted upon ourselves and, in turn, *given the veneer of inevitability*. It is precisely inevitability that *The Wire* is so passionately contesting.

By seeing and hearing the rhymes of *The Wire* over the course of a five-season narrative arc, we are reminded that the show is a visual poem of the city-state of Baltimore, while remaining resonant with any other community in crisis in our country and beyond. Simon's avowed understanding of *The Wire* in the context of Greek tragedy reminds us that, for the Athenians who watched the plays of Sophocles or heard the epics of Homer, the dramatic settings of cities such as Thebes, Corinth, and Troy could always be made to rhyme with the setting of Athens. *The Wire*'s rhyming of characters, injustices, and institutions really argues that we need to keep staging the plays that speak truth to power, even at the price of heartbreak—that we need to keep singing the songs that matter, especially in times when people increasingly seem to be, in Simon's words, "worth less and less" (Pearson and Andrews 2009).

So if *The Wire* is the postmodern *Iliad* of Baltimore, the "rhymes" of the final "verses" frame the series as an unfinished narrative poem that does not merely draw on the fatalism of ancient Greece but also makes a muckraking, politically agitating, and progressive call to arms in the tradition of Upton Sinclair and others. The rhyming narrative of *The Wire* is, in fact, a formal exercise in denying the false closure of all finales and "final words" on things that matter. If Simon set out to subvert the genre of the classic police procedural—where "closing the book" on a case is always the goal—then he did so in part by refusing to give us the kind of finale we are conditioned as viewers to think we want. In this light, *The Wire*'s last episode is just as much an "antifinale" finale as David Chase's smash cut to black in the last episode of *The Sopranos* (1999–2007). Perhaps the key difference here is that Chase's beautifully orchestrated finale reflects *The Sopranos*' modernist, art-house existentialism at its finest, whereas Simon's approach is decidedly more classical in inspiration and execution.

I am reminded of a statement loosely yet not definitively attributed to Mark Twain: "History doesn't repeat; *at best*, it *sometimes* rhymes" (my emphasis). Twain himself was fascinated by history's echoes and its half-heard rhymes in the past. As David Rosenberg and Tony Grafton explore so brilliantly in *Cartographies of Time* (2012), for Twain "the minor events of history are valuable, although not always showy and picturesque" (199). In his preface to one edition of *Paradise Lost*, John Milton famously defended his choice in that iconic epic *not* to rhyme, referring to "the troublesome and modern bondage of rhyming" ([1667] 2012, 2). For Milton, rhyming was poetically lazy and directly reflective of the continued bondage of the English people to the idea of monarchy after the Restoration. Yet his embrace of blank verse was still, in essence, an embrace of a form that rejected the sing-song formula of literal rhyming but retained the capacity to link lines and thoughts to one another, to see patterns of life and language where they might be found. A slightly more cynical take on rhyming can be found in *The Mating Mind* (2001), where evolutionary psychologist Geoffrey Miller posits that poetry is a system of rules and constraints that are adopted "as a display of verbal intelligence and creativity" (379) and, thereby, as a marker of implicit evolutionary desirability and fitness. For Miller, rhymes are first and foremost showy and attention-seeking mating rituals.

Ultimately, however, I think David Simon's project strives to transcend Twain, Milton, and Miller's conceptions of rhyming. At its best, *The Wire* never comes off as narratively showy for its own sake, although the viewers of its original broadcast at times bordered on self-congratulatory for watching it; certainly, there was a reason *The Wire* ended up in the now infamous weblog *Stuff White People Like* (n.d.). At heart, though, *The Wire* is less about narrative pride than about sociological and political urgency. It is in this antiauthoritarian spirit that David Simon constructed the historio-graphical and narrative rhymes of *The Wire*, which are never literal equiva-lences but haunting echoes from the poetry of ever-meaner streets. These are rhymes that even Milton might appreciate, for they have the power of epic and the sorrow of tragedy.

What distinguishes *The Wire* is how it obstinately refuses to provide us with any overarching explanation for the decay it chronicles—as Simon puts it, *The Wire* "is a drama that offers multiple meanings and arguments" (2000). Although there are swipes at George W. Bush's Iraq War and other policies, the show hardly sees in Bush or our collective moment the origin of social ills that clearly go much deeper into our shared past. *The Wire* depicts many characters that we hold accountable for their destructive choices, but it never suggests there is any one moral fulcrum on which the crisis of the city-state can be leveraged. Criminalized addiction, the crude politicization of urban decline and racism, and the systemic war on the underclass are clearly complex stories; yet so too is every character on *The Wire*, to the point where our sympathies inevitably turn to the community itself as an organism in crisis. Although the show at times embraces a strange sort of urban natural-ism, it also attempts to enter the hearts and heads of all those it chronicles. Simon and his collaborators treat the culture, language, and way of life of the show's communities and institutions neither as crude propagandists nor as neutral anthropologists. Perhaps a helpful analogy is to think about how *The Wire* evokes Howard Zinn's *A People's History of the United States* ([1980] 2015); it might be illuminating to think of *The Wire* as a "people's history of the war on drugs."

The Wire also has historiographical roots in broader patterns of meaning making. The pioneering work of sociologist Eviatar Zerubavel on "collective memory and the social shape of the past" in his book *Time Maps* (2004) is especially instructive here. Zerubavel gives us a theoretical framework for understanding the "socio*mental* topography" of our shared, communal cognition of the past (1). In exploring "mnemonic communities" over the centuries in various social and geographical contexts, Zerubavel pointedly reminds us that "far from being a strictly spontaneous act, remembering is also governed by unmistakably social *norms of remembrance* that tell us what we should remember and what we should essentially forget" (5).

It is in this light that *The Wire* is a polemical effort to contest and transform those norms of remembrance and forgetting as they relate to the urban underclass of America. In particular, the finale shows us the tragic rhymes of a dying Baltimore but precisely does not leave us hostage to what Zerubavel calls "mnemonic typification" or "recurrence narratives." The finale is not some cyclical, sociopolitical *Groundhog Day* (Harold Ramis, 1993); rather, the show is asking us not to be satisfied or jaded by that trope. If anything, it denies the aura of inevitability surrounding predatory capitalism by exposing the social construction of that mythology in our own collective choices—the first and most egregious of which is blindness. It is no accident that in the series finale the newly clean and sober Bubbles is one of the few figures of hope in the series, captured in that simple yet beautiful image of him climbing the stairs from exile in his sister's basement to sit with her at her dinner table. In considering whether to let a newspaper reporter talk about his long road and his many pains, Bubbles reads a line from Kafka that serves as the epigraph to Simon and Burns's landmark book *The Corner* (1998): "You can hold yourself back from the sufferings of the world, that is something you are free to do and it accords with your nature, but perhaps this very holding back is the one suffering you could avoid." This "holding back" is the self-inflicted blindness of the tragic Oedipus figure that is the contemporary state and its citizenry.

To conclude, I would like to invoke one last voice in my own rhyming exercise: Michel de Certeau. *The Wire*'s intricately crafted portrait of a city-state in freefall calls us to bear witness to subject-citizens tracking what de Certeau calls in *The Practice of Everyday Life* (1988) "the thicks and thins of an urban 'text' they write without being able to read" (93). The complex and overdetermined social spaces traced by *The Wire*'s Baltimoreans—rebounding on one another like so many unknowing billiard balls—make of them "unrecognized poems in which each body is an element signed by many others" (de Certeau 1988, 93). Above all, what *The Wire* critiques are those practices of "blindness" by which we fail to see our profound interconnectedness at every level. As de Certeau reminds us, even "objects and words . . . have hollow places in which a past sleeps, as in the everyday acts of walking, eating, going to bed—in which ancient revolutions slumber" (1988, 108). This revolutionary potential in the everyday (and in the *documenting* of the everyday) is *The Wire*'s rejoinder to the modern city under late capitalism as a space of disproportional surveillance and power. Reluctant subjects of what Roland Barthes (1983) in a different context dubbed an "empire of signs," we nonetheless remain able and duty bound to contest that empire on the ground—and, first of all, in our imaginations.[7]

References

Barthes, Roland. 1983. *Empire of Signs*. Translated by Richard Howard. New York: Hill & Wang.

De Certeau, Michel. 1988. *The Practice of Everyday Life*. Translated by Steven Rendall. Berkeley: Univ. of California Press.

Dignan, Andrew, Kevin B. Lee, and Matt Zoller Seitz. 2008. "Extra Credit [Parts 1–5]: *The Wire*—a Close Analysis of the [Seasons 1–5 Title Sequences]." "Moving Image Source," Museum of the Moving Image. At http://www.moving imagesource.us/articles/extra-credit-part-1-20080728.

Du Bois, W. E. B. [1903] 1999. *The Souls of Black Folk*. New York: Norton.

Johnson, Clark, dir. [2008] 2011. "-30-." *The Wire*, season 5, episode 10. Aired Mar. 9, 2008, HBO. Written by David Simon and Ed Burns. On *The Wire: The Complete Series*. Los Angeles: HBO Studios. DVD.

Miller, Geoffrey. 2001. *The Mating Mind: How Sexual Choice Shaped the Evolution of Human Nature*. New York: Anchor.

Milton, John. [1667] 2012. *Paradise Lost*. 3rd ed. Edited by Gordon Teskey. New York: Norton.

Pearson, Jesse, and Philip Andrews. 2009. "Interview with David Simon." *Vice*, Dec. 1. At http://www.vice.com/read/david-simon-280-v16n12.

Rosenberg, Daniel, and Anthony Grafton. 2012. *Cartographies of Time: A History of the Timeline*. Princeton, NJ: Princeton Univ. Press.

Sepinwall, Alan, and Matt Zoller Seitz. 2016. *TV (the Book): Two Experts Pick the Greatest American Shows of All Time*. New York: Grand Central Publishing.

Simon, David. 2000. "*The Wire*: A Dramatic Series for HBO." Sept. 6. At http://kottke.org.s3.amazonaws.com/the-wire/The_Wire_-_Bible.pdf.

———. 2011. "Commentary on '-30-.'" On *The Wire: The Complete Series*. Los Angeles: HBO Studios. DVD.

Simon, David, and Ed Burns. 1998. *The Corner: A Year in the Life of an Inner-City Neighborhood*. New York: Broadway Books.

Stuff White People Like. n.d. At https://stuffwhitepeoplelike.com. Accessed Aug. 1, 2016.

7. I would be remiss if I did not emphasize the intellectual, professional, and personal debt I owe to the late David Lavery, a model of television scholarship for a generation. He was the first to encourage me to publish seriously about television, and he is sorely missed by many contributing to this volume.

Talbot, Margaret. 2007. "Stealing Life: The Crusader behind *The Wire*." *New Yorker*, Oct. 22. At http://www.newyorker.com/magazine/2007/10/22/stealing -life.

Zerubavel, Eviatar. 2004. *Time Maps: Collective Memory and the Social Shape of the Past*. Chicago: Univ. of Chicago Press.

Zinn, Howard. [1980] 2015. *A People's History of the United States*. Reissue ed. New York: Harper.

70

Xena: Warrior Princess

AMANDA POTTER

On June 8, 2001, Xena the Warrior Princess died on US television. This female hero with a dark past had spent six seasons traveling the ancient world fighting on the side of good with her female friend and sidekick Gabrielle. After all her adventures, she knowingly walked into a battle she knew she could not win and was killed brutally. After burying her armor before the battle, in order to set aside her old life for the last time, in this way echoing her actions in the first episode of the series, "Sins of the Past," Xena taught Gabrielle "the pinch"—a technique to stop a victim's blood from flowing to the brain, which, if not reversed, will cause death. Xena withheld this knowledge from Gabrielle throughout the series, and so teaching it to her at this moment signified that Xena now believed Gabrielle was ready to take over for her. Xena then walked into battle alone, was bombarded with arrows, then attacked by Samurai swordsmen, and finally decapitated. All this happened in the first five minutes of the series finale, "A Friend in Need II."[1] Thus began the controversial ending to a groundbreaking show. Viewers' reception of this final episode was varied and, for many, deeply emotional.

Xena: Warrior Princess (1995–2001) began as a spin-off from *Hercules: The Legendary Journeys* (1995–99),[2] an action series set in ancient Greece and featuring a male hero, Hercules, and his male sidekick, Iolaus. The character of Xena, played by New Zealand actress Lucy Lawless, is introduced in the first season of *Hercules* as a "femme fatale" and evil warlord who wants to kill Hercules, and, in the original story line for the three-episode

1. All references to *Xena* episodes, including the finale, come from *Xena: Warrior Princess* 2001–2.

2. All references to episodes in *Hercules* come from *Hercules: The Legendary Journeys* 2003.

story arc Xena is to become a good character but then die in battle at the end of "Unchained Heart" (Weisbrot 1998, 12). Because Xena proved popular with viewers, however, she gained a six-year reprieve in her own series. "Unchained Heart" ends with Xena telling Hercules, "There's so much in my life I have to make amends for. I've got to get started." This is where *Xena: Warrior Princess* begins, with Xena's quest for redemption. The first episode of the series, "Sins of the Past," starts with Xena burying her armor, symbolically putting aside her past as an evil warlord, but she later retrieves it in order to use it to fight on the side of good after meeting would-be bard Gabrielle (Renee O'Connor), who will become her sidekick. Xena and Gabrielle then set out on their adventures, championing the deserving and privileging the needs of family and friends over desire for power, wealth, and glory. Together they travel across the ancient world from Greece to Rome, Egypt, Great Britain, China, India, and Scandinavia, finally ending up in Japan (known in the series as "Jappa").

From the beginning, *Xena* was different from *Hercules* and other contemporary series of the 1990s because its protagonist is a female action hero. The series was first broadcast in 1995, more than a year before *Buffy the Vampire Slayer* (1997–2003) hit the small screen, and, at the time, *Xena* was the only popular adventure, action, fantasy, or science fiction show being broadcast that featured female leads without male counterparts.[3] As well as being female, Xena is not a traditional hero like Hercules: she had previously been, according to series cocreator R. J. Stewart, "a monster" (quoted in Hayes 2003, 10), and she spends the series attempting to atone for her dark past. Xena's sidekick, Gabrielle, is also repeatedly referred to in the series as her "soul mate," and the series became famous for its lesbian subtext. Although series creators continued to keep fans guessing as to the exact nature of the relationship between the protagonists, many later episodes play on the subtext, and "A Friend in Need, Part II" (6.22) includes a long kiss between Gabrielle and the ghost of Xena. In the 1990s, the character of Xena was attractive to both male and female viewers of differing ages and sexual orientations. However, her costume—short-skirted leather armor and metal breastplate, leaving Lucy Lawless's long legs exposed—was problematic for some feminist critics, who applauded the existence of the female action hero

---

3. Principal female characters did exist in series before *Xena*, but they were partnered with a male character, as in *The X-Files* (1993–2002), or were part of an ensemble cast, as in the *Star Trek* series *Deep Space Nine* (1993–99). For a discussion of early action heroines on television, see Inness 1998, 31–49.

but questioned whether she could be both feminist icon and sex symbol at the same time (see, for example, Kastor 1996 and Minkowitz 1996).

Although in the story proper Xena was born and raised in the Greek village of Amphipolis, her origins as a character are in the East. Series co-creator Rob Tapert was influenced by Hong Kong cinema, in particular the title character of the film *The Bride with White Hair* (Ronny Yu, 1993), when conceiving his character (Weisbrot 1998, 5–6). The *Hercules* episode "The Gauntlet" (1.12) features a sequence taken from this earlier film, in which Xena is forced to walk through a "gauntlet" of soldiers wielding arms. In *Xena: Warrior Princess*, an important incident in Xena's past in the ancient East is shown in flashback in "The Debt II" (3.7). Following her crucifixion by Caesar, the warlord Xena traveled to China (known as "Chin"), where she met Lao Ma, wife of the Chinese emperor, who taught Xena that she should "live for others" and "serve others," not just herself. Although Xena does not adopt these values until later in her life, her final act of self-sacrifice in "A Friend in Need, Part II" is the ultimate act of serving others, and this act takes place in the East, Japan.

In "A Friend in Need, Part I," Xena is recruited by a monk to help the ghost of Akemi, a Japanese princess who had been Xena's friend when Xena was an evil warlord. Akemi's ghost has been imprisoned by the demon Yodoshi, the soul eater, and forced to lure people to their deaths so that Yodoshi can take their souls. In life, Yodoshi had been Akemi's evil father, whom Akemi had killed before killing herself, an act that "broke [Xena's] heart." Xena must be dead in order to defeat Yodoshi, but she can be brought back to life by having her ashes sprinkled in the Fountain of Strength on Mount Fuji. In "A Friend in Need, Part II," Gabrielle attempts to save Xena by retrieving and burning her body and taking her ashes to Mount Fuji. However, after defeating Yodoshi, Xena must remain dead so that the souls of those Yodoshi has taken can achieve a state of grace, including the souls of forty thousand villagers who died in a fire caused by Xena in the past, when she was grieving for Akemi. Xena chooses to stay dead, and so Akemi's ghost tells her, "You've redeemed me. You've redeemed them. You've redeemed yourself." Xena's six-season journey toward redemption is over. The episode and series end with Gabrielle, now a traveling warrior, sailing off on new adventures, Xena's spirit watching over her.

By 2001, much had happened to Xena, and so she had become a different character from the Xena who first appeared in *Hercules* in 1995, primarily because she atoned for her past crimes with her many heroic acts in life. Some viewers and critics therefore considered her redemptive death unnecessary and even as undermining what had gone before. In her reaction to the episode, one of the 2,290 fans who responded to an online poll on the series finale was incredulous: "For six years, Xena has tried to amend her dark past, and this was her final reward?" ("Disappointed" 2001). Critic Sara Crosby found Xena to be one of a sequence of action heroines "snapped into sacrificial victims" on our television screens, along with Max in *Dark Angel* (2000–2002) and Buffy (2004, 169). A *Xena* fan echoed this sentiment in her short and shouty comment that the series ending "SEEMS LIKE ANOTHER CLASSIC/SEXIST CASE OF A STRONG INDEPENDENT WOMAN BEING SLAPPED DOWN" ("Group Therapy" 2001). US historian Kathleen Kennedy also found the ending less than satisfying because until this final episode, the boundary-crossing series had not conformed to any one ideology. Xena had rejected both the violence of Rome and the pacifism of the cult of love, yet in the series finale she, as martyr, adopts "Roman/Christian messianic paradigms" even though her act of redemption takes place in the East (2007, 327).

Following an advance screening of the series finale, Rob Tapert and R. J. Stewart, who held joint credits for writing the episode, responded to fans' questions about "A Friend in Need, Part II," arguing that Xena could redeem herself only through self-sacrifice. Tapert explained that Xena was a "war criminal" and that her "redemption was withheld" throughout the series until "A Friend in Need" (Fitz 2001). To Tapert, Xena's death was inevitable from the beginning. Stewart added that "the ultimate redemption for Xena here is not to be brought back to life," so she must not only die but also remain dead (Baermer 2001). I hoped throughout the series finale that Gabrielle would succeed in bringing Xena back to life, but, despite Gabrielle's race against time to achieve this, this hope was dashed in the final minutes, an outcome that felt somewhat unfair—to Gabrielle, to Xena, to me, to other viewers.

The need for Xena to die did resonate with some fans; for example, according to one fan, "the season ended the only way that it could—with Xena paying the ultimate price for her past sins" ("Group Therapy" 2001). Many other fans instead hoped for a "sunset scene" in which Xena and Gabrielle would end the series together (Clark 2001). "A Friend in Need, Part II" does set up expectations that a happy ending could be achieved by having Xena return from the grave, particularly because she is killed so early in the final episode and Gabrielle finds a potential solution to bring her back to life. However, a "sunset" ending had already been played out in the series finale of *Hercules: The Legendary Journeys*, "Full Circle," in which Hercules and

Iolaus walk off together along the beach into the sunset, as well as in the *Xena* comic episode immediately preceding the finale, "Deja Vu All Over Again," in which the reincarnations of Xena and Gabrielle drive off into the sunset together. Large numbers of fans, whether they loved or hated the ending, wanted to write about their experiences in watching it, so the editor of *Whoosh*, fansite and "birthplace of the International Association of *Xena* Studies," Kym Taborn, received 373 article submissions for a special "Group Therapy" issue responding to the series finale, as opposed to the usual "5–10 submissions per month" (Taborn 2001). "A Friend in Need, Part II" stands out as a powerful and thought-provoking, if not always popular, ending to *Xena: Warrior Princess*, and it gave many fans the opportunity to reevaluate what the series meant to them. And the season finale has proved not to be the end of Xena after all. Plans for a new series of *Xena* were announced in 2016 with the promise of a main-text lesbian relationship between Xena and Gabrielle (see Frizzell 2016). This project subsequently stalled. However, in 2018 a new *Xena: Warrior Princess* comic series is being published by Dynamite. This series, written by Meredith Finch (2018), starts with Xena and Gabrielle meeting for the first time and offers the opportunity for Xena's heroic journey to begin all over again. So Xena does not have to stay dead after all.

References

Baermer [*sic*]. 2001. "A Report from the Museum of Radio and Television." *Whoosh*, June 19. At http://www.whoosh.org/road/mtr2001.

Clark, L. A. 2001. "Adventures in the Stunned Trade: Comments on the Final Episode of *Xena: Warrior Princess*." *Whoosh* 59 (Aug.). At http://www.whoosh.org/issue59/clark59.html.

Crosby, Sara. 2004. "The Cruellest Season: Female Heroes Snapped into Sacrificial Heroines." In *Action Chicks: New Images of Tough Women in Popular Culture*, edited by Sherrie A. Inness, 153–78. New York: Palgrave Macmillan.

"Disappointed" (fan comment). 2001. *Whoosh* 59 (Aug.). At http://www.whoosh.org/issue59/letter59h.html#disappointed302_352.

Finch, Meredith. 2018. *Xena: Warrior Princess*. Vol. 4, no. 1. Mt. Laurel, NJ: Dynamite.

Fitz, Paddy. 2001. "Slumming (and Slimming) in Beverley Hills." *Whoosh*, June 19. At http://www.whoosh.org/road/mtr2001/fitz.html.

Frizzell, Nell. 2016. "Xena: Lesbian Warrior Princess—Have the Rules of TV Just Been Rewritten?" *Guardian*, Mar. 15. At https://www.theguardian.com/tv-and

-radio/tvandradioblog/2016/mar/15/xena-lesbian-warrior-princess-have-the
-rules-of-tv-just-been-rewritten.

"Group Therapy." 2001. *Whoosh* 59 (Aug.). At http://www.whoosh.org/issue59
/letter59h.html#group130_150.

Hayes, K. Stoddard. 2003. *"Xena: Warrior Princess": The Complete Illustrated
Companion*. London: Titan.

Hercules: The Legendary Journeys. 2003. Troy, MI: Anchor Bay. DVD.

Inness, Sherrie A. 1998. *Tough Girls: Women Warriors and Wonder Women in
Popular Culture*. Philadelphia: Univ. of Pennsylvania Press.

Kastor, Elizabeth. 1996. "Woman of Steel: Television's Warrior Xena is a Superhero-
ine with Broad Appeal." *Washington Post*, Sept. 21. At https://www.washington
post.com/archive/lifestyle/1996/09/21/woman-of-steel/6f6c61e0-c13c-4eed-89
8e-4e36102edcc4/.

Kennedy, Kathleen. 2007. "Xena on the Cross." *Feminist Media Studies* 7, no. 3:
313–32.

Minkowitz, Donna. 1996. "Xena: She's Big, Tall, Strong—and Popular." *Ms.* 7, no.
1: 74–77.

Taborn, Kym Masera. 2001. "The Mojo That Once Was and Poll Results." *Whoosh*
59 (Aug.). At http://www.whoosh.org/issue59/editor59.html.

Weisbrot, Robert. 1998. *"Xena: Warrior Princess": The Official Guide to the
Xenaverse*. New York: Doubleday.

Xena: Warrior Princess. 2001–2. London: Universal Playback. DVD.

71

The X-Files

"The Truth"

LORNA JOWETT

The finale of *The X-Files* (1993–2002) is often included in lists of the worst series finales ever, with many seeing the finale of the penultimate season, the eighth, as the "real" ending of the series. The series has since been continued with a film (*The X-Files: I Want to Believe* [Chris Carter, 2008]), a six-episode season 10 in 2016 and a ten-episode season 11 in 2018, so the status of "The Truth" (episodes 9.19 and 9.20) as the series finale is retroactively in question.[1] Series creator and writer of the season 9 finale, Chris Carter, stated that he wanted "to be able to wrap things up for the fans who have been there from the beginning . . . [and] to go out with a series of very, very strong episodes that are going to pull a lot of threads together from the last nine years" (quoted in Brown 2013, 7), and its director, Kim Manners, comments in *The Complete Collector's Edition* DVD set that the final scene of "The Truth" is a perfect ending given that *The X-Files* "was really a series about frustration" (Manners 2007).

As noted, the finale was written by Carter, who is credited with writing sixty-five episodes of *The X-Files* (as well as with cowriting the film and writing and directing several episodes in 2016 and 2018), and directed by veteran Kim Manners (who is credited with directing fifty-one episodes of the series—a gravestone with Manners's name on it appears as a tribute in the third episode in 2016)—and it might therefore have been seen to be in safe hands. Carter, as Stacey Abbott and Simon Brown point out, "had never produced a television show before" (2013, 2), yet *The X-Files* signaled

---

1. All references to episodes of *The X-Files*, including "The Truth," come from *The X-Files: The Complete Collector's Edition* 2007.

changes in the television landscape in the 1990s, and it drew on significant predecessors as well as influencing subsequent series. Its usefulness as a case study for examining the expansion of US television markets at the time—including the rise of the Fox network and its move into one-hour drama (see Johnson 2005) as well as the trend in series designed as cult or "quality," aimed at niche audiences and encouraging greater viewer engagement—has made *The X-Files* the subject of several academic studies. Catherine Johnson argues that "the representation of the fantastic in *The X-Files* offered the possibility for the visual flourishes and stylistic distinctiveness which were particularly valuable for Fox as markers of difference and indicators of quality" (2005, 101) at a time when many critics and viewers considered Fox "scattershot and lowbrow" (Soter 2002, 115).

The series undoubtedly made Carter's name, and others who worked on it have since been involved with major or critically acclaimed television series in the same vein as *The X-Files*, including James Wong (*American Horror Story* [2011–]), Howard Gordon (*Homeland* [2011–]), John Shiban (*Supernatural* [2005–]), Michelle MacLaren (*The Walking Dead* [2010–]), and Vince Gilligan (*Breaking Bad* [2008–13]). Likewise, lead actors Gillian Anderson and David Duchovny may be familiar now, but at the time the series debuted, neither was well known. As with the crew, many *X-Files* actors have gone on to feature in other "cult" or "quality" television series, their appearances often capitalizing on what Jeffrey Bussolini calls the "intertextuality of casting" (2013).

As Johnson observes, *The X-Files* is important to fan studies, too: "*The X-Files* was actively produced by Fox as a cult series designed to attract the fan–consumer taste market" (2005, 100), and fans of the series became known as "X-Philes." The series drew attention for its fandom as it was airing in the 1990s, and Bertha Chin highlights that "X-Philes are often considered to be among the first group of fans" to establish a virtual fan community by early adoption of the Internet, actively "appropriating list-servs and forums to perform their fan identities" (2013, 87).

At the time the series was broadcast, it tapped into the cultural climate of the late twentieth century, drawing heavily on UFOlogy and conspiracy theory to the point that it made "alien abduction and colonisation an integral part of the cultural discourse of the 1990s" (Abbott and Brown 2013, 1). The series mixed fantasy (in particular horror and science fiction) with crime drama and employed a material realism to ground its fantastic elements in familiar, mundane settings. "In *The X-Files*," observes Jan Delasara, "immediacy and verisimilitude are achieved through the use of selective scenic detail and the foregrounding of realities that viewers recognize as emblematic of life in the 1990s, such as Mulder and Scully's omnipresent cell phones and computers" (2000, 19). Delasara also notes that despite *The X-Files*' generic hybridity, "it seldom seem[ed] to violate generic boundaries" but rather "stretch[ed] them," with several episodes exploiting "the close relationship between the grotesque and the humorous" (58). The story lines of individual episodes were frequently taken from news headlines, extrapolating current scientific research and technological development. Moreover, the series engaged with the evolution of feminism and postfeminism through the character of Dana Scully, whose influence is often cited in studies of gender representation on TV.

The X-Files also experimented with long-form structure, combining episodic narratives with season arcs and increasingly featuring bubble episodes to provide novelty within a familiar format (see Abbott 2010; Jowett 2013). These innovative episodes were integrated into the overall fabric of the series through their thematic preoccupation with truth and lies, revelation and concealment, as well as through distinctive aesthetics. The series combined form and content. Helen Wheatley identifies "densely layered images and montage-style flashbacks and flashforwards" as "key stylistic markers of Gothic television in the 1990s" (2006, 177), and it is easy to see how these markers apply to *The X-Files*. Influenced by film noir, the series used lighting and chiaroscuro to emphasize how visual imagery is implicated in constructing "the truth," and Manners's commentary on the season 9 finale picks out at least one "beautifully lit scene" in which Scully visits the captive Mulder (Manners 2007). Industry developments also contributed to the series' qualities: Johnson points out how the series "[took] advantage of the decreasing costs of special effects technology and advances in computer graphics to create its own exciting set pieces" (2005, 106).

Any long-running series is likely to disappoint at some stage. Moreover, as Clare Burdfield summarizes, "finales are notoriously hard. . . . The problem is that a lot is expected from these finales, years of plotlines and character development need to be boiled down to one, pivotal episode. We want closure, both narrative and emotional, the chance to say goodbye to characters we have spent possibly hundreds of hours with, and the overall themes and tone of the series to be reinforced. So it's not a surprise so many shows seem to fall down at this final hurdle" (2016). The two-episode finale, "The Truth," fulfills some of these expectations. Organized largely as a courtroom drama, it seems to attempt the narrative and emotional closure Burdfield refers to. Mulder departed the series at the end of season 8, yet he returns in these episodes and is soon on trial for murder. The series' conspiracy-theory narrative is central, and Manners describes the final episodes as highly demanding for the actors, "especially when [they] were basically telling the story of nine years of *The X-Files*" (2007). Calling witnesses enables a clip-show approach, revisiting key points in the series' long history as well as bringing back some notable characters. The DVD booklet introducing the ninth season describes it as "a tribute of sorts to the fascinating characters who breathed life into the show's nine-year run," noting that "many fan favorites appeared in the special two-hour finale" (*The X-Files* 2007). Several of these returning characters had been killed in previous seasons but appeared as Mulder's hallucinations, and "fan favorites" include Covarrubias, Krychek, Rohrer, Kersch, the Cigarette Smoking Man, the Lone Gunmen, Gibson Praise, and X.

For many viewers, however, the characters who really "breathed life" into *The X-Files* were Scully and Mulder, reunited again in these (apparently) final episodes, having been separated during season 8. The combination of the two as series leads was part of *The X-Files'* attraction for viewers, as seen by falling audience numbers after Mulder left the series (see Brown 2013). Manners's commentary dwells on "The Truth" as a reunion of *The X-Files* "family," thus sidestepping the consequences of Duchovny's leaving and his character's exit for the series' loyal audience (and thus also avoiding the fact that bringing Mulder back did not lure that audience in to watch the finale). Just as Scully is an iconic female character, representing the changing role of women in TV drama—and in society—Mulder is a "zeitgeist icon" (Laura Jacobs, quoted in Delasara 2000, 102). The series had always provided "room to question the central narrative voice—in this case, both Mulder's and the FBI's," argues Delasara (2000, 80).

Many episode and season arcs demonstrate this, yet, for some, the series allowed alternative perspectives only to a point. "The television episodes regularly deny Scully the vision of the paranormal that they provide the viewer," note Rhonda Wilcox and J. P. Williams, suggesting that Mulder's interpretation is generally validated or presented as the "correct" reading of events (1996, 117). Carter continually stated his investment in Scully as an independent woman ("I will never write a 'woman in distress,' unable to take care of herself" [quoted in Soter 2002, 125]), and *The X-Files* was praised for avoiding the lone-male-hero premise common to science fiction (Ken Tucker, cited in Soter 2002, 148). Certainly, positioning Scully as the rational, scientific sceptic and Mulder as the emotion-driven believer served to disrupt existing conventions of character gendering, and Anderson's "intensity and seriousness" (Chris Carter, quoted in Soter 2002, 117) played a part in her character's popularity. The chemistry between the series' stars served to lighten its often dark tone (see Soter 2002), yet the sexual tension between the two leads and the way it was handled in the final stages of the televised narrative arguably undermined Scully. In the finale, Scully cries in Mulder's arms, pleading for his support, while Mulder's adherence to his beliefs is presented as noble individualism: "What's really on trial here is the truth." Fan fiction continuations of the narrative, points out Emily Wills, "can provid[e] an opportunity for Scully to be both a scientific hero and a mother—a dual capability simply impossible in [the] canon" (2013), suggesting that although many fans were invested in the relationship, they also valued Scully's agency and autonomy.

Simon Brown sees season 9 as the culmination of a gradual shift that "changes the key character traits of Mulder and Scully, downplaying their personal investment in the mysteries they explore" as new characters John Doggett (Robert Patrick) and Monica Reyes (Annabeth Gish) are brought on board, a shift that he interprets as the producers "attempting to reconfigure *The X-Files* as a procedural drama," effectively rebooting the series midflow (2013, 20). Disappointingly, this shift meant that "the clear heterosexual trajectory of *The X-Files* itself" (Silbergleid 2003, 53) was mobilized to provide the narrative and emotional closure Burdfield (2016) identifies as expected of a finale. Scully and Mulder's heteronormative romance provides the hope and emotional warmth that a dark and unresolved conspiracy narrative needs to offer its audience and, Robin Silbergleid (2003) points out, reassures the audience that the horrific interventions suffered by Scully have not negated her humanity. Humanity in "The Truth" is aligned with heterosexual romantic fulfillment, and the episode ends with Scully and Mulder embracing. Although season 10 in 2016 did not reunite Scully and Mulder as a heteronormative couple, season 11 did show them in the kind of romantic and sexual relationship fans had imagined. Nostalgia and investment might encourage viewers to watch the revived series, yet set against Gillian Anderson's performance as Stella Gibson in the BBC series *The Fall* (2013–), the Scully and Mulder dynamic in 2016 and 2018 looks rather dated.

Those who see the season 8 finale as the "real" ending of the series might argue that it offers a more coherent and satisfying conclusion, yet this finale, too, reinforces heteronormative ideals: the closing scene shows Scully, Mulder, and baby William finally together as a family and the two agents kiss. This scene provides the emotional closure Burdfield (2016) identifies and a form of narrative closure, as does "The Truth," yet it does not reinforce "the overall themes and tone of the series," another expectation she cites as integral to a series finale. Certainly, to me, both the season 8 finale and the season 9 finale betray the tone of the series, suggesting as they do that heteronormative romance and family cancel out the quest for the "truth" that the series' characters have devoted years to. The themes and tone of *The X-Files* meant it was never going to be tied up in a neat conclusion: almost every episode had an open ending, leaving questions and possibilities rather than conclusions and certainty. That the season 9 finale fails to satisfy indicates, as Manners (2007) notes, fidelity to the series' main driver: frustration. *The X-Files* has undoubtedly had an influence on subsequent television drama, and its decline, its "finale," and its revival/s continue to serve as significant examples of the evolution of serial drama, complete with both pleasures and frustrations.

References

Abbott, Stacey. 2010. "Innovative TV." In *The Cult TV Book*, edited by Stacey Abbott, 91–99. London: I. B. Tauris.

Abbott, Stacey, and Simon Brown. 2013. "Introduction: The Truth Is (Still) Out There: *The X-Files* Twenty Years On." In "The Truth Is Out There: The *X-Files* 20 Years On," special issue of *Science Fiction Film and Television* 6, no. 1: 1–6.

Brown, Simon. 2013. "Memento Mori: The Slow Death of *The X-Files*." *Science Fiction Film and Television* 6, no. 1: 7–22.

Burdfield, Clare. 2016. "Avoiding Disappointment—Judging a TV Show by Its Finale." *CSTonline*, May 12. At https://cstonline.net/avoiding-disappointment-judging-a-tv-show-by-its-finale-by-claire-burdfield/.

Bussolini, Jeffrey. 2013. "Television Intertextuality after *Buffy*: Intertextuality of Casting and Constitutive Intertextuality." *Slayage* 10, no. 1 [35]. At http://www.whedonstudies.tv/uploads/2/6/2/8/26288593/bussolini_slayage_10.1.pdf.

Chin, Bertha. 2013. "The Fan–Media Producer Collaboration: How Fan Relationships Are Managed in a Post-series *X-Files* Fandom." *Science Fiction Film and Television* 6, no. 1: 87–99.

Delasara, Jan. 2000. *PopLit, PopCult, and "The X-Files": A Critical Exploration.* Jefferson, NC: McFarland.

Johnson, Catherine. 2005. *Telefantasy*. London: BFI.

Jowett, Lorna. 2013. "'Mulder, Have You Noticed That We're on Television?' X-Cops, Style, and Innovation." *Science Fiction Film and Television* 6, no. 1: 23–38.

Manners. Kim. 2007. "Episode Commentary on 'The Truth.'" On *The X-Files: The Complete Collector's Edition*. Beverly Hills, CA: Twentieth Century Fox Home Entertainment. DVD.

Silbergleid, Robin. 2003. "'The Truth We Both Know': Readerly Desire and Heter-
onarrative in *The X-Files*." *Studies in Popular Culture* 25, no. 3: 49–62.

Soter, Tom. 2002. *Investigating Couples: A Critical Analysis of "The Thin Man,"
"The Avengers," and "The X-Files."* Jefferson, NC: McFarland.

Wheatley, Helen. 2006. *Gothic Television*. Manchester, UK: Manchester Univ.
Press.

Wilcox, Rhonda, and J. P. Williams. 1996. "'What Do You Think?': *The X-Files*,
Liminality, and Gender Pleasure." In *"Deny All Knowledge": Reading "The
X-Files,"* edited by David Lavery, Angela Hague, and Marla Cartwright,
99–120. Syracuse, NY: Syracuse Univ. Press.

Wills, Emily Regan. 2013. "Fannish Discourse Communities and the Construction
of Gender in *The X-Files*." *Transformative Works and Cultures* 14. At http://
journal.transformativeworks.org/index.php/twc/article/view/410/404.

The X-Files: The Complete Collector's Edition. Beverly Hills, CA: Twentieth Century Fox Home Entertainment. DVD.

Conclusion

The End Is the Beginning Is the End
(with Apologies to the Smashing Pumpkins)

DOUGLAS L. HOWARD

For all that television endings have meant to us—and nearly all of the finales that you have just read about are, in one way or another, cultural milestones of sorts—changes in the way that we watch television now and this age of streaming, multiplatform "peak TV"[1] could mean the end of them, thus bringing me here, appropriately enough, to the finale of the finale, "the last," in Billy Corgan's words, "of a line of lasts" (The Smashing Pumpkins 1996). As of the writing of this conclusion in 2017–18, in fact, a number of TV critics are already pointing to what may be our waning interest in finales, a death-rattle playing out on our flatscreens, tablets, and iPhones. Looking back on the past year in TV, *Guardian* critic Jack Seale wonders if finales "die[d] a death" in 2017 (2017), and *Vulture* writer Matt Zoller Seitz similarly believes that they are "no longer the be-all and end-all of TV storytelling" (2017). Whereas Martha Nochimson made headlines for asking David Chase "whether Tony [Soprano] was dead" in a *Vox* piece in 2014, seven years after *The Sopranos* went dark, both Seale and Seitz agree that we don't seem to be obsessing about *Girls* or *The Leftovers* (2014–17) in the same way or "[carrying those endings] around with [us] for years," as Seitz puts it, "like sweet vindication or a festering grudge" (2017). And that's a good thing, he argues, and a sign of how the medium is evolving (and of how we, as viewers, are evolving with it) because both we and the showrunners

---

1. FX CEO John Landgraf coined this term at a Television Critics Association press tour in 2015, when he predicted "that 2015 or 2016 [would] represent peak TV in America" (quoted in Rose and Guthrie 2015).

are no longer so unhealthily fixated on "the power and perfection of the ending" (Seitz 2017), to the point where we all lose sight of the possibilities in storytelling, in performance, in the medium as an art form. If we are becoming more savvy consumers of media, perhaps we are outgrowing our need for the end?

Although a significant portion of this change stems, according to Seitz, from the way showrunners approach their shows and a deliberate turn away from "the endgame," there's also the reality of what he calls "the atomization" of the TV audience: "we don't watch in large enough numbers [any-more] to slam the brakes on the national conversation" (2017). When we had to worry about new programming only from a handful of broadcast net-works or even only from those networks and a few cable channels, a series finale such as the one for *M*A*S*H* or *Friends* or even Johnny Carson's last *Tonight Show* was almost mandatory viewing. Networks could prepare and program for it; they virtually conceded the time slot to *Seinfeld* when it fin-ished in 1998.[2] As *New York Times* correspondent John Koblin reports on the industry now, though, and puts the change in audience numbers in per-spective, "A show with ratings that would have prompted cancellation not long ago can be the source of some relief these days—the viewership is not *that* bad, after all, goes the rationale" (2017).[3] And that industry problem is a finale problem inasmuch as that drop in numbers means that any finale is less of a "spectacle" and less urgent than it was in the past; there's not the same kind of cultural peer pressure to be there for the moment. Whether the hype created the desire in us or helped to fuel it, when Sam Malone poured his last drink and Jerry and his friends went off to prison, we didn't just want to be there; we needed to be there. We missed something if we weren't, something that would not come again, something that we could never get

2. According to Jay Bobbin, the networks' respect for the *Seinfeld* finale was such that in "a sweeps month typically marked by new programming, ABC [repeated] the Clint East-wood movie *Unforgiven*, while Fox [had] encore installments of *The World's Wildest Police Videos* and [*When*] *Animals Attack*. CBS [countered] with the season finales of *Promised Land* and *Diagnosis Murder*, but *Diagnosis* star Dick Van Dyke said, 'I'd expect that most people will see our episode during summer reruns'" (1998). Perhaps even more bizarre, "the cable channel TV Land [stopped] regular programming for an hour and [hung] out a sign saying it [would] be back after the 'Seinfeld' finale" (James 1998).

3. As yet another sign of the times, at a recent Television Critics Association press tour FX CEO John Landgraf "expressed wonder that any viewers in the current media environ-ment make time for series television" (Holloway 2018).

back. Will we feel the same sense of urgency when Midge Maisel tells her last joke or those creepy *Riverdale* kids graduate? If Seitz is right, we won't; those days, those feelings, and the experience of those finales are gone.

Alan Sepinwall, who collaborated with Seitz on *TV (the Book)* (2016), sees the same writing on the wall, but for different reasons. For Sepinwall, recent trends in television programming, exemplified by the return of *Will & Grace* in 2017 and the new *Roseanne* in 2018, point to the outright rejection of the "definitive" finale in favor of softer endings, series revivals, and the lucrative possibility of reengaging a ready-made fan base. Although some of the most popular and most powerful finales "are great," he writes, "precisely because they're definitive," writers now are less inclined to give their characters those last rites, "just in case that Netflix money might roll in 10 or 15 years down the line" (2017). (In this context, even "definitive" is no longer definitive. Consider the recent example of *Prison Break* (2005–9). Main character Michael Scofield dies and is buried in the finale in 2009, but the revival of the series in 2017 brings him back to life and puts him in a Middle Eastern prison.) And given what Koblin says about the decline in ratings expectations, even a portion of *Roseanne*'s audience from the 1990s could make it a hit by today's standards.[4] So who wouldn't want to roll the dice on one more season of *Gilmore Girls* or take one more shot at the truth on *The X-Files*?

Zoe Williams, however, suggests that TV might, among other things, be feeling the ill effects of zombie culture, where revivals are commonplace. Inasmuch as the narratives of shows such as *The Walking Dead* inherently rely on the premise that death is not the end, Williams argues, then "how [can we] want [or expect] a definitive finish" from the shows themselves (2017)? Going back to what C. Lee Harrington says about how we use "discourses of death and dying" to describe the ends of television series (2012, 580), if we have already accepted the idea that our favorite characters can

---

4. The *Roseanne* reboot certainly was a ratings hit—as Dana Feldman reports in *Forbes*, it "set all kinds of records, starting with the nine-episode 10th season premiere, which scored the largest-ever Total Viewer Live plus seven-day increase for any single telecast on any network in the history of television" (2018)—but ABC canceled the show in response to actress Roseanne Barr's racist tweet about former Obama adviser Valerie Jarrett. According to *TMZ*, however, the network may still take a chance on yet another reboot and "has been exploring the possibility of rebranding the show [around] Sara Gilbert's character, Darlene" ("ABC 'Roseanne' Reboot" 2018).

live on, albeit as flesh-eating monsters, and if we are already breaking or undermining those discourses, then why wouldn't we accept our favorite shows as "walkers," even if they disappoint and horrify us in their return?

Then, of course, there's the experience of streaming a finale or seeing it as part of a weekend or week-long binge-watch. In a recent *CST* post (Howard 2017), I talked about the value of second-to-last episodes as fuel for the imagination and how they set up our expectations for the finale.[5] Where networks in the past had control over when we watched and how long we had to wait for those shows, time that they took advantage of by promoting those episodes and building the hype and the audience, streaming diffuses that control because our relationship with time and order on series TV has changed. We are no longer as beholden to the networks to determine when we watch or in what order we watch or how we experience the narrative.[6] We could conceivably begin watching *Seinfeld* now by streaming the finale first, start a *Gilmore Girls* marathon with the final four words of the revival, and then kick off a *How I Met Your Mother* binge by meeting Ted Mosby's wife, all with little or no fanfare and no media hype surrounding the "event." And even if enough of us were to watch the same episode to pose a challenge to the record books, "we don't," as Seitz states, "all watch . . . at the same time [anymore]" (2017) or, for that matter, in the same way or even the same kind of episode. (And whereas broadcast viewers experience the show with commercials, streaming audiences can see it commercial free.) The convenience of streaming has broken down or is, at least, reshaping the communal nature of the viewing experience,[7] and the industry's attempt to cater to individual preferences may increasingly be giving way to audiences made up of individuals.

5. "With the penultimate viewing," I noted, "we . . . collaborate with the series and create in our minds the ideal ending, the one that best suits our sense of what [the series] was and what it meant to us" (Howard 2017).

6. In chapter 65 of this volume, Adam Ochonicky's description of the new *Twin Peaks* finale, whose own preoccupation and play with time suggests a self-reflexive awareness of its status as a streaming on-demand media product, could be a metaphor for any episode (including the finale) in any series now, given how all episodes have been detached from specific moments in time through streaming: each episode (finale) exists in "a constant elsewhere that is forever out of time but somehow still present."

7. According to Justin Grandinetti, the communal experience still exists and has been "perpetuated via social media, blogs, and other online mediums," but audiences who make use of these outlets have had to adapt to these changes in temporality and the increased potential for plot spoilers within these communities (2017, 28).

There's also the matter of watching the finale as part of a series of episodes in quick succession. Even if we watch the episodes in order, does the finale mean as much and affect us in the same way if we see it as part of a five-hour binge? Does it have the same impact? Do we experience it psychologically and aesthetically as a separate entity or unit? I binged the last few episodes of *Sense8* (2015–18), and, in some ways, the individual "sitting" defined my experience as much as, if not more than, the episodes themselves. Netflix contributed to that feeling through its "postplay" feature, in which the closing credits are cut back and the next episode starts just as the previous one is ending.[8] The finale, as a result of this feature, seemed like part of one long episode to me, and I didn't have those forced breaks in the narrative and network commercials to reinforce the episodic nature of my viewing. While I was immersed in the plotlines and the world of the show, I certainly didn't have time to digest or savor what I was watching, to reflect on what I had seen, or to prepare for the episode that I was about to see.[9]

And if all of the episodes appear simultaneously, is the value of the finale diminished in that way as well? By making entire seasons available to audiences at once, services such as Netflix again not only undermine the idea of order—viewers are not bound by the network to watch episodes in any kind of numerical sequence—but they eliminate the separation between episodes that could, if only on a psychological level, make us value one episode over the other. We don't necessarily see the finale as the end of some great narrative or viewing experience, the "dessert" that comes after we have enjoyed the rest of the meal; rather, all of the food comes at the same time. A streaming service also doesn't advertise or promote the finale in the same way as a broadcast network. Although it may mention that a season is available, it doesn't place any special emphasis on the final episode. Netflix, for example, doesn't highlight the *Mad Men* finale in any way on its website or even indicate that it is the series finale. It just lists it as another episode, with the episode number and title.

8. As Djoymi Baker explains, this postplay feature was added in 2012 but was made optional in 2014, when subscribers complained that it "spoilt the pace and mood [of their viewing]" (2017, 40).

9. Netflix viewer Steve Portugal was critical of the postplay feature when it was first introduced largely for these reasons and considered the credits part of his viewing experience, when he "[savored] the moment of reflection, the mood, whatever it [was], that the artist [had] put into the content and [when he let] the music and the emotion take [him] further" (quoted in Gilbert 2012).

All of these arguments make me think that this collection will become an unintentional retrospective on the TV finale and its heyday, now a thing of the past. In this mindset, I see myself channeling some inner curmudgeon as I stream future finales, desperately clinging to nostalgic visions of the episodes that gave rise to these chapters and grumbling to anyone who will listen about how "they don't make 'em like they used to." But although this sounds like the beginning of the end (or the end of the end), it may just be the state of the finale in transition.[10] Even if current finales aren't drawing those *Fugitive* and *M*A*S*H* finale ratings, there is still a need for them, financially as well as psychologically. In fact, if anything, as Todd VanDerWerff points out, there are actually more finales on TV and elsewhere now, as much because of the dramatic increase in the number of shows themselves as because of our perpetual desire for closure: "Because the advent of streaming has made serialized dramas more valuable to their studios as complete sets, with beginnings, middles, and ends, more and more low-rated shows are running three, four, or even five seasons and getting the chance to thoughtfully wrap up their stories" (2017). A finale lets potential viewers know that they will be engaging in something amounting to a complete narrative or, at least, in the showrunner's fully realized vision for the series. Regardless of how much the showrunners hedge their bets at the end, there is still something attractive about a story in its entirety or, at least, the illusion of one.

And endings, in some form, obviously still matter to viewers, even in this streaming age, as the recent example of *Sense8* indicates. Netflix canceled the Lana Wachowski, Lilly Wachowski, and J. Michael Straczynski sci-fi ensemble drama at the end of a tense second season in 2017, just as Wolfgang was being tortured by BPO and the group had kidnapped its nemesis, Whispers, in response. For all of the talk about dwindling audience numbers, the *Sense8* fans mobilized, in Lana Wachowski's words, "like the fist of Sun" (quoted in Strause 2017) and moved Netflix to end the series with a two-and-a-half hour finale in June 2018 that leaves the heroes celebrating, orgiastically, at Nomi and Amanita's wedding in Paris.

As much as the medium is changing, I can't imagine that we will completely be doing away with finales on series television. (In some ways, that would be a step backward to those pre-*Fugitive* days of television that left the

---

10. According to Frank Kermode, even transition is part of the apocalyptic paradigm and yet another fiction that "register[s] the conviction that the end is immanent rather than imminent" (2000, 101). So in attempting to deflect all of this talk about the end of the finale, I may ultimately be reinforcing a narrative pattern of ending.

castaways stranded on Gilligan's Island.) After all, our beginnings and endings define us as a culture and help us, as Frank Kermode puts it, "to make sense of [our] span" (2000, 7), so why should television (and our "imaginative investment" in it [Kermode 2000, 17]) be any different? And though we may be reviving and re-ending our TV shows and hesitating to make those endings so definitive—even zombies can be put down for good with a well-placed double tap[11] or headshot—this trend could speak to the need to revive and redefine who and what we are and our uncertainty in making that (re)definition so permanent. According to researcher Emily Roach, our current focus on open-ended closure—which, as I mentioned in the introduction and as this collection repeatedly illustrates, is not exactly something new[12]—could work as a "progressive" rejection of heteronormative narratives, where "people get married and have kids and settle into a suburban lifestyle" (quoted in Williams 2017). Because we are rewriting our own stories and reconstructing our own sense of cultural identity, of course we want our television shows to reinforce those revisions by allowing for multiple possibilities rather than valuing one version of domestic or social order over another. But Roach expects that even in such stories we will see some kind of resolution, even if it has only to do with "the most obvious element" or basic plot point (quoted in Williams 2017), and Williams admits that, amid these other types of endings, she "miss[es] closure" (2017), a lament that Sepinwall (2017) appears to share. Given how television responds to trends and caters to audiences, perhaps, if enough people feel this way, we will find ourselves in the near future turning to our platforms for something more pointed—a more apocalyptic apocalypse—as either a cultural statement of affirmation or out of some nostalgic desire for an order that no longer exists (if it ever did in the first place) because those ends help to justify our means and serve as an expression of who and what we are or would like to be.

This brings me to that point in the book that I have been both anticipating and dreading. Even now, I see the paradox of it, that there will be more beyond it, for you to consider, for us to talk about, just as what it means is, I hope, different now than what it was at the beginning, in the introduction, when I tried to deny it and said (or outright promised, really)

---

11. Readers are invited to review main character Columbus Ohio's rules for surviving the zombie apocalypse in *Zombieland* (Ruben Fleischer, 2010).

12. Willa Paskin also makes this argument—that all television finales come with loose ends that "are freedom . . . for us" (2017). In those incomplete moments in the narrative, our imaginations have free reign to fill in the gaps with what feels right to us.

that this wouldn't happen. And yet it did, over and over again. Nevertheless, the physical reality of space brings me to it and demands it, irrevocable and inevitable in its moment. But, as I said earlier, this is what you came here for. So, without further ado, this is the end . . . and the beginning . . .

References

"ABC 'Roseanne' Reboot Green Light Could Come This Week!!!" 2018. *TMZ*, June 4. At http://www.tmz.com/2018/06/04/abc-roseanne-reboot-announcement-imminent/.

Baker, Djoymi. 2017. "Terms of Excess: Binge-Viewing as Epic-Viewing in the Netflix Era." In *The Age of Netflix: Critical Essays on Streaming Media, Digital Delivery, and Instant Access*, edited by Cory Barker and Myc Wiatrowski, 31–54. Jefferson, NC: McFarland.

Bobbin, Jay. 1998. "'Seinfeld' Will Exit with a Big Goodbye." *Daily Press (TV)*, May 10. At https://www.newspapers.com/image/238238734.

Feldman, Dana. 2018. "While 'Roseanne' Reboot Is Ratings Gold, Not All Hits Should Make a Comeback." *Forbes*, Apr. 10. At https://www.forbes.com/sites/danafeldman/2018/04/10/while-roseanne-reboot-is-ratings-gold-not-all-hits-should-make-a-comeback/#1be4f879738c.

Gilbert, Jason. 2012. "Netflix's 'Post-play' Feature Will Suck You into More TV Show Marathons." *Huffington Post*, Aug. 16. At https://www.huffingtonpost.com/2012/08/16/netflix-unveils-post-play_n_1789111.html.

Grandinetti, Jason. 2017. "From Primetime to Anytime: Streaming Video, Temporality, and the Future of Communal Television." In *The Age of Netflix: Critical Essays on Streaming Media, Digital Delivery, and Instant Access*, edited by Cory Barker and Myc Wiatrowski, 11–30. Jefferson, NC: McFarland.

Harrington, C. Lee. 2013. "The *Ars Moriendi* of US Serial Television: Towards a Good Textual Death." *International Journal of Cultural Studies* 16, no. 6: 579–95.

Holloway, Daniel. 2018. "FX's John Landgraf: Peak TV Was Media-Circus 'Sideshow' in 2017." *Variety*, Jan. 5. At http://variety.com/2018/tv/news/peak-tv-1202654457/.

Howard, Douglas L. 2017. "In Praise of Penultimates." *CSTonline*, Nov. 24. At https://cstonline.net/in-praise-of-penultimates-by-douglas-howard/.

James, Caryn. 1998. "CRITIC'S NOTEBOOK: All Right, Goodbye Already! Parting Is Such Sweet Sitcom." *New York Times*, May 12. At http://www.nytimes.com/1998/05/12/arts/critic-s-notebook-all-right-goodbye-already-parting-is-such-sweet-sitcom.html.

Kermode, Frank. 2000. *The Sense of an Ending: Studies in the Theory of Fiction*. With a new epilogue. New York: Oxford Univ. Press.

Koblin, John. 2017. "On Network TV, the Gap between a Hit and a Dud Is Shrinking." *New York Times*, May 14. At https://www.nytimes.com/2017/05/14/business/media/fall-shows-2017-tv.html.

Nochimson, Martha. 2014. "Did Tony Soprano Die at the End of *The Sopranos*?" *Vox*, Aug. 27. At https://www.vox.com/2014/8/27/6006139/did-tony-die-at-the-end-of-the-sopranos.

Paskin, Willa. 2017. "Is It Still Possible for a TV Show to Have a Satisfying Ending—or End at All?" *Slate*, Dec. 21. At http://www.slate.com/arts/2018/01/the-daily-show-slams-the-other-late-night-shows-for-being-too-factual.html.

Rose, Lacey, and Marisa Guthrie. 2015. "FX Chief John Landgraf on Content Bubble: 'This Is Simply Too Much Television.'" *Hollywood Reporter*, Aug. 7. At https://www.hollywoodreporter.com/live-feed/fx-chief-john-landgraf-content-813914.

Seale, Jack. 2017. "Why TV Finales Didn't Matter in 2017." *Guardian*, Dec. 17. At https://www.theguardian.com/culture/2017/dec/21/why-tv-finales-didnt-matter-in-2017.

Seitz, Matt Zoller. 2017. "TV Is Moving Away from Finale Fever—Which Is Making for Better TV." *Vulture*, June 11. At http://www.vulture.com/2017/06/do-tv-series-finales-matter-anymore.html.

Sepinwall, Alan. 2017. "Will TV Finales Stop Mattering?" *Uproxx*, Aug. 3. At http://uproxx.com/sepinwall/will-and-grace-revival-ignoring-series-finale/.

The Smashing Pumpkins. 1996. "The Beginning Is the End Is the Beginning." *Rarities and B-Sides*. Virgin, 2005. CD.

Strause, Jackie. 2017. "'Sense8' Two-Hour Finale Set at Netflix." *Hollywood Reporter*, June 29. At https://www.hollywoodreporter.com/live-feed/sense8-two-hour-finale-set-at-netflix-1017948.

VanDerWerff, Todd. 2017. "The Delicate Art of the TV Series Finale." *Vox*, Oct. 17. At https://www.vox.com/culture/2017/10/17/16462246/series-finale-best-worst-tv-halt-and-catch-fire-americans.

Williams, Zoe. 2017. "Too Closure for Comfort: The Death of Definitive TV Endings." *Guardian*, Apr. 24. At https://www.theguardian.com/tv-and-radio/2017/apr/24/tv-endings-breaking-bad-walking-dead-big-little-lies.

Contributors ✦ Index

Contributors

Stacey Abbott is reader in film and television studies at the University of Roehampton. She is the author of *Celluloid Vampires* (2007) and *Angel* (2009) as well as coauthor, with Lorna Jowett, of *TV Horror: Investigating the Dark Side of the Small Screen* (2013). She is also the editor of *The Cult TV Book* (2010) and general editor of the Investigating Cult TV series at I. B. Tauris.

Kim Akass is senior lecturer in film and television at the University of Hertfordshire. She is a cofounding editor of the journal *Critical Studies in Television*, the managing editor of *CSTonline* (www.cstonline.tv), and coeditor (with Janet McCabe) of the Reading Contemporary TV series. She has published widely on US TV and is currently working on the manuscript "From Here to Maternity: Representations of Motherhood on US TV."

Karin Beeler is professor and chair of the English Department at the University of Northern British Columbia. She is the author of *Seers, Witches, and Psychics on Screen* (2008). She has also coedited *Children's Film in the Digital Age: Essays on Audience, Adaptation, and Consumer Culture* (2015, with Stan Beeler) and *Investigating "Charmed": The Magic Power of TV* (2007, with Stan Beeler).

Stan Beeler teaches film and television studies in the English Department at the University of Northern British Columbia. His publications include *Reading "Stargate SG-1"* (2006, with Lisa Dickson); *Investigating "Charmed": The Magic Power of TV* (2007, with Karin Beeler); *Dance, Drugs, and Escape: The Club Scene in Literature, Film, and Television since the Late 1980s* (2007); and *Children's Film in the Digital Age: Essays on Audience, Adaptation, and Consumer Culture* (2015, with Karin Beeler).

David Bianculli has been a TV critic since 1975, currently runs the website tvworthwatching.com, and serves as a TV critic and guest host for NPR's *Fresh Air*. He has written three books on television and its impact—*Teleliteracy: Taking Television Seriously* (1992), *Dictionary of Teleliteracy: Television's 500 Biggest Hits, Misses, and Events* (1996), and *The Platinum Age of Television: From "I Love Lucy" to*

"The Walking Dead," How TV Became Terrific (2016)—as well as *Dangerously Funny: The Uncensored Story of "The Smothers Brothers Comedy Hour"* (2009). His articles, columns, and reviews have appeared in several books, in such magazines as *TV Guide, Broadcasting & Cable,* the *New York Times Book Review, Rolling Stone, Variety, Film Comment,* and *Television Quarterly,* and (syndicated) in hundreds of daily newspapers such as the *New York Times.* He now teaches TV and film history and appreciation as a full professor at Rowan University.

Keith Brand is chair of the Radio, TV, and Film Department at Rowan University, where he teaches courses in sound communication and radio production. A board member of the Association of Independents in Radio and PhillyCAM, he has more than twenty-five years of broadcast radio experience as host of WXPN's program *Sleepy Hollow* in Philadelphia and produces features for NPR's programs *All Things Considered, Weekend Edition Saturday,* and *Justice Talking.* His publications include articles in the *Journal of Radio Studies* and the *Journal of Radio and Audio Media.*

Bill Brioux is a leading Canadian media critic and writes a weekly column for the Canadian Press. He has published articles in the *Toronto Star, Hello! Canada,* and *Movie Entertainment* magazine; is the author of *Truth and Rumors: The Reality behind TV's Most Famous Myths* (2008); and blogs regularly at brioux.tv.

Clinton Bryant has an MA in English from the University of Vermont, specializing in Southern Gothic literature and popular culture. In addition, he is a creative writer whose work has been published in several magazines, including *Pomona Valley Review* and *Red Fez.*

Cynthia Burkhead is associate professor and chair in the English Department at the University of North Alabama. In addition to *Dreams in American Television Narratives* (2013) and *Joss Whedon: Conversations* (2011, coedited with David Lavery), she has authored or coedited books on John Steinbeck and *Gray's Anatomy.*

Jeffrey Bussolini is associate professor of sociology-anthropology and women's studies at the City University of New York. He is the editor and translator of *The Philosophical Ethology of Dominique Lestel* (2017), *The Philosophical Ethology of Vinciane Despret* (2017), and *The Philosophical Ethology of Roberto Marchesini* (2017). His article "Michel Foucault's Influence on the Work of Giorgio Agamben" appears in *A Foucault for the 21st Century* (2009). He has also published extensively on television series such as *Buffy the Vampire Slayer* and *Firefly.*

Michele Byers is a professor at Saint Mary's University in Halifax, Nova Scotia. She has published extensively in the areas of television and identity in journals such as *Atlantis*, *Canadian Ethnic Studies*, *Shofar*, *Culture*, and *Theory & Critique* as well as in such books as *The Essential Cult TV Reader* (2009), *You Should See Yourself: Jewish Identity in Postmodern American Culture* (2006), and *Programming Reality: Perspectives on English-Canadian Television* (2008). Byers is the editor of *Growing Up "Degrassi": Television, Identity, and Youth Cultures* (2005) and coeditor of *"Dear Angela": Remembering "My So-Called Life"* (2007, with David Lavery), *On the Verge of Tears: Why the Movies, Television, Music, Art, and Literature Make Us Cry* (2010, with David Lavery), and *"The CSI Effect": Television, Crime, and Governance* (2009, with Val Johnson). Her most recent work involves the study of television and ethnicity.

Shelley Cobb is associate professor of film and English at the University of Southampton. She has published widely on women filmmakers, film adaptation, celebrity culture, and chick flicks and is currently principal investigator of the project "Calling the Shots: Women and Film Culture in the UK, 2000–2015," funded by the UK Arts and Humanities Research Council. Her books include *Adaptation, Authorship, and Contemporary Women Filmmakers* (2015) and the edited collection *First Comes Love: Power Couples, Celebrity Relationships, and Cultural Politics* (2016).

Amy M. Damico is professor in the School of Communication at Endicott College in Beverly, Massachusetts, and is the faculty adviser to the Endicott Scholars honors program. She is coauthor of *21st-Century TV Dramas: Exploring the New Golden Age* (2016, with Sara E. Quay).

Mark Dawidziak has written or edited about twenty-five books. He has been a theater, film, and television critic for almost forty years. The TV critic at the *Cleveland Plain Dealer* since 1999, he is the author of three books about landmark TV series: *The "Columbo" Phile* (1989), *The "Night Stalker" Companion* (1997), and, most recently, *Everything I Need to Know I Learned in "The Twilight Zone"* (2017). Also an internationally recognized Mark Twain scholar, he has written or edited five Twain-centric books, including *Mark My Words: Mark Twain on Writing* (1996) and *Horton Foote's "The Shape of the River": The Lost Teleplay about Mark Twain* (2003). Working the spooky side of the street, he has written a horror novel (*Grave Secrets: The Kolchak Papers* [1994]), nonfiction books (*The Bedside, Bathtub, & Armchair Companion to "Dracula"* [2008]), plays, short stories, and comic book scripts. An adjunct professor at Kent State University, he is the cofounder of Ohio's Largely Literary Theater Company.

Dean DeFino is professor of English and director of film studies at Iona College. His publications include *The HBO Effect* (2013) and *Faster, Pussycat! Kill! Kill!* (2014).

David Scott Diffrient is associate professor of film and television at Colorado State University. He is the author of a book on *M*A*S*H* in the TV Milestones series and editor of *Screwball Television: Critical Approaches to "Gilmore Girls"* (2010, Syracuse University Press).

Michael Donovan is professor in the Radio, TV, and Film Department at Rowan University.

Trisha Dunleavy is associate professor in media studies at Victoria University of Wellington, New Zealand. Her research interests center on multiplatform television; creative industries (TV and film); high-end TV drama; American, British, and New Zealand television; and TV narrative, aesthetics, and complexity. Her major publications are *Ourselves in Primetime: A History of New Zealand Television Drama* (2005), *Television Drama: Form, Agency, Innovation* (2009), *New Zealand Film and Television: Institution, Industry, and Cultural Change* (2011) with Hester Joyce, and *Complex Serial Drama and Multiplatform Television* (2018).

Gary R. Edgerton is professor of creative media and entertainment at Butler University. He has published eleven books and more than eighty-five essays on a variety of television, film, and culture topics in a wide assortment of books, scholarly journals, and encyclopedias. He also coedits the *Journal of Popular Film and Television*.

Sam Ford consults with organizations on storytelling, audience engagement, and sustainable innovation strategies. He is also a research affiliate with MIT Comparative Media Studies/Writing, an instructor with Western Kentucky University's Popular Culture Studies Program, and a Knight News Innovation Fellow with Columbia University's Tow Center for Digital Journalism. With Abigail De Kosnik and C. Lee Harrington, he is coeditor of *The Survival of Soap Opera: Transformations for a New Media Era* (2011). He has written about soap operas for *Transformative Works and Cultures*, *In Media Res*, the *Wall Street Journal*, *Fast Company*, *Portfolio*, and a range of other publications and has taught semester-long courses on the genre at MIT and Western Kentucky University.

Teresa Forde is senior lecturer in film and media at the University of Derby. She has published on subjects such as memory, time travel, science-fiction soundtrack, the body and technology, and fantasy film and television. Her most recent publication is a character study of Rory Williams from *Doctor Who* for the edited collection *Who Travels with the Doctor? Essays on the Companions of Doctor Who* (2016). Forde is interested in film and television, modes of exhibition, archiving memories and experiences, and transmedia texts. She also cocurated a gallery exhibition on the artist Marion Adnams (December 2017–March 2018) and produced a video installation for the show.

Lincoln Geraghty is reader in popular media cultures in the School of Media and Performing Arts at the University of Portsmouth. He serves as editorial adviser for the *Journal of Popular Culture*, *Reconstruction*, the *Journal of Fandom Studies*, and the *Journal of Popular Television*. Geraghty was recently appointed as a senior editor for the new online open-access journal *Cogent Arts and Humanities*. He is author of *Living with "Star Trek": American Culture and the "Star Trek" Universe* (2007), *American Science Fiction Film and Television* (2009), and *Cult Collectors: Nostalgia, Fandom, and Collecting Popular Culture* (2014). He has edited *The Influence of "Star Trek" on Television, Film, and Culture* (2008), *Channeling the Future: Essays on Science Fiction and Fantasy Television* (2009), *The "Smallville" Chronicles: Critical Essays on the Television Series* (2011), *The Shifting Definitions of Genre: Essays on Labeling Film, Television Shows, and Media* (2008, with Mark Jancovich), and, most recently, *Popular Media Cultures: Fans, Audiences, and Paratexts* (2015). He is currently serving as editor for the multivolume *Directory of World Cinema: American Hollywood* (2011, 2015).

Eric Gould is a designer and writer in Boston. He is a former instructor at the Boston Architectural College and Wentworth Institute of Technology. He is an associate editor at tvworthwatching.com, where he writes about television, art, and culture.

Gary Gravely is instructor of English and humanities at Roane State Community College in Harriman, Tennessee. He received his PhD from Middle Tennessee State University in 2015. After growing up as a kid obsessed with the multiverse of DC Comics, he was easily seduced into the web of possible-worlds narrative theory, which was the centerpiece of his dissertation. Aside from his classroom duties, Gravely enjoys reading historical biographies, following the University of Kentucky basketball program, feeding his addiction to comic books, and binge-watching television with his wife, Laura.

Stephanie Graves is an adjunct instructor of English at the University of North Alabama. She completed her MA in English at Middle Tennessee State University, where her concentration was film and television studies. Her research interests include the grotesque, the Southern Gothic, postmodernism, and gender and queer studies. A native southerner, she particularly enjoys writing about herself in the third person.

Ensley F. Guffey is an author and historian of American popular culture. He has published peer-reviewed scholarly essays on *Breaking Bad*, *Buffy the Vampire Slayer*, *Farscape*, and *Marvel's The Avengers*, and he writes regular columns on films, television, and comic books for BiffBamPop.com and FreakSugar.com. With his wife, K. Dale Koontz, Guffey is the coauthor of *Wanna Cook? The Complete, Unofficial Companion to "Breaking Bad"* (2014) and *Dreams Given Form: The*

Unofficial Companion to the Universe of "Babylon 5" (2017). He is currently working with Samira S. Nadkarni on an academic collection focusing on war and military studies in the works of Joss Whedon.

Hannah Hamad is senior lecturer in media studies at the University of East Anglia and author of *Postfeminism and Paternity in Contemporary US Film: Framing Fatherhood* (2013). She is also the editor of the forum section of *Celebrity Studies Journal* and has published widely on gender, postfeminism, and neoliberalism in popular culture.

Karen Hellekson is an independent scholar based in Maine. She has published on science fiction, TV, and fan studies. She is founding coeditor of the academic journal *Transformative Works and Cultures*.

Dana Heller is dean of the College of Arts and Sciences at Eastern Michigan University. She writes about film and television and is the author of numerous articles on topics related to literature, popular culture, LGBTQ studies, and American studies. She is also the author or editor of eight books, most recently *Hairspray* (2011) and *Loving "The L Word": The Complete Series in Focus* (2013).

Lynne Hibberd is a senior lecturer in media and cultural studies at Leeds Beckett University. Her publications include chapters in *Media International Australia* (2010), *The Handbook of Gender, Sex, and Media* (2013), *Reframing Disability?* (2014), and *Ageing, Popular Culture, and Contemporary Feminism* (2014) as well as journal articles in *Feminist Media Studies* and *Critical Studies in Television*.

David Hinckley vividly remembers watching the original television broadcasts of *Davy Crockett* and badgering his parents into buying him a coonskin cap, which was really rabbit fur. Some years later he went to work at the *New York Daily News*, where he has been television critic for the past eight of his thirty-five years. He still has the coonskin cap, which, like him, is slightly worse for wear.

Douglas L. Howard is academic chair of the English Department on the Ammerman Campus at Suffolk County Community College. He is the editor of *"Dexter": Investigating Cutting Edge Television* (2010) and the coeditor of *The Essential "Sopranos" Reader* (2011) and *The Gothic Other: Racial and Social Constructions in the Literary Imagination* (2004). He has also contributed essays, columns, and book chapters to various publications, including *This Thing of Ours: Investigating "The Sopranos"* (2002), *Reading "The Sopranos"* (2006), *Reading "Deadwood"* (2006), *Milton in Popular Culture* (2006), *Reading "24"* (2007), *Modern and Postmodern Cutting Edge Films* (2008), *Revisioning 007* (2009), *The Essential*

Cult Television Reader (2009), *On the Verge of Tears* (2010), *Interrogating "The Shield"* (2012, Syracuse University Press), and the e-journal *CSTonline*.

Zeke Jarvis is associate professor at Eureka College. He is the author of the prose books *So Anyway . . .* (2014), *In a Family Way* (2015), and *Lifelong Learning* (2018) as well as of the reference texts *Make 'Em Laugh: American Historians of the 20th and 21st Century* (2015) and *Silence in the Library: Banned and Challenged Books* (2017).

Deborah Jermyn is a reader in film and television at the University of Roehampton. She has published widely on women, feminism, and popular culture, including numerous pieces on women and TV crime drama and ageing femininities in the media. Her books include *Sex and the City* (2009), *Prime Suspect* (2010), and *Nancy Meyers* (2017).

Erika Johnson-Lewis teaches in the Humanities Department at St. Petersburg College. Her publications include chapters in *Cylons in America* (2008) and *Looking for "Lost"* (2011).

Lorna Jowett is reader in television studies at the University of Northampton, where she teaches some of her favorite things, including horror, science fiction, and television, sometimes all at once. She is coauthor with Stacey Abbott of *TV Horror: Investigating the Dark Side of the Small Screen* (2012), author of *Dancing with the Doctor: Dimensions of Gender in the New "Doctor Who" Universe* (2017) and *Sex and the Slayer: A Gender Studies Primer for the "Buffy" Fan* (2005), as well as editor of the collection *Time on TV* (2016). She has published many articles on television, film, and popular culture, with a particular focus on genre and representation.

When **K. Dale Koontz** discovered Joss Whedon's series *Buffy the Vampire Slayer* when she should have been studying for the bar exam, the die was cast. (She passed the bar, so she has something to fall back on, just in case.) In addition to teaching communication and film courses at Cleveland Community College in Shelby, North Carolina, Koontz has presented original work examining popular culture in locations ranging from Boiling Springs, North Carolina, to Istanbul, Turkey. In addition to contributing to a number of edited collections, including the recent book *Reading Joss Whedon* (2014), she is the author of *Faith and Choice in the Works of Joss Whedon* (2008). In 2010, she was the only American keynote speaker at the Fourth Biennial Slayage Conference on the Whedonverses. With Ensley F. Guffey, she is the coauthor of the critically and commercially successful book *Wanna Cook? The Complete, Unofficial Companion to "Breaking Bad"* (2014) as well as of *Dreams*

Given Form: The Unofficial Guide to the "Babylon 5" Universe (2017). Koontz can be reached via Twitter at @KDaleKoontz and on her blog, UnfetteredBrilliance (at http://www.unfetteredbrilliance.blogspot.com), where she posts about new and classic movies and television.

Alice Leppert is assistant professor of media and communication studies at Ursinus College. Her work has appeared in the journals *Cinema Journal*, *Genders*, *Celebrity Studies*, *In Media Res*, *Cinema Journal Teaching Dossier*, and *In the Limelight* as well as in the books *Under the Microscope: Forms and Function of Female Celebrity* (2011), *First Comes Love: Power Couples, Celebrity Kinship, and Cultural Politics* (2015), and *Cupcakes, Pinterest, and Ladyporn: Feminized Popular Culture in the Early 21st Century* (2015). She also serves as the book review editor for *Film Criticism*.

Renee Middlemost is an early-career researcher and lecturer at the University of Wollongong. Her PhD thesis, "Amongst Friends: The Australian Cult Film Experience," examines the audience participation practices of cult-film fans in Australia. Her forthcoming publications reflect her diverse research interests, including a chapter on cult film and nostalgia in *The Routledge Guide to Cult Cinema* (2019) and an essay on the antihero persona of Jason Statham.

Brett Mills is senior lecturer in television and film studies at the University of East Anglia. He is the author of *Television Sitcom* (2005), *The Sitcom* (2009) and *Creativity in the British Television Comedy Industry* (2016). Between 2012 and 2015, he conducted the project "Make Me Laugh" (www.makemelaugh.org.uk), funded by the UK Arts and Humanities Research Council, working with writers, producers, directors, and other practitioners who make television comedy to explore their creative process.

Joanne Morreale is associate professor in the Media and Screen Studies Department at Northeastern University. Her scholarship involves history and criticism of television and advertising. She is most recently author of *The Dick Van Dyke Show* (2015) and coauthor of *Advertising and Promotional Culture: Case Histories* (2018).

Jonathan Nichols-Pethick is professor of media studies at DePauw University, where he also serves as the director of the Pulliam Center for Contemporary Media. He is the author of *TV Cops: The Contemporary American Television Police Drama* (2012).

Asokan Nirmalarajah has a PhD in American literature and culture from the University of Cologne in Germany. His dissertation, "Gangster Melodrama: *The*

Sopranos and the Genre Tradition" (2011), reevaluates the historical significance of *The Sopranos* with respect to the tradition of the American gangster genre by re-reading the television series and the gangster film as advanced takes on the popular mode of American melodrama. He has taught literature, film, and television and currently works as chief editor of the website Bild der Frau.

Martha P. Nochimson has had a busy and varied career. She created and chaired the Film Studies Program at Mercy College, where she taught for twenty-four years. Taking time off intermittently between 1984 and 1990 to write for five network daytime soap operas, she also taught screenwriting for eleven years at the Tisch School of the Arts at New York University. She was an editor for *Cineaste* magazine for six years and is the author of eight books, including *World on Film: An Introduction* (2010), *David Lynch Swerves: Uncertainty from "Lost Highway" to "Inland Empire"* (2013), and *The Wiley-Blackwell Companion to Wong-Kar Wai* (2016). Since 1995, she has been an associate of the Columbia University seminar "Film and Interdisciplinary Interpretations." She has appeared on American, Canadian, and French television to talk about film and television and is a "talking head" in the HBO tribute film in celebration of the fifteenth anniversary of *The Sopranos*. One of the aspects of her work as a film and television scholar that she cherishes most is the many interviews she has been privileged to conduct with some of the most exciting artists working in the media, including David Chase, David Lynch, and David Simon. She is now working on a book about series television.

Adam Ochonicky completed his PhD at the University of Wisconsin–Milwaukee and is currently a full-time lecturer of English at the University of Wisconsin–Oshkosh, where he teaches courses on topics such as horror, surveillance cinema, science fiction, and regionalism. He is the author of *Nostalgic Frontiers: Spatiality, Violence, and the Midwest in Film* (2018). His work has appeared in *Screening the Past*, the *Quarterly Review of Film and Video*, *Nineteenth-Century Literature*, and *In Media Res*. He also serves as the media review editor for *Middle West Review*.

Lynnette Porter is professor in the Humanities and Communication Department at Embry-Riddle Aeronautical University. She has authored or coauthored seventeen books to date, most of them about television series or films. She is a huge fan of Captain Jack and Ianto Jones as well as of Barrowman siblings John and Carole and actor Gareth David-Lloyd (all of whom, she brags, she has had the pleasure of interviewing).

Amanda Potter is a research fellow with the Open University in the United Kingdom, where she wrote her PhD dissertation on viewer reception of classical myth on television in *Xena: Warrior Princess* and *Charmed* in 2014. She is interested in how viewers engage with the classical world through television series, particularly through fan fiction. She has published on *Xena*, *Charmed*, *Doctor Who*, *Torch-wood*, and *Rome* and has forthcoming publications on *Spartacus*.

Elizabeth L. Rambo is associate professor of English at Campbell University, specializing in medieval literature. She coedited *Buffy Goes Dark: Essays on the Final Two Seasons of "Buffy the Vampire Slayer" on Television* (2009, with Lynne Y. Edwards and James B. South) and has published essays on *Buffy*, *Angel*, *Firefly*, and *Sugarshock!* Her medieval scholarship deals with Celtic studies, Arthurian legends, and medievalism in pop culture. She is a charter member of the Whedon Studies Association.

Mitchell E. Shapiro, a professor in the School of Communication at the University of Miami for the past thirty-five years, is currently the director of honors (and former academic associate dean). He is a renowned scholar and educator, researching television programming from both empirical and historical perspectives for the past forty years. In addition to numerous book chapters and journal articles, he has authored nine books, the most recent of which, *The Top 100 American Situation Comedies: An Objective Ranking* (2015), was featured on *Live with Kelly and Michael*. Shapiro has served as a consultant for television and radio stations in South Florida and around the nation. He advises stations about all aspects of business operations, from market and audience to on-air talent to program acquisition and scheduling. He has appeared numerous times on local and national television and radio as an expert in broadcast media.

Douglas Snauffer is a freelance writer who has contributed articles to such publications as the *Akron Beacon Journal* and *Starlog* magazine. He has authored several books, including *Crime Television* (2006) and *The Show Must Go On* (2008); and as a scriptwriter, he has contributed to programs on the Syfy Channel.

Stephen Spignesi is the author of close to seventy books and a practitioner in residence at the University of New Haven, where he teaches composition and literature and has been nominated for an Excellence in Teaching Award. Spignesi is considered an authority on the work of Stephen King, the history of the Titanic, the music and history of the Beatles, *The Andy Griffith Show*, *ER*, the work of Woody Allen, Robin Williams, George Washington, and the American presidents and Founding Fathers. Spignesi's book *JFK Jr.* (1999) was a *New York Times* best seller. His book *The Complete Stephen King Encyclopedia* (1993) was nominated for a Bram Stoker Award. Spignesi was christened "the world's leading authority on Stephen King" by *Entertainment Weekly* magazine and appears in the ITV documentary *Autopsy: Robin Williams* (2015). His novel *Dialogues* (2005) was hailed as a reinvention of the psychological thriller.

Nikki Stafford is the author of television companion guides to *Sherlock*, *Lost*, *Buffy the Vampire Slayer*, *Angel*, *Alias*, and *Xena*. She has appeared on TV and radio as a pop-culture pundit and has been quoted by several media outlets, including the *New York Times*, *USA Today*, *EW.com*, the *Globe and Mail*, the *Washington Post*, and many others. She has been a keynote speaker at several academic conferences and occasionally manages to update her TV blog, *Nik at Nite*. She lives in London, Ontario.

Jeff Thompson is associate professor of English at Tennessee State University in Nashville. He is the Rondo Award–nominated author of *The Television Horrors of Dan Curtis: "Dark Shadows," "The Night Stalker," and Other Productions, 1966–2006* (2009); *House of Dan Curtis: The Television Mysteries of the "Dark Shadows" Auteur* (2010); and *Nights of Dan Curtis: The Television Epics of the "Dark Shadows" Auteur* (2016). He has written about *Dark Shadows* for fanzines, books, magazines, websites, and academic presentations. At home, Jeff has a *Dark Shadows* guest bedroom, a Joan Bennett wall, and a *Psycho* bathroom.

Robert J. Thompson is the Trustee Professor of the Newhouse School of Public Communications at Syracuse University, where he is also director of the Bleier Center for Television and Popular Culture. He has written or edited six books on American TV.

Sue Turnbull is professor of communication and media studies at the University of Wollongong, where she is discipline leader for Creative Industries and director of the Research Centre for Texts, Culture, and Creative Industries. Her current research includes a study of television use among migrants and the transnational career of the TV crime drama. Her recent publications include *The Media and Communications in Australia* (2014, with Stuart Cunningham) and *The Television Crime Drama* (2014). Sue is joint editor of *Participations: Journal of Audience and Reception Studies* and a frequent media commentator on television and radio in Australia who also writes on crime fiction for the *Sydney Morning Herald* and *The Age*.

Jason P. Vest is professor of English in the Division of English and Applied Linguistics at the University of Guam. His publications include *Future Imperfect: Philip K. Dick at the Movies* (2007, 2009); *The Postmodern Humanism of Philip K. Dick* (2009); *"The Wire," "Deadwood," "Homicide," and "NYPD Blue": Violence Is Power* (2010); and *Spike Lee: Finding the Story and Forcing the Issue* (2014). He lives and works in Mangilao, Guam.

Barbara Villez is emeritus professor at University of Paris 8, where she taught courses on common law and legal translation as well as on television representations of law and justice and comparative legal practices seen through images. She is associate researcher at the Institute for Advanced Judicial Studies in Paris, where she directs the program on images of justice and the seminar "Justices, Images, Languages, Cultures." She is also responsible for a network of scholars on television series at the Laboratoire communication et politique of the Institut de recherche interdisciplinaire en sciences sociales (University Paris Dauphine and the National Research Center). She has written numerous articles on television legal series, often comparing televised representations of law in France and the United States. Her book *Séries télé: Visions de la justice* (2005), translated and updated in English as *Television and the Legal System* (2009) retraces more than sixty years of television courtroom dramas in these two countries. Her most recent book is *"Law & Order," New York Police judiciaire: La justice en prime time* (2014).

Joseph S. Walker lives in Indiana, where he teaches literature and composition. In recent years, he has published work on *The Sopranos*, *Mystery Science Theater 3000*, *Arrested Development*, and a variety of other television shows and films. In addition to his work as a cultural critic, he is an active member of the Mystery Writers of America, and his fiction has appeared in *Alfred Hitchcock's Mystery Magazine*, *The First Line*, and a number of other publications.

Ronald Wilson is lecturer in the Film and Media Studies Department at the University of Kansas. He teaches courses in film theory, popular culture, and film genres. His most recent publications include *The Gangster Film* (2014) and *Cop Shows: A Critical History of Police Dramas on Television* (2015).

J. Jeremy Wisnewski is an author and philosopher who earns his keep doing philosophy with undergraduates at Hartwick College. He has published twelve allegedly nonfiction books, all of which seem suspicious in retrospect. He is currently at work on philosophically informed literary fiction.

Katheryn Wright is assistant professor of interdisciplinary studies at Champlain College. Her book *The New Heroines: Female Embodiment and Technology in 21st Century Popular Culture* (2016) examines how teen and young-adult heroines are models for posthuman subjectivity. She has also published articles and book chapters on media convergence, screen cultures, and biopolitics.

Paul R. Wright took his doctorate in comparative literature from Princeton University. He has taught at Princeton, Osaka University in Japan, and Villanova University. Wright is currently codirector of the Honors Program and associate professor of English at Cabrini University. His main area of research is Renaissance cultural history, including humanism, Machiavelli, and Milton. Wright also works in film and media studies, offering courses on television as narrative art and publishing on television shows such as *The Sopranos* and *Deadwood*. He is currently at work on a book-length study of Machiavelli's *Florentine Histories* as well as on an edited volume on television auteurs.

Bill Yousman earned his doctorate in communication from the University of Massachusetts at Amherst. His area of focus is media studies. He is the former managing director of the Media Education Foundation and the current director of the Graduate Program in Media Literacy and Digital Culture at Sacred Heart University, where he is an assistant professor in the School of Communication and Media Arts. His research focuses on media literacy education and the construction of racial ideologies in media images and narratives. He has published numerous essays in peer-reviewed journals and anthologies. His first book, *Prime Time Prisons on U.S. Television: Representation of Incarceration*, was published in 2009. His most recent book is *The Spike Lee Enigma: Challenge and Incorporation in Media Culture* (2014).

Lori Bindig Yousman is associate professor in the School of Communication and Media Arts at Sacred Heart University. She earned her doctorate in communication at the University of Massachusetts–Amherst, where she was awarded the title of university fellow as an incoming student in 2004. Her research interests include cultural studies, critical television studies, and media literacy, with a focus on the construction and commodification of young femininity. In addition to contributing to a number of edited volumes, Yousman is the coauthor of *"The O.C.": A Critical Understanding* (2013) and author of *"Dawson's Creek": A Critical Understanding* (2008) and *"Gossip Girl": A Critical Understanding* (2015).

Index

Actors and characters of featured shows are listed under the shows' main entries.